Common European Legal Thinking

Hermann-Josef Blanke · Pedro Cruz Villalón · Tonio Klein · Jacques Ziller
Editors

Common European Legal Thinking

Essays in Honour of Albrecht Weber

Editors

Hermann-Josef Blanke
University of Erfurt
Erfurt, Germany

Pedro Cruz Villalón
Court of Justice of the European Union
Luxembourg, Luxembourg

Tonio Klein
University of Applied Sciences for
Administration and Public Management in
the State of Lower Saxony
Hannover, Germany

Jacques Ziller
Università di Pavia
Pavia, Italy

ISBN 978-3-319-19299-4 ISBN 978-3-319-19300-7 (eBook)
DOI 10.1007/978-3-319-19300-7
Springer Cham Heidelberg New York Dordrecht London

Library of Congress Control Number: 2015949078

Printed on acid-free paper

Springer International Publishing AG Switzerland is part of Springer Science+Business Media (www.springer.com)

Preface

Common European Legal Thinking emanates from the existence of a shared European legal culture as especially reflected in the existence of a common European constitutional law. It denotes a body of individual constitutional principles – written and unwritten – that represent the common heritage of the constitutions of the Member States. Taking into account the two major European organisations, the Council of Europe and especially the European Union, the essays of this *Festschrift* discuss a range of constitutional principles, including the rule of law, democracy, and the exercise of political power in a multilevel system which recognises fundamental rights as directly applicable and supreme law. Other essays examine the value of pluralism, the commitment of private organisations to uphold public values, principles or rules, and the objectives and methods of a transnational science of administrative law. These articles highlight the fact that the *Ius Publicum Europaeum Commune* is "politically" in the making, which can often be seen in the shape of general legal principles. The publication recognises the role of *Albrecht Weber* as a forerunner of *Common European Legal Thinking*.

After his legal studies at the Universities of Munich, Frankfurt, Geneva and Würzburg and the completion of his second state examination, *Albrecht Weber* received his Ph.D. in 1972 with a study on the status of UN civil servants in the United States – Privileges and Immunities ("Der UN-Beamte in den USA"). He then worked as an assistant to Dr. Dr. h.c. *Hugo J. Hahn* (1927–2010), professor of public law and international public law. Professor Hahn decisively influenced and shaped *Albrecht Weber*'s academic thinking and research interests, including monetary law. In 1980, the jubilee qualified as a professor at the University of Würzburg with a book on protection provisions and economic integration ("Schutznormen und Wirtschaftsintegration", 1982). He was awarded the *venia legendi* for European, International and German and Foreign Public Law, all of which he inspired with his ideas and research during his time as an active university professor (1982–2010).

An important part of his academic work was the law relating to aliens, migration and refugees, which is interrelated with public international and now also European law. Upuntil his retirement as an active university professor in 2010, the jubilee has worked at the Institute for Research on Migration and Intercultural Studies (IMIS) at the University of Osnabrück, as well as for the Council on Migration (Berlin) and the Association of the Study of the World Refugee Problem (AWR) – not only for academic reasons, but also motivated by a Christian sense of responsibility.

Having been assigned the status of Private Lecturer (*Privatdozent*), from 1980 to 1982 *Albrecht Weber* worked as an academic assistant to the then president of the German Federal Constitutional Court, Prof. Dr. h.c. *E. Benda*. Under his guidance he experienced the practice of German "constitutional jurisdiction" in the so-called "Third Senate",[1] which strongly and sustainably shaped his thinking and his academic writing on constitutional law. The first reflection of this experience was the first edition in the 1980s, edited together with *Ch. Starck*, of a comparative law study on constitutional jurisdiction in Western Europe ("Verfassungsgerichtsbarkeit in Westeuropa", 1986/90). Analysing constitutional jurisdiction and judicial review always comprises the question of whether a national legal order guarantees the procedure of "constitutional complaint". As a consequence, from the mid-1990s the jubilee has worked on questions of substantial protection of fundamental rights in a DFG-funded project on "Fundamental Rights in Europe and North America" (2001).

From 1982 to 2010, *Albrecht Weber* was full professor for public law at the Faculty of Law of the University of Osnabrück and a member of the executive board of the Institute for European Law. His interest in foreign public law, comparative law and European law is also reflected by the number of occasions when he was invited as a visiting professor to universities in Europe and all over the world, including Montreal (McGill University, 1987), where he worked on language arrangements and minority protection, Aix-Marseille (1990, 1995 and 2003), Paris (Sorbonne, 1999, 2003) and Pisa (2000).

Since the early 1990s, *Albrecht Weber* has conducted multiannual research programmes on comparative constitutional law at the University of Seville, as well as with the Faculty of Law of the University of Aix-Marseille. For many years he has been participating as a valued dialogue partner in the *Table ronde internationale de justice constitutionnelle* (Aix-Marseille University). It was there that he was confronted with the thinking of French constitutional lawyer *Louis Favoreu*, the "missionnaire du droit constitutionnel". After the end of the division of Europe in the 1990s, *Albrecht Weber* was a consultant to the European Union's TACIS Projects in Russia (1998–2000) and Poland (2000).

Three books, published one shortly after the other, were decisive for the jubilee's work since the late 1990s. At first he referred back to international public law and together with *M. Schweitzer* co-authored a handbook in 2004, co-funded by the Fritz Thyssen Foundation, on the practice of the Federal Republic of Germany in inter-

[1] "Third Senate" is the unofficial name for the around 70 research assistants working at the Court. According to Art. 13.1 of the Rules of Procedure of the Court, the research assistants "shall assist the judges to whom they have been assigned in their official duties" and they "shall take instructions from such judge". At present, every judge is assigned four assistants, mostly judges from the different judicial branches. In 1984, the so-called "Third Senate" paid tribute to the imaginary *Friedrich G. Nagelmann* with an anthology of excellent legal essays, thus parodying the genre of a *liber amicorum*.

national public law ("Handbuch der Praxis des Völkerrechts in der Bundesrepublik Deutschland"). This casebook is intended to help those involved in the practical application of public international law and therefore need quick and immediate access to its sources and interpretation. In the same year a comparative law book was published on fundamental rights as guaranteed in the national legal orders of the Western world. Its case-law approach should help in accessing fundamental rights jurisprudence in other legal orders. This work again documents the jubilee's strong interest in the human rights jurisprudence of the highest courts.

As an outcome of the decades of comparative research, in 2010, the year of his retirement as an active university professor, *Albrecht Weber* published a book on comparative constitutional law in Europe ("Europäische Verfassungsvergleichung"). It contains a study on the "essentials" of the Western European constitutions and thus is a comprehensive fundamental guide of German academic writing for the comparison of constitutional law. At the same time this study can be perceived as a basic work on the foundations of a European Constitution (in the making).

Albrecht Weber's work bears evidence of a truly European lawyer and researcher in law with a broad analytical approach to international public law. It provides valuable insights and impetus for research on European law – in recent years especially with regard to the legal developments in European Economic and Monetary Union – and for comparative constitutional law. Together with the authors, the editors of this *Liber Amicorum* congratulate the jubilee on the occasion of his 70th birthday on July 20, 2015. Ad multos annos!

Erfurt/Luxembourg/Hannover/Pavia in April 2015

Herm.-J. Blanke
Pedro Cruz Villalón
Tonio Klein
Jacques Ziller

Foreword by the Board of the Institute for Migration Research and Intercultural Studies (IMIS) of the University of Osnabrück

Migration has long constituted a central element of societal change. People's spatial mobility has changed the world in the last centuries. Countless examples attest to the tremendous influence of labour and settlement migration, nomadism, mobility related to education or training, the historical slave trade and contemporary human trafficking, refugee movements, expulsion, and deportation. These have shaped the composition of populations as well as the development of labour markets, political systems, cultural identities and religious orientations. Moreover, migration will continue to be a central societal issue with high political significance in the future, as indicated by the current debates related to further (very unevenly distributed) world population growth, the aging of the wealthy "Northern" societies, climate change, the socio-political and legal challenges of migration, and the lack of skilled labour for increasingly complex, internationally and tightly interconnected "knowledge societies".

For the last quarter of a century, the Institute for Migration Research and Intercultural Studies (IMIS) of the University of Osnabrück has focused its scientific interests on the diverse aspects of spatial mobility and intercultural encounters in history and the present. Prof. Dr. *Albrecht Weber* was one of the founders of IMIS in 1991, when it evolved out of the 1989 "Working Group on Migration Research and Intercultural Studies", of which *Albrecht Weber* was also a participant. This interdisciplinary institute was founded at a time in which migration research in Germany was still figuring out how to position itself and just starting to explore interdisciplinary approaches. During its founding period, the core of IMIS was constituted by *Albrecht Weber*, who brought in his expertise as a law researcher, as well as four other legal cooperation members representing the fields of history, education, psychology, and sociology.

The Institute for Migration Research and Intercultural Studies was the first institute in this field to be established with a set, long-term staff and budget at a German university. This institute quickly attracted the interest of other departments within the university, so that the number of participating researchers as well as the spectrum of disciplines grew. Currently the participants at IMIS come from the following fields and research areas: ethnology, geography, history, intercultural pedagogy, intercultural management, art history, political science, psychology, legal studies, religious studies, sociology, language and literature studies, as well as economics.

From the beginning, IMIS has aimed to support the consolidation and networking of interdisciplinary research as well as the dialogue between science and praxis. This has been accomplished with basic research, publications, public events, and scientific advising. Because of its long-term and intensive research activities as well as its broad spectrum of interdisciplinary exchange, IMIS has become a transregionally and internationally well-known and recognized research institute.

From the beginning *Albrecht Weber* helped construct and develop this institute, which profited significantly from his legal-scientific expertise. Since 1995 one focus of scientific activities in IMIS revolved around the interdisciplinary research training group "Migration in Modern Europe". Its establishment and development over the first ten years was made possible in part with the funding application support of *Albrecht Weber*, including two successful application extensions. During this period, about 50 doctoral students and post-docs took part in the interdisciplinary training of this program, funded by the German Research Foundation (DFG). Since 2004 IMIS has also offered basic academic training with its interdisciplinary master's program "International Migration and Intercultural Relations" (IMIB). Until his retirement Prof. Dr. *Albrecht Weber* taught the fundamental concepts and questions of migration law to master's students from all over the world and from diverse fields of study.

Albrecht Weber's scientific research achievements at IMIS include numerous publications, especially in the research fields of immigration law, aliens law, citizenship law, and asylum law. With his expertise, *Albrecht Weber* contributed especially to the establishment and development of IMIS' long-term research focuses "Migration – Nation State – Welfare State: Germany and Europe" as well as "Immigration Policy and Legislation: Germany in the International Context". An early and important reference point in IMIS' history was the IMIS-Conference "Germany as a Land of Immigration in the European Union: Development Demands and Regulation Possibilities", funded by the Volkswagen Foundation and the European Union Commission and led by *Albrecht Weber*. The conference papers for this were published in 1997 as Volume 5 of *IMIS-Schriften*. *Albrecht Weber* also led the major research project "Basic Rights in the Constitutional Judicature of Europe and North America", which examined basic rights in 25 legal systems. In this context special attention was given to those basic rights, which applied to the free movement of persons and goods, protection from political persecution, and asylum.

Albrecht Weber's intensive and many-sided activities on the issues of migration and integration stretched far beyond Osnabrück. Especially important was his long-term involvement on the board of the "Committee for Migration" (RfM), founded in 1995/96 as a nationwide network of scientists who deal with questions of migration and integration. He was also involved in the many activities of the head committee of the international Association for the Study of the World Refugee Problem (AWR). Also numerous guest professorships (for instance, at the McGill University in Montreal/Canada in 1987, at the University of Marseille III/Aix-en-Provence in

1990 and 1995, at the Sorbonne in 1999 and 2003, as well as at the University of Pisa in 2000) constituted landmarks in *Albrecht Weber*'s international research activities.

Prof. Dr. *Albrecht Weber*'s devoted efforts to these issues were of fundamental importance for the establishment and further development of IMIS and of migration research more generally. From the beginning, he dedicatedly contributed his law studies expertise in the context of the institute's pursuits. He also supported the sometimes difficult everyday communication regarding the diverse concepts, approaches, and perspectives which make up interdisciplinary migration research. The further development of the institute was also buttressed by his various contacts within the university. With his nationally and internationally highly regarded scientific projects and publications, his international teaching activities, and his work in scientific organizations, *Albrecht Weber* has made an essential contribution to the institute's networks and to the establishment of migration research as a discipline in the academic landscape. Wc thank him very warmly in the name of IMIS.

Jochen Oltmer
Andreas Pott

Abbreviations

AEUV	Vertrag über die Arbeitsweise der Europäischen Union (Treaty on the Functioning of the European Union – TFEU)
AG	Advocate General
AJIL	American Journal of International Law
ANI	National Integrity Agency
AöR	Archiv für Öffentliches Recht
Art.	Article(s)
BCBS	*Basel Committee* on Banking Supervision
BCE	Banque centrale européenne
BGBl.	Bundesgesetzblatt
BL	Basic Law (German Constitution = Grundgesetz)
Br.-Drs.	Bundesratsdrucksache
Bt.-Drs.	Bundestagsdrucksache
BVerfG	Bundesverfassungsgericht (German Federal Constitutional Court)
BVerfGE	Entscheidung des Bundesverfassungsgerichts (Decision of the German Federal Constitutional Court)
BV-G	Bundesverfassungsgesetz (Austrian Constitution)
CEDAW	Committee on the Elimination of Discrimination against Women
CEDH	Convention européenne des droits de l'homme Cour européenne des droits de l'homme
CEECs	Central and Eastern European Countries
CEFTA	Central European Free Trade Agreement
cf.	compare
CFA	Chartered Financial Analyst
CFI	Court of First Instance
CISA	Convention implementing the Schengen Agreement
cit.	cited
CJEU	Court of Justice of the European Union
CJUE	Cour de justice de l'Union européenne (Court of Justice of the European Union)

CMLR (CMLRev.)	Common Market Law Review
CoC	Code of Conduct
CoE	Council of Europe
CoR	Committee of the Regions
COSAC	Conference of Community and European Affairs Committees of Parliaments of the European Union
CVM	Consultation and Verification Mechanism
DDR	Deutsche Demokratische Republik (GDR – German Democratic Republic)
DG	Directorate-General
DNA	National Anti-Corruption Directorate
Doc.	Document
DÖV	Die Öffentliche Verwaltung
DVBl.	Deutsches Verwaltungsblatt
EC	Treaty establishing the European Community/European Community/European Communities
ECB	European Central Bank
ECHR	European Convention on Human Rights and Fundamental Freedoms
ECJ	European Court of Justice ("Luxembourg Court"), see also CJEU
ECR	European Court Reports
ECSC	European Coal and Steel Community
ECtHR	European Court of Human Rights ("Strasbourg Court")
Ed.	editor
Eds.	editors
edn.	edition
EEC	European Economic Community
EFSF	Europäische Finanzstabilisierungsfazilität
EFSM	Europäischer Finanzstabilisierungsmechanismus
e. g.	exempli gratia (for example)
EJIL	European Journal of International Law
ELJ	European Law Journal
ELRev.	European Law Review
EMU	Economic and Monetary Union
EP	European Parliament
EPL	European Public Law
ERT	European Round Table (of Industrialists)
ESM	Europäischer Stabilitätsmechanismus/European Stability Mechanism
ESMV	Vertrag zur Errichtung des Europäischen Stabilitätsmechanismus
ETA	Euskadi Ta Askatasuna (Basque separatist organisation)
et al.	et alii/aliae (and others)
et seq(q).	et sequens, et sequentes (and the following page/s)

EU	European Union
EUCFR	European Union Charter of Fundamental Rights
EuConst	European Constitutional Law Review
EuGH	Gerichtshof der Europäischen Union (European Court of Justice – ECJ)
EuGRZ	Europäische Grundrechte Zeitschrift
EuR	Europarecht
EuZW	Europäische Zeitschrift für Wirtschaftsrecht (Frankfurter Allgemeine Zeitung)
ex p.	ex parte
EZB	Europäische Zentralbank (European Central Bank)
FAZ	Frankfurter Allgemeine Zeitung
FCC	Federal Constitutional Court
fn.	footnote
GC	General Court (part of the CJEU) Grand Chamber/Grande Chambre
GDP	Gross Domestic Product
GG	Grundgesetz (German Basic Law)
GOBR	Geschäftsordnung des Bundesrats (Rules of Procedure of the German Bundesrat)
IAMLADP	International Annual Meeting on Language Arrangements, Documentation and Publications
ibid.	ibidem (at the same place)
ICANN	Internet Corporation for Assigned Names and Numbers
id.	idem (the same)
i. e.	id est (that is)
ILM	International Law Materials
IMF	International Monetary Fund
ISO	International Organization for Standardization
IT	information technology
i. V. m	in Verbindung mit (in conjunction with)
IWF	Internationaler Währungsfonds
JCMS	Journal of Common Market Studies
JSC	Justice Select Committee
JZ	Juristen Zeitung
KfW	Kreditanstalt für Wiederaufbau (reconstruction loan corporation)
LfE	Licence for Europe
MEP	Member of the European Parliament
N.B.	Nota bene (lat.) – note well
NGO	Non-Governmental Organization
NJW	Neue Juristische Wochenschrift
No.	Number
NPLD	European Network to Promote Linguistic Diversity
NVwZ	Neue Zeitschrift für Verwaltungsrecht

OECD	Organization for Economic Cooperation Development
O.J.	Official Journal
O.J. C	Official Journal (Communications)
O.J. L	Official Journal (Legislation)
OMT	Outright Monetary Transactions
OUP	Oxford University Press
p.	page(s)
PACE	Police and Criminal Evidence Act
para	paragraph
passim	here and there mentioned
PGD	Preimplantation Genetic Diagnosis
PND	prenatal diagnostics
PUF	Presses Universitaires de France
RCC	Romanian Constitutional Court
RDCE	Revista de Derecho Constitucional Europeo
RDUE	Revue de droit de l'Union européenne
RMC	Revue du Marché Commun
RTDeur/RTDE	Revue trimestrielle de droit européen
RZB	Raiffeisen Zentralbank Österreich
scil.	scilicet (namely)
SCM	Superior Council of Magistracy
Sec.	Section
seq.	sequens (following page)
seqq.	sequentes (following pages)
ser.	Series
SME	Small and Medium-sized Enterprise
StabMechG	Gesetz zur Übernahme von Gewährleistungen im Rahmen eines europäischen Stabilisierungsmechanismus (Stabilisierungsmechanismusgesetz)
STC	Sentencia del Tribunal Constitucional (judgment of the Spanish Constitutional Tribunal)
StGB	Strafgesetzuch (German Penal Code)
TCE	Treaty establishing a Constitution for Europe
TDM	Text and Data Mining
TEU	Treaty on European Union as amended by the Treaty of Lisbon
TFEU	Treaty on the Functioning of the European Union
TFUE	Traité sur le fonctionnement de l'Union européenne
TTIP	Transatlantic Trade and Investment Partnership
TUE	Traité sur l'Union européenne
UK	United Kingdom
UN(O)	United Nations Organisation
UNFPA	United Nations Population Fund
UNTS	United Nations Treaty Series
US	United States
v/v.	versus (against)

VCLT	Vienna Convention on the Law of Treaties (1969)
Vol.	Volume
VSKS	Vertrag über Stabilität, Koordinierung und Steuerung in der Wirtschafts- und Währungsunion
VVDStRL	Veröffentlichungen der Vereinigung der Deutschen Staatsrechtslehrer
WHO	World Health Organization
WTO	World Trade Organisation
ZaöRV	Zeitschrift für ausländisches öffentliches Recht und Völkerrecht

Contents

List of Authors

Dr. iur. utr. Dr. h.c. Rainer Arnold Emeritus Professor of Public Law and European Law, University of Regensburg, Germany. Corresponding Member of the Academy of Sciences of Bologna, Membre associé de l'Académie internationale de droit comparé, Fellow of the European Law Institute

Dr. iur. Javier Barnes Professor of Administrative Law, University of Huelva, Spain

Dr. iur. Hermann-Josef Blanke Professor of Public Law and International Public Law, University of Erfurt, Germany

Prof. Reimer von Borries, LL.M. (Columbia University New York) former Head of Division at the Federal Ministry of Finance (FRG), Honorary Professor, University of Osnabrück, Germany

Robert Böttner, B.A., LL.M. assistant at the Chair for Public Law, International Public Law and European Integration, University of Erfurt, and assistant to the Professor for German and International Economic Law, Leipzig University of Applied Sciences (HTWK), Germany

Dr. iur. José Manuel Moreira Cardoso da Costa Emeritus Professor of Public Law, University of Coimbra, justice (1983–1986) and former President (1989–2003) of the Portuguese Constitutional Court

Dr. iur. Dr. h.c. mult. Vlad Constantinesco Emeritus Professor, University Robert-Schuman (Strasbourg), France, Professor at the College of Europe (Bruges 1982–1992, Natolin since 2006)

Dr. iur. Franz Cromme former State Secretary for Lower Saxony, lecturer at the Viadrina European University, Frankfurt/Oder, Germany

Dr. iur. Pedro Cruz Villalón Professor of Constitutional Law, Universidad Autónoma de Madrid (Spain), Justice (1992–1998) and President (1998–2001) of the Spanish Constitutional Court, Advocate-General of the Court of Justice of the European Union (since 2009)

Dr. Dr. iur. Dr. h.c. mult. Francis Delpérée Emeritus Professor, Catholic University of Louvain, Member of the House of Representatives of Belgium (since 2014), President of the International Academy of Constitutional Law, Belgium

Dr. iur Dr. h.c Eberhard Eichenhofer Professor of Social Security Law and Civil Law, Friedrich-Schiller-University Jena, Germany

Dr. iur. Dr. h.c. mult. Francisco Fernández Segado Professor of Constitutional Law, Complutense University (Madrid), Spain

Dr. iur. Dr. h.c. Michel Fromont Emeritus Professor, University Paris I Panthéon-Sorbonne, France, former Professor at German Universities

Dr. iur. Diana-Urania Galetta Professor of Administrative Law, University of Milan, Italy

Dr. iur. Lech Garlicki Professor for Constitutional Law, Warsaw University, former Justice at the Constitutional Court of the Republic of Poland (1993–2001) and former judge at the European Court of Human Rights (2002–2012)

Dr. iur. Ulrich Häde Professor of Law, Administrative, Financial and Monetary Law, European University Viadrina, Frankfurt (Oder), Germany

Margot Horspool Emeritus Professor of European and Comparative Law, University of Surrey, visiting Professor at Queen Mary University and Notre Dame University, London, United Kingdom

Prof. Dr. Tonio Klein University of Applied Sciences for Administration and Public Management in the State of Lower Saxony, Hannover, Germany

Dr. iur. Jörg Luther Professor of Public Law, University of Piemonte Orientale “A. Avogadro”, Italy

Dr. theol. Reinhold Mokrosch Emeritus Professor of Protestant Theology, Practical Theology and Religious Pedagogics, Founder of the Centre for Empirical Research in Values, University of Osnabrück, Gemany

Dr. iur. Dr. h.c. mult. Peter-Christian Müller-Graff Professor of Civil Law, Commercial Law and Corporate Law, Ruprecht-Karls-University Heidelberg, Germany

Jaime Nicolás Muñiz, MA Spanish MA in Law and German master’s degree in social science, former Senior Civil Servant in high-level positions in the Spanish State Administration, Deputy and Acting Director at the Centro de Estudios Constitucionales and the public broadcasting corporation RTVE, fomer Head of the Presidential Office at the Council of State, for twenty years Associate Professor of Constitutional Law at the University Carlos III in Madrid, Spain

Dr. phil. habil. Arnim Regenbogen philosopher and associate Emeritus Professor, Institute of Philosophy, Department of Humanities, University of Osnabrück, Germany. Member of the interdisciplinary research group “Value Education”

Dr. iur. Thierry Renoux Professor of Constitutional Law, Paul Cézanne University of Aix-Marseille, France

Dr. iur. Dr. h.c. Karl-Peter Sommermann Professor of Public Law, Political Theory and Comparative Law, German University of Administrative Sciences, Speyer, Gemany

Daniel Spichtinger, Mag. phil. (Vienna), MA (Bath) Senior Policy Officer "Open Access", European Commission, DG Research and Innovation, Brussels, Belgium

Dr. phil. Manfred Spieker Professor of Christian Social Science, University of Osnabrück, Germany

Dr. iur utr. Christian Starck Emeritus Professor of Public Law, University of Göttingen, President of the Göttingen Academy of Sciences and Humanities, Germany

Dr. iur. Dr. h.c. mult. Klaus Stern Emeritus Professor of Public Law, University of Cologne, former judge at the Constitutional Court of North Rhine-Westphalia, Germany

Dr. iur. Rudolf W. Strohmeier Deputy Director General at DG Research and Innovation of the EU-Commission in Bruxelles, Belgium, Member of the European Academy of Sciences and Arts

Dr. iur. Dr. h.c. Christian Tomuschat Emeritus Professor of Public Law, International Public Law and the Law of the European Union, Humboldt-University Berlin, Germany, member of the Institut de droit international, President of the OSCE Court of Conciliation and Arbitration (since 2013)

Dr. iur. Carlos Vidal Prado Professor of Constitutional Law, National Distance University, Madrid, Director of the Secretary General for the Universities, Ministry of Education, Spain

Dr. iur. Franz Zehetner Professor of Public Law, Vienna University of Technology, Austria

Dr. iur. Jacques Ziller Professor of the Law of the European Union, University of Pavia, Italy

James Otis and *The Writs of Assistance* Case (1761)

Francisco Fernández Segado

1 Introduction: A Brief Approximation to the Dictum in *Bonham's Case*

The dictum pronounced by Chief Justice *Edward Coke* in *Bonham's Case* (1610) is well known by any constitutional law specialist. Nevertheless, I would like to discuss the basis upon which *Coke* formulated the constitutional theory of judicial review of legislation.

On April 30, 1606 *Thomas Bonham* was cited before the president and censors of the Royal College on a charge of practising medicine in London without a certificate to practise from the Royal College. Bonham was a Doctor of Philosophy and Physic, having graduated from Cambridge University. He did not, however, hold any degree or certificate from the Royal College. He was fined one hundred shillings and further forbidden – under pain of imprisonment – to practise medicine until he was first properly admitted to the Royal College.

The Royal College of Physicians was a unique institution in early modern England.[1] Chartered in 1518 under Cardinal Wolsey's Chancellorship, the College was founded by three royal physicians and three London physicians, all with academic doctorates of medicine. By an Act of Parliament confirming their charter passed during the reign of *Henry VIII*, the College had gained the right to sit as a court itself in order to judge all other practitioners. It had the power to admit those academically qualified to membership, to grant licenses to those without academic qualifications but proven practical experience, and to punish those practising negligently and/or without license. A statute of Queen Mary's first Parliament also allowed the officers of the College to imprison offenders at their pleasure. The juridical authority of the College thus flew in the face of the common law assumption that to practise medicine one needed only the consent of the patient.[2] Moreover, the College's power of medical licensing overlapped with one of the bishop's authority

[1] Cook 2004, p. 129.
[2] Cook 2004, p. 130.

H.-J. Blanke et al. (eds.), *Common European Legal Thinking*,
DOI 10.1007/978-3-319-19300-7_1

to grant licenses to physicians and surgeons, in addition to conflicting with the other universities' ability to issue licenses for the practice of physic and surgery (ancillary to their powers to grant degrees).

Bonham took the position that since he was a Doctor of Medicine at Cambridge University, the Royal College of Physicians had no jurisdiction whatsoever over him. As a consequence of this stance, Bonham was imprisoned for seven days. This case then, as it was brought before Justice *Coke*, was an action for false imprisonment by *Bonham* against *Henry Atkins*, *George Turner*, *Thomas Moundford*, and *John Argent*, doctors in physic, and *John Taylor* and *William Bowden*, both yeomen (leading members of the Royal College of Physicians). According to *Smith*[3], the defendants pleaded the Letters Patent dated from the 10th year of the reign of *Henry VIII*, which gave them the powers as a College to impose fines on practitioners in London who had not been duly admitted to practice medicine by them.

Coke analyses whether a doctor of physic of one university or another, be by the Letters Patents, and by the body of the Act of 14 Henry VIII, is restrained to practise Physic within the City of London. His reply is:

> They (the members of the Royal College) did rely upon the Letter of the grant, ratified by the said Act of 14 H. VIII which is in the negative, *scil. Nemo in dicta civitate et cetera exerceat dictam facultatem nisi ad hoc per praedict' praesidentem et communitatem, et cetera admissus sit, et cetera.* And this proposition is a general negative, and *Generale dictum est generaliter intelligendum;* and *nemo* excludeth all; and therefore a Doctor of the one University or the other, is prohibited within this negative word *Nemo.* And many cases were put, where negative Statutes shall be taken *stricte et exclusive,* which I do not think necessary to be recited.[4]

But later, *Coke* adds with a significant emphasis:

> The University is *Alma mater,* from whose breasts those of that private College have sucked all their science and knowledge (which I acknowledge to be great and profound) but the Law saith, *Erusbecit lex filios castigare parentes:* the University is the fountain, and that and the like private Colleges are *tanquam rivuli,* which flow from the Fountain, *et melius est petere fontes quam sectari rivulos.*[5]

Coke puts forth five arguments in support of his holding that the College had not properly exercised their general powers. The fourth argument is the true keystone in which *Coke* uttered what many[6] believe to be his most controversial dictum:

> The Censors cannot be Judges, Ministers, and parties; Judges, to give sentence or judgment; Ministers, to make summons; and Parties, to have the moiety of the forfeiture, *quia aliquis non debet esse Judex in propria causa, imo iniquum est aliquem sui rei esse judicem:* and one cannot be Judge and Attorney for any of the parties.

The idea that it takes three persons, a plaintiff, a defendant, and a judge, to make a case and reach a judgment, was clear to the earliest writers on English law[7],

[3] Smith 1966, p. 302.
[4] *Bonham's Case* may be seen in Sheppard 2003, p. 270.
[5] Sheppard 2013, p. 272.
[6] E. g. Bowen 1957, p. 315.
[7] Fleta had already written in this respect: "Est autem iudicium trinus actum trium personarum ad minus, actoris, iudicis et rei, sine quibus legitime consistere non potest", cf. Yale 1974, p. 80.

and implicit in such a proposition was the understanding that a judgement was not properly attainable unless the three persons of the trinity were kept distinct. On the matter, *Henry de Bracton*, in his very outstanding book *De legibus et consuetudinibus angliae,* wrote that a judge should be disqualified on such grounds as kindred, enmity or friendship with a party, or because he was subordinate in status to the party, or had acted as his advocate. However, this seems to have been borrowed from the doctrines of canon law, and while the church courts clearly applied these provisions for recusation of the *suspectus iudex,* there seems no case in which the yearbook lawyers who referred to *Bracton* had borrowed these principles.[8]

Of course, a fundamental idea of this nature has long been enshrined in the maxim that no one may be judge in his own cause. *Coke* adopted this notion into his reasoning. Just after the above-mentioned argument, he added in his celebrated dictum*:* "And it appeareth in our Books, that in many Cases, the Common Law doth control Acts of Parliament, and sometimes shall adjudge them to be void: for when an Act of Parliament is against Common right and reason, or repugnant, or impossible to be performed, the Common Law will control it, and adjudge such Act to be void."[9]

Many have considered this passage to be the birth certificate of judicial review of legislative acts. For Plucknett, a distinguished professor from Harvard University, *Coke*'s solution was in the idea of a fundamental law which limited Crown and Parliament. What that law was, was a question as difficult to answer as it was insistent – and, as subsequent events showed, capable of surprising solutions.[10] The nearest we find is the assertion of the paramount law of "reason". For the rest, the common lawyer's "reason" is left in as much uncertainty as he himself ascribed to the Chancellor's equity. Moreover, *Coke* was prepared to advance medieval precedent for his theory and it has thus evoked the criticism of later investigators. In Plucknett's opinion, *Coke*'s theory reaches its final expression in *The Case of the College of Physicians.* Nevertheless, Plucknett acknowledges that *Coke*'s challenging of both Crown and Parliament has provoked controversy up to his own time.[11]

Conversely, the interpretation given by *Thorne* is very different. *Coke*'s dictum is considered as a maxim of statutory interpretation. According to *Thorne*[12], *Coke*'s fourth argument was directed toward an interpretation of the statute which on its face seemed to make Bonham's imprisonment lawful. As the question of the legality of *Bonham*'s imprisonment was the only question before the Court, *Coke*'s fourth point is, according to Thorne, not a dictum, but a material portion of his argument. And finally, though *Coke*'s fourth argument is phrased in very wide terms, it foresees no statute as void because of a conflict between it and common law, natural law, or higher law, but simply a refusal to follow a statute as absurd on its face.

[8] Yale 1974, p. 81.

[9] Sheppard 2013, p. 275.

[10] Plucknett 1926–1927, p. 31.

[11] Plucknett 1926–1927, p. 34.

[12] Thorne 1938, p. 547 et seq.

In order to settle the matter, one may say that the interpretation given to his dictum in the American colonies would be the main characteristic of the constitutional theory of judicial review of legislation. *Sherry* may have correctly written that it seems to be widely accepted that *Coke* was one of the primary sources of the American institution of judicial review.[13] Likewise, *Schwartz* has underlined *Coke*'s fundamental contribution to American constitutionalism. He stated the supremacy of law in terms of positive law, and it was in such terms that the doctrine was of such importance to the Founders of the American Republic: "When they spoke of a government of laws and not of men, they were not indulging in mere rhetorical flourish."[14] Of course, there were other philosophical influences on the Founders, including *Locke*, continental Enlightenment philosophers, radical English Whigs, and the Scottish Common Sense School.[15]

It is necessary not to forget the peculiar political circumstances of the colonies, which were already quite predisposed against the British Parliament as it had been seen as an organ of oppression; such a situation would make it possible that *Coke*'s dictum soon be incorporated into the arsenal of weapons used to oppose the English Parliament. Therefore, the *Writ of Assistance Case* and the figure of *James Otis* are paradigmatic.

2 The Great Impact upon Juridical Colonial Thought by the Doctrine Established by Chief Justice Edward Coke in *Bonham's Case*

2.1 *Coke*'s juridical thinking would have a very remarkable impact on the colonies that went far beyond the doctrine of judicial review. The men of the American Revolution fed their appetite for new ideas by way of *Coke*'s writings, particularly his *Institutes*. Even more, for the Americans of the eighteenth century, *Coke* was the contemporary colossus of the law – "our juvenile oracle", *John Adams* termed him in an 1816 letter – who combined in his own person the position of highest judge, commentator on the law and leader of the parliamentary opposition to royal tyranny. It also contributed to considering *Coke* (whose more evident manifestation was his knowledge of ancient law) as a true antiquarian.[16] Furthermore, he contributed greatly to the opening of new fields of knowledge, always seen from his own viewpoint as genuine defender of the rule of law.

Coke's dictum was easily accessible since it appeared in the *Abridgments*[17] which were frequently studied by the lawyers of the colonies. It was repeated

[13] Sherry 1992–1993, p. 174.

[14] Schwartz 1993, p. 5.

[15] Michael 1990–1991, p. 427 et seqq.

[16] "(H)is learning, antiquarian to the core, opened up vistas and past crises as history scarcely could." Mullet 1932, p. 471.

[17] Most scholars agree that the three more important *Abridgments* were those of Bacon 1736, Viner 1741–1756 and Comyn's *Digest* 1762, cf. McGovney 1944–1945, p. 7.

in the *Abridgments* of *Viner*, *Bacon* and *Comyns* and as *Goebel* tells us,[18] *Coke*, *Strange*, *Keble* and *Salked* were frequently cited in common law cases, even into the late eighteenth century, and a lot of American law came out of *Bacon*'s and *Viner*'s *Abridgments.* In addition, a significant number of the colonial lawyers were educated in England. According to *Kramer*,[19] there was a time when it was popular to read *Sir Edward Coke*'s opinion in *Bonham's Case* and his reports of the proceedings in *Prohibitions Del Roy* and *Proclamations* as an early, albeit failed, effort to establish something along the lines of modern judicial review. In this respect, *Mullett*[20] reminds us that *Coke*'s reputation was even more gilded in the eighteenth century when he was the lamp by which young Aladdins of the law secured their legal treasures. Six weeks with him alone was sufficient to secure *Patrick Henry*'s admittance to the Virginia Bar. *Thomas Jefferson* must have spent a much longer time dutifully studying *Coke*'s writings. "I do wish", he wrote, "the devil had old *Coke*, for I am sure I never was so tired of an old dull scoundrel in my life." But in the days of the Revolution, *Jefferson* was more charitable, preferring the whiggish virtues of *Coke* to the "honeyed Mansfieldism" of *Blackstone*.

Examples of the influence of *Coke* upon colonial politicians and lawyers are manifold. *Jefferson* said that *Coke*'s *Commentary upon Littleton* "was the universal elementary book of law students and a sounder Whig never wrote, nor of profounder learning in the orthodox doctrines of … British liberties."[21] *John Adams* gained the belief from *Coke* that common law was common right, and the subject's best birth right, and without it there was no right. The law, he further argued, provided a remedy for every wrong and delighted in so doing. Particularly, the common law was a defence against the Stamp Act, for *Coke* himself had once held that acts of Parliament that were unreasonable should be judged void. *Samuel Adams*, who lost his desire to be a lawyer after a brief experience with the *Institutes,* found in *Coke* an irreproachable authority for questioning parliamentary supremacy with particular reference to taxation. The dictum that Parliament could not tax the Irish *quia milites ad Parliamentum non mittunt* was applied to America. *Mullett*[22] reminds us that *Coke*'s eulogy of *Magna Charta* as declaratory of the fundamental laws and liberties was interpreted to mean that an act of Parliament contrary to it was void whether *Coke* had "expressly asserted it or not." Finally, *Adams* found in *Coke* proof that colonies ought not to be ruled tyrannically.

The influence of *Coke* on other important pamphleteers of the epoch is also remarkable. *John Rutledge*, an important personage of South Carolina in the revolutionary era, wrote that *Coke*'s *Institutes* seem almost the grounds of our law. *John Dickinson* who ultimately became a home ruler, found in *Coke* justification for the theory that subjects ought not to have to contribute to wars outside the realm. *James Wilson*, Supreme Court Justice since 1789, was the most exhaustive colonial student

[18] Goebel, Jr. 1954, p. 455.
[19] Kramer 2001–2002, p. 24 et seq.
[20] Mullet 1932, p. 458.
[21] Schwartz 1993, p. 5.
[22] Mullet 1932, p. 468.

of *Coke*,[23] and it was from *Calvin's Case* that *Wilson* derived the blanket defence of colonial claims, namely that the colonies were not bound by English statutes.

The meaning of the dictum in *Bonham's Case* in colonial America was unequivocal. The germinal idea had evolved in colonial America and was effectuated in the doctrine that a court could void an act promulgated by a legislative assembly subject to a higher law when the court found that the law had transgressed its boundaries. Going even further, *Hall* writes[24] that in the eighteenth century, leaders of the incipient American Revolution extracted from *Coke*'s opinion that a judicially enforceable higher law limited their imperial masters' authority. This had important practical implications for judicial review because it meant that judges could legitimately claim a policy-making role without the necessity of direct popular support.

The dictum became the most important source of the concept of judicial review. In due time, *Coke*'s theory of parliamentary supremacy under the law was wholly merged into the notion of legislative supremacy. In 1915, *Smith*[25] reminds us of a committee report to the New York State Bar Association: "In short the American Revolution was a lawyers' revolution to enforce *Lord Coke*'s theory of the invalidity of Acts of Parliament in derogation of the common right and of the rights of Englishmen." *Lord Coke*'s theory of the supremacy of the fundamental law, while not engrafted to or enshrined in the English common law itself, did travel the seas and find fertile ground for ready expression in the American colonies.

2.2 The theory established in *Bonham's Case,* or at least its interpretation in the English colonies, would find in them an appropriate setting for its revival. The supremacy of a fundamental law found faithful supporters in the colonists beyond the Atlantic Ocean. According to *Corwin*,[26] the Cokian doctrine corresponded exactly to the contemporary necessities of many of the colonies in the earlier days of their existence, which explains how it represented the teaching of the highest of all legal authorities before *Blackstone* appeared on the scene.

Of course, the theory of legislative supremacy so ardently argued by *Blackstone* and shared by the Whigs, did not originally mean that legislative assemblies would exist for the elaboration of the laws, the settling of the politics or the integration of the different interests of a society becoming ever more commercialised. During the Glorious Revolution, the dogma of legislative supremacy was primarily aimed at preventing an arbitrary monarch from unilaterally making decisions without parliamentary consent. When this theory was transferred to the colonies, its meaning was made more patent: in order to provide for every executive's unilateral action, the governor, appointed from London, should guarantee that the expression of popular consent was what should really give legitimacy to the law. Conversely, the British Parliament found itself far from being the idealised hero of the colonists, who so far away from it considered it a distant body lacking comprehension for their problems

[23] Mullet 1932, p. 470.
[24] Hall 1985, p. 4.
[25] Smith 1966, p. 313; Boudin 1928–1929, p. 223. The only disagreement between both scholars is the date; whereas Boudin dates the report to 1915, Smith dates it as 1917.
[26] Corwin 1925, p. 515.

and in whose deliberations they no longer participated. Similarly, the deeply rooted ideal of the existence of a fundamental law, alongside the refusal to deal with Parliament's arbitrariness, in addition to a certain fear of abuse of power of colonial legislative assemblies would make the juridical colonial world turn its eyes towards *Coke* and his theory of judicial review. Even more, the colonists would come to the great English Chief Justice in order to ground their creed that this fundamental law warranted rights such as those of "no taxation without representation" or "trial by jury".

Coke had spoken of something beyond human invention; *Blackstone*, on the other hand, knew of no such limit on human law-makers.[27] The American lawyers, fervent followers of *Coke* for a long time, now found themselves faced with the theories of *Blackstone*. They placed all their confidence in *Coke*'s doctrine, which does not indicate that *Blackstone*'s influence was fugacious. As *Wood* tells us, it would be a devastating logic if we think that almost all eighteenth-century Englishmen on both sides of the Atlantic had recognised something called fundamental law;[28] it was a guide to the moral rightness and constitutionality of ordinary law and politics. Even a despot such as *Cromwell* could confidently declare a century and half before the *Marbury v. Madison* opinion that "[i]n every government there must be something fundamental, something like a *Magna Charta* which would be inalterable." And the colonists on the other side of the Atlantic found *Coke*'s ideas very attractive inasmuch as they synchronized with their view of what ought to be the law.

For that reason it is not surprising that during the revolutionary war the theoretical basis for judicial review was grounded in the constant appeals of the colonists for a higher law in order to support particular laws of the British Parliament or the King's provisions as being null and void. In this way, the North American system of judicial review "is nothing more than the absence of any special system"[29] and was closely linked with the colonial experience, and therefore prior to independence.

Coke's doctrine would be followed by the great dogmatic constructions of *Vattel*, *Burlamaqui* and *Pufendorf*, to mention but a few scholars. Their theories coincided with the less elegant, but equally fruitful *Coke*'s dicta. Namely, *Vattel*'s "The Constitution of the State, and the Duties and Rights of the Nation in this Respect"[30] is of particular interest in this regard.

According to *Vattel*, legislation was limited not only by the natural law but by any norm that the people would include in their constitution. For the Swiss theorist, respect for the constitution was as decisive as was respect of the law. "The constitution of a State and its laws are the foundation of public peace, the firm support of political authority, and the security for the liberty of the citizens. But this constitution is a mere dead letter, and the best laws are useless if they be not sacredly observed. It is therefore the duty of a Nation to be ever on the watch that the laws be

[27] Black 1987–1988, p. 694.
[28] Wood 1999, p. 794.
[29] Grant 1954, p. 189.
[30] Vattel 1964/1758, p. 17 et seqq.

equally respected, both by those who govern and by the people who are to be ruled by them." *Vattel* mints the idea that the written constitution is the basis, the ground of all public authority, and at the same time he makes clear the distinction between the fundamental law and ordinary laws. With regard to the question of legislative power in relation to the constitution, *Vattel* answers in astonishing modernity:

> The question arises whether their power extends to the fundamental laws, whether they (the legislative power) can change the constitution of the State. The principles we have laid down lead us to decide definitely that the authority of these legislators does not go that far, and that the fundamental laws must be sacred to them, unless they are expressly empowered by the nation to change them; for the constitution of a State should possess stability; and since the Nation established it in the first place, and afterwards confided the legislative power to certain persons, the fundamental laws are excepted from their authority. It is clear that the society had only in view to provide that the State should be furnished with laws enacted for special occasions, and with that object it gave to the legislators the power to repeal existing civil laws, and such public ones as were not fundamental, and to make new ones. Nothing leads us to think that it wished to subject the constitution itself to their will. In a word, it is from the constitution that the legislators derive their power; how, then, could they change it without destroying the source of their authority?[31]

Impeccably, the last reflection about the constitution's modification by the legislative is very conclusive since *Vattel* underlines that the constitution is a higher law, a superior law with regard to ordinary law and therefore it is a norm limitative of the legislative power's intervention. This idea would be further developed by *Alexander Hamilton*'s number LXXVIII of the *Federalist Papers*.

The transcendence of these theories would be enormous since, as *Plucknett* tells us,[32] it was due to the reception of *Vattel*'s theoretical discussions and also to the firm faith that "what my Lord Coke says in *Bonham's Case* is far from any extravagance" that we owe him the idea of the bold experiment of making a written constitution which should have judges and a court (the Supreme Court) for its guardians.

3 Approximation to the Figure of James Otis and to Some Other Personages of the Case

3.1 *James Otis* was born in 1725 at West Barnstable, in the spur of Massachusetts that bounded Cape Cod Bay. From 1739 to 1743 he attended Harvard College, and in 1748 he began his practice of law at Plymouth. That southern area of the province was his father's stamping-ground as a lawyer, and no doubt the influence of *Otis* senior helped him get started. He seems to have made reasonable progress, for as early as May 1751 the Superior Court on circuit in Bristol appointed him "attorney for the Lord the King at this Term, the Attorney General being assent".[33]

[31] Vattel 1964/1758, p. 19.

[32] Plucknett 1926–1927, p. 70.

[33] Smith 1978, p. 312 et seq.

In 1756 *Otis* was made a justice of the peace for Suffolk County, but this was largely an honorific mark of social advance.

In 1757 *Thomas Pownall* was appointed to the governorship of the province. The good relations between *Otis* and *Pownall* possibly meant nothing so much as a shared interest in the classics. His early taste for the genre had never left *Otis*. As late as 1760 he published *The Rudiments of Latin Prosody with a Dissertation on Letters and the Principles of Harmony in Poetic and Prosaic Composition.* A century after, *Tyler* considered the work as "a book which shows that its author's natural aptitude for eloquence, oral and written, had been developed in connection with the most careful technical study of details. No one would guess ... that it was written by perhaps the busiest lawyer in New England."[34]

A short time before ceasing to practise law, in the fall of 1760, *Pownall* endorsed *Otis* for acting Advocate General. After *Pownall*'s demission, *Otis* still performed as Advocate General in the period of Governor *Hutchinson*'s caretaker administration, until Governor *Bernard* arrived on the scene. At first, there was no antipathy between the two men since *Otis* was not yet in politics. In 1761, he had swung into opposition against the governor, and the custom house, as *Smith* writes, was in the thick of the roughest common law assault the Vice-Admiralty Court had undergone in thirty years. In the elections of May 1761, the previously apolitical government lawyer had become one of the representatives for Boston in the House of Representatives and leader of an incipient anti-court party.

It is not exactly known when *Coke* resigned as Advocate General, but it can hardly have been later than the 24th of December 1760, for that day he was spokesman for the petition to the Assembly against lawful fees in the Vice-Admiralty Court. *Otis* was already situated in open conflict as opposed to the Vice-Admiralty Court. Relating how he had been asked to support the writ of assistance, the abstract shows *Otis* going on to speak of his resignation as acting Advocate General:

> I was solicited to argue this cause as Advocate-General, and because I would not, I have been charged with a desertion of my office; to this charge I can give a very sufficient answer, I renounced that office, and I argue this cause from the same principle; and I argue it with the greater pleasure as it is in favour of British liberty ...[35]

These words convey the impression that it had been on account of the writ of assistance that he quit; even that he quit specifically in order to argue against it. If this was true, it would enhance even more the historical importance of the writs of assistance controversy, for when *Otis* moved out of the establishment circle and into opposition, a force of unique impact was loosed upon the pre-revolutionary American scene. But if *Otis* had sacrificed his job solely because he objected to arguing for the writ of assistance, one wonders why he did not say so more clearly and positively. The proposition is that *Otis*'s resignation was precipitated by hostile influences bearing down from on high.

---

[34] Tyler 1897, p. 37; cited by Smith 1978, p. 314.
[35] Smith 1978, p. 323.

3.2 It is worth mentioning something about *Hutchinson*, a very outstanding personage in the case and also in the history of Massachusetts. *Hutchinson* was destined to be the last civilian governor of the province of Massachusetts-Bay. Born in 1711, after his graduation from Harvard College in 1727 he spent several years exclusively in the family merchant business. His career as a public man appears to have begun in 1737, when he became a selectman of the town of Boston. Soon afterward he was elected to the province's House of Representatives. In 1740 *Hutchinson* went to England to argue the cause of Massachusetts in a boundary squabble with New Hampshire. In 1742 he was back in America and again in the House of Representatives, of which he was soon to be speaker. In 1749 he was elected, by the House itself, to the other branch of the General Court, the Council. Like the House of Representatives, the Council was a legislative branch of the General Court, the overall organ of government under the Massachusetts province charter; but it also did duty as the consultative body to whom the Governor looked for advice and consent in matters of executive action. In 1752, *Hutchinson* became a judge.

An important assignment for our personage was his appointment as one of the Massachusetts representatives at the Albany conference in 1754: the plan for a colonial union produced at that abortive gathering owed much to the work of *Hutchinson*.

At the end of his life *Hutchinson* wrote an outstanding work, *The History of the Colony and Province of Massachusetts-Bay.*

The customs officer whom *Hutchinson* came upon at the warehouse was *Charles Paxton*. *Paxton* was also to have a considerable future in the events leading to the American Revolution, if only for his part in the appointment and the affairs of the ill-starred American board of customs commissioners under the Townshend legislation of 1767. According to *Sabine*,[36] "as far as individual men are concerned... Charles Townshend, in England, and Charles Paxton, in America, were among the most efficient in producing the Revolution". *Paxton* was born in New England in 1708. In his early twenties he was appointed marshal of the Vice-Admiralty Court at Boston. The responsibilities of the post – broadly, the execution of the court's decrees – involved *Paxton* naturally in the common law imbroglios that broke out between the court and the merchants around this time.

According to *Smith*,[37] *Paxton* went about his rewarding duties with such energy and resource that for an instant one might wonder whether Boston was not under visitation by the reincarnate spirit of *Edward Randolph*, its custom house tormentor of seventy years before. But *Paxton* was no *Randolph*. The architect of the customs regime in the colonies had been a man of considerable force of character. *Paxton* was above all a pussyfooter. To the world at large *Paxton* may have been "no man's friend"; but his relations with *Thomas Hutchinson* seem always to have been cordial. Indeed, in his account of the warehouse incident, *Hutchinson* referred to himself as a friend of *Paxton*.

[36] Sabine 1854, p. 154; cited by Smith 1978, p. 99.
[37] Smith 1978, p. 100 et seq.

4 The *Writ of Assistance* Case (1761)

In this case, *Coke*'s conviction reaches its zenith. As *Berger*[38] says, *Coke*'s statement became a rallying cry for Americans in 1761 when it was resoundingly invoked by *Otis*. *Schwartz* writes that the influence of *Coke* may be seen at all of the key stages in the development of the conflict between the Colonies and the mother country.[39] The *Writ of Assistance* case constitutes a historical milestone of the biggest transcendence in the revolutionary historical process that will ultimately culminate in the independence of the United States.

4.1 The Writ of Assistance's Institute

Under the common law, the judge-made jurisprudence that characterised the English legal system; the only things for which a legal search was available were for suspected stolen goods. If a legal search for anything else were to be recognized in the common law courts, it had to be legislated for in Parliament. Legislation for the legal search of smuggled goods in England was on the statute book when Parliament sought to duplicate the English customs regime in the colonies in 1696. Particularly in point were the two enactments of 1660 (*Act to prevent Frauds and Concealments of His Majesty's Customs*) and 1662 (*Act of Frauds*).

1660 appears to have been the first time that legislation for power of customs search was found necessary. With the Act of 1660 it would be legally possible to track down "any goods for which custom, subsidy or other duties" were "due or payable by virtue of the Act passed this Parliament", such goods having been "landed or conveyed away without due entry thereof first made, and the customer or collector, or his deputy agreed with". "Oath thereof" had to be made before the Lord Treasurer, a baron of the Exchequer, or the "Chief Magistrate of the ... place where the offence shall be committed, or the place next adjoining thereunto", who would issue out a warrant to any person or persons, thereby enabling him or them with the assistance of a sheriff, justice of peace or constable, to enter into any house in the day-time where such goods are suspected to be concealed, and in case of resistance to break open such houses, and to seize and secure the same goods; and all officers and ministers of justice are hereby required to be aiding and assisting thereunto.

It is worthwhile to observe in some detail how common law sentiment affected the shaping of the legislative provision that first made mention of a customs writ of assistance. This was Sect. 5 (2) of the Act of Frauds of 1662, which read as follows:

> And it shall be lawful to or for any Person or Persons, authorized by Writ of Assistance under the Seal of his Majesty's Court of Exchequer, to take a Constable, Headborough or other Public Officer inhabiting near unto the Place, and in the Day-time to enter, and go into

[38] Berger 1974, p. 25.
[39] Schwartz 1993, p. 5.

> any House, Shop, Cellar, Warehouse or Room, or other Place, and in Case of Resistance, to break open Doors, Chests, Trunks and other Package, there to seize, and from thence to bring, any Kind of Goods or Merchandize whatsoever, prohibited and uncustomed, and to put and secure the same in his Majesty's Storehouse, in the Port next to the Place where such Seizure shall be made.

Smith[40] emphasises that a right to use force was essential if a power of entry to search for smuggled goods were to serve its purpose effectively. Section 5 (2) therefore neutralised the prospect of judicial disallowance of force by specifically providing for force.

Particularly significant was the limitation of Sect. 5 (2) power of entry to daylight hours; in this limitation the influence of common law thinking is reflected. *Sir Matthew Hale* commented on the common law provisions for power of entry:

> It is fit that such warrants to search do express, that search be made in the day-time, and tho I will not say they are unlawful without such restriction, yet they are very inconvenient without it, for many times under pretence of searches made in the night robberies and burglaries have been committed, and at best it causes great disturbance.[41]

Furthermore, this provision made the writ of assistance possible not only for the uncustomed goods.

In the colonies the documents – variously called writs or warrants of assistance – were known long before the controversies, first in Massachusetts and later almost everywhere else by the middle of the eighteenth century. However, while Sect. 5 (2) of the Act of Frauds of 1662 may have fretted customs officers in America into trying to mock up something similar, the 1662 Act did not apply in America in those early years until the passage of the Act of Frauds of 1696.[42]

In American colonial history responsibility for enforcement of the acts of navigation and trade still lay to some degree with governors. For the most part powers and duties of enforcement were however vested in the customs organization, presided over by the board of customs commissioners in London. The writ of assistance signified a seizure and that interpretation stuck. Needless to say that in pre-revolutionary Massachusetts it was not in the provincial courts of common law that condemnation could be obtained; the juryman was as unhelpful as ever. No one, *Smith* reminds us,[43] knew better than *Edward Randolph* – an Englishman of some fame in early American history, first appointed collector of customs in the region of

---

[40] Smith 1978, p. 25.

[41] Smith 1978, p. 26.

[42] Section 6 of the *Act of Frauds* of 1696 reads as follows: "And for the more effectual preventing of Frauds, and regulating Abuses in the Plantation Trade in America, be it further enacted by the Authority aforesaid, That all Ships coming into, or going out of, any of the said Plantations, and lading or unlading any Goods or Commodities, whether the same be His Majesty's Ships of War, or Merchants Ships, and the Masters and Commanders thereof, and their Ladings, shall be subject and liable to the same Rules, Visitations, Searches, Penalties and Forfeitures, as to the entering, lading or discharging their respective Ships and Ladings, as Ships and their Ladings, and the Commanders and Masters of Ships, are subject and liable unto in this Kingdom, by virtue of an Act of Parliament made in the fourteenth Year of the Reign of King Charles the Second, intituled, *An Act for preventing Frauds, and regulating Abuses in His Majesty's Customs*".

[43] Smith 1978, p. 53.

New England (1676) and later promoted surveyor general of customs (1692) – the frustrations of a customs officer seeking condemnation of a seizure before an American jury. *Randolph* was entrusted with resolving this question. It seems that his idea was not for Vice-admiralty jurisdiction but for colonial courts of Exchequer. This formula was rejected. Thus, the condemnation jurisdiction that sustained the regime of seizure was in the Boston Court of vice-admiralty. This Court had its origin in the system of colonial Vice-Admiralty Courts inaugurated soon after the Act of Frauds of 1696, and was in trouble practically from the start. It quickly found an enemy in the courts of common law. With the establishment of a proper admiralty jurisdiction, the provincial common law courts stood to lose much of their ordinary marine business and they did not delay in making their displeasure felt.

In Massachusetts the merchants had the inveterate habit of having an arrogant disdain for the provided requirements of the customs and navigation's legislation. This proclivity was habitually known as smuggling. By the end of the 1750s it was commonplace for Boston newspapers to carry advertisements by the register of Vice-Admiralty Court about custom house seizures, either calling upon an unknown owner to put in a defence against condemnation proceedings, or telling of the condemnation of a seizure and offering the goods for sale.

4.2 The Facts of the Case

4.2.1 A concise description[44] demands a reminder that in 1759 the British ministry received dispatches from General Amherst, announcing the conquest of Montreal and the consequent annihilation of the French government in America. They immediately conceived the design, and passed a resolution subjecting the English colonies of these territories in the north to the unlimited authority of Parliament. This objective required the gathering of resources. With this view and intention they sent orders and instructions to the collector of the customs in Boston, *Charles Paxton*, to apply for the civil authority for writs of assistance, to enable the customs house officers to command all sheriffs and constables to help them break open houses, stores, shops, cellars, ships, bales, trunks, chests, casks, and packages of all sorts, in the search for goods, wares, and merchandise, which had been imported against the prohibitions or without paying the taxes imposed by certain acts of Parliament, called the Acts of Trade. For justification, it was alleged that the special search warrants had been ineffective.

Prior to the above-mentioned date, the Superior Court of Massachusetts had already granted several writs of this character. In March 1760, the Court granted two writs of assistance, one in Boston and another in Salem. Furthermore, after the death of *King George II* (25th October 1760), it was necessary to request the Superior Court of Massachusetts to grant some new writs of assistance in the name of *George III*, since the old writs ceased to be good six months after the death of

[44] For the facts cf. Grinnell 1917, p. 443 et seqq.

a monarch.[45] Although in March 1760 the granting of the two above-mentioned writs would not provoke a public refusal, ten months afterwards the situation was different and public dissent was massive and clamorous.

Under these circumstances, *Paxton* began his operations in Boston. For obvious reasons, he instructed his deputy collector in Salem, Mr. *Cockle*, to apply by petition to the Superior Court in November 1760 for writs of assistance. Chief Justice *Sewall* expressed great doubts of the legality of such a writ, and of the authority of the Court to grant it. After consultation the Court ordered the question be argued at the next February term (1761) in Boston.

In the meantime *Sewall* died, and Lieutenant Governor *Hutchinson* was appointed Chief Justice of the Court. *Adams* writes[46] that everyone knew that this appointment was made for the purpose of deciding the question in favour of the Crown.

An alarm was spread far and wide, because this could not have been more incompatible with the conception of the colonists, since the writs infringed on their maxim that "a man's house is his castle". Thus, the merchants of Salem and Boston immediately applied to the advocate *Pratt*, who refused and to *Otis* and *Thatcher*, who offered to defend them. Great fees were offered, but *Otis*, and, according to *John Adams*, also *Thatcher*, would accept of none. "In such a cause", said *Otis*, "I despise all fees."

4.2.2 The hearing began in February 1761. *Hutchinson*, in his *History of Massachusetts-Bay,* describing the progress of the hearing before himself and his fellow judges, tells of an objection to writs of assistance that were "of the nature of general warrants". The existence of precedents for writs of this kind was conceded, "but it was affirmed, without proof, that the late practice in England was otherwise, and that such writs issued upon special information only". To this there was appended a footnote: "The authority was a London magazine".[47] As *Smith* writes,[48] if *Hutchinson* had made this footnote a little more communicative, the illumination it affords to the origins of the *Writs of Assistance* case would have shone forth long ago. The reference was not to some unidentified periodical from London but to a quarterly publication carrying topical and general interest, *The London Magazine.* Particularly in point was an article in the issue of March 1760.

This article was concerned with an act that had recently been passed at Westminster "for the more effective prevention of the fraudulent importation of cambrics and French lawns". In the words of the act, cambrics and French lawns which had been improperly brought into Great Britain "shall be forfeited, and shall be liable to be searched for and seized in like manner as other prohibited and uncustomed goods are ...". When this legislation was still going through Parliament, the article re-

[45] McLaughlin 1935, p. 25.
[46] Grinnell 1917, p. 445.
[47] The *London Magazine* article was copied in full in the *Boston Evening-Post* for 19 January 1761, in nice time for the public hearing on writs of assistance only four or five weeks ahead. But it would have been circulated privately long before that.
[48] Smith 1978, p. 132.

lated, merchants trading in draperies petitioned the House of Commons that "they might have leave to be heard by their counsel" in protest against the measures envisioned in the bill, notably with regard to search of premises.[49] The merchants got their hearings, but the bill went through anyway. Consisting as they did simply of a blanket adoption of pre-existing provisions for search and seizure of "prohibited and uncustomed goods", they struck the *London Magazine* writer as a subject for explanatory comment, including a brief disquisition upon the writ of assistance.

In the above-mentioned publication it was reported[50] that on the 21st May, several merchants, wholesale drapers, and traders in linens in the city of London, whose names were thereunto subscribed, presented a petition to the House, alleging:

> That by the Bill then depending, all persons who should have any cambrics or French lawns in their possession after the time to be therein limited, were subject to several penalties and forfeitures, all warehouses and dwelling-houses were made liable to search, and the persons accused, directed to be held to special bail without any previous accusation upon oath, and in case of any doubt with respect to the species or quality of the goods, or where the same were manufactured the proof was to lie upon the owner, and not upon the prosecutor; and that the petitioners conceived, several of the provisions in the said bill, if the same should be passed into a law, would be greatly detrimental to the petitioners and other traders in linens.

The publication argued in the following manner:

> It is very true, that by our laws of customs and excise, there are many houses and places in this kingdom which may be entered and searched by an officer whenever he pleases, and without any accusation upon oath, or so much as a suspicion upon oath; but then those houses or places are such as in obedience to some act of parliament, have been entered by the possessor, as a house or place where he made or kept such goods as were by that act subjected to a duty; for as to any other house or place he might be possessed of, no officer can enter or search it, without a writ of assistance from the Exchequer, or a warrant from the commissioners, or from a justice or justices of the peace.
>
> As to a writ of assistance from the Exchequer, in pursuance of the Act of the 13th and 14th of Charles II. cap. 11. I believe it never was granted without an information upon oath, that the person applying for it has reason to suspect that prohibited or uncustomed goods are concealed in the house or place which he desires a power to search; and as to a search warrant from the commissioners, or a justice or justices of the peace, we must, from the Act of the 10th of his late Majesty, cap. 10, and the Act of the 11th of the same reign, cap. 30, conclude that they ought, before granting such a warrant, to have such an information: nay, that information ought to set forth the informer's grounds of suspicion; and if those grounds appear to be groundless, no such warrant ought be granted; for if such a warrant should be granted without any reasonable or solid ground of suspicion, and no such goods should upon search be found, I am apt to suspect, that an action would lie against the grantors, and that the plaintiff, in that action would recover damages & costs.

It is no wonder that *Hutchinson* would make such a reference to the above-mentioned information because the underlying question in the judicial controversy was the lawfulness of the general search warrants.

---

[49] Smith 1978, p. 133.

[50] The extract of the *London Magazine* may be seen in Smith 1978, p. 537 et seqq.

4.2.3 *Jeremiah Gridley*, in name of the Crown, said everything that could be said in favour of *Cockle*'s petition, but it all depended on the answer to the question "if the Parliament of Great Britain is the sovereign legislature of all the British empire".[51]

Thatcher followed him on the other side, and argued with the softness of manners, the ingenuity and cool reasoning, which were remarkable in his amiable character.

But *Otis*, in the words of *Adams*,[52] was "a flame of fire", with a promptitude of classical allusions, a depth of research, a rapid summary of historical events and dates, a profusion of legal authorities, a prophetic glance of his eyes into futurity, and a torrent of impetuous eloquence, he buried away everything before him. At the sight of so extraordinary a plea, *Adams* would express his prediction that "American independence was then and there born".

4.2.4 *Adams* was present for the entire trial and joined *Hutchinson* in compiling his impressions about the development of the trial.[53] "That council chamber," wrote John Adams over half a century after the event "was as respectable an apartment as the House of Commons or the House of Lords in Great Britain ... In this chamber, round a great fire, were seated five Judges, with Lieutenant Governor *Hutchinson* at their head, as Chief Justice, all arrayed in their new, fresh, rich robes of scarlet English broadcloth; in their large cambric bands, and immense judicial wigs."[54] For it was in this chamber that *Otis* delivered his landmark attack in *Lechmere's Case* against general writs of assistance. It inspired *Adams* deeply, whose great ability soon conferred him an importance comparable to that one of his master. It is not surprising that *Adams* was one of the leaders of the opposition to the Stamp Act of 1765. Later he always remained belligerent in the face of those British actions that he esteemed to the detriment of the colonists' liberties. The second President of the United States frequently reiterated that the case was the true starting point of the movement towards independence. He stated that *Otis*'s plea "breathed into this nation the breath of life", adding that "then and there the child Independence was born." And as *Corwin* would add near a century and half after, "he might well have added that then and there American constitutional theory was born."[55] *Otis* went straight back to *Coke*, as the Supreme Court Justice *Gray* would additionally write in an 1865 comment: "His main reliance was the well-known statement of Lord Coke in *Bonham's Case*." In *Gray*'s words, *Otis* "denied that (Parliament) was the final arbiter of the justice and constitutionality of his own acts; and ... contended that the validity of statutes must be judged by the courts of justice; and

[51] Grinnell 1917, p. 445.
[52] Grinnell 1917, p. 446.
[53] Smith collects in an Appendix of his book (*Appendix* I) the Notes written by John Adams, under the following title: "John Adams's contemporaneous notes of the writs of assistance hearing in February 1761". Smith 1978, p. 543 et seqq. As "*Appendix* J" of the same book is collected which Smith letters as "John Adams's Abstract", p. 548 et seqq.
[54] Schwartz 1993, p. 5 et seq.
[55] Corwin 1910–1911, p. 106.

thus foreshadowed the principle of American constitutional law, that it is the duty of the judiciary to declare unconstitutional statutes void."[56]

4.3 The Brilliant Otis's Plea

4.3.1 The hard core of the problem that *Otis* faced in the case was the extent to which the concept of "constitution" could be conceived of as a limitation on the power of law-making bodies. *Otis* faced the question in an epoch in which the doctrine of legislative supremacy was still dominant at least in England, although such a doctrine scarcely reflected the real juridical thinking in the colonies. Nevertheless, the primacy between the English judicial organs of the legislative supremacy's doctrine and the composition of the Superior Court of Massachusetts explain why *Otis* would, by no surprise, lose the suit.

Concerning the intervention for the Crown by *Jeremiah Gridley*, *Adams* reveals[57] that *Gridley* mainly argued that the granting of the writs was legal because it was protected by statutory norms, adding immediately after: "And the power given in this Writ is no greater Infringement of our Liberty than the Method of collecting Taxes in this Province. – Every Body knows that the Subject has the Privilege of House only against his fellow Subjects, not vs. the King either in matters of Crime or fine."[58]

In his attack on the general search warrant, *Otis* acknowledged firstly the lawfulness of some kind of writs, particularly the special writs. His basic position is the following:

> I will proceed to the subject of the writ. In the first, may it please your Honours, I will admit, that writs of one kind, may be legal, that is, special writs, directed to special officers, and to search certain houses & c. especially set forth in the writ, may be granted by the Court of Exchequer at home, upon oath made before the Lord Treasurer by the person, who asks, that he suspects such goods to be concealed in those very places he desires to search. The Act of 14th Car. II. which Mr. Gridley mentions proves this. And in this light the writ appears like a warrant from a justice of the peace to search for stolen goods. Your Honours will find in the old book, concerning the office of a justice of peace, precedents of general warrants to search suspected houses. But in more modern books you will find only special warrants to search such and such houses especially named, in which the complainant has before sworn he suspects his goods are concealed; and you will find it adjudged that special warrants only are legal.[59]

Otis subsequently argued that the controversial writs were not in agreement with the mentioned precedents since they are of the nature of general writs, not special writs. For *Otis*, a form of writ of assistance "special" to the occasion would be acceptable. In his "History of Massachusetts-Bay" *Thomas Hutchinson* recorded:

---

[56] Schwartz 1993, p. 6.

[57] "John Adams's contemporaneous notes of the writs of assistance hearing in February 1761" in Smith 1978, p. 543 et seqq.; "John Adams's Abstract" in Smith 1978, p. 548 et seqq.

[58] Smith 1978, p. 545.

[59] Smith 1978, p. 331.

> It was objected to the writs, that they were of the nature of general warrants; that, although formerly it was the practice to issue general warrants to search for stolen goods, yet, for many years, this practice had been altered, and special warrants only were issued by justices of the peace, to search in places set forth in the warrants; that it was equally reasonable to alter these writs, to which there would be no objection, if the place where the search was to be made should be specifically mentioned, and information given upon oath. The form of a writ of assistance was, it is true, to be found in some registers, which was general, but it was affirmed, without proof, that the late practice in England was otherwise, and that such writs issued upon special information only.[60]

The Bostonian advocate emphasised the argument that only special warrants are legal. It is significant that *Otis* would be well-disposed toward the acceptance of the questioned writs of assistance in case of their transformation into special warrants. As to the unlawfulness of a general warrant, *Adams*'s *Notes* contain the following:

> This Writ is against the fundamental Principles of Law. – The Privilege of the House. A Man, who is quiet, is as secure in his House, as a Prince in his Castle – notwithstanding all his Debts, & civil processes of any Kind. – But for flagrant crimes, and in Cases of great public Necessity, the Privilege may be (encroached?) on. – For Felonies an officer may break, upon Process, and oath. – i. e. by a Special Warrant to search such a House, (susp.) sworn to be suspected, and good Grounds of suspicion appearing.[61]

According to *Otis*, in the first place, the writ is universal, being directed "to all and singular justices, sheriffs, constables and all other officers and subjects &c." i. e. to every subject in the king's dominions; everyone with this writ may be a tyrant. In the next place, it is perpetual; there is no return, a man is accountable to no person for his doings, every man reigns secure in his petty tyranny, and spreads terror and desolation around him. In the third place, a person with this writ, in the daytime may enter all houses, shops, etc. at will, and command all to assist. As *Smith*[62] reminds us, the source for this was the Superior Court's 1755-type writ, which spoke of the customs officer and his men searching "at his or their will" and "in the day time". But the accentuation is odd. That the power of entry and search with writ of assistance was available only in the daytime and not round the clock was a point in its favour, one would have thought. For that reason, *Otis* would have done better to confine his emphasis to "at will", for he was trying to point out that entry of houses and so forth with the general writ of assistance was entirely at the discretion and pleasure of the holder. Fourthly, by this not only deputies, etc. but even their menial servants are allowed to lord it over us. What is this but to have the curse of Canaan with a witness on us, to be the servant of servants, the most despicable of God's creation? Consequently, *Otis* would qualify the general search warrant as "the worst instrument of arbitrary power; the most destructive of English liberty and the fundamental principles of law that ever was found in an English law-book".[63]

---

[60] Smith 1978, p. 332.
[61] Smith 1978, p. 339, 544.
[62] Smith 1978, p. 343.
[63] Haines 1932, p. 59.

4.3.2 In his defence of the Bostonian merchants, a century and half after *Bonham's Case,* and in his attack against the general writs of assistance, *Otis* finally invoked *Coke*'s holding which he had become familiar with through the *Bacon* and *Viner* "Abridgments". In *Adams*'s summary of the crucial position of *Otis* it reads: "As to acts of Parliament. An act against the Constitution is void: an act against natural Equity is void: and if an act of Parliament should be made, in the very words of the petition, it would be void. The Executive Courts must pass such Acts into disuse".[64] The duty of the courts of ruling laws null and void, had as a base the consideration about which "the reason of the common law controls every law of Parliament", which was not the case but which *Coke* had already pointed out. In his reasoning he affirmed that "the writ is against the fundamental principles of law (...) the privilege of house".[65]

It fits that *Otis* did not use the actual words from *Bonham's Case.* Though clearly his "Reason of the Common Law to control an Act of Parliament" corresponds to *Coke*'s dictum, it is not quite the same. According to *Smith,*[66] it suggests a sharpening of focus by which something else from *Coke* is brought into view: his report of *Prohibitions del Roy,* in 1607. In any case, on *Otis*'s argument that a writ of assistance search should be preceded by a specific court determination, a general writ, which by its nature precluded such process, could be protested as making the customs officer *iudex in propria causa.*

But what was the "constitution" which an act of Parliament could not infringe? In the opinion of *Bailyn,*[67] *Otis*'s answers were ambiguous, and proved to be politically disastrous. The main authority for his statement in the writs case that an act of Parliament against the constitution was void was *Coke*, reinforced by later judges expounding the great Chief Justice's dictum. But according to *Thorne*, in that pronouncement *Coke* had not meant "that there were superior principles of right and justice which Acts of Parliament might not contravene".

Opposite to such a consideration, it is necessary to say that *Otis* doesn't seem to have been confined to *Coke*'s authority because there is no doubt that he seemed to have in mind also another dictum, one that *Lord Hobart* expressed in *Day v. Savadge:* "Even an act of Parliament made against natural equity, as to make a man judge in his own case, is void in itself."[68] The appearance of the canon of the natural equity that *Otis* links in an inextricable way with the immutable principles of reason and the justice, leaves no doubt about this last influence since *Hobart* converted the principle *nemo iudex in propria causa* in canon of the natural equity, and this, at

[64] Corwin 1928–1929, p. 149 et seqq., 365 et seqq.

[65] Letter from John Adams to William Tudor, dated March 29th, 1817, cf. Grinnell 1917, p. 446 et seq.

[66] Smith 1978, p. 359.

[67] Bailyn 1976, p. 176 et seq.

[68] Additionally, Otis mentioned another no less known jurisprudential holding, that of Lord Holt in the case *City of London v. Wood* (1702): "What my Lord Coke says in Dr. Bonham's case in his 8 Rep. is far from any extravagancy, for it is a very reasonable and true saying, that if an act of Parliament should ordain that the same person should be party and judge, or what is the same thing, judge in his own cause, it would be a void act of Parliament.".

the same time, is the standard through which to judge if a law of Parliament was respectful with those principles of law and justice which had so taken root in the common law and which personified this fundamental law.

When *Otis* argued that the general writs of assistance were contrary to the "fundamental principles of law", I think he wanted to express that the laws of Parliament were limited by the fundamental principles of British freedom[69], and he used the word "constitution" probably as used in Britain at the time. To him, the British constitution must have been something real and tangible, fairly direct and conclusive in its limitations. The logical conclusion from his statement is that an unconstitutional law is not necessarily a bad law, or an inappropriate law, or even a law running counter to endeared traditions; an unconstitutional law is not a law at all. From this optic, *Otis*'s argument is so impressive and so prophetic of the constitutional system which was to come that we are in danger of overestimating its actual effect or of thinking of him as the creator of a fundamental American doctrine.[70] We can well believe, however, that the doctrine was as precocious as it was prophetic, though it was by no means altogether without historical background. It was for the moment ahead of its time.

Nevertheless, scholars such as *Bowen*[71] critically stated that the English justice system would have been astonished at the uses to which *Bonham's Case* was put. Even if we admit that *Otis* and his followers went far beyond anything *Coke* had intended, *Otis* made something similar to *Coke*: "Let us now peruse our ancient authors, for out of the old fields must come the new corne."[72] That is precisely what Americans have done in using *Coke* as the foundation for the constitutional edifice which, starting with *Otis*'s argument, they have erected.

Nevertheless, there is no doubt about the great impact of *Otis*'s position. As *Berger* reminds us,[73] sound or not, *Coke*'s statement became a rallying cry for Americans in 1761 when it was resoundingly invoked by *Otis*. If an Act of Parliament had the effect claimed for it, it would be "against the Constitution" and therefore void, an argument that *Adams*, concurring with *Otis*, repeated in opposition to the Stamp Act. On the 12th of September, 1765, Governor *Hutchinson*, referring to the opposition to the Stamp Act, wrote as follows: "The prevailing reason at this time is, that the act of Parliament is against *Magna Charta*, and the natural rights of Englishmen, and therefore, according to Lord Coke, null and void"[74], in adding afterwards: "This, taken in the latitude the people are often enough disposed to take it, must be fatal to all government, and it seems to have determined great part of the colony to oppose the execution of the act with force."[75] And as regards to the doctrine of judicial review, *Nelson* reminds us that, although not without their ambiguities, the *Writ of Assistance* case appeared at least to some

[69] McLaughlin 1935, p. 26.
[70] McLaughlin 1935, p. 27.
[71] Bowen 1957.
[72] Schwartz 1993, p. 6.
[73] Berger 1974, p. 25.
[74] Corwin 1910–1911, p. 106.
[75] Plucknett 1926–1927, p. 63.

American lawyers in the 1780s as a clarion call for judicial review and a clear challenge to the then dominant doctrine of legislative supremacy.[76]

In the margin of the previous reflections, *Otis*'s argument in the *Writs of Assistance* case is also perhaps the main piece of evidence for the claim that *Bonham's Case* was a significant source of colonial thinking about judicial review and an important building block in its development. According to *Kramer*,[77] such a consideration contrasts with the following fact: while *Bonham's Case* makes an occasional appearance, its absence from the case law and literature of the 1770s and 1780s is striking. It is why *Kramer* relativizes the specific weight of *Coke*'s opinion: "So far as I could tell, there is little basis for believing that Coke's opinion had much of anything to do with the development of an argument for judicial review, whatever it later became the American judicial mythology." This is an appraisal that I don't share.

The fact that *Coke*'s dictum should be revived as described, provoked very significant adherences. In a letter to Justice *Cushing* in 1776, *Adams* wrote: "You have my hearty concurrence in telling the jury the nullity of acts of Parliament. I am determined to die of that opinion, let the *ius gladii* say what it will."[78] This seems to have been the prevailing opinion, when in 1779 Massachusetts framed what became the model for the various state constitutions. *Adams* should have an outstanding role close to *Jefferson* in the preparation of the more important documents and it is logical to suppose that at the basis of the American constitutional law he would try to establish the point of view of *Coke* as it had been implicitly seen in Boston by *Otis*. As *Elliott* tells us, in this memorable instrument is found the first embodiment of the conception of three co-ordinate departments of government. With the preconceived idea of judicial power, it was inevitable that the duty of construing and protecting the new constitution should fall to the courts; and this seems to have been the intent of the men who drafted the constitution.[79]

Cushing, Justice of the first United States Supreme Court, in 1776, addressed a jury in Massachusetts, urging them to ignore such a law of the British Parliament as contrary to the fundamental law and for that reason null and void. The *Otis* formulation would be brought up often in the course of the political and juridical pre-revolutionary discussions. In 1773, a Boston newspaper reproduced the famous dictum. Otherwise, the *Writ of Assistance* case created a state of opinion that would later have a concrete reflection in the Massachusetts Bill of Rights whose article XIX begins as follows: "Every person has a right to be secure from all unreasonable searches and seizures of his person, his houses, his papers, and all his possessions."[80]

---

[76] Nelson 2000, p. 36.
[77] Kramer 2001–2002, p. 31.
[78] Elliott 1890, p. 232.
[79] Elliott 1890, p. 232 et seq.
[80] The Massachusetts Constitution, 1780 may be seen in Chafee, Jr. 1963, p. 237 et seqq.

4.4 The Suspension of the Trial and the Posterior Court's Sentence (November, 1761)

Coming back to the development of the trial we must be made aware that after the plea of *Otis*, according to the version given by *Hutchinson* in his *History of Massachusetts-Bay,* some of the judges manifested well-founded doubts. "The court", tells us *Hutchinson*, "was convinced that a writ or warrant, to be issued only in cases where special information was given upon oath, would rarely, if ever, be applied for, as no informer would expose himself to the rage of the people." Otherwise, "the statute of the 14th Charles II authorised issuing writs of assistance from the court of Exchequer in England. The statutes of the 7th and 8th of William III required that aid to be given to the officers of the customs in the plantations, which was required by law to be given in England." "Some of the judges, notwithstanding, from a doubt whether such writs were still in use in England, seemed to favour the exception, and, if judgment had been given, it is uncertain on which side it would have been. The chief justice was, therefore, desired, by the first opportunity in his power, to obtain information of the practice in England, and judgment was suspended."[81] The impression next conveyed by the *History* is of *Hutchinson*'s perplexed colleagues asking him to send to England for what really was the practice there. This perspective is a little at odds with *Hutchinson*'s account in a private letter written October 1st, 1765:

> In the year 1761 application was made by the Officers of the customs to the superior court of which I was then chief justice for writs of assistance. Great opposition was made ... and the court seemed inclined to refuse to grant them but I prevailed with my brethren to continue the cause until the next term & in the meantime wrote to England & procured a copy of the writ & sufficient evidence to the practice of the Exchequer there.[82]

Hutchinson wrote a letter dated March 5th, 1761, to *William Bollan*, still nominally Advocate General in the Boston Vice-Admiralty Court, lately displaced absentee collector of customs at Salem and Marblehead and since 1746 resident in Great Britain as the Massachusetts agent. *Bollan* sent him a copy of the writ of assistance taken out of the Exchequer, with a note thereon, setting for the manner of its issuing. At the sight of the reply, the writ was undoubtedly still in use in contemporary England.

On November 12th, two days before the Superior Court went back to the *Writ of Assistance* case, several letters and accompanying papers from agent *Bollan* were considered in the Council and the House of Representatives. What these were about is not stated in the records; but it is not impossible that one of them was *Bollan*'s letter to *Hutchinson* on the English writ of assistance.

On November 14th, 1761 the Superior Court of Massachusetts "entr'd up Judgment according to the verdicts and then adjourned to Wednesday next". The *Boston Gazette* from November 23th wrote: "Wednesday last, a Hearing was had before the Hon. Superior Court ... upon a Petition of the Officers of the Customs for a Writ of

[81] Smith 1978, p. 387.
[82] Smith 1978, p. 386.

Assistance ...". The completion of the *Writ of Assistance* case seems to have been all there was for the court on November 18th. In his *History of Massachusetts-Bay, Hutchinson* is very laconic in the account of the decision: "The chief justice was ... desired ... to obtain information of the practice in England, and judgment was suspended. At the next term, it appeared that such writs issued from the Exchequer, of course, when applied for; and this was judged sufficient to warrant the like practice in the province".[83] *Otis* could be mistaken in his empirical appreciation but this didn't weaken its juridical argument.

According to *Quincy*'s summary of the hearing's development from November 18th, 1761[84], *Hutchinson* reminded the court that the custom house officers had frequently applied to the Governor for this writ, and have had it granted by him, and therefore, though he had no power to grant it, the argument of non-user had been removed. *Gridley* minimised the transcendence of the writs arguing that "this is properly a writ of assistants, no assistance; not to give the officers a great power, but as a check upon them. For by this they cannot enter into any house, without the presence of the sheriff or civil officer, who will always be supposed to have an eye over and be a check upon them." In contrast, *Otis* reaffirmed his position:

> Let a Warrant come from whence it will improperly, it is to be refused, and the higher the Power granting it, the more dangerous. The Exchequer itself was thought a Hardship in the first Constitution ... It is worthy Consideration whether this Writ was constitutional even in England; and I think it plainly appears it was not; much less here, since it was not there invented till after our Constitution and Settlement. Such a Writ is generally illegal.

The hearing finished with the unanimous decision of the judges that the writ might be granted and soon after the writ was effectively granted. The only argument specifically mentioned in the *Boston Gazette* from November 23rd affords confirmatory evidence of where the emphasis in the November debate lay: "that such Writs by Law issued from the Court of Exchequer at home; and that by an Act of this Province, the Superior Court is vested with the whole Power and Jurisdiction of the Exchequer; and from thence it was inferr'd, that the Superior Court might lawfully grant the Petition".[85]

It is unnecessary to mention the political dissatisfaction with the result of the *Writ of assistance case,* which found expression a few weeks later in the province legislature. On February 20th, 1762, the Council set down a bill for the concurrence of the House of Representatives "for the better enabling the Officers of his Majesty's Customs to carry the Acts of Trade in Execution". Far from "better enabling" customs officers, the bill was designed to promote the very sort of frustration urged for them by *Otis* a month before. The general writ of assistance recently affirmed and issued by the Superior Court would be displaced by a "Writ or Warrant of Assistance" good for the one sworn occasion only.

---

[83] Smith 1978, p. 395.

[84] "Report of the resumed writs of assistance hearing, 18 November 1761, by Josiah Quincy junior", reprinted in Smith 1978, p. 556 et seqq.

[85] Smith 1978, p. 402 et seq.

The *writs of assistance bill* did not pass into law; Governor *Bernard* vetoed it and declared the bill to have been "so plainly repugnant and contrary to the Laws of England ... that if I could overlook it, it is impossible it should escape the penetration of the Lords of Trade ..."[86] According to *Smith*,[87] there was more to his delay in killing the bill than his report to the Board of Trade could have respectably disclosed. His chronic money problems gave him a special interest in maximizing the efficiency of customs law enforcement. The wider the liberty of customs officers to search out seizures the greater the personal profit to the Governor, from his entitlement to one-third of the proceeds. Whether or not *Bernard* had had a hand in his friend *Cockle*'s application for a writ of assistance in October 1760, and to whatever extent his appointment of *Hutchinson* to the Superior Court had been aimed at a satisfactory decision on this, the writ of assistance at last affirmed by the Superior Court was rich in promise of gubernatorial gravy. A legislative bill to displace this invaluable instrument by something that rendered effective customs search impossible and extinguished *Bernard*'s rosy expectations of augmented income was doomed from the start.

References

Bailyn, B. (1976). *The Ideological Origins of the American Revolution* (13th edn.). Cambridge (Massachusetts): The Belknap Press of Harvard University Press.

Berger, R. (1974). *Congress v. the Supreme Court* (2nd edn.). Cambridge (Massachusetts): Harvard University Press.

Black, B. A. (1987–1988). An Astonishing Political Innovation: the Origins of Judicial Review. *University of Pittsburgh Law Review*, *49*, 691–697.

Boudin, L. B. (1928–1929). Lord Coke and the American Doctrine of Judicial Power. *New York University Law Review*, *6*, 223–246.

Bowen, C. D. (1957). *The Lion and the Throne. The Life and Times of Sir Edward Coke* (pp. 1552–1634). London: Hamilton.

Chafee, Z. Jr. (Ed.). (1963). *Documents on Fundamental Human Rights. The Anglo-American Tradition*. New York: Atheneum.

Cook, H. J. (2004). Against Common Right and Reason: The College of Physicians v. Dr. Thomas Bonham. In A. D. Boyer (Ed.), *Law, Liberty and Parliament. Selected Essays on the Writings of Sir Edward Coke* (pp. 127–149). Indianapolis: Liberty Fund.

Corwin, E. S. (1910–1911). The Establishment of Judicial Review (I). *Michigan Law Review*, *9*(4), 102–125.

Corwin, E. S. (1925). The Progress of Constitutional Theory between the Declaration of Independence and the Meeting of the Philadelphia Convention. *The American Historical Review*, *30*(3), 511–536.

Corwin, E. S. (1928–1929). The "Higher Law" Background of American Constitutional Law (I and II). *Harvard Law Review*, *42*(2 and 3), 149–185 and 365–409, respectively.

---

[86] Smith 1978, p. 426.
[87] Smith 1978, p. 427 et seq.

Elliott, C. B. (1890). The Legislatures and the Courts: the Power to Declare Statutes Unconstitutional. *Political Science Quarterly*, *5*(2), 224–258.

Ferguson, J. R. (1979). Reason in Madness: The Political Thought of James Otis. *The William and Mary Quarterly*, *36*(2), 194–214. 3rd Series

Fernández Segado, F. (2013). *La evolución de la justicia constitucional*. Madrid: Dykinson.

Goebel Jr., J. (1954). Ex Parte Clio (Book Review). *Columbia Law Review*, *54*, 450–483.

Grant, J. A. C. (1954). Judicial Control of Legislation. *The American Journal of Comparative Law*, *3*(2), 186–198.

Grey, T. C. (1977–1978). Origins of the Unwritten Constitution: Fundamental Law in American Revolutionary Thought. *Stanford Law Review*, *30*(5), 843–893.

Grinnell, F. W. (1917). The Constitutional History of the Supreme Judicial Court of Massachusetts from the Revolution to 1813 (chapter IV of "The Anti-Slavery Decisions of 1781 and 1783 and the History of the Duty of the Court in Regard to Unconstitutional Legislation"). *Massachusetts Law Quarterly*, *2*(5), 437–456.

Haines, C. G. (1932). *The American Doctrine of Judicial Supremacy* (2nd edn.). Berkeley: University of California Press.

Hall, K. (1985). *The Supreme Court and Judicial Review in American History. Bicentennial Essays on the Constitution*. Washington, D.C: American Historical Association.

Kramer, L. D. (2001–2002). We the Court (The Supreme Court 2000 Term. Foreword). *Harvard Law Review*, *115*(1), 5–169.

McGovney, D. O. (1944–1945). The British Origin of Judicial Review of Legislation. *University of Pennsylvania Law Review*, *93*(1), 1–49.

McLaughlin, A. C. (1935). *A Constitutional History of the United States*. New York, London: D. Appleton Century Company.

Michael, H. K. (1990–1991). The Role of Natural Law in Early American Constitutionalism: Did the Founders Contemplate Judicial Enforcement of "Unwritten" Individual Rights? *North Carolina Law Review*, *69*, 421–490.

Mullet, C. F. (1932). Coke and the American Revolution. *Economica*, *38*, 457–471.

Nelson, W. E. (2000). *Marbury v. Madison. The Origins and Legacy of Judicial Review*. Lawrence: University Press of Kansas.

Nelson, W. E. (2002). Marbury v. Madison and the Establishment of Judicial Autonomy. *Journal of Supreme Court History*, *27*(3), 240–256.

Plucknett, T. F. T. (1926–1927). Bonham's Case and Judicial Review. *Harvard Law Review*, *40*, 30–70.

Schwartz, B. (1993). *A History of the Supreme Court*. New York, Oxford: OUP.

Sheppard, S. (Ed.). (2003). *The Selected Writings and Speeches of Sir Edward Coke*. Indianapolis (Indiana): Liberty Fund.

Sherry, S. (1992–1993). Natural Law in the States. *University of Cincinnati Law Review*, *61*, 171–222.

Smith, G. P. I. I. (1966). Dr. Bonham's Case and the Modern Significance of Lord Coke's Influence. *University of Washington Law Review*, *41*, 297–314.

Smith, M. H. (1978). *The Writs of Assistance Case*. Berkeley, Los Angeles, London: University of California Press.

Thorne, S. E. (1938). Dr. Bonham's Case. *Law Quarterly Review*, *54*, 543–542.

De Vattel, E. (1964). *The Law of Nations or the Principles of Natural Law Applied to the Conduct and to the Affairs of Nations and of Sovereigns*. New York, London: Oceana Publication Inc., Wildy & Sons Ltd. translation of the edition of 1758 by Charles G. Fenwick; reprinted

Wood, G. S. (1999). The Origins of Judicial Review Revisited, or How the Marshall Court Made More out of Less. *Washington and Lee Law Review*, *56*, 787–817.

Yale, D. E. C. (1974). Iudex in propria causa: An Historical Excursus. *The Cambridge Law Journal*, *33*, 80–96.

European Essentials: A Contribution to Contemporary Constitutional Culture

A research proposal, revisited

Pedro Cruz Villalón

Back in 2007, I engaged in a research proposal as part of an eventually unsuccessful application for a post in a European academic institution. It bore the title "European Essentials: A contribution to contemporary constitutional culture". Years later, having been asked to contribute to the present collective volume in honour of *Albrecht Weber* under the general heading "Common European Legal Thinking", my thoughts soon went back to those few pages, as they could be viewed as a plausible exercise in common legal thinking at European scale.

As I managed to retrieve the text from my files I had a mixture of impressions: Its content appeared to me to be at the same time both old and new. On the one hand, the basic underlying idea of a normative layer of exceptional resistance, under whatever circumstances, to partial derogations of the Constitution appeared alive as ever. On the other hand, *the name* itself could be questioned: "Essentials" might not be the proper, indeed the most adequate, word any more. Instead, another word, that of "identity", or better still "identities", could aspire to better convey that same idea. Worse still: How did I manage to speak about the subject – apart from an occasional appearance – while letting the word "identity" show up hardly at all? The text might already be old from the very beginning ... But I think it is time to let it – apart from small alterations[1] – speak for itself:

* * *

1 Foundations of the European Constitutional Culture

It should be readily accepted that Comparative Public Law somehow alters its nature when its object comes to be what it is being called the "European constitutional space" (*R. Bieber*[2]). This is clearly so when the space alluded to is that of the

The opinions expressed herein are strictly personal to the author.

[1] A short number of footnotes have been added.
[2] Bieber and Widmer 1995.

H.-J. Blanke et al. (eds.), *Common European Legal Thinking*,
DOI 10.1007/978-3-319-19300-7_2

European Union, rather less so in the case of the Council of Europe (European Convention of Human Rights). Particularly in the first case we are confronted with a well-known plurality (multilevel) of legal orders, reciprocally conditioned by means of a set of substantive and procedural mechanisms (*I. Pernice*[3]). The outcome is a combination of basic coincidences and singular identities (*A. v. Bogdandy*[4]), be it national or European in the narrow sense.

The phenomenon doesn't lack antecedents in different federation processes of the past,[5] which nonetheless have only a limited value for the contemporary process of European integration. It is debatable whether the term "Comparative Law" is still valid in the European scene, or whether a more suitable one should be found (in the way of "integrative" law, or something of the sort). Whatever the case, it seems undisputed the emergence of a *ius publicum europaeum*[6] in which "comparison" still has a decisive role to play.[7] Public Law concepts or notions may certainly have *different* meanings in the legal orders of the different European states, but there is a fast growing probability that they have the *same*, or very similar meaning in most of them (*J. Ziller*[8]).

In this context the research proposal opts for the category "constitutional culture" (*P. Häberle*[9]), in preference to other related categories, such as the above-mentioned "constitutional space", as well as the more familiar "acquis", "patrimonio" (*A. Pizzorusso*[10]) or even "common traditions". The notion of "constitutional culture" offers the advantage of emphasizing the dynamic dimension of the process, more intensely so than the more neutral "space" or the seemingly more established notions of acquis, patrimonio, or traditions. "Constitutional culture", on the other hand, demands interdisciplinarity more compellingly than other notions. Up to a certain degree, "constitutional culture" smoothes "the Channel divide" in Public Law[11]. The research proposal acknowledges the viability of a long-term research programme centred on the notion "European constitutional culture".

The reference to "Foundations" ("Grundlagen") finally may aptly identify the level where the inquiry ("visualisation") on this European constitutional culture is needed. The term itself points in the direction of abstraction. A research project centred on the notion "European constitutional culture" immediately calls for a reference to the term "foundations". The project obviously does not pretend to engage in very specific questions right away. Rather, the subject matter of the research proposal ("European essentials") should fit in this "foundations" level.

---

[3] Pernice 1999, p. 703.
[4] Bogdandy 2003, p. 156.
[5] Elleser 1928; Reißfelder 1959; Pleines 1973.
[6] von Bogdandy, Cruz Villalón and Huber 2007.
[7] The hundreds of "notes de recherche", internal comparative studies undertaken within the ECJ, bear witness to it.
[8] Ziller 2005, p. 452.
[9] Häberle 1994.
[10] Pizzorusso 2002.
[11] Loughlin 2003; Loughlin 2010.

2 "Essentials": An *Essential* Component of Contemporary Constitutional Culture

Throughout its bicentennial history and mainly on the occasion of responding to different challenges, (written) Constitutions have come to self-recognise a "core" in their content – "essentials" – aspiring to enhanced stability, and usually also to a higher form of legitimacy or social consensus.

In order not to get lost in a jungle of circumstances, I will strictly confine myself to what are arguably the three most illustrious challenges producing this effect that have been known up to the present: emergency situations, constitutional changes and integrations processes, it should be added, by order of appearance. Each of these challenges has sooner or later prompted the Constitutions to allow for the introduction in their content of the adequate provisions. But the ensuing constitutional provisions are always self-contained, in no way related to each other, since they tackle quite heterogeneous challenges.

Nonetheless they have something in common: all three of them tend to affect the empire of the Constitution and, at the same time, all of them may define a "no go zone", that is, an at all events preserved core or set of constitutional "essentials", placed beyond the reach of these situations. And all three set up an extraordinary type of power: The emergency power(s), the amending power, the "integration power".

It is not at all the case that all three challenges are to be placed at the same or even at a similar level. As such "challenges", they are quite distinct in themselves, the first having almost inevitably negative connotations, in sharp contrast with the other two. The only thing that is relevant to the purpose of the project is that all three may indirectly appear as *purveyors* of constitutional "essentials". They all frequently make explicit what is to be considered unaffected by these processes: What is not to be affected by emergency powers, what is not to be within reach of the amending power, what is not to be included in the integration process. And, in doing so, all of them contribute together, in each given constitutional order, to give expression to *the core* of the Constitution.

It cannot be said that, at the moment, there exists a ready at hand term to identify the phenomenon, which undoubtedly adds up to the somewhat obscure title heading this research proposal. There is good reason to emphasise the tentative character of the term (taken from a dictum by President *Herzog* when recapitulating on the European Convention 1999–2000)[12]. Other expressions could convey the same idea in other languages, such as "Verfassungskern" (*P. Pernthaler*[13]); they may even be more telling, but they fail to transmit their formulation through a plurality of usually key notions, as arguably essential components in themselves of contemporary constitutional culture. But one should be forewarned against the notion that these "essentials" belong to a qualitative different dimension, in terms of suprapositivity

[12] Herzog 2001, p. 44.

[13] Pernthaler 1998.

or even the Law of Nature. The notion of "essentials" should thus rely on the comparative – relative – side: *higher* stability, *stronger* legitimacy, *superior* consensus.

This is not to say that this inner differentiation of the Constitution (constitutional asymmetry?) was to be wholly unknown up until the present. The phenomenon has always been there, from the outset of constitutionalism. Suffice it to mention the differentiation between "Declaration of Rights" and "Frame of Government", or between "Déclaration des Droits" and "Constitution" on either side of the Atlantic. From a perspective that today we might call "identitary", article 16 of the *Déclaration* of 26th August of 1789 also points to some essential components, but the example could be misleading (*G. Stourzh*[14]).

Two hundred years later, through a process of long duration, accelerated in modern times, the cases of constitutionally protected "essentials" multiply themselves, becoming more varied. Each and every one of these purveyors of "essentials" is sufficiently known. New should be the uniting of them under the same magnifying glass. What is new is – again – rather the plurality of purveyors, sources or channels through which one enters into this zone of enhanced constitutional resistance. It is the diversity of "generating instances" of "the essential" that allows, now arguably more than ever, to proceed through accumulation: Formulations of "essentials" become particularly abundant, so facilitating observation.

2.1 The oldest source of "essentials" is the case of constitutional provisions confronting emergency situations, singularly political instability. The liberty vs. security dilemma is as old as the Constitution itself. The need to temporally suspend a set of constitutional contents – in lieu of the entire Constitution – as a way of preserving the constitutional order as a whole has been argued since the beginning of the constitutional era. Well known is the long process through which the emergency provisions found their way into the Constitution, and so came to be constitutionally recognised. But the focus was traditionally oriented to what came to be identified as the temporally "suspended" spaces, not the preserved ones, even in these emergency situations. Be it as it may: most Constitutions define today, normally by default, spaces "emergency-proof". And international treaties on human rights (Art. 15 ECHR) occasionally allow for the States to suspend some of the rights therein declared, while excluding some of them from whatever suspension.

During the second half of the 20th century the recourse to declarations of emergency situations was to be seen as a constitutional relic, in open contrast to the period previous to World War II. Nevertheless, *September 11* and its aftermath have changed dramatically this state of things. Emergency legislation has recovered unexpected centre stage, sometimes affecting even the core of the Constitution. The occasional discussion on the legitimacy of torture even if restricted to uppermost, truly dramatic, exceptional situations, illustrates best the phenomenon.

2.2 The second indirect source of "essentials" in order of appearance is that of the material limits to the amending power. The process has again been a long one. To

[14] Stourzh 1987, p. 78; Stourzh 1976, p. 397.

begin with, only gradually did an amending power emerge as different from the ordinary legislative power. And apart from limitations *ratione temporis*, it was only in a much later moment that material limitations to the amending power appear. Then the true material limits to the amending power are the absolute ones, that is, the ones allowing for no change of the core of the Constitution under no circumstances whatsoever. The most conspicuous example is of course Art. 79.3 of the German Basic Law, depicting the "eternal", or "perennial", Constitution. But there are other cases in which material limits to the amending power are only circumstantial, that is, requiring for instance exceptionally high majorities in Parliament, or other devices: they should also be considered. The flourishing of these material limits to the amending power may be occasionally explained by the perception of a "dark self" by some political communities, that is, the fear present in many polities to the "domestics devils".

2.3 The third and most recent purveyor of "essentials" is regional integration, and only sporadically "devolution" (Spain). European integration is indirectly providing an unprecedented complex, while bidirectional set of "essentials" ("reciprocal metaconstitutional provisions"[15]). The paradigmatic case is that of the pair formed by Art. 6.1 TEU and Art. 23 of the German Basic Law. In waiting is Art. 2 of the Treaty establishing a Constitution for Europe,[16] while many other State Constitutions have followed the German example identifying their own "essentials".

3 European Constitutional "Essentials"

There is no doubt that "essentials" – taken from these different sources – matter in the understanding of a given constitutional order. But, when applied to the European space, "essentials" matter particularly, both the "essentials" of the Union and that of the States. There is, arguably, a *practical* need to get acquainted with "essentials" in Europe, since they have come to represent one of the keystones of European integration. But there is also a more far-reaching need for a common position in Europe vis-à-vis emergency situations. And again a caveat should be pronounced: The search in this case is not primarily for *distinct* European "essentials", ready to be confronted with other regional identities; the search is ultimately intended as a contribution to present day – global – constitutional culture.

The proposed research should develop in the three following steps:

First Step: "The Law of Essentials". By such should be understood a) the ensemble of legal, normally constitutional provisions and, as the case may be, judicial decisions (Italy, France, Germany) signalling a "no go zone", be it by emergency, amending or integration powers (*substantive* law of essentials); and b) the norms providing for the safeguard of the core constitutional arrangements (*instrumental*

[15] See Cruz Villalón 2003 = Cruz Villalón 2004, p. 65.

[16] Art. 2 TEU.

law of essentials). Safeguards may be of *political* nature (Art. 7 TEU). But the key role should belong to the Judiciary: Are the courts in a position to review the respect of the outer limits of the emergency, the amending and the integration powers? Comparative work in this first step should allow us to know which one of the States have one of more descriptions of their constitutional core, and which State Constitutions, and how far, allow for the Judiciary to effectively protect it against the said powers.

Second step: "The Culture of Essentials". Here is where the notion of "constitutional culture" comes into play. But already the singular form "culture" is problematic. Anyway, "essentials" do not exist in some exterior world, out of time and space. Their necessary stability does not prevent them from change (new "essentials" may surge – death penalty, gender discrimination –, some may die out – primacy of the self-decided legal order). Space plays also a decisive role. And immediately: What is the role of the Legislative here, what that of the Judiciary in shaping the constitutional essentials? Essentials are not free of "interpretation", singularly judicial interpretation: In their written form, they are most frequently, though not always, expressed in abstract terms (rule of law, human dignity; but then again, on the other side, proscription of slavery, or of torture), terms that are most frequently "subject" to interpretation (N.B. Are there special conditions for the interpretation of essentials? How is proportionality supposed to behave here?)

Furthermore, the enhanced legitimacy and consensus around "essentials" should express itself in the form of enhanced support by the civil society: This is crucial in the case of States that broadly lack a "law of essentials" in the above-mentioned sense, but have nevertheless a solid notion of essentials (Great Britain, the Netherlands). Here some help from political scientists is direly needed.

Third and final step: "The Europe of Essentials". This is obviously the time for conclusions. What is the "faith" of Europe as a whole, constitutionally speaking? Or the "faiths", for that matter? How does it give expression to its deepest community convictions? How and how far is it ready to defend them? At the end, we should be in a position to offer, certainly not yet a general picture of the state of the constitutional culture in Europe, but hopefully a well-founded analysis of one of its crucial components.

* * *

Eight years after I wrote them, the previous pages present me, first, with an opportunity for reflection, almost a task of introspection: a reflection on my own way of approaching constitutional law, a reflection on how a project – even when it concerns categories that appear permanent – can "age" after a few years, a reflection, finally, on the possibility of "thinking in common" about constitutional law at European Union constitutional level. It is with a good deal of uncertainty about whether there is any point in this endeavour, and, I fear, in a rather disorganised (somewhat chaotic) manner, that I have decided to put down in writing a few of the thoughts that have occurred to me as a result of reading those pages. I only hope that they will be received kindly by their main intended recipient, *Albrecht Weber*, when tribute is paid to his academic career in which comparative law, in particular European comparative law, has played such an important role.[17]

The research I proposed at that time centred as a whole around an expression, "Constitutional Essentials", whose scope was far from clear.[18] Nor did the subtitle help to give it a meaning that could be transposed to or used in a precise manner in the sphere of constitutional law. In any event, that was how I always imagined it, in English. As in the case of another quite similar term, "fundamentals", that noun does not exist in the languages with which I am most familiar, but I can imagine it perfectly integrated into my language, imported thus from English.[19] At first sight, that type of wording, without even needing to be framed more accurately yet, appears to belong to the sphere of cultural sciences[20] – constitutional cultural sciences in this case – rather than to the sphere of positive law. And, of course, as the proposed research develops it will eventually lead to constitutional culture. However, the starting point, as I conceived it, is the sphere of positive law, the sphere of "written" constitutions, so to speak.

The purpose was to start from the empirical inquiry into the fact that, often enough, it is possible to identify in constitutional texts a difference in the effectiveness of their provisions depending on how they behaved in response to a variety of, so to speak, "specific" situations. As I shall explain below, those situations have very little in common. However, they do all share one feature: in all those situations, one witnesses a difference in the "behaviour" of the various provisions comprising a particular Constitution. It was thus possible to refer to the "added value" of certain components of a Constitution by comparison with "the rest" of its provisions.

The circumstances which could render operational that difference in the application of constitutional components might be hugely varied, as already known. Likewise, the specific consequences for the application or effectiveness of one or other provision might also be varied. What allowed me to conceive a common *name* to designate all those varied situations was the fact that it was possible to single out normative components with the capacity to assert their effectiveness in response to situations which, however, might affect the "normativity" of the rest.

In short, what mattered to me was that all those situations, governed by the Constitution in such terms that gave rise to "asymmetrical" situations in the effectiveness of the different constitutional provisions, made it possible to identify what I proposed categorising as "constitutional essentials", in other words, the ultimate foundation of the political community.

---

[17] To cite but a few works: Weber 1989; Weber 2007a; Weber 2007b; Weber 2010.

[18] As a more recent example of abundant recourse to the notion ("essential requirements", also "material core") in constitutional decision making, see Czech Constitutional Court, Pl. ÚS 27/09 (Decision of 10 September 2009) – *Constitutional Act on Shortening the Term of Office of the Chamber of Deputies*, English version: http://www.usoud.cz/en/decisions/?tx_ttnews%5Btt_news%5D=468&cHash=44785c32dd4c4d1466ba00318b1d7bd5

[19] To my knowledge it is possibly *Herm.-J. Blanke* who has incorporated the notion in 2002, preferring the Latin, "Essentialia einer europäischen Verfassungsurkunde": Blanke 2002.

[20] Häberle 1998.

As an operational category in constitutional law, "constitutional essentials" refers to certain components of the respective Constitution which are capable of demonstrating a greater capacity to assert their effectiveness in response to specific situations, by comparison with the rest of the constitution.

The fact that I started my academic career with a comparative historical study of one of the said situations – a study of the process of "constitutionalisation" states of emergency in the 19th century[21] – may have contributed to the outline of my proposal. The suspension of certain constitutional guarantees in emergency situations revealed, by default, the existence of other guarantees the application of which remains unaffected in an emergency situation. It is surely the Germans who have the most accurate term for denoting that difference in the application of constitutional provisions in response to emergency situations governed by the Constitution: "notstandsfeste Verfassung"; in other words, the Constitution resistant to the emergency situation.

Of course, the foregoing implies that it is not "the whole" of the Constitution ("l'empire de la Constitution") that is suspended in a state of emergency. In any event, the constitutional regulation of states of emergency can in itself serve as an illustration of how to implement the transition from the field of positive law to the field of constitutional culture. In fact, the choice to respond to emergency situations with a limited suspension of the Constitution also reveals those components of the Constitution which the political community is not prepared to withdraw even in such emergency situations. In other words, this type of regime may make it possible to identify that which constitutes the very legitimacy of the constitutional order; its *raison d'être*, ultimately.

Thus, the constitutional culture of the bourgeois liberal State of the 19th century was able to demonstrate clearly, in response to emergency situations, the "non-essential nature" of the public freedoms granted by the Constitution, compared with the foundations of bourgeois society (security, property). An analysis of the instruments which constitutional States use today to combat, in particular, the threat of terrorist attacks also reveals the difference between what, in terms of rights and freedoms, may be sacrificed in emergency situations and what should never be given up under any circumstances. The difference is that emergency situations today are much more complex in nature.

However, emergency situations are not the only conceivable situation in which it is possible to discover "asymmetrical" situations within a Constitution, as far as its resilience is concerned. The same pattern is repeated vis-à-vis the power to review the Constitution, at least in some constitutional systems. The Constitution may reveal a number of absolute limits on the possibilities for its amendment. Or it may provide for more than a single constitutional amendment procedure. In both cases, the motivation is the same: the identification of an "area" of the Constitution which is beyond the reach of the power of review or, at least, may be amended only by means of a procedure more laborious than normal. The political community (at least to the extent that it continues to be represented in the historical constituent

[21] Cruz Villalón 1980.

assembly) prohibits itself from withdrawing certain constitutional components. Or, alternatively, it enables a minority to block a constitutional amendment which might be desired by the majority. And that is all based on the strong belief that certain provisions of the Constitution must aspire to a higher degree of permanence.

The third and final field of research I proposed at the time is specifically European. It can be described simply as the field of the limits of European integration as it arises either directly from constitutional provisions or from constitutional case-law. This is without doubt the part most in need of updating. It is striking that one category, that of "identity", is virtually absent from my project of eight years ago, even though that category has acquired a degree of prominence for it to aspire to displace the notion of "essentials". This is not, of course, the time to present that category, even in the most elementary terms.[22] What is important in the notion of "identity", be it "national" or "constitutional", is that European integration makes it possible to identify within the Constitution the components over which the political community in question seeks to retain control, thereby excluding any situation of "heteronomy".

The limitation of the research to those three cases seems rather unsatisfactory to me today. Other cases could have been included already at the time but I shall refer only to one of them: the transnational or "cross-border" effectiveness of rights. As is well known, the notion is that there are certain essential components of rights and freedoms which a political community may not jeopardise, in particular, by agreeing to surrender a person to the authorities of another State, either through extradition or through another channel. The Spanish Constitutional Court (*Tribunal Constitucional*) coined a specific term – the "contenido absoluto" ("essence") of the fundamental right – to refer to those components, during my time as a member of that court.[23] Over the years, the Spanish Constitutional Court referred that issue to the Court of Justice of the EU, leading to the *Stefano Melloni* case[24].

Be that as it may, the first part of the proposal ("The Law of Essentials") seems to me now to be excessively focused on positive law; in short, on the written Constitution. Admittedly, the "unwritten" Constitution plays today a marginal role at European Union constitutional level, but not to the extent that that its presence was not envisaged in the identification of the essential components of a Constitution, by one means or another. At the same time, however, it is necessary to acknowledge that the line which, in theory, must separate "The Law of Essentials", as I have described it, from "The Culture of Essentials" is rather difficult to draw in the case of the unwritten Constitution. Lastly, in so far as the notion of "constitutional essentials" was intended to be used to identify certain components of the written Constitution, the inclusion of cases of unwritten constitutions could have been dysfunctional.

---

[22] Sáiz Arnáiz and Alcoberro Llivina 2013; de Boer 2013; Jovanovic 2013; Konstantinides 2010–2011, p. 195.

[23] Spanish Constitutional Court (Tribunal Constitucional), STC 91/2000 (Decision of 30 March 2000) – *Paviglianiti* (in Boletín Oficial del Estado núm. 107, de 4 de mayo de 2000, p. 99 et seqq.), https://www.boe.es/boe/dias/2000/05/04/pdfs/T00099-00118.pdf

[24] Case C-399/11, *Melloni* (ECJ 26 February 2013).

The challenge of defining a "culture of essentials" based on data collected through a comparative study of the *written* Constitutions of a large or small number of Member States of the European Union now seems to me to be more problematic than it did eight years ago. There can be no doubt that that data can be used to work extensively on the task of identifying those components having "enhanced legal force", which, in the main, are replicated in the different systems analysed, and those components appearing as minority components. Similarly, a diachronic analysis can be carried out, for example, of the generalisation of the abolition of the death penalty and its possible inclusion among the components endowed with enhanced legal force.

Of course, all this is in no way a trivial task. And, as a category applicable to *positive* constitutional law, I also think that that outcome would have been worth the effort. In short, it still is, to my knowledge, a research that has not been undertaken, at least in the form explained above. The difficulty arises, as I see it now, when I proposed a dual recourse to the category, both for the Constitution "as law" and for the Constitution "as culture".[25]

I find the reason, as I see it today, simple to explain. Fairly frequently, and almost unavoidably, written Constitutions are now chronically *lagging behind* the constitutional culture. When I say "constitutional culture", I am referring to the whole set of constitutional beliefs that a political community either shares or is in the process of discussing publicly. In any event, written Constitutions – whether they were drawn up a few or many years ago – today give a clearly insufficient picture of a constitutional culture (or even, by default, "lack of culture") which must confront issues and challenges that are often totally new.

The most significant challenges faced by political communities in this second decade of the 21st century (bioethics, big data, migration flows, to give just two or three examples) must be "thought about" in terms of constitutional culture. By this I mean that the foundations of our political societies will be those resulting from the way in which we face up to those phenomena. In that connection, I am of the view that the progress which our societies are capable of making in terms of "constitutional culture" need to go ahead and pave the way for constitutional – written – law. It is highly unlikely for a constitutional assembly to be so far-sighted as to include those components in a written Constitution in a sufficient manner, and furthermore to endow those components with a particular resilience to the specific situations described above.

Therefore, if this is to be the correct way of approaching the "culture of – constitutional – essentials" in today's world, and specifically in Europe, the difficulty and, arguably, the insufficient nature of its analysis from the *formalised* perspective which I used as a starting point are clear.

In short, the definition of constitutions as "living instruments", in the terms in which that notion is applied to the European Convention on Human Rights, should allow the *emerging* constitutional culture, in the terms indicated, to be incorporated into the normative Constitution. The greater legitimacy of constitutional compo-

[25] Cruz Villalón 2006, p. 525.

nents, their greater claim to enhanced resilience, is possibly no longer the result of formalised constitutional guarantees.

Finally, "The Europe of Essentials". I did not say so explicitly eight years ago but it is clear that, in this closing part, the European Union must be given priority over the Europe of the Council of Europe. I do not mean by this that the larger area covered by the State parties to the European Convention on Human Rights could not have been the focus of research of this kind. Today, however, it seems to me to be more urgent, as a question of common European legal thinking, to focus on the "constitutional essentials" of the European Union.

The connection between the previous part and this final part is undoubtedly the concept of "common constitutional traditions". Just as the European Union was "inspired" by the constitutional traditions of the Member States when it constructed the edifice of rights and freedoms within the Union, "constitutional essentials", as identified in the constitutions of the Member States, must also pave the way for the construction of this category at European Union level.

In that regard, it seems to me to be urgent to position ourselves at European Union level, rather than Council of Europe level, owing to the prominence which the concept of "identity", whether qualified as "national" or "constitutional", has been acquiring in the European Union over the eight years to which I am referring. And perhaps the most urgent need is for an enhanced reflection on "*European* identity".

As a constitutional category, I cannot hide my clear preference for the term "essentials" over the term "identity". The concept of "identity" always brings to the forefront an element of particularity, of singularity, which, to my mind, is to some extent unnecessary, and to some extent unsuitable. If it were possible to free "identity" from that burden of "particularity", I would have no difficulty at all in abandoning the concept of "essentials".

In setting out the "values" on which the Union "is founded" and declaring those values to be "common" to the Member States, it is clear that Art. 2 TEU is formulating, albeit in very general terms, what constitutes "the Europe of Essentials". As such, it might perhaps also be said that Art. 2 TEU is setting out a description of the identity of Europe. In that case, however, the following question arises: vis-à-vis what or whom must the identity of the Union be asserted: Vis-à-vis the Member States? Vis-à-vis States that are "only" members of the Council of Europe? Vis-à-vis *others*, as distinct from the aforementioned?

It would then be a matter of ascertaining whether the Union, for its part, needs to operate using the concept of identity for itself and for its own benefit, since that concept has become so firmly rooted in the very perception of the Member States of their position in relation to the Union. In other words, whether it makes sense that the Union, in return, should also appropriate the category of identity with the same aim; that is, as a way of defining its position and its autonomy in relation to the Member States.

In principle, that does not seem to me to be the correct response to the difficulties which the concept of identity may create, in so far as it refers to the Member States, in the constitutional architecture of the Union. In any event, I do not wish to stray from my main point: Whether it is possible or useful to include the category of "constitutional essentials" at Union level.

In that connection, for example, the Treaties provide for multiple procedures by which they may be amended, and the Court of Justice has had occasion to consider them.[26] I fear, however, that that route would involve little progress towards the objective in point. It makes more sense that the identification of "constitutional essentials" within the European Union should be "inspired" by the constitutional traditions common to the Member States.

And, quite possibly, not only in relation to the more or less empirical data provided by constitutional texts themselves, but also in relation to the public debate, at national level, concerning what I referred to above as the "*emerging* constitutional culture".

At the end of this brief commentary on a research proposal that is about to return to my archive, I am left with the conviction that a Constitution must be inextricably two things: It must be *law* and it must be *culture*: the conviction that the core of what constitutes us Europeans as political communities should materialise, as essentials, in both respects – that of constitutional law and that of constitutional culture. In these early days of 2015, in light of the sharpening of the concerns over the recurrent episodes of terrorism and of the resulting debate on the available constitutional options, a great deal of effort of reasoning in that regard does not seem to me to be necessary.

References

Bieber, R., & Widmer, P. (Eds.). (1995). *L'espace constitutionnel européen/Der europäische Verfassungsraum/The European constitutional area*. Zurich: Schulthess Juristische Medien.

Blanke, H.-J. (2002). Essentialia einer europäischen Verfassungsurkunde. *Thüringer Verwaltungsblätter*, 9/2002, 197–203, 224–232.

de Boer, N. (2013). *Constitutional identity, fundamental rights and the issue of divergent rights standards in the EU*. Utrecht: University of Utrecht.

von Bogdandy, A. (2003). *Europäische und nationale Identität: Integration durch Verfassungsrecht*. Veröffentlichungen der Vereinigung der Deutschen Staatsrechtslehrer, vol. 62, pp. 156–193). Berlin: De Gruyter.

von Bogdandy, A., Cruz Villalón, P., & Huber, P. H. (Eds.). (2007). *Handbuch Ius Publicum Europaeum* vol. 1. Heidelberg: C. F. Müller.

Cruz Villalón, P. (1980). *El estado de sitio y la Constitución. La constitucionalización de la protección extraordinaria del Estado (1789–1878)*. Madrid: Centro de Estudios Constitucionales.

Cruz Villalón, P. (2003). El papel de los Tribunales Constitucionales nacionales en el futuro constitucional de la Unión. In N. Colneric et al. (Ed.), *Une communauté de droit. Festschrift für Gil Carlos Rodríguez Iglesias* (pp. 271–282). Berlin: Berliner Wissenschafts-Verlag.

Cruz Villalón, P. (2004). *La Constitución inédita. Estudios ante la constitucionalización de Europa*. Madrid: Trotta.

[26] See in particular, Case C-370/12, *Pringle* (ECJ 27 November 2012), and the Opinion of AG Kokott of 26 October 2012 in that case.

Cruz Villalón, P. (2006). Constitución y cultura constitucional. In P. Cruz Villalón (Ed.), *La curiosidad del jurista persa y otros estudios sobre la Constitución* (2nd edn., pp. 525–534). Madrid: Centro de Estudios Políticos y Constitucionales.

Elleser, K. (1928). *Die Verfassungs-Autonomie der deutschen Länder und ihre Reichsrechtlichen Beschränkungen*. Mannheim: Peuvag druckerei-filiale.

Häberle, P. (1998). *Verfassungslehre als Kulturwissenschaft*. Berlin: Duncker & Humblot.

Häberle, P. (1994). *Europäische Rechtskultur. Versuch einer Annäherung in zwölf Schritten*. Baden-Baden: Nomos.

Häberle, P. (2009). *Europäische Verfassungslehre* (6th edn.). Baden-Baden: Nomos.

Herzog, R. (2001). Die Grundrechtscharta als Nukleus einer Europäischen Verfassung?. In Herbert-Quandt-Stiftung (Ed.), *Europas Verfassung – Eine Ordnung für die Zukunft der Union* Sinclair-Haus-Gespräche, (vol. 16, pp. 44–51). Bad Homburg: Herbert-Quandt-Stiftung. http://www.herbert-quandt-stiftung.de/files/publications/europas_verfassung_38_a66aad.pdf

Jovanovic, M. (2013). *Identity, political and human rights culture as prerequisites of constitutional democracy*. The Hague: Boom Eleven International.

Konstantinides, T. (2010–11). Constitutional identity as a shield and as a sword, *Cambridge Yearbook of European Legal Studies*, *13*, 195–218.

Loughlin, M. (2003). *The Idea of Public Law*. Oxford: OUP.

Loughlin, M. (2010). *Foundations of Public Law*. Oxford: OUP.

Pernice, I. (1999). Multilevel Constitutionalism and the Treaty of Amsterdam: European Constitution-making revisited. *CMLR*, *36*, 703–750.

Pernthaler, P. (1998). *Der Verfassungskern. Gesamtänderung und Durchbrechung der Verfassung im Lichte der Theorie, Rechtsprechung und europäischen Verfassungskultur*. Vienna: Manz.

Pizzorusso, A. (2002). *Il patrimonio costituzionale europeo*. Bologne: Il Mulino.

Pleines, W. (1973). *Homogenität in einer europäischen bundesstaatlichen Verfassung auf Grund der Erfahrungen mit der Homogenität in deutschen Bundesstaaten*. Kiel: University Publication.

Reißfelder, M. (1959). *Verfassungsautonomie und Verfassungshomogenität der deutschen Einzelstaaten in den Verfassungssystemen seit 1815*. Frankfurt/Main: University Publication.

Sáiz Arnáiz, A., & Alcoberro Llivina, C. (Eds.). (2013). *National constitutional identity and European integration*. Cambridge: Intersentia.

Stourzh, G. (1976). Die Konstitutionalisierung der Individualrechte. Zum 200. Jahrestag der "Declaration of Rights" von Virginia vom 12. Juni 1776. *JZ*, 31. Jahrg., Nr. 13, 397–402.

Stourzh, G. (1987). Die Begründung der Menschenrechte im englischen und amerikanischen Verfassungsdenken des 17. und 18. Jahrhunderts. In E.-W. Böckenförde, & R. Spaemann (Eds.), *Menschenrechte und Menschenwürde. Historische Voraussetzungen – säkulare Gestalt – christliches Verständnis* (pp. 78–90). Stuttgart: Klett Cotta.

Weber, A. (1989). *Richterliche Verfassungskontrolle in Lateinamerika, Spanien und Portugal*. Baden-Baden: Nomos.

Weber, A. (2007a). *Verfassungsgerichtsbarkeit in Mittel und Osteuropa*. Baden-Baden: Nomos.

Weber, A. (2007b). *Verfassungsgerichtsbarkeit in Westeuropa* (2nd edn.). Baden-Baden: Nomos.

Weber, A. (2010). *Europäische Verfassungsvergleichung*. Munich: C. H. Beck.

Ziller, J. (2005). National constitutional concepts in the new Constitution for Europe. *European Constitutional Law Review*, *1*(2), 247–271.

Common Legal Thinking in European Constitutionalism: Some Reflections

Rainer Arnold

1 Common Legal Thinking and the Integration Process

Common legal thinking in Europe is mainly a fruit of European integration. In general, legal thinking means the principal approaches to law which are reflected in the understanding of legal texts, which determine the value concepts and the balance of their conflicts, which influence the methodology of interpretation, which are relevant for the degree of acceptance of constitutional and international or supranational law in the interpretation of ordinary law, and which are the basis of the readiness to get inspired by conceptual solutions stemming from a different legal order and much more.

These principal approaches to law are significantly visible in jurisprudence but also in academic discussion and in political action, in particular in the processes of constitutional reforms and in basic ordinary legislation. It seems that jurisprudence, notably constitutional and "transnational" jurisprudence produced by national constitutional or supreme courts as well as by multinational regional courts, in Europe by the courts in Strasbourg and Luxembourg, is most important for the analysis of common legal thinking.

Constitutional law in a formal as well as in a functional sense is the main indicator of a common legal thinking. Functional constitutional law can also exist in multinational integration areas, in the form of international treaties, however with a substantially basic and therefore constitutional content. Common legal thinking in integration areas can therefore be sufficiently perceived only if the various layers of constitutional law are taken into consideration in a holistic view.[1]

Legal thinking in a national context, at least in the field of constitutional law, is to a great extent based on domestic traditions, rooted in the particular cultures and corresponding to the values of a society. In the era of regional integration and globalisation national systems have abandoned their isolation, voluntarily or in view of the indispensability of transnational cooperation, and "opened" their sovereignty

[1] Häberle 2011; Weber 2010, p. 1–4.

H.-J. Blanke et al. (eds.), *Common European Legal Thinking*,
DOI 10.1007/978-3-319-19300-7_3

relativising the exclusiveness of the national normative regime on their territories.[2] Common legal thinking develops with a significant intensity in integration areas where a *communitarisation* of politics, economy and other fields takes place. The more this process advances, the more law and legal thinking approximate. The model of such a far-reaching opening process is the supranational system of the European Union.

The EU as a regional integration area promotes common legal thinking to a high degree due to its supranational structure and its broad competence spectrum which potentially covers nearly all the fields related to a State. The harmonising mechanisms and processes within the Union are numerous: harmonisation or at least approximation of law, the orientation towards common values, the preliminary question system for uniform interpretation, the multinational decision process creating common law with participation of the various Member States, etc.

Legal thinking in this sense refers to the sphere of EU-related matters while the question of a *European* common legal thinking refers to a broader area which includes the purely national fields under the aspect of common national principles as well as the impact of the European Convention of Human Rights (ECHR).

Common principles based on a common value orientation can also be found on the universal level, in particular in the context of the Human Rights Covenants and of the Charter of the United Nations. These universal principles are recognised by the international community as a consequence of their outstanding importance for peaceful coexistence. Cooperation in the globalised world can only be assured if it is based on universal principles such as the respect of human rights or of the legal obligations resulting from international treaties and in particular from the UN Charter. If these principles are violated, globalised cooperation, namely in the economic field, is seriously hindered. Universal principles (as a fruit of common legal thinking) and international cooperation, which is also a sort of integration, albeit a loose one, are reciprocally connected.

It must be admitted that universal principles are much more exposed to relativism resulting from regional cultural diversity[3] than common regional principles in integration areas with a (relatively) coherent culture and tradition. However, divergences in legal thinking exist to a certain degree also in such consolidated areas.

2 The European Constitutional Area as a Basis of Common Legal Thinking

2.1 The European Constitutional Area: Definition

The identification of European legal thinking requires analysis of the European constitutional area as a whole. It seems that the various levels of constitutional law in Europe are interwoven and form a sort of normative and functional unit. This indi-

[2] German FCC, 2 BvL 52/71 (Order of 29 May 1974)–*Solange I* (in BVerfGE 37, 271 [280]).
[3] Arnold 2013.

cates a conceptual coherence of basic ideas in an institutionally connected system. The European constitutional area is not identical with the European Union but includes the ECHR. The EU forms the institutionalised integration area while the conceptual integration area, containing the basic values of constitutional law, fundamental and human rights as well as the rule of law, includes the signatories of the ECHR.

It is evident that the institutionalised integration area of the EU characterised by supranationality is more consolidated and therefore a field of stronger *communitarisation* of the legal orders composing it. The integration process also leads to common legal thinking in the infrastructure of the ordinary legislation where harmonisation even creates uniform law. The consequence is not only common but uniform legal thinking in these fields.

2.2 Vertical Impacts and Horizontal Influences in the European Constitutional Area

A distinction can be made between *vertical impacts* and *horizontal influences*[4]. Vertical impact means the normative obligation to follow a superior legal order. The EU Member States have to respect the EU law primacy, and even more, by a transfer of internal competences to the supranational institutions they have opened their formerly closed legal orders and accepted the existence of EU law together with national law on their territories.[5] The vertical normative impact of supranational on national law is evident.

A similar vertical impact can be stated for the relationship between the Council of Europe Member States, among them all the EU members, and the ECHR. The Convention, in its form an international treaty but in substance constitutional law, is of binding force for the signatories. Even if the mechanisms of this relationship are basically international, they are functionally supranational.

The influence of Member States' concepts on legal thinking and shaping of EU law is significant. The general principles of EU law in the basic constitutional fields of fundamental rights and rule of law elements are based on a common constitutional tradition, as Art. 6.3 TEU says. This corresponds to a long tradition in community law which dates back to the origins of formulating fundamental rights by the European judges.[6] The EU Charter of Fundamental Rights which has been established as an autonomous part of the EU primary law, has not abandoned this connection. The mentioned Art. 6.3 TEU amalgamates national, supranational and conventional concepts by making reference to both national and conventional guarantees. Furthermore, the EU functionally connects the EU guarantees with national constitutional jurisprudence as well as with the interpretation of the ECHR by the Strasbourg Court (Art. 52.3 and 4 EUCFR). It results from this normative pivot that

[4] Arnold 1997, p. 673–694.

[5] German FCC, 2 BvL 52/71 (Order of 29 May 1974)–*Solange I* (in BVerfGE 37, 271 [280]).

[6] Rideau 2010, p. 248–251.

the vertical impact of national legal thinking as expressed in national constitutional concepts exists to a considerable extent.

It can be seen that the ECHR exerts influence on EU law which has a normative basis in the mentioned article even before the EU's formal accession to the Convention. Once accomplished, the accession will create full subordination and a vertical normative impact of the ECHR on the EU legal order. However, the influence of national concepts on the interpretation of the ECHR is less manifest as the same influence with regard to EU law.

It should be mentioned in this context that the accession has been severely threatened by the Court of Justice's negative opinion of 18 December 2014. The Court puts forward the argument that "the specific characteristics and the autonomy of EU law" are not duly safeguarded by the accession agreement in particular because there is no mechanism foreseen to coordinate the concepts of articles 53 ECHR and 53 EUCFR which threatens "primacy, unity and effectiveness of the EU law".[7] Furthermore the principle of mutual trust seems to be endangered; accession could "upset the underlying balance of the EU and undermine the autonomy of EU law".[8] In addition, the advisory opinion mechanism foreseen by Additional Protocol No. 16 to the ECHR could, in the Court's opinion, be contrary to the obligation of the Member States' courts to make requests for preliminary rulings to the Court of Justice of the EU.[9] Furthermore, the Court fears that its monopoly of deciding on controversies enshrined by Art. 344 TFEU could be undermined.[10] Additional doubts have been formulated by the Court concerning the co-respondent mechanism as well as to the prior involvement procedure.[11]

The Court's opinion has aroused[12] and will arouse in the future vehement debates on the question whether these arguments are well founded. The review mechanism of the ECHR is based on the control under European standards of rights and respects also a certain margin of appreciation of the Council of Europe's Member States. This will also be applied to the European Union. It seems that a solution to the questions raised by the Court will take a long time so that harmonization of fundamental rights protection in Europe will not be attained in the near future.

A *horizontal mutual influence* takes place, to a certain extent, between the States themselves, with significant intensity between the EU members through the intermediation in particular of the supranational jurisprudence, and, with less intensity but also to a considerable degree, with and between the other Member States of the Council of Europe. This latter process of transfer takes place in particular through the common impact of the ECHR on the national legal orders, institutionally reinforced by the individual complaint before the ECtHR.

---

[7] Opinion 2/13, *Accession to the ECHR* (ECJ 18 December 2014) para 189.
[8] Opinion 2/13, *Accession to the ECHR* (ECJ 18 December 2014) para 191, 194.
[9] Opinion 2/13, *Accession to the ECHR* (ECJ 18 December 2014) para 196.
[10] Opinion 2/13, *Accession to the ECHR* (ECJ 18 December 2014) para 214.
[11] Opinion 2/13, *Accession to the ECHR* (ECJ 18 December 2014) para 258, summary.
[12] See for example Fuchs 2015 and Michl 2014.

A direct State-to-State transfer of concepts occurs mainly by a "judicial dialogue" [13]or, in the legislative process, by a sort of "political dialogue" in the sense that models which are adequately experienced in other countries are integrated into the own legal order. The horizontal judicial dialogue is based on a transfer of the persuasive authority of foreign jurisprudence, a voluntary process which requires the existence of legal similarities in a relatively homogeneous context of legal tradition. Homogeneity in an integration area, particularly in a supranational system, is conducive to a conceptual transfer by dialogue. The interpretation of undetermined notions as regularly used in constitutions in their basic provisions can be enriched by such horizontal dialogue.

On a pluri-national level interpretation impulses can also arise from transnational texts such as the ECHR. Horizontal and vertical transfer possibilities can compete; the vertical transfer will be preferred in general because of the binding character of the transnational text. The horizontal state-to-state approach is subsidiary to the vertical approach; i. e. the former only applies if the interpretation of value-oriented provisions is left to the national sphere or the transnational text does not cover the case in question.

In conclusion it can be said that legal thinking in a pluri-level integration system has a tendency to converge by vertical and horizontal conceptual transfers. This occurs on the basis of institutionalisation (vertical transfer) or of persuasion (horizontal transfer).

2.3 *Conceptual Transfer*

The development of common legal thinking is a process of intellectual integration with varying velocity. It is a reciprocal, inter-cultural process with the result of a conceptual Europeanisation.

Transfer is the keyword for the development of common legal thinking. It is a process which regularly takes place between different legal orders, of states or of internationally determined entities (as the supranational EU) or normative systems (as the ECHR). Transfer within a legal order, e. g. within a State, is possible, in particular within federal systems from one of the constituent parts of the Federation to the other. This type of "internal" transfer has to be distinguished from the regular type of "external" transfer which is relevant in our context.

A transfer can lead to a total or partial reception of a foreign concept or can have a guiding function with a directive influence on the own interpretation of norms or on the balancing of conflicting values, in particular fundamental rights. The main examples are indefinite terms in constitutional provisions, predominantly fundamental rights and rule of law elements. Constitutional argumentation is to some extent result-related; the important aspects of the transfer refer in particular to the

[13] Judicial dialogue takes place also between the ECtHR and the national constitutional courts, Blanke 2012, p. 186.

definition of the terms which are at the basis of the concept, determining its contents and limits as well as to the results of balancing, such as for example to the balancing between freedom and security or personality rights and public interest.

The process of transfer can be clearly analysed when national concepts are transferred to the EU legal order. As normative concepts, they remain part of the law to which they originally belong. As soon as the concepts are integrated into a different legal order, they have to be adapted to its structure and finalities, an adaptation which potentially entails changes in content and function. The transferred concept is destined to form a functional unit with the rest of the new legal order. This methodological approach has been clearly defined by the *Internationale Handelsgesellschaft* decision of the ECJ[14] for the recognition of unwritten general principles of community law as fundamental rights or rule of law guarantees. What the ECJ has expressed in this decision is a general rule for the integration of a transferred concept into another legal order.

The transfer is carried out by the instruments of the receiving order (in case of a judicial transfer by the decision of a court of this order, in case of a normative transfer by shaping the own legislation in accordance to this concept). It is not a normative but an intellectual transfer. The judicial or normative process of reception is effectuated by the institutions and with the means of the receiving order and results in the judicial application or the creation of own law.

Transfers can have a *genuine*, *primary* function, such as the interpretation of an own law concept according to the understanding of the parallel concept in a different legal order, or it can have a *secondary* function, a control or review function, if the interpretation of the own legal concept is to be controlled for its compatibility with guarantees established by a different legal order. An example for the former is the interpretation of national in accordance with supranational law, a widespread instrument for avoiding or diminishing conflicts between the two legal orders. An example for the latter is the impact of the ECHR on the interpretation of a national concept in a review case and the subsequent national interpretation in conformity with the Strasbourg solution. Common legal thinking in the sense of this second case also shows elements of the first category. It seems that the interpretation of German fundamental rights in the light of the Strasbourg jurisprudence as a general rule, developed by the German Federal Constitutional Court (FCC),[15] embodies an aspect of the primary as well as of the secondary transfer type: on the one hand, it responds to the control function of the ECtHR and expresses the readiness of national values as formulated by the German Basic Law (BL) to comply with the Convention. This is, according to the FCC, a consequence of the commitment to inviolable and inalienable human rights, as contained in Art. 1.2 BL[16], and of an internationalised concept of the rule of law. It includes a preventive reaction to a possible review by the Strasbourg Court.

---

[14] Case 11-70, *Internationale Handelsgesellschaft* (ECJ 17 December 1970) para 4.

[15] German FCC, 2 BvR 1481/04 (Order of 14 October 2004) para 62 et seq.–*Görgülü* (in BVerfGE 111, 307 [317]).

[16] Blanke 2012, p. 187, 190–191, also with reference to the Italian jurisprudence.

3 Common Tendencies in European Constitutional Law as a Reflection of Common Legal Thinking

There are four major tendencies in constitutional law in Europe: the individualisation, the constitutionalisation, the internationalisation and the (vertical and horizontal) separation of powers.[17] They find their expression mainly in jurisprudence and in constitutional reforms. Corresponding processes take place on various levels of constitutional law, i. e. the national, the supranational and the conventional level, and they are homogeneous, at least to a considerable degree. These developments are necessarily based on a common European constitutional thinking.

3.1 Individualisation on the National Level

One of the most striking tendencies is the growing importance of the individual not only in politics but also in law, especially in constitutional law.[18] The protection of the individual by fundamental rights is in the centre of modern constitutional law based on the idea of human dignity which is either expressly formulated in the Constitution or is an implicit element of it. In European constitutionalism human dignity has increasingly become a written fundamental guarantee with specific importance for the judiciary not only in Germany but also in Central and Eastern Europe[19]. It corresponds to this tendency that human dignity as a fundamental principle and right has been introduced into the EUCFR and placed, as in the German Basic Law, at the top of the fundamental rights list[20]. This seems to be an ideological signal for the "anthropocentric" character of modern constitutionalism and the indispensability of the complete and efficient protection of the individual's basic rights. Human dignity, notwithstanding the difficulties in defining it in all aspects, is the core value for the protection of the individual, thus being the basis of any other fundamental right. Without any doubt, dignity is also inherent in the ECHR even if the Convention text refers to it only indirectly by its Art. 3.

The protection of the individual by fundamental rights is a requirement of the common anthropocentric approach in European constitutionalism, and therefore an expression of common legal thinking. It is evident that the common conviction does not cover the details, but refers to the principle, i. e. the idea to protect the individual efficiently by constitutional guarantees, an idea which is linked to the respect of the person and therefore basically to human dignity.

---

[17] Arnold 2004, p. 733–751.

[18] The issue of substantive and functional efficiency of fundamental rights protection cannot be fully elaborated in this context due to its complexity. For a more detailed analysis see Arnold 2015, p. 3–10.

[19] Zakariás and Benke 2012, p. 44–67.

[20] See for an analysis of the European system of fundamental rights protection Blanke 2012, p. 157–232; Stern 2006, p. 169–184; with specific regard to the EUCFR see also Grabenwarter and Pabel, in Blanke and Mangiameli (2013), Art. 6 TEU, para 16–39.

It is common constitutional thinking in Europe that fundamental rights protection must achieve an optimal standard, both in substance and accessibility. All kinds of dangers, present or future, known or unknown, should be covered, a protection task which has to be fulfilled as far as possible by judicial interpretation. This task corresponds to the evolutionary, "living" character of the Constitution[21]. Furthermore, restrictions of fundamental rights, in particular from the legislator, must be prevented from becoming excessive. Proportionality, which in Europe has become a flexible, well operable instrument at the end,[22] even on a universal scale, and the guarantee of the essence of a fundamental right are mechanisms to satisfy the primordial principle of individual freedom.

3.2 Individualisation on the Supranational and Conventional Level

The same basic ideas and the same methodological orientation can be found on the supranational and conventional level. The principle of "effet utile" is well known through the jurisprudence of the European courts[23] and the judicial task to ensure a comprehensive coverage of the protection by interpretation is clearly recognised. The judicial approach to both the EUCFR and the ECHR, is dynamic and therefore takes account of the ongoing evolution. In particular, the recent jurisprudence on data protection is significant for this[24].

Furthermore, proportionality and the guarantee of the essence of fundamental rights are well implemented on these two levels. The express limits for restrictions of fundamental rights in Art. 52.1 EUCFR correspond to the current standards in European constitutionalism. These limits have already been formulated in the jurisprudence of the ECJ, notably in the *Hauer* case.[25] With regard to proportionality, the jurisprudence of the Strasbourg court has developed a detailed system for the balancing of conflicting values using formula such as "pressing social need", etc.[26]

3.3 Constitutionalisation: Common Legal Thinking in the New Rule of Law Concept

The rule of law is the core of constitutional law, a sort of constitutional *Grundnorm*. It corresponds to common legal thinking in Europe that the constitution is

[21] Berti 1990, p. 234 et seq.

[22] Institut Louis Favoreu 2010; Meyer-Ladewig 2012, p. 239–240.

[23] Potacs 2009, p. 465–487; Appl. No. 15318/89, *Loizidou v Turkey* (ECtHR 23 March 1995) para 72.

[24] Case C-131/12, *Google* (ECJ 13 May 2014) para 68 et seq., 98.; Case C-212/13, *František Ryneš* (ECJ 11 December 2014) para 28.

[25] Case 44/79, *Hauer* (ECJ 7 February 1973) para 23.

[26] Meyer-Ladewig 2006, Art. 8, para 42–43a.

recognised as the "supreme law of the land", the basic legal order of the State, with primacy over all branches of public power, including the legislator.[27] This new, substantive rule of law concept[28] embraces not only legality of executive and judicial action, the attributes of the original formal rule of law concept, but also *constitutionality*. It is value-oriented and fundamental rights are necessarily linked to it. Law is conceived as the instrument to achieve justice. The Constitution being the basis, legislation puts it into effect in detail. Public power shall not only be bound by the law (i. e. any law whatsoever, as it was meant under the former "formal" rule of law doctrine), but by constitutional law and legislation which is conform to it. This is how the rule of law encompasses a requirement of justice, not to mention that constitutional law consists of written norms and unwritten values and principles inherent in it.

The new approach has been clearly expressed by the French *Conseil Constitutionnel*: "La loi n'exprime la volonté générale que dans le respect de la Constitution"[29]; i. e. only legislation which conforms to the Constitution can be regarded as the expression of the will of the people pronounced by their representatives in Parliament. Primacy of the Constitution is accepted by common legal thinking in Europe.

In a significantly growing number of States primacy is safeguarded by constitutional courts. The development of constitutionalism since the second half of the 20th century demonstrates the triumph of the Austrian model of constitutional justice, the creation of constitutional courts, distinct from ordinary supreme courts, with the power to declare legislation unconstitutional in case of non-conformity with the Constitution. This is based on an advanced concept of rule of law the necessity or desirability of which seems to correspond with a widespread conviction in Europe. The emerging judicial review of compatibility of ordinary law with the Constitution is characteristic for the new democracies in Central and Eastern Europe, countries which all (with the exception of Estonia) have implemented the Austrian model of constitutional justice.[30] The review of legislation is its core element and of high importance for transformation. Also in more traditional systems in Europe, judicial review of legislation is increasing, sometimes, as in Scandinavian states, through the initiation of ordinary courts not willing to apply legislation which they qualify as unconstitutional. The new Finnish Constitution of 1999 gives, against a long-lasting tradition, the courts the competence not to apply legislation in case of "evident conflict" with the Constitution. The Swedish Instrument of Government permits a decentralised judicial review of legislation by its revised Art. 14 of Chap. 11, even if conflict with the Constitution is not evident. Norway has been carrying out such a review for a long time.[31] On the basis of an increasing common perception of how the primacy of the Constitution shall be put into effect,

---

[27] Tanchev 2013, p. 261–256.

[28] For the philosophical and historic foundations of Rule of Law, of "imperium legis" (p. 49) see Sellers 2014, p. 3–13 as well as Kirste 2014, p. 29–43.

[29] French Constitutional council, Decision n°85–197 DC (23 August 1985) para 27.

[30] Brunner 1993, p. 819–826; Luchterhand 2007, p. 259–356; Arnold 2003, p. 99–115; Arnold 2006, p. 1–21.

[31] Smith 2000, p. 11–13.

existing constitutional justice has been consolidated or enlarged (see France with the introduction of an *a posteriori* review of legislation[32], Belgium where the *Cour d'arbitrage* was converted into a constitutional court[33]) or even a constitutional court was created (as in Luxembourg[34]).

In the United Kingdom, the supreme constitutional dogma of sovereignty of Parliament[35] is the traditional theoretical barrier against the challenge of Westminster legislation by courts, but in the last decades this doctrine has been considerably weakened. The processes responsible for the beginning transformation of this extremely restrictive dogma are in particular: devolution with the establishment of parallel powers to Westminster Parliament[36], installation of the mechanisms of the Human Rights Act,[37] and *Factortame* jurisprudence[38]. It has to be noted that in the UK, in contrast to the continental constitutional systems, there is no written constitution in a single document, but functional constitutional law does exist and consists of legislation, jurisprudence and (not normatively binding) conventions. Parliamentary legislation is at the top of the internal normative hierarchy. Legislation with basic contents cannot be made unchangeable by successive legislation because, in view of the sovereignty doctrine, Parliament cannot bind its successor. Judicial review of legislation as it has developed on the continent is therefore not compatible with the UK doctrine.

Despite this exceptional situation, common legal thinking in Europe clearly adheres to the new concept of rule of law accepting the primacy of the Constitution over the legislator and promoting judicial review, preponderantly through particular constitutional courts in accordance with the Austrian model which has developed towards a "European" model.

Constitutional justice is not only taking place on the national level but also within the EU. Supranational legislation, as it is well known, is reviewed, on submission, by the Court of Justice of the EU. Primary law is "the basic constitutional charter", as the court formulated in an Opinion.[39] Secondary law has to conform to it, otherwise it could be declared void. National courts when applying EU secondary law and esteeming it incompatible with EU primary law have to initiate preliminary ruling proceedings according to Art. 267.2 lit. b TFEU. The modern concept of the rule of law is rooted in the supranational order and has been specified by the jurisprudence of the ECJ[40] under the influence of the constitutional tradition in the Member States. The connection between fundamental rights and the rule of law is clearly expressed by both the preamble of the EUCFR and the ECHR.

---

[32] Ardant and Mathieu 2010, p. 129–132; Fabbrini 2008, p. 1297–1312.

[33] Verdussen 2012.

[34] Kill 2005.

[35] Dicey 1967, p. 39–85.

[36] Deacon 2012.

[37] Kavanagh 2009.

[38] Jowell and Oliver 2011.

[39] Opinion 2/13, *Accession to the ECHR* (ECJ 18 December 2014). See also Balaguer 2012: "(pre)constitutional nature of the EU" (p. 258), "material constitutionalisation of the Union" (p. 267); more sceptic, D'Atena 2012, p. 12: "the existence of a 'constitution' in Europe was (and is) undeniable, despite the absence of a constitutional Charter".

[40] Pech 2009.

The ECHR has primordial importance for the evolution of the rule of law and its value-oriented dimension. It has evolved into a "constitutional instrument" and has established a "European public order"[41] and therefore essentially contributed to a common European rule of law thinking. It is manifest that its enforcement mechanism is characterised by international law and does not allow it to intervene directly into the internal sphere of the signatory States with annulment verdicts. However, in many signatory States (France, Art. 55 Const., Poland, Art. 91 Const., Slovenia, Art. 8 Const., Czech Republic, Art. 10 Const., etc.) the ECHR has primacy over ordinary legislation with the consequence that the national courts apply the conventional guarantees and not the contradicting national legislation. This is a sort of functional legislation review under the aspects of the European constitutional order of the Convention. This has a significant effect on the implementation of the rule of law which does not only mean the rule of national law but also of international law. It can also be stated that even in a traditional system where legislation review by constitutional justice has not or not fully accepted the primacy of the ECHR, international orders have propulsive force towards the judicial control of the legislator.

3.4 Internationalisation

The third basic tendency in European constitutionalism is *internationalisation*. Common legal thinking in the era of globalisation is rooted in the awareness that political and economic action is no longer predominantly nation-centred but embedded in the international community, which is reflected in the internal legal order in many ways. The modern state is an "open state" which is willing to cooperate with other subjects of public international law. Sovereignty is no longer a shield to defend the national sphere against the impacts from outside but has become a bridge to the global forum. *Transnationality* replaces nationality in more and more respects and promotes *integration* which is a step further towards institutionalised cooperation in varying intensity. The members of the EU have opened their statehood[42] to a far-reaching degree and established *supranationality*, a specific form of internationalisation.

3.4.1 International Law in the Internal Order

The national constitutional order reflects in many ways the need for adaptation to international law. The respect of general and specific international law is clearly expressed by the Constitutions. In a majority of countries international treaties prevail over ordinary legislation. In countries with a transformation system as in Germany,

[41] Appl. No. 15318/89, *Loizidou v. Turkey* (ECtHR 23 March 1995) para 70 et seqq.

[42] German FCC, 2 BvE 2/08, 2 BvE 5/08, 2 BvR 1010/08, 2 BvR 1022/08, 2 BvR 1259/08, 2 BvR 182/09 (Judgment of 30 June 2009) para 220, 225, 240, 340 – *Lissabon-Vertrag* (in BVerfGE 123, 267).

international treaties only have the rank of ordinary federal legislation (cf. Art. 59.2 BL). Interpretation in favour of international law helps to maintain primacy of the treaty over national law. This is particularly significant in the field of human and fundamental rights. According to constitutional jurisprudence German fundamental rights have to be interpreted in the light of the ECHR and the jurisprudence of the Strasbourg court.[43]

3.4.2 Supranationality and Constitutional Identity

The supranational character of EU law comprises three elements: the autonomy of the EU legal order established by a transfer of national competences, the direct effect of this law in the internal national order and finally the primacy of EU law over national law.[44]

The basis for a transfer of competences is enshrined in the Constitution itself which allows and fosters it. However, primacy over national constitutional law is, according to widespread legal thinking in the Member States, not without limits. Supranational law must not be incompatible with the national *constitutional identity*.[45] The core elements of the national constitutional order as an authentic expression of the fundamental legal culture of the society shall be kept untouched. This corresponds to an adequate understanding of what a union, a community, is and complies with the principle of "unity by diversity". The jurisprudence seems to define constitutional identity as the rights and principles which cannot be changed even by constitutional reform. This is at least the approach of the German and the Czech Constitutional Court (referring to Art. 9.2 Const.)[46]; similar limits can be found in the jurisprudence of other countries if they do not generally deny EU law primacy over national constitutional law, as in Poland[47] and Lithuania[48].

These limits are not contrary to the idea of inter- and supranationalisation but contribute to harmonising the national and multinational order and to establishing an adequate equilibrium between both. This is in line with the obligation of the EU and its institutions to respect the national identities of the Member States (Art. 4.2 TEU). The identity concept of the EU includes the national "fundamental

[43] German FCC, 2 BvR 1481/04 (Order of 14 October 2004) para 62 – *Görgülü* (in BVerfGE 111, 307), German FCC, 2 BvR 2365/09 (Judgment of 4 May 2011) para 86, 88 et seqq.– *Sicherungsverwahrung* ("preventive custody") (in BVerfGE 128, 326).

[44] Case 6/64, *Costa/E.N.E.L.* (ECJ 15 July 1964).

[45] German FCC, 2 BvE 2/08, 2 BvE 5/08, 2 BvR 1010/08, 2 BvR 1022/08, 2 BvR 1259/08, 2 BvR 182/09 (Judgment of 30 June 2009) para 216, 218 et seq., 228, 235, 240–242, 331 et seq., 336, 339 et seq., 364, 369 – *Lissabon-Vertrag* (in BVerfGE 123, 267). See also Blanke, in Blanke and Mangiameli (2013), Art. 4 TEU, para 18–34; 50–61 (national jurisprudence); 65–71 (position of the ECJ). For the development of a European identity see Lepsius 2006, p. 23 et seqq.

[46] Czech Constitutional Court, Pl.ÚS 19/08 (Decision of 26 November 2008) – *Lisbon*, para 59.

[47] Polish Constitutional Court, K 18/04 (Decision of 11 May 2005).

[48] Lithuanian Constitutional Court, 17/02-24/02-06/03-22/04 (14 March 2006); Lithuanian Constitutional Court, 30/03 (Decision of 21 December 2006) para III/9.4; Lithuanian Constitutional Court, 47/04 (Decision of 8 May 2007) para II/3.

constitutional structures" and therefore comprises the constitutional identity of each Member State. It has to be noted that supranationality expresses the *EU perspective* of national and constitutional identity of a Member State, however not that of the Member State itself. The competence to define it and to assert an infringement by a *national* authority remains within the national constitutional court while the exclusive competence to declare EU secondary law incompatible with constitutional identity in the *EU perspective* and to annul it or to stop its application belongs to the supranational courts. National constitutional courts have to initiate preliminary ruling proceedings before the ECJ for the review of EU secondary law on its incompatibility with Art. 4.2 TEU.

The supranationalisation of large fields of national competences on the level of ordinary law has been well accepted. The same process for the constitutional order is more in dispute. It seems to be a predominant opinion that safeguarding core elements of the national constitutional order is necessary in order to maintain national statehood and a basic constitutional culture.

In conclusion it can be stated that legal thinking in Europe is highly influenced by European integration and the acceptance of the societies regarding the supranational structure of the EU which is state-like in its instruments.

The more societies are integrated, the more they develop a common legal thinking. The state as the most integrated political system homogenises legal thinking by the existence of a normative hierarchy with the Constitution at the top. To a large degree, the EU assumes the functions of the Member States and is, in this respect, similar to a state. The EU is based on common values as they are enshrined in the TEU and the EUCFR. It is manifest that this considerably fosters the evolution of common convictions in the field of law. The own legal traditions of the Member States compete with the emerging supranational legal thinking. It is a question of *subsidiarity* how far particular national approaches are recognised. This problem concerns common legal thinking in a multinational community as such, i. e. in the EU as well as in the ECHR. To which extent margins of appreciation must be admitted to the national legal cultures is a question of the adequate equilibrium between common and particular legal thinking. Both are necessary in a multinational community.

3.5 Separation of Powers

Separation of powers in a vertical and horizontal sense is a further tendency of European constitutionalism. It cannot be treated here in detail. Subnational territorial organisation in federal and regional systems is a widespread phenomenon in Europe. In its different aspects the structures vary considerably. Vertical separation of powers and strengthening of democracy also on the subnational levels are the main impulses. For this reason self-governing bodies elected through universal suffrage are typical. The degree of autonomy varies; however, it can roughly be said that matters which genuinely concern a subnational territorial entity (region, province, local community, etc.) are regularly attributed to this entity for autonomous decision, that means without interference by the state or another subnational territorial entity. Control of legality often remains centralised.

Horizontal separation of powers encompasses various phenomena, in particular the shift of decision-making competences from the traditional institutions such as Parliament to (transnational) administrative bodies or the privatisation of public authority. As common principles have not yet been clearly developed on this nevertheless important subject, it shall not be enlarged upon in this context.

4 Conclusion

Common legal thinking in Europe is progressively developing. This process is mainly value-oriented: the increasing importance of fundamental rights on the basis of human dignity, of the rule of law in an advanced form which focuses on the constitutional review of the legislator, and of the intensive and multiple impacts of inter- and supranational law as the basis for integration into an "ever closer union" in Europe.

Manifold vertical and horizontal transfer processes between the different legal orders in Europe are the instrumental framework for this convergence process in legal thinking. The inherent dynamics can give impulses for the evolution of a common European legal and constitutional culture. However, as in every integration process, advancement has to be adequately balanced with respect for individual tradition and particularity. Subsidiarity consolidates integration. Common legal thinking has always been aware of the particular cultural sources at its base; this is an enrichment and not a deficit.

References

Ardant, P., & Mathieu, B. (2010). *Institutions politiques et droit constitutionnel* (22nd edn.). Paris: L.G.D.J.

Arnold, R. (1997). L'exposition des constitutions européennes aux influences externes. In J. Miranda (Ed.), *Perspectivas constitucionais nos 20 anos da constituição de 1976* (pp. 673–694). Coimbra: Coimbra editora.

Arnold, R. (2003). *Constitutional Courts of Central and Eastern European Countries as a Dynamic Source of Modern Legal Ideas* Tulane European & Civil Law Forum, 2003. (pp. 99–115). New Orleans: Tulane University School of Law.

Arnold, R. (2004). *Interdependenz im europäischen Verfassungsrecht. Essays in Honour of Georgios I. Kassimatis*. Athens/Bruxelles/Berlin: Sakkoulas/Bruylant/Berliner Wissenschaftsverlag. Alivizato et al. (ed.committee)

Arnold, R. (2006). Strukturen der Verfassungsgerichtsbarkeit in den neuen Demokratien Mittel- und Osteuropas. *Zeitschrift für öffentliches Recht*, *61*, 1–21.

Arnold, R. (Ed.). (2013). *The Universalism of Human Rights*. Dordrecht: Springer.

Arnold, R. (2015). *In Essays in Honour of Friedhelm Hufen*

Balaguer Callejón, F. (2012). The Relations Between the EU Court of Justice and the Constitutional Courts of the Member States. In H.-J. Blanke, & S. Mangiameli (Eds.), *The European Union after Lisbon* (pp. 251–278). Berlin, Heidelberg: Springer.

Berti, G. (1990). *Interpretazione costituzionale* (2nd edn.). Padova: CEDAM.

Blanke, H.-J. (2012). The Protection of Fundamental Rights in Europe. In H.-J. Blanke, & S. Mangiameli (Eds.), *The European Union after Lisbon* (pp. 159–232). Berlin/Heidelberg: Springer.

Blanke, H.-J., & Mangiameli, S. (Eds.). (2013). *The Treaty on European Union (TEU). A Commentary*. Berlin, Heidelberg: Springer.

Brunner, G. (1993). Die neue Verfassungsgerichtsbarkeit in Osteuropa. *Zeitschrift für ausländisches öffentliches Recht und Völkerrecht, 53*(4), 819–870.

D'Atena, A. (2012). The European Constitution's Prospects. In H.-J. Blanke, & S. Mangiameli (Eds.), *The European Union after Lisbon* (pp. 3–18). Berlin, Heidelberg: Springer.

Deacon, R. (2012). *Devolution in the United Kingdom* (2nd edn.). Edinburgh: Edinburgh University Press.

Dicey, A. V. (1967). *An Introduction to the Study of the Constitution. With an Introduction by E.C.S. Wade* (10th edn.). London: Macmillan.

Fabbrini, F. (2008). Kelsen in Paris: France's Constitutional Reform and the Introduction of A Posteriori Constitutional Review of legislation. *German Law Journal, 9*(10), 1297–1312.

Fuchs, T. (2015). *Das EMRK-Gutachten. EuGH, Gutachten 2/13 (Gutachten zum EMRK-Beitritt) vom 18. Dezember 2014. DeLuxe Europarecht aktuell 01/2015*. https://www.rewi.europa-uni.de/de/forschung/projekte/deluxe/archiv_2015/01_2015_EMRK_Gutachten/DeLuxe_EMRK-Gutachten.pdf

Häberle, P. (2011). *Europäische Verfassungslehre* (7th edn.). Baden-Baden: Nomos.

Institut Louis Favoreu (2010). *Le juge constitutionnel et la proportionnalité. Annuaire International de Justice Constitutionnelle* vol. XXV. Paris/Marseille: Economica/Presses universitaires d'Aix-Marseille.

Jowell, J., & Oliver, D. (Eds.). (2011). *The Changing Constitution* (7th edn.). Oxford: OUP.

Kavanagh, A. (2009). *Constitutional Review under the UK Human Rights Act*. Cambridge: University Press.

Kill, G. (2005). Luxembourg. In Council of Europe (Ed.), *Constitutional Courts and European Integration*. Science and technique of democracy. Vol. 36, pp. 115–130. Strasbourg: Council of Europe.

Kirste, S. (2014). Philosophical Foundations of the Principle of the Legal State (Rechtsstaat) and the Rule of Law. In J. R. Silkenat, J. E. Hickey Jr., & P. D. Barenboim (Eds.), *The Legal Doctrines of the Rule of Law and the Legal State (Rechtsstaat)* (pp. 29–43). Berlin, Heidelberg: Springer.

Lepsius, R. M. (2006). The ability of a European Constitution to forge a European identity. In H.-J. Blanke, & S. Mangiiameli (Eds.), *Governing Europe under a Constitution* (pp. 23–35). Berlin, Heidelberg: Springer.

Luchterhand, O. (2007). Generalbericht: Verfassungsgerichtsbarkeit in Osteuropa. In O. Luchterhand, C. Starck, & A. Weber (Eds.), *Verfassungsgerichtsbarkeit in Mittel- und Osteuropa. Teilband I: Berichte* (pp. 295–356). Baden-Baden: Nomos.

Meyer-Ladewig, J. (2006). *Europäische Menschenrechtskonvention. Handkommentar* (2nd edn.). Baden-Baden: Nomos.

Meyer-Ladewig, J. (2012). The Rule of Law in the Case Law of the Strasbourg Court. In H.-J. Blanke, & S. Mangiameli (Eds.), *The European Union after Lisbon* (pp. 233–249). Berlin, Heidelberg: Springer.

Michl, W. (2014). *Thou shalt have no other courts before me, VerfBlog*. http://www.verfassungsblog.de/thou-shalt-no-courts/ (Created 2014/12/23)

Pech, L. (2009). The Rule of Law as a Constitutional Principle of the European Union. *Jean Monnet Working Paper, 04/09*, 1–79.

Potacs, M. (2009). Effet utile als Auslegungsgrundsatz. *Europarecht*, Vol. 44, 465–487.

Rideau, J. (2010). *Droit institutionnel de l'Union européenne* (6th edn.). Paris: L.G.D.J.

Sellers, M. (2014). What Is the Rule of Law and Why Is It So Important?. In J. R. Silkenat, J. E. Hickey Jr., & P. D. Barenboim (Eds.), *The Legal Doctrines of the Rule of Law and the Legal State (Rechtsstaat)* (pp. 3–13). Berlin, Heidelberg: Springer.

Smith, C. (2000). Judicial review of parliamentary legislation: Norway as a European pioneer. *Amicus Curiae*, 32, 11–13. http://sas-space.sas.ac.uk/3780/1/1355-1498-1-SM.pdf

Stern, K. (2006). From the European Convention on Human Rights to the European Charter of Fundamental Rights: The prospects for the protection of human rights in Europe. In H.-J. Blanke, & S. Mangiiameli (Eds.), *Governing Europe under a Constitution* (pp. 169–184). Berlin, Heidelberg: Springer.

Tanchev, E. (2013). Rule of Law and State Governed by Law. In G. G. Harutyunyan (Ed.), *New Millennium Constitutionalism: Paradigms of Reality and Challenges* (pp. 251–278). Yerewan: NJHAR.

Verdussen, M. (2012). *Justice constitutionnelle*. Bruxelles: Larcier.

Weber, A. (2010). *Europäische Verfassungsvergleichung*. München: C.H. Beck.

Zakariás, K., & Benke, K. (2012). La dignité humaine dans la jurisprudence des cours constitutionnelles de l'Allemagne, de Hongrie et de la Roumanie. In Cour Constitutionnelle de la Roumanie (Ed.), Le Bulletin de la Cour Constitutionnelle. *Études. Jurisprudence. Communications* (vol. No. 2/2012, pp. 44–67).

A Perspective of EU Constitutional Law

A Dynamic Constitutional Treaty and the Specific Constitutional Elements of the Association of Sovereign States

Franz Cromme

Albrecht Weber sought, through his teaching and research, a path towards European integration, primarily by way of a sustainable European constitutional law. He also accompanied and helped other scientists to this endeavour, such as the author of this essay. The three different editions of the book[1] about a "Constitutional Treaty of the European Union" (published in three editions in 1987, 2003, and 2010) clarify the dynamic development of European primary and constitutional law, in addition to discussing possible visions of the future. *A. Weber* wrote critical, realistic and supplementary critiques[2] for each of the three editions. He was also amenable to the opportunity to engage in dialogues, whether they be brief or long.

In the past few years, the sometimes theoretical and idealistic discussions about European constitutional law have become increasingly progressive and realistic in their point of view. In conjunction with the sovereign financial debt crisis, this perspective has further increased since the Treaty of Lisbon entered into force.[3] On this topic, an overview of the perspective of EU constitutional law from the book "Die Zukunft des Lissabon-Vertrages"[4] (The Future of the Treaty of Lisbon – hereinafter: "Draft 2010")[5] ought to be examined. This book will be updated and expanded by 2015. This overview encompasses all organs, "working methods", and policies of the EU. It will be kept as brief as possible. However, in order to expand the discussion, some digressions (excurses) will have to be incorporated, above all the up-to-date "specific constitutional elements"[6] and the currently applicable "association of sovereign States" (*Staatenverbund*). This perspective should promote and supplement the *Common European Legal Thinking* at the Union level.

[1] Cromme 1987, p. 13–84; Cromme 2003, p. 27–277; Cromme 2010, p. 25–319.

[2] Weber 1988, p. 800; Weber 2005, p. 561; Weber 2011, p. 88.

[3] Cf. Blanke and Mangiameli 2011.

[4] Cromme 2010, p. 25–319.

[5] The headings of this essay will include corresponding references to the "Draft 2010" (= Cromme 2010).

[6] Cromme 1997, p. 1–56.

H.-J. Blanke et al. (eds.), *Common European Legal Thinking*,
DOI 10.1007/978-3-319-19300-7_4

1 Introduction[7]

1.1 The Majority for European Unification Versus the Missing Consensus on Some Important Questions

Despite much backlash, the majority of European citizens favour further European unification. A long-term goal for the European Union could be something like "The United States of Europe", which could be achieved by using the proven and easily transferable constitutional models from federal states such as Germany and the United States. Nevertheless, one crucial development of the EU into a federal state is not yet possible to ascertain, for the reason that lasting consensus still has not been reached as to important questions regarding the economy, society and the state. This is particularly apparent in the financial culture,[8] and to some extent in the administration, justice, and democracy culture as well. And the new British reform-considerations must be kept in mind.

1.2 Excursus A: Democratic Decisions by Majority or with Consent of a Large Majority

The principle of majority rule is regarded by theorists and practitioners alike as an essential – even self-evident – procedural element of a true democracy. It has made democracy in the Member States both operational and successful, in addition to resolving basic questions of economic and social affairs within the EU.

However, conferring the principle of majority rule onto everyone, especially regarding financial decisions of the EU, would be premature in the forthcoming phase of development. This transfer would neglect the democratically theoretical prerequisite of majority rule, namely minimum homogeneity[9] and fundamental consensus.[10] A large part of the EU would be dominated without its consent. Even the former Commission President *M. Barroso* declared in Brussels on 9 October 2012 that the European states have a different "financial culture".[11] However, if clear consensus cannot be reached in one area, then on a case by case basis, there needs to be either consensus by unanimity or by way of a "large majority". This already applies to the large, individual decisions that are made within the ESM System.

[7] Cromme 2010, p. 104/105,109,110,113 (Art. 1 I, IV, Art. 8, Art. 49, IV) and explanations p. 107, 115–118, 189/90.

[8] Quotation of Barroso, M., *Frankfurter Allgemeine Zeitung/dpa,* 12.10.2012, p. 14 and 5.4.2013 p. 6 et seq.

[9] Nohlen and Schultze 2002, p. 432.

[10] Cromme 2012b, p. 12; Cromme 2013b, p. 33.

[11] Quotation of Barroso, M., *Frankfurter Allgemeine Zeitung/dpa,* 12.10.2012 p. 14 and 5.4.2013 p. 6, 7; cf. *Frankfurter Allgemeine Zeitung*, 22.4.2013, p. 18, with regard to the political term culture (*Kultur*) Nohlen and Schultze 2002, p. 469 No. 3.

It also appears that an agreement by all participating European states with regard to consensus is necessary, including the convergence and restructuring programme that was proposed by the European Council.

According to remarks made by the governments of key states (and also according to the case law of the German Constitutional Court[12] regarding ESM), there are no signs that the currently unresolved macroeconomic problems will be resolved principally by way of intergovernmental measures (excepting newly created supranational banking oversight). This would nonetheless have to happen in accordance with the rights of the European Parliament as well with the *aquis communautaire* (primarily with regard to the communitised competition system of EU internal markets and the autonomy of the ECB), and it would additionally have to conform to the Commission's decidedly politically stable control rights (not just according to the supranational Six Pack, etc., but also according to the ESM Treaty and the Fiscal Pact).

Regardless, EU primary law will ultimately advance towards the German Federal Constitutional Court's concept of *Staatenverbund*, or as coined by Federal Chancellor *A. Merkel*, the so-called "union method". Gradually, a trend counter to the Community method will develop once again.

1.3 The Steps to Unification

Nevertheless, if one were to attempt to achieve the European "United States" as a federal state, then one more hurdle would still need to be cleared: the state identities of the EU states, as they are understood by the German Constitutional Court,[13] would no longer be guaranteed; in Germany, for example, a national referendum would be needed (Art. 146 GG). Thus, for the time being, it should only be envisaged as a medium-term perspective[14] of integration in advance of a European "federation" (or a reinforced "association of sovereign States").

As a first major step, this goal should be realised according to a constitutional convention (in perhaps 5–10 years), namely through new EU primary law/constitutional law. Because one would have to envisage additional long-term phases of development, it would be necessary to clarify the development perspective of the new constitutional law (up to the conceivable limit of the loss of state identity). An additional constitutional process would obviously be needed. The EU's proposed new constitutional law must set forth effective rules for the ensuing longer development phases, primarily for the period after its entry into

[12] German Federal Constitutional Court (Bundesverfassungsgericht), 2 BvE 6/12, et al. (preliminary ruling of 12 September 2012; judgment of 18 March 2014) – *ESM Treaty*.

[13] German Federal Constitutional Court (Bundesverfassungsgericht), 2 BvE 2/08 et al. (judgment of 30 June 2009) para 233 et seqq. – *Lisbon*: integration limit (German: "Integrationsschranke").

[14] Comprehensive: Sommermann 2013, p. 708 et seqq.; to federation (German: "Föderation"): von Bogdandy 2001, p. 157 et seqq.; Fischer 2000, p. 171, 179 et seq.; short term measures: see below Part IV.

force, such as that which will be discussed in Part IV, "The Development of the European Union and the Development of the Constitutional Treaty".

Even on this long road to a "federation in development", the Member States would still, for all intents and purposes, remain the "masters of the treaties". New primary law (in conjunction with the national constitutions) should also have constitutional status. It could be given the designation of "basic treaty", or more fittingly, "constitutional treaty" (*Verfassungsvertrag*). The new primary law/constitutional treaty should be "exempt" according to "institutional laws" (*verfassungsausführende Gesetze*, following the French model); and it should succinctly[15] reflect the constitutional core of the current and evolving European Union law. Above all, in its Part I ("The Principles"), it should be made clear and coherent for interested citizens.

1.4 Excursus B: The Constitutional Treaty – its Exemptions According to "Institutional Laws"

In 2004, the European Constitutional Convention approved a draft of a "Treaty Establishing a Constitution for Europe", but it was ultimately rejected by referendums in both France and the Netherlands. However, the text of the draft still did not reach the level of a "self-supporting"[16] constitution (which was desired by many);[17] thus the Member States still remain the "masters of the treaties" with regard to this draft. The Treaty of Lisbon also declined to use the word "constitution". The complete phrase "constitutional treaty" should nonetheless be sufficiently clarified regarding the remaining constitutional sovereignty of the Member States. It can also be concluded that even today the European people would have no objection to a "constitutional treaty" (within the European "constitutional union" – *Verfassungsverbund*)[18] assuming it did not supersede, but rather coexisted parallel to the national constitutions.[19] The term "constitutional treaty" (*Verfassungsvertrag*) was coined by *Carl Schmitt*.[20] At that time, however, this term still had not yet established a link to a scarcely conceivable European constitutional law. The phrase "constitutional treaty" was first introduced to the European literature and discussion in 1987.[21]

Owing to the preeminent importance of constitutional law, a constitution as well as a constitutional treaty should be kept short and succinct. The aim of the *Dehane*, *Simon* and *von Weizsäcker* commission[22] was on the one hand to "succinctly" contractually establish the principles of European constitutional law, and on the other

[15] Cromme 2010 (with transitional regulations) Art. 9 I, II, V; Expl. p. 109–10, 311–12.

[16] Böckenförde 1991, p. 29 et seqq., 38.

[17] Cromme 2010, p. 106; Cromme 2009, p. 177, 180.

[18] Pernice 2001, p. 148, 163 et seqq.

[19] Cromme 2010, p. 105.

[20] Schmitt 1928, p. 63, 69, 367, 371.

[21] Cromme 1987.

[22] Dehaene et al. 1999.

hand to structure the multitude of additional rules of European primary law in a flexible way and as a result be able to liberate required changes from the necessity of a treaty amendment (or unanimity). This goal could not be achieved by the extensive Treaty of Lisbon (with its equal components of TEU and TFEU). Accordingly, an instrument of French constitutional law ought to be used, specifically its institutional law (Art. 34 and 46 of the French Constitution).

The institutional laws (*lois organiques*; *verfassungsausführende Gesetze*)[23] serve primarily to streamline the breadth of the constitutional treaty and to improve the intelligibility of the summarised texts of the constitution. They must be limited according to the "content, purpose and extent" of the authority granted by the constitutional treaty; they also require the "large majority" of the European Parliament and the European Council (with greater involvement of the national parliaments).[24]

1.5 The Concept for the EU Constitutional Law

In terms of content, the proposed constitutional treaty envisages graduated (in each specific department) levels of integration of constitutional law of the proposed "federation in development". These would fall between the Treaty of Lisbon and the distantly conceivable European federal state in the hierarchy.

The constitutional treaty should be characterised by the following principles:

a) the value of the Charter of Fundamental Rights as constitutional law of the Union (as in the TCE/Treaty of Lisbon) and also as establishing basic principles for the Member States,
b) the fundamental competence-competence of the Member States,
c) the same importance of supranational action of the Union and the intergovernmental cooperation of States – graded according to policy areas and with precedence of the already established (enumerative) supranational competences,
d) the gradual development of the constitutional treaty (even in accordance with the convention process) on the basis of existing community and union law, and as a general rule, with the principle of subsidiarity and a moderate increase of supranational competences,
e) the equal decision-making power of the European Parliament and the European Council/Council of Ministers with regard to Union legislation,
f) the blanket application of the principle of majority rule in the European Council/Council of Ministers in supranational affairs,
g) the application of the consensus principle (unanimous or by a "large majority" with "constructive abstention" of the minority) for the cooperation of the states in the frame of the European Council/Council of Ministers,
h) the involvement of national parliaments,
i) the preservation of the identity of the Member States as states.

[23] Cromme 2010 Art. 9, Expl. p. 110–11, 147–48 (with handling and transitional regulations Art. 156 I, II; Expl. p. 311/12); Cromme 2003, Art. 12a.
[24] Cromme 2010: Art. 20 III.

1.6 Excursus C: The Further Development of the "Specific Constitutional Elements of the Association of Sovereign States"[25]

According to the principles of the proposed new constitutional treaty, the competence-competence of the Member States and the provisionally equal importance of supranational and international acting can above all be considered important specifics regarding the association of sovereign States. Lately, this has also applied to the (evolving) participation of the national parliaments in decisions of the Council of Ministers at the EU level as well as to the (recently further developed by the German Constitutional Court) obligation to safeguard the national identity[26] of the Member States.[27]

Of particular importance are some additional specific constitutional elements, such as the equal rank of national and European fundamental rights, citizenship rights of the EU that were derived from national citizenship rights, as well as the "binding cooperation"[28] of Member States in the realm of foreign policy (Art. 28 and 31 TEU). Furthermore, the cooperative relationship between the ECJ and the national constitutional courts as well as the concept of the "ever-closer Union" are also important.

Moreover, there are other constitutional elements, that are demanded to be modified, such as the European Parliament as a "parliament of the people", but that is not apportioned according to the populations of the various states – or conversely, constitutional elements that could still be developed, such as the constitutional convention as a regular institute of innovation, in addition to the connection between supranational and intergovernmental actions,[29] or the prohibition of horizontal financial compensation.[30]

In which direction, and with which specific constitutional elements the development of EU constitutional law proceeds, remains to be seen. Many things can be complex and difficult to classify.[31] The German Federal Constitutional Court's case law with regards to the association of sovereign States should not be seen as an obstacle in the way of further development of EU constitutional law: The Court's general descriptions of the association of sovereign States are still not very extensive and detailed; they therefore leave a great deal open for future interpretation. For example, the German Constitutional Court ranks the "ever-closer Union"[32] as

[25] Cromme 1997, p. 1–56 (Critique: Weber 1998, p. 103).
[26] German Federal Constitutional Court (Bundesverfassungsgericht), 2 BvE 2/08 et al. (judgment of 30 June 2009) para. 233 et seqq. – *Lisbon*.
[27] cf. Cromme 1997, p. 6: "Erhaltung eines Kernbereiches der Souveränität".
[28] Cromme 2012a, p. 215; see below Excursus D.
[29] Cromme 2012a, p. 209 et seqq.
[30] Cromme 2012a, p. 215; Cromme 2010: Art. 140 II; Expl. p. 297 et seq. (= Art. 157 IV 1st edn., Cromme 1987).
[31] Cromme 2012a, p. 214.
[32] German Federal Constitutional Court (Bundesverfassungsgericht), 2 BvR 2134/92, 2 BvR 2159/92 (judgment of 12 October 1993) – *Maastricht*.

being one of the most important elements, because it is carried out through "public authority"[33] (as a supranational element). In addition, the court also stressed the importance of the "state-organised" nations[34] in the "sovereign permanent" states[35] (as an intergovernmental element). Both these elements were joined together through the Treaty of Maastricht. In its Maastricht ruling (as well as in the Lisbon ruling), the German Federal Constitutional Court relatively openly characterised the EU as an association of sovereign States and in accordance with the German Basic Law.

The association of sovereign States (or the "federation in development") is accordingly not a fixed "ideal type", but rather is an actual "real type", [36] and is thus appropriately designated for "flexible systems".[37] At any rate, an analysis of EU constitutional law should not be fixated on the "state model"[38] or the "federal state model".

2 Proposals for a Constitutional Treaty of the EU (Parts I, II, III, IV)

2.1 Part I – The Principles[39]

The fundamental elements of the new primary law/constitutional law should adhere to the comprehensive and basic standards of the Treaty of Lisbon. Chief among these elements are values, fundamental rights, objectives, and Union citizenship as it is derived from state citizenship.

The European Charter of Fundamental Rights, which, in conjunction with the constitutions of the Member States, has its own significance, should survive as a stand-alone constitutional charter (according to the British model), and should also be valid and protected as an equally important part of constitutional law alongside the EU constitutional treaty.

With the principle of subsidiarity comes the ability to check whether competences of the union can be reduced. The national identity of the Member States, particularly with regard to their "basic functions" (Art. 4 TEU), should not merely be "respected" but should also be "guaranteed".

[33] German Federal Constitutional Court (Bundesverfassungsgericht), 2 BvE 2/08 et al. (judgment of 30 June 2009) – *Lisbon*.

[34] German Federal Constitutional Court (Bundesverfassungsgericht), 2 BvR 2134/92, 2 BvR 2159/92 (judgment of 12 October 1993) para 108 – *Maastricht*.

[35] German Federal Constitutional Court (Bundesverfassungsgericht), 2 BvE 2/08 et al. (judgment of 30 June 2009) – *Lisbon*.

[36] According to Larenz 1991, p. 221–22, 463, 465; Cromme 1997, p. 5–6.

[37] Larenz 1991, p. 469.

[38] Grimm 1995, p. 587 and there notes 28, 50 (to Cromme 1987). With the same view Blanke and Böttner in this Volume.

[39] Cromme 2010, Art. 1 IV,V – Art. 2 u.3; Expl. p. 127–28, 134–35 – Art. 6; Expl. p. 144–45 – Art. 7; Expl. p. 118, 133.

Because of the current inconsistencies[40] regarding the legal personality of the EU, a clarification is needed, especially in relation to the inclusion (but only in the medium term) of increased intergovernmental actions in the EU: "The Union has legal personality. The states act in conjunction with one another, as well as with the Union. The European Union, through its institutions, possesses a single institutional framework for the Union's undertakings and for the cooperation between states".

With respect to relations between Member States, their external solidarity ("The Principles" – Part I), should especially be emphasised, namely via a mutual assistance obligation that is more apparent than in Art. 42.7 TEU (in addition to obligations under the NATO Treaty).

Pertaining to the scope of EU constitutional law "for an indefinite period of time", a comprehensive constitutional principle of sustainability (*Nachhaltigkeit*) should be set forth in Part I and should be emphasised, not just for environmental law, but also for fiscal management and the entire legislation and administration.

2.2 *Part II – The Institutions and Functioning of the EU*

2.2.1 European Parliament and Legislation[41]

In a uniform electoral law, an incremental distribution of seats should be introduced according to the population of the states (with a small "adjustment" for small and medium-sized states).

Laws originating from the "ordinary legislative procedure" (Art. 289.1 TFEU) should also be referred to as "laws" of the EU. Under these laws, the right of initiative should lay not only with the Commission, but also with the Parliament and the Council of Ministers. Important laws[42] should be introduced formally and concurrently by the European Parliament and by the national parliaments. And along with the consultation of the national parliaments, the European Parliament as well as the (now in parliamentary form) European Council/Council of Ministers should decide these laws.

It will be necessary to have "direct regulations" for the European Council/Council of Ministers, in particular in the areas of foreign and defence policy, as well as domestic policy in addition to the regulations implemented by the Commission on the basis of law.

Given the increasing "binding cooperation" between Member States within the European Council/Council of Ministers, above all in the areas of foreign policy and financial policy (Art. 28, 31, 36 TEU), it is now more self-evident that the opinion of the European Parliament *must* be taken into account (Art. 23.3 GG).

---

[40] Geiger, in Geiger et al. (2010), Art. 47 TEU para 1–3; Cromme 2010, Expl. p. 134–35.

[41] Cromme 2010: Art. 11 Alternative; Expl. p. 153–54; (similar to the Council of Ministers: Art. 26 III) – Art. 13, 20, 24 II, 33, 61; Expl. p. 155–57, 220–21; cf. Art. 23.3 GG.

[42] Especially institutional laws; see above Excursus B.

2.2.2 European Council and Council of Ministers[43]

The (newly formed) European Council respectively the Council of Ministers will continue to play an important role with regard to decisions, co-decisions, and the right of participation of the Member States in government functions (especially in foreign policy), as well as in administrative functions (for example with restricted comitology). In addition to these operational responsibilities, the right of co-decision in the Union should be given to the Council of Ministers. In this way, the tasks of the Member States in the EU can be pooled and coordinated with each other. In any case, a second chamber comprising members of national parliaments along with the European Council/Council of Ministers, should be avoided.[44] However, the involvement of the national parliaments should not only be left to national constitutional law and the different national practises, but also should be largely determined by European constitutional law.

At the same time, the Council formations should be restructured (Laeken Declaration), and the former European Council and Council of Ministers should be joined together as a newly styled "European Council". In its role as law maker of the EU, the European Council should be "parliamentised" and modelled after the German *Bundesrat*: several members of government (deciding uniformly for each state) would be delegated to the "plenum", depending on the number of inhabitants in each state. Other than the heads of government, two to six Ministers (or their representatives) would be active in the "new" European Council, for a total of over 120 members of government. There they would vote essentially according to the double voting rights provided for in the Treaty of Lisbon.

Certain operational tasks should remain under the authority of specific departments within the Council of Ministers and these departments should have decision-making powers (i. e. "special committees" such as a foreign affairs council, defence council, council for national security, fiscal council). In the wake of the former European Council, the political and strategic leadership of the entire European Council/Council of Ministers should be overtaken by a "council of heads of state and government" (*Rat der Staats- und Regierungschefs*) – under the chairmanship of the President of the European Council.

2.2.3 The European Commission[45]

Compared to the reformed European Council/Council of Ministers as the focus of the Member States regarding the leadership of the EU (as an organ of the supranational Union as well as a "borrowed" organ for the cooperation and the "binding cooperation" between the Member States), the unity[46] of the Union should be

[43] Cromme 2010: Art. 25, 26 I, II, III, 29, 30, 32; Expl. p. 161–64, 173–74.

[44] With the same view Blanke and Böttner in this Volume.

[45] Cromme 2010: Art. 37–39; Expl. p. 179 – Art. 34 and 42; Expl. p. 176–77.

[46] Regarding the EU as a connection of states and of a supranational union cf. Pechstein and Koenig 2000, para 92; Cromme 2010, p. 27 et seqq., note 175 – Regarding the "equality of the

equally represented by the European Parliament "in tandem" with the European Commission. Parliament and the Commission should cooperate both politically and personally. The Commission should thereby become less bureaucratic, but remain guardian of the Treaties. Its importance became more relevant during the financial crisis due to its control measures and other executive powers. Conversely, the Commission should be under a legal and political obligation according to the principle of subsidiarity to phase out and reduce excessive activities at the task level of the Member States.

From now on, the Commission President should be elected directly by the European Parliament; the members of the Commission (including the "European Foreign Minister" and the "European Finance Minister"), should be appointed by the President of the Commission, each with subsequent consent of the European Council. The President of the Commission should be strengthened in his role, such as to determine the guidelines of the policy of the Commission, or even being able to dismiss members of the Commission. With regard to the function of the Commission as guardian of the Treaties, it is important to keep in mind the limited right of appeal that the European Council (respectively the Parliament) has. Moreover, introducing a constructive vote of no confidence ought to be considered.

Additionally, a voting member of the Commission from each Member State should be appointed. However, only half of the Commission members should be head of a department (including the coordinating Vice President); the other Commissioners would have supplementary deputies and representative functions (following the Bavarian model).

The Commission can also, so far as is necessary, be charged with the enforcement of intergovernmental contract law (on the basis of "binding cooperation"). Along with actions for breach of the Treaties brought before the ECJ, additional competences of the Commission (together with the Council of Ministers) should be created for better administrative enforcement and better implementation of Union law in the Member States.

2.2.4 The European Court of Justice[47]

The institutional arrangements for the ECJ and other courts can remain essentially the same. The "cooperative relationship" between the ECJ and the national constitutional courts should be encouraged.[48] Regardless, a partially expanded jurisdiction of the EU should be planned (especially in the enforcement of the principles for the States as laid out in Part I), as well as for the implementation of the agreements between the Member States on the basis of "binding cooperation". The latter particularly applies to the obligations of states in the areas of macroeconomic finance- and economic policy.

Member States before the treaties and regarding the differentiated integration as well the opt-outs (above Great Britain and Turkey): Cromme 2007, p. 821 et seqq.

[47] Cromme 2010: Expl. p. 189–90.

[48] Cromme 2010: Expl, p. 187–88.

2.2.5 Cooperation Between the States and the Institutions of the Union[49]

In many areas, preference has been given to supranational regulations aimed at equal treatment of all EU States, in addition to those aimed at legal precision. In contrast, however, the cooperation between states within the framework of the European Council/Council of Ministers (with participation of the European Parliament) should no longer be concealed or denied, but rather regulated in a general manner within a special subsection of primary law/constitutional law.

The "binding cooperation" of the "willing states" in foreign policy (with "constructive abstention" of up to one-third of Member States under Art. 28, 31, 36 TEU) should be facilitated and developed with respect to procedure (for example, also with regard to a small number of *dissenting* votes). It should also be tasked in the areas of freedom, security and justice, but above all in financial and stability policy and in growth, structure and convergence policy (which is currently under development). The general primacy of supranational competence (achieved through existing primary law) would remain as it is.

This (notably also operational) "binding cooperation" needs to be distinguished from "enhanced cooperation" (closer cooperation; *verstärkte Zusammenarbeit*) which more generally includes middle and small-sized groups of states. However, the principle of binding cooperation aspires for consensus from all or a large part of the Member States. The enhanced cooperation should remain in the text of the Treaty of Lisbon, as it refers to the permanent transfer of supranational competences.

2.2.6 Excursus D: "Binding Cooperation" of the EU States According to Applicable Law

The concept of a European association of sovereign States agrees with the case law of the German Federal Constitutional Court and is authoritative for Germany.[50] The details are not yet entirely set in stone, thus it can (as stated) be developed for the purpose of further European integration. In the Convention's draft of a treaty for a European constitution, an attempt was made to supplant or even deny the importance of intergovernmental cooperation at the European level. This cooperation, however, remains a reality even under the Treaty of Lisbon, especially in the arena of foreign policy.

At the same time, the EU's association of sovereign States created specific constitutional elements of the EU. One of these is the binding "resolutions" of the EU states in the realm of foreign and security policy, with the special feature of the so-called constructive abstention for individual states (according to Art. 28, 31, and 36 TEU). These resolutions are already established law. No Member State can be majority-dominated by this specific intergovernmental action (based upon the

[49] Cromme 2010: Art. 53, 54, 59; Expl. p. 131–32, 214–18.

[50] German Federal Constitutional Court (Bundesverfassungsgericht), 2 BvE 2/08 et al. (judgment of 30 June 2009) headnote 1, para 229 – *Lisbon*.

consensus of as many states as possible). Rather, in this case, a "resolution" of a "large majority" is only legally binding on those Member States voting in favour of it. This large majority is achieved when not more than one-third of the states (with concurrent participation of the EU population) abstain from voting. The loyal "constructive abstention" applies to this minority. One should speak here of a "binding cooperation"[51] at the government level. In some cases, even an already qualified majority of the Council of Ministers (with opposing votes) is sufficient.

This binding cooperation between Member States in the realm of foreign policy, which the European Parliament is also consulted on, is considered a little-examined constitutional element of European law.[52] It should, at least, prevent blocking by small blocking minorities and should also indicate the threshold of when we can speak of clear consensus.[53] Regardless, larger EU states could hardly be outvoted, as neither could large groups within middle and small-sized states. Conversely, individual states from the minority could use their right of proposal to get a decision of a large majority. More general insights into the changing formation of coalitions with the European Council and Council of Ministers can be obtained by the so-called cooperative game theory and by actual EU case studies.

Binding cooperation formally came into play during the Kosovo War. This however did not happen during the Libya crisis even though a more differentiated and sustainable decision was objectively possible for the Europeans; only a partially satisfactory result was achieved, though informally. Binding cooperation involves organised joint decisions of the individual Member States within the framework of the Council of Ministers. More success may be found in the area of foreign policy under the applicable law, but only if the "willing" states were to demand solidarity and leadership, and the irresolute states were to participate gradually, at least partially. The presently already applicable "binding cooperation" would gain overall importance and would be more widely practised, if it (as proposed), would be further developed in regards to procedure and then transferred to other areas of expertise.

2.3 *Part III – The Policies of the EU*[54]

The rules of the internal market (especially according to the pervious EEC Treaty) can remain as they are in essence (in the above-mentioned focus on the core of the constitution). More detailed regulations of primary law (especially in the TFEU) would be acquired by the applicable "institutional laws" (*lois organiques*; *verfassungsausführende Gesetze*) or be transferred via transitional arrangements (Part IV).

[51] Cromme 2010: Expl. p. 131, 196; Cromme 2012a, p. 215; Cromme 2003: Art. 69a; Expl. p. 194.

[52] Terhechte, in Schwarze (2009), Art. 12 TEU para 2, 3; Cromme 2010: Expl. p. 197 with further reference.

[53] Regelsberger & Kugelmann, in Streinz (2012), Art. 31 TEU para 9.

[54] Cromme 2010: Art. 82 III, 156; Expl. p. 204–05, 210–11, 241–243.

In other departments, the intergovernmental cooperation between the states initially increased (especially after the financial crisis, both within and outside the institutions of the Union). This intergovernmental cooperation should safeguard the core of the national constitutional law and the identity of the states (according to the view of some states and their citizens). However, in the new constitution-treaty of the "federation in development" (and furthermore in the subsequent constitutional process under Part IV) an additional "communitisation" (*Vergemeinschaftung*) of supranational actions could be possible (incrementally, for example, after having considered the necessity of a decisive common foreign policy and after the emergence of a common finance culture).

2.3.1 Foreign Policy[55]

The "common foreign policy" of the Treaty of Lisbon is characterised by a juxtaposition of intergovernmental and supranational action.[56] The merging of both parts requires a holistic and complete way of thinking and an appropriate allocation of roles between the Member States and the institutions of the Union.

The "special foreign policy" of the Union is essentially already supranational, especially in the areas of foreign trade and developmental policy, alongside the trade and arms embargo and finally with regard to international treaties (in all areas of Part III of the TFEU). It is equivalent in importance to the other "general foreign policy", especially the classic "political" foreign and security policy.

This "general foreign policy" (including the non-contractual duty of external relations) is still intergovernmental, however. Here, there should be some further changes in the development of constitutional law. Firstly, one can achieve more progress with a further restriction on unanimity in the Council of Ministers by expanding the (already mentioned) "binding cooperation" between the "willing" states according to the applicable Art. 28, 31 and 36 TEU. In addition, there is an already proposed new remedy at law in the ECJ.

It should be emphasised (more so than in Art. 18 and 41 TEU), that the "European Foreign Minister" (as Vice President of the Commission, Chairman of the Foreign Affairs Council and head of the European External Action Service) coordinates the intergovernmental and the supranational foreign policy and controls it together with the Member States. He should also be responsible for the use of external funds from the EU budget. But above all he must ensure that the "general foreign policy" will be reinforced by way of an effective "special foreign policy" of the Union. Indeed, the foreign minister of the EU is in all (also "mixed") negotiations essentially also the negotiator of the EU.

In consequence of its increasingly coordinating and controlling role, the "critical mass" of competence must be achieved, so that the "high representative" for Foreign

[55] Cromme 2010: Art. 59 II Expl. p. 216–219.

[56] Art. 18.1, 18.2, 18.3, Art. 24.1 (3), Art. 40 TEU on the one hand and Art. 18.4, 40 TEU, Art. 218 TFEU on the other hand.

Affairs can now be named and accepted as the "EU Foreign Minister". He would be appointed by the President of the Commission and confirmed by the European Council (like other members of the Commission). Prior to the appointment of the Minister of Foreign Affairs, however, the President of the Commission must adjust an agreement with the President of the European Council, who would still retain his (primarily representative) role in European foreign policy.

2.3.2 Defence[57]

With the (almost exclusive) intergovernmental defence policy of the TEU, there needs to be a new set of intergovernmental and supranational competences (also in the interest of a growing division of responsibilities between the States), especially in the joint European armaments,[58] in order to increase efficiency of the various national armaments while lowering the costs. In this way, the EU could increase its importance in relation to the United States, Russia and China with regard to security policy and the protection of European interests.

In the possible event that the United States partially pulls out of Europe as well as out of the European NATO Organisation, the creation of a permanent military command structure of the EU in Europe will have to be considered, even for further missions outside Europe. However, as long as EU foreign and security policy depends upon the (still to be improved) "binding cooperation" between the States, those states' troops are subject to their jurisdiction. The States must still retain their rights, even with respect to the decision to place their troops under the EU guide units (as it is currently with NATO). Within this European context, the parliamentary reservation in Germany can indeed become more effective.

2.3.3 Internal Market, Agriculture, Energy, Transportation, Labour and Social Affairs, Environment, Euratom, Research[59]

As we have seen, the different areas of EU law relating to the internal market can remain, but in a condensed form. A protectionist "industrial policy" for the benefit of individual sectors and in individual States should be further excluded. The same should also apply to the EU's foreign trade. However, (cooperative, market and cost-oriented) innovative EU actions to maintain and extend the European position in global free trade should be possible.

In some areas of the internal market, insufficient supranational competences of the Union will need to be amended and updated, for instance in energy policy (especially for a Europe-wide, market-driven supply security), and in environmental policy (e. g. for the abolition of unanimity in the Council of Ministers on international climate protection treaties).

[57] Cromme 2010: Art. 72, 73, 77a; Expl. p. 229–30, 234–236, 238.

[58] Cromme 2003: Art. 94.1, 2, 3; Expl. p. 209–10.

[59] Cromme 2010: Art. 82 I, 85, 91, 104, 106, 113 IV; Expl. p. 240, 246 – energy: Art. 104; Expl. p. 265–66, 287–88 – environment: Art. 119, 120; Expl. p. 277–283, 287–88.

While there are limits on the Union's social policy (including the German Constitutional Court's case law regarding identity), the free labour market, on the other hand, should include the wage formation process (differentiated by region, while respecting the role of the social partners), and requires partial European governance through an expanding "deepened economic and monetary union".

2.3.4 Macroeconomic and Monetary Union[60]

2.3.4.1 Intergovernmental and Supranational Competences

Apart from the European Central Bank, the general "coordination of economic policies" is essentially regulated through intergovernmental means (Art. 121 et seqq. TFEU) – but only in principle. To a large part supranational powers were in development during the financial crisis (for example with the Six Pack, but also with the banking union related to systematically important banks), but especially in the latter, because individually precise regulations are required. In the new European primary law/constitutional law, the legal basis for these supranational regulations should be clarified and partially expanded upon and supplemented with executive competences of the "European Finance Minister". Also, the supplementary intergovernmental agreements and institutions (such as the Fiscal Pact, ESM Funds, and the bank funds) should be adapted with the national law and integrated into the text of the constitution.

The European Central Bank requires a concentration of its "core functions" on "monetary policy" (especially with regard to the funding of Member States and to the so-called TARGET 2 loans). Furthermore, it should be made clear that the ECB (until further notice?) can take over extensive duties in the area of EU banking supervision. Completion and control of the stability and growth policies requires an overarching coordination (especially through the planned limited "reform treaties" between the Union and countries in crisis for the convergence in the EU and structural improvement in those countries), namely through the new "binding cooperation" in an intergovernmental (only macroeconomic) "economic government".[61]

2.3.4.2 Excursus E: Autonomous Powers in the System: The ECB, the "Invisible Hand" of the Financial Markets and the Social Partners

How does the independent ECB, as we have understood it so far and as we now observe it, fit in with a (coordinating or even "overarching") European economic government? How does it fit in with the new redesigned, consistent economic

---

[60] Cromme 2010: Art. 94, 97; Expl. p. 252–53, 257–58; up to date additions: Calliess 2013, p. 785 et seqq.; Cromme 2013, p. 594 et seqq.

[61] Also feasible in the short term; see below Part IV (at the end); Cromme 2014, p. 448, 455–56.

system of the EU? A controversial topic is the "unlimited" purchase of government bonds by the ECB – next to that at the same order of magnitude are the so-called TARGET2 loans from the ECB to the national central banks, which one could characterise as overdrafts between national central banks with unlimited overdraft protection. Both financing aids of the ECB are considered by some experts, as well as by policy, as a fast and flexible addition to EMS assistance in the Euro zone. As a corrective measure, a (controversial) nexus between bond purchases and ESM procedure, in addition to other further requirements is intended, even with a partial policy link (which would need to be limited).

On the one hand, the ECB is an independent and without "braking" control of the European Parliament and the national parliaments; on the other hand, however, it is expressly legally limited by the "monetary policy" and by the primary objective of price stability. It is not yet sufficiently clear in the legal sense to what extent the interest rate policy and the credit policy belong to the monetary policy. After all, it is conceivable that the German *Bundestag* or the institutions of other Member States would intervene in the event of an increasing risk of inflation or increasing loss of interest rate. In the event that the ECB overextends its authority regarding monetary policy one could "block" this, using other areas of the stability systems, namely in extreme cases at releases of ESM guarantees. One could also demand and assert a clarification of the term "monetary policy", and that a procedural limitation of indirect acquisition of state bonds in addition to a limit on TARGET2 loans would be set. This clarification would be achieved in any case through an amendment of the statutes of the ECB, or by a change in EU primary law in accordance with simplified procedure (Art. 48.6 TEU) – and thus probably without referendums in the States.

On the one hand, the "smoothing" of troubled international money markets is one of the tasks of the central banks. On the other hand, the German Constitutional Court, in its first ruling on the ESM, pointed out that the ECB may also not unrestrictedly acquire assets (government bonds) on the secondary market. Economists and lawyers should understand the grounds for the reasoning of the court as one of the most important statements of the court: according to the ruling, the ECB may not "target financing of states, which is independent from the capital markets".[62] Neither the global private sector nor the worldwide state budgets can finance themselves with their own resources or subsidies "from above"; if necessary, their funds must also be supplemented through the capital market. And this must also be controlled by the interest rates. These aspects highlight the fact that the macroeconomic system of the EU is not only dependent upon the diverse organisation of the state action of the Member States and of the EU, but also that the "invisible hand" of the (disciplined by the state) capital market is constitutionally protected.

Similarly, the same applies to the (mostly silent) role that the wage policy could have in the recovery of the European economy, especially in respect to the debtor states. The wage determination process (*Lohnfindung*) is part of the free labour

[62] German Federal Constitutional Court (Bundesverfassungsgericht), 2 BvE 6/12 et al. (preliminary ruling of 12 September 2012) para 278; cf. Art. 120, 124 TFEU.

market. However, it is largely entrusted to the autonomous social partnership of trade unions and employers' associations. It is constitutionally protected in Germany and the EU. There still remains a limited scope for a cautious, but not just declamatory, wage policy of the Member States and the Union; and the wage policy must recognise the social partners as responsible key players. The EU must act despite, and because of, the cultural differences in Northern and Southern Europe regarding social partnerships. However, detailed government-imposed wage levels are extremely unlikely, but are perhaps possible in the medium term as guidelines or directives for wage increases. The goal must be a uniform, but regionally differentiated labour market that is supported by social protection policies.

2.3.4.3 Excursus F: Growth in the Indebted Countries through Structured Reform and Economic Development

It is not just about stable finances and a functioning labour market, but also about new economic and political chances for both the crisis States and also for the EU. It will be necessary to develop current aid measures of the ESM and the ECB, as well as the on-going state budget beyond a new concept for the economic and growth policies of the EU, and to realise (initially as an intergovernmental concept) an eventual way to a simplified amendment of EU Treaties (Art. 48.6 TEU).

This last building block of the EU's economic policy could only be realised as a small supranational part within the framework of the current EU Treaties. In addition to the aforementioned wage policy, the rules of convergence would have to be created in the entire EU area (temporarily only in the Euro zone), which still has diverse economic areas. In order to complete this internal development policy of the EU, a programme of limited duration and scope would need to be built, namely a convergence, structure, rehabilitation and solidarity programme. Approaches can be seen (in Part IV) in the Fiscal Pact and the *Van Rompuy* report of October 2012 to the European Council.[63] As part of this package, it is important to ponder gradual structural changes of economic and labour law, the tax system, and the economically relevant administration in those states which need to be rehabilitated – but ultimately, it is for the benefit of the workers and those groups which are most socially vulnerable.

In order to implement this temporary restructuring plan – as it is cautiously called in the Van Rompuy report – "limited, temporary, flexible, and targeted" funds will be needed; this is blurred in the October 2012 report by talk of "fiscal capacity". On the one hand, the many and sometimes small-scale funding resources should be estimated in the EU budget (probably in a partial budget for the Euro zone) and be appropriated individually by the Commission. As a general rule, the services, together with the restructuring conditions, should be contractually agreed to between the Commission and the individual states.

[63] Van Rompuy 2012, p. 34 et seqq.

On the other hand, the availability and the gradual release of these considerable financial resources would only be possible with the consent of the Member States regarding a fund (similar to the ESM and bank funds), because only the EU states as a whole have the ability to procure additional funds, and they especially have the ability to take out larger loans, so long as they are not themselves hit hard by the financial crisis.

2.3.4.4 Excursus G: The Intergovernmental Macroeconomic "Economic Government"

In addition to the completion of the financial and stability union (including the banking union), a new labour market policy and in particular a new growth policy also emerged. For these related tasks, the described legally "binding cooperation" [64] according to Art. 28, 31, 36 TEU (which should be further developed procedurally) should be conferred on the entire financial policy as well as the macroeconomic policy.[65] A comparable (so far only de facto) cooperation at the governmental level would be practised in the stability policy, in the "resolutions" of the Fiscal Pact, and in the ESM Treaty within the framework of the European Council.

The economic government would be formed in a similar, but legally binding way, which would be established through an amendment of the TFEU. It would not be an additional EU institution, but rather a part and component of the Council of Ministers/European Council[66] with a special "method of operating". It would consist of heads of government and ministers of all governments of the Member States whose currency is the Euro or who honestly wish to join the Euro area. The European Parliament would have a right to be consulted.

This new intergovernmental joint economic government has, in relation to the Member States, a functional overarching responsibility in all macroeconomic areas, of the supranational law of the EU. The law on the internal market would not be called into question.

This "government" would not be able to pass any laws. However, in addition to various operative measures (such as the general economic policy or for the amendment of the stability policy), it would above all determine binding long-term planning of the future convergence policy, as well as work on the development of relevant structural policies with respect to the aforementioned treaties that the Union has with the crisis countries. The legally binding resolutions must in principle be made by consensus; otherwise the "large majority" of the states (as explained)[67] must work with the binding nature of the decision for the "willing" states; namely accompanied by the minority's fulfilment of the duty of loyalty.

[64] See above Excursus D.
[65] Cromme 2010: Art. 94 IV.
[66] See above Sect. 2.2.2 (European Council and Council of Ministers).
[67] See above Excursus D.

The economic government would either supplement or replace the currently existing Euro Group. As needed, it could meet together with the members of the Council of Ministers that do not belong to the Euro zone, and could coordinate decisions regarding common interests; the same especially applies to the consultation of the entire Council of Ministers with respect to co-decisions in supranational legislation. The introduction of an economic government would also follow the previous French proposal. Additionally important: since there would be no "expansion of the Union" but rather only more cooperation between states, the simple procedure for the amendment of a treaty (Art. 48.6 TEU) would suffice[68] and holding state referendums would not be necessary.

An overarching new Art. 121 TFEU is conceivable:

> Common Economic Government:
>
> (1) In the European Council and in the Council[69] of the governments of those Member States whose currency is the Euro (or those who have declared a willingness to adopt the Euro with the approval of their national parliaments) in connection with the European Commission adjust their common action in the conjuncture, employment and growth policies as well as in the stability and budget policies. Principles, general guidelines and common strategies shall be fixed in the European Council, as well as additional in the Council of Ministers guidelines, necessary operative and executive measures, common positions regarding foreign policy and recommendations for necessary laws and necessary agreements of implementation between the Member States.
>
> (2) Decisions according to Paragraph 1 are binding; Articles 28 (2), 32 (1) and 36 of the Treaty on European Union shall apply analogous.

2.3.5 Areas of Freedom, Security and Justice[70]

In domestic and legal policy, there are (similar to the macroeconomic economic and monetary union) some possible precise supranational regulations, in particular for the (limited) legislation on the harmonisation of civil and criminal law, and for the cooperation of the police and judicial authorities in the Member States. Here it can remain largely unchanged with regards to the provisions of the Treaty of Lisbon.

The executive competences of the Union in the areas of immigration and border policy should be developed in connection with specific development aid in the countries of origin.

In addition to the supranational competences, there must be an overarching "binding cooperation" within the framework of the European Council/Council of Ministers for the operative cooperation and the further development of new concepts in the areas of freedom, security and justice. Above all, the entirety of Art. 67 through 89 TFEU should be replaced with a concise and systematic version.[71]

---

[68] Cromme 2012a, p. 215.

[69] Distinguish here "European Council" and "Council of Ministers" according to the current setting; to the new formation proposed here see above Sect. 2.2.2 "European Council and Council of Ministers".

[70] Cromme 2010: Art. 143, 144, 146, 151, 152; Expl. p. 298–302.

[71] Monar 2008, p. 397: The Regulations of Articles 67–89 TFEU "speaks of the Principles of Transparency Scorn".

2.3.6 Budget and Finance and the Union[72]

The budgetary law of the supranational Union can be implemented in the new constitutional law. However, it must be closely linked with the overriding macroeconomic finance policy of the Union and the States (in the context of a reinforced economic and currency union). Also, the borrowing of money by the Union, which has long been practised, albeit secretively to the primary law, should be legalised, clarified and limited under strict rules.

Also some tighter rules regarding the tasks of the Commission in the interest of economy and efficiency appear necessary, from eventual emergency budgets to the implementation of the budget. Structural aid for agriculture and the economy (with appropriate conditions) should be retained. However, persistent and comprehensive financial compensation (based on the German model) should explicitly be excluded.

Art. 311.2 TFEU speaks of the "Union's own resources", whereby only the currently existing tax on Union personnel earned this designation. Art. 311 TFEU provides for "new categories of own resources" and for implementing measures for "special legislative procedures" that correspond basically to a unanimous treaty amendment for the simplified treaty amendment procedure (Art. 48.6 TEU). This provision can be included in the corresponding general provisions in Part IV for the further "development of the EU and the development of the constitutional treaty". Early major shifts in the EU's financial constitution do not appear realistic (at any rate, not as a hurdle for the next big step towards a new European constitutional law).

The new constitutional law could provide a specific further competence of the Union from the outset in matters of taxation, provided there is a qualified majority, namely for harmonisation and implementation measures in the existing system (such as improving the uniform tax base) or for instance making an eco-tax (a steering tax/ecological incentive tax) or a market-stabilising financial transaction tax.[73]

2.4 Part IV – The Development of the EU and the Development of the Constitutional Treaty[74]

2.4.1 The Masters of the Treaties and the Constitution Convention

As was pointed out in the introduction, the desired new constitutional law of the "federation in development" has not yet been accomplished. Rather, further steps in the development of the EU and of the constitutional treaty as an essential element

[72] Cromme 2010: Art. 94 I, 95 I II, 133,136; Expl. p. 288, 294–95 – Art. 133, 135, 140 I, II, III and Art. 140 IV; Expl. p. 291, 297–98 – Art. 132 I, III; Expl. p. 289–90.

[73] If necessary, initially as "enhanced cooperation".

[74] Cromme 2010: Art. 8, 155, 156, 159, 172–74; Expl. p. 309, 310–313, 316–319; Cromme 2003, Art. 188 III, IV; Expl. p. 276.

of the new constitutional law should be considered in Part IV. Further developments are still within the purview of the Member States as the masters of the Treaties, especially with the participation of the Parliament, the European Council, and the Commission.

Regardless, the constitutional convention should not[75] be the controlling instrument for individual small steps with respect to the organic development of the still incomplete new constitutional law. Rather, the "simplified treaty amendment procedure" according to Art. 48.6 TEU must now be accepted as a more normal procedure, which will be finished through the ratification by the states. However, the European Council should reach a preliminary amendment decision not just after consultation with the European Parliament, but rather with its consent.

The constitutional convention should be considered much more an "organ of innovation", and should, but only for longer intervals (or for specific reasons), develop comprehensive and far-reaching amendments for a mature and broad constitutional law, with the approval in the ratification procedure in the Member States.

With regard to this special significance of the convention, it ought to be considered whether a concluding decision by a "large majority" of the European Council and the European Parliament would be sufficient.[76] This single exception to the unanimity principle (or the principal of amendment of primary law through contract) must be adopted with the approval of all states from the outset in accordance with the new constitutional law; only then would it be accepted from the beginning. The abolition of the unanimous vote is only compatible with sovereignty of the Member States, because the States that vote against an amendment will still have the right (since the Treaty of Lisbon) to withdraw from the EU. In this context, the right of withdrawal from the EU should be eliminated under the new constitutional law (except for withdrawal according to convention procedure). This is because the EU was created to last in perpetuity ("for an indefinite period of time").

For future constitutional conventions, there are certainly some important and innovative topics which are not yet ripe for the proposed new constitutional law, but which may be possible later within the framework of the development of the constitutional treaty (in the sought-after "federation of states") and without the loss of state identity.[77] For example, some of these topics are the aforementioned "own resources" of the Union, the desire for more authority in the realm of foreign relation policy and tax law, and a more thorough macroeconomic economic and monetary union, in addition to the rules of the European veto law in the United Nations and participation in international disarmament.

---

[75] Cromme 1987, p. 82; Cromme 2005, p. 36, 50–51.

[76] Cromme 2003, Art. 188 III, IV; Cromme 1997, p. 45: right to withdraw.

[77] Sommermann 2013, p. 708 et seqq.

2.4.2 Start with Minor Changes to Primary Law – Create a Concurrent Impetus for Progressive Integration

In light of the medium and long-term perspective of European constitutional law (with a constitutional treaty in approximately five to ten years and "development of the constitutional treaty" in subsequent stages), early first steps for the further development of the EU are both possible and necessary. This applies to the possible necessity[78] for clarification regarding the banking union and the monetary policy of the ECB, but above all to the proposed introduction of an intergovernmental macroeconomic "economic government".[79] These limited changes to primary law can be enforced in simplified procedures (Art. 48.6 TEU) because they do not include an "expansion" of the (supranational) Union.[80]

The "masters of the Treaties" should demonstrate a constitutional concept within the framework of the proposed (narrow) change – just an extensive "perspective for EU constitutional law". In this context, the soon-to-be limited change to the Treaties can be understood as momentum for the future of European constitutional law as well as a "yes" to the EU and the Euro.

References

Blanke, H.-J., & Mangiameli, S. (Eds.). (2011). *The European Union after Lisbon – Constitutional, Economic and External Actions*. Berlin: Springer.

Böckenförde, E.-W. (1991). *Staat, Verfassung, Demokratie: Studien zur Verfassungstheorie und zum Verfassungsrecht*. Frankfurt a. M.: Suhrkamp.

v. Bogdandy, A. (2001). Grundrechtsgemeinschaft als Integrationsziel? *JZ*, *56*(4), 157–171.

Calliess, C. (2013). Die Reform der Wirtschafts- und Währungsunion als Herausforderung für die Integrationsarchitektur der EU – Europa- und Verfassungsrechtliche Überlegungen. *DÖV*, *20*, 785–794.

Cromme, F. (1987). *Verfassungsvertrag der Gemeinschaft der Vereinigten Europäischen Staaten*. Delmenhorst: Riek.

Cromme, F. (1997). *Spezifische Verfassungselemente des Staatenverbundes: Bausteine für die Europäische Union*. Berlin: Köster.

Cromme, F. (2002). Verfassungsvertrag der Europäischen Union – Begriff und Konzept. *DÖV*, *14*, 593–600.

Cromme, F. (2003). *Verfassungsvertrag der Europäischen Union: Entwurf und Begründung* (2nd edn.). Baden-Baden: Nomos.

Cromme, F. (2005). Spezifische Bauelemente der europäischen Verfassung. *Europarecht*, *40*(1), 36–53.

Cromme, F. (2007). Die primärrechtliche Absicherung der Einheit der EU bei der differenzierten Integration – Die Entwicklung bis zum Brüsseler Mandat. *Europarecht*, *42*(6), 821–828.

[78] See above Excursus E.

[79] See above Excursus G; Cromme 2014, p. 448, 455–56.

[80] See above Excursus G.

Cromme, F. (2009). Juristische Irrlichter auf dem Wege zum Europäischen Verfassungsvertrag und zum Lissabon-Vertrag. *DÖV*, *5*, 177–180.

Cromme, F. (2010). *Die Zukunft des Lissabon-Vertrages: ein kurzgefasster und dynamischer Verfassungsvertrag* (3rd edn.). Baden-Baden: Nomos.

Cromme, F. (2012a). Eine Konsequenz aus der Krise: Fortentwicklung der EU als Staatenverbund? – Verknüpfung intergouvermentalen und supranationalen Handelns. *DÖV*, *6*, 209–216.

Cromme, F. (2012b). Letter to the Editor. *Der Spiegel*, *38*(17.09.2012), 12.

Cromme, F. (2013a). Vom ESM und Fiskalpakt zu einem makroökonomischen Rechtssystem der EU. *DÖV*, *15*, 594–599.

Cromme, F. (2013b). Letter to the Editor. *Frankfurter Allgemeine Zeitung*, *33*(12.4.2013), p. 33.

Cromme, F. (2014). Die Einführung einer Wirtschaftsregierung der EU – ein Impuls für die fortschreitende Integration. *Europarecht*, *49*(4), 448–458.

Dehaene, J.-L., Simon, D., & von Weizsäcker, R. (1999). *Die institutionellen Auswirkungen der Erweiterung: Bericht an die Europäische Kommission*. Luxembourg: European Commission.

Fischer, J. (2000). Vom Staatenverbund zur Föderation. Gedanken über die Finalität der Europäischen Integration. In Walter Hallstein-Institut für Europäisches Verfassungsrecht (Ed.), *Verfassungsrechtliche Reformen zur Erweiterung der Europäischen Union* (pp. 171–181). Baden-Baden: Nomos.

Geiger, R., Kahn, D.-E., & Kotzur, M. (Eds.). (2010). *EUV/AEUV. Kommentar* (5th edn.). Munich: Beck.

Grimm, D. (1995). *Braucht die EU eine Verfassung?* Munich: Carl-Friedrich-von-Siemens-Stiftung.

Larenz, K. (1991). *Methodenlehre der Rechtswissenschaft* (6th edn.). Berlin: Springer.

Monar, J. (2008). Die Vertragsreformen von Lissabon in den Bereichen Inneres und Justiz: verstärkte Handlungsfähigkeit, Kontrolle und Differenzierung. *Integration*, *31*(4), 379–398.

Nohlen, D., & Schultze, R.-O. (Eds.). (2002). *Lexikon der Politikwissenschaft* vol. Band 1: A-M. Munich: Beck.

Pechstein, M., & Koenig, C. (2000). *Die Europäische Union* (3rd edn.). Tübingen: Mohr Siebeck.

Pernice, I. (2001). Europa und nationales Verfassungsrecht. Bericht von Prof. Dr. Ingolf Pernice. *Veröffentlichungen der Vereinigung der Deutschen Staatsrechtslehrer*, *60*, 148–193.

Van Rompuy, H. (2012). *Auf dem Weg zu einer echten Wirtschafts- und Währungunion* Brussels, 12 October 2012.

Schmitt, C. (1928). *Verfassungslehre*. Munich: Duncker & Humblot.

Schwarze, J. (Ed.). (2009). *EU – Kommentar* (2nd edn.). Baden-Baden: Nomos.

Sommermann, K.-P. (2013). Integrationsgrenzen des Grundgesetzes und des europäischen Verfassungsverbundes: Brauchen wir eine neue Verfassung? *DÖV*, *18*, 708–714.

Streinz, R. (Ed.). (2012). *EUV/AEUV* (2nd edn.). Munich: Beck.

Weber, A. (1988). Buchbesprechung Franz Cromme: „Verfassungsvertrag der Gemeinschaft der Vereinigten Europäischen Staaten. *DVBl*, *103*(16), 800–801.

Weber, A. (1998). Buchbesprechung Franz Cromme: „Spezifische Verfassungselemente des Staatenverbundes: Bausteine für die Europäische Union. *DVBl*, *113*(23), 1303.

Weber, A. (2005). Buchbesprechung Franz Cromme: „Verfassungsvertrag der Europäischen Union: Entwurf und Begründung. *DVBl*, *120*(9), 561–562.

Weber, A. (2011). Buchbesprechung Franz Cromme: „Die Zukunft des Lissabon-Vertrages: ein kurzgefasster und dynamischer Verfassungsvertrag". *DVBl*, *126*(2), 88–89.

One State, one Seat, one Vote? Accommodating Sovereign Equality to International Organizations

Christian Tomuschat

1 Introduction

Sovereign equality of States is one of the ground rules of the international legal order, set forth in Art. 2 (1) of the UN Charter and confirmed in principle 6 of the Friendly Relations Declaration of the UN General Assembly of 1970 (Res. 2625[XXV]). When dealing with one another outside a specific legal framework, all States are legally endowed with the same rights. They all are entitled to be respected as independent entities, they all may enter into international relationships by concluding treaties with other nations, and the regime of international responsibility applies also to all of them, irrespective of their factual power in economic or military terms.[1] This is the great gift which the international legal order makes to smaller States, an act of faith according to which right takes precedence over might. According to a famous dictum by *Emeric de Vattel*:

> Un Nain est aussi bien un homme, qu'un Géant: Une petite République n'est pas moins un Etat souverain que le plus puissant Roïaume.[2]

Sovereign equality should not be a hollow proposition. Obviously, it requires in particular *bona fide* compliance on the part of the powerful actors on the international stage. But respect for their minor partners also benefits them since it generates a climate of understanding and cooperation susceptible of ensuring peace in the world and thereby at the same time solidifying their dominant positions.

When States enter into international agreements with a view to establishing frameworks of cooperation through international organizations, equality cannot be the pervading *Leitmotiv* for the composition of the relevant institutions tasked with performing the responsibilities conferred on the organization concerned. Account must be taken of the different degrees of factual capacity of the participating Mem-

[1] For a comprehensive study of sovereign equality see Kooijmans 1964. Assessment of this seminal work after half a century by Nijman and Werner 2012, p. 6–12.

[2] Vattel 1758, p. 11, § 18. His dictum was more a postulate than a description of political realities in the 18th and 19th centuries: see Mosler 1949.

H.-J. Blanke et al. (eds.), *Common European Legal Thinking*,
DOI 10.1007/978-3-319-19300-7_5

ber States.[3] An international organization entrusted with securing international peace and security, for example, would be blind to realities and hopelessly ineffective if it ventured to assign the same responsibilities to Andorra, Monaco, or San Marino as to major powers like the United States, China, or Russia. Therefore, the governments convening in San Francisco at the end of World War II with a view to building a new world organization agreed on the establishment of a privileged organ, the Security Council, with five permanent members as key elements holding a right of veto on all matters of substance. This bold architectural design was conceived alongside the basic rule of sovereign equality albeit at first glance in open contrast with the latter rule. Obviously, the drafters were aware of the empirical necessity to bolster the lofty principle of non-recourse to armed force (Art. 2 [4] UN Charter) by a factual counterweight. Their seemingly ambiguous approach to sovereign equality shows persuasively that this principle does not constitute a rule of *jus cogens*, to be respected under any circumstances.[4] Only if a small State were to be denied on principle its legal capacity as a State might considerations pertaining to *jus cogens* come into play. Generally, the international community is free to give its institutional arrangements the shape deemed appropriate for the objectives to be pursued.[5] The privileged position as a permanent member of the Security Council is matched by increased responsibilities.[6] Effectiveness and efficiency must not be impeded by formalistic reasoning. The international legal order has been shaped by States with a view to furthering their mutual interests and not as an instrument of blockade.[7]

When the process of European integration started with the European Coal and Steel Community (ECSC) in 1951/2, the principle "one State – one seat" was to a great extent translated into the founding Treaty. In particular, each of the six participating States was allocated one seat on the Council and one seat on the Court of Justice,[8] whereas some modification was introduced for the High Authority where the big producers, France, Germany, and Belgium, received two seats each. It needs not be explained that the original alliance of six Western European States has in the meantime grown to a voluminous multi-faceted actor comprising 28 States and that further accessions to this bloc are expected – not in the near future, but in a midterm perspective of five to twenty years. A European Union of 33 to 35 States, therefore, is not a far-away vision, but a concrete expectation that must be taken into account in policy planning for the future of Europe. Are the European institutions really viable if composed of 35 members among whom protracted processes

[3] See generally Cogan 2009, p. 223 et seq.; Dunoff 2012, p. 110; Efraim 2000.

[4] See, e. g., Orakhelashvili 2006, p. 50–53.

[5] In spite of some hesitations, this is also recognized by Kooijmans 1964, p. 240–243. Boutros-Ghali 1960, p. 68, speaks of "égalité technique" as opposed to "égalité inter-etatique". For an overview of the adjustment of sovereign equality to the requirements of International Organizations see Dunoff 2012.

[6] Kooijmans 1964, p. 281.

[7] Preuß 2008.

[8] However, the two Advocates-General were attributed to France and Germany. A seventh judge was added with a view to avoiding split votes, see below Sect. 2.4.

of accommodation of interests are inevitable? But which other structure can be envisaged as an alternative to the traditional model? In particular, how can democratic legitimacy be ensured? The following considerations will attempt to shed some light on the solutions that might be desirable for a large-scale Europe that has lost the vestiges of its original features as a purely Western construction. In this perspective, the EU institutions will be examined one by one with a view to ascertaining their suitability as the building blocks of a governmental entity that must satisfy the most variegated requirements. The basic assumption of this analysis will be that the sovereign nation State has not (yet) yielded its place to constructions according to which the process of Europeanization and globalization has made such historical roots obsolete, replacing them with a spirit of European or cosmopolitan patriotism as suggested by *Jürgen Habermas*.[9] In any event, the actual political practice still conceives the world in terms that hold on to classical templates where the State remains the guarantor of fair distribution of the benefits of international cooperation.

2 The Institutions of the European Union

When the Treaty establishing the ECSC was elaborated,[10] reliance on the classic principle of sovereign equality caused no major problem. To be sure, the six participating States were unequal in size and economic significance, Luxembourg as the smallest Member State having even much less than one million inhabitants, but the launching of the Community initiative went far beyond any purely economic reasoning where narrow selfish interests were to be balanced. All participating States viewed the merger of the coal and steel industries in their respective territories as another step on the path of reconciliation after the horrors of World War II whereby the former enemies of the Third Reich extended their hands to the recovering Western part of Germany, the newly created Federal Republic of Germany. It would have been inconceivable, at that time, to provide for any kind of discriminatory regime to the detriment of the smaller States, except for institutional configurations where some differentiation imposed itself *par la nature des choses*. In addition, within a group of six like-minded States prospects for agreement in all decision-making processes seemed to be free from any risks. Lastly, the powers of the ECSC were fairly limited, confined, as the name indicated, to the coal and steel sector. No need, therefore, was seen to provide in the ECSC Treaty for a power centre analogous to the UN Security Council, where the Federal Republic of Germany would of course have had to play a leading role alongside France.[11]

---

[9] Habermas 2011, p. 54 and passim. See discussion by Scicluna 2012, p. 442–4.

[10] The Treaty was signed on 18 April 1951, it entered into force on 23 July 1952.

[11] However, at the practical level the negotiations on the number of members of the High Authority and the Court were not easy, see Condorelli Braun 1972, p. 16–25.

2.1 From the Assembly of the ECSC Treaty to the European Parliament

The establishment of an international organization with genuine decision-making powers was a truly revolutionary step at the beginning of the 1950s. Until then, the model-type of an international organization did not exceed a purely consultative role. In particular, the League of Nations had not been provided with autonomous powers independent from the will of individual Member States although in some instances it was entrusted with administering certain territorial units (Danzig and Saar) in the implementation of the Paris Peace Treaties of 1919. The Council of Europe followed faithfully the example set by the League of Nations while the United Nations had already embarked on a new course by conferring true powers of decision on the Security Council in the field of international peace and security. Yet the most innovative feature of the ECSC was the additional authority it held to directly impose rights and obligations on private undertakings, those active in the coal and steel sector. That derogation from the all-encompassing legislative power of national parliaments was recognized as so fundamental that some democratic legitimation was deemed necessary in order to remain in conformity with the new constitutions that had been framed under the auspices of the recently reinvigorated democratic principle. Accordingly, during the negotiating process on the Schuman Declaration of 9 May 1950 it soon became clear that some kind of parliamentary body would be a necessary complement of the institutional structure.[12] That body received the name of Assembly. The Art. 20 ECSC Treaty provided that the Assembly should consist of "représentants des peuples des États réunis dans la Communauté".[13] But it continued by stating in Art. 21 (1) that the "delegates" (*délégués*) were to be designated by the respective national parliaments once a year among their members, or should be elected by direct universal suffrage. Obviously, the term "delegates" was badly chosen since it suggested that the members of the Assembly might be subject to orders imparted to them by someone – possibly by their national bodies of origin. However, the Assembly was not a diplomatic conference composed of governmental representatives, but a true parliamentary body with members accountable only to their own conscience.

There could be no doubt that for the distribution of seats in the Assembly the principle of mechanical equality could not apply inasmuch as the basic parameter of democracy is the individual human being. Accordingly, some ponderation had to take place. The three largest States – France, Germany, and Italy – each received 18 seats. Belgium and the Netherlands were treated on a level of parity with 10 seats each, and finally Luxembourg obtained a contingent of 4 seats. Any observer could perceive immediately that a compromise between the principle of sovereign equality and the democratic principle had been struck. Had the negotiators opted for strict demographic proportionality, Luxembourg would not have received a single

[12] Mosler 1966, p. 376–379.
[13] The only authentic language of the Treaty was French (Art. 100).

seat, a monstrously perverse idea in a federal unit where all participating States must be present in all institutions. This concept of degressive proportionality has been maintained over the years. This is not the place to retrace the developments from the ECSC Assembly over the Parliamentary Assembly of the EEC to today's European Parliament as the outgrowth of direct elections. Suffice it to observe that degressive proportionality is now enshrined in Art. 14.2 TEU. There can be no doubt that this principle works to the benefit of the smaller Member States. In particular the minimum threshold of six members per Member State provides the basis for a representation even of Luxembourg and Malta with a small group of deputies who will normally reflect the breadth of the pluralistic profile of these nations.

Criticisms challenging degressive proportionality, underlining that a Luxembourger will have a roughly ten times larger stake in the European Parliament than a German or a French citizen, are not aware of the logic inherent in the federal structure of the European Union. In particular the German Federal Constitutional Court held, in its judgment on the constitutionality of the Lisbon Treaty, that the scheme chosen for the European Parliament could be condoned *à la rigueur* in respect of an international entity as the European Union but lacked a truly democratic character.[14] It thereby embraced a rigid yardstick of democracy without regard for the circumstances of its institutional context. Following its advice would be tantamount to making the larger Members States the masters of the integration process by marginalizing, even overpowering the demographically inferior Member States. No valid grounds can therefore be adduced to support the contention advanced by the German Federal Constitutional Court that there is room for the principle of sovereign equality only in the "State house" but not in the complementary parliamentary body. It is true that in the United States, in particular, each one of the 50 component States sends two representatives to the Senate while for the House of Representatives only the number of voters is taken into account. However, domestic arrangements cannot serve as the guiding example for the institutions of an entity at international level where first of all the consent of all members must be secured.

Under the regime introduced by the Lisbon Treaty, the distribution of seats constitutes again a balance between the principle of sovereign equality and the democratic model. While under the EEC Treaty the number of members allocated to each State had been numerically and unchangeably fixed in the text of the Treaty itself (Art. 138), the Treaty of Amsterdam provided for some flexibility (Art. 190 [2]). A further step was taken by the Treaty of Lisbon which now enables the European Council to proceed with regard to each electoral period to a new distribution of the seats in accordance with demographic developments (Art. 14.2 TEU). According to the present scheme, which was determined by the European Council on 28 June 2013,[15] the former equality between the larger Member States, which was already given up in view of the elections in 1990, has been definitively aban-

[14] German Federal Constitutional Court (Bundesverfassungsgericht), 2 BvE 2/08 (30 June 2009) para 284–288; 2 BvR 1390/12 (18 March 2014) para 161.

[15] European Council Decision 2013/312/EU *establishing the composition of the European Parliament*, O.J. L 181/57 (2013).

doned. Germany now comes in first place with 96 seats, followed by France with 74 seats and Italy and the United Kingdom with 73 seats each. Thus, the system has become "more democratic". It seems that the principle of degressive proportionality has found general acceptance notwithstanding the overrepresentation it grants to the smaller Member States.[16] This is the price which apparently must be paid to ensure internal harmony in a federal unit.

2.2 *The Council*

From the very beginning, the intergovernmental institution of the Council was meant to link the new supranational entity to its Member States. However, the Special Council of Ministers, in abbreviated form the Council, was not mentioned as the first one in the list of institutions in the ECSC Treaty (Art. 7). Although conceived as the instrument through which national governments were to coordinate the policies of the ECSC, it did not have the same importance as today since most of the decision-making powers were specifically and narrowly circumscribed in the Treaty itself so that the High Authority, when empowered to take action, lacked any broad margin of discretion for political choices. Art. 27 ECSC Treaty stipulated that each Member State was to send one of the members of its government to the Council. This rule has been maintained for more than six decades. Today, Art. 15.2 TEU provides that the European Council, the EU's major policy-setting organ, "shall consist of the Heads of State or Government of the Members States, together with its President and the President of the Commission". Likewise, Art. 16.2 TEU identifies the Council, the institution for the management of current EU matters, as made up of "a representative of each Member State at ministerial level".

From the very beginning, this configuration amounted to a considerable advantage for the smaller Member States. At the same time, it was also clear that some kind of adjustment had to take place in order to reflect, with regard to political decision-making, the factual differences between the Member States. Following blindly the one State – one vote rule would have constituted an unfair discrimination to the detriment of the larger Member States. Accordingly, already the ECSC Treaty provided for weighted voting concerning the decisions of the Council. Decisions could be adopted by a majority vote of four against two, provided, however, that the majority included "the vote of the representative of one of the States which produces at least twenty percent of the total value of coal and steel produced in the Community" (Art. 28 [3]). Only one of the two major members, France and Germany, could therefore be overruled – a contingency which never seems to have happened. Over the years, the early formula had of course to be adapted to the transformation

[16] For a statistical breakdown of voters per one member of the European Parliament see http://en.wikipedia.org/wiki/Apportionment_in_the_European_Parliament

of the ECSC first into the European Economic Community, then into the European Community, and lastly into the European Union.

Under the regime introduced by the Treaty of Lisbon, the European Council takes its decisions, unless provided otherwise, by consensus (Art. 15.4 TEU). Consensus, as is well known, must be distinguished from unanimity.[17] If consensus is to be reached, all sides must negotiate in a spirit of understanding and compromise. Whoever persistently blocks a consensus may act in perfectly legal exercise of its rights but may disqualify itself as a loyal partner in the common undertaking. Thus, the advantage for smaller States is more apparent than real. In the long run, they are unable to maintain their divergent positions if not supported by a significant number of other dissenting Member States.

As far as the Council is concerned, the TEU has redefined the qualified majority. Art. 16.4 provides:

> As from 1 November 2014, a qualified majority shall be defined as at least 55 % of the members of the Council, comprising at least fifteen of them and representing Member States comprising at least 65 % of the population of the Union.
>
> A blocking minority must include at least four Council members, failing which the qualified majority shall be deemed attained.

Many sophisticated considerations have gone into this calculation which, additionally, has been slightly modified for a transitional period until 31 March 2017 according to Protocol No. 36 to the Treaty of Lisbon. The text clearly shows that the drafters were fully aware of the importance of voting rules. This insistence on some kind of fair distribution of voting power should not be stigmatized as an ill-conceived attempt to secure national interests. Any kind of supranational government must also seek to attain a high degree of democratic legitimacy, which is possible only if the individual citizen is taken as the basic parameter, with the appropriate modifications within a federal entity. On the whole, the "one State – one vote" criterion is still the dominant feature of the voting regime in that the four largest Member States – Germany, France, Italy, and the United Kingdom – are each counted with a coefficient of 29, without any distinction as to the number of inhabitants. In practice, voting procedures are generally eschewed. The Council seeks to reach its decisions by consensus to the extent possible.

A close look is also warranted into the presidency of the Council, as provided for by Art. 16.9 TEU. According to this rule, the Presidency of the Council shall be held by Member State representatives "on the basis of equal rotation". Currently, a time schedule exists which fixes the Presidency until 2020.[18] Realizing that this rule carries with it heavy responsibilities, efforts were undertaken as from 1999 to ensure better coordination between succeeding Presidencies.[19] In 2006, following a German initiative, the COREPER adopted the format of "team Presidencies" lasting 18 months. The first team Presidency operated between Germany, Portugal

---

[17] Wolfrum and Pichon 2012, para 3.

[18] Council Decision 2009/908/EU *laying down measures for the implementation of the European Council Decision on the exercise of the Presidency of the Council, and on the chairmanship of preparatory bodies of the Council*, O.J. L 322/28 (2009).

[19] On the relevant practice see Jensen and Nedergaard 2014, p. 1035 et seq.

and Slovenia from January 2007 to June 2008 with some success, while the subsequent team Presidency between France, the Czech Republic, and Sweden ran into major controversies.[20] Eventually, in 2009 the Lisbon Conference adopted a Declaration (No. 9) according to which the Presidency shall be entrusted to groups of three Member States for periods of 18 months each, which does not detract from the fact that there will always be one main actor who shall discharge the relevant functions for a period of six months. This modulation of the principle enshrined in Art. 16.9 TEU alleviates the concerns relating to the assignment of the speaker's role to States that may be regarded as light weights on the international stage. In particular at the United Nations, the Presidency will many times have to express the political views of the EU.[21] Does it matter who takes the floor?[22] According to the European philosophy, the contingencies of the rotation system must be disregarded. A statement by a French diplomat in the General Assembly is supposed to have the same value as the statement of the representative of a smaller member, which we may call Ruritania for the sake of simplicity. Clearly, one has to defend the right of new Member States to take part in all decision-making processes in which the EU is involved. Nevertheless, the stature of the EU must be appropriately reflected in its representatives. It is tempting to say that the institutional backing of any person who is empowered to take the floor in an international body on behalf of the EU makes the authority of the relevant statement. This is, however, a view from the inside. From the outside, the delegation of the power of official articulation to persons from smaller countries may be viewed rather as a sign of weakness than a sign of cohesive solidarity and strength. Further empirical studies are needed to clarify whether the principle of absolute parity in external relations should be preserved as such or requires some kind of overhaul.

2.3 *The Commission*

The executive institution called upon to push forward the integration process, today the European Commission, had been given the name of High Authority under the ECSC Treaty (Art. 9). The High Authority was conceived as the embodiment of the common European interest, expected to counterbalance any attempts at unilaterally pursuing one-sided national interests. From the very outset, the number of the members of the High Authority was differentiated. The largest producers of coal and steel (France, Germany, Belgium) received two seats on the High Authority while the three remaining members had to content themselves with one seat each.[23] Art. 9 (5) ECSC Treaty stated explicitly that the members of the High Authority had

[20] Jensen and Nedergaard 2014, p. 1041–2.

[21] See, e. g., statement by Lithuanian delegate *Murmokaite* in the General Assembly on the relationship between the Human Rights Council and the General Assembly, 18 December 2013, UN doc A/68/PV.70, p. 11.

[22] This aspect is not considered by Gehring et al. 2013, p. 849 et seq.

[23] On the negotiating process see Condorelli Braun 1972, p. 16–25.

to abstain from all conduct "incompatible with the supranational character of their functions", a key formulation which later disappeared from the text of the Treaties when the executive organs of the three European Communities were merged in 1967. Indeed, the High Authority was the central element of the French Schuman Declaration of 9 May 1950.[24]

Given the statistical breakdown, the configuration of the Authority amounted again to a massive discrimination in favour of the smaller States although the inequality had been compensated for to some extent by the additional seats for the large producing nations. But this was not deemed to constitute an unfair advantage precisely because the members of the High Authority were formally characterized as supranational agents, as servants of the *bonum commune* of Europe. Internally, the differences in stature deriving from the national background of the members were compensated through an artful distribution of responsibilities. In fact, the first two Presidents of the High Authority were French nationals.

With the shift from the ECSC to the European Economic Community (EEC) and the European Atomic Community (EAC) in 1958 and the further increase in the membership of the European integration process in the following years, new approaches were tested. Under the Rome Treaties, the three large Member States (France, Germany, Italy) were upgraded by the allotment of two Commissioners each (Art. 157 [1] EEC Treaty).[25] This formula was extended to the ECSC when in 1967 a Single Commission was established (provisionally 14, then 9 members). The subsequent enlargement process was characterized each time by the addition of one new Commissioner per new member, the United Kingdom however being raised to the "upper class" by the allocation of two Commissioners, a promotion which in 1985 also Spain was able to achieve (17 Commission members as from 1 January 1986). The Maastricht Treaty provided for a composition of 20 members in view of the expected accession of a group of new Member States.

At that stage, the perspective changed. It became progressively difficult to bring about suitable arrangements for the assignment of functions among the members of the Commission. At the same time, it emerged that holding a post of European Commissioner gave the home States of the office holders a considerable amount of influence in the processes of mutual accommodation. The Amsterdam Treaty did the courageous step of reducing the number of Commissioners to one national per Member State as from 1 May 1999, which implied the abolition of the prime hitherto granted to the larger States. Trying to find a compromise between the requirement of efficiency and the desire for adequate national representation, the Treaty of Lisbon provided furthermore for a reduction of the number of Commission members, as from 1 November 2014, to two thirds of the number of Member States. As for the criteria of selection, Art. 17.5 (2) stated:

> The members of the Commission shall be chosen from among the nationals of the Member States on the basis of a system of strictly equal rotation between the Member States, reflecting the demographic and geographical range of all the Member States.

[24] See Mosler 1966; Reuter 1953, p. 23–35, 51–57.

[25] Luxembourg, lacking a nuclear industry, was not represented on the Commission of the EAC.

This proviso was not to the pleasure of all governments, in particular those who until 1999 had held a permanent second post. It also led to an acrimonious debate in Ireland. Large parts of the population feared that Ireland would soon become a victim of its impact. This debate influenced greatly the outcome of a referendum on the Treaty of Lisbon which Ireland was obligated to hold in accordance with Art. 29 of its Constitution. On 12 June 2008, the referendum came out with a negative answer. The Irish electorate rejected the draft Treaty. In order to save the reform process, the European Council promised to the Irish public that use would be made of the enabling clause ("unless the European Council, acting unanimously, decides to alter this number") permitting a departure from the envisioned cut. Being reassured by this promise, the Irish electorate then approved the Treaty of Lisbon in a second referendum on 2 October 2009. Finally, the European Council took the decision on the continuity of the existing system of composition of the Commission on 22 May 2013.[26] Accordingly, the new Commission that took office on 1 November 2014 was composed of 28 members.

It does not come as a surprise that one finds in the description of the competences of the new Commissioners a lot of overlap. Thus, *Maroš Šefčovič* from Slovakia heads the portfolio on the "Energy Union" while *Miguel Arias Cañete* from Spain has to deal with "Climate Action and Energy"; *Andrus Ansip* from Estonia is responsible for the "Digital Single Market" while *Günther Oettinger* from Germany has been assigned the desk for "Digital Economy and Society". It stands to reason that the Commissioners concerned will have to work in close cooperation with one another in order to avoid frictions and parallel work. Anticipating the threat of never-ending disputes over competences, President *Jean-Claude Juncker* has introduced a new hierarchical structure. In addition to the High Representative of the Union for Foreign Affairs and Security Policy, he has chosen six Vice-Presidents whose task it will be to coordinate the work of the other Commissioners with regard to certain clusters of subject-matters.[27] As stated in the relevant document explaining the reasons underlying the new architecture, the intention is not to create different classes of Commissioners, first-class Commissioners with directive powers and second-class Commissioners who have to follow the guidelines imparted to them not only by President *Juncker* himself but also by the responsible coordinator. It has also been emphasized that the basic structure of decision-making has not been changed: the Commission shall remain a collegial body where every member has the same voting power. However, it remains to be seen whether the unprecedented design will prove fruitful or will rather give rise to obstacles impeding the decision-making process. In this regard, it is striking to note that apart from the High Representative, the former Italian Foreign Minister *Federica Mogherini*, who was appointed by the European Council with the agreement of the President of the Commission (Art. 18.1 TEU), all the other Vice-Presidents have their origins in smaller

[26] European Council Decision 2013/272/EU *concerning the number of members of the European Commission*, O.J. L 165/98 (2013).

[27] See Commission Document, 10 September 2014, http://europa.eu/rapid/press-release_IP-14-984_en.htm

countries, four of them even in countries that pertain to the EU only since 2004 (*Andrus Ansip*, Estonia; *Valdis Dombrovskis*, Latvia; *Kristalina Georgieva*, Bulgaria; *Maroš Ševčovič*, Slovakia). Only the First Vice-President, *Frans Timmermans* (Belgium) comes from a country with a long-standing tradition of European integration. None of the Commissioners from the three largest Member States alongside Italy (France, Germany, United Kingdom) has been given a coordinating role. President *Juncker* hopes to bring about "a dynamic interaction of all Members of the College, breaking down silos and moving away from static structures".[28]

The new architecture of the Commission constitutes an intelligent move to break away from a horizontal structure where the Commissioners reported exclusively to the President of the Commission, each one working alone without any institutional link with the neighbouring portfolios. But it implies a lopsided inclination in favour of the smaller Member States. It cannot be expected that Commissioners from a powerful Member State will easily follow the advice/directives given to them by the responsible coordinator from a country with little experience in European matters. Major difficulties are lying ahead in case the EU should admit further members from Eastern Europe. It is almost certain that a Commission of 33 or 35 members would become almost unmanageable since no rational criteria could be imagined justifying the parcellation of the EU's competences into tiny bits and pieces to fit such an extended number of portfolios. Remedial action must therefore be seriously envisaged. The original thrust of Art. 17.5 TEU, i. e. reduction of the number of Commissioners to two thirds of the number of Member States, should be restored. In this regard, experiences from the World Bank and the International Monetary Fund could be drawn upon. In both institutions, the number of votes held by the Member States is calculated in accordance with their capital share. Executive Directors, if not appointed by the larger share holder States, invariably act for a couple of Member States.

Obviously, finding the right balance is difficult and requires a high degree of imagination. On the one hand, the EU is a federal unit, which means that none of the Member States may be permanently excluded from the relevant decision-making processes. Smaller States cannot simply be shoved aside. The larger States, on the other hand, should not be granted the faculty of ruling the EU as they see fit. Thus, some compromise solution is inevitable. In any event, the present structure has shown its weaknesses precisely in the formation of the *Juncker* Commission. A structural preponderance of the smaller States does not show the true face of Europe. Fortunately, it has never been envisaged to include as full members the European micro-States Andorra, Monaco and San Marino.[29] Should that have been done, the untenableness of the one State – one seat principle would have emerged

[28] See Commission Document, 10 September 2014, p. 1 (http://europa.eu/rapid/press-release_IP-14-984_en.htm).

[29] Special agreements, in particular on a customs union, have been concluded with Andorra and San Marino.

immediately.[30] To some extent, the organizational framework of an international organization must reflect the characteristic features of its members. In particular, where governmental powers are exercised, democratic legitimacy is an indispensable requirement.

2.4 The Court of Justice

It stands to reason that the Court of Justice had also to become an element of the fine-tuning of the distribution of seats among the different Member States. One might imagine, somewhat naïvely, that nationality does not play any role for judges in international courts. In an individual opinion in the famous case of *Nicaragua v. United States*, Judge *Manfred Lachs* indicated in a few words the main requirements an international judge has to comply with: "A judge [. . .] is bound to be impartial, objective, detached, disinterested and unbiased." At the same time he expressed the trust that the judges in the case at hand had been able to fulfil these expectations.[31]

This is a statement inspired by the most respectable and noble trust in the righteousness of the members of the judicial profession.[32] It would indeed be wrong to say in a straightforward way that *M. Lachs* is disproven by realities. However, his words need to be seen within the general framework of the prevailing arrangements for the architecture of international courts and tribunals. Wherever one casts a glance at the relevant regulations, one invariably finds that the States involved in international disputes attach great importance to seeing a judge of their nationality on the bench, be it as ordinary members of the court concerned or as an *ad hoc* judge specifically appointed for the case under review if a national judge is lacking on that body. At the ICJ recourse to the method of appointing an *ad hoc* judge is the method provided for by the Statute (Art. 31). In the ECtHR a rule obtains that makes the presence of the judge of the nationality of the respondent State obligatory for all Chamber decisions (Art. 26 [1] of the Rules of Court);[33] apparently, Committee decisions have not been placed under this rule on the assumption that Committees of the ECtHR are solely engaged in routine matters. The same system can be found under the American Convention on Human Rights for the Inter-American Court of Human Rights (Art. 55). In other words, States see a necessity of ensuring some kind of "representation" – which cannot be true representation because that would be incompatible with the independence of a judge – when they are involved in a proceeding. Some flexibilization has been introduced, however, by the Statute of the CJEU since 1979 (Art. 16). Where chambers are formed, the requirement that

[30] See also the Commission Communication, *EU Relations with the Principality of Andorra, the Principality of Monaco and the Republic of San Marino Options for Closer Integration with the EU*, COM/2012/0680 final/2, para 5.5.

[31] International Court of Justice. *Military and Paramilitary Activities in and against Nicaragua (Nicaragua v. United States of America)* (Judgment of 27 June 1986), ICJ Reports 1986, p. 158.

[32] In the same vein Kelsen 1944, p. 213.

[33] Challenging this rule Dzehtsiarou and Coffey 2014, p. 274, 295.

a national judge from the Member State involved in the proceeding concerned does not apply, not even with regard to the Grand Chamber.

The question why such insistence on a national judge is still prevalent in the statutes of present-day international courts notwithstanding the appeal to the *bona fide* discharge of their duties by all the members of a judicial body requires elucidation. At first glance, one might assess the national judge as a person expected to defend the interests of his/her home country. However, this seems to be a totally erroneous explanation. A judge behaving like a counsel acting for his/her country would immediately disqualify him/herself. He/she would not be listened to by his/her colleagues. Sometimes, regular judges feel compelled to write excessive individual opinions rallying behind their home State[34] – and receive resolute criticism.[35] *Ad hoc* judges, in particular, must be extremely careful in presenting their reasoning *lege artis* without any excessive partisan zeal in order to be accepted as true interlocutors in a dispute to be settled by the best argument. The configuration prevailing in arbitral bodies where each party nominates or appoints one of the arbitrators and where only the umpire plays a totally independent role may be different; here, pressure weighs heavily on the government-appointed arbitrators to espouse the case of their "patrons" to the full extent. In a collegial body, however, the challenge is to win a majority for one's own standpoint. By taking one-sided positions, a judge would rather achieve counter-productive results. Lastly, a judge having acquired a reputation as a staunch defender of his/her country's interests is prone to jeopardizing his/her chances for re-appointment which, in the case of the European Union, must be done by common accord of the governments of the Member States (Art. 253 TFEU).

Therefore, another explanation has a much higher degree of plausibility. National judges are generally well-informed about the legal position in their countries of origin. They constitute precious resources as far as the structure and complexities of their domestic legal orders are concerned. Thus, they can ensure that no judgment is based on misunderstandings of municipal rules or specific factual circumstances. Of course, they are also in a position to explain the submissions of their governments should some doubts arise.[36] Conversely, this means that national governments may be confident that their submissions are adequately assessed without any fatal misinterpretation. This has nothing to do with any kind of partisan mishandling of cases.

Lastly, in recent times it has been increasingly emphasized by many writers, in particular by *A. von Bogdandy* and *I. Venzke*, that the judicial function pertains inherently to the exercise of governmental powers that need democratic legitimacy.[37] Only if judgments handed down at international level can be seen as being retrace-

---

[34] Dissenting opinion of Judge M. Schwebel in *Military and Paramilitary Activities in and against Nicaragua (Nicaragua v. United States of America)* (Judgment of 27 June 1986), ICJ Reports 1986, p. 259–527.

[35] Hohmann and de Waart 1987, p. 162; Highet 1987, p. 1, speaks of "one of the most closely reasoned and yet impassioned dissenting opinions ever to be appended to a decision of the Court".

[36] See Tomuschat 2006, p. 183–4.

[37] von Bogdandy and Venzke 2012, p. 7–41; von Bogdandy and Venzke 2014, p. 152 and passim.

able to the grass-roots level can they claim legitimacy like any other acts of public power. This requirement must be felt all the more intensely in the case of judicial bodies that take an active role in developing the law as could be witnessed in the past in respect of the Court of Justice.[38] Law-making in a purposive manner cannot be justified as being nothing else than accomplishment of the ordinary judicial task. Increasingly, however, Western societies place their trust in judicial bodies for the settlement of all kinds of disputes, even disputes the essence of which pertains rather to the political domain. To date, the well-foundedness of this trust has been spared any major crisis test.[39]

The consequences to be drawn from the premise of international judges as lawmakers for the presence of national judges in international judicial bodies are rather ambiguous. Should one proceed from the assumption that any act performed by an international court must have its ultimate roots in the population of each and every Member State of the institutional framework of which the court concerned is a constitutive element, then the one State – one seat model is the perfect legal reflection. Every individual would then have to recognize the relevant judicial acts as fully in conformity with his/her democratic right of self-determination. Conversely, however, such a narrow understanding, as it underlies notably the jurisprudence of the German Constitutional Court,[40] would seriously hamper the building of institutions at world-wide level where the simple one State – one seat rule exceeds the limits of its operability. A court with 193 judges would constitute a monstrosity without any internal cohesion. It is a simple empirical fact – and thereby also a normative building block – that the international community has long since come to acknowledge, within the framework of the United Nations, organs with limited membership that are entrusted with far-reaching powers. Obviously, the Security Council is the most prominent case in point. The Security Council derives its authority from the acts by which the UN Member States have ratified the Charter – acts that sometimes lie decades back in the past. It may seem awkward that the assent to the conferral of vital powers should remain the continuing source of legitimacy forever, without any need for confirmation or renewal. *Pacta sunt servanda* has undeniably a face with harsh traits. Eventually, however, it is not immutable. In the last analysis, a State is free to leave the United Nations under the conditions ventilated at the San Francisco founding conference.[41]

The necessity of reducing the numbers of judges to a level where decision making according to judicial methods proper is still possible, in such a way that every single judge may present his/her arguments as an individual without any need for parliamentary voting procedures being introduced, has been acknowledged at world level, on the American and the African continent. The ICJ is composed of 15 judges, the Inter-American Court of Human Rights has been maintained at a

---

[38] See generally von Bogdandy and Venzke 2011.

[39] See critical comment by Tomuschat 2005.

[40] See German Federal Constitutional Court, 2 BvE 2/08 (30 June 2009) para 244–272 – *Lisbon*.

[41] Declaration of interpretation of the founding conference of San Francisco, reprinted in Goodrich and Hambro 1949, p. 143.

level of 7 judges, and the African Court of Human Rights is made up of 11 judges. Clearly, the functional requirements have taken precedence everywhere except in Europe where, both at the CJEU and the ECtHR, the one state – one seat rule is maintained.[42]

The big disadvantage of sprawling courts, where even the tiniest member has a word to say, is that they inevitably become unrepresentative of the social background from which they emerge. The over-representation of smaller States entails also a cultural shift. Legal issues are predominantly viewed from the perspective of those smaller States which is generally not the same as that of larger and more powerful States. Judges, although doing their best to be impartial and unbiased, cannot elude the cultural imprint they have undergone and are still subjected to in their societies of origin. Accordingly, democratic legitimacy requires some ponderation in favour of the population factor.

All concerns about equitable regional distribution could be discarded if without any empirical verification international judges could be deemed automatically to develop a "cosmopolitan" understanding of law and justice. This has been claimed by quite a number of authors,[43] and it also underlies the reflections of *A. von Bogdandy* and *I. Venzke*. One may agree that for a judge to delink him/herself from national thinking habits and prejudices is an ideal to be constantly pursued.[44] Conversely, this ideal must be confronted with the systemic expectation that members of an international court are appointed or elected as representatives of a regional civilization with its specific particularities. Nobody is totally free from the traces of his/her upbringing and education – and indeed should not be so. *Posner* and *Yoo* even go so far as to maintain that independent judges cannot be effective[45] – a contention that lacks solid underpinnings and is generally rejected.[46] Even in the European environment, however, concerns have been voiced that anxieties of not being re-nominated for another term of office may affect the mental independence of a judge.[47]

The Court of Justice started within the ECSC with seven judges. The point of departure was that each of the original Member States should be provided with one judge. But since instances of a split vote can never be excluded, it was thought preferable to establish a court with seven judges, the seventh judge to be distributed somewhat at random, the Netherlands holding a second post from 1952 to 1958

---

[42] The situation of the two courts is not the same. The CJEU is part of a system for common action, whereas the ECtHR is mandated to supervise compliance with human rights in individual countries.

[43] Amtenbrink 2008, p. 21–24; Dannenbaum 2013, p. 101 et seq. Conceptual foundations developed by Gordon 2012.

[44] On the manifold grounds which may motivate an international judge see Cogan 2007/8, p. 433–439.

[45] Posner and Yoo 2005, p. 72. Cogan 2009, p. 236, speaks of a "myth" of independence of international judges.

[46] See, e. g., Benvenisti and Downs 2011, p. 1059; von Bogdandy and Venzke 2014, p. 219; Cogan 2007/8, p. 414; Mackenzie and Sands 2003, p. 275.

[47] Malinovský 2013, p. 126, 129. Other threats to a judge's independence have been described by Benvenisti and Downs 2011, with special regard to the ICJ.

allocated to them for the benefit of a leading trade union representative (*Jos Serrarens*).[48] Currently, the CJEU has 28 judges, an accurate reflection of the membership of the EU.[49] It need not be mentioned specifically that with this composition the bench is grossly unbalanced to the benefit of the smaller Member States.[50] This state of affairs must cause concern inasmuch as the Court of Justice, notwithstanding its mandate to ensure respect for the law (Art. 19.1 TEU), has emerged as one of the dynamic actors involved in bringing the European legal order to systemic perfection.

From the very inception, however, some kind of equilibrium was established by the institution of the Advocate-General, provided for not in the ECSC Treaty itself but in the Protocol on the Statute of the Court of Justice (Art. 10). Following criteria of economic relevance, the two posts of Advocate-General were initially always allocated to a French and a German lawyer. In 1973, after the accession of the United Kingdom, the number of Advocates-General was increased to four, to be shared among the four large Member States (France, Germany, Italy, and United Kingdom).[51] According to the rhythm of new accessions the number of Advocates-General rose as well. In 1981, with the admission of Greece, the number reached five so that one post could be reserved for a smaller Member State, another post was added as a consequence of the accession of Spain and Portugal in 1985, and in 1995 the level of eight Advocates General was attained.[52] It is interesting to note that as from that moment a precise regulation as to the distribution of the available seats was introduced: the five large Member States obtained one post of Advocate-General each while the other Member States were to share the remaining three posts in turn.[53] Art. 252 TFEU maintained the number at eight, providing at the same time that the Council, acting unanimously, may further increase the number. In Declaration No. 38 attached to the Final Act of the Lisbon Conference, the Member States expressed at the same time their willingness to allocate one permanent seat to Poland should the number of Advocates-General be raised to eleven. When on 25 June 2013 such a decision was indeed adopted, it was understood that the next – ninth – Advocate-General would indeed be a Polish national.[54] Accordingly, a Polish Advocate-General, *Maciej Szpunar*, was appointed on 16 October 2013.

It is obvious that in respect of the distribution of the posts of Advocates-General the general calculation system was from its very inception framed differently from the simple one State – one seat system applied for the judges. Thus, the lack of

[48] According to a general understanding, the seventh judge had to be close to the trade union movement.

[49] Art. 19.2 TEU. Regarding the General Court, this provision specifies that it shall include "at least one judge per Member State".

[50] Criticism by Alter 1998, p. 137; defence of the system by Michel 2010, p. 10–12.

[51] Council Decision of 1 January 1973 *increasing the number of Advocates-General*, O.J. L 2/29 (1973).

[52] For details see Lenaerts 2014, p. 16.

[53] Joint Declaration of 1 January 1995 on Article 31 of the Decision adjusting the instruments concerning the accession of the new Member States to the EU, O.J. L 1/221 (1995).

[54] Council Decision 2013/336/EU of 25 June 2013 *increasing the number of Advocates-General of the Court of Justice of the European Union*, O.J. L 179/92 (2013).

balance in the judicial system resulting from the over-representation of the smaller States can be balanced to a certain extent. It is a matter of common knowledge that, although the opinions of the Advocates-General are not binding, constituting no more than well-informed advice, the Court generally follows their assessment of the pending cases.[55] No such counter-weight exists regarding the General Court, which is not assisted by Advocates-General. However, one finds again elements of ponderation in the Civil Service Tribunal of the CJEU, a judicial panel of the General Court, where instructions are given as to the selection of the seven judges. In Art. 3(1) of Annex 1 to the Council Decision establishing the Tribunal[56] it is specified that "when appointing judges, the Council shall ensure a balanced composition of the Tribunal on as broad a geographical basis as possible from among nationals of the Member States and with respect to the national legal systems represented".

Here, the guiding criterion could not be the economic strength of the Member States inasmuch as all cases brought before the Civil Service Tribunal come from staff members of the EU, who are all equal, without any regard for their nationality. Accordingly, national dividing lines or rivalries do not exist. Significantly enough, here the focus is on the national legal systems encountered among the Member States. Functional necessities were the driving force behind the limitation of the number of judges. For judicial bodies, the number of seven seems to favour a climate of careful consideration and discussion. In any event, providing for a higher number of judges in respect of staff disputes would amount to an unjustifiable exaggeration.

2.5 *The European Central Bank*

The ECB is a latecomer on the European stage. It owes its coming into being to the decision taken at the Maastricht summit to introduce a common monetary policy whose core element is the euro. The legal foundations of the ECB are laid down in Art. 127 to 133 TEU as well as in Protocol No. 4 on the Statute of the European System of Central Banks and of the European Central Bank. Pursuant to Art. 10 of this Protocol, the Governing Council of the ECB shall comprise the members of the Executive Board of the ECB (six persons) and the governors of the national central banks of the Member States whose currency is the Euro (19 States as from January 2015). Art. 10.2 provides that "each member of the Governing Council shall have one vote". Any observer must remain almost incredulous noting this rule. The ECB is the key actor in the common financial market brought about by the Maas-

[55] Famous is the opinion of AG *Maduro* in the *Kadi* case, who devised an outcome which the Court followed closely: Case C-402/05 P, *Kadi* (opinion of AG Maduro of 16 January 2008; ECJ judgment of 3 September 2008). In the ground-breaking Case 6/64, *Costa v. ENEL* (ECJ 15 July 1964), by contrast, Advocate-General *Roemer* (Opinion of 25 June 1964) remained on orthodox positions.

[56] Council Decision 2004/752/EC, Euratom of 2 November 2004 *establishing the European Union Civil Service Tribunal*, O.J. L 333/7 (2004).

tricht Treaty, with a tremendous power on the economies of all Member States. Contrary to the task assigned to the judicial system of the EU to "ensure that in the interpretation and application of the Treaties the law is observed" (Art. 19.1 TEU), the members of the ECB have an undeniable policy-making function. Where in earlier instruments such functions were established at European level, the drafters took generally care, as shown above, to provide for some ponderation of the votes, in particular in the Council. Here, on the other hand, even the smallest Euro State was given the same stature as to France and Germany, the two States that have to shoulder the main burdens entailed by the common monetary policy. Estonia, Latvia and Malta were placed on a footing of parity with national economies whose dimensions exceed theirs by coefficients of up to 100, and Cyprus and Greece, countries that are running huge deficits in their budgets, enjoy also the same statutory rights as all the other Euro States. Obviously, the interests of countries with chronic debts are fundamentally opposed to the interests of the countries seeking to keep the Euro trustworthy as indicated in the mission assigned to the ECB (Art. 127.1 TFEU). It is no wonder, therefore, that grave internal disputes have emerged within the ECB.

It is hard to guess on what grounds the negotiators of the more potent Member States originally agreed to such a regime which flies in the face of the rule that powers and burdens have to correspond to one another. Germany and France may have felt some kind of moral obligation to ensure fairness of treatment to the smaller nations. However, in financial matters such generosity is misplaced not only from an economic perspective, but also under the auspices of the democratic principle. It can hardly be justified to confer on a group of States whose population does not amount to half of the aggregate of the French and German population the right to overrule the largest economies of the Euro zone. It may well be that in practice many decisions of the ECB are taken by consensus.[57] But it has also emerged in recent times that deep-going tensions have preceded many of the strategic decisions taken with regard to interest rates and the increase of the amounts of central bank financial resources made available to the commercial banks. Expert knowledge may justify some distance from parliamentary accountability, a concept which underlies Art. 88 of the German Basic Law as well, where the independence of the *Bundesbank* is guaranteed. However, to leave the course of action to be steered to some banking experts who are neither representative of the peoples on whose behalf they act nor can be made accountable according to usual democratic patterns leads the EU on a path where legitimacy is successively eroded. The conclusion is inevitable that a big mistake was committed when originally the Statute of the ECB was negotiated.

Fortunately, the *problématique* was soon recognized in the practice of ECB. Concerns emerged that with the increase in the membership of the Euro zone conducting business in the Governing Council of the ECB would become unmanageable. Therefore the Council adopted an amendment to the ECB Statute providing that the governors' voting rights would be cut and would have to be exercised in rotation

---

[57] Stressed by the ECB on its website, https://www.ecb.europa.eu/ecb/orga/decisions/govc/html/faqvotingrights.en.html

according to a pre-determined schedule as soon as 16 States would have joined the Euro area.[58] This regulation was continued under the Lisbon Treaty but modified before its entry into force by an increase of the ceiling to 18.[59] As of 1 January 2015 this has been exceeded with the accession of Lithuania to the Euro zone. The governors are split up into two groups according to their strength in terms of GDP. The first group shall comprise the governors of the five strongest States while the second group shall consist of the remaining governors. Four votes shall be allocated to the first group while the second group (14 governors) shall hold 11 votes.

Surprisingly enough, in the relevant legal literature the strangeness of the voting pattern was mostly only noted as a fact of life that deserves no further commentary.[60] The system had apparently reached such a high degree of sophistication since it was launched in 1993 that the drafters overlooked the essentials of sound institutional underpinnings. It is true that the new regime may be regarded as softening the imbalance to some extent but does not really cure the ill. It mainly took into account the discomfort produced by too high a number of members in the Governing Council but not the imbalance in the relationships among the participating States. The only reliable check against an overpowering of the larger States by the smaller States is the presence of the members of the Executive Board in the Governing Council. In the choice of the members of the Executive Board, the economic weight of the Euro zone States is consistently taken into consideration. Germany, France and Italy have always been represented on the Executive Board. Current events show, however, that the President of the ECB can enter into deep-impact understandings and alliances with the smaller States of the EU in a way that distorts the requirement of truly representative decision-making.

It is true that Art. 130 TFEU, confirmed by Art. 7 of the ECB Statute, sets forth that the members of the ECB shall be independent. They shall neither seek nor take instructions from any European or national body. However, this independence can in no way be compared to judicial independence. The governors of the national central banks are chosen as representatives of their national economies. There is no pre-determined objective they are bound to follow. What guides them is their personal assessment of what serves best the common European and their specific national interests. In this light, the structural imbalance obtains an even deeper impact.[61]

---

[58] Decision 2003/223/EC of the Council, meeting in the composition of the Heads of State or Government of 21 March 2003 *on an amendment to Article 10.2 of the Statute of the European System of Central Banks and of the European Central Bank*, O.J. L 83/66 (2003). A model calculation was presented by Bénassy-Quéré and Turkish 2009, p. 25–53.

[59] ECB Decision 2009/5/EC of 18 December 2008 *to postpone the start of the rotation system in the Governing Council of the European Central Bank (ECB/2008/29)*, O.J. L 3/4 (2009).

[60] Chevallier-Govers, in Blanke and Mangiameli (2013), Art. 13 TEU para 50; Palm, in Grabitz et al. (2014), Art. 283 TFEU para 8; Potacs, in Schwarze (2012), Art. 283 TFEU para 1.

[61] A call for "denationalization" of members of the Governing Council of the ECB has been made by Heisenberg 2003.

3 Conclusions

It is hard to draw general conclusions after this cursory study of the key institutions of the EU as to their composition. Invariably, compromises have to be found between, one the one hand, equality of the Member States and, on the other hand, equality of citizens according to democratic parameters. No recipes for absolutely fitting distribution schemes can be given. However, generally over-representation of the smaller States in conformity with the principle: one State, one seat and one vote, has become the outstanding feature, notwithstanding manifold efforts to curb this trend.[62] Care must be taken to ensure that with the further increase of the membership of the EU the balance be better adjusted. The situation prevailing at the ECB requires deep-going reform. For other institutions like in particular the Court of Justice it would be clearly preferable to reduce the number of members down to a size where every member is constrained to conceive of his/her role as that of a true servant of the *bonum commune europaeum*, without any national strings linking him/her back to the country of origin. One must be afraid, though, that the tremendous caseload will render any such initiative nugatory.

References

Alter, K. J. (1998). Who are the 'Masters of the Treaty'? European Governments and the European Court of Justice. *International Organization*, *52*(1), 121–147.

Amtenbrink, F. (2008). The Multi-Dimensional Constitutional Legal Order of the European Union – a Successful Case of Cosmopolitan Constitution-Building? *Netherlands Yearbook of International Law*, *39*, 3–68.

Bénassy-Quéré, A., & Turkish, E. (2009). The ECB Governing Council in an Enlarged Euro Area. *JCMS*, *47*(1), 25–53.

Benvenisti, E., & Downs, G. W. (2011). Prospects for the Increased Independence of International Tribunals. *GLJ*, *12*(5), 1057–1081.

Blanke, H.-J., & Mangiameli, S. (Eds.). (2013). *The Treaty on the European Union (TEU). A Commentary*. Heidelberg: Springer.

Bodansky, D. (1999). The Legitimacy of International Governance: A Coming Challenge for International Environmental Law? *AJIL*, *93*(3), 596–624.

von Bogdandy, A., & Venzke, I. (2011). Beyond Dispute: International Judicial Institutions as Lawmakers. *GLJ*, *12*(5), 979–1004.

von Bogdandy, A., & Venzke, I. (2012). In Whose Name? An Investigation of International Courts' Public Authority and Its Domestic Justification. *EJIL*, *23*(1), 7–41.

von Bogdandy, A., & Venzke, I. (2014). *In wessen Namen? Internationale Gerichte in Zeiten globalen Regierens*. Berlin: Suhrkamp.

Boutros-Ghali, B. (1960). Le principe d'égalité des Etats et les Organisations Internationales. *Recueil des cours*, *100*(II), 1–73.

[62] See generally criticism by Bodansky 1999, p. 614.

Cogan, J. K. (2007/8). Competition and Control on International Adjudication. *Virginia Journal of International Law*, *48*, 411–450.

Cogan, J. K. (2009). Representation and Power in International Organization: The Operational Constitution and its Critics. *AJIL*, *103*(2), 209–263.

Condorelli Braun, N. (1972). *Commissaires et juges dans les Communautés européennes*. Paris: Pichon & Durand-Auzias.

Dannenbaum, T. (2013). Nationality and the International Judge: The Nationalist Presumption Governing the International Judiciary and Why It Must Be Reversed. *Cornell International Law Journal*, *45*(1), 77–184.

Dunoff, J. L. (2012). Is Sovereign Equality Obsolete? Understanding Twenty-First Century International Organizations. *Netherlands Yearbook of International Law*, *43*, 99–127.

Dzehtsiarou, K., & Coffey, D. K. (2014). Legitimacy and Independence of International Tribunals. An Analysis of the European Court of Human Rights. *Hastings International and Comparative Law Review*, *37*, 271–322.

Efraim, A. D. (2000). *Sovereign (In)equality in International Organizations*. The Hague et al: Martinus Nijhoff.

Gehring, T., Oberthür, S., & Mühleck, M. (2013). European Actorness in International Institutions. *JCMS*, *51*(5), 849–865.

Goodrich, L. M., & Hambro, E. (1949). *Charter of the United Nations* (2nd edn.). Boston: World Peace Foundation.

Gordon, G. (2012). Legal Equality and Innate Cosmopolitanism in Contemporary Discourses. *Netherlands Yearbook of International Law*, *43*, 183–203.

Grabitz, E., Hilf, M., & Nettesheim, N. (Eds.). (2014). *Das Recht der Europäischen Union: Kommentar*. Munich: Beck.

Habermas, J. (2011). *Zur Verfassung Europas: Ein Essay*. Berlin: Suhrkamp.

Heisenberg, D. (2003). Cutting the Bank Down to Size: Efficient and Legitimate Decision-making in the European Central Bank after Enlargement. *JCMS*, *41*(3), 397–420.

Highet, K. (1987). Evidence, the Court, and the Nicaragua Case. *AJIL*, *81*(1), 1–56.

Hohmann, H., & de Waart, P. J. I. M. (1987). Compulsory Jurisdiction and the Use of Force as a Legal Issue: The Epoch-Making of the International Court of Justice in Nicaragua v. United States of America. *Netherlands International Law Review*, *34*, 162–191.

Jensen, M. D., & Nedergaard, P. (2014). Uno, Duo, Trio? Varieties of Trio Presidencies in the Council of Ministers. *JCMS*, *52*(5), 1035–1052.

Kelsen, H. (1944). Principle of Sovereign Equality of States as a Basis for International Organization. *Yale Law Journal*, *53*(2), 207–220.

Kooijmans, P. H. (1964). *The doctrine of the legal equality of states: An inquiry into the foundations of international law*. Leiden: Sythoff.

Lenaerts, K. (2014). *EU Procedural Law*. Oxford: OUP.

Mackenzie, R., & Sands, P. (2003). International Courts and Tribunals and the Independence of the International Judge. *Harvard International Law Journal*, *44*(1), 271–286.

Malinovský, J. (2013). Les écueils de la reconduction des juges internationaux. In J.-F. Akandji-Kombé (Ed.), *L'homme dans la société internationale. Mélanges en honneur du Professeur Paul Tavernier* (pp. 121–139). Brussels: Bruylant.

Michel, V. (2010). Les juridictions des Communautés européennes. In H. Ruiz Fabri, & J.-M. Sorel (Eds.), *Indépendance et impartialité des juges internationaux* (pp. 9–30). Paris: Pedone.

Mosler, H. (1949). *Die Großmachtstellung im Völkerrecht*. Heidelberg: Lambert Schneider.

Mosler, H. (1966). Die Entstehung des Modells supranationaler und gewaltenteilender Staatenverbindungen in den Verhandlungen über den Schuman-Plan. In E.von Caemmerer, H.-J. Schlochauer, & E. Steindorff (Eds.), *Probleme des europäischen Rechts. Festschrift für Walter Hallstein* (pp. 355–386). Frankfurt: Vittorio Klostermann.

Nijman, J. E., & Werner, W. G. (2012). Legal Equality and the International Rule of Law. *Netherlands Yearbook of International Law, 43*, 3–24.

Orakhelashvili, A. (2006). *Peremptory Norms in International Law*. Oxford: OUP.

Posner, E. A., & Yoo, J. C. (2005). Judicial Independence in International Tribunals. *California Law Review, 93*(1), 1–74.

Preuß, U. K. (2008). Equality of States. Its Meaning in a Constitutionalized Global Order. *Chicago Journal of International Law, 9*(1), 17–50.

Reuter, P. (1953). *La Communauté européenne du charbon et de l'acier*. Paris: Librairie générale de droit et de jurisprudence.

Schwarze, J. (Ed.). (2012). *EU-Kommentar* (3rd edn.). Baden-Baden: Nomos.

Scicluna, N. (2012). When Failure isn't Failure: European Union Constitutionalism after the Lisbon Treaty. *JCMS, 50*(3), 441–456.

Tomuschat, C. (2005). Das Europa der Richter. In J. Bröhmer (Ed.), *Internationale Gemeinschaft und Menschenrechte. Festschrift für Georg Ress* (pp. 857–874). Köln: Carl Heymanns.

Tomuschat, C. (2006). National Representation of Judges and Legitimacy of International Jurisdictions: Lessons from ICJ to EC. In I. Pernice, J. Kokott, & C. Saunders (Eds.), *The Future of the European Judicial System in a Comparative Perspective* (pp. 39–57). Baden-Baden: Nomos.

de Vattel, E. (1758). *Le droit des gens ou principes de la loi naturelle*. London.

Wolfrum, R., & Pichon, J. (2012). Consensus. In R. Wolfrum (Ed.), *The Max Planck Encyclopedia of Public International Law* (vol. II, pp. 673–678). Oxford: OUP.

La Conciliation Entre la Primauté du Droit de l'Union Européenne et l'Identité Nationale des Etats Membres: Mission Impossible ou Espoir Raisonné?

Vlad Constantinesco

> Un des plus grands défis pour les juristes depuis le début du XXe siècle a été de penser la hiérarchie des normes et le pluralisme des ordres juridiques au-delà et en-deçà des Etats nations.[1]

La question des rapports entre le droit de l'Union et les droits des Etats membres est centrale, non seulement pour assurer le plus efficacement possible, l'égale validité du droit de l'Union dans tous les ordres juridiques nationaux, mais aussi comme l'un des critères possibles pour définir la nature juridique de l'Union européenne, oscillant entre Etat fédéral, Confédération d'Etats ou Fédération, sans compter, aussi, la solution d'une nature *sui generis,* peu satisfaisante en théorie, mais que la réalité observable impose le plus souvent.

Les quelques lignes qui suivent se veulent un hommage à *Albrecht Weber*, cet éminent collègue et ami dont l'ouverture d'esprit, la curiosité, l'ont entraîné vers ces nouveaux territoires scientifiques que sont le droit européen et ses articulations avec les droits nationaux, ainsi qu'en témoigne son magistral ouvrage comparatiste: *Europäische Verfassungsvergleichung*.[2] La présente contribution ne prétend évidemment pas épuiser le sujet, mais plus simplement l'éclairer par quelques considérations générales qui montreront comment une question qui au départ se présentait de manière plutôt simple, est aujourd'hui devenue – sous la pression de multiples facteurs – une question complexe, mais aussi une question controversée, qui demeure ouverte.

Car la manière dont cette question se règle – comme la nature de l'instance qui la règle et le niveau auquel elle est réglée – déterminera le degré d'effectivité du droit de l'Union dans les ordres juridiques nationaux, ainsi que la nature de l'ordre juridique qui est le sien.

Il peut sembler assez extraordinaire, aujourd'hui, que les rédacteurs des traités de Paris et de Rome n'aient pas consacré une disposition expresse des traités constitutifs à régler cette question – à la différence des constitutions établissant des

---

[1] Halperin 2004, p. 340.

[2] Weber 2010, p. 401 et seq en particulier.

H.-J. Blanke et al. (eds.), *Common European Legal Thinking*,
DOI 10.1007/978-3-319-19300-7_6

Etats fédéraux.[3] Cette prudente discrétion – ou ce traitement par prétérition – peuvent s'expliquer par la commune volonté des Etats fondateurs de ne pas dessiner avec des traits trop accusés la nature de la structure qu'ils créaient: il aurait été prématuré, et maladroit, de dévoiler d'emblée l'horizon politique – qui ne pouvait qu'être incertain et indéterminé – d'une construction au premier chef économique, technique – voire technocratique – et plutôt élitiste.

Du coup, ce silence allait laisser la place à d'autres protagonistes que les Etats fondateurs des Communautés européennes pour préciser les rapports entre le droit communautaire (aujourd'hui, droit de l'Union) et les droits nationaux. Parmi ces autres protagonistes, les plus importants seront par ordre d'apparition, d'abord la Cour de justice et sa jurisprudence fondatrice (celle qui a posé le principe de primauté dans l'arrêt *Costa c. ENEL*)[4] *J. Ziller*[5] fait observer à juste titre que le terme employé par la Cour de justice dans l'arrêt *Costa c. ENEL,* dans sa rédaction initiale en français, est celui de *prééminence*, alors que la version allemande, par exemple utilise le mot *Vorrang*, beaucoup plus explicite et beaucoup plus fort. Il ajoute: "È solo di recente che si è consolidato l'uso della parola *primauté* in francese, e 'primato' in italiano." A ce protagoniste central – mais qui ne possède pas l'*utima ratio* d'annuler ou de déclarer inapplicable au litige une disposition du droit national contraire au droit de l'Union –, s'en sont ajoutés d'autres. Au premier chef, les constituants nationaux lors des révisions constitutionnelles jugées nécessaires pour rendre compte des progrès de l'intégration européenne, mais aussi les juridictions nationales – *juges de droit commun du droit de l'Union*, selon la formule consacrée –, avec, en particulier, les juges constitutionnels et les juridictions suprêmes des différents ordres juridictionnels nationaux.

On est donc passé d'une situation de centralité (une seule autorité pour fonder le principe de primauté et pour en décrire les conséquences et les limites – le mode d'emploi – à l'usage des juridictions nationales) à une situation de concurrence (une pluralité de centres décisionnels investis d'une compétence qui les conduit à se prononcer non seulement sur un conflit entre une règle du droit de l'Union et une règle nationale, mais aussi sur la règle de conflit elle-même). Il y a donc aujourd'hui une pluralité de locuteurs, et ce changement de panorama rend plus complexe le contexte dans lequel seront définis les rapports entre droit de l'Union et doit nationaux (Sect. 1).

Si la primauté, telle qu'initialement conçue par la Cour de justice, revêt un caractère absolu (tout le droit de l'Union l'emporte sur tout le droit interne contraire), le fait que la réalisation concrète de la primauté dépende aujourd'hui d'une multiplicité d'instances vient incontestablement la relativiser. Témoin de cette évolution, la notion d'*identité nationale* que l'on peut considérer comme un infléchissement à la primauté du droit de l'Union (Sect. 2).

---

[3] Cf. par exemple Art. VI § 2 de la constitution des Etats-Unis d'Amérique (1787) ou Art. 31 de la Loi fondamentale allemande (1949).
[4] Affaire 6/64, *Costa c. ENEL* (CJCE 15 juillet 1964).
[5] Ziller 2013, p. 247.

1 Un Changement de Panorama

Le constat d'une multiplicité d'acteurs qui auront leur mot à dire en ce qui concerne les rapports entre le droit de l'Union et tel droit national est banal, mais il faut commencer par lui (Sect. 1.1), avant d'aborder un autre élément qui a conduit à modifier le panorama juridique européen: la multiplicité des textes susceptibles d'entrer en conflit (Sect. 1.2). A travers cette démarche, on observera que c'est la diffusion de la protection des droits de l'homme – ou des droits fondamentaux de la personne (on considèrera ici que les deux expressions sont équivalentes) – aussi bien dans le droit de l'Union que dans les constitutions des nouveaux Etats membres de l'Union européenne et du Conseil de l'Europe qui a été sans doute le facteur déterminant pour compliquer la question des rapports entre droit de l'Union et droits nationaux.

1.1 Des Instances Multiples

S'agissant de l'Union européenne, la Cour de justice continue de jouer un rôle prééminent depuis son arrêt fondateur rendu dans l'affaire *Costa c. ENEL.* Ceci s'explique certainement par le fait que la Cour reçoit les questions préjudicielles envoyées par les juridictions nationales, la procédure de renvoi préjudiciel étant le canal le plus efficace pour permettre à la Cour de se prononcer sur l'incompatibilité entre une disposition du droit national et une norme du droit de l'Union, mais aussi de déterminer quelles doivent être, dans ce cas, les obligations pesant sur le juge national.[6] Les autres deux juridictions qui forment, avec la Cour de justice, l'institution judiciaire de l'Union européenne: le Tribunal et le Tribunal de la Fonction Publique, n'ont pas, compte tenu de leurs compétences, à se prononcer sur la compatibilité de mesures nationales avec le droit de l'Union.

Mais tous les Etats membres de l'Union le sont également du Conseil de l'Europe, et à ce titre, sont aussi Hautes Parties contractantes à la Convention européenne des droits de l'homme. Si la CEDH ne lie pas encore formellement l'Union européenne – le principe de l'adhésion de l'UE à la CEDH est affirmé dans l'art. 6.2 TUE, tel qu'il résulte du traité de Lisbonne, mais les négociations, plus complexes qu'il n'y pouvait paraître au départ, n'ont pas encore à ce jour abouti – on doit néanmoins se poser la question du sort d'un acte national pris en exécution d'un acte de l'Union, et donc conforme à ce droit, mais qui pourrait être contraire aux droits garantis par la CEDH. La solution apportée par l'arrêt *Bosphorus*[7] pourrait ici servir de repère et garantir, jusqu'à preuve du contraire

[6] Affaire 106/77, *Administration des Finances de l'Etat c. S. A. Simmenthal* (CJCE 9 mars 1978) Rec. 1978, p. 629.

[7] Req. n° 45036/98, *Bosphorus Airlines Hava Yolları Turizm ve Ticaret Anonim Şirketi c. Irlande* (CEDH GC 30 juin 2005):.

"155. De l'avis de la Cour, une mesure de l'Etat prise en exécution de pareilles obligations ju-

– présomption simple –, que le droit national, s'il est conforme au droit de l'Union, ne contrevient pas aux droits garantis par la CEDH.

Enfin, il faut introduire dans ce panorama juridictionnel l'ensemble des juges nationaux: ce sont eux qui vont avoir à faire vivre le principe de primauté, car l'effectivité de ce principe dépendra en dernière instance de la manière dont ils répondront – plus ou moins complètement – aux exigences du principe de primauté, telles que la Cour de justice les a définies. Parmi ces juges nationaux, une attention particulière doit être accordée aux juges constitutionnels. Etablis par la constitution, c'est-à-dire par l'acte juridico-politique de valeur la plus élevée dans l'ordre juridique interne, ils doivent aussi, certes en vertu de leur compétence découlant de leur propre constitution mais aussi en leur qualité de juge de droit commun du droit de l'Union, donner au droit de l'Union la prévalence sur le droit national contraire, tout en faisant application de sa constitution dont les termes ne sont pas toujours les plus explicites. Il est évident que cette mission sera encore plus difficile si le droit national en cause est telle disposition de la constitution elle-même!

1.2 Des Textes Multiples

Le souci de garantir les droits fondamentaux, apparu d'abord en droit interne, puis au plan universel avec la Déclaration universelle des droits de l'homme de 1948, trouve aussi à s'incarner dans des instruments régionaux dont le plus perfectionné est bien la CEDH, qui organise un contrôle juridictionnel international en cas de

---

ridiques doit être réputée justifiée dès lors qu'il est constant que l'organisation en question accorde aux droits fondamentaux (cette notion recouvrant à la fois les garanties substantielles offertes et les mécanismes censés en contrôler le respect) une protection à tout le moins équivalente à celle assurée par la Convention (*M. & Co.*, décision précitée, p. 152, démarche à laquelle les parties et la Commission européenne souscrivent). Par 'équivalente', la Cour entend 'comparable': toute exigence de protection 'identique' de la part de l'organisation concernée pourrait aller à l'encontre de l'intérêt de la coopération internationale poursuivi (paragraphe 150 ci-dessus). Toutefois, un constat de 'protection équivalente' de ce type ne saurait être définitif: il doit pouvoir être réexaminé à la lumière de tout changement pertinent dans la protection des droits fondamentaux.
156. Si l'on considère que l'organisation offre semblable protection équivalente, il y a lieu de présumer qu'un Etat respecte les exigences de la Convention lorsqu'il ne fait qu'exécuter des obligations juridiques résultant de son adhésion à l'organisation.
Pareille présomption peut toutefois être renversée dans le cadre d'une affaire donnée si l'on estime que la protection des droits garantis par la Convention était entachée d'une insuffisance manifeste. Dans un tel cas, le rôle de la Convention en tant qu' 'instrument constitutionnel de l'ordre public européen' dans le domaine des droits de l'homme l'emporterait sur l'intérêt de la coopération internationale (*Loizidou c. Turquie* (exceptions préliminaires), arrêt du 23 mars 1995, série A no 310, pp. 27–28, § 75).
[...] 165. Dans ces conditions, la Cour estime pouvoir considérer que la protection des droits fondamentaux offerte par le droit communautaire est, et était à l'époque des faits, 'équivalente' (au sens du paragraphe 155 ci-dessus) à celle assurée par le mécanisme de la Convention. Par conséquent, on peut présumer que l'Irlande ne s'est pas écartée des obligations qui lui incombaient au titre de la Convention lorsqu'elle a mis en œuvre celles qui résultaient de son appartenance à la Communauté européenne (paragraphe 156 ci-dessus).".

violation par un Etat partie des droits qu'elle énonce. On sait comment la Cour de justice des Communautés européennes a progressivement accordé le rang de *principes généraux du droit* communautaire aux droits fondamentaux, tels qu'il résultent des traditions constitutionnelles communes des Etats membres, mais aussi des instruments internationaux auxquels ils sont parties.

Les droits garantis par la CEDH font donc ainsi, par le truchement des principes généraux, leur entrée dans le droit communautaire, mais, parallèlement à ce mouvement jurisprudentiel, l'Union européenne a entrepris, d'une part, de se donner sa propre déclaration des droits fondamentaux: la *Charte des droits fondamentaux de l'Union européenne* (2000), et, d'autre part, de devenir partie contractante à la CEDH. Si la protection des droits fondamentaux incombe d'abord à chaque Etat – leurs constitutions énonçant ces droits fondamentaux et organisant les recours en inconstitutionnalité les protégeant –, leur qualité simultanée d'Etat membre de l'Union, tenus en tant que tels à l'observance de la *Charte*, et d'Etat partie à la CEDH, créent les conditions d'interférences normatives complexes, que l'adhésion de l'Union à la CEDH ne simplifiera pas nécessairement.

La dernière révision introduite par le traité de Lisbonne (2009) introduit la *Charte des droits fondamentaux de l'Union européenne* dans le droit originaire. La *Charte* se voit octroyer la même valeur juridique que les traités, par l'art. 6.1 TUE. Elle a commencé, avant même son incorporation au droit originaire,[8] à être appliquée par la Cour de justice.

L'art. 52 de la Charte vise à régler les problèmes relatifs à son champ d'application,[9] tandis que son art. 53[10] s'occupe de préciser le niveau de protection assuré par la Charte, en cherchant à préserver l'autonomie des différents textes protecteurs des droits fondamentaux (le droit de l'Union, le droit international et les conventions auxquelles l'Union ou tous ses Etats membres sont parties, la CEDH, et *last but not least* les constitutions des Etats membres) ainsi que le niveau de protection établis par chacun de ces textes. L'existence de la Charte et

[8] Pour la première apparition de la Charte dans la jurisprudence de la Cour de justice, voir Burgorgue-Larsen 2006. Lire aussi sous cet arrêt le commentaire de Brodier 2006.

[9] Art. 52 Charte des droits fondamentaux: "1. Les dispositions de la présente Charte s'adressent aux institutions, organes et organismes de l'Union dans le respect du principe de subsidiarité, ainsi qu'aux États membres uniquement lorsqu'ils mettent en œuvre le droit de l'Union. En conséquence, ils respectent les droits, observent les principes et en promeuvent l'application, conformément à leurs compétences respectives et dans le respect des limites des compétences de l'Union telles qu'elles lui sont conférées dans les traités.
2. La présente Charte n'étend pas le champ d'application du droit de l'Union au-delà des compétences de l'Union, ni ne crée aucune compétence ni aucune tâche nouvelles pour l'Union et ne modifie pas les compétences et tâches définies dans les traités.".

[10] Art. 53 Charte des droits fondamentaux: "Aucune disposition de la présente Charte ne doit être interprétée comme limitant ou portant atteinte aux droits de l'homme et libertés fondamentales reconnus, dans leur champ d'application respectif, par le droit de l'Union, le droit international et les conventions internationales auxquelles sont parties l'Union, ou tous les États membres, et notamment la Convention européenne de sauvegarde des droits de l'Homme et des libertés fondamentales, ainsi que par les constitutions des États membres.".

des droits qui y sont énoncés ne devrait pas diminuer les garanties offertes par les autres textes, nationaux ou internationaux qui coexistent avec elle.

Mais comment concilier cette affirmation avec le principe de primauté du droit de l'Union, dont la Charte fait partie? Tel est l'objet de l'arrêt rendu, sur renvoi préjudiciel formé par le *Tribunal Constitucional* espagnol, par la Grande Chambre de la Cour de justice de l'Union européenne, dans l'affaire *Melloni*.[11] Au cœur des questions posées par le juge constitutionnel espagnol à la Cour se trouve évidemment l'interprétation qu'il convient de donner de l'art. 53 de la Charte, en ce qui concerne les interférences entre le niveau de protection offert par la constitution et les obligations, découlant en l'espèce de la décision-cadre 2002/584 sur le mandat d'arrêt européen, telle que modifiée par la décision-cadre 2009/299.

La réponse de la Grande Chambre est particulièrement nette:

> 56. À cet égard, la juridiction de renvoi envisage d'emblée l'interprétation selon laquelle l'article 53 de la Charte autoriserait de manière générale un État membre à appliquer le standard de protection des droits fondamentaux garanti par sa Constitution lorsqu'il est plus élevé que celui qui découle de la Charte et à l'opposer, le cas échéant, à l'application de dispositions du droit de l'Union. Une telle interprétation permettrait, en particulier, à un État membre de subordonner l'exécution d'un mandat d'arrêt européen délivré en vue d'exécuter un jugement rendu par défaut à des conditions ayant pour objet d'éviter une interprétation limitant les droits fondamentaux reconnus par sa Constitution ou portant atteinte à ceux ci, quand bien même l'application de telles conditions ne serait pas autorisée par l'article 4 bis, paragraphe 1, de la décision-cadre 2002/584.
>
> 57. Une telle interprétation de l'article 53 de la Charte ne saurait être retenue.
>
> 58. En effet, cette interprétation de l'article 53 de la Charte porterait atteinte au principe de la primauté du droit de l'Union, en ce qu'elle permettrait à un État membre de faire obstacle à l'application d'actes du droit de l'Union pleinement conformes à la Charte, dès lors qu'ils ne respecteraient pas les droits fondamentaux garantis par la Constitution de cet État.
>
> 59. Il est, en effet, de jurisprudence bien établie qu'en vertu du principe de la primauté du droit de l'Union, qui est une caractéristique essentielle de l'ordre juridique de l'Union [. . .], le fait pour un État membre d'invoquer des dispositions de droit national, fussent-elles d'ordre constitutionnel, ne saurait affecter l'effet du droit de l'Union sur le territoire de cet État [. . .].

Comme le note *A. Da Fonseca*:

> Se fondant sur le principe de primauté, la Cour de justice rappelle qu'un Etat membre ne peut invoquer des dispositions nationales, même d'ordre constitutionnel, pour faire obstacle à l'application du droit de l'Union. L'article 4 bis, § 1, étant conforme à la Charte, et de surcroît ne laissant aucune marge d'appréciation aux Etats membres, ces derniers ne peuvent en aucun cas entraver l'exécution d'un mandat d'arrêt européen par l'application de leurs standards nationaux.[12]

Le rappel du principe de primauté, dont l'autorité s'étend aux dispositions de la constitution nationale, vient ainsi plus que relativiser la portée de l'art. 53 de la Charte. Cette solution se fonde certes sur le fait que la Cour a estimé les dispositions

---

[11] Affaire C-399/11, *Stefano Melloni c. Ministerio Fiscal* (CJUE 26 février 2013). Voir en particulier: Benlolo Carabot 2013; Weiler 2013; Da Fonseca 2014.

[12] Da Fonseca 2014.

en cause de la décision-cadre n'étaient pas contraires à la Charte, cependant, comme le souligne *R. Mehdi*:

> Par son rigorisme, la lecture que la Cour retient, dans l'affaire Melloni, du principe de primauté, conduit inévitablement à neutraliser les dispositions de l'article 53 de la Charte et à priver le juge de la faculté d'invoquer le traitement plus favorable qui pourrait être accordé à une personne sur la base des dispositions constitutionnelles.[13]

Ainsi est-on fondé à se demander si:

> Does this mean that EU Member States can never set higher national standards of fundamental rights in all situations governed by EU law? [...] Of course not. In accordance with settled case law of the CJUE in others areas of EU law, Member States can still go beyond what is required by EU law, but only to the extent that subject matter has not been completely regulated by the Union.[14]

Mais si la règlementation européenne est complète, comme c'est le cas en l'espèce, l'invocation du droit national, fut-il constitutionnel, ne peut pas mettre en cause la primauté du droit de l'Union. Comment celle-ci s'accommoderait-elle de l'invocation du respect d'une disposition qui exprimerait l'identité nationale d'un Etat membre?

2 Primauté et Respect de l'Identité Nationale de l'Etat Membre

La mention selon laquelle l'Union respecte l'identité nationale de ses Etats membres, inscrite aujourd'hui à l'art. 4.2 TUE, dans la version donnée par le traité de Lisbonne (2009), figurait déjà dans le traité de Maastricht (1991). Mais le TUE dans sa rédaction actuelle, énonce nombre de points qui ne se trouvaient pas dans le traité de Maastricht. Ainsi, il est d'abord précisé que l'identité nationale des Etats membres est "inhérente à leurs structures fondamentales politiques et constitutionnelles", et aussi, "y compris en ce qui concerne l'autonomie locale et régionale". Il y a là comme une "réserve de souveraineté", le droit de l'Union ne pouvant pas affecter l'ordre constitutionnel et administratif des Etats membres; les réserves aux traités multilatéraux doivent être, selon la Convention de Vienne sur le droit des traités (1981), être acceptées par tous les Etats parties au traité et ne pas aller à l'encontre de l'objet et du but du traité. De plus, l'art. 4.2 TUE indique encore que l'Union "respecte les fonctions essentielles de l'Etat, notamment celles qui ont pour objet d'assurer son intégrité territoriale, de maintenir l'ordre public, et de sauvegarder la sécurité nationale. En particulier, la sécurité nationale reste de la seule responsabilité de chaque Etat membre".

L'insistance mise à souligner que les fonctions régaliennes traditionnellement reconnues aux Etats membres ne peuvent pas faire l'objet d'immixtions procédant du droit de l'Union répond au souci des Etats membres de garder la main sur ces domaines qui sont au cœur de leur souveraineté.

---

[13] Mehdi 2013.

[14] Franssen 2014.

L'ensemble de cette disposition confirme, avec d'autres indices (ainsi le droit de retrait prévu par l'art. 50 TUE), que la construction d'ensemble de l'Union obéit – pour partie au moins – à la figure de la Confédération d'Etats – reposant sur le maintien de la souveraineté au niveau des Etats membres et non à celle de l'Etat fédéral, qui supposerait un déplacement des souverainetés vers l'échelon fédéral. D'autres indices, par exemple la centralisation de la politique monétaire, orienteraient vers l'Etat fédéral. Nous avons toujours soutenu la thèse de la nature mixte de l'Union européenne, même si nous en reconnaissons volontiers les limites et si nous ne méconnaissons pas les objections qui pourraient lui être faites. La catégorie de la *Fédération*, dont l'exploration a été magistralement faite par *O. Beaud*[15] ne nous semble pas convenir pour qualifier l'Union européenne, comme nous l'avons développé ailleurs.[16]

Que nous dit cette disposition des rapports entre le droit de l'Union et les droits des Etats membres? Peut-on, à l'instar de la primauté, la considérer comme une règle de conflit ou comme une exception au principe de primauté? (La Déclaration n° 17, annexée aux traités constitutifs par le traité de Lisbonne, et relative à la primauté, renvoie à la jurisprudence de la Cour et reproduit un avis du Service juridique du Conseil, du 22 juin 2007, qui rappelle les termes de l'arrêt Costa c. ENEL. Cette Déclaration ne possède pas de valeur contraignante.)

L'Union "respectc", *die Union «achtet»,* les mots choisis par les rédacteurs de cette disposition ne peuvent pas se traduire facilement en termes de rapports entre normes juridiques. Deux acceptions pourraient toutefois être proposées.

La première consiste à dire que l'Union – et son droit – tiennent compte de l'identité nationale de ses Etats membres dans l'élaboration de ses propres normes. Ceci est d'autant plus compréhensible que, comme l'indique l'art. 2 TUE, l'Union est fondée sur un certain nombre de valeurs fondamentales, et que ces valeurs sont communes aux Etats membres. Le mécanisme d'alerte précoce ou préventive introduit par le protocole sur le rôle des parlements nationaux, en ce qui concerne la surveillance du respect du principe de subsidiarité dans les propositions de la Commission, institue un mécanisme qui devrait aboutir à ce "respect" des identités nationales, en appelant la Commission à modifier ou à retirer sa proposition. Dans ces cas, le conflit de normes est en quelque sorte éliminé avant même son possible surgissement: aussi ne peut-on pas considérer que l'art. 4.2 TUE constitue, si l'on suit cette première hypothèse, une véritable règle de conflit. Il serait plutôt une règle destinée à prévenir le conflit de normes.

La seconde verrait dans cette disposition une "réserve de souveraineté", c'est-à-dire un "renvoi à la compétence nationale". Mais, figurant dans le droit originaire de l'Union et au frontispice que sont ses dispositions liminaires, cette "reserve" présente un caractère paradoxal car il appartiendrait à la Cour de justice, compétente pour l'interpréter, d'en indiquer les contours et l'intensité. Aussi bien ne s'agit plus alors d'une "réserve de souveraineté" ou d'un "renvoi à la compétence nationale",

[15] Beaud 2007.

[16] Constantinesco 2002; voir également Lejeune 2009.

aux sens habituels de cette expression.[17] Il n'en demeure pas moins que les auteurs des traités ont cru utile de donner ce socle juridique à d'autres dispositions, plus anciennes, du droit originaire[18] qui témoignent aussi de la même tendance: soustraire un élément jugé important du droit national à l'emprise du droit de l'Union. L'art. 4.2 TUE jouerait ainsi le rôle d'une *lex generalis,* tandis que les autres dispositions du TFUE qui s'y rattachent ressortissent de la catégorie des *leges speciales.*

La notion d'identité nationale est également présente dans la jurisprudence des juridictions constitutionnelles nationales: c'est de là, même, qu'elle a surgi pour désigner les dispositions de la constitution nationale qui sont, selon les termes de Monsieur *P. Mazeaud*, dans le discours de présentation des vœux du Conseil constitutionnel qu'il présidait alors, le 3 janvier 2005, au président de la République: "cruciales" et "distinctives":

> Oui, en raison du consentement constitutionnel et populaire dont il a bénéficié, le droit communautaire est d'effet direct et prévaut, en cas de conflit, sur nos normes nationales, y compris, dans la généralité des cas, sur nos règles constitutionnelles. Mais non, le droit européen, si loin qu'aillent sa primauté et son immédiateté, ne peut remettre en cause ce qui est expressément inscrit dans nos textes constitutionnels et qui nous est propre. Je veux parler ici de tout ce qui est inhérent à notre identité constitutionnelle, au double sens du terme "inhérent": crucial et distinctif. Autrement dit: l'essentiel de la République.[19]

Dans un certain nombre de décisions le Conseil constitutionnel[20] a estimé qu'au sommet de l'ordre juridique français il ne peut y avoir que la constitution, en particulier dans les domaines inhérents à son identité constitutionnelle. L'identité constitutionnelle est ainsi un rempart qui devait préserver l'ordre juridique français contre les effets d'une norme de l'Union qui serait susceptible de l'affecter. En d'autres termes, l'identité constitutionnelle – qui se rattache au *décisionnisme* – perturbe la logique *normativiste* selon laquelle la Cour de justice a construit les rapports entre droit de l'Union et droits nationaux: revanche de *C. Schmitt* sur *H. Kelsen*, en quelque sorte! On lira avec intérêt *G. Lebreton* 2009[21] qui écrit notamment: "Pour le Conseil constitutionnel, comme pour le célèbre penseur allemand, l'autorité souveraine est celle qui impose sa volonté dans les cas décisifs. En l'occurrence, le constituant français reste le seul maître du pouvoir de modifier l' 'identité constitutionnelle de la France', car la décision du 27 juillet 2006 interdit aux autorités communautaires de porter atteinte à celle-ci 'sauf à ce que le constituant y ait consenti'."

La réticence du Conseil constitutionnel français à admettre la prévalence du droit de l'Union sur la constitution[22] est partagée par d'autres juridictions constitution-

---

[17] Constantinesco 2010.

[18] Ainsi les Art. 36, 45, 52, 65, 72, 202 et 276 TFUE.

[19] Mazeaud 2005.

[20] Conseil Constitutionnel, décision n° 2004-496 DC (10 juin 2004); Conseil Constitutionnel, décision n° 2007-560 DC (20 décembre 2007). Cette dernière décision contient la formule suivante au considérant n° 19: "Considérant, en premier lieu, que la transposition d'une directive ne saurait aller à l'encontre d'une règle ou d'un principe inhérent à l'identité constitutionnelle de la France, sauf à ce que le constituant y ait consenti.".

[21] Lebreton 2009, p. 389.

[22] On consultera Constantinesco & Pierré-Caps 2013, en particulier p. 231.

nelles d'autres Etats membres. Ainsi que le constatait déjà le dédicataire de ces Mélanges en 2010:

> Während der EUGH seit der Entscheidung in der Rechtsache *Costa/ENEL* den Vorrang des Unionsrechts nicht nur gegenüber nationalem Gesetzesecht, sondern auch Verfassungsrecht statuiert hat, wird dies nur von wenigen Verfassungstexten gestützt und von der überwiegenden Mehrheit der Verfassungsgerichte, bzw. obersten Gerichthöfe nicht geteilt.[23]

Le peu d'empressement des pouvoirs constituants nationaux à inscrire dans la norme fondamentale de l'Etat la primauté du droit de l'Union sur les constitutions elles-mêmes s'explique facilement: ce serait reconnaître officiellement et formellement que l'Etat a cessé d'être souverain et que son statut est devenu par une telle clause celui d'un Etat membre d'une structure fédérale. Les juridictions constitutionnelles, qui tirent leur titre à juger de la constitution, peuvent difficilement admettre la prévalence sur la constitution d'une norme extérieure à celle-ci, car cela serait mettre en cause la supériorité de la constitution – même si c'est en vertu de la constitution que cette norme internationale a pu être négociée, signée et ratifiée –, et donc du titre qui fonde leur compétence. Aussi assiste-t-on à des distinguos subtils, comme celui du Tribunal constitutionnel espagnol qui oppose la *primauté* du droit de l'Union, dans son champ de compétences ou dans sa sphère d'application, qui s'applique à tout le droit national, y compris à la constitution, à la *suprématie* de la constitution dans tous les domaines, hormis ceux où le droit de l'Union dispose de la primauté.[24]

Que dire, s'il s'agit, en guise de conclusion, de répondre à la question posée par le titre de cette contribution: *concilier la primauté et l'identité nationale: mission impossible ou espoir raisonné?* Peut-être évoquer les limites du dialogue entre les juges, qui, semble-t-il est arrivé au terme des accommodements possibles – les techniques selon lesquelles se sont construits ces accommodements sont répertoriées par *J. Ziller*[25] auquel on renverra pour de plus amples précisions et références –, chacun (le juge de l'Union, les juges constitutionnels nationaux) demeurant sur ses positions, celles-ci se justifiant par la logique qui a présidé à leur création, chacun de ces juges recherchant, sauf exception, à ménager les autres, sans compromettre sa mission nationale. On cite généralement la décision de la Cour constitutionnelle de la République tchèque du 31 janvier 2012 "in that case there were excesses on the part of a European Union body, that a situation occurred in which an act by a European body exceeded the powers that the Czech Republic transferred to the European Union under Art. 10a of the Constitution; this exceeded the scope of the transferred powers, and was ultra vires"[26] et a considéré comme tel un arrêt antérieur de la Cour de justice de l'Union. Les raisons d'une telle mise à l'écart du droit de l'Union seraient à rechercher dans des conflits entre les pouvoirs publics tchèques.[27] Chaque

---

[23] Weber 2010, p. 401.

[24] Cf. Burgorgue-Larsen 2005.

[25] Ziller 2013, p. 257 et seq.

[26] Cour constitutionnelle de la République tchèque (Ústavní soud České republiky), Pl. ÚS 5/12, Slovak Pensions (31 janvier 2012).

[27] Pour plus de détails voir Ziller 2013, p. 266; voir également Constantinesco 2013, p. 119; Kovar 2014, p. 375.

juge a ainsi édifié des garde-fous à la primauté du droit de l'Union, qu'il s'agisse des *contre limites* du juge italien, de l'*identité constitutionnelle*, pour le juge français ou, pour le juge allemand, après les raisonnements des arrêts *Solange*, l'invocation des principes de la *démocratie représentative* et de l'*Etat fédéral*, opposables à la primauté du droit de l'Union. Resterait à délimiter le critère permettant de dégager, parmi les textes constitutionnels ou de valeur constitutionnelle, les principes opposables à la primauté du droit de l'Union. Une piste possible, qui ne vaut que pour certaines constitutions rigides, mènerait aux dispositions que la constitution déclare intangibles ou insusceptibles de révision celles que la doctrine allemande appelle les *Ewigkeitsklauseln*, même si les histoires constitutionnelles des pays d'Europe nous enseignent que rien n'est éternel. Nous ne pouvons entrer dans cette discussion ici.

La parole devrait revenir au "politique", car seule une décision politique pourrait ordonner de manière efficace les rapports entre ordres juridiques européens et nationaux. Ce qui signifie non seulement une décision souhaitée par les gouvernements des Etats membres, mais aussi une décision soutenue par leurs peuples.

A l'heure où la morosité, la défiance et le scepticisme envers l'Union européenne gagnent les opinions publiques, une telle perspective semble relever de l'utopie ou du vœu pieux. Pourtant, n'est-il pas de la responsabilité de ceux qui nous gouvernent de prendre conscience – et de faire comprendre à leurs électeurs – que l'Union ne pourra pas subsister (et c'est la première condition qu'elle doit remplir pour progresser) si elle ne devient pas plus efficace tout en devenant mieux connue, mieux comprise, mieux et davantage réclamée? Vaste chantier à entreprendre d'urgence si l'on ne veut pas que l'Union européenne rejoigne, dans les livres d'histoire du futur, la longue liste des entreprises politiques avortées. Mais les "politiques" lisent-ils les Mélanges?

References

Beaud, O. (2007). *Théorie de la Fédération*. Paris: PUF.

Benlolo Carabot, M. (2013). Mandat d'arrêt européen: la protection des droits fondamentaux subordonnée aux exigences de la primauté du droit de l'Union européenne. *Lettre « Actualités Droits-Libertés » du CREDOF*, 22 mars 2013. http://wp.me/p1Xrup-1IV. Accessed 9 February 2015

Brodier, H. (2006). Premier visa pour la Charte des droits fondamentaux de l'Union européenne dans l'arrêt de la CJCE validant la directive relative au regroupement familial.*L'Europe des libertés,* 21. http://leuropedeslibertes.u-strasbg.fr/article.php?id_article=297&id_rubrique=40. Accessed 9 February 2015

Burgorgue-Larsen, L. (2005). La déclaration du 13 décembre 2004. *Cahiers du Conseil constitutionnel,* 18. http://www.conseil-constitutionnel.fr/conseil-constitutionnel/francais/nouveaux-cahiers-du-conseil/cahier-n-18/la-declaration-du-13-decembre-2004-dtc-n-1-2004-br.51927.html. Accessed 16 February 2015

Burgorgue-Larsen, L. (2006). L'apparition de la Charte des droits fondamentaux dans la jurisprudence de la Cour de justice des Communautés, note sous l'arrêt du 27 juin 2006, Parlement européen c. Conseil, aff. C-540/03. *AJDA*, 2286.

Constantinesco, V. (2002). Europe fédérale ou fédération d'états-nations. In R. Dehousse (Ed.), *Une constitution pour l'Europe?* (pp. 115–150). Paris: Presses de Sciences Po.

Constantinesco, V. (2010). La confrontation entre identité constitutionnelle européenne et identités constitutionnelles nationales: convergence ou contradiction? Hiérarchie ou contrepoint?. In J.-C. Masclet, H. Ruiz Fabri, C. Boutayeb, & S. Rodrigues (Eds.), *L'Union européenne: Union de droit, Union des droits. Mélanges en l'honneur de Philippe Manin* (pp. 79–94). Paris: Pedone.

Constantinesco, V. (2013). La souveraineté est-elle soluble dans l'Union européenne? *L'Europe en formation*, *368*, 119–135.

Constantinesco, V., & Pierré-Caps, S. (2013). *Droit constitutionnel* (6th edn.). Paris: PUF.

Da Fonseca, A. (2014). *Le Tribunal constitutionnel espagnol et la Cour de justice: un dialogue d'apparat autour de l'affaire Melloni? 30 mars 2014.* http://www.gdr-elsj.eu/2014/03/30/cooperation-judiciaire-penale/le-tribunal-constitutionnel-espagnol-et-la-cour-de-justice-un-dialogue-dapparat-autour-de-laffaire-melloni/. Accessed 12 February 2015

Franssen, V. (2014). Melloni as a wake-up call – setting limits to higher national standards of fundamental rights' protection. *European Law Blog,* 10 mars 2014. http://europeanlawblog.eu/?p=2241. Accessed 12 February 2015

Halperin, J.-L. (2004). *Histoire des droits en Europe de 1750 à nos jours*. Paris: Flammarion.

Kovar, R. (2014). La souveraineté nationale est-elle soluble dans l'Union européenne?. In F. Berrod, J. Gerkrath, R. Kovar, C. Mestre, V. Michel, S. Pierré-Caps, D. Ritleng, & D. Simon (Eds.), *Europe(s), Droit(s) européen(s). Une passion d'universitaire. Liber Amicorum en l'honneur du professeur Vlad Constantinesco* (p. 375). Bruxelles: Bruylant.

Lebreton, G. (2009). L'identité constitutionnelle de la France. In C. Leveleux-Teixeira, A. Rousselet-Pimont, P. Bonin, & F. Garnier (Eds.), *Normes et normativité. Etudes d'histoire du droit rassemblées en l'honneur d'Albert Rigaudière* (p. 381). Paris: Economica.

Lejeune, Y. (2009). L'Etat fédéral est-il une bonne clé pour comprendre le fédéralisme? Un commentaire du livre d'Olivier Beaud: Théorie de la Fédération. *Revue belge de droit constitutionnel*, *2*, 207–230.

Mazeaud, P. (2005). Discours de présentation des vœux du Conseil constitutionnel au président de la République le 3 janvier 2005. *Cahiers du Conseil constitutionnel,* 18. http://www.conseil-constitutionnel.fr/conseil-constitutionnel/francais/nouveaux-cahiers-du-conseil/cahier-n-18/voeux-du-president-du-conseil-constitutionnel-m-pierre-mazeaud-au-president-de-la-republique.51930.html. Accessed 16 February 2015

Mehdi, R. (2013). *Retour sur l'arrêt Melloni: quelques réflexions sur des usages contradictoires du principe de primauté. 29 mars 2013.* http://www.gdr-elsj.eu/2013/03/29/cooperation-judiciaire-penale/retour-sur-larret-melloni-quelques-reflexions-sur-des-usages-contradictoires-du-principe-de-primaute/. Accessed 16 February 2015

Weber, A. (2010). *Europäische Verfassungsvergleichung*. München: C.H. Beck.

Weiler, J. H. H. (2013). Editorial. Human Rights: Member State, EU and ECHR Levels of Protection. *EJIL*, *24*(2), 472–475.

Ziller, J. (2013). *Diritto delle politiche e delle istituzioni dell'Unione europea*. Bologna: Il Mulino.

The Portuguese Constitution and European Union Law

Four Notes

José Manuel M. Cardoso da Costa

1 A few years ago[1] we examined the topic in the title in writing, tackling it from the two perspectives in which it might be raised (each, of course, being necessarily connected to the other): that of the relationship (which may be termed material-functional) between the two normative complexes, considered in themselves; and that of the relationship (which may be termed organic-functional) likely to become established between the court systems from which, ultimately, the respective types of remedy are to be sought, namely the Portuguese Constitutional Court and the European Court of Justice.

Since then, the context in which the issue arises has changed significantly, especially as regards European Union law: leaving aside the relatively unimportant Treaty of Nice, the process of establishing a "Constitution for Europe" failed but, through the Treaty of Lisbon, the new Treaty on European Union and the Treaty on the Functioning of the European Union were approved and entered into force on 1 December 2009; and, more recently, spurred on by the current financial situation of the euro area and the lessons that experience of the single currency have yielded, and following measures that have been taken meanwhile to remedy the situation and the crisis which resulted in some States participating in the currency (among them, Portugal), the "Treaty on Stability, Coordination and Governance in the Economic and Monetary Union" was approved and ratified by 25 Member States and entered into force on 1 January 2013. But with regard to the Portuguese Constitution, matters are also not exactly on the same footing (at least from a formal point of view), given the addition (which will be discussed later) that takes into account precisely the foreseeable development of the Union's basic law, introduced by the revision that took place in 2004.

Is it the case that, in view of these changes, we shall have to modify the conclusions that were advanced in the articles referred to above? And moreover: will there be other notable aspects of the implications of EU law for the Portuguese constitutional framework, and for its application, which should be considered and analysed?

[1] Costa 1998, p. 1363 et seqq.; later developed and turned into Costa 2000, p. 193 et seqq.

H.-J. Blanke et al. (eds.), *Common European Legal Thinking*,
DOI 10.1007/978-3-319-19300-7_7

It is to these questions that we seek to give an initial and very succinct answer in the notes that follow.

2 Although the primacy of EU law over ordinary domestic law has long since been established, in the legal systems of the Member States and in its scope, a similar unquestioned primacy is nonetheless surely far from being accepted, in the same domestic law and its corresponding practice, over constitutional law – over the *Constitution* itself. As we know, this is the Luxembourg Court's understanding, and has been so for a while; but the same approach cannot be presumed on the part of those domestic courts (constitutional courts and the like) to which oversight of their respective constitutions is mainly and more specifically entrusted, as is certainly shown by the case law, and recent case law at that, from one of the most influential among them, namely the German *Bundesverfassungsgericht* (Federal Constitutional Court).

In Portugal, the issue had not yet arisen in practice when we first approached it; and neither has it arisen to date. This means that we can only continue to consider and analyse it at a theoretical and doctrinal level.

From this point of departure (i. e. without being able nor having to take any position in advance from the case law), the view we held was, in short, that if the primacy of national constitutional law was to continue to be recognised domestically, it could not in any event ignore the European commitment also expressly assumed by it (Art. 7.6), a commitment entailing the acceptance by the Portuguese State of the law resulting from the transfer of powers to the then Community by agreement between its Member States. Now, this should mean that, in the event of an (albeit unlikely) conflict between Community rules and domestic constitutional requirements, the application of the former should not always be rejected, but rather that this would only occur in the case of a flagrant and entirely unacceptable clash with the fundamental values and principles of the Constitution. To that end we covered ourselves by invoking the leeway offered by the "tolerance" which the Constitution itself already provided for in the text of the chapter on its relationship with international law (Art. 277.2). And we added that where, all this notwithstanding, the Community law provision had to be overruled, such a result should not be arrived at without first determining its exact meaning and scope (or perhaps by determining its invalidity) by having recourse to "preliminary reference" to the Court of Justice.

We could now (retrospectively) reformulate the view thus stated by saying that no hierarchical relationship between the Portuguese Constitution and the Treaty was to be posited (merely by virtue of EU membership) such that – we once again resort to the well-known *Kelsen*ian term – the latter has displaced the former in the pyramid of rules; and by adding that this should not prevent the possibility of any kind of trade-off in the application of one or the other in the case where Union law and the national Constitution come into actual or potential conflict – a trade-off that should not be the task of the national or Union courts acting in isolation, but rather a collaboration between the two.[2] All of this is, after all, consistent with and in ways anticipates and has points of convergence with the concept, which has meanwhile been put forward increasingly by various authors, of a necessary "inter-constitutionality" corresponding to a "multi-level" and "networked" constitutionalism – as the model, according to the authors, best suited to expressing the stage reached in this area by the European Union and its Member States (without however analysing and questioning here the deeper meaning of this concept and without committing to any one of its possible implications).

We believe that the understanding described above still obtains today, at least in its broad outlines.

As pointed out, the great and (given the nature of the text that it was part of) fundamental "innovation" that the Constitutional Treaty would have introduced, as regards the primacy of EU law, was the express enshrining of the principle in its very first and emblematic precepts, on the "Definition and Objectives of the Union": Art. I-6, indeed, states without any qualification that "The Constitution and law adopted by the institutions of the Union in exercising competences conferred on it shall have primacy over the law of the Member States". This proclamation (which – it will also be recalled – raised serious reservations, from more than one quarter) was eventually not included in the TEU as adopted by the Treaty of Lisbon – to which was simply attached a Declaration that "The Conference recalls that, in accordance with well settled case law of the Court of Justice of the European Union, the Treaties and the law adopted by the Union on the basis of the Treaties have primacy over the law of Member States, under the conditions laid down by the said case law". Nothing therefore changed the status of Union law concerning the "formal" source

[2] This is, we believe, the crucial point. In fact, the most problematic aspect is not so much the side of the question that we have labelled material-functional – since in this regard, the TEU itself is based on the major legal values common to the Member States (Art. 2) and on the safeguarding of the constitutional traditions specific to each of them (Art. 4.2); the more difficult aspect is really knowing whether the guarantee of harmonisation thus postulated between EU law and national constitutions should be reserved exclusively to the ECJ or whether it must be shared with constitutional courts (or the supreme courts) of the Member States. We declare a preference for the latter, in the belief that although it may entail some cost in terms of instability or ambiguity, this will finally match the cost of the similarly unstable balance, a balance left deliberately unresolved, which continues to characterise, institutionally, the European Union as a political formation. For a similar opinion, see Ramos 2005, p. 375 et seq., 394 et seq.

Thus, taking into account what has just been mentioned, we think a similar response should be given today to the issue that parallels the one addressed in the main text, and that we had merely referred to in our previous article: the issue of a rule being made or a decision taken by an organ of the Union, allegedly *ultra vires*, i. e. beyond the functions and powers permitted by the Treaties. Here also our tendency, at least, is to favour the view that the possibility of intervention of the domestic courts (especially constitutional) in the question should not be categorically excluded, although the main word belongs, of course, to the ECJ. As is well known, it is precisely such issues that the German FCC has concluded that it possesses jurisdiction to hear. As for the Portuguese case, and in the absence of any established judicial practice related to the issue, it may however be added that the view advanced here may perhaps now find extra support in Art. 8.4 of the Constitution, as it expressly makes the domestic applicability of EU laws, with the force that it recognises them to have, dependent on them having been "issued by its institutions, in the exercise of their respective powers" (cf. *infra*, in the main text).

(which the case law continued to be) of the principle of primacy – notwithstanding the Declaration's undeniable and substantial effect of enhancing recognition of this principle, together with the removal of any doubt about its validity.

In terms of Portuguese constitutional law, however, something very significant had already occurred in this regard. It was that, in anticipation of a successful conclusion of the ratification process of the Constitutional Treaty and its entry into force, the Portuguese constitutional legislation was amended in advance to reflect the position so emphatically proclaimed in Art. I-6 of the intended Treaty (thus sidestepping in advance the difficulties that were to be raised): this was given effect in 2004 by the inclusion, in Art. 8 of the Portuguese Constitution, of a new provision (Art. 8.4) which reads as follows: "The provisions of the treaties governing the European Union and the rules adopted by its institutions, in the exercise of their respective powers, are applicable to domestic law, in terms as defined by EU law, with respect for the fundamental principles of the democratic rule of law". The Treaty establishing a Constitution for Europe finally foundered; but the rule in the Portuguese Constitution, to which it admittedly gave birth, remains in force – whence the fact that among those constitutions of Member States that we are aware of, this is the one (not to say the only one to do so in this way) that most directly addresses the issue of incorporating EU law into the domestic system and, by the reference to the same law defining its terms, acknowledges its primacy.

Now it appears – if we see things as they are – that the terms in which the Portuguese Constitution came to embrace the primacy of EU law only confirm the general drift of the reading we have already advanced of its implications for domestic constitutional law itself, which we recalled at the outset. Indeed, insofar as it ensures the domestic application of EU law "in terms as defined" by it, then, given also the way the ECJ has interpreted and applied it, the effect is of course to ensure its primacy and we do not see how, as a matter of principle, the extension of this also to constitutional laws can be resisted; with the sole proviso, however, that the application of EU law in domestic courts must not lead, in any event, to the disregarding of the "fundamental principles of the democratic rule of law", which means nothing more than that the primacy of EU law cannot be allowed to override what in the final analysis is the essential and irreducible core of the Constitution.[3]

That said, it should just be added that the new constitutional provision obviously does not and could not get us any further forward as to how the Portuguese Constitutional Court would proceed, were it to find itself faced with the critical situation of having to refrain from applying a rule of EU law because it was incompatible with that irreducible core of the democratic rule of law, as conceived by the Constitution that its task is to uphold. Therefore nothing precludes us from continuing to think that, in this case, the Court should not take that step without first referring to the

[3] As for the definition of that core, we believe that it cannot be derived from any generic concept of the "democratic rule of law", but rather from the way the Portuguese Constitution conceives and fashions it (perhaps with its own idiosyncrasies and singularity), and certainly not by restricting itself to the sphere of fundamental rights: indications of principle may be provided by the list of "material limits" for constitutional revision, in accordance with Art. 288.

Court of Justice the "preliminary question" of the interpretation or validity of the rule in question.

3 The relationship of EU law to domestic constitutional law is not limited, however, to the issues we have so far considered. There is another aspect – and that is the question whether the latter does after all extend its own guarantee to the application of the former at domestic level, with precedence over the corresponding ordinary legislation, and if so, whether or not the court (i. e. the Constitutional Court) primarily devoted to protecting the Constitution should also take over the protection of that primacy.

To clarify the point: what is at stake is that, where the reception of EU law, with the primacy that it confers on itself, into domestic law is automatically provided for and assured by the Constitution, it may well be said that non-recognition of such primacy by the legislature or by a national court (either directly, or else by applying an incompatible domestic provision) will at the same time lead to a violation of the relevant constitutional principle (i. e. the principle which is the domestic source of that primacy), that is, to an "unconstitutionality", and as such be liable to scrutiny by the court and according to the procedures specifically provided for.

Now, in the Portuguese legal system – as we have just seen – the principle of "automatic" reception of immediately applicable EU law, and its consequent primacy, is directly expressed at the constitutional level. Moreover, it might be maintained (as we ourselves maintained in the article that we have been taking as a point of reference) that the principle was already there, even before the addition, mentioned above, of Art. 8.4 of the Portuguese Constitution: it was already to be found in Art. 8.3 (expressed in general terms, but essentially addressing the country's integration into the EEC) which states that "the rules adopted by the competent organs of the organisations to which Portugal belongs apply directly in national law, provided this has been established in the appropriate constitutive treaties". The addition of paragraph 4 therefore served only to make things clearer, not so much in terms of the direct applicability of EU law, but rather as to its primacy.

Therefore, one could raise the question of whether or not the concept of "unconstitutionality", with the resulting effects at the level of the court's competence and procedure,[4] should be applied to the situation where a domestic provision is contrary to EU law. But the answer to that question should be firmly in the negative, and for two reasons: firstly, because, to qualify the situation thus, we would surely be facing a kind of "indirect unconstitutionality", the examination of which would generally (so we would argue) be outside the jurisdiction of the Constitutional Court; secondly, and decisively, because the assumption, by the Constitution, of Portugal's integration into the EEC could only be understood in a global sense, to the fullest extent and with all its implications, including at institutional level, so

[4] While we cannot develop the point in all its detail and with all its implications, it should nevertheless be noted that the problem in question (which has been raised in practice, cf. infra) was, under the Portuguese system of judiciary review of legislation, fundamentally one of finding out if a person affected could lodge an "appeal on constitutionality" to the Constitutional Court, based on the application by a lower court of a domestic provision contrary to EU law.

that there being, under the Treaty, a specific judicial body for ensuring compliance with Community law, it would not make sense and would even be incongruous that a similar domestic body (the Constitutional Court) intervenes to the same effect.

We are also certain that the addition of paragraph 4 to Art. 8 of the Constitution in no way affects this understanding: indeed it only serves to reinforce it.

More important than our doctrinal point of view, however, is the fact that the Portuguese Constitutional Court has arrived at the same conclusion and has tenaciously adhered to it in decided cases – both before and after the explanatory paragraph was added to the Constitution. This goes to show, therefore, that the Court does not consider itself to be specifically suited to the function of ensuring the primacy of EU law (of being the "guardian" of EU law): This primacy should be ensured by the other domestic courts and, as a last resort, the ECJ.

4 These – as set out above – are the two aspects of the issue surrounding the relationship of Portuguese constitutional law with EU law that we should reconsider in the light of the development of the former in this respect arising from the revision made to the Constitution in 2004.

But, in truth, there is – we believe – also a third level of this relationship that cannot be overlooked: a subtler and more complex problem, concerning the extent to which EU law (and decisions taken by EU bodies in applying it) can or should influence a judgment on the compliance of domestic law with the Constitution itself.

At stake here is neither whether the effectiveness of a rule of EU law may be nullified at the domestic level on the grounds of incompatibility with the national constitution, nor whether a domestic legal provision can or should be judged "unconstitutional" because it is contrary to EU law: what is at issue is rather whether constraints imposed on the domestic legislature by EU law (or by measures founded on its application), which narrow its scope for choosing solutions (its margin of legislative freedom), should not be included among the factors to consider (particularly by the Constitutional Court) when reaching a finding of the unconstitutionality or otherwise (with respect to the national Constitution) of laws passed by the domestic legislature.

The question has become acutely topical in Portugal in recent years – due to the programme of measures and targets that the country has undertaken to overcome the financial crisis it finds itself in, measures and targets set out in the Memorandum of Understanding (as successively revised) concluded in 2011 with the European Commission, the European Central Bank and the International Monetary Fund (commonly known as the "troika"). In fact, the programme forced the adoption of particularly stringent measures into law, in various areas, but in particular with respect to wages (especially for public employees) and allowances for pensioners – measures that were repeatedly submitted for consideration by the Constitutional Court which in turn declared them unconstitutional, in broad and crucial respects. Now, in defence of the legitimacy of such measures, the Court was reminded precisely of the fact that these laws were passed in the immediate context of the programme referred to above and also, in particular, in accordance with the rules of EU law concerning the budget balance and the level of indebtedness of Member States.

It is not our intention, nor would it be feasible, to analyse and discuss the relevant case-law here.[5] Limiting ourselves, therefore, to noting that this case law was not, in general, particularly germane to the problem stated, we will point out only that posing this problem is certainly pertinent and justified – especially when the question of unconstitutionality (as was the case) has been put in the light of the great "formal" (in a certain sense) principles of the Constitution, such as the principle of equality or the principle of proportionality. When these are at stake, we really fail to see how the constraints arising from EU membership and those imposed by EU law can be ignored: without taking them into consideration – either in a judgment founded on the equality principle or by assessing the appropriateness, necessity or proportionality of a legislative measure – not only is the adjudicating body failing to consider a "reality principle" (one that judicial decisions should never ignore) but it also side-lines that other legal order which (with support from the Constitution itself) constrains the domestic legislature, namely EU law. For all these reasons it seems to us that this will be – for those who want to have the question put in these terms – a suitable terrain for "inter-constitutionality" within the framework of a "multi-level" and "networked" constitutionalism.

It is clear, however, that by posing the problem just addressed in the way we did, we are of course detracting from the possibility of removing it on the basis of the consideration that such rules of EU law (or decisions taken in applying it) are themselves, ultimately, inconsistent with the national Constitution. This, of course, is also a theoretically possible course to take, but if we do so we will have reverted to the question we started with. In any event, we do not believe that the problem can or always has to be posed in the form of a dilemma in this way: rather we think that situations may well arise where the national legislature's freedom of action is constrained by EU legal rules, without the question (theoretical or otherwise) of the compatibility of these with the national constitution having to be posed in earnest.

5 It only remains to focus on one last point – one that now concerns an obligation that the EU Member States that are parties to this Convention have taken on through the "Treaty on Stability, Coordination and Governance in the Economic and Monetary Union" – commonly known as the Budget Treaty.

The obligation created by this instrument that is taken into account here is that which binds the Contracting Parties to introduce into the domestic legal system of

[5] This has provoked an extended and intense doctrinal debate (in addition, predictably, to an intense political debate, heavily reported in the media): for the former see the different views expressed in the collection of articles in Ribeiro and Coutinho 2014 and Novais 2014. Note however that the constitutional issues raised by the financial crisis has given rise to widespread interest amongst scholars, in particular in the *IXth IACL World Congress of Constitutional Law*, which took place in Oslo in June 2014, where two of the workshops were indeed devoted to the topics of "Social Rights and the Economic Crisis" and "Constitutions and Financial Crisis": the papers presented there (including Portuguese ones and others dealing with the case of Portugal) are still available on the website www.uio.no/wccl

each, one year at the latest after the entry into force of the Treaty, "provisions of binding force and permanent character, preferably constitutional, or otherwise guaranteed to be fully respected and adhered to throughout the national budgetary processes", through which compliance is guaranteed, again by each one of them, with the budgetary balance rule, as defined by the Treaty, and its corollaries (Art. 3.2, with reference to paragraph 1, and Art. 8 dealing with the non-fulfilment of the obligation).

The Portuguese State has now complied with this obligation by passing Law No. 3/2013 of 2013, which embodied the seventh amendment to the Budget Framework Law (Law No. 91/2001 of 20 August), in particular by giving a new wording to Art. 12-C of this Framework Law.

Although some voices were heard advocating the incorporation of the Treaty's budgetary balance rule into the constitutional text itself,[6] this was not, as it turns out, the route taken. Rather, it was understood that the incorporation of the rule in the Budget Framework Law already satisfied the alternative requirement of the Treaty that this rule must be included at least in a provision by which compliance could be fully assured during the process of presentation, discussion and approval of the annual budget.

To conclude, what should be noted here is that such an understanding is entirely acceptable, given the fact that the Budget Framework Law comes within the category of laws to which the Portuguese Constitution attributes an "enhanced value" in the sense of being laws that are "legal prerequisites of other laws" (cf. Art. 112.3 of the Constitution) and cannot therefore be modified by them. That is the unanimous (we suppose) opinion of the scholars; and, although it has not received the explicit imprimatur of the Constitutional Court, neither has it been rejected, and one can even say that it has been implicitly accepted by that Court (see, in particular, Judgment no. 374/2004[7]). Indeed, in accordance with the provisions of Art. 106.1 of the Constitution, the annual budget law must be "prepared, organised, enacted and implemented [. . .] in accordance with the appropriate framework law" – which no doubt means that its mandatory provisions cannot be called into question case by case during each annual budget process: this is precisely the minimum that the Budget Treaty requires, in the alternative which provides for the incorporation of the budgetary balance rule into domestic law.

References

Cardoso da Costa, J. M. M. (1998). O Tribunal Constitucional Português e o Tribunal de Justiça das Comunidades Europeias. In A. Varela, D. F. do Amaral, J. Miranda, & J. J. G. Canotilho (Eds.), *Ab Uno ad Omnes: 75 anos da Coimbra Editora: 1920–1995* (pp. 1363–1380). Coimbra: Coimbra Editora.

[6] As we know, this is the position in Germany with the parallel rule in Art. 115 BL (German BL, *Grundgesetz*) – which, as we also know, was the source of inspiration for Art. 3 of the Treaty.

[7] Constitutional Court of Portugal, Acórdão n.º 374/2004 (26 May 2004), http://www.tribunalconstitucional.pt/tc/acordaos/20040374.html

Cardoso da Costa, J. M. M. (2000). Le Tribunal constitutionnel portugais et les juridictions européennes. In P. Mahoney, F. Matscher, H. Petzold, & L. Wildhaber (Eds.), *Protection des droits de l'homme: la perspective européenne/Protecting Human Rights: The European Perspective: Mélanges à la mémoire de/Studies in memory of Rolv Ryssdal* (pp. 193–211). Cologne et al.: Heymanns.

Moura Ramos, R. M. (2005). O Tratado que estabelece uma Constituição para a Europa e a posição dos Tribunais Constitucionais dos Esstados-Membros. In *In Estudos em Homenagem ao Conselheiro José Manuel Cardoso da Costa* (vol. II, pp. 365–395). Coimbra: Coimbra Editora.

Novais, J. R. (2014). *Em Defesa do Tribunal Constitucional*. Coimbra: Almedina.

de Almeida Ribeiro, G., & Coutinho, L. P. (Eds.). (2014). *O Tribunal Constitucional e a Crise – Ensaios Críticos*. Coimbra: Almedina.

International Law, Law of the European Union and National Constitutional Law

Christian Starck

1 Introduction: Hierarchy of Norms and Competence

There is no relation in the shape of a strict hierarchy of norms between the three legal orders which are mentioned in the heading. For international law and national constitutional law, this is a matter of common knowledge. The hierarchy or grading of norms regularly arises from an allocation of competences. Internally, this is given by constitutional law. As an example I refer to Art. 31 BL [Basic Law for the Federal Republic of Germany], which reads as follows: "Federal law shall take precedence over Land law." At first view this Article seems to establish a strict hierarchy of federal law over Land law. But by looking at the regulations of competence for legislative powers in the Basic Law, it becomes clear, that there is Land law which cannot be overridden by federal law, because the Federation lacks the legislative powers. If the Federation regulated in the field of Land legislative powers, then its laws would be void in default of legislative powers. Therefore, no federal law would exist that could override Land law. Only in the field of concurrent legislative powers (Art. 72.1/2, 74 BL) – newly besides some exceptions (Art. 72.3 BL) – the sentence "Federal law shall take precedence over Land law" applies. Within the legal order of the Federation or a state a strict hierarchy between the constitution and the laws and those and legal regulations is valid.

Legal hierarchies in a constitutional democracy are based on the primacy of the constitution *and* on the democratic derivation of state authority. The directly democratically legitimised parliament enacts the laws in the scope of which government bodies can, due to empowerment (Art. 80.1 BL), issue regulations. In the relation of the legislation of the Federation and states democratic relations of derivability of equal value exist, which are updated in accordance with the division of competence under federal constitutional law.[1] The constitution-amending federal legislator can, within certain limits (Art. 79.3 BL), dispose of the division of competence between

[1] German Federal Constitutional Court, 2 BvN 1/69 (Order of 29 January 1974) – *Landesgrundrechte* (in BVerfGE 36, 342 [361 et seq.]); to the relationship of federal constitutional law to state constitutions cf. Badura 1995, p. 112 et seq.

H.-J. Blanke et al. (eds.), *Common European Legal Thinking*,
DOI 10.1007/978-3-319-19300-7_8

federal state and states by amending the Basic Law (Art. 79.1/2 BL). The federal state is hierarchically superior to the states to the extent of its competence. Therefore, competence determines upon hierarchy. This is likewise an expression of federalism in which the Federation has got the "Kompetenz-Kompetenz" [the power to change the division of competence between the Federation and the Länder] which expresses its internal sovereignty.

Now to my topic "International Law, Law of the European Union and National Constitutional Law". I start – still introductory – with a few clarifications to the three legal categories.

1.1 ***International Law*** is the law of the international community, which consists in treaties and customs which have strengthened in law; added to that are "the basic principles of law recognised by civilized nations".[2] This law, which applies between the states – inter nationes –, is based on the agreement of states through treaties, through action and through mutual conviction. Instances which uphold the law are the organs of the United Nations, which can, however, rarely enforce the law, and, with a better self-assertion, the regional institutions under international law, such as the Council of Europe with the European Court of Human Rights.

1.2 ***Law of the European Union*** represents international treaties of the Member States of the European Union (primary European Law) and the law which is set based on these treaties by the organs of the European Union (secondary European Law). Between the treaty law and the law set by the organs of the European Union an evident hierarchy exists – as the grading in primary and secondary European Law already indicates. The secondary Union Law has to remain within the limits of the treaties, internally comparable to the relationship between constitutional law and ordinary law. The Court of Justice of the European Union is assigned to preserve the law through the interpretation and application of the treaties (Art. 19.1 sentence 2 TEU).

1.3 ***National constitutional law*** as the highest internal source of law (precedence of the constitution!) is essential for the exercise of public authority inwards and outwards. Therefore, it regulates the conclusion of international treaties (Art. 59 BL), which, also when in the shape of contract law regarding the European Union, have to stay within the limits of the constitution.[3] Usually, international treaties have force of law below the constitution. This means that the rule *lex posterior derogat legi priori* applies, meaning that the new law displaces the old treaties. Taking this rule into account, the legislator has to make sure that new laws comply with international treaties, which have been concluded previously, or has to try to adapt the treaty to the planned new legislation through negotiations between the government

[2] Cf. Art. 38.1 of the Statute of the ICJ.

[3] Kempen, in von Mangoldt et al. (2010), Art. 59, para 98 et seq.; Rauschning, in Kahl et al. (2009), Art. 59, para 103 et seq.

and the contracting party, so that internal law and obligations of international law remain in harmony.[4]

Art. 25 BL declares the general rules of international law to be an integral part of federal law, which take precedence over all acts. Only the general principles of international law and international customary law, to the extent that it contains general rules, take part in this hierarchy of international law over non-exclusive federal law.[5]

For the development of the European Union, Art. 24.1 BL and the special regulation of Art. 23.1 BL, which was incorporated into the BL in 1992, allow to transfer sovereign powers. So far as the Basic Law is thereby alerted in content, the proceeding of the amendment of the Basic Law applies. Furthermore, Art. 23.1 BL contains limitations in terms of content for the acts of delegation, and therefore binds the legislator at the conclusion of corresponding international treaties. The protection of constitutional law rests on the Federal Constitutional Court.[6]

After these introductory considerations to the hierarchy of norms and to competence, I would like to go into detail in the following. First, I will discuss the relationship between international treaties and national constitutional law, mainly using the example of the European Convention on Human Rights (Sect. 2). Thereafter, I take a look at supranationality, which is created through international treaties of sovereign States, whereby the sovereignty of the Member States in the European Union requires special attention (Sect. 3). The strict hierarchy of norms within the law of the European Union conduces to secure the sovereignty of the Member States (Sect. 4). In the last section, I deal with the relationship between national fundamental rights and fundamental rights of the European Union (Sect. 5).

2 International Treaties and National Constitutional Law Using the Example of the ECHR

International law is an important instrument of the states enabling cooperation between them. Normally, treaties are concluded for that purpose. In the Vienna Convention on the Law of Treaties[7] reference is made to the principles of the United Nations (Preamble, Art. 1, 2 UN Charter), including the sovereign equality and independence of states, non-intervention in internal affairs of states, the prohibition of the use of force as well as the universal respect for and protection of human rights and fundamental freedoms for all.

In German constitutional law international treaties, which regulate the political relationship of the Federation or refer to objects of federal legislation, require the

[4] On this problem see the example of a current case of tax law cf. Krumm 2013, p. 364 et seq.

[5] Koenig, in von Mangoldt et al. (2010), Art. 25, para 20 et seq.; Cremer 2013a, para 10–18; Geiger 2002, p. 164 et seq.

[6] See, for instance, German Federal Constitutional Court, 2 BvE 2/08 et al. (Judgment of 30 June 2009) – *Lissabon-Vertrag* (in BVerfGE 123, 267 et seqq.).

[7] Of 23 May 1969, in force by 27 January 1980 (BGBl. 1985 II, p. 926).

approval or participation of the body responsible for the federal legislation in the given situation in the form of federal law (Art. 59.2 BL). The treaty which creates international law is an expression of sovereignty and equality of the states. Internally, according to German constitutional law the directly democratically legitimised parliament is responsible for concluding the act of sovereignty, which then is executed outwards by the Federal President (Art. 59.1 sentence 2 BL). Just as a private person enters a contract with one or several other private persons and thereby creates law, states conclude treaties with one another as a legal basis for collaboration of any kind and create international law.

The protection of human rights that is guaranteed in regional international law through the European Convention on Human Rights (ECHR) raises a problem of hierarchy. The Convention as international treaty law stands below the fundamental rights of the BL. But the Federal Republic has obligated itself to recognise the jurisdiction of the European Court of Human Rights (ECtHR) (Art. 46 ECHR). Individuals can apply to the ECtHR for review of German legal acts, which have already been examined on the benchmark of the German fundamental rights, on the measure of the ECHR.

Recently, the situation where the ECtHR judged a decision of the Federal Constitutional Court to be a violation of human rights, emerged in a legal dispute between *Princess Caroline of Hanover* (née of Monaco) and the Federal Republic of Germany, which passed as a legislation between the princess and a publishing house through all court instances. It concerned balancing the freedom of the press with personality rights; the ECtHR interpreted this differently to the Federal Constitutional Court with regard to the concept of a "person of contemporary history", the information value to the press organisation, and determination of exactly what is a private sphere.[8] The level of hierarchy between the Basic Law and the ECHR as an international treaty has in fact been reversed. This is why Germany – a country in which the ECHR has the rank of ordinary law – comprehensively ensures that no law or judgment infringes the human rights of the ECHR as interpreted by the ECtHR.

The Federal Constitutional Court has, without explicitly responding to the problem of ranks, stated in reference to previous decisions[9]: "[T]he guarantees of the Convention influence the interpretation of the fundamental rights and constitutional principles of the Basic Law. The text of the Convention and the jurisdiction of the European Court of Human Rights serve, on the level of constitutional law, as guides to interpretation in determining the content and scope of fundamental rights and constitutional principles of the Basic Law, provided that this does not lead to a restriction or reduction of protection of the individual's fundamental rights under the Basic Law – and this the Convention itself does not desire (Art. 53 ECHR)."

[8] See, extensively, Starck 2006a, p. 76 et seqq. = Starck 2006b, p. 85 et seqq.

[9] German Federal Constitutional Court, 2 BvR 1481/04 (Order of 14 October 2004) – *Görgülü* (in BVerfGE 111, 307 [317]), with reference to 2 BvR 589/79, 2 BvR 740/81, 2 BvR 284/85 (Order of 26 March 1987) – *presumption of innocence* (in BVerfGE 74, 358 [370]); German Federal Constitutional Court, 2 BvR 1462/87 (Order of 14 November 1990) – *condition of probation* (in BVerfGE 83, 119 [128]).

The fundamental rights of the Basic Law can – without difficulties – be interpreted in order that they comply with the ECHR.[10]

Another example comes from family law. In 2003, the Federal Constitutional Court considered § 1626a of the German Civil Code, which makes mutual parental care for an illegitimate child solely conditional on the mother's will, as not infringing Art. 6.2 BL.[11] The ECtHR decided differently in a German case[12] in 2009, based on Art. 8 and 14 ECHR, which say nothing about parental rights, but on the legal development in other European states.[13] A margin of discretion would exist for the national legislator when regulating parental care, but it narrows, if a general European standard can be found. In 2010, subsequent to this decision, the Federal Constitutional Court declared § 1626 (1) Civil Code as incompatible with Art. 6.2 BL and thus unconstitutional.[14] The Federal Constitutional Court moves in line with the European Court of Human Rights in a new, very extensively reasoned interpretative approach.[15]

In this case the result may be convincing. But generally you have to ask, how does the ECtHR determine a common European standard? How can one reason that this achieves a normative status? Let us take another example: Since 1959 the Federal Constitutional Court has steadily decided that marriage in the sense of the Basic Law is a union of a man and a woman in a generally inextricable long-term relationship[16], a structural principle which is withheld from the legislator's power of disposition.[17] Should this become different, if the ECtHR finds that the stage of development in other European states also acknowledges same-sex union as marriage? The example shows that there are limits to the adaptation to actual European standards.

---

[10] Frowein 1992, para 7, 24 et seq.

[11] German Federal Constitutional Court, 1 BvL 20/99, 1 BvR 933/01 (Judgment of 29 January 2003) – *right of custody* (in BVerfGE 107, 150 [169 et seq.]).

[12] Appl. No. 22028/04 *Zaunegger v. Germany* (ECtHR 3 December 2009).

[13] See the list in German Federal Constitutional Court, 1 BvR 420/09 (Order of 21 July 2010) – *joint custody* (in BVerfGE 127, 132 [139 et seq.]).

[14] German Federal Constitutional Court, 1 BvR 420/09 (Order of 21 July 2010) – *joint custody* (in BVerfGE 127, 132 [145 et seq.]).

[15] German Federal Constitutional Court, 1 BvR 420/09 (Order of 21 July 2010) – *joint custody* (in BVerfGE 127, 132 [146–162]).

[16] German Federal Constitutional Court, 1 BvR 205/58 (Judgment of 29 July 1959) (in BVerfGE 10, 59 [66]); 1 BvR 636/68 (Decision of 4 May 1971) – *Spanier-Entscheidung* (in BVerfGE 31, 58 [82]); 1 BvR 16/72 (Order of 11 October 1978) – *Transsexueller* (in BVerfGE 49, 286 [300]); 1 BvL 136/78, 1 BvR 890/77, 1 BvR 1300/78, 1 BvR 1440/78, 1 BvR 32/79 (Judgment of 28 February 1980) – *Ehescheidung* (in BVerfGE 53, 224 [245]); 2 BvL 27/81 (Order of 8 March 1983) (in BVerfGE 63, 323 [330]); 1 BvF 1/01, 1 BvF 2/01 (Judgment of 17 July 2002) – *gleichgeschlechtliche Lebenspartnerschaft* (in BVerfGE 105, 313 [345]); 2 BvR 1397/09 (Order of 19 June 2012) – *Lebenspartnerschaft Beamter* (in BVerfGE 131, 239 [259]); 2 BvR 909/06 (Order of 7 May 2013) para 86 – *Ehegattensplitting* (in BVerfGE 133, 377 et seqq.).

[17] German Federal Constitutional Court, 2 BvL 27/81 (Order of 8 March 1983) (in BVerfGE 63, 323 [330]).

Art. 10.2 of the Spanish Constitution of 1978 explicitly demands:[18] "Provisions relating to the fundamental rights and liberties recognised by the Constitution shall be construed in conformity with the Universal Declaration of Human Rights and international treaties and agreements thereon ratified by Spain." Similarly reads Art. 16.2 of the Portuguese Constitution of 1976. In these countries the constitution itself regulates the precedence of international human rights declarations to which the country has acceded. But the cited constitutional provisions may indeed only concern the normative substance of the declarations and not the stage of development of the states which have acceded to the Convention on Human Rights.

Besides that, it can come to a legally secured primacy of application of the liberties of the ECHR, if the European Court of Justice (ECJ) reviews the application of community law by national authorities and adduces Art. 6.2 and 6.3 TEU[19] as a fundamental legal principle.[20] An accession of the European Union to the European Convention on Human Rights is planned. The draft of a respective agreement is present,[21] but in Opinion 2/13 the CJEU has declared this agreement not compatible with Article 6.2 TEU or with Protocol (No 8) relating to Article 6.2.[22]

3 Supranationality and Sovereignty

The cooperation between states can be so close, that international institutions are established. Already in the initial version of the Basic Law from 1949 it was intended in Art. 24.1 that the Federation can assign sovereign powers to international institutions by law.[23] Thereby the path was paved from cooperation to integration, from internationality to supranationality. Supranationality means that the state transfers sovereign powers and that the supranational public authority can issue sovereign acts, which are directly effective in the contracting states, i. e. also in Germany. The concession of sovereign powers to supranational institutions entails that their exercise in particular is no longer always dependent on the will of the Member State.

Sovereign rights are transferred by law. This organisational reservation of statutory powers requires that the content and extent of the assigned sovereign rights are

[18] Las normas relativas a los derechos fundamentales y a las libertadas que la Constitución reconoce se interpretarán de conformidad con la Declaración Universal de Derechos Humanos y los tradados y acuerdos internationales sobre las mismas materias ratificados por España.

[19] They read as follows: (2) "The Union shall accede to the European Convention for the Protection of Human Rights and Fundamental Freedoms. Such accession shall not affect the Union's competences as defined in the Treaties." (3) "Fundamental rights, as guaranteed by the European Convention for the Protection of Human Rights and Fundamental Freedoms and as they result from the constitutional traditions common to the Member States, shall constitute general principles of the Union's law.".

[20] Cremer 2013b, para 135 et seq.

[21] See Polakiewicz 2013, p. 472 et seq.

[22] Opinion 2/13, *Accession to the ECHR* (CJEU 18 December 2014).

[23] Vogel 1964.

definite.[24] Since the act of transfer of sovereignty creates a new hierarchy, which withdraws competence from the parliament and obliges the *Bundestag* to executive legislation, when directives are issued by institutions of the European Union (Art. 288.3 TFEU), a sufficient certainty of the transfer of sovereignty is necessary. This is especially apparent in cases where legal acts are issued by majority decisions in the Union's institutions.[25]

Art. 23 BL is a special provision for European integration, which was already well advanced on the basis of Art. 24 BL (the Federation may by law transfer sovereign powers to international organisations). The aim of Art. 23.1 sentence 1 BL is the realisation of a united Europe. Already in the initial version of the Preamble of the Basic Law it reads: "... inspired by the determination to promote world peace as an equal partner in a united Europe".[26] In order to achieve this goal, "the Federal Republic of Germany shall participate in the development of the European Union that is committed to democratic, social and federal principles, to the rule of law, and to the principle of subsidiarity, and that guarantees a level of protection of basic rights essentially comparable to that afforded by this Basic Law" (Art. 23.1 sentence 1 BL). To meet the objective of integration the Federation can transfer sovereign powers by a law with the consent of the *Bundesrat* (Federal Council of Germany).

The basis of the European Union is international treaties. The Member States of the European Union maintain their sovereignty, which is an expression of self-determination of the respective constitutive people. The Member States remain "masters of the treaties", as the Federal Constitutional Court never gets tired of pointing out.[27] This is strongly expressed in the Lisbon-Judgment of the Federal Constitutional Court[28] and summarised in the guiding principles:[29] The European Union is an association of sovereign states [Staaten(ver)bund], which "remain sovereign", that is established on a lasting basis, a "treaty union of sovereign states", which are still responsible for "the political formation of economical, cultural and social circumstances", for the living conditions of their citizens, especially for the range of self-responsibility and the personal and social security, which is protected by

[24] German Federal Constitutional Court, 2 BvR 2134, 2159/92 (Judgment of 12 October 1993) – *Maastricht* (in BVerfGE 89, 155 [183–188]); 2 BvE 2/08 et al. (Judgment of 30 June 2009) – *Lissabon-Vertrag* (in BVerfGE 123, 267 [355]); 2 BvE 13/13 et al. (Order of 14 January 2014) para 48 (in BVerfGE 134, 366).

[25] Classen, in von Mangoldt et al. (2010), Art. 24, para 9 et seq.

[26] See Starck, in von Mangoldt et al. (2010), preamble, para 40 et seq.

[27] German Federal Constitutional Court, 2 BvE 2/08, 2 BvE 5/08, 2 BvR 1010/08, 2 BvR 1022/08, 2 BvR 1259/08, 2 BvR 182/09 (Judgment of 30 June 2009) – *Lissabon-Vertrag* (in BVerfGE 123, 267 [349]); in settled case-law see German Federal Constitutional Court, 2 BvR 687/85 (Order of 8 April 1987) – *Kloppenburg* (in BVerfGE 75, 223 [242]); 2 BvR 2134, 2159/92 (Judgment of 12 October 1993) – *Maastricht* (in BVerfGE 89, 155 [200]) (supported by the will of the Member States). See also Badura 1995, p. 116.

[28] German Federal Constitutional Court, 2 BvE 2/08 et al. (Judgment of 30 June 2009) – *Lissabon-Vertrag* (in BVerfGE 123, 267 [339 et seq.]).

[29] German Federal Constitutional Court, 2 BvE 2/08 et al. (Judgment of 30 June 2009) – *Lissabon-Vertrag* (in BVerfGE 123, 267).

fundamental rights. Further, the court names such like political decisions, which are in particular dependent on cultural, historical and linguistic understanding. This should also include the mentality of the population, of whose inclusion at the issuing of law the theory of legislation provides information to us.

The transfer of sovereign powers to the European Union (Art. 23.1 sentence 2 BL) has led to some confusion in the German and foreign legal literature and case-law: The Czech constitutional court speaks of a division of sovereignty, of the "concept of shared – 'pooled' – sovereignty [. . .] which is difficult to classify in political science categories".[30] A few think that sovereignty as a term of constitutional and international law has become obsolete,[31] others plead in favour of a federative sovereignty of the Union.[32] It is likewise inadequate to assume an abeyance of sovereignty.[33] The Federal Constitutional Court has opposed this by repeatedly describing the Member States as masters of the treaties.[34]

You have to free yourself from the idea that the transfer of sovereign powers to a supranational union withdraws sovereignty in whole or in part from the state that carries out the transfer through an international treaty, meaning that the state, which is the actor, gives up its sovereignty. The conclusion of an international treaty, which binds the state legally, is an act of sovereignty. Just as I do not give up my liberty when joining an association or a trading company and agree to the thereby underlying obligations, the state does not give up its sovereignty when transferring sovereign powers, or better competences[35] or authorisations[36] to a supranational union for collective exercise, even if it is many and important sovereign powers.

The European Union is still based on the democratically legitimised will of the Member States. Their persisting sovereignty[37] also shows up in the right to leave the European Union (cf. Art. 50 TEU). How could a state after giving up its sovereignty still be able to leave the European Union! If sovereignty was divided or in a state of abeyance, then sovereign states, which were able to conclude international treaties on the transfer of further sovereign powers, on new tailoring of already transferred sovereign powers or on revocation of individual sovereign powers[38], would not exist

---

[30] Cited from Ley 2000, p. 165.

[31] Ipsen 1972, p. 101; Ipsen 1992, para 19; Denninger 2000, p. 1125; Kokott 2002, p. 21 et seq.

[32] Dreier 1988, Col. 1208; Everling 1993, p. 942 et seq.

[33] Ipsen 1992, para 19; Schönberger 2004, p. 104, et seq. on the basis of the theory of federation by Schmitt 1928 p. 363, 372 et seq., who presumes a "substantial equality" and an "ontological conformity" of the Member States (p. 376); Schmitt has, in the course of his remarks, the German Reich, a federal state, in mind, which was founded in 1871; further particulars on references in Starck 2005, p. 722 et seq. (footnotes 36–38).

[34] German Federal Constitutional Court, 2 BvE 2/08 et al. (Judgment of 30 June 2009) – *Lissabon-Vertrag* (in BVerfGE 123, 267 [349 et seq.]); Classen, in von Mangoldt et al. (2010), Art. 23, para 3; differently Pernice, in Dreier (2006), Art. 23 para 36 (with further annotations).

[35] See Art. 88-1 of the French Constitution.

[36] Rights of decision-making, Chapter X § 5 Swedish Constitution.

[37] Steinberger 1991, p. 16 et seq.; Schmitz 2001b, p. 237 et seq.; Hillgruber 2002, p. 1077 et seq.; Hillgruber 2004, para 61–74; Randelzhofer 2004, para 33 et seq.

[38] German Federal Constitutional Court, 2 BvE 2/08 et al. (Judgment of 30 June 2009) – *Lissabon-Vertrag* (in BVerfGE 123, 267 [350]): The steps of integration have to be limited in subject through the pact of tranfer and in principle revocable.

anymore. At the same time, this would mean the discharge of international law as a basis for European integration and the transition into a dynamic European law, which should lead to a European federal state law.

Against this the Federal Constitutional Court has rightly said in 2009 in the Lisbon-judgment on the understanding of sovereignty of the Basic Law:[39] Sovereign statehood is freedom which is organised by international law and committed to it. Sovereign statehood stands for a pacified area and the order guaranteed therein on the basis of individual freedom and collective self-determination. The Federal Constitutional Court points out that the Basic Law seeks European integration and an international order of peace. The text says: "It is true that the Basic Law grants the legislature powers to engage in a far-reaching transfer of sovereign powers to the European Union. However, the powers are granted under the condition that the sovereign statehood of a constitutional state is maintained on the basis of an integration programme according to the *principle of particular limited authorisation* and respecting the Member States' *constitutional identity*, and that at the same time the Member States do not lose their ability to politically and socially shape living conditions on their own responsibility."[40]

In practice this is secured through cooperation between the Federal Constitutional Court and the European Court of Justice, as the Federal Constitutional Court has underlined several times. In its request for a preliminary ruling of 14 January 2014 to the European Court of Justice,[41] concerning the European Central Bank, this relationship of cooperation is outlined as follows: "In their cooperative relationship, it is for the Court of Justice to interpret the act. On the other hand, it is for the Federal Constitutional Court to determine the inviolable core content of the constitutional identity, and to review whether the act (in the interpretation determined by the Court of Justice) interferes with this core." Therewith, the Federal Constitutional Court has the last word concerning the validity of legal acts of the institutions of the European Union with regard to Germany. In the concrete case the European Court of Justice will have to closely review the measures of the European Central Bank on its compatibility with the bank's competences. The measures will, in the interpretation of the Court, then be reviewed by the Federal Constitutional Court by the mentioned standards of the Basic Law.

The Federal Constitutional Court says on the limits of authorisation of Art. 23.1 sentence 1 BL: "The Basic Law does not grant powers to bodies acting on behalf of Germany to abandon the right to self-determination of the German people in the form of Germany's sovereignty under international law by joining a federal state. Due to the irrevocable transfer of sovereignty to a new subject of legitimation that goes with it, this step is reserved to the directly declared will of the German people alone." The Federal Constitutional Court points out that single sovereign

[39] German Federal Constitutional Court, 2 BvE 2/08 et al. (Judgment of 30 June 2009) – *Lissabon-Vertrag* (in BVerfGE 123, 267 [346]).

[40] Emphasis added. German Federal Constitutional Court, 2 BvE 2/08 et al. (Judgment of 30 June 2009) – *Lissabon-Vertrag* (in BVerfGE 123, 267 [347]), also to the following.

[41] German Federal Constitutional Court, 2 BvE 13/13 et al. (Order of 14 January 2014) para 27 (in BVerfGE 134, 366).

rights may only be transferred when defined. A transfer in such a way that further authority of the European Union can be derived from it, is unconstitutional. In particular, the transfer or utilisation of a "Kompetenz-Kompetenz"[42] is forbidden. These principles are established in the treaties as a mirror image: conferred competences (Art. 5.1 TEU) and the European Union's obligation to preserve the national identity of its Member States (Art. 4.3 TEU).

4 Hierarchy within the Law of the European Union

With that we have arrived at the precedence of primary Union law (international law) over secondary Union law. The institutions of the European Union, i. e. the European Parliament, the European Council, the Council, the Commission, the Court of Justice (Art. 13 et seq. TEU) owe their existence to the international treaties, which founded the European Union, and are bound in their actions to the stipulated assignments and authorisations. From this, a strict hierarchy follows. Nonetheless, the institutions of the Union, including the Court of Justice, perform an expansion of competence through development of the law referring to the implied powers doctrine and the rule of *effet utile* of international treaty law. The Federal Constitutional Court takes note of this,[43] but warns against a gradual transition of responsibility for integration to institutions of the European Union, especially through the European Court of Justice, which was previously regarded as the engine of integration.[44]

The integration cannot develop its dynamic from the inside, but is reliant on integrative steps of the Member States, the "masters of the treaties". "Implied powers" has to be within the scope of the limited conferred competence. Everything else is an assumption of competence. The same applies for *effet utile*, which is no clause to optimise competence. *Effet utile* can only claim validity of the interpretation of a limited conferred competence insofar as otherwise the interpretation of the authorisation would make it practically meaningless.[45] Hereto I cite a statement of *K. F. Gärditz* and *Ch. Hillgruber*[46]: "An expanding interpretation of a (limited) competence of the Union, which is solely justified by the useful integrating effect *('effet utile')*, allegedly connected therewith, gives virtually reasons [...] to the supposition of an obvious transgression of competence."

[42] To this a chain of judgments: German Federal Constitutional Court, 2 BvR 1107/77, 2 BvR 1124/77, 2 BvR 195/79 (Order of 23 June 1981) – *Eurocontrol I* (in BVerfGE 58, 1 [37]); 2 BvR 2134, 2159/92 (Judgment of 12 October 1993) – *Maastricht* (in BVerfGE 89, 155 [187, 192, 199]); 2 BvE 6/99 (Judgment of 22 November 2001) – *NATO Strategy* (in BVerfGE 104, 151 [210]); 2 BvE 2/08 et al. (Judgment of 30 June 2009) – *Lissabon-Vertrag* (in BVerfGE 123, 267 [349]); 2 BvE 6/12 et al. (Judgment of 12 September 2012) – *ESM, fiscal compact* (in BVerfGE 132, 195 [238 et seq.]).

[43] German Federal Constitutional Court, 2 BvE 2/08 et al. (Judgment of 30 June 2009) – *Lissabon-Vertrag* (in BVerfGE 123, 267 [351]).

[44] See with further particulars Walter 2009, p. 258 et seq.; Streinz 2008, para 164, 566.

[45] Potacs 2009, p. 474 et seq.

[46] Gärditz & Hillgruber 2009, p. 877.

In the context of implied powers and *effet utile* stands Art. 352 TFEU, which contains a supplementary clause on competence, that covers, compared to the predecessor norm of Art. 308 EC, which was limited to a treaty-immanent development of the achievement of targets within the common market,[47] all policy areas of the treaties (exception: foreign and security policy, Art. 352.4 TFEU). Therein, the Federal Constitutional Court sees a blanket empowerment, which would allow a substantial alteration of the treaty without the approval of parliaments of the Member States and concludes: the German representative in the Council may not declare formal approval on behalf of the Federal Republic of Germany of a corresponding legislative proposal of the Commission as long as the German *Bundestag* and *Bundesrat* have not ratified it according to Art. 23.1 sentences 2 and 3 BL.[48]

Here, the question regarding hierarchy and competence arises so clearly, that the Federal Constitutional Court, with reference to previous own decisions, speaks of a "transgression of limits when utilising the authorities of the European Union" and consistently arrogates *ultra vires* review to itself:[49] "In the case that legal protection cannot be obtained at Union level, the Federal Constitutional Court examines, if legal acts of the European institutions and establishments, while ensuring the principle of subsidiarity under the law of the Community and the Union (Art. 5.1 sentence 3 and Art. 5.3 TEU), keep within bounds of their powers, which have been conferred through limited competence."

For the question concerning hierarchy and competence this means, that the primacy of Union law only applies by and within the scope of the continuing constitutional authorisation. Therefore, a relative primacy is present, which only applies within the scope of transferred competence. The legal act of transfer, which is constitutionally authorised, stands hierarchically above the law which is created by the institutions of the European Union, because the European Union is no federal state, which is equipped with "Kompetenz-Kompetenz".

The international treaties, which constitute competence, are measures for the decisions of the European Court of Justice, which has been created and given competence through the treaties itself. Through the EEC treaty judicial power was not assigned to the Community for a boundless extension of competence, as the Federal Constitutional Court already said in 1987.[50] The Court of Justice could and would have to determine "legal instruments transgressing the limits" of the Commission or the Parliament in a proceeding before it and declare them illegal. If it does not do so,

---

[47] German Federal Constitutional Court, 2 BvE 2/08 et al. (Judgment of 30 June 2009) – *Lissabon-Vertrag* (in BVerfGE 123, 267 [394]), subsequent to Oppermann 2005, para 68.

[48] German Federal Constitutional Court, 2 BvE 2/08 et al. (Judgment of 30 June 2009) – *Lissabon-Vertrag* (in BVerfGE 123, 267 [395]).

[49] German Federal Constitutional Court, 2 BvR 1107/77, 2 BvR 1124/77, 2 BvR 195/79 (Order of 23 June 1981) – *Eurocontrol I* (in BVerfGE 58, 1 [30 et seq.]); 2 BvR 687/85 (Order of 8 April 1987) – *Kloppenburg* (in BVerfGE 75, 223 [235, 242]); 2 BvR 2134, 2159/92 (Judgment of 12 October 1993) – *Maastricht* (in BVerfGE 89, 155 [188]) ("ausbrechender Rechtsakt" [legal instrument transgressing the limits]).

[50] German Federal Constitutional Court, 2 BvR 687/85 (Order of 8 April 1987) – *Kloppenburg* (in BVerfGE 75, 223 [242]).

it has to accept that the Federal Constitutional Court does it with the consequence that corresponding acts of the European Union are not applicable in Germany. This competence to review, which is constitutionally reasoned and is not contrary to the principle of openness towards European Law [*Europarechtsfreundlichkeit*] of the Basic Law and the principle of loyal cooperation (Art. 4.3 TEU), is necessary to safeguard the "fundamental political and constitutional structures of sovereign statehood of the members at progressing integration"[51] and to protect the Member States from gradually easing into a European federal state.

In 2010, the Federal Constitutional Court found once again that Union law remains dependent on a contractual transfer and authorisation.[52] Therefore the Union's institutions including the ECJ remain, for an extension of their powers, reliant on alterations to the treaty, which the Member States make and take the responsibility for in the scope of their authorisations. Indeed, the Federal Constitutional Court sees the risk, that *ultra vires* review of national constitutional courts could endanger the Union law's primacy, but also the risk of an extension of competence contrary to the treaty. A pro-European *ultra vires* review would ask for the assessment of an action of the European Union which is obviously contrary to the competence, and being of great importance, whereto several German Professors on public law can be cited. The Federal Constitutional Court appropriately limits the competence on the development of law of the ECJ to the completion of programmes as provided for in the treaty, the closure of gaps and the solution of contradictions in values. New basic political decisions and a structural transfer of competence are forbidden.[53]

The Federal Constitutional Court refers to the different procedures in which it can exercise its scrutiny role.[54] Interesting is the Court's suggestion to create a new procedure, which is especially tailored to *ultra vires* review and an identity check. The introduction of such a new procedure would send an important signal towards the Union's institutions and in particular to the ECJ, already the respective considerations of the Federal Constitutional Court are a clear warning.

[51] German Federal Constitutional Court, 2 BvE 2/08 et al. (Judgment of 30 June 2009) – *Lissabon-Vertrag* (in BVerfGE 123, 267 [354]), with reference to 2 BvR 2236/04 (Judgment of 18 July 2005) – *European arrest warrant* (in BVerfGE 113, 273 [296]); also for significant and stark transgressions of competence Kokott 1994, p. 233; Isensee 1997, p. 1255 et seq.; different view Schmitz 2001b, p. 285 et. seq., according to which the constitutional law of the Member States is subjected to the decisions of the European Court of Justice without limitations.

[52] German Federal Constitutional Court, 2 BvR 2661/06 (Order of 6 July 2010) – *Honeywell* (in BVerfGE 126, 286 [302 et seqq.]), also to the following.

[53] German Federal Constitutional Court, 2 BvR 2661/06 (Order of 6 July 2010) – *Honeywell* (in BVerfGE 126, 286 [306]).

[54] German Federal Constitutional Court, 2 BvE 2/08 et al. (Judgment of 30 June 2009) – *Lissabon-Vertrag* (in BVerfGE 123, 267 [354 et. seq.]).

5 National Fundamental Rights and Fundamental Rights of the European Union

The fundamental freedoms of Union law are included in the following guarantees: free movement of goods (Art. 28 et seq. TFEU), free movement of workers (Art. 45 et. seq. TFEU), freedom of establishment (Art. 49 et. seq. TFEU), freedom to provide services (Art. 56 et. seq. TFEU) and free movements of capital and payments (Art. 63 et. seq. TFEU). At first, these fundamental freedoms are rights of equality in the sense that at the presence of cross-border matters nationals of the Member States of the European Union have to be treated as equal to own nationals of the concerned Member State.

Furthermore, by now the fundamental freedoms of the Union law act as real rights to freedom, to which they have gradually developed through the jurisdiction of the European Court of Justice.[55] This implies an influence of Union law on German law, as regulations, which are without distinction applicable to nationals and foreigners, are reviewed for their compatibility with the Union law's principle of proportionality. The argumentation of the European Court of Justice is not only oriented on rights of equality, as in accordance to the treaty, but also on rights of freedom, as a citation from the *Gebhard* decision proves: It follows from the Court's jurisdiction that "national measures liable to hinder or make less attractive the exercise of fundamental freedoms guaranteed by the Treaty must fulfil four conditions: they must be applied in a non-discriminatory manner (1), they must be justified by imperative requirements in the general interest (2), they must be suitable for securing the attainment of the objective which they pursue (3), and they must not go beyond what is necessary in order to attain it (4)."[56]

This statement means that internal proportionality examinations can, in cross-border cases, be reviewed independently by the European Court of Justice and the conclusions of the examinations can interfere with the outcome under national law.[57] For example, beer that does not meet the German purity standard legally laid down may be imported into Germany from another Member State[58] and someone with a qualification certificate of another Member State may practise his profession in Germany. The fundamental freedoms can thereby lead to a disadvantage for Germans.

When reviewing the proportionality of restrictions, the European Court of Justice has to take the underlying policies of the concerned state into consideration, for example health policy, which is within the responsibility of the Member States and where the Union may only take additional measures. A harmonisation is explicitly precluded in Art. 168.5 TFEU. It is, again, a problem of competences.

[55] Case 8/74, *Dassonville* (ECJ 11 July 1974); Case 107/83, *Klopp* (ECJ 12 July 1984); Case C-55/94, *Gebhard* (ECJ 30 November 1995).
[56] Case C-55/94, *Gebhard* (ECJ 30 November 1995) para 37.
[57] Examples in Starck 2007, p. 17 et seq., 40 et seq.
[58] Case 178/84, *Reinheitsgebot* (ECJ 12 March 1987).

The European Union exercises public powers, which have been assigned to it by the Member States. Under German constitutional law, public power is only allowed to be transferred, if a level of protection of basic rights essentially comparable to that afforded by the Basic Law is guaranteed (see Art. 23.1 sentence 1).[59] Regarded as fundamental rights under Community law were, based on the case-law of the European Court of Justice[60], human dignity, human integrity, the right to respect for private and family life, the inviolability of the home, the protection of the confidentiality of correspondence with the lawyer, of medical secrecy and of personal data, the freedom of religion and the freedom of movement. Further: the basic right of communication, the freedom to choose and practise an occupation, the freedom of association, the basic right of ownership, rights of equality and basic procedural rights.

The Charter of Fundamental Rights of the European Union (EUCFR), which was proclaimed in the year 2000 in Nice and became valid law in 2009, pools the Member States' common concepts of fundamental rights.[61] It applies with equal ranking to the international treaties on the European Union (Art. 6.1 [1] TEU). The competences of the Union as defined in the treaties are in no way extended through the provisions of the Charter (Art. 6.1 sentence 2 TEU, Art. 51.1 EUCFR). The fundamental rights of the Charter are only binding to the institutions of the European Union and to the Member States when implementing Union law (Art. 51.1 EUCFR). The competences of the Member States may not be touched in the application of the Union's fundamental rights.

* * *

I have tried to make clear,

- that you can only agree on a hierarchy of norms on the basis of an order of competences,
- that integration goes a substantial step further than cooperation,
- but that integration does not yet establish a new statehood.

References

Badura, P. (1995). Supranationalität und Bundesstaatlichkeit durch Rangordnung des Rechts. In C. Starck (Ed.), *Rangordnung der Gesetze* (pp. 107–122). Göttingen: Vandenhoeck & Ruprecht.

[59] German Federal Constitutional Court, 2 BvL 52/71 (Order of 29 May 1974) – *Solange I* (in BVerfGE 37, 271 [280 et seq.]); 2 BvR 1107/77, 2 BvR 1124/77, 2 BvR 195/79 (Order of 23 June 1981) – *Eurocontrol I* (in BVerfGE 58, 1 [30 et seq.]); 2 BvR 197/83 (Order of 22 October 1986) – *Solange II* (in BVerfGE 73, 339 [376]); 2 BvR 2134, 2159/92 (Judgment of 12 October 1993) – *Maastricht* (in BVerfGE 89, 155 [174 et seq.]).

[60] Cf. Rengeling 1993.

[61] Schmitz 2001a, p. 833 et seq.

Cremer, H. J. (2013a). Allgemeine Regeln des Völkerrechts. In J. Isensee, & P. Kirchhof (Eds.), *Handbuch des Staatsrechts* 3rd edn. vol. XI Heidelberg: C.F. Müller.

Cremer, H. J. (2013b). Entscheidung und Entscheidungswirkung. In O. Dörr, R. Grote & T. Marauhn (Eds.), *EMRK/GG – Konkordanzkommentar zum europäischen und deutschen Grundrechtsschutz* (2nd edn. vol. II, p. 2053–2147). Tübingen: Mohr Siebeck.

Denninger, E. (2000). Vom Ende nationalstaatlicher Souveränität in Europa. *Juristenzeitung*, vol. 55, 1121–1126.

Dreier, H. (1988). Souveränität. In Görres-Gesellschaft (Ed.), *Staatslexikon* vol. IV Freiburg i. Br.: Herder.

Dreier, H. (2006). *Grundgesetz Kommentar* (2nd edn.). vol. II. Tübingen: Mohr Siebeck.

Everling, U. (1993). Überlegungen zur Struktur der Europäischen Union und zum neuen Europaartikel des Grundgesetzes. *DVBl*, vol. 108, 936–947.

Frowein, J. A. (1992). Übernationale Menschenrechtsgewährleistungen und nationale Staatsgewalt. In J. Isensee, & P. Kirchhof (Eds.), *Handbuch des Staatsrechts* vol. VII Heidelberg: C.F. Müller.

Gärditz, K. F., & Hillgruber, C. (2009). Volkssouveränität und Demokratie ernst genommen. Zum Lissabon-Urteil des BVerfG. *JZ*, vol. 64, 872–880.

Geiger, R. (2002). *Grundgesetz und Völkerrecht* (3rd edn.). Munich: C. H. Beck.

Hillgruber, C. (2002). Souveränität – Verteidigung eines Rechtsbegriffs. *JZ*, vol. 57, 1072–1080.

Hillgruber, C. (2004). Der Nationalstaat in übernationaler Verflechtung. In J. Isensee, & P. Kirchhof (Eds.), *Handbuch des Staatsrechts* 3rd edn. vol. II Heidelberg: C.F. Müller.

Ipsen, H.-P. (1972). *Europäisches Gemeinschaftsrecht*. Tübingen: Mohr Siebeck.

Ipsen, H.-P. (1992). Deutschland in den Europäischen Gemeinschaften. In J. Isensee, & P. Kirchhof (Eds.), *Handbuch des Staatsrechts* vol. VII Heidelberg: C.F. Müller.

Isensee, J. (1997). Vorrang des Europarechts und deutsches Verfassungsvorbehalte. In J. Burmeister (Ed.), *Verfassungsstaatlichkeit: Festschrift für Klaus Stern zum 65. Geburtstag* (pp. 1239–1268). Munich: C. H. Beck.

Kahl, W. et al. (Ed.). (2009). Bonner Kommentar zum Grundgesetz. *Loose leaf*. Heidelberg: C.F. Müller.

Kokott, J. (1994). Deutschland im Rahmen der Europäischen Union. *Archiv des öffentlichen Rechts*, *119*, 207–237.

Kokott, J. (2002). Die Staatsrechtslehre und die Veränderung ihres Gegenstandes. Konsequenzen von Europäisierung und Internationalisierung. *Veröffentlichungen der Vereinigung der Deutschen Staatsrechtslehrer*, *63*, 7–40.

Krumm, M. (2013). Legislativer Völkervertragsbruch im demokratischen Rechtsstaat. *Archiv des öffentlichen Rechts*, *138*, 363–410.

Ley, I. (2000). Brünn betreibt die Parlamentarisierung des Primärrechts. *JZ*, vol. 55, 165–173.

von Mangoldt, H., Klein, H. H., & Starck, C. (Eds.). (2010). *Kommentar zum Grundgesetz* (6th edn.). Munich: Vahlen.

Oppermann, T. (2005). *Europarecht* (3rd edn.). Munich: C. H. Beck.

Polakiewicz, J. (2013). Der Abkommensentwurf über den Beitritt der Europäischen Union zur Europäischen Menschenrechtskonvention. *EuGRZ*, vol. 40, 472–482.

Potacs, M. (2009). Effet utile als Auslegungsgrundsatz. *EuR*, vol. 44, 465–487.

Randelzhofer, A. (2004). Staatsgewalt und Souveränität. In J. Isensee, & P. Kirchhof (Eds.), *Handbuch des Staatsrechts* 3rd edn. vol. II Heidelberg: C.F. Müller.

Rengeling, H.-W. (1993). *Grundrechtsschutz in der Europäischen Gemeinschaft*. München: C. H. Beck.

Schmitt, C. (1928). *Verfassungslehre*. Munich/Leipzig: Duncker & Humblot.

Schmitz, T. (2001a). Die EU-Grundrechtscharta aus grundrechtsdogmatischer und grundrechtstheoretischer Sicht. *JZ*, vol. 56, 833–843.

Schmitz, T. (2001b). *Integration in der supranationalen Union: das europäische Organisationsmodell einer prozeßhaften geo-regionalen Integration und seine rechtlichen und staatstheoretischen Implikationen*. Baden-Baden: Nomos.

Schönberger, C. (2004). Die Europäische Union als Bund. *Archiv des öffentlichen Rechts*, *129*, 81–120.

Starck, C. (2005). Allgemeine Staatslehre in Zeiten der Europäischen Union. In K. Dicke et al. (Ed.), *Weltinnenrecht. Liber Amicorum Jost Delbrück* (pp. 711–726). Berlin: Duncker & Humblot.

Starck, C. (2006a). Das Caroline-Urteil des Europäischen Gerichtshofs für Menschenrechte und seine rechtlichen Konsequenzen. *JZ*, vol. 61, 76–81.

Starck, C. (2006b). *Praxis der Verfassungsauslegung II*. Baden-Baden: Nomos.

Starck, C. (2007). *Rechtliche Bewertung der Niederlassungsfreiheit und des Fremdbesitzverbots im Apothekenrecht*. Baden-Baden: Nomos.

Steinberger, H. (1991). Der Verfassungsstaat als Glied einer Europäischen Gemeinschaft. *Veröffentlichungen der Vereinigung der Deutschen Staatsrechtslehrer*, *50*, 9–55.

Streinz, R. (2008). *Europarecht* (8th edn.). Heidelberg: C.F. Müller.

Vogel, K. (1964). *Die Verfassungsentscheidung des Grundgesetzes für eine internationale Zusammenarbeit*. Tübingen: Mohr Siebeck.

Walter, K. (2009). *Rechtsfortbildung durch den EuGH. Eine rechtsmethodische Untersuchung ausgehend von der deutschen und französischen Methodenlehre*. Berlin: Duncker & Humblot.

Who Amends the German Basic Law? The EU's Influence on Equal Rights for Same-Sex Registered Civil Partners in German Jurisprudence

Tonio Klein

1 Introduction

It should be clear how to answer this question by looking at Art. 79 of the Basic Law (BL) that clearly and unequivocally stipulates that the Basic Law may only be amended by a law which explicitly does so and which is approved by two thirds of the Members of the *Bundestag* and two thirds of the votes of the *Bundesrat* (i. e. both Houses of the legislature). But if "amendment" is taken to include a substantive change of meaning rather than a mere change of the wording, the answer is less evident. However, it should be clear beyond reasonable doubt that one is not limited to the conception of the creators of the Basic Law, as adopted in 1949.[1] As *J. Limbach*, the former President of the Federal Constitutional Court (FCC), pointed out: "the legal order is nor without gap and contradiction, neither written in unambiguous language nor unaffected by social change. This applies especially to constitutional law which operates as a fundamental legal order not aiming at detailed regulation."[2] Thus, *Montesquieu*'s famous dictum that the judge is nothing but "the mouth that pronounces the words of the law"[3] has to be wrong.[4] This is known best by the person in whose honour this festschrift is conceived and written. *Albrecht Weber* has worked among other things with the classical sources of the General Theory of the State during his teaching at the University of Osnabrück. Moreover, before becoming a professor, he was an academic assistant to *E. Benda*, the former president of the FCC, in the 1970s – a time when the Court made many decisions that caused

[1] The more so as this BL is often ambiguous, heterogeneous and not easy to interpret – to take one example: whether the right to life in Art. 2.2 sentence 1 BL encompasses unborn life: Anderheiden 2006, p. 7; Gas 2012, p. 311 et seq.

[2] Limbach 1996, para 15: "weder ist die Rechtsordnung lückenlos, widerspruchsfrei, sprachlich eindeutig noch gegenüber dem sozialen Wandel erhaben. Das gilt in besonderem Maße für das Verfassungsrecht, das sich durch eine geringe Regelungsdichte auszeichnet und nicht den Anspruch auf Lückenlosigkeit erhebt" (my translation).

[3] Montesquieu 1758, p. 327.

[4] Hirsch 2004, II. 1.; Limbach 1996, para 15.

H.-J. Blanke et al. (eds.), *Common European Legal Thinking*,
DOI 10.1007/978-3-319-19300-7_9

tremendous controversy.[5] Social change may have its influence on the outcome of a judicial institution, as well as the personality of individual judges and both may bring about at least a de facto amendment of the Basic Law. Consider, for example, Justice *P. Kirchhof*'s "Halbteilungsgrundsatz" (which may be translated as "principle of equal shares", i. e. between the State and the individual, considering the fruit of one man's economic activity): According to Art. 14.2 BL, "Property entails obligations. Its use shall also serve the public good." *Kirchhof* gave the word "also" ("zugleich", i. e. "at the same time") the meaning of "in equal shares"[6]; which was clearly not intended by the founders of the BL.[7] A famous example considering European integration was given in the "Maastricht" judgment of the FCC. No one expected that Art. 38.1 BL ("Members of the German Bundestag shall be elected in general, direct, free, equal and secret elections") should not only confer the rights expressly stated, but also an individual and legally enforceable right that the *Bundestag* should prevent substantial competences from being transferred to the EU.[8]

Notwithstanding this example, the FCC is generally favourable to European integration, as is the Basic Law in its Art. 23.[9] Sometimes, the FCC's jurisprudence is even more influenced and inspired by EU law than some people would like. *A. Weber*, however, was always receptive to such tendencies and interested in them, for they are closely linked to the question of methods of interpreting the law, especially constitutional law. This has always evoked a positive response from him, not only from an EU law perspective, but also as a result of his interest in comparative constitutional law, which made him always ready to look beyond the conventional methods of interpreting the law and consider influences such as EU law, as well as foreign constitutional law, international law and European Human Rights Law in the broader sense of the term. Thus, one may note here the influence of EU fundamental rights on German Jurisprudence, in particular the doctrine of "interpretation

---

[5] Cf. Limbach 1996, para 3.

[6] German FCC, 2 BvL 37/91 (Order of 22 June 1995) para 52 – *Halbteilungsgrundsatz* (in BVerfGE 93, 121 et seqq.).

[7] Cf. Sacksofsky 2006, p. 661 et seq.; Sauer 2006. Consequently, in translations of the BL made for and published by the Government or the Bundestag, one may find the English term "also" and the French term "en même temps": Federal Ministry of Justice and Consumer Protection: Basic Law for the Federal Republic of Germany (2014), translation by Tomuschat and Currie, http://www.gesetze-im-internet.de/englisch_gg/englisch_gg.html#p0079 (any direct BL quote in this text is taken from this translation); German Bundestag: Loi Fondamentale pour la République Fédérale d'Allemagne (2012), translation by Autexier et al., http://www.bundestag.de/blob/189762/f0568757877611b2e434039d29a1a822/loi_fondamentale-data.pdf

[8] German FCC, 2 BvR 2134, 2159/92 (Judgment of 12 October 1993) – *Maastricht* (in BVerfGE 89, 155 [171 et seq.]), criticised by numerous scholars, e. g. Gassner 1995, p. 429 et seqq.; Häde 1993, p. 2457 et seq.; Hobe and Wiegand 1994, p. 1 et seq.; Tomuschat 1993, p. 489 et seqq.

[9] E. g. German FCC, 2 BvE 2/08 et al. (Judgment of 30 June 2009) para 220 – *Lissabon-Vertrag* (in BVerfGE 123, 267 et seqq.): "The German constitution is directed towards opening the sovereign state order to peaceful cooperation of the nations and towards European integration"; cf. also para 240: "the principle of the BL's openness towards European Law (*Europarechtsfreundlichkeit*)".

in accordance with the directives" ("richtlinienkonforme Auslegung"[10]). This will lead to reflections on how far the "Europeanisation" of national constitutional law has already gone and if in fact the EU may, at least indirectly, amend the Basic Law.

A. Weber, in his farewell lecture, decisively opposed *R. Herzog*'s and *L. Gerkens*'s appeal to "stop" the European Court of Justice, specifically because of the court's assessing a (not yet enforced) prohibition of discrimination on the ground of age to be a "general principle of law".[11] Subsequently, he is credited with favouring the FCC in the context of further steps towards the implementation of a *written* EU clause (Art. 21 of the Charter of Fundamental Rights, EUCFR) in national constitutional law. Furthermore, his general interest in matters of actual social significance has been made clear in many discussions with both colleagues and his academic assistants; we have in particular discussed and held lectures on controversially received decisions of the FCC. Therefore, I hope that the treatment of the FCC's jurisprudence on same-sex registered couples raises his interest, for both of these aspects may be found in it. Last but not least, the FCC's convergence (almost a de facto equalisation) of registered civil partnership and marriage raises the fundamental question of the separation of powers, seen as a serious and real danger by *B. Rüthers*. If "marriage", as conceived in Art. 6.1 BL ("Marriage and the family shall enjoy the special protection of the state.") is to include same-sex marriages, contrary to what was intended at the time of the adoption of the BL, it should be the responsibility of the legislature and not of the judiciary to change it, and the legislature should explicitly amend the Basic Law in that sense.[12] Conversely, Art. 21.1 of the EUCFR contains a prohibition of discrimination based on "sexual orientation". Does this have a binding effect on the BL, directly or indirectly, or serve at least as an inspiration and influence on its interpretation?

2 The Starting Point: The National Legislator's Will and the Emergence of Art. 21.1 of the Charter of Fundamental Rights

2.1 The Relevance of the Negative Intention of the Constitution-Making Body: No Requirement of Interpretation in the Original Sense!

The FCC has consistently stated that "marriage" means a legal union or status of persons of different sexes.[13] But this interpretation is not necessarily valid forever,

[10] Kühling 2014, p. 481 et seqq.; Tonikidis 2013, p. 598 et seqq.

[11] Weber 2012, p. 307 et seqq.; cf. Herzog and Gerken 2008; cf. Case C-144/04, *Mangold* (ECJ 22 November 2005); Herrmann 2006, p. 69 et seq.

[12] Rüthers 2013.

[13] German FCC, 1 BvR 205/58 (Judgment of 29 July 1959) (in BVerfGE 10, 59 [66]); 1 BvR 636/68 (Decision of 4 May 1971) – *Spanier-Entscheidung* (in BVerfGE 31, 58 [82]); 1 BvR 16/72 (Order of 11 October 1978) – *Transsexueller* (in BVerfGE 49, 286 [300]);

bearing in mind that the FCC was never hostile to a dynamic approach in interpreting the BL, as *Limbach* in particular has emphasised.[14] One must bear in mind that "historical" interpretation is one method among others, but not the only method. *Rüthers* is, of course, right in assuming that in 1949, the question whether married couples may be of the same sex was simply not something the creators of the Basic Law had in mind. In other words, the question was not answered in the negative, it was not even imagined.[15] But this is as natural as we, in our time, do not know and cannot know the social issues of the year 2075. Social change is not only natural, but in most cases broadly accepted, if not ardently desired and later welcomed. Some examples may be given. Since its enactment in 1949, the Basic Law contains the following provisions: "Human dignity shall be inviolable" (Art. 1.1 BL), "All persons shall be equal before the law" (Art. 3.1 BL), "Marriage and the family shall enjoy the special protection of the state" (Art. 6.1 BL). But in that year, nobody had and could have possibly considered the human dignity of transsexuals or embryos *in vitro*, or indeed the status of same-sex married couples or any other form of equal treatment of homosexuals. In a broader sense, it was common knowledge that fundamental rights were of limited applicability and subject to various pre-conditions which nowadays are considered no longer relevant. In former times, it was a common assumption which did not have to be written in the Constitution that some people (such as pupils, minors, prisoners, soldiers and civil servants) were subject to a "special relationship of subordination" ("besonderes Gewaltverhältnis"), conferring on them what may be called second-class fundamental rights. The right to physical integrity (Art. 2.2 sentence 1 BL) did not apply to pupils and minors, their corporal punishment by teachers, parents and instructors being not only widely practised, but almost unquestioned. The right to privacy of correspondence (Art. 10.1 BL) did not apply to prisoners, until in 1972, a famous FCC order put an end to that.[16] Some fundamental rights did not fully apply to civil servants, formerly considered as mere executioners of the public authority's will[17] and thus as the State itself and not as individuals who may oppose their fundamental rights *against* the State. And even if this had been fundamentally contested more than half

1 BvL 136/78, 1 BvR 890/77, 1 BvR 1300/78, 1 BvR 1440/78, 1 BvR 32/79 (Judgment of 28 February 1980) – *Ehescheidung* (in BVerfGE 53, 224 [245]); 2 BvL 27/81 (Order of 8 March 1983) (in BVerfGE 63, 323 [330]); 1 BvF 1/01, 1 BvF 2/01 (Judgment of 17 July 2002) – *gleichgeschlechtliche Lebenspartnerschaft* (in BVerfGE 105, 313 [345]); 2 BvR 1397/09 (Order of 19 June 2012) – *Lebenspartnerschaft Beamter* (in BVerfGE 131, 239 [259]); 2 BvR 909/06 (Order of 7 May 2013) para 86 – *Ehegattensplitting* (in BVerfGE 133, 377 et seqq.).

[14] Limbach 1996, para 1 et seqq.

[15] Cf. Michael 2010, p. 3538 et seq.; Rüthers 2013.

[16] German FCC, 2 BvR 41/71 (Order of 14 March 1972) – *Strafgefangenenentscheidung* (in BVerfGE 33, 1 et seqq.).

[17] The image of a civil servant as being "just a cog in the State's clockwork" (Rad im Uhrwerke des Staates), originating from Gönner 1808, p. 208 et seq., was evoked as late as 1992 and maintained in 2005 by Depenheuer: Depenheuer 2005, para 19; Depenheuer 1992, p. 405; criticised by Leuze 1998, p. 188. A more general, critical approach to an alleged resurrection of the institution of "special relationship of subordination" ("besonderes Gewaltverhältnis") is given by Sachs 2004, p. 209 et seqq.

a century ago, who would possibly have foreseen that someday, a Muslim would apply to be appointed to the teaching profession at a public school (i. e. as a civil servant) and challenge the decision that her declared intention to wear, in the name of freedom of religion (Art. 4.1/2 BL), a headscarf at school and in lessons means that she is unsuited for the office?[18] It was not before 2001 that *E. W. Böckenförde* could state the following: "The idea that on entry into the status of a civil servant, one has to surrender his fundamental rights 'at the door', as was still accepted in 1949, is overcome without any question."[19]

According to *G. Dürig*, ladies' wrestling could not benefit from fundamental rights' protection for in 1958, he considered it to indicate a "tastelessness" which should cause one "to be ashamed of oneself".[20] Nowadays, by contrast, ladies' wrestling is an Olympic sport.

These examples give a vivid demonstration that anyone intending to interpret the Basic Law in the exact sense of its founders' will and in the context of formerly accepted moral values, should be ready to go back in time, since many of its underlying moral values have not only changed considerably, but with common consent. Social change is as inevitable as natural and therefore should not in general be dismissed. *Rüthers* is right in emphasising the importance of an "original intention of a provision".[21] But he turns into an insurmountable criterion of legal interpretation what is no more (but also no less) than a starting point.

In his interpretative approach, *Rüthers* approaches the US doctrine of "originalism", according to which the Constitution should be interpreted in accordance with its original meaning – that is, the meaning it had at the time of its enactment.[22] Even applied to Germany, this doctrine is, as we have seen, highly questionable, but it becomes much more indefensible and almost absurd when applied to States with much older constitutions. The Fourteenth Amendment of the U.S. Constitution (1868) granted all persons equal protection of the laws,[23] but this was far from requiring equal treatment of races, which, in the field of public education, was not

---

[18] Cf. German FCC, 2 BvR 1436/02 (Judgment of 3 June 2003) – *Kopftuchurteil* (in BVerfGE 108, 282 et seqq.).

[19] Böckenförde 2001,1 BvR 471/10 (order of 27 January 2015) – *Kopftuchbeschluss* (in: Die Öffentliche Verwaltung, 68, p. 471 et seqq.), p. 725: Die Rede von den Grundrechten, die "beim Eintritt ins Beamtenverhältnis, wie man noch nach 1949 meinte, an der Türe 'abgegeben' werden", sei eindeutig überwunden (my translation).

[20] Dürig, in Maunz and Dürig (1958), Art. 1 Abs. I para 28: "Geschmacklosigkeit", "Bei Damenringkämpfen schämt man sich" (my translation).

[21] Rüthers 2013.

[22] Cf. Heun 2008, p. 233 et seqq.; Kahn 2001, p. 574 et seqq.; brief overview in http://www.sandiego.edu/law/centers/csco/; its significance for the *Tea Party*: Foley 2012, p. 167 et seqq.

[23] Section 1. All persons born or naturalized in the United States, and subject to the jurisdiction thereof, are citizens of the United States and of the State wherein they reside. No State shall make or enforce any law which shall abridge the privileges or immunities of citizens of the United States; nor shall any State deprive any person of life, liberty, or property, without due process of law; nor deny to any person within its jurisdiction the equal protection of the laws. http://en.wikipedia.org/wiki/Fourteenth_Amendment_to_the_United_States_Constitution

applied or enforced until the U.S. Supreme Court's landmark judgment (1954) in *Brown v. Board of Education*.[24]

Many things self-evident today were seen quite differently some years ago without this being necessarily enshrined in a written legal document. For example, it was commented on regarding the Prussian police and public order law in the 19th century that it does not have to be written law that it be forbidden to smoke in public but that it is permitted to drop litter in the street. Today, it is exactly the contrary which is supposed to be equally obvious.[25] The same is true for the French Declaration of Human and Civil Rights (1789): These rights were not intended to be applicable to a substantial part of society, notably women and Jews.[26] Today, it is exactly this Declaration which is not only seen as a landmark in Human Rights Law, but which is also directly applicable and enforceable in French Constitutional Law. It has been incorporated in the Constitution of the 5th Republic[27] – with, of course, a general applicability to all human beings (or, for some rights, all citizens). This illustrates that originalism is a dangerous and misleading doctrine.

2.2 The Genesis of the Suspect Criterion of "Sexual Orientation" in Art. 21.1 of the Charter of Fundamental Rights

When in 1999 the Charter was drawn up by a Convention consisting of a representative from each EU Member State and from the European Commission, as well as Members of the European Parliament and of national parliaments, the prohibition of discrimination based on the ground of sexual orientation was not unknown to the Convention's members. For example, the post-apartheid Constitution of the Republic of South Africa was drafted under constructive advice from scholars worldwide, notably from Germany.[28] The fact that this Constitution contained a non-discrimination clause on those lines evoked no one's anger or astonishment, except for two (out of 400) representatives of the fundamentalist *African Christian Democratic Party* in the Constitutional Assembly.[29] Although EU Member States did not have

[24] Supreme Court of the United States, Nos. 1, 2, 4 and 10 – October Term 1953 (Judgment of 17 May 1954 – *Brown vs. Board of Education*), 1953347 U.S. 483 (1954), http://caselaw.lp.findlaw.com/scripts/getcase.pl?navby=CASE&court=US&vol=347&page=483

[25] Kirchhof, P.: Speech on the occasion of his honorary doctorate at the University of Osnabrück, 23 June 2006; speech on the occasion of the 25-year existence of the Faculty of Law at the University of Osnabrück, 5 November 2005. Both speeches are unpublished but were attended by the author.

[26] Kirchhof (cf. supra).

[27] Cf. Preamble of the Constitution of 4 October 1958: "The French people solemnly proclaim their attachment to the Rights of Man and the principles of national sovereignty as defined by the Declaration of 1789".

[28] Gas 2002, p. 37 et seqq.

[29] Green 1996, col. 375 et seqq.: "we have strong objection to the inclusion of the words 'sexual orientation', which is aimed at giving a lifestyle of homosexuality and lesbianism constitutional recognition. [...] The Bible teaches that homosexuality and lesbianism are sins which people

such a clause before the proclamation of the Charter in 2000,[30] it had been included in the constitutions of some of the German *Länder*.[31] The principal discussions in the Convention concerned matters other than the "sexual orientation" criterion (e. g. the prohibition of discrimination on the ground of age, which was more controversial in both jurisprudence and legal debate in both Germany and the EU).[32] Although it was criticised by some German scholars,[33] the Convention was finally able to adopt the clause outlawing discrimination on grounds of sexual orientation without difficulty or controversy. Later, Germany likewise adopted and ratified the Lisbon Treaty, which conferred on the Charter the status of directly applicable EU primary law. In summary, it must be said that the provision's genesis was far less complicated than its academic discussion and reception. This is supposedly an explanation for the fact that the FCC gave his reasoning on the impact of the clause in German Constitutional Law in very few words, notwithstanding the substantial impact and consequences of its decision in the case to be discussed.

3 The Influence of the European Charter in the FCC's Decision Concerning the Unequal Treatment of Marriage and Registered Civil Partnerships with Regard to Survivors' Pensions ("Hinterbliebenenversorgung")

Although the question to what extent Art. 51 EUCFR directly binds the Member States[34] was not raised in the case under discussion, the FCC accepted Art. 21 EUCFR as well as other norms of International Human Rights Law as sources (among others) for the interpretation of Art. 3 BL: "A strict standard of review in connection with unequal treatment relating to sexual orientation, which approaches the standard applied in connection with other prohibitions of discrimination, is also in line with the development of European law. Both Art. 13 of the EC Treaty and Art. 21.1 of the Charter of Fundamental Rights (ECtHR) of the European Union include sexual orientation in the group of prohibitions of discrimination. The case-law of the European Court of Human Rights also requires just as 'serious grounds' to justify differentiations based on sexual orientation as for those based on sex (ECHR, judgment of 24 July 2003 – no. 40.016/98 – Karner v. Austria, *Österreichische Juristen-*

---

voluntarily choose to commit [. . .] there is a possibility for homosexuals to leave their sinful life. It is not a permanent condition.".

[30] Since 2005: Chap. 1 Art. 2.4, Chap. 2 Art. 12 Constitution of Sweden; since 2004: Art. 13.2 Constitution of Portugal.

[31] Art. 10.2 Constitution of Berlin (since 1995); Art. 12.2 Constitution of Brandenburg (since 1992); Art. 2.3 Constitution of Thuringia (since 1993); cf. Hölscheidt, in Meyer (2014), Art. 21 para 10.

[32] Hölscheidt, in Meyer (2014), Art. 21 para 23 et seqq.

[33] Streinz, in Streinz (2011), Art. 21 EUCFR para 4, footnote 8; Tettinger 2001, p. 1013.

[34] Cf. Barsch and Garms 2014, p. 54; Kingreen, in Calliess and Ruffert (2011), Art. 51 EUCFR; Ogorek 2014, p. 954 et seqq.; Ruffert 2014, p. 662 et seqq.; Thym 2013, p. 889 et seqq.

Zeitung 2004, p. 36 (38) with further references).”[35] Sexual orientation is de facto made equivalent to the other prohibited grounds in Art. 3.3 BL, for they all describe both personal and unchangeable characteristics. It is clear that the brief reasoning concerning EU law does not necessarily carry sufficient weight for the establishment of a new technique of interpretation. But on the other hand, this may be due to the assumption (yet to be proven) that the analogous application of Art. 3.3 BL when being discriminated against because of sexual orientation does not evoke any dogmatic difficulty. This assumption will be tested by a comparison of two doctrines concerning the interpretation of national law.

4 Interpretation of National (Constitutional) Law in Accordance with the European Charter – a Corollary of the Doctrine of Interpretation of National Law in Accordance with the Directives?

Not only is the doctrine of interpretation of national law in accordance with the directives (“richtlinienkonforme Auslegung”) well established in German jurisprudence, but this is also the case with the doctrine of interpretation of national law in accordance with the European Charter. Both are founded on the general principle of loyalty towards the EU (“Unionstreue”) as contained in Art. 4.3 TEU and Art. 23.1 BL[36] and on the supremacy of EU law.[37] But this is not so evident when it comes to interpreting national fundamental rights affected by *national* authority, for Art. 51 of the Charter explicitly limits the directly binding effect of the European Charter in this case. A de facto binding effect may thus unlawfully enlarge the Union’s competences and could, according to German case law, be considered as a “legal instrument transgressing the limits” (“ausbrechender Rechtsakt”), otherwise called an “ultra vires” act. In other words, this may be an act exceeding EU competences under the principle of conferral and the principle of subsidiarity as elaborated in Art. 5 TEU and thus transgressing the limits of the powers granted with a view to European integration (“Integrationsermächtigung”) by the *Bundestag*.[38] Although not only the legislature, but also the executive and even the judiciary are subject to review under the principle of *ultra vires* review, it is, in our case, the FCC’s order in the above-mentioned “survivors’ pensions” case which may constitute an *ultra*

[35] German FCC, 1 BvR 1164/07 (Order of 7 July 2009) para 88 – *Hinterbliebenenversorgung* (in BVerfGE 124, 199 et seqq.).

[36] E. g. German FCC, 2 BvE 2/08 et al. (Judgment of 30 June 2009) para 240 – *Lissabon-Vertrag* (in BVerfGE 123, 267 et seqq.): “principle of sincere cooperation” (Art. 4.3 TEU) and “the principle of the Basic Law’s openness towards European Law (*Europarechtsfreundlichkeit*)” (Art. 23.1 BL).

[37] Jarass 2013, p. 36.

[38] Cf. German FCC, 2 BvE 2/08 et al. (Judgment of 30 June 2009) para 240 – *Lissabon-Vertrag* (in BVerfGE 123, 267 et seqq.); for former reference see German FCC, 2 BvR 2134, 2159/92 (Judgment of 12 October 1993) para 106 – *Maastricht* (in BVerfGE 89, 155 et seqq.).

vires act, i. e. an act of the same body that claims competence for *ultra vires* review. Notwithstanding the fact that the "survivors' pensions" order and the jurisprudence concerning *ultra vires* review emerge from the two different chambers of the FCC and that one may see substantial differences between the "eurosceptical" Second Chamber and the "europhile" First Chamber,[39] it is most unlikely that the FCC will quash its own decisions. In addition, one has to emphasise that the assumption of a doctrine of interpretation of national law in accordance with the European Charter is far from being unlawful when understood in the context of the following principle: If more than one way to interpret a provision of the Basic Law exists, one has to choose the one which is consistent with the European Charter. This is exactly what applies with regard to the doctrine of interpretation of national law in accordance with the directives: If more than one way to interpret a national provision exists, one has to choose the one which is consistent with the relevant EU directive.

5 Evaluation of the Outcome: Should Same-Sex Registered Civil Partners Have the Same Rights as Married Couples?

Rüthers correctly points out that equal treatment only may be given to "equal" persons and that the question whether persons are equal in the sense of "comparable" is inextricably linked to a cultural imprint which may be found implicitly or explicitly in the answer.[40] But in our time, the "cultural imprint" shows in the fact that "sexual orientation" is contained in Art. 21.1 EUCFR as an explicit form of prohibited discrimination. Remember that this is not the will of a few aspiring reformers, but the will of all 28 EU Member States, which adopted and ratified this provision without difficulty.[41] Bearing in mind that these States and their peoples belong to various religious traditions, and that conceptions according to which homosexuality is a sinful aberration and not a personal condition are deeply rooted in some of them, it is of paramount importance that the Member States and their peoples (directly or through their representative bodies) unanimously agreed on the provision.

Nevertheless, equal treatment may lead to a de facto right to marry for homosexuals, which is, by some scholars, seen critically, for in Germany, Art. 6.1 BL contains not only the right to marry, but also an institutional guarantee ("Institutsgarantie") of marriage: "Marriage and the family shall enjoy the special protection of the state." Marriage and the family being linked in this provision, one may argue that marriage is the nucleus of the family which is the nucleus of society and that therefore "special" protection has to be given to couples who are, at least potentially, able to reproduce. This being biologically impossible for homosexuals, one may ask whether granting rights of married couples to them may endanger pop-

[39] Cf. Michael 2010, p. 3542.

[40] Rüthers 2013.

[41] Cf. supra, 2.2.

ulation and social coherence, particularly in times of demographic change and low fertility rates in many EU Member States.

Conversely, marriage is not solely aimed at reproduction. In a State that is founded on the values of respect for human dignity, freedom, democracy, equality, the rule of law and respect for human rights (cf. Art. 2 TEU, Art. 20.1, 28.1 BL), state authorities are generally prohibited from controlling the reasons for the decision of two individuals to get married. In Germany, a man and a woman may do so without legal obstacles, apart from those contained in §§ 1303 et seqq. German Civil Code (*Bürgerliches Gesetzbuch*).[42] The problems of forced marriages and unconsummated marriages are not discussed here. Apart from such cases, the decision to marry is a personal choice, affecting the core identity and therefore not subject to public control. Couples may marry because they love each other and want to have children, because they love each other, but do not intend to reproduce, in order to save taxes, in order to hide the homosexuality of a spouse, in order to satisfy a demand from parents, in order to "legalise" a long-lasting concubinage before meeting the creator, because although they do not love each other they have sufficient affection to care for each other, because one spouse was offered a barrel of beer by some friends or lost a bet – the list is endless. In many cases, the will to reproduce is of minor importance, and it is clear that the state may not require a couple to provide evidence of their capacity to reproduce before granting a certificate of marriage. Thus, it is far from being obvious that homosexuals should not – albeit directly or indirectly – benefit from the rights of married persons.

It must be added that in our time, the nexus of marriage and reproduction is nothing but a general assumption with many exceptions. And most of the exceptions concern heterosexual, not homosexual couples, which may be seen in the data provided by the latest German mini-census: In 2011, 11.783,000 couples without children (albeit married or not) lived in Germany, compared to 11.710,000 "families" (i. e. married couples with children, unmarried couples with children, lone parents). Of those couples without children, 83.5 % were married, compared to 69.8 % of the "families",[43] so that in fact more than half of all married couples are without children, amounting to a total of 9.838,805 married couples. Even bearing in mind that some of them will reproduce later, the number greatly exceeds the number of registered civil partners which amounted to 27,000 in the same year.[44] Therefore, the "nucleus" aspect makes denying homosexuals equal rights even more questionable, if not absurd. No one would, for example, deny heterosexuals the right to marry who are so far advanced in years that their capacity to reproduce is undoubtedly non-existent. As regards fertility, it is impossible to see a "funda-

[42] http://www.gesetze-im-internet.de/bgb/ (German); http://www.gesetze-im-internet.de/englisch_bgb/index.html (English).

[43] Federal Statistical Office, Statistical Yearbook 2012, p. 33, https://www.destatis.de/EN/Publications/Specialized/Population/StatYearbook_Chapter2_5011001129004.pdf?__blob=publicationFile

[44] Federal Statistical Office, Statistical Yearbook 2012, p. 38, https://www.destatis.de/EN/Publications/Specialized/Population/StatYearbook_Chapter2_5011001129004.pdf?__blob=publicationFile

mental biological difference"[45] between aged heterosexual couples and homosexual couples.

Last but not least, imagine the following situation: A man and a woman marry and think about whether to have children or not. Will the resulting decision in any way be influenced by *other* couples' legal status and the benefits emerging thereof? Will they deliberately decide against children for the sole reason that with equal treatment of homosexuals, they will have nothing less, but homosexuals will have something more? This is quite unrealistic, for couples will primarily consider their *own* situation. While homosexuals are better off, heterosexuals are not worse off. There is no absolute amount of rights and benefits in this context, and granting rights and benefits to someone does not imply that they are somehow taken away from someone else.[46] This is also the reason why one has to oppose[47] the traditional doctrine of "requirement of distance" ("Abstandsgebot"), supposed to be grounded in the wording of Art. 6.1 BL ("Marriage and the family shall enjoy the *special* protection of the State", my emphasis) as well as in the guarantee of the institution ("Institutsgarantie") of marriage in the same Article: Other legal institutions of partnership are said to keep a distance to marriage,[48] but as was demonstrated, the FCC was right in definitively rejecting this doctrine, which is far from being indisputably enshrined in the Basic Law even at the time of its origin.[49] Contrary

---

[45] This being *Rüthers*'s reason for denying equal treatment to homosexuals; Rüthers 2013.

[46] Hölscheidt, in Meyer (2014), Art. 21 para 41.

[47] As do, among others: German FCC, 1 BvF 1/01, 1 BvF 2/01 (Judgment of 17 July 2002) para 101 – *gleichgeschlechtliche Lebenspartnerschaft* (in BVerfGE 105, 313 [348]); Barsch and Garms 2014, p. 61 et seqq.; Beck 2010, p. 12; Epping 2015, para 513; Freytag 2012, p. 451; Grünberger 2010, p. 203.

[48] Government of Saxony, Government of Thuringia, cf. German FCC, 1 BvF 1/01, 1 BvF 2/01 (Judgment of 17 July 2002) para 19 et seq. – *gleichgeschlechtliche Lebenspartnerschaft* (in BVerfGE 105, 313 et seqq.); Diederichsen 2000, p. 1843; di Fabio 2003 p. 993; Isensee 2011, para 205; Krings 2000, p. 405 et seqq.; Scholz and Uhle 2001, p. 398; cf. Barsch and Garms 2014, p. 56 et seqq.

[49] German FCC, 1 BvF 1/01, 1 BvF 2/01 (Judgment of 17 July 2002) para 101 – *gleichgeschlechtliche Lebenspartnerschaft* (in BVerfGE 105, 313 [348]): "In the debates on Art. 6.1 of the Basic Law, the question of the protection of new ways of life also played a substantial role (on this, cf. the contributions of Helene Weber, in: *Protokoll der 21. Sitzung des Hauptausschusses*, p. 240, and Elisabeth Selbert, in: *Protokoll der 43. Sitzung des Hauptausschusses*, pp. 552–553). Here, in particular the argument that the special protection of the family excluded the equal treatment of illegitimate children in Art. 6.5 BL (cf. Weber and Süsterhenn in: *Protokoll der 21. Sitzung des Hauptausschusses*, 242–243) was unsuccessful. If Mangoldt, as rapporteur, in his Written Report on Art. 6.1 BL finally noted that this fundamental right was scarcely more than a declaration in the case of which it was not really evident what effect it had as directly applicable law (*Anlage zum stenographischen Bericht der 9. Sitzung des Parlamentarischen Rates*, p. 6), then this reflects that although there was agreement on subjecting marriage and the family to constitutional protection, there was no clarification as to what this means in detail for its relationship to other ways of life. At all events, a requirement of distance cannot be based on this.".
This was confirmed directly or indirectly by many subsequent decisions such as the "survivors' pensions" order and expressly in 2013 in an interview by the Court's vice president F. Kirchhof: "The Basic Law does not contain a requirement of distance", cf. Die Welt, 15 May 2013, http://www.welt.de/newsticker/news2/article114486335/Verfassungsgerichts-Vize-kritisiert-Bayern-wegen-Homo-Ehe.html (my translation).

to *Rüthers*, even originalism does not lead to a requirement of distance. The FCC is on the right track in closing the gap between homosexual and heterosexual couples.

6 Evaluation of the Impact of EU Law

Is there a *general* imperative that all national law has to be interpreted and applied in the light of the European Charter? This may only be a rebuttable presumption, for anything else would overstretch the scope of application of the European Charter, contrary to its Art. 51. Nevertheless, the general principle of loyalty towards the EU ("Unionstreue") as contained in Art. 4.3 TEU and the principle of the Basic Law's receptiveness towards European Law ("Europarechtsfreundlichkeit")[50] require that such a doctrine is applied subject to the following conditions:

- *The wording of the European Charter is unequivocal.* Concerning homosexuality, this is the case with regard to the prohibition of discrimination on the ground of "sexual orientation" in Art. 21.1 EUCFR.
- *The national provision in question does not explicitly exclude the possibility that the Charter should be "read in" and should prevail in the interpretation of the national provision.* This condition is satisfied when Art. 6.1 BL is correctly seen as not containing a "requirement of distance" which would lead to an exception from the general principle of non-discrimination in Art. 3 BL. Although this is a question of major controversy[51], it is sufficient that the requirement of distance is not an explicit and unequivocal obstacle to the application of Art. 21 EUCFR, i. e. *in dubio pro Europa*. In other words: Art. 3.3 BL specifies explicit grounds where discrimination is prohibited, but does not exclude others. Although this was not how the Article was intended to be read[52] (unlike Art. 21.1 EUCFR, it does not contain words on the lines of "any ground such as ..."), analogous application is at least not explicitly excluded. Therefore the above-mentioned rule applies with the following specification: *If more than one way to interpret a national provision exists without violating its unambiguous wording, one has to choose the interpretation which is consistent with the relevant Charter provision.* It may be added that the general Art. 3.1 BL may serve as a residual norm ("Auffangnorm") for any grounds of discrimination not contained in Art. 3.3 BL and that Art. 3.1 BL shall be applied with the same strict scrutiny as Art. 3.3 BL if a ground such as sexual orientation is equivalent to those grounds encompassed by Art. 3.3 BL.[53]
- *A conflicting norm in EU law of the same rank does not exist.* In the same-sex civil partnership cases, one may ask whether Art. 9 EUCFR may be evoked for it guarantees the right to marry and the right to found a family "in accordance with

[50] E. g. German FCC, 2 BvE 2/08 et al. (Judgment of 30 June 2009) para 240 – *Lissabon-Vertrag* (in BVerfGE 123, 267 et seqq.).
[51] Cf. supra, 5.1.
[52] E. g. Dürig and Scholz, in Maunz and Dürig (1996), Art. 3 para 27 et seq.
[53] Cf. supra, 3.

the national laws governing the exercise of these rights".[54] This may be seen as not requiring the Member States to extend the institution of marriage to same-sex couples on the basis of Art. 21.1 EUCFR. Conversely, the provision does not explicitly or indirectly prevent Member States from doing so, for marriage is not necessarily to be seen as exclusively reserved for two people of different sexes.[55] Moreover, what was said in reference to the "requirement of distance" is also true with regard to Art. 9.1 EUCFR: This Article not requiring, but permitting the requirement of distance, the decision whether to uphold it or not may be determined by Art. 21.1 EUCFR which is thus the decisive provision to which Art. 9.1 EUCFR is subject. The above-mentioned condition has to be interpreted in the following terms: *An uncontestably and thus coercively conflicting norm in EU law of the same rank does not exist.*

7 Conclusion

Who amends the Basic Law? It may be the EU, for Art. 3.3 BL was conceived as containing an exclusive list of grounds for strict scrutiny, which has been enlarged by the ground of sexual orientation as contained in Art. 21.1 EUCFR. But who "amends" the EU Treaties? The Member States as "masters of the Treaties". In some cases, EU law may dynamically develop and thus go far beyond the "masters'" intention. But for the most part, this danger of overstepping the national legislators' conferral of powers and rules is greatly over-estimated. Specifically, the (de facto) incorporation of sexual orientation in Art. 3.3 BL is not legal prestidigitation, but required by the clear wording of Art. 21.1 EUCFR which Member States unanimously and definitively agreed. The interpretation of national law – even constitutional law – in accordance with the European Charter may lead to a substantial "change in the meaning of fundamental rights through European integration" ("Grundrechtswandel kraft europäischer Integration").[56] In the "survivors' pensions" order, the FCC has made a decisive, but probably not final step in the right direction.

A. *Weber* has always favoured the convergence of national and European fundamental rights,[57] and should therefore be assumed to acclaim this method of interpreting the law. But will he also acclaim the consequences, i. e. the de facto equalisation of same-sex civil partnerships and heterosexual marriages? To be honest, I do not know and I have not asked him. In our numerous discussions on matters

[54] Cf. Barsch and Garms 2014, p. 54 et seqq.; Kingreen, in Calliess and Ruffert (2011), Art. 9 EUCFR para 3.
[55] Freytag 2012, p. 451; Tettinger and Geerlings 2005, p. 425.
[56] Michael 2010, p. 3537 et seqq.; see p. 3542 where he acclaims this kind of interpretation of the BL in German FCC, 1 BvR 1164/07 (Order of 7 July 2009) para 88 – *Hinterbliebenenversorgung* (in BVerfGE 124, 199 et seqq.).
[57] Cf., for example, Weber's article on whether the EUCFR may lead to a "European Constitution": Weber 2000, p. 537 et seqq.

of general political and social interest (which, for a broad-minded scholar on [comparative] constitutional law, European law and International [Human Rights] Law like him, are always inextricably linked to their legal and scientific aspects), we sometimes disagreed. But he has always shown great interest in and openness to the positions of both colleagues and assistants. Being an Emeritus Professor since 2010, *A. Weber* has never ceased to work with his human thirst for knowledge and scientific curiosity. In dealing with an actual and highly controversial topic, this contribution expresses my deep wish that this will long continue in the years to come.

References

Anderheiden, M. (2006). *Gemeinwohl in Republik und Union*. Tübingen: Mohr Siebeck.

Barsch, L. & Garms, K. (2014). *Der besondere Schutz der Ehe und die Gleichstellung der eingetragenen Lebenspartnerschaft. Ein nicht nur rechtliches Spannungsverhältnis*. Unpublished bachelor thesis, available via tonio.klein@nsi-hsvn.de.

Beck, V. (2010). Standpunkt zum Beschluss des BVerfG vom 21.07.2010. *Neue Juristische Wochenschrift aktuell, 36*, 12–14.

Böckenförde, E.-W. (2001). “Kopftuchstreit” auf dem richtigen Weg? *Neue Juristische Wochenschrift, 54*, 723–728.

Calliess, C., & Ruffert, M. (Eds.). (2011). *EUV/AEUV. Das Verfassungsrecht der Europäischen Union mit Europäischer Grundrechtecharta. Kommentar*. Munich: Beck.

Depenheuer, O. (1992). Die “volle persönliche Verantwortung” des Beamten für die Rechtmäßigkeit seiner dienstlichen Handlungen – Zum Spannungsverhältnis zwischen Eigenverantwortung und Verwaltungshierarchie. *Deutsches Verwaltungsblatt, 107*, 404–413.

Depenheuer, O. (2005). Das öffentliche Amt. In J. Isensee, & P. Kirchhof (Eds.), *Demokratie – Bundesorgane (§ 36)* Handbuch des Staatsrechts der Bundesrepublik Deutschland, vol. III Heidelberg: C.F. Müller.

Diederichsen, U. (2000). Homosexuelle – von Gesetzes wegen? *Neue Juristische Wochenschrift, 53*, 1841–1844.

Di Fabio, U. (2003). Der Schutz von Ehe und Familie: Verfassungsentscheidung für die vitale Gesellschaft. *Neue Juristische Wochenschrift, 56*, 993–998.

Epping, V. (2015). *Grundrechte*. Berlin: Springer.

Foley, E. P. (2012). *The Tea Party. Three Principals*. Cambridge, New York, Melbourne, Madrid, Cape Town, Singapore, Sao Paulo, Delhi, Tokyo, Mexico City: Cambridge University Press.

Freytag, C. (2012). Lebenspartnerschaftsgesetz, Eheschutzgebot und Differenzierungsverbot. *Die Öffentliche Verwaltung, 65*, 445–455.

Gas, T. (2002). *Affirmative Action in der Republik Südafrika. Unter Berücksichtigung verfassungsvergleichender Bezüge*. Baden-Baden: Nomos.

Gas, T. (2012). *Gemeinwohl und Individualfreiheit im nationalen Recht und Völkerrecht*. Hamburg: Maximilian.

Gassner, U. M. (1995). Kreation und Repräsentation. Zum demokratischen Gewährleistungsgehalt von Art. 38 Abs. 1 S. 1 GG. *Der Staat, 34*, 429–453.

Gönner, N. T. (1808). *Der Staatsdienst aus dem Gesichtspunkt des Rechts und der Nationalökonomie betrachtet: nebst der Hauptlandespragmatik über die Dienstverhältnisse der*

Staatsdiener im Königreiche Baiern; mit erläuternden Anmerkungen. Landshut: Krüll. http://bavarikon.de/de/bookviewer/kpbO-BSB-MDZ-00000BSB10373905_00001

Green, L. M. (1996). Speech. In Republic of South Africa (Ed.), *Debates of the Constitutional Assembly. 29 March to 11 October 1996* (vol. 3, col. 373–377). Cape Town: Creda Press.

Grünberger, M. (2010). Die Gleichbehandlung von Ehe und eingetragener Lebenspartnerschaft im Zusammenspiel von Unionsrecht und nationalem Verfassungsrecht – Das Urteil des BVerfG zu VBL-Hinterbliebenenversorgung. *Familie – Partnerschaft – Recht, 16*, 203–208.

Häde, U. (1993). Das Bundesverfassungsgericht und der Vertrag von Maastricht. Anmerkungen zum Urteil des Zweiten Senats von 12. 10. 1993 – 2 BvR 2134/92, 2 BvR 2159/92. *Betriebs-Berater, 48*, 2457–2463.

Herrmann, Chr. (2006). Die negative unmittelbare Wirkung von Richtlinien in horizontalen Rechtsverhältnissen. Erwiderung auf T. Gas, Gastkommentar. Heft 24/2005, p. 737. *Europäische Zeitschrift für Wirtschaftsrecht, 17*, 69–70.

Herzog, R., & Gerken, L. (2008). *Stoppt den Europäischen Gerichtshof. Frankfurter Allgemeine Zeitung, 8 September 2008.* http://www.cep.eu/fileadmin/user_upload/Pressemappe/CEP_in_den_Medien/Herzog-EuGH-Webseite.pdf

Heun, W. (2008). Originalism als Interpretationsmethode im US-amerikanischen Verfassungsrecht. In R. Wahl (Ed.), *Verfassungsänderung, Verfassungswandel, Verfassungsinterpretation. Vorträge bei deutsch-japanischen Symposien in Tokyo 2004 und Freiburg 2005* (pp. 233–248). Berlin: Duncker & Humblot.

Hirsch, G. (2004). *Der Richter im Spannungsfeld von erster und dritter Gewalt.* http://www.jura.uni-erlangen.de/fachbereich/fotoalbum/2004-1/rede-hirsch.htm

Hobe, S., & Wiegand, B. (1994). Die Maastricht-Entscheidung des Bundesverfassungsgerichts. *Thüringer Verwaltungsblätter, 3*, 204–213.

Isensee, J. (2011). Das Grundrecht als Abwehrrecht und als staatliche Schutzpflicht. In J. Isensee, & P. Kirchhof (Eds.), *Allgemeine Grundrechtslehren (§ 191)* Handbuch des Staatsrechts des Bundesrepublik Deutschland, vol. IX Heidelberg: C.F. Müller.

Jarass, H. D. (2013). Zum Verhältnis von Grundrechtecharta und sonstigem Recht. *Europarecht, 48*, 29–44.

Kahn, P. W. (2001). Verfassungsgerichtsbarkeit und demokratische Legitimation. *Jahrbuch des öffentlichen Rechts der Gegenwart, Neue Folge 49*, 571–586.

Kühling, J. (2014). Die richtlinienkonforme und die verfassungskonforme Auelegung im öffentlichen Recht. *Juristische Schulung, 54*, 481–490.

Krings, G. (2000). Die "eingetragene Lebenspartnerschaft" für gleichgeschlechtliche Paare – der Gesetzgeber zwischen Schutzabstandsgebot und Gleichheitssatz. *Zeitschrift für Rechtspolitik, 33*, 409–415.

Leuze, D. (1998). Das allgemeine Persönlichkeitsrecht des Beamten. *Zeitschrift für Beamtenrecht, 46*, 187–196.

Limbach, J. (1996). *Das Bundesverfassungsgericht als politischer Machtfaktor. Humboldt Forum Recht, 12/1996, 1, = Humboldt Forum Recht, 1996, 70,* http://www.humboldt-forum-recht.de/deutsch/12-1996/beitrag.html.

Maunz, T. & Dürig, G. (Eds.) (1958–2014). *Grundgesetz. Kommentar*. Munich: Beck.

Meyer, J. (Ed.). (2014). *Charta der Grundrechte der Europäischen Union*. Baden-Baden: Nomos.

Michael, L. (2010). Lebenspartnerschaften unter dem besonderen Schutze einer (über-)staatlichen Ordnung. Legitimation und Grenzen eines Grundrechtswandels kraft europäischer Integration. *Neue Juristische Wochenschrift, 63*, 3537–3542.

Montesquieu, C. (1758). *De l'Esprit des Lois*. Geneva: Barillot & Fils, complete work: http://classiques.uqac.ca/classiques/montesquieu/de_esprit_des_lois/de_esprit_des_

lois_tdm.html, concretely quoted passage: http://fr.wikisource.org/wiki/Page:Montesquieu_Esprit_des_Lois_1777_Garnier_1.djvu/501.

Ogorek, M. (2014). Bindung der Mitgliedsstaaten an die Unionsgrundrechte bei der Beschränkung von Grundfreiheiten. *Juristische Arbeitsblätter*, *46*, 954–956.

Ruffert, M. (2014). Europarecht: Anwenungsbereich der Grundrechte in der GRCh. *Juristische Schulung*, *54*, 662–664.

Rüthers, B. (2013). *Wer herrscht über das Grundgesetz? Frankfurter Allgemeine Zeitung, 17 November 2013*. http://www.faz.net/aktuell/politik/die-gegenwart/deutschland-wer-herrscht-ueber-das-grundgesetz-12668461.html

Sachs, M. (2004). Wiederbelebung des besonderen Gewaltverhältnisses? *Nordrhein-Westfälische Verwaltungsblätter*, *18*, 209–214.

Sacksofsky, U. (2006). Halbteilungsgrundsatz ade – Scheiden tut nicht weh. *Neue Zeitschrift für Verwaltungsrecht*, *25*, 661–662.

Sauer, O. (2006). Abschied vom Halbteilungsgrundsatz. Das Bundesverfassungsgericht stärkt die Gestaltungsfreiheit des Steuergesetzgebers. *Forum Recht* 04_2006, p. 131–133. http://www.forum-recht-online.de/2006/406/406sauer.pdf

Scholz, R., & Uhle, A. (2001). "Eingetragene Lebenspartnerschaft" und Grundgesetz. *Neue Juristische Wochenschrift*, *54*, 393–400.

Schwarze, J. (1994). Europapolitik unter deutschem Verfassungsrichtervorbehalt. Anmerkungen zum Maastricht-Urteil des BVerfG vom 12.10.1993. *Neue Justiz*, *48*, 1–5.

Streinz, R. (Ed.). (2011). *EUV/AEUV: Vertrag über die Europäische Union und Vertrag über die Arbeitsweise der Europäischen Union*. Munich: Beck.

Tettinger, P. J. (2001). Die Charta der Grundrechte der Europäischen Union. *Neue Juristische Wochenschrift*, *54*, 1010–1015.

Tettinger, P., & Geerlings, J. (2005). Ehe und Familie in der europäischen Grundrechtsordnung. *Europarecht*, *40*, 419–440.

Thym, D. (2013). Die Reichweite der EU-Grundrechte-Charta – Zu viel Grundrechtsschutz? *Neue Zeitschrift für Verwaltungsrecht*, *32*, 889–896.

Tomuschat, Chr. (1993). Die Europäische Union unter der Aufsicht des Bundesverfassungsgerichts. *Europäische Grundrechte-Zeitschrift*, *20*, 489–496.

Tonikidis, S. (2013). Grundzüge der richtlinienkonformen Auslegung und Rechtsfortbildung. *Juristische Arbeitsblätter*, *45*, 598–604.

Weber, A. (2000). Die Europäische Grundrechtscharta – auf dem Weg zu einer europäischen Verfassung. *Neue Juristische Wochenschrift*, *53*, 537–544.

Weber, A. (2012). Auf der Suche nach dem Europäischen Juristen. *Jahrbuch des öffentlichen Rechts der Gegenwart*, *Neue Folge 60*, 307–316.

Multilevel Protection of Fundamental Rights in Europe: The Case of Spain

Carlos Vidal Prado

1 Introduction

Internationally, like in Europe, a culture of human rights has gradually been built, in the framework of what some have called "international law of constitutional States," and which Rawls rechristened as "The Law of Peoples".[1] This was the grounding of a generalised awareness in regard to the necessary international protection of rights and freedoms, and, specifically, their judicial protection, much more efficient than diplomatic protection, which prevailed until a few years ago. However, we cannot refer to a universal culture, since democracies are still in the minority, and there are a number of totalitarian regimes in which fundamental rights are violated daily. These regimes are a reality that are stubbornly contemptuous of the more than one hundred international instruments, including declarations and treaties, concerning human rights, that have been adopted since 1945, as well as the creation of an abundance of bodies for the promotion thereof.

One might say, like *Pedro Nikken*,[2] that the Universal Declaration of Human Rights (1948), the International Convention on Civil and Political Rights (1966), the International Convention on Economic, Social and Cultural Rights (1966) and the European Convention on Human Rights (1950) together form a veritable International Human Rights Charter, which has been followed by a number of specific declarations, such as those concerning women, children, the disabled, the use of torture, racial discrimination, etc., as well as the Charter of Fundamental Rights of the European Union, which one might see as the dogmatic part of the Union's "material constitution".

The same author rightly asserts that the defining trend in international developments in this regard is that of their progressive nature, in terms of both the number and content of the rights envisaged and the efficiency and vigour of the procedures to protect them: the declarations were followed by treaties; the treaties by the creation of bodies to foster and protect rights; and finally, legal bodies were set up,

[1] Rawls 1993, p. 36 et seqq.; Rawls 1999, § 2.
[2] Nikken 1987.

H.-J. Blanke et al. (eds.), *Common European Legal Thinking*,
DOI 10.1007/978-3-319-19300-7_10

which are considerably more efficient. Nevertheless, this efficiency still depends largely on national guarantees.

Along with this successive increase in the safeguarding of rights in Europe and globally, there has been another new phenomenon in Spain, which has also signalled the birth of a degree of new protection, which one might consider to be within the sphere of each autonomous region.

The recent reforms of the Statutes of Autonomy have introduced into these statutes an entirely new section: a declaration of rights. This refers primarily, though not only, to social rights, but it also includes civil rights. Supposedly, the aim is to increase the guarantees of these rights. Spain's Autonomous Regions are the key to the country's social State, since competences in the spheres of education, healthcare and social welfare have essentially been transferred to the Autonomous Regions. The aim of the new wording is to increase public social policies, from which it will be possible to deduce subjective rights in respect of various kinds of benefits, these rights always being legally binding.

The controversy this has generated in Spain stems, essentially, from the fear that this varying level of guarantees in the nation's various territories may lead to inequality of treatment among Spanish citizens, simply by virtue of living in one region or another.[3] We will examine this issue later in this work.

In short, we may sustain that rights are a kind of national, international and supranational public order (even in their various territorial levels, in composite States like Spain), that legitimise the emergence of institutions and jurisdictions in these spheres for their protection, which can entail a potential erosion of internal state autonomy in this terrain, and even empowerment for international intervention in those States that gravely breach human rights. However, the efficiency of international protection of rights, and specifically their jurisdictional protection, still depends to a greater or lesser degree on States' internal guarantees, according to whether this internationalisation is presided over by a treaty to which States are or are not signatories, or whether we are talking about supranationalisation culminating in a larger entity of which the States are members. But the State guarantee is still indispensable.[4] And, in this connection, the efficacy of this international protection will also depend on the internal levels of rights guarantees. In some States, these levels will be higher than stipulated by international standards, so international protection will have an almost imperceptible influence internally, due to being unnecessary.

To refer to this development of the protection of rights in different spheres, the expression "multilevel" is often used, and it is also applied to the interaction between areas and constitutions, especially within Europe.[5] That is why we have used it in the title of this work.

---

[3] Díez-Picazo 2006; Caamaño 2007. Concerning the role of local and regional authorities and of the Committee of the Regions in the multilevel protection of the fundamental rights, cf. the Committee of the Regions Study 2014.

[4] "The State is still the centre of reference for the recognition and protection of rights", Balaguer 2008, p. 134.

[5] Pernice 1999; Pernice and Kanitz 2004; D'Atena and Grossi 2004; Bilancia 2006; Di Federico 2011.

Perhaps one of the main achievements of the Lisbon Treaty was that it managed to "rescue" the Charter of Fundamental Rights from among the elements of the failed European Constitutional Treaty, including it as a binding catalogue in the Union's primary Law, albeit indirectly (and despite the regrettable exclusion clauses implemented by Poland, the UK and the Czech Republic). From a symbolic standpoint, and in order to raise its visibility among citizens, it would have been considerably more appropriate to include it in the Treaty itself, but at least it has been confirmed as legally binding.[6]

The European continent is endowed with one of the most sophisticated systems for the protection of fundamental rights worldwide. Over the same geographical space there are several diverse sets of normative orders, each with its own laws and institutions for the protection of fundamental rights: including a national (in Spain, we could say regional and national), a supranational and an international level.[7]

We shall now examine in more detail the clause of the Spanish Constitution opening it to the international protection of rights (Sect. 2), and discuss these rights in relation to the European spheres of protection, the one referring to the European Council (Sect. 3) and to the European Union itself (Sect. 4). We shall then give an overview of the new statutes of autonomy, which now envisage a catalogue of rights (Sect. 5), and we shall outline our conclusions (Sect. 6).

2 The Clause of Art. 10.2 of the Spanish Constitution Opening it to International Agreements and Treaties

The Spanish Constitution describes a State model open to the international sphere, in terms of the possibility of both assigning to supranational bodies the exercise of competencies deriving from the Constitution (art. 93) and the assumption of the contemporary paradigm of the protection of fundamental rights, incorporating international human rights law into Spain's own legislation. Accordingly, as the doctrine has properly evidenced, Spain is an internationally integrated State.[8] This is projected particularly in the sphere of fundamental rights, since, as is well known, according to Art. 10.2 of the Spanish Constitution "the rules concerning fundamental rights and freedoms recognised by the Constitution shall be interpreted in accordance with the Universal Declaration of Human Rights and the international treaties and agreements ratified by Spain in these matters".

As *J. González Campos* has shown, this precept is actually a constitutional "mandate" for the correct interpretation of fundamental rights recognised in the Constitution,[9] an interpretation that serves to "identify the meaning of rules that are almost always characterised by being controversial, vague, open, indeterminate".[10]

[6] Tajadura 2010, p. 25.
[7] Fabbrini 2010, p. 9 et seqq.
[8] Torres del Moral 2010, p. 109 et seqq.
[9] González Campos 1999, p. 42 and p. 47.
[10] Sáiz Arnáiz 2008, p. 193.

With regard to the effects of this interpretative clause of Art. 10.2 of the Spanish Constitution, the doctrine and the Constitutional Court consider that this channel does not facilitate the inclusion of new fundamental rights to our legislation (the proper channel would be Art. 96 of the Constitution, whereby international treaties – also those that recognise new rights – form a part of our legislation; having said that, these new rights to be included in Spanish legislation would not be fundamental in nature). What would be possible is to incorporate into rights that are already recognised (in other words, already present in the Constitution) "aspects not explicitly provided in the Constitution".[11] In this regard, *L. M. Díez-Picazo* has gone so far as to assert that "it is reasonable to conceive of international treaties on human rights as rules which, in a way, materially develop Title I of the Constitution".[12]

With regard to the scope of this interpretative clause, we must begin by noting that application of the rule contained in Art. 10.2 of the Spanish Constitution concerning the interpretation of fundamental human rights that may be protected (which broadly coincide with civil and political rights) is beyond all doubt, with the consequence that, in this interpretation, respect for Art. 10.2 of the Spanish Constitution "authorises and even advocates" using case law of the European Court of Human Rights in application of the European Convention on Human Rights of 1950, as the Constitutional Court was quick to point out.[13] This implies that, in the delimiting of the content of the rights by the Constitutional Court in its 30 years of activity, the doctrine of the Court of Strasbourg has taken on special significance,[14] and has been largely incorporated by our Constitutional Court into the constitutional system of rights.

It has been said that the Constitutional Court has used the interpretative rule of Art. 10.2 of the Constitution in a manner rather confined to the rights of Chap. 2 of the aforementioned Title I, and among them in particular those of Sect. 1, namely those that may be upheld through appeal for constitutional protection.[15] However, it could be used for the interpretation of all those rights recognised in Title I of the Constitution that may be reflected in the form of a recognised right in an international treaty ratified by Spain, at least provided the treaty in question includes some jurisdictional mechanism (hence, with some body with the capacity to authoritatively interpret the aforementioned rights, and impose that interpretation in a binding manner on States signing the treaty).

[11] Sáiz Arnáiz 2008, p. 196.

[12] Díez-Picazo 2003, p. 153 et seq.

[13] Cf. for example, the Spanish Constitutional Court Judgment No. 36/1984 (14 March 1984), II. 3.: "Art. 10.2 of the Spanish Constitution's reference to the Universal Declaration of Human Rights and to the international treaties and agreements in this connection ratified by Spain for the interpretation of constitutional rules regarding fundamental rights and public freedoms, authorises and indeed advocates, referring [. . .] to the doctrine established by the ECtHR". However, this does not mean that the Constitutional Court has always assumed the doctrine of the ECtHR, and in every area. In this regard, in Spanish Constitutional Court Judgment No. 236/2007 (7 November 2007), the Court expressly states (II. 11.) some differences of criteria between the two courts, highlighting the contrast between the respective lines of case law in relation with the existence or otherwise of a "right to family life".

[14] García de Enterría 1990; Vidal Prado 2001.

[15] Sáiz Arnáiz 2008, p. 195.

3 The Protection of Rights Within the Sphere of the Council of Europe

3.1 The European Convention on Human Rights (ECHR) and Case Law of the European Court of Human Rights

It is widely known that both the Rome Convention of 1950 and the European Social Charter include jurisdictional mechanisms that help guarantee the rights recognised in those texts, and that they may therefore also influence the interpretation of these rights inside Spain. Doubts are not raised in Spain with regard to the consideration of the European Convention on Human Rights within the sphere of the interpretative clause of Art. 10.2, it even having been stated that the ECHR imposes a "European public order",[16] or that it is capable of generating a European public space – because it integrates and is comprised – of rights and freedoms.[17]

In interpreting the rights recognised by the Rome Convention, "the European Court of Human Rights has taken on the role of quasi-constitutional body in Europe in the field of human rights",[18] on the one hand, as the Strasbourg court's rulings are binding on States, and, on the other, because through its rulings the court shapes the content and limits of the rights set forth in the ECHR. In this regard, the Court itself has expressly stated that its rulings serve not only to resolve the matters put to it, but more broadly to clarify, protect and develop the rules of the ECHR and thus contribute to the way States uphold their commitments as signatories.[19]

This broadness granted by the European Court of Human Rights to its interpretative role connects it with the purpose of the ECHR, by asserting that, as a regulatory treaty, it is necessary, furthermore, to establish which is the most suitable interpretation to achieve the purpose and comply with the objective of this treaty, and not that which would provide a more limited scope to the commitments of the signatories.[20]

Hence, the doctrine refers to the interpretative effect of the judgments[21] of the Strasbourg court, which implies that, in countries that have signed the ECHR, constitutional rules on fundamental rights may only operate autonomously in those sectors that have not yet been touched by Strasbourg case law.[22] As a result, European Court of Human Rights case law links national legal operators (starting with the Constitutional Court) in respect of the essential or minimum content of the fundamental rights that have also been recognised in the Rome Convention.[23]

Although, logically, the level of guarantee of the Spanish Constitution is higher than that of the European Convention, if a ruling from the European Court considers

---

[16] Fernández Sánchez 1987, p. 56.

[17] García Roca and Santolaya 2005, p. 21–23.

[18] Ripol Carulla 2007, p. 33.

[19] Appl. No. 5310/71, *Ireland v. The United Kingdom* (ECtHR 18 January 1978).

[20] Appl. No. 2122/64, *Wemhoff v. Germany* (ECtHR 27 June 1967).

[21] Fernández Sánchez 1987, p. 138. In Spanish: "efecto de cosa interpretada de las sentencias".

[22] Díez-Picazo 2006, p. 18.

[23] Fossas 2008, p. 174. Aláez rejects this opinion, and takes the view that the interpretation of the ECtHR cannot alter the dogma of fundamental constitutional rights. Cf. Aláez 2009.

that an infra-constitutional Spanish court is contrary to the Convention, its effects, according to *P. J. Tenorio*, must be to render that internal rule unconstitutional.[24] The problem is that the Strasbourg court is not formally competent in the control of "conventionality", and, accordingly, its decision cannot result in the expulsion of that rule from the legal order, so it will continue to be valid, although the courts should not apply it, once the European Court of Human Rights has declared it to be contrary to the ECHR. What these Spanish bodies should do, in the event of being faced with the potential application of this rule, is to raise the issue of unconstitutionality with Spain's Constitutional Court for the relevant purposes. Henceforth, Spain's highest court might then agree with the European Court of Human Rights, but it might not, in which case the Spanish rule would remain in the legislation, not only as a valid rule, but as an applicable rule, even contrary to the criterion of the European Court of Human Rights. Evidently, in such a case, the European Court of Human Rights is likely to impose penalties on the Spanish State. All of this unless the legislator has acted beforehand to reconcile the two legal orders, which would be an even more likely scenario.

Spain has been condemned by the European Court of Human Rights on various occasions, but it is not among the worst offenders in this regard, with the United Kingdom having received the largest number of penalties, some of which resulting from cases of traditional corporal punishment.

If one of the purposes of enforcing Protocol number 11 was to avoid undue delays in processing complaints, it was soon evident that, not only was this goal unattainable, but that delays are actually longer now, almost certainly because of the steady increase in the number of complaints. So, paradoxically, the European Court of Human Rights is not complying with Art. 6.1 of the ECHR, while at the same time it frequently punishes States for taking too long to resolve judicial proceedings. The entry into force of Protocol number 14 is expected to alleviate this problem, or at least that is the hope.

3.2 *The European Social Charter*

We must reasonably sustain that the interpretative clause of Art. 10.2 of the Spanish Constitution also operates with respect to the social rights recognised in the international treaties signed by Spain, to the extent that we have a quasi-jurisdictional body like the European Committee of Social Rights that offers, albeit partially, an authorised interpretation of the rights recognised in the European Social Charter.

It is possible to conclude this based on the revised text of the European Social Charter, which establishes a mechanism for collective complaints of a jurisdictional nature, in application of which the European Committee of Social Rights issues judgments that are binding upon States (the so-called "conclusions"). It is true that the Committee's conclusions are not directly binding, but that does not prevent them

[24] Tenorio 1997, p. 166.

from being quasi-jurisdictional,[25] and, accordingly, it has been possible to say that the European Committee of Social Rights makes law.[26] Evidently, these decisions by the European Committee of Social Rights directly affect, in the first instance, the State that has been subject to the collective complaint, but its interpretative effects on rights recognised by the European Social Charter extend to all signatory States, so that – in this interpretative aspect of constitutional rights – it is to a degree irrelevant whether or not a State has formulated reservations with regard to the adoption of the system of collective complaints. As *J. Quesada* points out in relation to our own legislation, "Even though Spain has not accepted the mechanism of collective complaints, all this means is that our country cannot be subject to a direct judgment through this channel. However, this does not mean that Spain can remain on the sidelines with respect to decisions adopted as a result of examining collective complaints".[27]

In any event, it should be mentioned that the Constitutional Court has distinguished between treaties and agreements that establish real legal commitments, that are binding (hard law), and those international agreements whose value is merely as guidance (soft law[28]). This distinction, in the material sphere we are considering herein, leads to a distinction between the Conventions of the Council of Europe (mainly, the ECHR and the European Social Charter),[29] which are clear examples of international hard law on human rights, and the resolutions and recommendations of the Council of Europe.

4 Rights Guarantees in the EU: The EU Charter of Fundamental Rights

The EU's evolution and development very soon raised the need to structure protection for fundamental rights within the sphere of European legislation, and the Court of Justice will be the first to respond.[30] The successive reforms of Treaties each in-

[25] Belorgey 2007.
[26] Belorgey 2007, p. 360.
[27] Jimena Quesada 2006, p. 65.
[28] According to Tammes, soft law is a phenomenon that has the characteristics of "law" in its directive effect to influence the will and restrict the liberty of those to whom [it] is addressed, but with the impression that something is missing in the legal or binding nature of the law as we know it from daily life. Cf. Tammes 1983.
[29] Accordingly, the Council of State has asserted that the conventions and agreements of the European Council have supra-legislative value in regard to the interpretation of fundamental rights and public freedoms, since the Constitutional Court, pursuant to Art. 10.2 of the Constitution, has interpreted the regulations relating to fundamental rights and freedoms that are recognised by the Constitution in accordance with the provisions of various European Council conventions. See *Report by the Council of State concerning the insertion of European law into Spanish legislation*, of 14 February 2008, p. 289.
[30] Vittorino 2003, p. 111.

corporated new mechanisms for protection, culminating in the inclusion of the EU Charter of Fundamental Rights.[31]

Much more intensely than in the international treaties mentioned previously, the EU Charter of Fundamental Rights is another element in the complex system to protect basic rights that is in place in Spain, like in any other Member State. It is worth highlighting how, although from the material standpoint the rights safeguarded by the Spanish Constitution and the European Charter might be identical, the development and exercise of these rights in national and European legislation may yield different results, in accordance with the provisions of Art. 53.1 of the Spanish Constitution and Arts. 52 and 53 of the Charter.

The fact that the rights are identical in their definition does not guarantee that, when interpreting them, the results will be the same. Taking into account Art. 52 of the Charter and Art. 53.1 of the Spanish Constitution, it is possible that their sphere of protection may be different. This is not merely a theoretical possibility, but the Luxembourg Court reiterated that from the moment a national regulation is included in the sphere of application of European law, it must be in accordance with the fundamental rights safeguarded by the Court of Justice.[32] The problem, in this specific case, is that the national regulation had been declared to conform to Spain's Constitution by the Constitutional Court,[33] so the judge ceased to apply the rule because it contradicts not the Spanish Constitution, but European law.

It is not problematic to have European control of national law from the standpoint of fundamental rights, but it is problematic that the legal systems compete against each other, and sometimes even ignore each other. Perhaps one solution is recognising the value of general principles of the European Convention on Human Rights and, specifically, the jurisdiction of the European Court of Human Rights.

Art. 6.3 of the Charter grants the rights and freedoms of the ECHR and those resulting from common constitutional traditions among Member States the value of general principles, making them a canon for interpretation for legal operators of the Charter. This is further strengthened by the provisions of Arts. 52.3 and 52.4 EUChFR. The European Charter makes the Rome Convention of 1950 a necessary minimum, essential content of the rights and freedoms of the Charter. Regardless of when the Convention was ratified by the EU, the legal protection offered by European law is and must be equivalent to that recognised by the Convention, as evidenced in the European Court of Human Rights' *Bosphorus* Ruling.[34]

The Nice Charter recognises the right to effective remedy before a court (Art. 47) and the Lisbon Treaty attributes to the European Union Court of Justice the mission of guaranteeing that remedy via its organisation into three institutions: the Court of Justice, the General Court and the Court of Auditors.

---

[31] Stern and Tettinger 2005; Stern and Tettinger 2006.

[32] Case C-81/05, *Anacleto Cordero Alonso v. Fondo de Garantía Salarial (Fogasa)* (ECJ 7 September 2006).

[33] Spanish Constitutional Court Judgment No. 306/1993 (30 November 1993).

[34] Appl. No. 45036/98, *Bosphorus* (ECtHR 30 June 2005) para 155 et seq.

So one might say that the European Union already has a systematised and coded catalogue of rights, with which European citizens will gain in both the quality and security of all components of the legal system. While, until now, the Court of Justice had to use the referrals for preliminary hearing by national courts to create case law regarding certain rights, it will be underpinned by its own Charter of Rights, also relying on the case law heritage of the Court of the European Council and national courts.

Both States and legal persons and entities can access European justice institutions asking for effective judicial remedy (the terminology used in the European Charter of Rights is the same terminology used in the Spanish Constitution, which in its Art. 24 guarantees effective judicial remedy).

Within the sphere of competency of the European Union, national courts must preferably apply EU law, also in the sphere of rights, provided the matters refer to the European sphere of competency. The Court of Justice has been grappling with the problem of applicable Law for many years now, attempting to use case law to supplement the absence of a specifically European table of rights. Naturally, the European founding treaties and the regulations and directives issued in regard to the matter in question are applicable. But at the end of 1969 the Court introduced a new element in its line of case law by taking into account for solving a case the general principles of European law concerning the fundamental rights of individuals.[35]

The question focuses on the identification of these principles. The Court believes that respect for fundamental rights is an integral part of the general principles of European law and that to safeguard this it is must take as inspiration the constitutional traditions common to Member States, rejecting measures incompatible with recognised and guaranteed fundamental rights guaranteed by these States' constitutions.[36] But the Court of Justice adds a further element integrating these principles: "International treaties for the protection of human rights on which Member States have collaborated or of which they are signatories" may also offer indications that it is advisable to take into account within the framework of EU law.[37] And this raised the issue of whether or not the European Convention on Human Rights was part of EU law. We should take into account that the States belonging to the Union are also signatories to the Convention.

Well, at least since 1975, the Court of Justice has used the Convention as an interpretative element for the protection of economic rights in Europe. Specifically, the Convention's requirement that any restriction of rights be justified by the needs of a democratic society has enabled the European Union's Court of Justice to overcome or limit the public order exception whereby sometimes its Member States oppose the application of a particular law in their countries.[38]

[35] Case 29/69, *Stauder v. City of Ulm* (ECJ 20 November 1969).

[36] Case 11/70, *Internationale Handelsgesellschaft* (ECJ 17 December 1970); Case 4/73, *Nold v. Commission* (ECJ 14 May 1974).

[37] The aforementioned judgment in the *Nold* case.

[38] Case 36/75, *Rutili* (ECJ 28 October 1975).

Having overcome the reticence to considering the Convention an integral part of European Union law, the Luxembourg Court understood that its competency must focus on the Union's own economic laws. Nevertheless, sometimes it has taken the Convention as the minimum level of protection of those economic laws.

Now, the European Union Charter of Fundamental Rights has simplified things, although the Convention and Strasbourg's case law will continue to be used, perhaps even more intensively, as a supplement and guide for interpretation. Accordingly, the Court of Justice uses all the aforementioned sources plus the Treaty of the European Union and the Treaty on the Functioning of the European Union, which contain relevant principles with respect to rights.

The problem is that there are two systems for guaranteeing rights in Europe, each with its corresponding court, and that an act of the Union cannot be appealed before the European Court of Human Rights because the latter is not a party to the Rome Convention.

A Court of First Instance resolves, without prejudice to subsequent appeals to the Court of Justice, direct complaints from persons and legal entities. The former's creation responds to the idea of easing the workload of the Court of Justice, enabling it to focus on the uniform interpretation of European Union law, and speeding up the legal process.

If the alleged breach of a right stems from an action by the Union, the person or legal entity affected can appeal directly to the Court of First Instance. But the plaintiff might also prefer to contest it before a national judge; in which case, the judge refers the case to the Court of Justice in order for it to interpret or assess the validity of the rule or action by the Union that is the subject of contention. Neither of these courts are courts of appeal or cassation of the national courts, and neither has the national competency in respect of rights that have been transferred – and nor may it be – to the Union. This protection system is circumscribed to the applicable Law described above.

If an internal action is contested, the proper channel is the national judge and subsequent referral for preliminary hearing, if appropriate, in the terms set forth above. But the internal judge may also directly apply European Union law in litigation between individuals if it is unquestionably applicable.

The incorporation onto this stage of the European Union Charter of Rights does not imply the mere addition of an autonomous element to the protection of rights. It is much more than that. The content, possibilities and restrictions of rights and freedoms are a result of the interplay of opening relationships established between the various sub-systems. European legislation must avail itself of the legal logic of rights and must seek to reach a reasonable consensus with regard to the proper working of the system.

Nevertheless, not everyone is optimistic regarding the real efficacy of the European Charter. *L. Favoreu* has described the mechanisms for guaranteeing rights in the specific sphere of European law, and in respect of the action of European bodies, as deficient. This is a reflection of the French pro-European doctrine that considers that there are not sufficient mechanisms to control EU actions. *Favoreu* even proposes that, if we really want a truly efficient European Charter of Rights that may be applied not only to national bodies, but to European ones, a specific recourse must be instituted. However, he also doubts that the Court of Justice, with its huge workload, can take on such a task, and so is sceptical about the effective application of the Charter.[39]

5 Declarations of Rights in Spain's Statutes of Regional Autonomy

As we have said, Spain's recently reformed Statutes of Regional Autonomy have added a new element: a declaration of rights. The aim is to increase the guarantees of those rights, from which it will be possible to deduce subjective rights in respect of various kinds of benefits, but always legally binding, since the Statutes of Autonomy are organic laws, subject to the Constitution.[40] In the words of *P. Cruz Villalón*, we must not forget that the drafter of the Constitution preconfigures and the legislator configures rights.[41] By preconfiguring, the drafter of the Constitution is establishing the framework in which the legislator may manoeuvre, respecting the essential content of law that is preconfigured by the Constitution. But, even if the legislator has not developed legislation, the law is also enforceable in its essential constitutional dimension.

The controversy this has generated in Spain stems, essentially, from the fear that this varying level of guarantees in the nation's various territories may lead to inequality of treatment among Spanish citizens, simply by virtue of living in one or other region. Consequently, exercising autonomous competencies must take into account a unitary nationwide status of citizen, based on the list of basic conditions of equality of the various rights regardless of territorial perspective (Art. 149.1 no° 1 of the Spanish Constitution).[42]

Most of the social rights are set forth in Spain's Constitution in chapter III of Title I, and they are not real fundamental rights but "Guiding principles of economic and social policy", except the right to education, which is among the fundamental rights. The others are those that, basically, are included in statutory declarations: the right to health, social services, employment rights (except the right to industrial action and belonging to a union), the rights of the elderly and of minors, the right to benefits derived from situations of dependency and disability, the right to a guaranteed citizen's income and the right to culture and heritage. However, these rights, while recognised in the Statutes, will be operative in accordance with the scope of the various competencies of the respective autonomous regions,[43] as the Constitu-

---

[39] Favoreu 2005, p. 252 et seq.

[40] Gavara de Cara 2010a, p. 79–127 ("La proyección social de la Constitución: una implementación multinivel"); Gavara de Cara 2010b.

[41] Cruz Villalón 1991, p. 134.

[42] González Pascual 2007, p. 106 et seq.

[43] In general, concerning relations between statutory rights and competencies in the Spanish case, cf. Gavara de Cara, Mateu Vilaseca and Vallès Vives 2010.

tional Court has highlighted. In this context, it is worth recalling that declarations of rights cannot imply the adoption of new competencies.[44]

In accordance with the competencies of each Autonomous Region,[45] the autonomous legislator will determine the scope of the statutory rights and their various degrees of regulatory specification. The aim of including the declarations of rights of the Statutes of Autonomy is to transform the guiding principles of economic and social policy provided in the Constitution into subjective rights, systematising in a single catalogue laws regulated via sector-specific autonomous laws and protecting new laws not regulated by the Constitution using autonomous competencies.[46]

The Constitutional Court has confirmed the establishment of rights in the Statutes produces a direct link between the public powers of the Region, as expressly stated in the statutory texts themselves. But, strictly speaking, these are not so much rules that generate laws, but mandates to the public powers that may end up generating real subjective public rights, always legally configured.[47]

In all cases, but especially in rights such as the right to education, which enjoys the maximum level of constitutional protection, in the event of a conflict between the autonomous regulation and the Constitution, it is evident that the Constitution shall always prevail, and the decision of subjective protection will ultimately correspond to the Constitutional Court.

Consequently, in the Statutes these social rights must be considered to be mandates to the legislator, linked to the competencies themselves, but not contributing too many new aspects, and not allocating new functions that might imply replacing the State legislator in the spheres described. Statutory declarations of rights, because of their high degree of reliance on competencies, do not contribute in terms of either law or competencies a new perspective on social rights, since, on the one hand, their real efficacy depends on the existence of a sufficient financial provision, but, on the other hand, transversal State competencies singularly in the social and civil sphere, might continue to act as a basis for reaching cooperation agreements with the Autonomous Regions to achieve a high degree of equality in terms of the enjoyment of social rights.

Despite the existence of the statutory declarations of rights and their purpose as a mechanism for interpreting and integrating competencies, the fact is that the development, application and interpretation of statutory rights may not be contrary to the rights recognised in the Constitution, in a dual sense: on the one hand, for the express identification in the Constitution, and, on the other hand, in relation to the rest of fundamental rights that may not be undermined or limited by the regional implementing regulations, since frequently some social rights are interlinked to other rights of personality or property.[48]

---

[44] Balaguer 2008, p. 140.

[45] Concerning social rights as competencies, cf. González Pascual 2007, p. 101 et seqq. Concerning social rights in Statutes of Regional Autonomies, cf. López Menudo 2009; De la Quadra-Salcedo 2008.

[46] Castellá 2004, p. 168.

[47] Spanish Constitutional Court Judgment No. 247/2007 (12 December 2007), II. 15.

[48] For example, Art. 8.3 of the Statute of Autonomy of Castilla y León provides that the statutory provisions regarding rights and freedoms (title I) may not be developed, applied and interpreted so

6 Conclusion

There is an abundance of catalogues of rights, both internally and internationally, at a time when it is already tough enough to resolve conflicts between the various sources of law, within a complex legal framework. *Favoreu* questions the opinion held by many that, the more rules to protect rights are approved, the greater the level of protection that will be attained. Indeed, he even asks whether the multiplication of regulations containing rights might not even weaken legal protection. For the French author, the various levels of protection of rights do not appear to imply a greater guarantee of their exercise and protection. Sometimes, with a single catalogue, as in the USA, a higher standard of protection may perhaps be attained. All this bearing in mind that the more catalogues and levels of protection, the more possible conflicts may arise between courts. Levels of protection, if accompanied by specific jurisdictional guarantees, also constitute different possibilities for appeal: in Spain, the Court of First Instance, the Higher Court of the Autonomous Region, the Supreme Court, the Constitutional Court, the European Court of Justice and the European Court of Human Rights. If the European Charter applies, as *L. Favoreu* says, only nationally, and not to actions by EU bodies, would this not make it a substantially useless regulation, from the legal standpoint?[49]

As we said at the beginning, the key aspect is still the level of guarantees offered by each State in its own territory. The efficiency of international rights protection will also depend on States' internal guarantees. And, in this connection, the efficiency of this international protection will also depend on the internal levels of rights guarantees. In some States, these levels will be higher than stipulated by international standards, so international protection will have an almost imperceptible influence internally, due to being unnecessary. A clear example of this scenario is the case of the outlawing of Batasuna, the political wing of the terrorist organisation ETA. This is a European case study for the "multilevel" protection of fundamental rights. It can be used to analyse the degree of protection of the right of political association inside Spanish territory (where there are two levels: that of the Constitution and that of the Law), and in the supranational European sphere (in this case, the ECHR). The Spanish Constitution only bans criminally illicit political parties, but it does not prevent other kinds of prohibition. The Organic Law on Political Parties includes provisions for banning political parties for reasons not directly linked to criminal activities too (basically if they refuse to condemn and reject violence and terrorist crimes, thereby effectively providing a refuge for such actions). The ECHR goes further, even accepting that parties might be banned for ideological reasons, albeit within certain limits. Accordingly, in this scenario the ECHR offers less protection to political associations than is offered by Spanish law, and the outcome

as to reduce or restrict fundamental rights recognised by the Constitution and by the international treaties and conventions ratified by Spain. Consequently, their functions and scope go considerably beyond their use as a mere parameter for control in the development of statutory rights.

[49] Favoreu 2005, p. 254–255.

of the appeal against its outlawing presented by *Batasuna* to the European Court of Human Rights was entirely logical, and in line with the Court's case law doctrine.[50]

The differences in standards of protection in a multilevel system such as the one that characterises the process of European integration need not be negative, but constitute a structurally necessary element of that process. However, it cannot be overlooked that there are some specific characteristics of each protection level that do not allow a generalised treatment of them. Just as internally, in Spain, the legislator (both State and regional) can increase or reduce the standard of protection, always within the framework of the Constitution, so can legal operators at European level. The problem is not the cohabitation or coexistence of different standards of protection, but how they are articulated. Consequently, the incorporation of the European Charter of Rights to primary European law implies a challenge going forward: finding a way to articulate the coexistence of the Charter and the European Convention for Human Rights, and with the Member States' national standards of protection.

References

Aláez Corral, B. (2009). Ideario educativo constitucional y respeto a las convicciones morales de los padres: a propósito de las Sentencias del Tribunal Supremo sobre Educación para la Ciudadanía. *El Cronista del Estado social y democrático de Derecho*, *5*, 24–33.

Balaguer Callejón, F. (2008). Constitucionalismo multinivel y derechos fundamentales en la Unión Europea. In E. Fernández García et al. (Ed.), *Estudios en homenaje al profesor Gregorio Peces-Barba* (vol. 2, pp. 133–158). Madrid: Dykinson.

Belorgey, J.-M. (2007). La Carta Social Europea del Consejo de Europa y su órgano de control: el Comité Europeo de Derechos Sociales. *Revista de Derecho Político*, *70*, 347–377.

Bilancia, P. (2006). Las nuevas fronteras de la protección multinivel de los derechos. *Revista de Derecho Constitucional Europeo*, *6*, 255–277.

Caamaño, F. (2007). Sí pueden (Declaraciones de Derechos y Estatutos de Autonomía. *Revista Española de Derecho Constitucional*, *79*, 33–46.

Castellá Andreu, J. M. (2004). *La función constitucional del Estatuto de Autonomía de Cataluña*. Barcelona: Institut d'Estudis Autonòmics.

Committee of the Regions, European Union (2014). *Multilevel Protection of the rule of law and fundamental rights – the role of local and regional authorities and of the Committee of the Regions* (study written by A. Marx et al.).

Cruz Villalón, P. (1991). El legislador de los derechos fundamentales. In A. P. López (Ed.), *La garantía constitucional de los derechos fundamentales* (pp. 125–137). Madrid: Civitas.

D'Atena, A., & Grossi, P. (2004). *Tutela dei diritti fondamentali e costituzionalismo multilivello. Tra Europa e Stati nazionali*. Milán: Giuffrè.

Díez-Picazo, L. M. (2003). *Sistema de derechos fundamentales*. Madrid: Civitas.

Díez-Picazo, L. M. (2006). Pueden los Estatutos de Autonomía declarar derechos, deberes y principios? *Revista Española de Derecho Constitucional*, *78*, 63–75.

[50] Appl. No. 25803/04 and 25817/04, *Batasuna* (ECtHR 30 June 2009). Cf. Rodríguez-Vergara Díaz 2010.

Fabbrini, F. (2010). The European Multilevel System for the Protection of Fundamental Rights: A 'Neo-Federalist' Perspective, *Jean Monnet Working Paper* 15/10, New York University School of Law. http://www.jeanmonnetprogram.org/papers/10/101501.html. Accessed 23 November 2014

Favoreu, L. (2005). I garanti dei diritti fondamentali europei. In G. Zagrebelsky (Ed.), *Diritti e Costituzione nell'Unione Europea* (p. 247). Rome: Edizioni Laterza.

Di Federico, G. (2011). Fundamental Rights in the EU: Legal Pluralism and Multi-Level Protection After the Lisbon Treaty. In G.Di Federico (Ed.), *The EU Charter of Fundamental Rights, Ius Gentium: Comparative Perspectives on Law and Justice* (vol. 8, pp. 15–54). Berlin: Springer.

Fernández Sánchez, P. A. (1987). *Las obligaciones de los Estados en el marco del Convenio Europeo de Derechos Humanos*. Madrid: Centro de Publicaciones del Ministerio de Justicia.

Fossas Espadaler, E. (2008). Cosa interpretada en derechos fundamentales: jurisprudencia del TEDH y jurisprudencia constitucional. *Revista Vasca de Administración Pública, 82*, 165–180.

García de Enterría, E. (1990). Valeur de la jurisprudence de la Cour Européenne des Droits de l'Homme en droit espagnol. In F. Matscher, & H. Petzold (Eds.), *Protecting Human Rights: The European Dimension/Protection des droits de l'homme: la dimensions européenne. Mélanges en l'honneur de Gérard J. WIARDA* (pp. 221–230). Cologne: Carl Heymanns.

García Roca, J., & Santolaya, P. (2005). *La Europa de los Derechos. El Convenio Europeo de Derechos Humanos*. Madrid: Centro de Estudios Políticos y Constitucionales.

Gavara de Cara, J. C. (2010a). *La dimensión objetiva de los derechos sociales*. Barcelona: Bosch.

Gavara de Cara, J. C., Mateu Vilaseca, M., & Vallès Vives, F. (2010b). Los derechos estatutarios en el sistema constitucional español: caracterización y consecuencias. In J. C. Gavara de Cara (Ed.), *Los derechos como principios objetivos en los Estados compuestos* (pp. 17–52). Barcelona: Bosch.

González Campos, J. D. (1999). Las normas internacionales sobre derechos humanos y los derechos fundamentales y libertades reconocidos en la Constitución Española (art. 10.2 CE). In P. Cruz Villalón, J. D. González Campos, & M. Rodríguez-Piñero (Eds.), *Tres lecciones sobre la Constitución* (p. 35). Sevilla: Megablum.

González, P. M. I. (2007). *El proceso autonómico ante la igualdad en el ejercicio de los derechos constitucionales*. Oñati: Instituto Vasco de Administración Pública.

López Menudo, F. (2009). Los derechos sociales en los Estatutos de Autonomía. *Revista Andaluza de Administración Pública, 73*, 71–190.

Nikken, P. (1987). *La protección internacional de los derechos humanos. Su desarrollo progresivo*. Madrid: Civitas & Instituto Interamericano de Derechos Humanos.

Pernice, I. (1999). Multilevel Constitutionalism and the Treaty of Amsterdam: European Constitution-Making revisited?, *Common Market Law Review*, 36, 703–750. http://www.whi-berlin.eu/documents/whi-paper0499.pdf. Accessed 23 November 2014

Pernice, I., & Kanitz, R. (2004). Fundamental Rights and Multilevel Constitutionalism in Europe, *WHI Paper* 7/04, March 2004. http://www.whi-berlin.de/documents/whi-paper0704.pdf. Accessed 23 November 2014

De la Quadra-Salcedo Janini, T. (2008). El régimen jurídico de los derechos sociales estatutarios. Reflexiones tras la STC 247/2007 de 12 de diciembre. *Revista General de Derecho Constitucional, 5*, 1–48.

Quesada, J. L. (2006). Retos pendientes del Estado social español: en especial, la ratificación de la Carta social europea revisada de 1996. *Nuevas Políticas Públicas Anuario multidisciplinar para la modernización de las Administraciones Públicas, 2*, 40–71.

Rawls, J. (1993). The Law of Peoples. *Critical Inquiry, 20*(1), 36–68.

Rawls, J. (1999). *The Law of Peoples*. Cambridge, MA: Harvard University Press.

Ripol Carulla, S. (2007). *El sistema europeo de protección de los derechos humanos y el derecho español*. Barcelona: Atelier.

Rodríguez-Vergara Díaz, A. (2010). Batasuna ante el Tribunal Europeo de Derechos Humanos: protección "multinivel" de derechos en Europa y régimen de los Partidos políticos en España. *Revista de Derecho Comunitario Europeo, 35*, 195–221.

Saiz Arnáiz, A. (2008). Art. 10.2 CE. La interpretación de los derechos fundamentales y los Tratados Internacionales sobre derechos humanos. In M. E. Baamonde, & M. Rodríguez-Piñero (Eds.), *Comentarios a la Constitución* (pp. 193–209). Madrid: Wolters Kluwer.

Stern, K., & Tettinger, P. J. (Eds.). (2005). *Die Europäische Grundrechte-Charta im wertenden Verfassungsvergleich*. Berlin: Berliner Wissenschafts-Verlag.

Stern, K., & Tettinger, P. J. (Eds.). (2006). *Kölner Gemeinschaftskommentar zur Europäischen Grundrechte-Charta*. Munich: C. H. Beck.

Tajadura, J. (2010). *El futuro de Europa. Luces y sombras del Tratado de Lisboa*. Granada: Comares.

Tammes, A. J. P. (1983). Soft law. In T. M. C. Asser Institute Staff (Ed.), *Essays on International and Comparative Law in Honour of Judge Erades* (pp. 187–195). The Hague: Martinus Nijhoff Publishers.

Tenorio Sánchez, P. J. (1997). La incorporación de la Convención Europea de Derechos del Hombre a los ordenamientos internos. In Y. Gómez (Ed.), *Los derechos en Europa* (pp. 153–170). Madrid: UNED.

Torres del Moral, A. (2010). *Estado de Derecho y democracia de partidos*. Madrid: Universidad Complutense de Madrid.

Prado, V. C. (2001). Corti Europee e giurisprudenza del Tribunal Constitucional spagnolo. *Rivista di Diritto Pubblico Comparato ed Europeo, 4*, 2073–2082.

Vittorino, A. (2003). La Cour de justice et les droits fondamentaux depuis la proclamation de la Charte. In N. Colneric, J.-P. Puissochet, D. Ruiz-Jarabo, & D. V. Edwards (Eds.), *Une Comunauté de Droit, Festschrift für Gil Carlos Rodríguez Iglesias* (pp. 111–126). Berlín: Berliner Wissenschafts-Verlag.

L'Allemagne, la France et l'Union Européenne: Dialogue ou Duel des Juges Constitutionnels?

Michel Fromont

Le fonctionnement et surtout le développement de l'Union européenne lancent un formidable défi aux juges constitutionnels nationaux. Alors que, selon le Préambule du traité de Maastricht instituant celle-ci et confirmé par le traité de Lisbonne, les États se sont déclarés « résolus à poursuivre le processus créant une union sans cesse plus étroite [. . .] dans la perspective des étapes ultérieures à franchir pour faire progresser l'intégration européenne », les juges constitutionnels ont toujours pour mission d'assurer la supériorité de la constitution nationale sur toutes les règles de droit applicables sur le territoire national et le respect de celle-ci par toutes les autorités exerçant leurs compétences sur ce territoire. Les juges constitutionnels éprouvent ainsi des difficultés à concilier leur mission de gardien de la constitution avec la suprématie du droit de l'Union européenne qui fut d'abord affirmée par le juge européen avant d'être confirmée par les traités.

Bien que les juges constitutionnels français et allemands aient globalement la même mission, la défense de la constitution nationale, ils sont appelés à statuer dans des contextes assez différents: les procédures suivies sont assez différentes et les règles constitutionnelles ne sont pas les mêmes. Il n'est donc pas étonnant que les jurisprudences constitutionnelles des deux pays soient en définitive assez éloignées les unes des autres malgré des traditions juridiques et une idéologie assez proches. Du moins en est-il ainsi selon nous lorsqu'il s'agit du contrôle de la constitutionnalité des traités européens ou de l'attitude des juges constitutionnels face à un acte de l'Union européenne. Seule les jurisprudences relatives à la constitutionnalité des lois de mise en œuvre des actes de l'Union européenne présentent une certaine similitude.

1 La Jurisprudence Relative à la Constitutionnalité des Traités Relatifs à l'Union Européenne

Historiquement, la question de la conformité à la constitution nationale s'est tout d'abord posée au sujet des traités instituant les Communautés européennes et

H.-J. Blanke et al. (eds.), *Common European Legal Thinking*,
DOI 10.1007/978-3-319-19300-7_11

l'Union européenne. Elle ne se pose pas tout-à-fait de la même façon selon que le traité est simplement un texte qui a été signé par les représentants des États négociateurs ou qu'il a été dûment ratifié: dans le premier cas, il s'agit simplement d'un projet d'engagement élaboré par les États signataires alors que, dans le second cas, le traité est entré dans l'ordre juridique international et lie tous les États qui ont procédé à sa ratification. Mais, dans la pratique, même en Allemagne où le contrôle de constitutionnalité peut s'exercer à l'encontre d'un traité déjà entré en vigueur, il s'est exercé en fait seulement entre le vote de la loi d'approbation et le dépôt des instruments de ratification, les partenaires de l'Allemagne ayant patienté le temps nécessaire pour que la question du respect de la constitution allemande soit résolue au préalable.

1.1 La Jurisprudence Constitutionnelle Allemande Relative aux Traités Européens

1.1.1 Les Procédures Utilisées

La Loi fondamentale n'a prévu aucune procédure spécifique pour le contrôle de la constitutionnalité des traités. De fait, les traités sont toujours contestés en contestant la loi d'approbation du traité, ce qui a pour conséquence de ne rendre possible la saisine de la Cour qu'après l'intervention du Parlement. Le contrôle s'exerce donc plusieurs mois après la signature du traité. Théoriquement, la loi ne peut être attaquée qu'après sa promulgation et ensuite, elle peut être contestée indéfiniment. Dans la pratique, la Cour constitutionnelle fédérale (*Bundesverfassungsgericht*) accepte d'être saisie avant la promulgation de la loi dès lors que celle-ci a été adoptée par les deux chambres,[1] ce qui gagne quelques jours; en outre, cette pratique permet en général au Président fédéral de différer la signature de la loi jusqu'au jour où la compatibilité du traité avec la constitution est formellement admise.

De plus, la Cour s'efforce de statuer relativement rapidement dans de telles hypothèses (9 mois pour le traité de Maastricht et 13 mois pour le traité de Lisbonne). Il existe toutefois un cas où la Cour a statué quelques 9 mois après l'entrée en vigueur des traités, celui des traités relatifs à la mise en place du Mécanisme européen de stabilité monétaire:[2] le Président fédéral a procédé au dépôt de ratification des traités non pas après que la Cour eut statué sur le fond des recours contestant la constitutionnalité des traités, mais dès que la Cour eut rejeté la demande d'ordonnance provisoire tendant à suspendre la procédure de ratification.[3]

[1] Cour Constitutionnelle fédérale allemande, 1 BvF 1/52 (décision du 30 juillet 1952) – *Traité sur l'Allemagne* (dans BVerfGE 1, 396 et seqq.).

[2] Cour Constitutionnelle fédérale allemande, 2 BvR 1390/12 (décision du 18 mars 2014) – *Traités relatifs au Mécanisme européen de stabilité* (dans NJW 2014, p. 1505).

[3] Cour Constitutionnelle fédérale allemande, 2 BvR 1824/12 (décision du 12 septembre 2012)– *Demande de suspension de la procédure de ratification des traités sur le Mécanisme européen de stabilité* (dans BVerfGE 132, 195). De fait les traités sont entrés en vigueur le 27 septembre 2012.

Enfin, dans la pratique, les lois relatives aux traités européens n'ont jamais été contestées après l'entrée en vigueur du traité européen. Malgré ces efforts pour atténuer les inconvénients du système allemand, l'Allemagne est souvent responsable du retard avec lequel les traités européens peuvent entrer en vigueur. De plus et surtout, l'extrême tardiveté de la saisine et donc du contrôle entraîne, selon nous, de grandes conséquences. En effet, la Cour est amenée à ne pas constater de violations de la constitution et à se contenter d'assortir la déclaration de conformité à la constitution de nombreuses interprétations conformes à la constitution qui sont de véritables réserves apportées unilatéralement à un traité international par l'un des États signataires.

Les titulaires du droit de saisine sont, comme pour une loi ordinaire, non seulement les principaux organes constitutionnels de la Fédération ou d'un *Land*, mais encore tout tribunal qui a des doutes sérieux sur la constitutionnalité de la loi d'approbation (c'est-à-dire, en pratique, du traité) et, depuis les arrêts relatifs aux traités de Maastricht et de Lisbonne,[4] tout citoyen allemand qui invoque l'atteinte portée à son droit de vote. Ce droit de vote, qui est consacré par l'article 38 de la Loi fondamentale[5] et est assimilable à un droit fondamental, peut donc faire l'objet d'un recours individuel porté devant la Cour constitutionnelle fédérale (*Verfassungsbeschwerde*).[6]

Or, la Cour a estimé que ce droit de vote n'avait pas seulement une signification procédurale, celle de permettre au citoyen de déposer un bulletin dans l'urne pour élire le *Bundestag*, mais aussi une signification matérielle: tout citoyen a droit à ce que l'assemblée qu'il élit exerce la plénitude de ses attributions. C'est évidemment un raisonnement bien hasardeux, car c'est un véritable tour de passe-passe qui bouleverse entièrement le recours individuel: au lieu d'être un moyen de défense des droits subjectifs des individus, il devient une action populaire permettant à tout citoyen de défendre le système démocratique de l'Allemagne et, en réalité, de défendre la souveraineté de la République fédérale. D'ailleurs, dans son arrêt relatif au traité de Lisbonne, la Cour constitutionnelle fédérale a employé 33 fois le mot « souveraineté » (*Souveränität*) qui est pourtant totalement absent de la Loi fonda-

---

[4] Cour Constitutionnelle fédérale allemande, 2 BvR 2134, 2159/92 (décision du 12 octobre 1993) – *Traité de Maastricht* (dans BVerfGE 89, 155); Cour Constitutionnelle fédérale allemande, 2 BvE 2/08 et al. (décision du 30 juin 2009) – *Traité de Lisbonne* (dans BVerfGE 123, 267). Noter que dans la deuxième affaire jugée, la Cour constitutionnelle fédérale était également saisie de litiges entre organes constitutionnels de la part de députés du *Bundestag*. Mais la Cour n'a admis la recevabilité de ces demandes que pour autant qu'elle faisait valoir que le traité privait le *Bundestag* de son droit d'autoriser toute intervention militaire (para 196–206), question qui n'a pas fait l'objet de longs développements dans la suite du jugement.

[5] Art. 38, Loi fondamentale (ci-après GG): « (1) Les députés du *Bundestag* allemand sont élus au suffrage universel, direct, libre, égal et secret [. . .] (2) Est électeur celui qui a dix-huit ans révolus [. . .] »

[6] Art. 93 GG: « (1) La Cour constitutionnelle fédérale statue: [. . .] 4a. sur les recours constitutionnels qui peuvent être formés par quiconque estime avoir été lésé par la puissance publique par l'un de ses droits fondamentaux ou dans l'un de ses droits garantis par les articles 20, al. 4, 33, 38, 101, 103 et 104 »

mentale.[7] D'une conception subjective du recours individuel, la Cour est passée à un recours de type objectif.

1.1.2 Les Règles de Fond Appliquées

La Cour constitutionnelle fédérale applique principalement l'article 23 de la Loi fondamentale qui est consacré à l'Union européenne depuis le 29 septembre 1990 dont l'alinéa 1 dispose: « (1) Pour l'édification d'une Europe unie, la République fédérale d'Allemagne concourt au développement de l'Union européenne [...] (2) A cet effet, la Fédération peut transférer des droits de souveraineté (*Hoheitsrechte*) par une loi approuvée par le Bundestag. (3) L'article 79, al. 2 et 3, est applicable à l'institution de l'Union européenne ainsi qu'aux modifications de ses bases conventionnelles et aux autres textes comparables qui modifient ou complètent la présente Loi fondamentale dans son contenu ou rendent possibles de tels modifications ou complements ».[8] En application de ce texte, toute loi autorisant la ratification d'un traité relatif à l'Union européenne ou autorisant l'adoption d'une décision modifiant celui-ci doit respecter « les principes énoncés aux articles 1 et 20 de la Loi fondamentale » (article 79, al. 3 de la Loi fondamentale) ce que la Cour constitutionnelle fédérale appelle l'identité constitutionnelle (*Verfassungsidentität*) de l'Allemagne.

Mais, comme la Cour constitutionnelle fédérale examine la question de la constitutionnalité du traité à travers la loi d'autorisation, elle se reconnaît implicitement le pouvoir de contrôler le respect de toutes les règles constitutionnelles par la loi d'approbation du traité. Toutefois, elle reste fidèle à la jurisprudence « Aussi longtemps » par laquelle elle s'interdit de contrôler le respect des droits fondamentaux sauf dans le cas où l'Union excéderait manifestement ses compétences (*ultra vires*). De ce fait, le contrôle principal exercé par la cour porte sur l'ampleur des pouvoirs transférés au nom de la défense de la démocratie allemande que garantit le droit d'élire le *Bundestag* qui est proclamé par l'article 38 de la Loi fondamentale. Ainsi, dans la décision relative au traité de Maastricht, la Cour constitutionnelle fédérale a estimé que le droit de vote des citoyens élisant le *Bundestag* serait vidé de sa substance si les transferts de compétences prévus par le traité et autorisés par la loi d'approbation n'étaient pas définis d'une façon suffisamment précise pour empêcher que des interprétations extensives privent de façon imprévisible le *Bundestag* d'une partie importante de ses compétences. Mais comme nous l'avons déjà noté, en exigeant le respect du droit de vote, la Cour veille en réalité au respect des compétences du *Bundestag* et donc, en définitive, au respect de la souveraineté de l'Allemagne.

---

[7] Lenz 2009.

[8] Extraits de l'article 79 GG: « (1) La Loi fondamentale ne peut être modifiée que par une loi qui en modifie ou en complète expressément le texte [...] (2) Une telle loi doit être modifiée par les deux tiers des membres du Bundestag et les deux tiers des voix du Bundesrat. (3) Toute modification de la présente Loi fondamentale qui toucherait à l'organisation de la Fédération en Länder, au principe de la participation des Länder à la législation, ou aux principes énoncés aux articles 1 et 20 est interdite »

Mais si la Cour a poussé le principe de son contrôle très loin, elle n'a exercé son pouvoir qu'avec modération: aucune clause du traité n'a été déclarée incompatible avec les règles constitutionnelles allemandes, ce qui s'explique selon nous par le caractère tardif de la saisine. En revanche, elle a souvent subordonné sa déclaration de conformité à la nécessité de *respecter les interprétations qui, selon elle, rendent le traité compatible avec le droit constitutionnel allemand*, mais qui sont en réalité des réserves unilatérales au traité. De plus, elle a assorti ces réserves de menaces en cas de non-respect par les autorités de l'Union européenne: une interprétation non conforme au droit allemand « n'aurait aucune force obligatoire pour l'Allemagne ».[9] En outre, elle a parfois imposé aux autorités allemandes des obligations précises: par exemple, dans la décision relative au traité de Lisbonne, elle a exigé que, pour l'exercice de certaines compétences pénales par l'Union européenne, une loi allemande approuve les décisions prises ou que, pour utiliser la procédure dite du frcin de secours prévue à propos de la sécurité sociale des travailleurs migrants, le représentant du gouvernement allemand n'agisse que sur instructions du Gouvernement allemand et éventuellement du *Bundesrat*.[10] A propos du traité instituant un Mécanisme européen de stabilité, la Cour a imposé aux autorités allemandes l'obligation de veiller au respect de leurs engagements financiers envers l'Union européenne afin que l'Allemagne ne soit pas privée de son droit de vote.[11]

En cette matière, la jurisprudence constitutionnelle française est bien différente, ce qui s'explique principalement par le fait que le contrôle de constitutionnalité s'exerce en général avant que le Parlement ait été saisi de la loi d'autorisation et qu'une déclaration d'inconstitutionnalité entraîne de ce fait des conséquences moins graves pour les relations avec les États partenaires.

1.2 La Jurisprudence Constitutionnelle Française Relative aux Traités Européens

1.2.1 Les Procédures Utilisées

La Constitution française a prévu une procédure spécifique pour le contrôle de la constitutionnalité des traités. Respectueuse de l'ordre international, elle a prévu une procédure exclusivement préventive. Selon l'article 54, « si le Conseil constitutionnel, saisi par le Président de la République, par le Premier Ministre, par le président de l'une ou l'autre assemblée ou par soixante députés ou sénateurs, a déclaré qu'un engagement international comporte une clause contraire à la Consti-

[9] Cour Constitutionnelle fédérale allemande, 2 BvR 2134, 2159/92 (décision du 12 octobre 1993) considérant 157 – *Traité de Maastricht* (dans BVerfGE 89, 155).

[10] Cour Constitutionnelle fédérale allemande, 2 BvE 2/08 et al. (décision du 30 juin 2009) considérants 352 à 366 et 400 – *Traité de Lisbonne* (dans BVerfGE 123, 267).

[11] Cour Constitutionnelle fédérale allemande, 2 BvR 1390/12 (décision du 18 mars 2014)–*Traités relatifs au Mécanisme européen de stabilité* (dans NJW 2014, p. 1505).

tution, l'autorisation de ratifier ou d'approuver l'engagement international en cause ne peut intervenir qu'après la révision de la Constitution ». Un tel système donne aux titulaires du droit de saisine la possibilité de contester la constitutionnalité du traité avant même qu'il ait été approuvé par le Parlement et au Conseil constitutionnel celle de déclarer inconstitutionnelle une clause du traité suffisamment tôt pour que le gouvernement puisse mettre en route une procédure de révision de la Constitution en vue de modifier celle-ci afin qu'il n'y ait plus d'incompatibilité entre la Constitution et le traité à ratifier. De ce fait, il présente l'immense avantage d'éviter toute contrariété possible entre la Constitution française et l'engagement international de la France.

De fait, ce système a bien fonctionné jusqu'à présent, car il a toujours permis de mettre en harmonie la Constitution avec les traités européens. Ainsi, la loi constitutionnelle du 25 juin 1992 a inséré dans la Constitution le titre XIV intitulé « Des Communautés européennes et de l'Union européenne ».[12] Depuis l'entrée en vigueur du traité de Lisbonne l'intitulé est simplement « De l'Union européenne ». A l'occasion de la signature des trois grands traités relatifs à la construction de l'Europe unie, trois lois constitutionnelles ultérieures ont été adoptées et promulguées en vue de mettre la Constitution en conformité avec le traité à ratifier compte tenu de la décision que venait de rendre le Conseil constitutionnel.[13] Leur contenu se trouve aujourd'hui formulé dans des termes très généraux par le premier article du titre XIV intitulé « De l'Union européenne »: « Article 88-1. La République participe à l'Union européenne constituée d'États qui ont choisi librement d'exercer en commun certaines de leurs compétences en vertu du traité sur l'Union européenne et du traité sur le fonctionnement de l'Union européenne signés à Lisbonne le 13 décembre 2007. » Cette formulation, qui remonte une loi constitutionnelle de 1992 (sous réserve de la suppression de la mention des Communautés européennes qui n'existent plus aujourd'hui) a été considérée comme suffisante pour justifier toutes les contrariétés pouvant exister entre les textes européens actuels et la Constitution française à une seule exception, l'attribution du droit de vote aux élections municipales aux citoyens de l'Union européenne résidant en France.[14]

1.2.2 Les Règles de Fond Appliquées

Bien que l'article 88-1 de la Constitution française autorise les transferts de compétences au profit de l'Union européenne sous la seule restriction du respect de la réciprocité, le Conseil constitutionnel a estimé qu'un traité ne pouvait pas trans-

---

[12] Loi constitutionnelle n° 95-554 du 25 juin 1992 (à la suite de la décision traité de Maastricht).

[13] Ces lois constitutionnelles sont: la loi n° 99-49 du 25 janvier 1999 (à la suite de la décision n° 97-394 DC du 31 décembre 1997 relative au traité d'Amsterdam), la loi n° 2004-505 DC du 1er mars 2005 (à la suite de la décision n° 2004-505 DC relative au traité établissant une constitution pour l'Europe et aujourd'hui remplacée par les lois ultérieures) et la loi n° 2008-103 du 4 février 2008 (à la suite de la décision n° 2007-560 du 20 décembre 2007 relative au traité de Lisbonne).

[14] Conseil constitutionnel (ci-après CC) n° 92-308 DC (9 avril 1992) *Traité de Maastricht*, considérants 21 à 27.

férer des compétences à l'Union européenne sans respecter certaines limites. Par conséquent, si le traité dépasse ses limites, le pouvoir constituant dérivé doit modifier la Constitution avant que l'engagement de la France ne devienne définitif. Ces limites sont, en l'état actuel de la jurisprudence, au nombre de trois.

La première limite est l'impossibilité pour le traité de contenir une clause contraire à une disposition explicite de la constitution: par exemple, dans la décision relative au traité de Maastricht, l'attribution du droit de vote aux seuls citoyens français (article 3 de la Constitution) ne peut pas être contredite par une disposition du traité attribuant aux citoyens de l'Union européenne un droit de vote aux élections municipales. Une modification de la Constitution a donc été nécessaire.[15]

La seconde limite est l'impossibilité de « remettre en cause les droits et libertés garantis par la Constitution ». Jusqu'à présent, le Conseil constitutionnel a toujours admis la compatibilité des traités européens avec les droits de l'homme que garantit la Constitution française. Par exemple, dans la décision relative au traité établissant une constitution pour l'Europe, le Conseil a admis la constitutionnalité du traité en faisant valoir qu'il n'y avait pas de différence notable entre les droits de l'homme garantis par la Constitution et la jurisprudence constitutionnelle françaises et les droits fondamentaux garantis tant par la Charte des droits fondamentaux de l'Union européenne que par la Convention européenne des droits de l'homme auxquels se référait explicitement le traité établissant une constitution pour l'Europe.[16]

Enfin la troisième limite est l'exigence que le traité ne porte pas atteinte aux « conditions essentielles d'exercice de la souveraineté »: en particulier, les compétences transférées ne doivent pas porter sur une partie notable des domaines réservés normalement à l'État détenteur de la souveraineté nationale tels que la politique monétaire, la justice, la police (par exemple, le contrôle aux frontières dans la décision relative au traité de Maastricht), la défense, la politique étrangère; en outre, dans cette appréciation des conditions essentielles d'exercice de la souveraineté nationale, le juge constitutionnel tient compte des modalités d'exercice des compétences transférées, en particulier des règles d'adoption de la décision de l'Union (selon que chaque État conserve ou non un droit de veto, le droit de choisir de ne pas être lié par la décision prise). C'est pour avoir dépassé ces limites que le Conseil constitutionnel a déclaré inconstitutionnelles diverses clauses contenues dans les traités d'Amsterdam,[17] dans le traité établissant une constitution pour l'Europe[18]

[15] CC, n° 92-308 DC (9 avril 1992) *Traité de Maastricht*, considérants 21 à 27. – Loi constitutionnelle du 25 juin 1992: Article 88-3 de la constitution: « Sous réserve de réciprocité et selon les modalités prévues par le traité sur l'Union européenne signé le 7 février 1992, le droit de vote et l'éligibilité aux élections municipales peut être accordé aux citoyens de l'Union résidant en France. Ces citoyens ne peuvent exercer les fonctions de maire et d'adjoint ni participer à l'élection des sénateurs. Une loi organique votée dans les mêmes termes par les deux assemblées détermine les conditions d'application du présent article. »

[16] CC, n° 2004-505 DC (19 novembre 2004) *Traité établissant une constitution pour l'Europe*, considérants 14 à 22.

[17] CC, n° 97-394 DC (31 décembre 1997) *Traité d'Amsterdam*, considérants 21 à 26, 27 à 30.

[18] CC, n° 2004-505 (19 novembre 2004) *Traité établissant une constitution pour l'Europe*, considérants 27 à 28, 29 à 32, 33 à 34, 35.

ou encore dans le traité de Lisbonne,[19] ce qui a provoqué chaque fois une modification de la Constitution.[20] En revanche, le Conseil constitutionnel a jugé que le traité sur la stabilité, la coordination et la gouvernance au sein de l'Union économique et monétaire ne comportait pas de clauses contraires à la Constitution.[21]

Du fait d'un aménagement très différent des procédures, le contraste entre l'attitude du juge constitutionnel allemand et celle du juge constitutionnel français est flagrant. En raison du fait que le contrôle de constitutionnalité s'exerce tardivement, le juge allemand est contraint à déclarer le traité conforme à la constitution, mais à assortir cette déclaration de constitutionnalité de réserves d'interprétation qui ont pour effet de ne jamais éliminer totalement toute contestation de la conformité du traité à la constitution. Au contraire, le juge français sait que sa déclaration d'inconstitutionnalité de certaines clauses du traité n'aboutira qu'à une modification de la constitution pour éliminer définitivement toute contestation.

2 La Jurisprudence Relative à la Constitutionnalité des Actes de l'Union Européenne

Les actes de l'Union européenne, principalement les actes normatifs, sont l'œuvre exclusive des organes de l'Union et ne sont donc pas des actes nationaux, quoique destinés à s'appliquer sur les territoires des États. Ils échappent donc en principe à tout contrôle des juges constitutionnels des États membres. C'est d'ailleurs ainsi que raisonne la Cour de justice de l'Union européenne (ci-après CJUE); en revanche, le juge constitutionnel allemand a imaginé un subterfuge assez audacieux pour se prononcer malgré tout sur la validité d'un acte de l'Union européenne: il reproche aux organes nationaux de ne pas avoir empêché son adoption en utilisant d'ailleurs assez largement les principes qu'il avait dégagés précédemment lors de l'examen de la constitutionnalité des traités européens.

2.1 La Jurisprudence Constitutionnelle Française Relative aux Actes de l'Union Européenne

2.1.1 Les Procédures Utilisées

Comme aucune procédure spécifique n'est prévue pour un contrôle éventuel de la constitutionnalité d'un acte de l'Union européenne, la seule procédure qui pourrait éventuellement être utilisée est l'exception d'inconstitutionnalité qui serait invo-

[19] CC, n° 2007-560 DC (20 décembre 2007) *Traité de Lisbonne*, considérants 18 à 19, 20 à 21, 23 à 24, 27.

[20] CC, n° 92-308 DC (9 avril 1992) *Traité de Maastricht*, considérants 27, 45 et 50.

[21] CC, n° 2012-653 DC (9 août 2012) *Traité de stabilité*, considérants 21, 28 et 30.

quée à l'occasion de l'examen d'un recours dirigé contre un acte émanant d'une autorité nationale mettant en œuvre un acte de l'Union européenne. Le Conseil constitutionnel a très tôt écarté une telle exception, non pas en se fondant sur une règle de procédure, mais en se fondant sur l'impossibilité d'apprécier la conformité à une constitution nationale d'un acte qui n'appartient pas à l'ordre juridique national et a, en conséquence, déclaré que les actes des Communautés européennes devaient respecter le droit communautaire.[22]

La seule question qui s'est posée est celle de savoir si le Conseil constitutionnel devait saisir la CJUE d'une question préjudicielle portant sur l'interprétation à donner, voire sur l'appréciation de conformité au droit de l'Union (traités institutifs et Charte des droits fondamentaux). Saisi d'une demande de contrôle abstrait a priori, le Conseil constitutionnel a fait valoir que la brièveté du délai durant lequel il doit rendre sa décision l'empêchait de saisir la CJUE.[23] En revanche, depuis quelques années, lorsqu'il est saisi d'une question prioritaire de constitutionnalité mettant en cause la règle nationale d'application d'un acte de l'Union et donc indirectement un acte de l'Union, le Conseil constitutionnel accepte de saisir la CJUE d'une question préjudicielle, car de la réponse à cette question dépendent la validité et la signification de la règle nationale d'application et il a statué ensuite en tenant compte de la réponse de la Cour.[24] La différence d'attitude du Conseil constitutionnel s'explique par le fait que dans le cadre d'un contrôle abstrait a priori, le Conseil constitutionnel ne dispose que d'un mois pour statuer[25] alors que, dans le cadre de la question prioritaire de constitutionnalité (qui est le résultat d'une hybridation entre l'exception d'inconstitutionnalité et le recours individuel pour violation d'un droit de l'homme), il dispose d'un délai de trois mois.[26]

2.1.2 Les Règles de Fond Appliquées

A l'occasion de l'examen de la constitutionnalité d'une règle nationale d'application d'un acte de l'Union, le Conseil constitutionnel peut ainsi être amené, non pas à déclarer non valable l'acte de l'Union contraire au droit constitutionnel français, mais, au contraire, à ne pas annuler la règle nationale dont l'inconstitutionnalité est due précisément à l'acte de l'Union qu'elle met en œuvre. De façon paradoxale, il

[22] CC, décision n° 77-90 DC (30 décembre 1977) *Règlement du Conseil des Communautés européennes du 17 mai 1977 établissant des dispositions communes pour l'isoglucose*, considérant 4.
[23] CC, décision n° 2006-540 DC (27 juillet 2006) *Droit d'auteur*, considérant 20: « Devant statuer avant la promulgation de la loi, le Conseil constitutionnel ne peut saisir la Cour de justice des Communautés européennes de la question préjudicielle prévue par l'article 234 du traité instituant la Communauté européenne. »
[24] CC, décision n° 2013-3P QPC, (4 avril 2013) *Mandat d'arrêt européen*, considérants 7 et 8 – Cas C-168/13 PPU (réponse de la Cour européenne à la demande du Conseil constitutionnel français) (CJUE 30 mai 2013) – CC, décision n° 2013-314 QPC, 14 juin 2013, (décision rendue après réception de la décision de la CJUE).
[25] Art. 61, al. 3, de la constitution.
[26] Art. 23-1 de la loi organique n° 2009-1523 du 10 décembre 2009 relative à l'application de l'article 61-1 de la constitution.

faut donc que l'acte de l'Union ait clairement entendu restreindre un droit garanti par la constitution nationale pour que la règle nationale d'application qui impose la même restriction à un droit constitutionnellement garanti échappe à la censure du juge constitutionnel.

Le seul cas où le Conseil constitutionnel se réserverait le droit d'annuler la mesure d'application de l'acte de l'Union contraire au droit constitutionnel français et empêcherait ainsi l'acte de l'Union de s'appliquer sur le territoire français serait le cas où l'Union porterait « atteinte à l'identité constitutionnelle de la France ». Comme le Conseil constitutionnel n'a pas encore eu l'occasion d'utiliser cette notion pour s'opposer à l'application d'un acte de l'Union, il est difficile d'en connaître le contenu véritable. Pour notre part, nous entendons par identité constitutionnelle de la France les règles républicaines traditionnelles auxquelles le peuple français est particulièrement attaché.

2.2 La Jurisprudence Constitutionnelle Allemande Relative aux Actes de l'Union Européenne

2.2.1 Les Procédures Utilisées

Comme la loi française, la loi allemande ne prévoit aucune procédure permettant de contester directement un acte de l'Union et, d'ailleurs, s'il y en avait une, elle serait une violation flagrante du droit de l'Union. Mais, comme le juge français, le juge allemand est tenté d'exercer son contrôle sur les actes de l'Union par le canal de l'exception d'inconstitutionnalité à l'occasion de l'examen de la constitutionnalité d'une mesure nationale d'application de cet acte. La Cour constitutionnelle fédérale a commencé très tôt à réclamer à son profit un tel droit de contrôle puisque dans la décision « Aussi longtemps I » (*Solange I*),[27] elle a revendiqué le droit de contrôler le respect des droits fondamentaux allemands par un acte de la Communauté européenne et elle n'y a renoncé que plus tard (*Solange II*),[28] estimant que la Communauté européenne avait établi entretemps un système garantissant une protection des droits fondamentaux équivalente, ce qui était d'autant plus remarquable qu'à cette époque, la Charte des droits fondamentaux de l'Union européenne n'était pas encore devenue partie intégrante du droit primaire de l'Union.

Mais à partir de la décision relative au traité de Maastricht, la Cour Constitutionnelle fédérale s'est mise à revendiquer de nouveaux pouvoirs de contrôle. Au nom de la garantie du droit de vote des citoyens allemands, elle a exigé que les organes de l'Union européenne n'excèdent pas les pouvoirs qui leur ont été transférés en particulier par le Parlement allemand et a donc revendiqué le pouvoir de déclarer

---

[27] Cour Constitutionnelle fédérale allemande, 2 BvL 52/71 (décision du 29 mai 1974) – *Solange I* (dans BVerfGE 37, 271).

[28] Cour Constitutionnelle fédérale allemande, 2 BvR 197/83 (décision du 22 octobre 1986) – *Solange II* (dans BVerfGE 73, 339).

inapplicable sur le territoire allemand les actes de l'Union qui sont *ultra vires*.[29] Elle a appliqué sa doctrine successivement aux règlements européens,[30] à une décision-cadre européenne,[31] une directive de l'Union,[32] une décision du Conseil des gouverneurs de la Banque centrale européenne (BCE).[33] Plus récemment, la Cour constitutionnelle fédérale a poussé l'audace jusqu'à contrôler le respect du droit de l'Union par la CJUE.[34]

Il est vrai que la Cour a toujours conclu par un rejet du recours son examen de la compatibilité des actes de l'Union avec le droit constitutionnel allemand, y compris l'obligation imposée aux organes de l'Union de respecter la délimitation des compétences transférées à l'Union par les autorités allemandes. Pour justifier ses décisions de rejet des recours, elle a constamment fait valoir que seule la violation manifeste et grave des règles de compétences s'imposant aux organes de l'Union. A plusieurs reprises, la Cour a également invoqué le nécessaire respect de l'identité constitutionnelle de l'Allemagne, mais elle ne lui a jamais accordé une grande importance bien que cette exigence repose en droit allemand sur des bases textuelles plus solides qu'en droit français du fait de l'existence de l'article 79, al. 3 de la Loi fondamentale selon lequel « est interdite toute modification de la Loi fondamentale qui toucherait à l'organisation de la Fédération en Länder, au principe de la participation des Länder à la législation ou aux principes énoncés aux articles 1 et 20 ».

Dans sa décision rendue le 18 mars 2014 à propos de la politique de l'euro, la Cour est-elle allée encore plus loin? Apparemment elle a parfaitement respecté les compétences de la CJUE puisqu'elle a pour la première fois posé une question préjudicielle en appréciation de la compatibilité de la décision des Gouverneurs de la BCE du 6 septembre 2012 avec diverses dispositions des traités européens et en interprétation de divers articles du traité sur le fonctionnement de l'Union européenne (TFUE).[35] Mais, en réalité, elle a longuement démontré que, selon elle, les articles 119 et 127 et seqq. du TFUE ainsi que les articles 17 et seqq. du statut de la BCE étaient violés par la décision des Gouverneurs de la BCE d'acheter des em-

---

[29] Cour Constitutionnelle fédérale allemande, 2 BvR 2134, 2159/92 (décision du 12 octobre 1993) considérant 157 – *Traité de Maastricht* (dans BVerfGE 89, 155); 2 BvE 2/08 et al. (décision du 30 juin 2009) – *Traité de Lisbonne* (dans BVerfGE 123, 267).

[30] Cour Constitutionnelle fédérale allemande, 2 BvL 1/97 (décision du 7 juin 2000) – *Marché commun des bananes* (dans BVerfGE 102, 147).

[31] Cour Constitutionnelle fédérale allemande, 2 BvR 2236/04 (décision du 17 juillet 2005) – *Mandat d'arrêt européen* (dans BVerfGE 113, 273). Voir aussi Cour Constitutionnelle fédérale allemande, 1 BvR 256/08, 1 BvR 263/08, 1 BvR 586/08 (décision du 2 mars 2010) – *Surveillance des communications électroniques* (dans BVerfGE 125, 260).

[32] Cour Constitutionnel fédérale allemande, 1 BvR 256/08, 1 BvR 263/08, 1 BvR 586/08 (décision du 13 mars 2007) – *Réglementation de l'émission des gaz à effet de serre* (dans BVerfGE 118, 79).

[33] Cour Constitutionnelle fédérale allemande, 2 BvR 2728/13 (décision du 14 janvier 2014) *Décision d'acheter à l'avenir des emprunts d'État* (dans BVerfGE 134, 366).

[34] Cour Constitutionnelle fédérale allemande, 2 BvR 2661/06 (décision du 6 juillet 2010) – *Honeywell (contrats de travail à durée déterminée)* (dans BVerfGE 126, 286).

[35] Cour Constitutionnelle fédérale allemande, 2 BvR 1390/12 (décision du 18 mars 2014) – *Traités relatifs au Mécanisme européen de stabilité* (dans NJW 2014, p. 1505).

prunts d'État sur le marché secondaire, et elle a même indiqué à la Cour européenne comment il faudrait interpréter cette décision de façon à la rendre compatible avec les traités européens et, par voie de conséquence, avec le droit constitutionnel allemand tout en évitant de la déclarer nulle.[36]

Ainsi la Cour Constitutionnelle fédérale semble vouloir pénétrer très loin dans le domaine normalement réservé à la CJUE, celui de l'interprétation du droit de l'Union et de l'appréciation de validité des actes de l'Union.

3 La Jurisprudence Relative à la Constitutionnalité des Lois Nationales de Transposition du Droit de l'Union Européenne

En signant et ratifiant les traités relatifs à l'Union européenne, les États membres se sont engagés à appliquer ou à mettre en œuvre les décisions de l'Union, spécialement les actes normatifs que sont les règlements de l'Union et surtout les directives de l'Union. S'ils ne le font pas, ils violent le droit de l'Union et la CJUE peut constater leur manquement. Quant aux juridictions constitutionnelles nationales, elles doivent veiller au respect de la constitution nationale principalement par les actes normatifs nationaux qu'il s'agisse des lois d'application ou des lois de transposition. Quelle est l'attitude des juges constitutionnels nationaux face à une loi nationale dont la question de conformité à la constitution nationale est posée au juge national?

3.1 La Jurisprudence Constitutionnelle Française Relative aux Actes de l'Union Européenne

3.1.1 Les Procédures Utilisées

En France, depuis le 1er mars 2010, le Conseil constitutionnel peut désormais être saisi de deux façons différentes de la question de la constitutionnalité d'une loi.

En premier lieu, le Conseil constitutionnel peut être saisi d'une demande de contrôle abstrait dans les quinze jours qui suivent le vote de la loi; la demande peut être faite par le Président de la République, le Premier Ministre, le Président du Sénat ou le Président de l'Assemblée nationale ou encore par soixante députés ou soixante sénateurs. Cette procédure a été utilisée une douzaine de fois soit pour contester la constitutionnalité de lois nationales mettant en œuvre des règlements européens, soit pour contester des lois nationales transposant des directives de l'Union.[37] Le

---

[36] Heun 2014, p. 331 et seqq.

[37] Un décompte grossier permet de recenser quatre décisions concernant des règlements (n° 70-39 DC du 19 juin 1970 et n° 2014-694 DC du 28 mai 2014) et 11 décisions concernant des directives (n° 94-348 DC du 3 août 1994, n° 98-400 DC du 20 mai 1998, n° 2004-496 DC du 10 juin 2004,

Conseil constitutionnel doit statuer dans un délai d'un mois; l'affaire ne donne pas lieu à une audience publique, mais seulement à un échange de prises de position écrites ou exceptionnellement orales entre les auteurs de la saisine, le Gouvernement et le membre du Conseil constitutionnel auquel a été confiée la fonction de rapporteur.

En second lieu, le Conseil constitutionnel peut être saisi d'une question prioritaire de constitutionnalité. C'est une procédure hybride qui présente certains caractères de la question préjudicielle puisqu'elle est posée par une juridiction ordinaire qui a des doutes sérieux sur la constitutionnalité de la loi qu'elle doit appliquer à un litige concret dont elle est saisie, des caractères du recours individuel pour violation d'un droit de l'homme garanti par la constitution puisqu'elle est provoquée par un justiciable qui prétend que la loi applicable porte atteinte à un droit que garantit la constitution et enfin des caractères d'une procédure abstraite puisque la juridiction initialement saisie de l'affaire ne peut pas elle-même poser la question, mais doit solliciter auprès de la juridiction suprême dont elle relève une décision de renvoi au Conseil constitutionnel. Depuis l'entrée en vigueur de la loi d'application de l'article 61-1 de la Constitution qui prévoit cette nouvelle procédure le 1er mars 2010, cette procédure a connu un grand succès puisque plus de 400 décisions ont été rendues sur des questions prioritaires de constitutionnalité. En revanche, le nombre d'affaires portant sur les lois d'application ou de transposition d'actes normatifs de l'Union européenne est encore assez petit: nous n'avons recensé que quatre cas.[38]

3.1.2 Les Règles Matérielles Appliquées

En France, le Conseil constitutionnel a amorcé sa jurisprudence principalement à propos des lois nationales transposant dans le droit national une directive (ou une décision-cadre) de l'Union européenne en rendant en 2004 quatre decisions;[39] puis, il l'a précisée et complétée en 2006[40] et depuis cette date il l'applique de façon régulièrement en n'y apportant que des variantes minims.[41]

n° 2004-497 du 1er juillet 2004, n° 2004-498 DC et n° 2004-499 DC du 29 juillet 2004, n° 2005-531 DC du 29 décembre 2005, n° 2006-540 DC du 27 juillet 2006, n° 2006-543 DC du 30 novembre 2006, n° 2008-564 DC du 19 juin 2008, n° 2011-631 DC du 9 juin 2011).

[38] Ces quatre décisions QPC sont: n° 2010-79 QPC (17 décembre 2010), n° 2011-217 QPC (3 février 2012), n° 2014-373 QPC (4 avril 2014), n° 2014-410 QPC (18 juillet 2014).

[39] Ces quatre décisions de 2004 sont: CC, n° 2004-496 DC (10 juin 2004) *Économie numérique*, n° 2004-497 (1er juillet 2004) *Communications électroniques*; n° 2004-498 DC (29 juillet 2004) *Bioéthique*; n° 2004-499 DC (29 juillet 2004) *Protection des données personnelles*.

[40] CC, n° 2006-540 DC (27 juillet 2006) *Droits d'auteur*; n° 2006-543 DC (30 novembre 2006) *Secteur de l'énergie*.

[41] CC n° 2008-564 DC (19 juin 2008) *Organismes génétiquement modifiés*; n° 2010-79 QPC (17 décembre 2010) *Protection subsidiaire d'un étranger*; n° 2011-631 DC (9 juin 2011) *Loi sur l'immigration*; n° 2012-659 DC (13 décembre 2012) *Financement de la sécurité sociale*; n° 2014-690 DC (13 mars 2014), *Droit de la consommation*; n° 2014-373 QPC (4 avril 2014) *Travail de nuit*; n° 2014-410 DC (18 juillet 2014) *Cogénération d'énergie thermique et électrique*.

La jurisprudence française repose assez largement sur l'interprétation de l'article 88-1 qui fut inséré dans la constitution par la loi constitutionnelle du 25 juin 1992. Cette insertion, ainsi que celle des trois articles suivants, s'est inscrite dans le cadre d'une révision constitutionnelle visant à faciliter la ratification du traité de Maastricht.[42] Néanmoins cette interprétation n'a pas tout à fait la même portée selon que le Conseil constitutionnel est saisi d'une demande de contrôle abstrait préalable à la promulgation de la loi ou d'une question prioritaire de constitutionnalité (qui n'est possible que depuis 2010).

Lorsqu'il est saisi d'une demande de contrôle abstrait a priori, le Conseil constitutionnel a interprété l'article 88-1 de la Constitution comme posant non seulement le principe de la participation de la République française à l'Union européenne, mais encore comme imposant aux pouvoirs publics français l'obligation de transposer les directives (ou les décisions-cadres qui leur sont assimilées) et, par voie de conséquence, comme lui donnant la compétence de vérifier si la loi soumise à son contrôle a bien pour objet de transposer la directive et si elle l'a fait correctement. Ainsi pour avoir « méconnu manifestement l'objectif d'ouverture des marchés concurrentiels de l'électricité et du gaz naturel fixé par les directives », le Conseil constitutionnel a déclaré « contraire à l'article 88-1 de la constitution » une partie de la loi relative au secteur de l'énergie.[43] Il se réserve aussi le droit de veiller au respect des « dispositions inconditionnelles » de la directive.[44] Bien qu'il s'agisse dans les deux cas d'une forme de contrôle du respect du droit de l'Union par la loi nationale, le Conseil constitutionnel a choisi, du moins jusqu'à présent, de ne pas saisir la Cour de justice de l'Union en cas de doute sur la compatibilité de la loi au regard des engagements européens; il s'en est justifié en invoquant son obligation de statuer dans un délai d'un mois lorsqu'il est saisi d'une demande de contrôle abstrait préalable à la promulgation.[45] En conséquence, « il ne saurait déclarer non conforme à l'article 88-1 de la Constitution qu'une disposition manifestement incompatible avec la directive qu'elle a pour objet de transposer ».[46]

En outre, sans avoir véritablement fourni de justification explicite, le Conseil constitutionnel a posé la règle selon laquelle « la transposition d'une directive ne

[42] Ces textes ont été complétés ou mis à jour par la suite, spécialement pour permettre la ratification du relative au traité établissant une constitution pour l'Europe (loi constitutionnelle du 1er mars 2005) et de Lisbonne (loi constitutionnelle du 23 juillet 2008): aujourd'hui la constitution comporte un titre nouveau, le titre XV intitulé « De l'Union européenne » qui contient pas moins de 7 articles numérotés de 88-1 à 88-7.

[43] CC, n° 2006-543 DC (30 novembre 2006) *Secteur de l'énergie*, considérant 9.

[44] CC, n° 2006-543 DC (30 novembre 2006), considérant 9: « La loi française de transposition serait contraire à l'exigence constitutionnelle qui résulte de l'article 88-1 de la constitution si elle [...] méconnaissait manifestement l'objectif [...] fixé par la directive que ses dispositions inconditionnelles. »

[45] Cet argument est peu convaincant, car la Cour de justice de l'Union a institué précisément une procédure d'urgence en novembre 2000.

[46] CC n° 2006-540 DC (27 juillet 2006) *Droits d'auteur*, considérant 20; n° 2006-543 DC (30 novembre 2006) *Secteur de l'énergie*, considérant 7; n° 2008-564 DC (19 juin 2008) *Organismes génétiquement modifiés*, considérant 45; n° 2010-605 DC (12 mai 2010) *Jeux de hasard*, considérant 18; n° 2011-631 DC (9 juin 2011) *Loi sur l'immigration*, considérant 45.

saurait aller à l'encontre d'une règle ou d'un principe inhérent à l'identité constitutionnelle de la France sauf à ce que le constituant y ait consenti ».[47] Pour avoir violé l'article 66 de la Constitution, le Conseil constitutionnel a ainsi déclaré inconstitutionnelle une disposition de l'article 56 de la loi sur l'immigration qui permettait de prolonger la rétention administrative d'un étranger sans intervention du juge.[48]

L'ensemble de cette jurisprudence est résumé dans une très récente décision du Conseil constitutionnel: « En l'absence de mise en cause d'une règle ou d'un principe inhérent à l'identité constitutionnelle de la France, le Conseil constitutionnel n'est pas compétent pour contrôler la conformité à la Constitution de dispositions législatives qui se bornent à tirer les conséquences nécessaires de dispositions inconditionnelles et précises d'une directive de l'Union européenne; en ce cas, il n'appartient qu'au juge de l'Union européenne, saisi le cas échéant à titre préjudiciel, de contrôler le respect par cette directive des droits fondamentaux garantis par l'article 6 du traité sur l'Union européenne. »[49]

En raison d'un cadre procédural différent, la jurisprudence du Conseil constitutionnel saisi d'une question prioritaire de constitutionnalité est un peu différente. En effet, seul le respect de « droits et libertés que la constitution garantit » peut être examiné par le Conseil constitutionnel. Le respect de « l'exigence constitutionnelle de transposition des directives ne relève donc pas des droits et libertés que la constitution garantit et ne saurait, par suite, être invoqué dans le cadre d'une question prioritaire de constitutionnalité ».[50] Le juge constitutionnel se refuse donc à contrôler si le législateur national a correctement transposé la directive européenne ou plus généralement mis en œuvre un acte de l'Union et peut seulement s'assurer que la loi ne porte pas atteinte à un droit garanti par la constitution nationale, du moins si l'acte de l'Union lui laissait une marge de liberté lui permettant de le respecter.

En revanche, probablement parce que le délai imparti au Conseil constitutionnel pour statuer sur une question prioritaire de constitutionnalité est de trois mois et non d'un mois comme dans le contrôle abstrait préalable, le Conseil constitutionnel accepte de saisir lui-même la CJUE d'une question préjudicielle en interprétation d'un acte de l'Union, ce qu'il a fait pour la première fois le 4 avril 2013 à propos de la décision-cadre sur le mandat d'arrêt européen afin de savoir si l'acte de l'Union laissait au législateur national une marge de liberté lui permettant de respecter le droit à l'intervention d'un juge quand la liberté individuelle est en cause.[51]

---

[47] CC n° 2006-540 DC (27 juillet 2006) *Droits d'auteur*, considérants 36 à 40, 50; n° 2006-543 DC (30 novembre 2006) *Secteur de l'énergie*, considérant 6; n° 2008-564 DC (19 juin 2008) *Organismes génétiquement modifiés*, considérant 44; n° 2010-605 DC (12 mai 2010) *Jeux de hasard*, considérant 18.

[48] CC n° 2011-631 DC (9 juin 2011) *Loi sur l'immigration*, considérant 76.

[49] CC, n° 2013-690 DC (13 mars 2014) *Droit de la consommation*, considérant 31.

[50] CC, n° 2010-605 DC (12 mai 2010) *Jeux de hasard*, considérant 19 (qui est en réalité un *obiter dictum*).

[51] CC, n° 2013-314 QPC (4 avril 2013) (saisine de la Cour européenne) considérant 7; Cas C-168/13 PPU (CJUE 30 mai 2013) (réponse de la Cour européenne); CC, n° 2013-314 QPC (14 juin 2013) (prise en compte de la réponse de la Cour européenne), considérants 7, 8 et 9.

Enfin, le juge français s'est généralement montré prudent et n'a conclu à une inconstitutionnalité que dans un nombre très restreint de cas. Dans le cadre du contrôle abstrait, on relève une douzaine de déclarations de non-conformité (partielle) à la constitution, ce qui est un nombre appréciable, mais un nombre très faible de réserves d'interprétation en vue de rendre conforme à la constitution la règle de droit examinée (un ou deux). Dans le cadre du contrôle concret (question prioritaire de constitutionnalité), qui n'a fonctionné qu'à partir de 2010, le nombre est encore très réduit et donc peu significatif.

3.2 La Jurisprudence Constitutionnelle Allemande Relative aux Actes de l'Union Européenne

3.2.1 Les Procédures Utilisées

En Allemagne, la Cour Constitutionnelle fédérale peut être saisie de la question de la constitutionnalité d'une loi d'application d'un règlement de l'Union ou de transposition d'une directive de l'Union dans le cadre de trois procédures: la demande de contrôle abstrait faite par une autorité politique après la promulgation de la loi, la demande de contrôle concret présentée par une juridiction contestant sérieusement la validité de la loi qu'elle doit appliquer au procès dont elle est saisie, enfin la demande d'une personne quelconque contestant un acte de l'État portant atteinte à un droit fondamental dont il est titulaire. Dans la pratique, les autorités politiques ne saisissent que rarement la Cour Constitutionnelle fédérale pour les raisons suivantes: les députés du *Bundestag* doivent être relativement nombreux pour présenter une demande de contrôle abstrait (un quart d'entre eux) et une grande partie d'entre eux est favorable à la construction de l'Europe et les gouvernements n'usent que très rarement de leur droit de saisine.[52] Quant au contrôle concret, la seule demande qui fut faite par un tribunal non constitutionnel fut rejetée par la Cour Constitutionnelle fédérale parce qu'il n'avait pas démontré que la réponse à la question était nécessaire à la solution du litige dont il était saisi, la possibilité d'une telle réponse dépendant de l'existence ou non d'une marge de liberté laissée au législateur par la directive de l'Union.

En revanche, la procédure du recours individuel pour violation d'un droit fondamental a été utilisée plus fréquemment. Si notre décompte est exact, la Cour a eu à juger cinq recours individuels contestant la constitutionnalité de lois relatives à l'application ou à la transposition de règlements ou de directives de l'Union. Ce faible nombre est d'autant plus surprenant que le recours individuel est devenu pra-

[52] Le seul cas de saisine par un Land (en l'espèce le Land de Saxe-Anhalt) est le suivant: Cour Constitutionnelle fédérale allemande, 1 BvF 1/05 (décision du 13 mars 2007) – *respect de la liberté d'exercer sa profession, du droit de propriété et du principe d'égalité devant la loi par la loi sur les émissions de gaz à effet de serre mettant en œuvre la directive 2006/87/CE* (dans BVerfGE 118, 79), analyse Fromont 2008, p. 1711.

tiquement une action populaire, puisque il est désormais ouvert à toute personne prétendant être lésée dans son droit à être gouvernée démocratiquement. De plus, en 2011, la Cour Constitutionnelle fédérale a encore élargi le domaine du recours individuel pour violation d'un droit fondamental puisque elle a accepté d'examiner un recours individuel contestant la constitutionnalité de l'interprétation que la Cour fédérale de justice (*Bundesgerichtshof*) avait donnée d'une loi transposant une directive européenne.[53]

Il est vrai qu'aux décisions relatives aux lois mettant en œuvre des décisions émanant d'organes de l'Union, il convient d'ajouter quelques décisions relatives à la mise en œuvre de traités européens qui sont d'ailleurs très célèbres, ayant concerné soit le traité de Lisbonne, soit les traités relatifs au sauvetage de l'euro.

3.2.2 Les Règles Matérielles Appliquées

La jurisprudence constitutionnelle allemande relative aux lois d'application ou de transposition de règlements ou de directives de l'Union comporte selon nous deux branches. La première est la jurisprudence relative aux droits fondamentaux proprement dits, c'est-à-dire des différentes libertés, des garanties de bonne justice et du droit à l'égalité. La seconde concerne la jurisprudence relative au respect du droit de vote (article 38 de la Loi fondamentale) et donc du principe de démocratie (ou selon la terminologie française, de la souveraineté nationale) telle qu'elle a été analysée précédemment à propos du contrôle de la constitutionnalité des lois d'approbation des traités européens.

Dans les affaires qui portent sur le respect d'un droit fondamental proprement dit par une loi nationale d'application ou de transposition ou encore par l'interprétation qu'en donne le juge national ordinaire, les droits fondamentaux invoqués jusqu'à présent ont été la liberté individuelle, le droit au secret de la correspondance, le droit d'exercer la profession de son choix et le droit de propriété. Comme en France, le contrôle du respect des droits fondamentaux par les lois nationales mettant en œuvre des décisions de l'Union est exclu chaque fois que le législateur n'a pas d'autre choix pour respecter l'acte de l'Union. En conséquence, il convient de distinguer deux séries de cas.

Dans le premier cas, l'acte de l'Union ne laisse au législateur allemand ou au juge allemand aucune marge de transposition ou d'interprétation: le législateur ou le juge national est alors un simple exécutant et, s'il y a atteinte portée aux droits fondamentaux allemands, il faut contester l'acte de l'Union lui-même devant le juge européen en faisant valoir que celui-ci viole les droits fondamentaux que garantit le droit de l'Union, ce qui suppose d'ailleurs que le droit fondamental en cause

[53] Cour Constitutionnelle fédérale allemande, 1 BvR 1916/09 (décision du 19 juillet 2011)-*Droit d'auteur* (dans BVerfGE 129, 78).

est garanti à la fois par le droit constitutionnel allemand et par le droit de l'Union européenne.[54]

Dans le second cas, l'acte de l'Union laisse au législateur allemand une marge de liberté lui permettant de ne pas porter atteinte aux droits garantis par la Loi fondamentale. La Cour Constitutionnelle fédérale doit alors contrôler elle-même la constitutionnalité de la loi qui a mis en œuvre l'acte de l'Union. Si la Cour juge que le législateur a effectivement utilisé la marge de liberté qui lui était laissée pour éviter de porter une atteinte inconstitutionnelle à un droit fondamental allemand, elle doit déclarer que la loi est conforme à la constitution; ce fut le cas pour la loi relative aux certificats d'émission de gaz à effet de serre.[55] Si, au contraire, la Cour juge que le législateur n'a pas su utiliser la marge de liberté qui lui était laissée par la directive pour éviter de porter à un droit fondamental une atteinte inconstitutionnelle, elle doit déclarer inconstitutionnelles les dispositions de la loi qui violent les droits fondamentaux allemands alors qu'il aurait pu l'éviter. C'est ce qui s'est produit à deux reprises dans des affaires retentissantes: la première concernait la transposition de la décision-cadre sur le mandat d'arrêt européen et la seconde les obligations imposées aux opérateurs de stocker pendant six mois des données relatives aux correspondances électroniques échangées sur leurs réseaux.[56]

Dans la seconde branche de la jurisprudence constitutionnelle allemande, il est reproché au législateur d'avoir porté atteinte aux compétences du législateur fédéral au-delà de ce qui est admissible. La Cour Constitutionnelle fédérale a déjà eu l'occasion de se prononcer à ce sujet dans plusieurs décisions relatives soit à des lois dites d'accompagnement et de mise en œuvre de traités européens venant modifier les traités constitutifs précédents ou de décisions importantes d'organes de l'Union,[57] soit à des lois dites d'application de règlements ou de transposition de

[54] Cour Constitutionnelle fédérale allemande, 1 BvR 1916/09 (décision du 19 juillet 2011) considérants 88–91 – *Droit d'auteur* (dans BVerfGE 129, 78).

[55] Cour Constitutionnel fédérale allemande, 1 BvR 256/08, 1 BvR 263/08, 1 BvR 586/08 (décision du 13 mars 2007) – *Réglementation de l'émission des gaz à effet de serre* (dans BVerfGE 118, 79). Le Sommaire (*Leitsätze*) contient la phrase: « La transposition de directives communautaires qui ne laissent aucune marge de transposition aux États membres, mais contiennent des dispositions impératives, ne doit pas être jugée au regard des droits fondamentaux, aussi longtemps que la Cour de justice des Communautés européennes assure une protection efficace des droits fondamentaux contre le pouvoir des Communautés qui doit être considérée comme équivalente à celle qui est impérativement exigée par la Loi fondamentale. »

[56] Cour Constitutionnelle fédérale allemande, 2 BvR 2236/04 (décision du 17 juillet 2005) – *Mandat d'arrêt européen* (dans BVerfGE 113, 273: droit d'un Allemand de ne pas être extradé et d'être jugé par un juge). – Cour Constitutionnelle fédérale allemande, 1 BvR 256/08, 1 BvR 263/08, 1 BvR 586/08 (décision du 2 mars 2010) – *Surveillance des communications électroniques* (dans BVerfGE 125, 260): droit au secret de la correspondance.

[57] Cour Constitutionnelle fédérale allemande, 2 BvE 2/08 et al. (décision du 30 juin 2009) considérant 406 – *traité de Lisbonne* (dans BVerfGE 123, 267): « La loi tendant à étendre et renforcer les droits du Bundestag et du Bundesrat dans les affaires de l'Union européenne viole l'article 38 GG dans la mesure où les droits de participation du Bundestag et du Bundesrat sont aménagés de façon insuffisante. » – Cour Constitutionnelle fédérale allemande, 2 BvR 987/10, 2 BvR 1485/10, 2 BvR 1099/10 (décision du 7 septembre 2011) considérant 133 – *Sauvetage de l'Euro* (dans BVerfGE 129, 124): « Le droit de vote garanti par l'article 38 GG n'est pas violé par la loi sur l'union monétaire et la stabilité financière ni par la loi sur la prise en charge de garanties dans

directives de l'Union.[58] Dans ces différentes affaires, la Cour était saisie de recours individuels de personnes prétendant être lésés dans leur droit fondamental à élire le *Bundestag* dans la mesure où les lois de mise en œuvre aboutissaient à restreindre les compétences du *Bundestag* et donc indirectement l'influence des citoyens allemands sur des secteurs importants de la politique économique allemande.

Cependant deux atténuations ont été apportées à cette jurisprudence hostile à tout développement de l'Union européenne qui n'aurait pas été préalablement prévu par un traité européen lui-même respectueux des principes constitutionnels déclarés intangibles par l'article 79, al. 3 de la Loi fondamentale.

La première atténuation résulte du fait que la Cour accepte de ne pas exercer un contrôle strict des atteintes portées aux compétences du *Bundestag*. Par exemple, dans sa décision du 7 septembre 2011, elle déclare que « la constatation de l'aliénation de l'autonomie budgétaire ... doit se borner aux violations évidentes ».[59] Dans cette décision, elle assortit toutefois la déclaration de conformité à la Loi fondamentale d'une réserve d'interprétation ainsi formulée: « la disposition selon laquelle le Gouvernement doit consulter la commission du budget du Bundestag » doit être interprétée « comme obligeant le Gouvernement fédéral à obtenir au préalable l'approbation de la commission ».[60] En réalité, la Cour procède dans ce cas à une véritable correction de la loi.

le cadre d'un Mécanisme européen de stabilisation. Le Bundestag n'a pas méconnu de façon contraire à la constitution ses compétences budgétaires et par là même le contenu substantiel du principe de démocratie. » – Cour Constitutionnelle fédérale allemande, 2 BvR 1390/12 (décision du 18 mars 2014) considérant 223 – *traités relatifs au Mécanisme européen de stabilité* (dans NJW 2014, p. 1505): « Les dispositions de la loi sur la création du Mécanisme européen de stabilisation et de la loi sur le financement du Mécanisme européen de stabilisation satisfont, du moins selon une interprétation conforme à la constitution, aux exigences découlant des articles 20, alinéa i, 20, alinéas 1 et 2 combinés avec l'article 79, alinéa 3 GG relatives aux droits de participation et aux possibilités d'influence du Bundestag afin d'assurer une gestion démocratique du Mécanisme européen de stabilité et la préservation de l'ensemble de sa compétence budgétaire. »

[58] Cour Constitutionnelle féderale allemande, 2 BvR 2728/13 (décision du 14 janvier 2014) considérant 99 – *Décision d'acheter à l'avenir des emprunts d'État* (dans BVerfGE 134, 366): « Les doutes portant sur la validité de la décision du Conseil de la Banque centrale européenne relative au rachat de titres d'État par la BCE (décision OMT) peuvent être éliminés selon la Cour en adoptant une interprétation conforme au droit de l'Union. Cela suppose que le contenu de la décision dans son ensemble réponde pour l'essentiel aux exigences exposées ci-dessus. » Voir aussi Heun 2014, p. 331 et seqq.

[59] Cour Constitutionnelle fédérale allemande, 2 BvR 987/10, 2 BvR 1485/10, 2 BvR 1099/10 (décision du 7 septembre 2011) considérant 130 – *Sauvetage de l'Euro* (dans BVerfGE 129, 124).

[60] Cour Constitutionnelle fédérale allemande, 2 BvR 987/10, 2 BvR 1485/10, 2 BvR 1099/10 (décision du 7 septembre 2011) considérant 141 – *Sauvetage de l'Euro* (dans BVerfGE 129, 124). Un exemple d'interprétation conforme à la constitution d'une loi d'accompagnement se trouve également dans Cour Constitutionnelle fédérale allemande, 2 BvR 1390/12 (décision du 18 mars 2014) considérants 223 et 229 – *Traités relatifs au Mécanisme européen de stabilité* (dans NJW 2014, p. 1505).

La seconde atténuation de cette jurisprudence est peut-être plus apparente que réelle. En effet, dans la décision rendue le 14 janvier 2014,[61] la Cour a estimé que les atteintes portées aux compétences économiques et financières du *Bundestag* étaient telles qu'elle a saisi elle-même la Cour de justice de questions préjudicielles. Mais, pour parvenir à cette décision, la Cour a démontré longuement qu'à ses yeux, la décision de la BCE violait diverses dispositions des traités européens, ce qui est contestable à un double titre. D'une part, la Cour ne se contente pas d'émettre des doutes sur la conformité de la décision au droit de l'Union, mais elle fait une démonstration très développée des violations du droit de l'Union commises par la BCE; elle semble disposée à ne s'incliner devant une décision contraire de la Cour de justice de l'Union que dans le cas où celle-ci procéderait à une interprétation restrictive de la décision contestée. D'autre part, elle abandonne sa jurisprudence précédente selon laquelle le juge national ne peut refuser l'application d'un acte des organes de l'Union que dans les cas où l'acte contesté est manifestement *ultra vires*, c'est-à-dire frappé d'un vice d'incompétence manifeste; or, en l'espèce, la thèse de l'incompatibilité avec le droit de l'Union et donc avec les transferts de compétence opérés par les traités est assez largement contestée et ne présente donc pas le caractère manifeste requis.

4 Conclusion

Si l'on compare le droit français et le droit allemand, ce sont surtout les différences institutionnelles qui frappent encore que les différences matérielles sont loin d'être négligeables.

Tout d'abord, en ce qui concerne les conditions d'exercice du contrôle de la constitutionnalité des traités européens, le contraste est grand entre les deux pays. En France, le contrôle peut s'exercer dès la signature du traité et s'exerce dans la pratique avant même que le Parlement donne son autorisation; cette relative précocité du contrôle permet au Conseil constitutionnel d'indiquer clairement les clauses du traité qui sont en contradiction avec la constitution alors en vigueur, ce qui laisse au titulaire du pouvoir constituant dérivé le temps nécessaire pour modifier la Constitution en vue de l'adapter au nouveau traité. En Allemagne, au contraire, le contrôle de constitutionnalité ne peut porter que sur la loi d'approbation après qu'elle a été adoptée par le Parlement; il est alors trop tard pour envisager à ce stade une modification de la constitution et, de fait, la seule modification de la Loi fondamentale qui a été effectuée pour adapter la constitution aux exigences de la construction européenne a eu lieu avant l'adoption de la loi d'autorisation.[62] C'est pourquoi la

[61] Cour Constitutionnelle fédérale allemande, 2 BvR 2728/13 (décision du 14 janvier 2014) – *Décision d'acheter à l'avenir des emprunts d'État* (dans BVerfGE 134, 366); voir aussi Heun 2014, p. 331 et seqq.

[62] La révision de la Loi fondamentale (nouvel article 23) a eu lieu le 21 décembre 1992 et le jugement de la Cour constitutionnelle fédérale relative au traité de Maastricht a été rendu le 12 octobre 1993.

Cour Constitutionnelle fédérale est amenée à toujours déclarer conforme à la constitution la loi approuvant le traité, mais sous réserve d'interprétations du traité. Cette pratique n'est guère satisfaisante, car la constitution ne fait pas toujours l'objet des adaptations nécessaires au bon fonctionnement de l'Union et les interprétations correctrices du juge constitutionnel allemand sont faites unilatéralement par le tribunal d'un seul État membre de l'Union européenne et sans que n'intervienne la CJUE.

En ce qui concerne le contrôle de la constitutionnalité des lois nationales mettant en œuvre les actes de l'Union européenne, les différences ne sont pas aussi importantes, mais elles sont loin d'être négligeables. C'est surtout le contrôle abstrait qui est assez différent: en France, le contrôle ne peut être déclenché que dans les quinze jours suivant l'adoption de la loi alors qu'en Allemagne, il ne peut être déclenché qu'après la promulgation de la loi. De plus, la pratique des saisines n'est pas la même: en France, les demandes de contrôle abstrait sont nombreuses et ont toutes été faites par des parlementaires alors qu'en Allemagne, le seul cas de demande de contrôle abstrait a été le fait du gouvernement d'un Land. Quant au contrôle concret, la différence majeure est la suivante: en France, la question prioritaire de constitutionnalité, qui est en quelque sorte une demande de contrôle concret pour violation d'un droit fondamental, a été assez peu utilisée de 2010 à 2014 en matière européenne, alors qu'en Allemagne, le recours individuel est pratiquement le seul utilisé et tend même à se transformer en action populaire, lorsque les requérants invoquent la violation de leur droit de vote et donc les atteintes portées aux prérogatives du *Bundestag*.

Si l'on compare les règles matérielles appliquées par le juge constitutionnel dans les deux pays, on constate que les thèmes sont en partie les mêmes: droits fondamentaux, identité constitutionnelle, respect de la souveraineté de l'État (souvent dissimulé sous les traits du principe de démocratie). En outre, pour le contrôle des lois mettant en œuvre les actes dérivés de l'Union européenne, les deux juridictions font la même distinction entre les actes de l'Union qui laissent aux autorités nationales une marge de liberté et ceux qui n'en laissent aucune pour décider si la loi de transposition est ou non contrôlable par le juge constitutionnel national.

Il existe toutefois une grande différence entre les deux pays: en droit allemand, l'article 79, al. 3 de la Loi fondamentale déclare intangibles le fédéralisme, la démocratie, la république, l'État de droit, la dignité de l'homme et l'obligation faite à toutes les autorités publiques de respecter et de protéger tous les droits fondamentaux.[63] De ce fait, toute la jurisprudence qui repose sur ces principes bénéficie de cette intangibilité. En conséquence, le titulaire du pouvoir constituant dérivé ne peut pas contredire cette jurisprudence et seule la Cour Constitutionnelle fédérale pourrait la modifier, ce qui donne une rigidité extraordinaire à la constitution et à la jurisprudence constitutionnelle allemandes, spécialement en matière européenne. Le contraste est grand avec le droit français dans lequel la constitution peut faire aisément l'objet de modifications en vue d'adapter la constitution aux nécessités

[63] L'article 79, al. 2 et 3 GG a d'ailleurs été déclaré expressément applicable aux traités européens par l'article 23, al. 1 GG tel qu'il a été inséré dans la Loi fondamentale par la loi constitutionnelle du 21 décembre 1992.

de la construction de l'Europe ou exceptionnellement pour contrer une jurisprudence du Conseil constitutionnel jugée inopportune, comme l'a montré l'adoption du nouvel article 53-1 par la loi constitutionnelle du 25 novembre 1995 en réaction à la décision du Conseil constitutionnel du 13 août 1993.[64]

Au-delà de cette comparaison des techniques juridiques, il faut constater que le juge constitutionnel a certes été institué pour protéger la constitution de son pays et qu'il est donc tout naturellement porté à la protéger contre toutes les atteintes qui seraient portées contre elle, même celles dues à la participation du pays à la construction d'une Europe unie. Néanmoins, le juge constitutionnel a le devoir d'accompagner une évolution qui vise à constituer un ensemble politique ayant un poids équivalent aux grandes puissances de ce monde, qu'il s'agisse de pays qui se sont déjà hissés aux toutes premières places, comme les Etats-Unis et le Japon ou de pays dits émergents tels que la Chine, l'Inde et le Brésil. C'est normalement au titulaire du pouvoir constituant dérivé de procéder à l'adaptation de la constitution à cette transformation. C'est ce qui se passe en France à l'occasion de la ratification des traités européens qui se sont succédés depuis 1958, mais qui ne s'est qu'imparfaitement produit en Allemagne, principalement en raison du principe d'intangibilité posé par la Loi fondamentale, mais aussi en raison des réticences du titulaire du pouvoir constituant dérivé lors de l'adoption du nouvel article 23 de la Loi fondamentale en 1992.

Compte tenu de ce que ces retouches apportées à la constitution sont parfois insuffisantes, d'autres facteurs ont aidé le juge constitutionnel à développer des jurisprudences plus accueillantes aux innovations apportées par la construction européenne. En premier lieu, il faut citer le principe, accepté par les deux pays, selon lequel l'État doit respecter ses engagements internationaux, ce qui permet de faire respecter certaines règles figurant dans les traités européens. En second lieu, il faut citer, en France, le principe de la supériorité des traités internationaux sur la loi et, en Allemagne, l'acceptation du caractère spécifique de l'Union européenne (ce qui ne bénéficie pas aux autres traités internationaux, même ceux du Conseil de l'Europe).

De plus, les traités européens les plus récents ont cherché à réserver une part d'influence aux droits nationaux dans le droit élaboré par l'Union elle-même comme le montrent divers articles du traité de Lisbonne sur le respect des droits de l'homme et de l'identité nationale.

[64] CC n° 93-325 DC (13 août 1993) *Loi relative à l'immigration*, considérants 81 à 107; Article 53-1 de la constitution insérée par la loi constitutionnelle du 25 novembre 1993: « (1) La République peut conclure avec les États européens qui sont liés par des engagements identique aux siens en matière d'asile et de protection des Droits de l'homme et des libertés fondamentales, des accords déterminant leurs compétences respectives pour l'examen des demandes d'asile qui leur sont présentées. (2) Toutefois, même si la demande n'entre pas dans leurs compétences en vertu de ces accords, les autorités de la République ont toujours le droit de donner asile à tout étranger persécuté en raison de son action en faveur de la liberté ou qui sollicite la protection de la France pour un autre motif. »

Ainsi un certain équilibre s'est établi pour l'instant entre les réticences face aux réductions apportées à l'autonomie des États membres et le besoin de créer « une union sans cesse plus étroite entre les peuples de l'Europe » (Préambule du traité de Lisbonne). Reste à savoir comment cet équilibre évoluera à l'avenir.

References

Fromont, M. (2008). La décision de la Cour constitutionnelle fédérale du 13 mars 2007. *Revue du droit public*, no. 6, 1711–1721.

Heun, W. (2014). Eine verfassungswidrige Verfassungsgerichtsentscheidung – der Vorlagebeschluss des BVerfG vom 14.1.2014. *Juristenzeitung*, 331–337.

Lenz, C.-O. (2009). Ausbrechender Rechtsakt. *Frankfurter Allgemeine Zeitung* (8.8.2009).

Die Rechtsprechung zur Eurokrise

Ulrich Häde

1 Einleitung

Der Euro ist die Währung von mittlerweile 19 Mitgliedstaaten der Europäischen Union (EU) und daher wesentlicher Gegenstand des deutschen und europäischen Währungsrechts. *Albrecht Weber* versteht sich sicher nicht nur als Währungsrechtler; dazu sind seine Interessen zu vielfältig. Während seiner Zeit (1974–1980) am Würzburger Lehrstuhl unseres gemeinsamen akademischen Lehrers *Hugo J. Hahn* kam er aber mit dem Währungsrecht in Berührung und hat es seither durch Publikationen begleitet. Erwähnt seien nur der Aufsatz „Die zweite Satzungsnovelle des Internationalen Währungsfonds und das Völkerrecht" in der 1977 erschienenen Festschrift für *F.A. Mann* sowie sein Beitrag „Die Währungsunion – Modell für ein Europa mehrerer Geschwindigkeiten?" in der 1997 von ihm federführend herausgegebenen Festschrift für *Hugo J. Hahn*.

Albrecht Weber war 1980–1982 wissenschaftlicher Mitarbeiter des damaligen Präsidenten des Bundesverfassungsgerichts *Ernst Benda*. Später befasste er sich als Autor mit der Rechtsprechung des Bundesverfassungsgerichts, so auch mit der Rechtsprechung zum Vertrag von Maastricht, der die Regelungen zur Währungsunion in den EG-Vertrag einfügte.[1] In den letzten Jahren meldet sich der Jubilar wieder häufiger zu währungsrechtlichen Themen zu Wort.[2] Mit Kritik und spürbarer Sorge analysiert er die Maßnahmen im Zusammenhang mit der Krise im Euro-Währungsraum, die seit 2010 durch ihre dramatische Zuspitzung und insbesondere den Beinahe-Staatsbankrott von Griechenland in den Mittelpunkt der öffentlichen Aufmerksamkeit rückte.

Dieser Beitrag nimmt diese Interessen auf und skizziert die Rechtsprechung des Bundesverfassungsgerichts und des Gerichtshofs der Europäischen Union (EuGH) zur Eurokrise. Ganz unvoreingenommen kann er nicht sein, da der Verfasser in den Verfahren vor dem Bundesverfassungsgericht Prozessbevollmächtigter der Bundesregierung war. Argumente von Beteiligten müssen allerdings nicht zwingend die

[1] Weber 1994, S. 53; Weber 1995, S. 421.

[2] Vgl. Weber 2011, S. 935; Weber 2012, S. 801; Weber 2013, S. 375.

H.-J. Blanke et al. (eds.), *Common European Legal Thinking*,
DOI 10.1007/978-3-319-19300-7_12

schlechteren sein. Darüber hinaus geht es hier nicht um eine eingehende Besprechung und Bewertung dieser Judikate, sondern nur um Hinweise auf wichtige Einzelaspekte. Diese Gerichtsentscheidungen wird man auch als Elemente auf dem Weg zu einem gemeinsamen juristischen Denken und Argumentieren in Europa verstehen dürfen.

2 Finanzkrise – Bankenkrise – Schuldenkrise – Eurokrise

Wann fing die Krise an und wie nennt man sie? Beide Fragen sind nicht leicht zu beantworten. Vor dem Beginn der Europäischen Wirtschafts- und Währungsunion gab es eine heftige Diskussion um Sinn oder Unsinn einer gemeinsamen Währung und auch darüber, welche Mitgliedstaaten der Währungsunion angehören sollten. Es war wohl mehr ein politisches als ein ökonomisch fundiertes Projekt, eine einheitliche Währung für Europa anzustreben und dabei Mitgliedstaaten in einer Schicksalsgemeinschaft zu vereinen, deren Mentalität und wirtschaftliches Handeln sehr unterschiedlich waren und noch sind.[3] Bei der Auswahl der teilnehmenden Mitgliedstaaten war man außerdem großzügiger, als es nach damaligem Recht erlaubt war.[4] Einen optimalen Währungsraum[5] bildet die Eurozone jedenfalls seit ihrem Entstehen wohl kaum.

Dass die Einführung der einheitlichen Währung erfolgte, ohne zugleich die Zuständigkeit für die allgemeine Finanz- und Wirtschaftspolitik auf die zentrale Ebene zu übertragen[6], mag ebenfalls zu einer gewissen Krisenanfälligkeit beigetragen haben. Die eingebauten Sicherungen wirken nicht zuverlässig. Artikel 126 AEUV schreibt zwar Haushaltsdisziplin vor, hat aber aufgrund von Umsetzungsmängeln nicht verhindern können, dass einige Mitgliedstaaten (immer noch) viel zu hoch verschuldet sind. Art. 125 AEUV, die sogenannte no-Bail-out-Regel, die ein Eintreten der Mitgliedstaaten für fremde Schulden verbietet, erzielt ebenfalls nicht den erhofften Effekt. Das liegt aber weniger an der angeblichen Verletzung dieser Vorschrift durch die Maßnahmen zur Krisenbewältigung. Vielmehr fehlte es diesem Haftungsverbot schon von vornherein an der erforderlichen Glaubwürdigkeit.[7] Die Kapitalmärkte behandelten deshalb alle Mitgliedstaaten zu lange gleich. Erst als im Zuge der Finanzkrise Zweifel am vorher trotz des Art. 125 AEUV unterstellten Bail-out aufkamen, gerieten einige Mitgliedstaaten, allen voran Griechenland, in akute Refinanzierungsprobleme.

Die Krise kam aus den Vereinigten Staaten und ging von verbrieften Immobilienkrediten aus.[8] Sie brachte Banken und Staaten ins Wanken. Die Begriffe Ban-

---

[3] S. dazu schon Häde 2012a, S. 35 f.
[4] Näher dazu Häde 1998, S. 1088.
[5] S. dazu Tavlas 1993, S. 663.
[6] S. dazu Hahn und Häde 2010, § 15, Rn. 2 ff.
[7] Vgl. schon Häde, in Calliess und Ruffert (1999), Art. 103 EGV, Rn. 6 f.
[8] S. dazu Hummer 2011, S. 237 ff.

ken-, Finanz- und Staatsschuldenkrisen erscheinen daher allesamt berechtigt.[9] In gewisser Weise geriet durch die krisenhafte Zuspitzung der Lage aber auch die gemeinsame Währung in Gefahr. Ob es eine akute Gefahr des Auseinanderbrechens der Eurozone gab oder ob nur einzelne Staaten in die Nähe eines Austritts aus ihr gerieten, wird man diskutieren können. Jedenfalls blieben die Ereignisse nicht ohne Auswirkungen auf die Währungsunion. Daher erscheint der Begriff „Eurokrise" als Kurzbezeichnung der komplexen Situation durchaus angemessen. Vorüber ist sie nicht, diese Krise.[10] Daher haben die bisherigen Maßnahmen zu ihrer Bewältigung ihre Bedeutung meist noch nicht verloren. Aus demselben Grund wirkt auch die Rechtsprechung, die sich mit diesen Maßnahmen zu beschäftigen hatte, in die Zukunft.

3 Judikate zur Eurokrise

3.1 Überblick

Das Bundesverfassungsgericht hatte seit 2010 mehrfach über Rechtsfragen im Zusammenhang mit der Eurokrise und Maßnahmen zu ihrer Bewältigung zu entscheiden. Einige Beschwerdeführer ließen es sich nicht nehmen, ihre Verfassungsbeschwerden und Anträge auf Eilrechtsschutz Anfang Mai 2010 sofort nach den ersten Maßnahmen und unter Pressebegleitung persönlich in Karlsruhe abzugeben.[11] Seither gab es weitere Verfassungsbeschwerden und auch Organstreitanträge. Im Einzelnen entschied das Bundesverfassungsgericht durch Urteil vom 7.9.2011 über Verfassungsbeschwerden gegen die Hilfen für Griechenland.[12] Am 28.2.2012 erließ es sein Urteil in einem Organstreitverfahren, in dem die Ausgestaltung der Beteiligungsrechte des Bundestages beanstandet worden war.[13] Über einen Organstreitantrag der Bundestagsfraktion Bündnis 90/Die Grünen im Zusammenhang mit der Unterrichtungspflicht der Bundesregierung aus Art. 23 Abs. 2 Satz 2 GG urteilte das Bundesverfassungsgericht am 19.6.2012.[14] Am 12.9.2012 erging die Entscheidung über Anträge auf einstweiligen Rechtsschutz, die sich insbesondere gegen völkerrechtliche Verträge (ESM-Vertrag, Fiskalvertrag) richteten.[15] Das Hauptsacheurteil

---

[9] Näher zu den Ursachen Blanke 2011, S. 406 f.; Ebner 2011, S. 117; Ohler 2011, S. 1061; Schulmeister 2011, S. 37; Wieland 2012, S. 213 f.

[10] Vgl. nur Schäfers 2014, S. 1: „Die Krise im Euroraum beherrscht zwar nicht mehr die Schlagzeilen, ist aber alles andere als gelöst.".

[11] http://www.welt.de/politik/deutschland/article7522608/Euro-Rebellen-klagen-gegen-Griechenland-Hilfe.html [29.9.2014].

[12] BVerfG, 2 BvR 987/10, 2 BvR 1485/10, 2 BvR 1099/10 (Urteil vom 7.9.2011) – *Euro-Rettungsschirm* (in BVerfGE 129, 124).

[13] BVerfG, 2 BvE 8/11 (Urteil vom 28.2.2012) – *Beteiligungsrechte Bundestag EFSF* (in BVerfGE 130, 318).

[14] BVerfG, 2 BvE 4/11 (Urt. v. 19.6.2012) – *Euro-Plus-Pakt* (in BVerfGE 131, 152).

[15] BVerfG, 2 BvE 6/12, 2 BvR 1390/12, 2 BvR 1421/12, 2 BvR 1438/12, 2 BvR 1439/12, 2 BvR 1440/12 (Urteil vom 12.9.2012) – *ESM, Fiskalpakt* (in BVerfGE 132, 195).

über die zugrunde liegenden Verfassungsbeschwerden und einen Organstreitantrag erließ das Bundesverfassungsgericht am 18.3.2014.[16]

Auch der EuGH hat sich bereits mit Aspekten der Eurokrise beschäftigt. In der Rechtssache *Pringle*[17] urteilte er am 27.11.2012 über die unionsrechtliche Zulässigkeit des Europäischen Stabilitätsmechanismus (ESM). Nicht Gegenstand dieses Beitrags sind noch laufende Verfahren, insbesondere jenes, in dem es um die Rechtmäßigkeit des von der Europäischen Zentralbank (EZB) angekündigten OMT-Programms zum Ankauf von Staatsanleihen geht. Das Bundesverfassungsgericht hat sich insoweit mit einem Vorabentscheidungsersuchen an den EuGH gewandt.[18] Der Gerichtshof hat darüber am 14.10.2014 mündlich verhandelt, bis zum Abschluss dieses Beitrags im Herbst 2014 aber noch keine Entscheidung gefällt.

3.2 Das Urteil vom 7.9.2011

3.2.1 Hilfen für Griechenland

Gegenstand des ersten Urteils sind Maßnahmen zur Bewältigung der im Mai 2010 akut gewordenen Krise. Griechenland verlor die Möglichkeit, Kredite an den Finanzmärkten aufzunehmen und stand vor dem Staatsbankrott. Daher beschlossen die Mitgliedstaaten der Eurozone, Griechenland durch koordinierte bilaterale Kredite im Gesamtumfang von 80 Mrd. € zu helfen.[19] Weitere 30 Mrd. € sagte der Internationale Währungsfonds (IWF) zu. In Deutschland erfolgt die Umsetzung der eingegangenen Verpflichtungen durch die Kreditanstalt für Wiederaufbau (KfW); deren Absicherung übernahm der Bund. Dazu ermächtigte das Gesetz zur Übernahme von Gewährleistungen zum Erhalt der für die Finanzstabilität in der Währungsunion erforderlichen Zahlungsfähigkeit der Hellenischen Republik[20] den Bund, Gewährleistungen für die Kredite der KfW an Griechenland in Höhe von bis zu 22,4 Mrd. € zu übernehmen.[21]

---

[16] BVerfG, 2 BvE 6/12, 2 BvR 1390/12, 2 BvR 1421/12, 2 BvR 1438/12, 2 BvR 1439/12, 2 BvR 1440/12, 2 BvR 1824/12 (Urteil vom 18.3.2014) – *ESM, Fiskalpakt* (in NJW 2014, 1505).

[17] Fall C-370/12, *Thomas Pringle* (EuGH 27.11.2012) (NJW 2013, 29 und EuZW 2013, 100).

[18] BVerfG, 2 BvE 13/13, 2 BvR 2728/13, 2 BvR 2729/13, 2 BvR 2730/13, 2 BvR 2731/13 (Vorlagebeschluss vom 14.1.2014) (in BVerfGE 134, 366).

[19] Vgl. Rat der Europäischen Union, Dokument 2492/10 vom 5.5.2010, Erklärung der Eurogruppe vom 2.5.2010, http://www.consilium.europa.eu/uedocs/cmsUpload/st02492.de10.pdf [29.9.2014].

[20] Währungsunion-Finanzstabilitätsgesetz (WFStG) vom 7.5.2010, BGBl. 2010 I S. 537. Näher dazu Brück et al. 2010, S. 2522.

[21] Zu den weiteren Einzelheiten dieses ersten Griechenland-Pakets s. Bonke 2010, S. 503 ff.; Häde 2011, S. 2 ff.

3.2.2 Der Rettungsschirm

Unmittelbar danach drohte weiteres Ungemach. Man befürchtete einen Dominoeffekt, der andere Mitgliedstaaten mitreißen könnte. Es kam darauf an, während eines Wochenendes und vor Öffnung der Märkte zu Wochenbeginn das drohende Chaos abzuwenden. Ob die schlimmen Folgen, die sich die Akteure damals für den Fall des Untätigbleibens wohl u. a. vom Präsidenten der EZB schildern ließen, tatsächlich eingetreten wären, lässt sich nicht überprüfen. Der Handlungsdruck war aber enorm. Daraufhin entstand der sogenannte Rettungsschirm. Mehrere Maßnahmen sollten gebündelt 750 Mrd. € an Hilfskrediten verfügbar machen.

Über den Europäischen Finanzstabilisierungsmechanismus (EFSM)[22] steuerte die EU 60 Mrd. € bei, 250 Mrd. € kamen vom IWF. Den größten Anteil (440 Mrd. €) stellten erneut die Mitgliedstaaten mit Euro-Währung zur Verfügung. Für die Vergabe der Hilfskredite gründeten sie die Europäische Finanzstabilisierungsfazilität (EFSF) in Form einer Aktiengesellschaft.[23] Mit dem Stabilisierungsmechanismusgesetz[24] ermächtigte der deutsche Gesetzgeber das Bundesfinanzministerium, Gewährleistungen in einer Höhe von bis zu 123 Mrd. € für Kredite zu übernehmen, durch die sich die EFSF die nötigen Mittel verschaffen wollte.

3.2.3 Materielle Aufladung des Art. 38 GG

Die sowohl gegen deutsche und europäische Rechtsakte sowie gegen weitere Maßnahmen der Krisenbewältigung gerichteten Verfassungsbeschwerden stützten sich auf Art. 38 Abs. 1, Art. 14 Abs. 1 und Art. 2 Abs. 1 GG.[25] Das Bundesverfassungsgericht beurteilte die Verfassungsbeschwerden gegen die beiden deutschen Gesetze als zulässig, „soweit sie auf der Grundlage von Art. 38 Abs. 1 Satz 1, Art. 20 Abs. 1 und Abs. 2 in Verbindung mit Art. 79 Abs. 3 GG eine Verletzung der dauerhaften Haushaltsautonomie des Deutschen Bundestages rügen“.[26]

Insoweit knüpft das Bundesverfassungsgericht an seine im Urteil vom 12.10. 1993 zum Vertrag von Maastricht entwickelte These an, dass Art. 38 GG „es im Anwendungsbereich des Art. 23 GG aus[schließe], die durch die Wahl bewirkte Legitimation von Staatsgewalt und Einflussnahme auf deren Ausübung durch die Verlagerung von Aufgaben und Befugnissen des Bundestages so zu entleeren, daß das demokratische Prinzip, soweit es Art. 79 Abs. 3 i. V. m. Art. 20 Abs. 1 und

---

[22] Verordnung (EU) Nr. 407/2010 des Rates vom 11.5.2010 *zur Einführung eines europäischen Finanzstabilisierungsmechanismus*, ABl. L 118/1.

[23] S. dazu Regling 2011, S. 261.

[24] Gesetz zur Übernahme von Gewährleistungen im Rahmen eines europäischen Stabilisierungsmechanismus (StabMechG), BGBl. 2010 I S. 627.

[25] BVerfG, 2 BvR 987/10, 2 BvR 1485/10, 2 BvR 1099/10 (Urteil vom 7.9.2011) – *Euro-Rettungsschirm* (in BVerfGE 129, 124 [138]).

[26] BVerfG, 2 BvR 987/10, 2 BvR 1485/10, 2 BvR 1099/10 (Urteil vom 7.9.2011) – *Euro-Rettungsschirm* (in BVerfGE 129, 124 [167]).

2 GG für unantastbar erklärt, verletzt wird."[27] Diese „Erfindung" des damaligen Berichterstatters *Paul Kirchhof* aus dem Jahr 1993 hat das Bundesverfassungsgericht auch im Urteil vom 7.9.2011 bestätigt und gegen Kritik verteidigt.[28] Artikel 38 Abs. 1 Satz 1 GG, der seinem Wortlaut nach nur vorschreibt, dass die „Abgeordneten des Deutschen Bundestages [. . .] in allgemeiner, unmittelbarer, freier, gleicher und geheimer Wahl gewählt" werden, soll es zugleich ausschließen, „die durch die Wahl bewirkte Legitimation von Staatsgewalt und Einflussnahme auf deren Ausübung durch die Verlagerung von Aufgaben und Befugnissen des Bundestages auf die europäische Ebene so zu entleeren, dass das Demokratieprinzip verletzt wird."[29] Grundsätzlich soll demnach jedem Einzelnen ein entsprechendes grundrechtsgleiches Recht zustehen, dessen Verletzung er im Wege der Verfassungsbeschwerde geltend machen kann.

Eine umfassende Kritik dieses Konzepts ist hier nicht zu leisten. Schon sein Ergebnis lässt aber Zweifel entstehen. Indem jeder Wahlberechtigte über die Verfassungsbeschwerde allein unter Berufung auf sein in der beschriebenen Weise materiell aufgeladenes Wahlrecht und daher ohne Betroffenheit in sonstigen Grundrechten eine Kontrolle deutscher Gesetze veranlassen kann, die zu Kompetenzverschiebungen zwischen den Mitgliedstaaten und der Europäischen Union führen, verschwimmt die Grenze zwischen Individualrechtsschutz und Normenkontrolle.[30] Da sich bei umstrittenen Maßnahmen stets ein Beschwerdeführer finden wird, schafft sich das Bundesverfassungsgericht zugleich eine Art Selbstbefassungsrecht in Angelegenheiten der Europäischen Union.[31]

Dieses Vorgehen kann man als Hinweis auf eine sehr tiefreichende Skepsis gegenüber den europäischen Eliten deuten, die den Prozess der europäischen Integration verantworten, sich dabei vielleicht zu einig sind und nicht genügend Rücksicht auf die Bürger und die nationalen Verfassungsstrukturen nehmen. Es mag auch durchaus eine gewisse befriedende Wirkung haben, wenn sich jedermann wegen Kompetenzübertragungen auf die europäische Ebene an das Bundesverfassungsgericht wenden kann. Dennoch bestehen erhebliche Bedenken, ob eine so gravierende Fortentwicklung des Art. 38 Abs. 1 GG und des verfassungsgerichtlichen Rechtsschutzsystems ohne Mitwirkung des verfassungsändernden Gesetzgebers zulässig sein kann.

Diese Bedenken werden stärker, je weiter das Bundesverfassungsgericht seine auf Art. 38 Abs. 1 GG gestützte Rechtsprechung ausdehnt. Denn es sind nicht nur deutsche Gesetze, die Gegenstand von allein auf das Wahlrecht gestützten Verfassungsbeschwerden sind. Stattdessen rücken im Zusammenhang mit den Stichwor-

---

[27] BVerfG , 2 BvR 2134/92, 2 BvR 2159/92 (Urteil vom 12.10.1993) – *Maastricht* (in BVerfGE 89, 155 [172]).

[28] BVerfG, 2 BvR 987/10, 2 BvR 1485/10, 2 BvR 1099/10 (Urteil vom 7.9.2011) – *Euro-Rettungsschirm* (in BVerfGE 129, 124 [169 f.]).

[29] BVerfG, 2 BvE 2/08, 2 BvE 5/08, 2 BvR 1010/08, 2 BvR 1022/08, 2 BvR 1259/08, 2 BvR 182/09 (Urteil vom 30.6.2009) – *Lissabon-Vertrag* (in BVerfGE 123, 267 [330]).

[30] Vgl. dazu auch Nettesheim 2011, S. 768 f.

[31] Vgl. schon Häde 2013, S. 255 f.

ten „Ultra-vires-Kontrolle“ und „Identitätskontrolle“ zunehmend auch Maßnahmen der Europäischen Union ins Blickfeld.[32]

3.2.4 Haushaltspolitische Gesamtverantwortung

Mit dem Urteil vom 7.9.2011[33] hat das Bundesverfassungsgericht seine Rechtsprechung in eine andere Richtung erweitert. Nach dem Wortlaut des Grundgesetzes bedürfen die Aufnahme von Krediten oder die Übernahme von Gewährleistungen „einer der Höhe nach bestimmten oder bestimmbaren Ermächtigung durch Bundesgesetz“ (Art. 115 Abs. 1 GG). Solche Gesetze lagen vor; gegen sie richteten sich die Verfassungsbeschwerden. Das Bundesverfassungsgericht stellte nun aber auf die „haushaltspolitische Gesamtverantwortung“ des Bundestages ab. Diese Budgetverantwortung dürfe er „nicht durch unbestimmte haushaltspolitische Ermächtigungen auf andere Akteure übertragen. Insbesondere darf er sich, auch durch Gesetz, keinen finanzwirksamen Mechanismen ausliefern, die – sei es aufgrund ihrer Gesamtkonzeption, sei es aufgrund einer Gesamtwürdigung der Einzelmaßnahmen – zu nicht überschaubaren haushaltsbedeutsamen Belastungen ohne vorherige konstitutive Zustimmung führen können, seien es Ausgaben oder Einnahmeausfälle.“[34] Das Wahlrecht sei „verletzt, wenn sich der Deutsche Bundestag seiner parlamentarischen Haushaltsverantwortung dadurch entäußert, dass er oder zukünftige Bundestage das Budgetrecht nicht mehr in eigener Verantwortung ausüben können.“[35]

Im Ergebnis sah das Bundesverfassungsgericht die haushaltspolitische Gesamtverantwortung, die man als besondere Ausprägung der schon lange in der Rechtsprechung bekannten Integrationsverantwortung[36] verstehen kann, und mit ihr das Wahlrecht aus Art. 38 Abs. 1 GG aber nicht als verletzt an. Deshalb wies es die Verfassungsbeschwerden insgesamt als unbegründet zurück. Trotz der hohen Summen, für die der Bund Gewährleistungen übernehmen sollte, sei eine Überschreitung der Belastungsgrenze nämlich nicht festzustellen. Eine unmittelbar aus dem Demokratieprinzip folgende Obergrenze für die Übernahme von Gewährleistungen könnte nur überschritten sein, wenn sich im Eintrittsfall die Gewährleistungen so auswirkten, dass die Haushaltsautonomie jedenfalls für einen nennenswerten Zeitraum nicht nur eingeschränkt würde, sondern praktisch vollständig leerliefe.[37] Das Bundesverfassungsgericht stellte fest: „Keines der angegriffenen Gesetze begründet

[32] Vgl. nur Häde 2012c, S. 163; Proelß 2011, S. 241.

[33] Zu diesem Urteil: Baumgart 2011, S. 450; Dechatre 2011, S. 303; Elicker & Heintz 2012, S. 141; Giegerich 2011, S. 642 ff.; Götz & Schneider 2012, S. 145; Pagenkopf 2011, S. 1473; Ruffert 2011b, S. 842.

[34] BVerfG, 2 BvR 987/10, 2 BvR 1485/10, 2 BvR 1099/10 (Urteil vom 7.9.2011) – *Euro-Rettungsschirm* (in BVerfGE 129, 124 [179]).

[35] BVerfG , 2 BvR 987/10, 2 BvR 1485/10, 2 BvR 1099/10 (Urteil vom 7.9.2011) – *Euro-Rettungsschirm* (in BVerfGE 129, 124 [177]).

[36] S. dazu die Beiträge in Pechstein 2012.

[37] BVerfG, 2 BvR 987/10, 2 BvR 1485/10, 2 BvR 1099/10 (Urteil vom 7.9.2011) – *Euro-Rettungsschirm* (in BVerfGE 129, 124 [183]).

oder verfestigt einen Automatismus, durch den der Deutsche Bundestag sich seines Budgetrechts entäußern würde. Derzeit besteht keine Veranlassung, einen unumkehrbaren Prozess mit nachteiligen Konsequenzen für die Haushaltsautonomie des Deutschen Bundestages anzunehmen."[38]

Das Urteil vom 7.9.2011 ist auch deshalb interessant, weil es eine Bemerkung enthält, an die sich das Bundesverfassungsgericht später nicht mehr festhalten lassen wollte. Diese Passage lautet:

> Die Rügen der Beschwerdeführer, ihre Grundrechte würden unmittelbar durch [...] den Aufkauf von Staatsanleihen Griechenlands und anderer Mitgliedstaaten des Euro-Währungsgebietes durch die Europäische Zentralbank verletzt, sind unzulässig, weil ihnen keine tauglichen Beschwerdegegenstände zugrunde liegen. Bei den angegriffenen Akten handelt es sich – unbeschadet anderweitiger Überprüfungsmöglichkeiten auf ihre Anwendbarkeit in Deutschland hin (vgl. BVerfGE 89, 155 [175]; 126, 286 [302 ff.]) – nicht um von den Beschwerdeführern angreifbare Hoheitsakte deutscher öffentlicher Gewalt im Sinne von Art. 93 Abs. 1 Nr. 4a GG und § 90 Abs. 1 BVerfGG.[39]

Eine Zeit lang danach sah sich das Bundesverfassungsgericht nicht mehr gehindert, sich ausführlich mit dem geplanten Ankauf von Staatsanleihen durch die EZB zu befassen.

3.3 Das Urteil vom 28.2.2012

3.3.1 Das Neunergremium

Das zweite Urteil betraf das sogenannte Neunergremium. Der § 3 Abs. 1 Satz 1 StabMechG in der nach dem Urteil vom 7.9.2011 geänderten Fassung[40] sah vor, dass die Bundesregierung „in Angelegenheiten der Europäischen Finanzstabilisierungsfazilität einem Beschlussvorschlag, der die haushaltspolitische Gesamtverantwortung des Deutschen Bundestages berührt, durch ihren Vertreter nur zustimmen oder sich bei einer Beschlussfassung enthalten [darf], nachdem der Deutsche Bundestag hierzu einen zustimmenden Beschluss gefasst hat." Abweichend davon regelte § 3 Abs. 3 Satz 1 StabMechG, dass die Beteiligungsrechte des Deutschen Bundestages in Fällen besonderer Eilbedürftigkeit oder Vertraulichkeit von einigen (in der Praxis neun) Mitgliedern des Haushaltsausschusses wahrgenommen werden sollten, die vom Deutschen Bundestag für eine Legislaturperiode gewählt werden. Zwei Abgeordnete der SPD-Fraktion im Deutschen Bundestag sahen durch diese Zuweisung von Kompetenzen des Bundestages an einige Mitglieder

[38] BVerfG, 2 BvR 987/10, 2 BvR 1485/10, 2 BvR 1099/10 (Urteil vom 7.9.2011) – *Euro-Rettungsschirm* (in BVerfGE 129, 124 [184]).

[39] BVerfG, 2 BvR 987/10, 2 BvR 1485/10, 2 BvR 1099/10 (Urteil vom 7.9.2011) – *Euro-Rettungsschirm* (in BVerfGE 129, 124 [175 f.]).

[40] Gesetz zur Änderung des Gesetzes zur Übernahme von Gewährleistungen im Rahmen eines europäischen Stabilisierungsmechanismus vom 9.10.2011, BGBl. I S. 1992.

des Haushaltsausschusses eine Verletzung ihres Abgeordnetenstatus aus Art. 38 Abs. 1 Satz 2 GG.[41]

Das Bundesverfassungsgericht gab ihrem Organstreitantrag mit Urteil vom 28.2.2012[42] unter Verweis auf das Demokratieprinzip statt, soweit „§ 3 Abs. 3 StabMechG die Antragsteller unter Verstoß gegen Art. 38 Abs. 1 Satz 2 GG in einem verfassungsrechtlich nicht gerechtfertigten Umfang von der Mitwirkung an der haushaltspolitischen Gesamtverantwortung des Deutschen Bundestages" ausschließe.[43] Als unmittelbares Repräsentativorgan des Volkes nehme der Bundestag seine Funktion „grundsätzlich in seiner Gesamtheit wahr, durch die Mitwirkung aller seiner Mitglieder [. . .], nicht durch einzelne Abgeordnete, eine Gruppe von Abgeordneten oder die parlamentarische Mehrheit."[44] „Bei der Ausübung des Budgetrechts und der Wahrnehmung seiner haushaltspolitischen Gesamtverantwortung" müsse „der Deutsche Bundestag die wesentlichen Entscheidungen selbst treffen."[45] Das habe „grundsätzlich durch Verhandlung und Beschlussfassung im Plenum" zu geschehen.[46] Das Bundesverfassungsgericht hob zwar das Selbstorganisationsrecht des Bundestages hervor, wies aber zugleich auf dessen Grenzen hin. „Soweit Abgeordnete durch Übertragung von Entscheidungsbefugnissen auf einen beschließenden Ausschuss von der Mitwirkung an der parlamentarischen Entscheidungsfindung ausgeschlossen werden sollen," sei „dies nur zum Schutz anderer Rechtsgüter mit Verfassungsrang und unter strikter Wahrung des Grundsatzes der Verhältnismäßigkeit zulässig."[47]

Im Ergebnis verwarf es deshalb die Regelung des § 3 Abs. 3 StabMechG als Verstoß gegen die Abgeordnetenrechte. Eilbedürftigkeit und Vertraulichkeit könnten den Ausschluss der meisten Bundestagsabgeordneten von Entscheidungen im Zusammenhang mit Maßnahmen der EFSF nicht rechtfertigen. Das Neunergremium darf seither nur noch tätig werden, wenn es um den Ankauf von Staatsanleihen durch die EFSF geht. Insoweit hat das Bundesverfassungsgericht nämlich eine Ausnahme zugelassen, weil „die Vorbereitung einer solchen Notmaßnahme, also auch deren Beratung und ein diesbezüglicher Zustimmungsbeschluss, absoluter Vertraulichkeit unterliegen" müssten.[48]

---

[41] Vgl. BVerfG, 2 BvE 8/11 (Urteil vom 28.2.2012) – *Beteiligungsrechte Bundestag EFSF* (in BVerfGE 130, 318 [320]).

[42] Zu diesem Urteil: Manger-Nestler 2012, S. 158; Moench & Ruttloff 2012, S. 1261.

[43] BVerfG, 2 BvE 8/11 (Urteil vom 28.2.2012) – *Beteiligungsrechte Bundestag EFSF* (in BVerfGE 130, 318 [34]).

[44] BVerfG, 2 BvE 8/11 (Urteil vom 28.2.2012) – *Beteiligungsrechte Bundestag EFSF* (in BVerfGE 130, 318 [342]).

[45] BVerfG, 2 BvE 8/11 (Urteil vom 28.2.2012) – *Beteiligungsrechte Bundestag EFSF* (in BVerfGE 130, 318 [345]).

[46] BVerfG, 2 BvE 8/11 (Urteil vom 28.2.2012) – *Beteiligungsrechte Bundestag EFSF* (in BVerfGE 130, 318 [347]).

[47] BVerfG, 2 BvE 8/11 (Urteil vom 28.2.2012) – *Beteiligungsrechte Bundestag EFSF* (in BVerfGE 130, 318 [350]).

[48] BVerfG, 2 BvE 8/11 (Urteil vom 28.2.2012) – *Beteiligungsrechte Bundestag EFSF* (in BVerfGE 130, 318 [363]).

3.3.2 Verbindung zum Urteil vom 7.9.2011

Diese große Zurückhaltung bei der Übertragung von Zuständigkeiten des Deutschen Bundestages auf ein kleines Gremium ist gut nachvollziehbar und sicher auch grundsätzlich berechtigt. Allerdings ist zu berücksichtigen, dass das Bundesverfassungsgericht die Kompetenzen des Bundestages im Zusammengang mit den Krisenbewältigungsmaßnahmen weit ausgedehnt hat. Der Bundestag ist an der Ausführung von Gesetzen beteiligt und nimmt damit exekutive Aufgaben wahr.[49] Das erklärt Zweifel daran, ob das Parlamentsplenum tatsächlich das geeignete Gremium ist, wenn sehr kurzfristige Entscheidungen zu treffen sind. Und dass sich Vertraulichkeit in einem so großen Kreis nicht stets gewährleisten lässt, dürfte ebenfalls auf der Hand liegen.

Wer die Errichtung des Neunergremiums als ein von vornherein zum Scheitern verurteiltes Unterfangen ansieht, sollte auch in die Erwägungen einbeziehen, dass eine Aussage des Bundesverfassungsgerichts im Urteil vom 7.9.2011 den Eindruck erwecken konnte, § 3 Abs. 3 StabMechG sei verfassungsrechtlich nicht zu beanstanden. Dort hatte das Bundesverfassungsgericht nämlich im Hinblick auf die ursprüngliche Fassung des Stabilisierungsmechanismusgesetzes ausgeführt:

> § 1 Abs. 4 des Gesetzes verpflichtet allerdings die Bundesregierung lediglich dazu, sich vor Übernahme von Gewährleistungen zu bemuhen, Einvernehmen mit dem Haushaltsausschuss des Deutschen Bundestages herzustellen, der ein Recht zur Stellungnahme hat (Satz 1 und 2). Sofern aus zwingenden Gründen eine Gewährleistung vor Herstellung des Einvernehmens übernommen werden muss, ist der Haushaltsausschuss unverzüglich nachträglich zu unterrichten, wobei die Unabweisbarkeit der Übernahme der Gewährleistung vor Herstellung des Einvernehmens eingehend zu begründen ist (Satz 3). Zudem ist der Haushaltsausschuss vierteljährlich über die übernommenen Gewährleistungen und die ordnungsgemäße Verwendung zu unterrichten (Satz 4). Mit diesen Regelungen allein wäre der fortdauernde Einfluss des Bundestages auf die Gewährleistungsentscheidungen durch verfahrensrechtliche Vorkehrungen – über die allgemeine politische Kontrolle der Bundesregierung hinaus – nicht sichergestellt. Denn diese Vorkehrungen würden – auch zusammen mit der Zwecksetzung, der Höhe des Gewährleistungsrahmens und der Befristung des Euro-Stabilisierungsmechanismus-Gesetzes – nicht verhindern, dass die parlamentarische Haushaltsautonomie in einer das Wahlrecht beeinträchtigenden Weise berührt wird.[50]

Daraus zog es den Schluss:

> Daher bedarf es zur Vermeidung der Verfassungswidrigkeit einer Auslegung des § 1 Abs. 4 Satz 1 des Euro-Stabilisierungsmechanismus-Gesetzes dahingehend, dass die Bundesregierung vorbehaltlich der in Satz 3 genannten Fälle verpflichtet ist, die vorherige Zustimmung des Haushaltsausschusses einzuholen.[51]

Mit der Formulierung „vorbehaltlich der in Satz 3 genannten Fälle" schien das Bundesverfassungsgericht ausdrücken zu wollen, dass es die Regelung dieses Sat-

[49] S. dazu Häde 2012b, S. 32 ff.

[50] BVerfG, 2 BvR 987/10, 2 BvR 1485/10, 2 BvR 1099/10 (Urteil vom 7.9.2011) – *Euro-Rettungsschirm* (in BVerfGE 129, 124 [185 f.]).

[51] BVerfG, 2 BvR 987/10, 2 BvR 1485/10, 2 BvR 1099/10 (Urteil vom 7.9.2011) – *Euro-Rettungsschirm* (in BVerfGE 129, 124 [186]).

zes 3 nicht beanstandete, sondern für verfassungskonform hielt. § 1 Abs. 4 Satz 3 StabMechG a. F. bestimmte:

> Sofern aus zwingenden Gründen eine Gewährleistung bereits vor Herstellung des Einvernehmens übernommen werden muss, ist der Haushaltsausschuss unverzüglich nachträglich zu unterrichten.

Im Ergebnis hatte das Bundesverfassungsgericht mehr oder weniger ausdrücklich akzeptiert, dass in bestimmten Fällen von Gewährleistungsübernahmen ein Gremium des Bundestages nur nachträglich informiert werden musste.[52] Die Regelung im neu gefassten § 3 Abs. 3 StabMechG, dass statt dieser nachträglichen Information des Haushaltsausschusses eine vorherige Zustimmung des Neunergremiums stattzufinden habe, kann man deshalb als eine Erweiterung der Beteiligungsrechte des Bundestages verstehen. So wollte das Bundesverfassungsgericht seinen kurzen Hinweis auf die „in Satz 3 genannten Fälle" dann aber doch nicht verstanden wissen.

3.4 Das Urteil vom 19.6.2012

Gegenstand des Urteils vom 19.6.2012[53] war die Unterrichtungspflicht der Bundesregierung aus Art. 23 Abs. 2 Satz 2 GG. Die Bundestagsfraktion Bündnis 90/Die Grünen rügte mit einem Organstreitantrag, die Bundesregierung habe den Deutschen Bundestag in seinem Recht aus dieser Vorschrift verletzt, indem sie ihm zwei Dokumente, die sich auf die Einrichtung des ESM bezogen, nicht übermittelte. Gerügt wurde außerdem, dass die Bundesregierung den Bundestag nicht vorab über die am 4.2.2011 öffentlich vorgestellte Initiative für den Beschluss eines Paktes für Wettbewerbsfähigkeit unterrichtet hat.[54]

Auch diese Entscheidung gehört in den Zusammenhang der Krisenbekämpfung. Die Mitgliedstaaten ergriffen nämlich nicht nur die bereits erwähnten Maßnahmen der akuten Nothilfe für Griechenland und einige andere Staaten (Portugal, Irland, Zypern), sondern verfolgten auch das Ziel, die Krise und ihre Ursachen dauerhaft zu bewältigen. In diesen Zusammenhang gehört der ESM, ein dauerhafter Krisenbewältigungsmechanismus in Form einer neuen internationalen Finanzinstitution mit eigener Rechtspersönlichkeit,[55] der auf der Grundlage des zwischen den Mitgliedstaaten der Eurozone geschlossenen Vertrags zur Errichtung des Europäischen Stabilitätsmechanismus (ESMV)[56] entstand.[57] Auch die zunächst als

---

[52] Zu diesem Vortrag BVerfG, 2 BvE 8/11 (Urteil vom 28.2.2012) – *Beteiligungsrechte Bundestag EFSF* (in BVerfGE 130, 318 [338 f.]).

[53] Zu diesem Urteil: Graf von Kielmansegg 2012, S. 654.

[54] BVerfG, 2 BvE 4/11 (Urt. v. 19.6.2012) – *Euro-Plus-Pakt* (in BVerfGE 131, 152 [153 f.]).

[55] Näher dazu Häde 2014, Rn. 8 ff.

[56] Vgl. das Gesetz zu dem Vertrag vom 2. Februar 2012 zur Einrichtung des ESM vom 13.9.2012, BGBl. II S. 981.

[57] Kritisch dazu Weber 2011, S. 938, der meint, der Weg in die Transferunion sei damit vorgezeichnet.

„Pakt für Wettbewerbsfähigkeit" bezeichnete, später „Euro-Plus-Pakt" genannte Vereinbarung zwischen den Mitgliedstaaten des Euro-Währungsgebiets[58] dient dazu, strukturelle Probleme anzugehen, die mit für diese Krise verantwortlich sind.

So unterschiedlich beide Vorgänge inhaltlich auch etwa hinsichtlich ihrer rechtlichen Verbindlichkeit sind, ist ihnen doch gemein, dass sie außerhalb des rechtlichen Rahmens der Europäischen Union stehen. Der ESM-Vertrag ist ein völkerrechtlicher Vertrag zwischen den Mitgliedstaaten mit Euro-Währung. Auch beim Euro-Plus-Pakt handelt es sich um eine Vereinbarung zwischen Mitgliedstaaten, die bewusst nicht innerhalb des EU-Rahmens vorgingen.[59] Daher war umstritten, ob Art. 23 GG auf solche völkerrechtlichen Maßnahmen im Umkreis der EU überhaupt anwendbar ist. Das Bundesverfassungsgericht entschied, dass auch der ESM-Vertrag und der Euro-Plus-Pakt den Angelegenheiten der Europäischen Union i. S. v. Art. 23 Abs. 2 Satz 1 GG zuzuordnen sind.[60] Erst daraus ergab sich dann, dass für diese Vereinbarungen auch die Unterrichtungsverpflichtung aus Art. 23 Abs. 2 Satz 2 GG gilt, die deutlich weiter geht als entsprechende Informationspflichten im Zusammenhang mit sonstigen völkerrechtlichen Vereinbarungen.

3.5 Das Urteil vom 12.9.2012

Zahlreiche Verfassungsbeschwerden und ein Organstreitantrag der Bundestagsfraktion Die Linke aus dem Jahr 2012 wandten sich erneut gegen Maßnahmen im Zusammenhang mit der Eurokrise. Der dauerhafte Krisenbewältigungsmechanismus ESM beruhte zwar auf einem völkerrechtlichen Vertrag, sollte aber auch durch eine Ergänzung des Art. 136 AEUV um einen neuen Abs. 3 im Unionsrecht abgesichert werden.[61] Darüber hinaus einigten sich die meisten EU-Mitgliedstaaten am 2.3.2012 auf den Vertrag über Stabilität, Koordinierung und Steuerung in der Wirtschafts- und Währungsunion (VSKS oder Fiskalvertrag).[62] Die deutsche Umsetzungs- und Begleitgesetzgebung[63] war Gegenstand der Verfassungsbeschwerden und des Organstreitantrags.

[58] Zur Entstehungsgeschichte BVerfG, 2 BvE 4/11 (Urt. v. 19.6.2012) – *Euro-Plus-Pakt* (in BVerfGE 131, 152 [168 ff.]). S. außerdem Obwexer 2012, S. 227 ff.; Ruffert 2011a, S. 1797.

[59] Vgl. Häde, in Kahl, Waldhoff & Walter (2012), Art. 88 Rn. 521.

[60] BVerfG, 2 BvE 4/11 (Urt. v. 19.6.2012) – *Euro-Plus-Pakt* (in BVerfGE 131, 152 [215, 223 f.]).

[61] Gesetz zu dem Beschluss des Europäischen Rates vom 25. März 2011 zur Änderung des Art. 136 des Vertrags über die Arbeitsweise der Europäischen Union hinsichtlich eines Stabilitätsmechanismus für die Mitgliedstaaten, deren Währung der Euro ist, vom 13.9.2012, BGBl. II S. 978.

[62] Gesetz zu dem Vertrag vom 2. März 2012 über Stabilität, Koordinierung und Steuerung in der Wirtschafts- und Währungsunion vom 13.9.2012, BGBl. II S. 1006.

[63] Gesetz zur finanziellen Beteiligung am Europäischen Stabilitätsmechanismus (ESM-Finanzierungsgesetz – ESMFinG) vom 13.9.2012, BGBl. I S. 1918.

3.5.1 Der ESM-Vertrag

Im Vordergrund standen die Angriffe gegen den ESM. Zweck dieser neuen internationalen Organisation ist es, „Finanzmittel zu mobilisieren und ESM-Mitgliedern, die schwerwiegende Finanzierungsprobleme haben oder denen solche Probleme drohen, unter strikten, dem gewählten Finanzhilfeinstrument angemessenen Auflagen eine Stabilitätshilfe bereitzustellen, wenn dies zur Wahrung der Finanzstabilität des Euro-Währungsgebiets insgesamt und seiner Mitgliedstaaten unabdingbar ist" (Art. 3 ESMV). Die Stabilitätshilfe kann insbesondere in Darlehen, aber auch in vorsorglichen Kreditlinien oder anderen Hilfen bestehen. Das maximale Darlehensvolumen des ESM beträgt 500 Mrd. €. Anders als bei der EFSF übernehmen die Mitgliedstaaten nicht nur Gewährleistungen. Vielmehr haben sie den ESM nach Art. 8 Abs. 1 ESMV mit einem Stammkapital in Höhe von 700 Mrd. € ausgestattet. 80 Mrd. € davon waren einzuzahlen, ansonsten handelt es sich um abrufbares Kapital. Am Stammkapital sind die Mitgliedstaaten im Verhältnis ihrer Anteile am Kapital der EZB beteiligt (§ 11 Abs. 1 ESMV). Deutschland trägt deshalb, wie im Anhang I zum ESM-Vertrag festgelegt, rund 27 %, also 190 Mrd. €.

Diese Summen sind so hoch, dass sie Sorgen auslösen können. In dem Verfahren vor dem Bundesverfassungsgericht ging es daher nicht zuletzt darum, ob das Eingehen dieser Verbindlichkeiten mit der haushaltspolitischen Gesamtverantwortung des Deutschen Bundestages vereinbar und letztlich vom Demokratieprinzip, auf das sich die Beschwerdeführer über Art. 38 Abs. 1 Satz 1 GG beriefen, noch gedeckt ist.

3.5.2 Eilrechtsschutz

Sämtliche Verfassungsbeschwerden wurden von Anträgen auf einstweiligen Rechtsschutz begleitet, die sich darauf richteten, „dem Bundespräsidenten bis zur Entscheidung über die jeweilige Hauptsache [zu untersagen], die von Bundestag und Bundesrat am 29. Juni 2012 als Maßnahmen zur Bewältigung der Staatsschuldenkrise im Euro-Währungsgebiet beschlossenen Gesetze auszufertigen und die mit ihnen gebilligten völkerrechtlichen Verträge zu ratifizieren."[64] Dem stand allerdings das Interesse entgegen, die vereinbarten Maßnahmen möglichst bald zur Krisenbewältigung einsetzen zu können. Insbesondere die Errichtung des ESM erschien erforderlich, um eine neuerliche Zuspitzung der fortdauernden Krise zu vermeiden. Von der Hinterlegung der deutschen Ratifizierungsurkunde hing das Inkrafttreten des ESM-Vertrags ab.

Nach der Rechtsprechung des Bundesverfassungsgerichts haben bei der Entscheidung über einstweilige Anordnungen „die Gründe, die für die Verfassungswidrigkeit der angegriffenen Maßnahmen vorgetragen werden, grundsätzlich außer Betracht zu bleiben, es sei denn, die in der Hauptsache begehrte Feststellung oder

[64] BVerfG, 2 BvE 6/12 et al. (Urteil vom 12.9.2012) – *ESM, Fiskalpakt* (in BVerfGE 132, 195 [197]).

der in der Hauptsache gestellte Antrag erwiese sich als von vornherein unzulässig oder offensichtlich unbegründet."[65] Jedenfalls vom Prinzip her erfolgt keine vorweggenommene Prüfung der Erfolgsaussichten in der Hauptsache. Daher ist meist das Ergebnis einer Folgenabwägung maßgeblich. Bei völkerrechtlichen Verträgen dürfte eine solche Abwägung grundsätzlich dafür sprechen, die Ratifizierung auszusetzen, weil ansonsten die Gefahr bestünde, dass ein Vertrag ratifiziert wird und in Kraft tritt, dessen Verfassungswidrigkeit sich u. U. erst im späteren Hauptsacheverfahren herausstellt. Im konkreten Fall hätte eine solche Verzögerung aber gravierende politische und ökonomische Folgen haben können.

Das Bundesverfassungsgericht befand sich daher in einem Dilemma. Es entschied auf Anregung der Bundesregierung,[66] einen Weg zu gehen, der von dem Vorgehen bei ähnlichen Verfassungsbeschwerden, insbesondere von dem im Zusammenhang mit den Anträgen gegen die Verträge von Maastricht und Lissabon abwich. Es stellte nämlich unter Verweis auf das schon länger zurückliegende Vorbild des Verfahrens zum Grundlagenvertrag mit der DDR[67] von 1973 bereits im Eilverfahren eine summarische Prüfung an, „ob die für die Verfassungswidrigkeit des angegriffenen Vertragsgesetzes vorgetragenen Gründe mit einem hohen Grad an Wahrscheinlichkeit erwarten lassen, dass das Bundesverfassungsgericht das Vertragsgesetz für verfassungswidrig erklären wird."[68]

3.5.3 Urteil mit Auflagen

Nach dieser Prüfung lehnte es mit seinem Urteil vom 12.9.2012[69] sämtliche Eilanträge ab, verband diese Entscheidung aber mit der Maßgabe, dass die Ratifikation des ESM-Vertrags nur erfolgen dürfe, wenn zugleich völkerrechtlich sichergestellt werde, dass Art. 8 Abs. 5 Satz 1 ESMV die Höhe der deutschen Zahlungsverpflichtungen tatsächlich auf die Summe von 190.024.800.000 € begrenzt. Ebenfalls sichergestellt werden sollte, dass andere Regelungen (Art. 32 Abs. 5, Art. 34 und Art. 35 Abs. 1 ESMV) „nicht der umfassenden Unterrichtung des Bundestages und des Bundesrates entgegenstehen."[70] Nachdem diese Auflagen durch eine gemeinsame interpretative Erklärung der Vertreter aller Vertragsparteien[71] erfüllt waren, konnten die Verträge ratifiziert werden und in Kraft treten.

[65] BVerfG, 2 BvE 6/12 et al. (Urteil vom 12.9.2012) – *ESM, Fiskalpakt* (in BVerfGE 132, 195 [232 m. w. N.]).
[66] BVerfG, 2 BvE 6/12 et al. (Urteil vom 12.9.2012) – *ESM, Fiskalpakt* (in BVerfGE 132, 195 [227]).
[67] BVerfG, 2 BvQ 1/73 (Beschluss vom 4.6.1973) – *Grundlagenvertrag* (in BVerfGE 35, 193 [196 f.]).
[68] BVerfG, 2 BvE 6/12 et al. (Urteil vom 12.9.2012) – *ESM, Fiskalpakt* (in BVerfGE 132, 195 [233]).
[69] Zu diesem Urteil: Müller-Franken 2012, S. 3161; Pilz 2012, S. 909; Ruffert 2012, S. 1050; Schorkopf 2012, S. 1273; Tomuschat 2012, S. 1431; Ukrow 2012, S. 417; van Ooyen 2012, S. 208.
[70] BVerfG, 2 BvE 6/12 et al. (Urteil vom 12.9.2012) – *ESM, Fiskalpakt* (in BVerfGE 132, 195 [196 f.]).
[71] Der Text findet sich in BGBl. 2012 II S. 1086 f.

3.5.4 Weiterentwicklung der Währungsunion

Inhaltlich erscheint im Hinblick auf dieses Urteil erwähnenswert, dass sich das Bundesverfassungsgericht in seiner Begründung auch zur Weiterentwicklung der Währungsunion positioniert hat. Aufgrund von Äußerungen von Mitgliedern des Zweiten Senats gegenüber der Presse[72] konnte der Eindruck entstehen, dass das Bundesverfassungsgericht kaum Spielraum für Änderungen sah. Umso wichtiger ist der folgende Hinweis im Urteil vom 12.09.2012:

> Die bisherige vertragliche Ausgestaltung der Währungsunion als Stabilitätsgemeinschaft bedeutet indes nicht, dass eine demokratisch legitimierte Änderung in der konkreten Ausgestaltung der unionsrechtlichen Stabilitätsvorgaben von vornherein mit Art. 79 Abs. 3 GG unvereinbar wäre. Nicht jede einzelne Ausprägung dieser Stabilitätsgemeinschaft ist durch die hier allein maßgeblichen Art. 20 Abs. 1 und Abs. 2 in Verbindung mit Art. 79 Abs. 3 GG garantiert.[73]

Das Bundesverfassungsgericht weist an dieser Stelle darauf hin, dass es schon in seinem Maastricht-Urteil ausgesprochen habe,

> dass eine kontinuierliche Fortentwicklung der Währungsunion zur Erfüllung des Stabilitätsauftrags erforderlich werden kann, wenn andernfalls die Konzeption der als Stabilitätsgemeinschaft angelegten Währungsunion verlassen werden würde (vgl. BVerfGE 89, 155 [205]). Wenn sich die Währungsunion mit dem geltenden Integrationsprogramm in ihrer ursprünglichen Struktur nicht verwirklichen lässt, bedarf es erneuter politischer Entscheidungen, wie weiter vorgegangen werden soll (vgl. BVerfGE 89, 155 [207]; 97, 350 [369]). Es ist Sache des Gesetzgebers, darüber zu befinden, wie etwaigen Schwächen der Währungsunion durch eine Änderung des Unionsrechts entgegen gewirkt werden soll.[74]

Auf diese Weise stellt das Bundesverfassungsgericht klar, dass durchaus noch Spielraum für eine verstärkte politische Union zur Ergänzung der Währungsunion besteht.

3.6 Das Urteil vom 18.3.2014

Den vorläufigen Abschluss der Rechtsprechung des Bundesverfassungsgerichts zur Eurokrise bildete das Hauptsacheurteil vom 18.3.2014.[75] Mit dieser Entscheidung wies das Gericht sämtliche Verfassungsbeschwerden und den Organstreitantrag gegen die Zustimmungs- und Begleitgesetze zur Änderung des Art. 136 AEUV, zum ESM-Vertrag und zum Fiskalvertrag zurück.[76]

---

[72] S. dazu Häde 2013, S. 259.
[73] BVerfG, 2 BvE 6/12 et al. (Urteil vom 12.9.2012) – *ESM, Fiskalpakt* (in BVerfGE 132, 195 [244]).
[74] BVerfG, 2 BvE 6/12 et al. (Urteil vom 12.9.2012) – *ESM, Fiskalpakt* (in BVerfGE 132, 195 [244]).
[75] S. dazu Manger-Nestler & Böttner 2014, S. 202.
[76] BVerfG, 2 BvE 6/12 et al. (Urteil vom 18.3.2014) – *ESM, Fiskalpakt* (in NJW 2014, 1505).

3.6.1 Erfüllung der Auflagen

Das Hauptsacheurteil stellte zunächst fest, dass durch die Haftungsbegrenzung nach Art. 8 Abs. 5 ESMV i. V. m. dessen Anhang II „sowie durch die gemeinsame Auslegungserklärung der Vertragsparteien des ESM-Vertrages vom 27. September 2012 (BGBl II S. 1086) und die gleichlautende einseitige Erklärung der Bundesrepublik Deutschland (BGBl II S. 1087) [. . .] hinreichend sichergestellt [ist], dass durch den Vertrag zur Einrichtung des Europäischen Stabilitätsmechanismus keine unbegrenzten Zahlungsverpflichtungen begründet werden.“[77] Da Art. 8 Abs. 5 Satz 1 ESMV dasselbe schon in kaum zu überbietender Deutlichkeit formulierte („Die Haftung eines jeden ESM-Mitglieds bleibt unter allen Umständen auf seinen Anteil am genehmigten Stammkapital zum Ausgabekurs begrenzt.“), erschien eine abweichende Auslegung ohnehin nicht naheliegend. Dennoch hatte das Bundesverfassungsgericht eine solche Auslegung gegen den Wortlaut für möglich gehalten und deshalb im Urteil vom 12.9.2012 die nun für ausreichend erachtete Klarstellung gefordert.[78]

3.6.2 Vorsorge für Kapitalabrufe

Das Urteil vom 18.3.2014 wies zwar alle Verfassungsbeschwerden und den Organstreitantrag als unzulässig oder unbegründet zurück. Das Bundesverfassungsgericht reicherte aber auch diese Entscheidung mit Aufforderungen an die Verfassungsorgane an. So stellte es fest:

> Der Gesetzgeber ist mit Blick auf die Zustimmung zu Artikel 4 Absatz 8 des Vertrages zur Einrichtung des Europäischen Stabilitätsmechanismus verpflichtet, haushaltsrechtlich durchgehend sicherzustellen, dass die Bundesrepublik Deutschland Kapitalabrufen nach dem Vertrag zur Einrichtung des Europäischen Stabilitätsmechanismus fristgerecht und vollständig nachkommen kann.[79]

Damit wandte es sich erneut den schon im Rahmen des Eilverfahrens besonders umstrittenen Bestimmungen zur Möglichkeit von Kapitalabrufen durch den ESM zu. Da der größte Teil des Stammkapitals des ESM nicht eingezahlt werden muss, aber abrufbar ist, sind bei Bedarf u. U. recht kurzfristige Abrufe vorgesehen (Art. 8 ESMV). Zugleich bestimmt Art. 4 Abs. 8 ESMV, dass ein säumiger Mitgliedstaat sein Stimmrecht nicht ausüben darf, bis die Zahlung erfolgt ist. Die Einschätzung, dass der ESM-Vertrag verfassungskonform ist, hat das Bundesverfassungsgericht aber nicht zuletzt darauf gestützt, dass der Deutsche Bundestag in der Lage ist, den deutschen Vertretern in den ESM-Organen vorzugeben, ob sie Maßnahmen des ESM zustimmen oder nicht. Da Deutschland bei allen wesentlichen Entscheidungen über eine Sperrminorität verfügt, entscheidet letztlich der Bundes-

[77] BVerfG, 2 BvE 6/12 et al. (Urteil vom 18.3.2014) – *ESM, Fiskalpakt* (in NJW 2014, 1505 [Ls. 1]).

[78] BVerfG, 2 BvE 6/12 et al. (Urteil vom 12.9.2012) – *ESM, Fiskalpakt* (in BVerfGE 132, 195 [255 f.]).

[79] BVerfG, 2 BvE 6/12 et al. (Urteil vom 18.3.2014) – *ESM, Fiskalpakt* (in NJW 2014, 1505 [Ls. 2]).

tag mit, ob der ESM z. B. Kredite an notleidende Mitgliedstaaten vergeben darf. Auf diese Weise kann er seine haushaltspolitische Gesamtverantwortung wahrnehmen.

Diese Legitimationskette zerbräche, wenn Deutschland in den Gremien des ESM sein Stimmrecht nicht ausüben könnte, falls es Kapitalabrufen nicht rechtzeitig Folge leistete. Das erklärt, warum das Bundesverfassungsgericht so viel Wert darauf legte, dass ein Verlust des Stimmrechtes unbedingt zu vermeiden ist. Deshalb verpflichtete das Gericht die deutschen Verfassungsorgane, „sicherzustellen, dass die gegenwärtig gegebene und verfassungsrechtlich geforderte Vetoposition der Bundesrepublik Deutschland auch unter veränderten Umständen erhalten bleibt“,[80] also etwa dann, wenn sich die Anteile am Kapital und am Stimmrecht aufgrund von Beitritten neuer Mitgliedstaaten ändern.

Die Beschwerdeführer hatten versucht, die Fähigkeit Deutschlands in Frage zu stellen, kurzfristigen Kapitalabrufen nachzukommen. Das Bundesverfassungsgericht folgte dem nicht, sondern stellte fest:

> Es ist derzeit haushaltsrechtlich ausreichend sichergestellt, dass die Bundesrepublik Deutschland sämtlichen für die Anwendung von Art. 4 Abs. 8 ESMV relevanten Zahlungsaufforderungen des Europäischen Stabilitätsmechanismus – bis zur Höhe ihres Anteils am genehmigten Stammkapital (Art. 8 Abs. 5 Satz 1 ESMV) – so rechtzeitig und umfassend nachkommen kann, dass eine Stimmrechtsaussetzung praktisch ausgeschlossen ist.[81]

Damit das auch künftig so bleibt, formulierte das Bundesverfassungsgericht die erwähnte Mahnung zur vorausschauenden Haushaltsplanung in Leitsatz 2 seines Urteils. Das ist einerseits so wichtig, dass es diese Hervorhebung rechtfertigt; andererseits handelt es sich dabei aber auch um eine haushaltspolitische und -rechtliche Selbstverständlichkeit, ist der Haushaltsgesetzgeber nach dem Grundsatz der Vollständigkeit des Haushaltsplans doch stets verpflichtet, alle voraussichtlichen Ausgaben zu berücksichtigen und für ihre Deckung Sorge zu tragen (Art. 110 Abs. 1 Satz 1 GG).[82]

3.7 Das Urteil des EuGH vom 27.11.2012

Die Urteile des Bundesverfassungsgerichts zum ESM und zu der Änderung des Art. 136 AEUV korrespondieren mit der Entscheidung des Gerichtshofs der Europäischen Union vom 27.11.2012 in der Rechtssache *Pringle*.[83]

---

[80] BVerfG, 2 BvE 6/12 et al. (Urteil vom 18.3.2014) – *ESM, Fiskalpakt* (in NJW 2014, 1505 [Ls. 4]).

[81] BVerfG, 2 BvE 6/12 et al. (Urteil vom 18.3.2014) Rn. 204 – *ESM, Fiskalpakt* (in NJW 2014, 1505).

[82] Vgl. auch BVerfG, 2 BvE 6/12 et al. (Urteil vom 18.3.2014) Rn. 210 – *ESM, Fiskalpakt* (in NJW 2014, 1505).

[83] Fall C-370/12, *Thomas Pringle* (EuGH 27.11.2012) (NJW 2013, 29 und EuZW 2013, 100). Zu diesem Urteil: Calliess 2013, S. 97; Epiney 2013, S. 614; Glaser 2013, S. 167; Nettesheim 2013, S. 14; Palmstorfer 2013, S. 215; Thym & Wendel 2012, S. 733; Weiß & Haberkamm 2013, S. 95.

3.7.1 Vereinbarkeit mit dem Unionsrecht

Auf Vorlage des irischen Supreme Court entschied der EuGH, dass der Beschluss 2011/199/EU des Europäischen Rates vom 25.3.2011 zur Änderung des Art. 136 des Vertrags über die Arbeitsweise der Europäischen Union hinsichtlich eines Stabilitätsmechanismus für die Mitgliedstaaten, deren Währung der Euro ist,[84] mit dem Unionsrecht vereinbar sei. Die Vorschriften des Unionsrechts stünden darüber hinaus dem zwischen den Mitgliedstaaten mit Euro-Währung geschlossenen ESM-Vertrag nicht entgegen.

Der EuGH stellte in diesem Zusammenhang fest, dass die Gewährung von Finanzhilfen durch den ESM nicht der Währungspolitik für die Mitgliedstaaten, deren Währung der Euro ist, zuzuordnen sei, für den Art. 3 Abs. 1 Buchst. c AEUV der Union die ausschließliche Zuständigkeit einräumt. Deshalb seien die Mitgliedstaaten grundsätzlich befugt, entsprechende vertragliche Regelungen außerhalb des EU-Rahmens zu vereinbaren.[85] Der Gerichtshof prüfte außerdem, ob das Unionsrecht Bestimmungen enthält, die dem ESM-Vertrag inhaltlich widersprechen könnten. Er ging insoweit auf Art. 2 Abs. 3, 119–121 und 126 AEUV ein. In keiner dieser Vorschriften sah er ein Hindernis für das vertragliche Vorgehen der Mitgliedstaaten.

3.7.2 Art. 125 AEUV

Erwähnt seien hier nur und vor allem die Ausführungen des EuGH zu Art. 125 AEUV, dessen Verletzung nicht nur in diesem Zusammenhang gerade in Deutschland immer wieder behauptet wurde. Interessant ist, dass der Gerichtshof die Vereinbarkeit von Finanzhilfen des ESM mit Art. 125 AEUV durchaus differenziert prüft. So stellt er fest, im Hinblick auf das Ziel des Art. 125 AEUV sicherzustellen, „dass die Mitgliedstaaten auf eine solide Haushaltspolitik achten",[86] sei „davon auszugehen, dass er der Union und den Mitgliedstaaten verbietet, finanziellen Beistand zu leisten, der zu einer Beeinträchtigung des Anreizes für den Empfängermitgliedstaat führen würde, eine solide Haushaltspolitik zu betreiben."[87] Demgegenüber verbiete „es Art. 125 AEUV nicht, dass ein oder mehrere Mitgliedstaaten einem Mitgliedstaat, der für seine eigenen Verbindlichkeiten gegenüber seinen Gläubigern haftbar bleibt, eine Finanzhilfe gewähren, vorausgesetzt, die daran geknüpften Auflagen sind geeignet, ihn zu einer soliden Haushaltspolitik zu bewegen."[88]

[84] ABl. 2011 L 91/1.
[85] Fall C-370/12, *Thomas Pringle* (EuGH 27.11.2012) Rn. 9 ff. (in NJW 2013, 29 und EuZW 2013, 100).
[86] Fall C-370/12, *Thomas Pringle* (EuGH 27.11.2012) Rn. 135 (in NJW 2013, 29 und EuZW 2013, 100).
[87] Fall C-370/12, *Thomas Pringle* (EuGH 27.11.2012) Rn. 136 (in NJW 2013, 29 und EuZW 2013, 100).
[88] Fall C-370/12, *Thomas Pringle* (EuGH 27.11.2012) Rn. 137 (in NJW 2013, 29 und EuZW 2013, 100).

Dieses Anknüpfen an das Ziel der Vorschrift und die Betonung der mit den Finanzhilfen verbundenen Auflagen führt im Ergebnis dazu, dass der EuGH weniger großzügig ist als einige Stimmen in der Literatur, die die Gewährung von Krediten schon von vornherein als nicht tatbestandsmäßig ansehen.[89] Diese leicht strengere Haltung des EuGH und das Einbeziehen des Zwecks von Art. 125 AEUV sind zu begrüßen. Das in der Vorschrift ausgesprochene Verbot darf nicht allein formal auf eine Haftung oder einen Schuldbeitritt im technischen Sinne beschränkt werden, weil damit seine Funktion verfehlt würde. Andererseits liegt unter den in Art. 136 Abs. 3 AEUV und im ESM-Vertrag genannten Voraussetzungen auch kein Verstoß gegen Art. 125 AEUV vor. Diese Vorschrift soll zwar die Haushaltsdisziplin stützen, nicht aber um den Preis der Gefährdung der gemeinsamen Währung. Insoweit ist Art. 125 AEUV zwar grundsätzlich weit auszulegen, sodass er auch freiwillige Hilfen erfasst.[90] In Situationen, in denen die kompromisslose Durchsetzung des Verbots, für Mitgliedstaaten einzutreten, die Euro-Währung gefährden würde, ist die Bestimmung aber teleologisch zu reduzieren. Für diesen Fall enthält Art. 125 AEUV eine Regelungslücke; ihm fehlt die erforderliche Ausnahmeklausel.[91]

4 Resümee und Ausblick

Die fünf Urteile des Bundesverfassungsgerichts und einige zusätzliche Entscheidungen in ihrem Umfeld (insbesondere über Eilanträge oder nicht angenommene Verfassungsbeschwerden)[92] haben grundlegende verfassungsrechtliche Fragen im Zusammenhang mit der Eurokrise geklärt und auf diese Weise Rechtssicherheit geschaffen. Für die Reichweite der Verfassungsbeschwerde gilt das noch nicht. Insbesondere im Hinblick auf die Frage, ob und unter welchen Voraussetzungen in Deutschland künftig jedermann nicht nur Maßnahmen der deutschen Staatsgewalt, sondern unter Hinweis auf Art. 38 Abs. 1 Satz 1 GG auch Sekundärrechtsakte der Europäischen Union angreifen kann, fehlt es bislang an dieser Klarheit. Ob die ausstehende Entscheidung über die Verfassungsbeschwerden gegen Maßnahmen der EZB, die das Bundesverfassungsgericht von den auf den ESM bezogenen Verfahren abgetrennt und zunächst dem EuGH vorgelegt hat,[93] insoweit Klärung bringt, bleibt abzuwarten. Der EuGH hat jedenfalls durch sein Urteil vom 27.11.2012 gezeigt, dass er bereit ist, Bedenken in den Mitgliedstaaten zu berücksichtigen und differenziert zu entscheiden.

[89] Vgl. z. B. Bandilla 2011, Rn. 11; Herrmann 2010, S. 415.
[90] Ebenso z. B. Calliess 2011, S. 260 ff.; Hafke 2010, S. 394 f.; Knopp 2010, S. 1779; Schorkopf 2011S. 339.
[91] S. dazu schon Häde 2010, S. 854 (859 ff.); Häde, in Kahl et al. 2012, Art. 88 Rn. 385 ff. m. w. N.
[92] Vgl. z. B. BVerfG, 2 BvE 8/11 (einstweilige Anordnung vom 27.11.2011) – *Beteiligungsrechte Bundestag EFSF* (in BVerfGE 129, 284).
[93] BVerfG, 2 BvE 13/13 et al. (Vorlagebeschluss vom 14.1.2014) (in BVerfGE 134, 366).

Literatur

Bandilla, R. (2011). Kommentierung von Art. 125 AEUV. In E. Grabitz, M. Hilf, & M. Nettesheim (Hrsg.), *Das Recht der Europäischen Union*. München: C. H. Beck.

Baumgart, J.-K. (2011). Die Zurückweisung der Verfassungsbeschwerden gegen Maßnahmen zur Griechenlandhilfe und zum Euro-Rettungsschirm. *Neue Justiz*, 450–454.

Blanke, H.-J. (2011). The European Economic and Monetary Union – between vulnerability and reform. *International Journal of Public Law and Policy*, *1*(4), 402–433.

Bonke, F. (2010). Die „Causa Griechenland": Rechtmäßigkeit der Krisenhilfen und Möglichkeit des Ausscheidens eines Mitgliedstaates aus der Europäischen Währungsunion. *Zeitschrift für Europarechtliche Studien*, 493–528.

Brück, M., Schalast, C., & Schanz, K.-M. (2010). Finanzkrise letzter Akt: Die deutschen Zustimmungsgesetze zur Griechenlandfinanzhilfe und zum Europäischen Stabilisierungsmechanismus. *Betriebsberater*, 2522–2527.

Calliess, C. (2011). Perspektiven des Euro zwischen Solidarität und Recht – Eine rechtliche Analyse der Griechenlandhilfe und des Rettungsschirms. *Zeitschrift für Europarechtliche Studien*, 213–282.

Calliess, C. (2013). Der ESM zwischen Luxemburg und Karlsruhe. Die Krise der Währungsunion als Bewährungsprobe der Rechtsgemeinschaft. *Neue Zeitschrift für Verwaltungsrecht*, *32*, 97–105.

Calliess, C., & Ruffert, M. (Hrsg.). (1999). *Kommentar zu EU-Vertrag und EG-Vertrag*. Neuwied: Luchterhand.

Dechatre, L. (2011). La décision de Karlsruhe sur le mécanisme européen de stabilité financière: Une validation sous condition et une mise en garde sibylline pour l'avenir. *Cahiers de droit européen*, *47*, 303–344.

Ebner, G. (2011). Ursprünge der Finanzkrise – fremdverschuldete und selbstverschuldete Komponenten. In W. Hummer (Hrsg.), *Die Finanzkrise aus internationaler und österreichischer Sicht* (S. 117–135). Innsbruck: Studienverlag.

Elicker, M., & Heintz, V.-P. (2012). Zum verfassungsrechtlichen Schutz des Geldwertes – Zugleich eine Besprechung der Entscheidung zur Griechenland-Hilfe. *Deutsches Verwaltungsblatt*, 141–144.

Epiney, A. (2013). Die Rechtsprechung des EuGH im Jahr 2012. *Neue Zeitschrift für Verwaltungsrecht*, 614–621.

Giegerich, T. (2011). *The Federal Constitutional Court's Deference to and Boost for Parliament in Euro Crisis Management*. German Yearbook of International Law, *54*, 639–657).

Glaser, A. (2013). Europäischer Gerichtshof. Anmerkung zum Urteil des EuGH, Plenum, vom 27.11.2012 - C-370/12. *Deutsches Verwaltungsblatt*, 167–169.

Götz, A., & Schneider, L. (2012). Das Bundesverfassungsgericht als Ersatzgesetzgeber – Methodische Bemerkungen zu dem Urteil des Bundesverfassungsgerichts vom 07.09.2011 in Sachen Finanzhilfen für Griechenland und Euro-Rettungsschirm. *Deutsches Verwaltungsblatt*, 145–148.

Graf von Kielmansegg, S. (2012). Parlamentarische Informationsrechte in der Euro-Rettung – Anmerkung zum ersten ESM-Urteil des BVerfG vom 19.06.2012. *Europarecht*, *47*, 654–666.

Häde, U. (1998). Zur Rechtmäßigkeit der Entscheidungen über die Europäische Wirtschafts- und Währungsunion. *Juristenzeitung*, *53*, 1088–1095.

Häde, U. (2010). Die europäische Währungsunion in der internationalen Finanzkrise – An den Grenzen europäischer Solidarität? *Europarecht*, *45*, 854–866.

Häde, U. (2011). Rechtsfragen der EU-Rettungsschirme. *Zeitschrift für Gesetzgebung*, *26*, 1–30.

Häde, U. (2012a). Die Europäische Währungsunion in schwerer See: Ist der Euro noch zu retten?. In Th. Giegerich (Hrsg.), *Herausforderungen und Perspektiven der EU* (S. 35–49). Berlin: Duncker & Humblot.

Häde, U. (2012b). *Euro-Rettung zwischen Exekutivprimat und Parlamentsvorbehalt*. Baden-Baden: Nomos.

Häde, U. (2012c). Grenzen bundesverfassungsgerichtlicher Ultra-Vires- und Identitäts-Kontrollen. In M. Pechstein (Hrsg.), *Integrationsverantwortung* (S. 163–174). Baden-Baden: Nomos.

Häde, U. (2013). Das Verständnis des Bundesverfassungsgerichts vom Kompetenzgefüge zwischen der EU und den Mitgliedstaaten. In T. M. J. Möllers, & F.-C. Zeitler (Hrsg.), *Europa als Rechtsgemeinschaft – Währungsunion und Schuldenkrise* (S. 245–259). Tübingen: Mohr Siebeck.

Häde, U. (2014). Der Europäische Stabilitätsmechanismus (ESM). In A. Hatje, & P.-C. Müller-Graff (Hrsg.), *Europäisches Organisations- und Verfassungsrecht* Enzyklopädie Europarecht, (1. Aufl., S. 891–903). Baden-Baden: Nomos.

Hafke, H. C. (2010). Rechtsbruch oder kreative Interpretation? – Fragen zur „Nothilfe" für strauchelnde Euro-Staaten. *Kreditwesen*, 393–397.

Hahn, H. J., & Häde, U. (2010). *Währungsrecht* (2. Aufl.). München: C. H. Beck.

Herrmann, C. (2010). Griechische Tragödie – der währungsverfassungsrechtliche Rahmen für die Rettung, den Austritt oder den Ausschluss von überschuldeten Staaten aus der Eurozone. *Europäische Zeitschrift für Wirtschaftsrecht*, *21*, 413–418.

Hummer, W. (2011). Von der amerikanischen „Subprime-Crisis" (2007) zum permanenten „Europäischen Stabilitätsmechanismus" (2013 ff.). In W. Hummer (Hrsg.), *Die Finanzkrise aus internationaler und österreichischer Sicht* (S. 231–389). Innsbruck: Studienverlag.

Kahl, W., Waldhoff, C., & Walter, C. (Hrsg.). (2012). *Bonner Kommentar zum Grundgesetz (Loseblatt)*. Heidelberg: C.F. Müller.

Knopp, L. (2010). Griechenland-Nothilfe auf dem verfassungsrechtlichen Prüfstand. *Neue Juristische Wochenschrift*, *63*, 1777–1782.

Manger-Nestler, C. (2012). Anmerkung zu BVerfG, Urteil v. 28.2.2012. *Neue Justiz*, 158–159.

Manger-Nestler, C., & Böttner, R. (2014). Anmerkung zu BVerfG, Urteil v. 18.3.2014. *Neue Justiz (NJ)*, 204–206.

Moench, C., & Ruttloff, M. (2012). Verfassungsrechtliche Grenzen für die Delegation parlamentarischer Entscheidungsbefugnisse – Zugleich Besprechung von BVerfG, Urteil vom 28.02.2012, 2 BvE 8/11, „Beteiligungsrechte des Bundestages/EFSF". *Deutsches Verwaltungsblatt*, 1261–1268.

Müller-Franken, S. (2012). Anmerkung zu BVerfG, Urteil v. 12.9.2012. *Neue Juristische Wochenschrift*, *65*, 3161–3162.

Nettesheim, M. (2011). „Euro-Rettung" und Grundgesetz. Verfassungsgerichtliche Vorgaben für den Umbau der Währungsunion. *Europarecht*, *46*, 765–783.

Nettesheim, M. (2013). Europarechtskonformität des Europäischen Stabilitätsmechanismus. *Neue Juristische Wochenschrift*, *66*, 14–16.

Obwexer, W. (2012). Das System der „Europäischen Wirtschaftsregierung" und die Rechtsnatur ihrer Teile: Sixpack – Euro-Plus-Pakt – Europäisches Semester – Rettungsschirm. *Zeitschrift für öffentliches Recht*, *67*, 209–251.

Ohler, C. (2011). Finanzkrisen als Herausforderung der internationalen, europäischen und nationalen Rechtsetzung. *Deutsches Verwaltungsblatt*, 1061–1068.

Pagenkopf, M. (2011). Schirmt das BVerfG vor Rettungsschirmen? *Neue Zeitschrift für Verwaltungsrecht*, *30*, 1473–1480.

Palmstorfer, R. (2013). Indirekter Bailout erlaubt, direkter Bailout verboten – Anmerkung zum Urteil des EuGH v. 27.11.2012, Rs. C-370/12 (Pringle). *Europarecht*, *47*, 215–224.

Pechstein, M. (2012). *Integrationsverantwortung*. Baden-Baden: Nomos.

Pilz, S. (2012). Europa auf dem Weg zur Stabilitätsunion? Der Fiskalvertrag im Lichte der Entscheidung des Bundesverfassungsgerichts. *Die Öffentliche Verwaltung*, 909–916.

Proelß, A. (2011). Zur verfassungsgerichtlichen Kontrolle der Kompetenzmäßigkeit von Maßnahmen der Europäischen Union: Der „ausbrechende Rechtsakt" in der Praxis des BVerfG. *Europarecht*, *45*, 241–263.

Regling, K. (2011). Aufgaben und Herausforderungen der EFSF. *Europäisches Wirtschafts- und Steuerrecht* , 261–265.

Ruffert, M. (2011a). The European Debt Crisis and European Union Law. *Common Market Law Review*, *48*, 1777–1805.

Ruffert, M. (2011b). Die europäische Schuldenkrise vor dem Bundesverfassungsgericht – Anmerkungen zum Urteil vom 7. September 2011. *Europarecht*, *45*, 842–855.

Ruffert, M. (2012). Europarecht und Verfassungsrecht: Verfassungskonformität von ESM-Vertrag und Fiskalpakt, einstweiliger Rechtsschutz. *Juristische Schulung*, 1050–1052.

Schäfers, M. (2014). Schwarze Null. *Frankfurter Allgemeine Zeitung*, (10.9.2014), 1.

Schorkopf, F. (2011). Gestaltung mit Recht. *Archiv des öffentlichen Rechts*, *136*, 323–344.

Schorkopf, F. (2012). „Startet die Maschinen" – Das ESM-Urteil des BVerfG vom 12.9.2012. *Neue Zeitschrift für Verwaltungsrecht*, *31*, 1273–1276.

Schulmeister, S. (2011). Ursachen der großen Krise und ihre Auswirkungen auf die Finanz- und Realwirtschaft. In W. Hummer (Hrsg.), *Die Finanzkrise aus internationaler und österreichischer Sicht* (S. 37–65). Innsbruck: Studienverlag.

Tavlas, G. S. (1993). The 'New' Theory of Optimum Currency Areas. *The World Economy*, *16*(6), 663–685.

Thym, D., & Wendel, M. (2012). Préserver le respect du droit dans la crise: la Cour de justice, le MES et le mythe du déclin de la communauté de droit – arrêt Pringle. *Cahiers de droit européen*, *48*(3), 733–757.

Tomuschat, C. (2012). Anmerkung zum Urteil des BVerfG vom 12.09.2012. *Deutsches Verwaltungsblatt*, 1431–1434.

Ukrow, J. (2012). Ein Rettungsschirm für das BVerfG? – Zum Urteil vom 12. September 2012. *Zeitschrift für Europarechtliche Studien*, 417–444.

van Ooyen, R. C. (2012). „„. . . mehr Demokratie wagen"? Bei der Euro-Rettung entdeckt das Bundesverfassungsgericht die parlamentarische Kontrolle der Außenpolitik. *Recht und Politik*, 208–213.

Weber, A. (1994). Die Wirtschafts- und Währungsunion nach dem Maastricht-Urteil des BVerfG. *Juristenzeitung* , 53–60.

Weber, A. (1995). Der Vertrag von Maastricht vor dem Verfassungsgericht – Einige rechtsvergleichende Anmerkungen zum Urteil des BVerfG vom 10.12.1993. In E. Klein (Hrsg.), *Grundrechte, soziale Ordnung und Verfassungsgerichtsbarkeit, Festschrift für Ernst Benda zum 70. Geburtstag* (S. 421–441). Heidelberg: C.F. Müller.

Weber, A. (2011). Die Reform der Wirtschafts- und Währungsunion in der Finanzkrise. *Europäische Zeitschrift für Wirtschaftsrecht*, *22*, 935–940.

Weber, A. (2012). Die Europäische Union auf dem Wege zur Fiskalunion? *Deutsches Verwaltungsblatt*, 801–806.

Weber, A. (2013). Europa- und völkerrechtliche Elemente der Gewährleistung von Haushaltsdisziplin in der Währungsunion. *Europarecht*, *47*, 375–388.

Weiß, W., & Haberkamm, M. (2013). Der ESM vor dem EuGH – Widersprüchliche Wertungen in Luxemburg und Karlsruhe? *Europäische Zeitschrift für Wirtschaftsrecht*, *24*, 95–99.

Wieland, J. (2012). Die Zukunft Europas – Krise als Chance. *Juristenzeitung*, *67*, 213–219.

General Principles of EU Law as Evidence of the Development of a Common European Legal Thinking: The Example of the Proportionality Principle (from the Italian Perspective)

Diana-Urania Galetta

1 On the General Principles of EU Law

1.1 The Development of General Principles of EU Law

While it is surely questionable whether the reference to "any rule of law" contained in Art. 263.2 TFEU[1] can be considered to be one of the bases for the development of the so-called general principles of EU law, it is conversely certainly the case that the provisions of Art. 340.2 TFEU are considered an essential point of reference in this context. This provision, which remained in essence unchanged in its wording since the Treaty of Rome (Art. 215.2 EEC), states in fact that: "In the case of non-contractual liability, the Union shall, in accordance with the general principles common to the laws of the Member States, make good any damage caused by its institutions or by its servants in the performance of their duties." This provision has been recently restated by Art. 41.3 EUCFR on the right to good administration.

The famous decision in 1957 of the Court of Justice in the case of *Algera* is indeed clear evidence of the fact that the Court has followed, since the very beginning of its case-law, the approach described in Art. 340 TFEU to a point far beyond the specific hypothesis contemplated by it (the non-contractual liability of the EEC). In the well-known case of *Algera* the central topic under discussion was, as a matter of fact, the possibility or not to withdraw an unlawful administrative act issued by a body of the European Coal and Steel Community. The Court of Justice, after declaring that

> "the possibility of withdrawing such measures is a problem of administrative law, which is familiar in the case-law and learned writing of all the countries of the community, but for the solution of which the treaty does not contain any rules" concluded that "unless the Court is to deny justice it is therefore obliged to solve the problem by reference to the

This paper is part of the publications related to project PRIN 2012 (2012SAM3KM) on Codification of EU Administrative Procedures.

[1] According to Art. 263.2 TFEU the CJEU shall have jurisdiction "on grounds of lack of competence, infringement of an essential procedural requirement, infringement of the Treaties or of any rule of law relating to their application".

H.-J. Blanke et al. (eds.), *Common European Legal Thinking*,
DOI 10.1007/978-3-319-19300-7_13

rules acknowledged by the legislation, the learned writing and the case-law of the Member States."[2]

Starting from this first, important ruling, the Court of Justice has been able to develop, over time, an organic body of general principles of EU law, many of which relate to the organisational structure and the activity of administrative bodies.[3]

1.2 Function and Material Sources of General Principles in European Union Law

As occurs in all national legal orders, also in EU legal order the main function of general principles of law has been, from the very beginning, to allow EU judges to fill in the gaps in EU legal order.[4] These gaps occur more often in that legal system than in domestic legal systems, because of the fact that the EU legal order follows the principle of conferral which is now expressly stated in Art. 5.2 TEU.[5]

The principle of conferral – according to its interpretation provided by the Court of Justice and to which even today, despite the express provision of the Treaty, it is necessary to refer to – means that the Union's action is based as much on the competences resulting specifically from the provisions of the Treaty, as on the competences that can be implicitly inferred from these provisions.[6] This corresponds, however, to a basic requirement for all international organisations and, *a fortiori*, for an organisation like the European Union, which exercises "responsabilités de puissance publique" and has the task of attaining objectives.[7]

In addition to this primary function there is also a second, very relevant function of the general principles of EU law which is also typical of national legal orders. The general principles of EU law aim at assisting judges (and public administrations) in the interpretation of written norms whose meaning is uncertain or unclear: this is the reason why such principles also are binding to Member States in the same way as primary law.[8]

In terms of the specific situation characterising general principles of law in the EU system there are, however, at least two important elements of differentiation, if compared with general principles of law within national legal orders.

---

[2] Joined Cases 7/56, 3/57–7/57, *Algera et al. v. Assemblée commune* (ECJ 10 July 1957). See more extensively in the Opinion of AG Lagrange of 14 June 1957.

[3] See Galetta 2013, para 4.

[4] See for all: Adinolfi 1994, p. 521.

[5] According to Art. 5.2 TEU, under the principle of conferral, "the Union shall act only within the limits of the competences conferred upon it by the Member States in the Treaties to attain the objectives set out therein. Competences not conferred upon the Union in the Treaties remain with the Member States".

[6] Case 45/86, *Commission v. Council* (ECJ 26 March 1987).

[7] In this sense Louis and Ronse 2005, p. 17.

[8] Ziller 2014, p. 351.

The first distinguishing feature of the general principles of law in the EU system is their potential source of origin: in the system of EU law a general principle of law can originate, in fact, from a much greater variety of material sources[9] than what normally would be the case for national legal orders.[10]

A general principle of EU law may, firstly, originate from sources of written law: provisions of the Treaties or of secondary legislation, which are regarded by the CJEU as manifestations of general principles. Sometimes the Court of Justice infers general principles of law from the "Treaty system", rather than from a single EU law provision. This is the case for the principles of primacy and of direct effect of EU law; but also for the principle of State liability for damage caused to individuals by breaches of EU law attributable to the State, which has been declared as a principle inherent in the system of treaties since the case of *Francovich*.[11]

A further hypothesis is when the existence of a general principle is inferred by the Court of Justice from the fact that such a principle applies in a certain number of national legal systems. Therefore, the principle is stated by the Court of Justice as a principle common to the laws of the Member States, as occurred, for example, in the above-mentioned *Algera* case.[12]

In this regard it is necessary to point out that the EU Court of Justice has never declared it to be necessary – for a general principle to be considered a general principle of EU law – that the principle concerned should be present in all, or even in most of the legal systems of the Member States.[13] It was in fact, at times, considered sufficient that the principle was present in only one of the systems examined, if it fitted well with achieving the objectives of the Treaties.[14]

Furthermore, the Court may refer to the case-law of the ECHR and consider it to be an expression of a general principle of law. In this regard, however, the Treaty of Lisbon has innovated in the way of an express provision, in Art. 6.3 TEU stating that "[f]undamental rights, as guaranteed by the European Convention for the Protection of Human Rights and Fundamental Freedoms and as they result from the constitutional traditions common to the Member States, shall constitute general principles of the Union's law" (wording taken also in Art. 48.3 EUCFR).

---

[9] On the fundamental distinction between material source and formal source of general principles see Ziller 2014, passim.

[10] See Galetta 2013, para 4.

[11] Joined Cases C 6/90 and C 9/90, *Francovich and Bonifaci* (ECJ 19 November 1991).

[12] Joined Cases 7/56, 3/57–7/57, *Algera et al. v. Assemblée commune* (ECJ 10 July 1957).

[13] See Tesauro 2013, p. 487 et seq.; see also Schwarze 2012, p. 118.

[14] In this regard a necessary point of reference is now Art. 52.4 EUCFR, stating that: "In so far as this Charter recognises fundamental rights as they result from the constitutional traditions common to the Member States, those rights shall be interpreted in harmony with those traditions". The Explanations to the Charter clarify then, in this specific regard, that "[t]he rule of interpretation contained in paragraph 4 has been based on the wording of Article 6, paragraph 3 of the Treaty on European Union and takes due account of the approach to common constitutional traditions followed by the Court of Justice [. . .]. Under that rule, rather than following a rigid approach of 'a lowest common denominator', the Charter rights concerned should be interpreted in a way offering a high standard of protection which is adequate for the law of the Union and in harmony with the common constitutional traditions".

Or, then and again, the Court of Justice refers to the general principles of international law as a material source of EU general principles.[15]

Nevertheless it is not, in my opinion, useful to design a classification of the general principles of EU law on the basis of their material source of origin. Such a classification would be, firstly, purely descriptive, as it would not have any concrete consequence (as we shall see below) as to the status and value of the principle. Secondly, it would be destined to undergo rapid aging, because of the continuous movement of general principles of EU law, from one material source of origin to another. In particular, it occurs very frequently that general principles "extracted" by the Court of Justice from the national laws of Member States, are later codified in primary EU law, or even incorporated into the rules of Treaties, moving in this way from one material source to another. This was for example the case – as we shall see in Sect. 2 – for the principle of proportionality, which is now partially codified in the Treaties.

This movement of general principles from one material source to another does not change their intimate nature, i. e. that of general principles of EU law. The Court of Justice has for example explicitly acknowledged this with regard to the individual's right to an effective remedy before a tribunal, stating that the latter is merely "the reaffirmation of the principle of effective judicial protection, which is a general principle of Community law stemming from the constitutional traditions common to the Member States".[16]

1.3 General Principles of EU Law as "Jurisprudential Norms" and Their Place in the Hierarchy of Sources

A second, very important element of differentiation of the general principles of EU law in relation to the general principles of national law is that – as has authoritatively been stated in academic literature – "[o]nly the Court of Justice is in a position to declare whether a norm has the status of a general principle of law with consequences in positive law. [...] Even if the 'masters of the treaties' enounce that a principle has the value of a general principle of EU law, it remains with the sole CJEU to interpret and apply such a norm, which therefore does not have a higher rank than other general principles of EU law".[17]

Another opinion according to which the recognition by the Court of Justice of a general principle is an important factor, but should not be considered as a *conditio sine qua non* for its existence,[18] is not convincing, as it is based on a kind of a "soft-

[15] See Hofmann et al. 2011, p. 75.

[16] Case C-221/09, *AJD Tuna* (ECJ 17 March 2011), where it refers also to its previous case-law in Case C-432/05, *Unibet* (ECJ 13 March 2007) para 37, and in Joined Cases C-402/05 P and C-415/05 P, *Kadi* (ECJ 3 September 2008) para 335.

[17] Ziller 2014, p. 351. In this same vein see already the remarks of Capotorti 1983, p. 409.

[18] See for example Prechal and de Leeuw 2008, p. 203.

law approach", which is contrary also to the fundamental need for transparency of the legal system of EU law.[19]

To express this in another way, it corresponds in my opinion to the most basic need for transparency of the legal system of EU law that until there is a ruling by the Court of Justice, which states that a certain principle should be regarded as a general principle of EU law, neither the textual data (in the case of a general principle contained in a rule of written law, even a rule contained in the Treaties), nor the statements of doctrine, Advocates General of the Court of Justice or of national Courts in this regard will ascertain the existence of the principle. This means that, in as far as general principles of EU law are concerned, the Court of Justice is the one holding the monopoly on their identification (i. e. creation within the EU legal order) and only its jurisprudence has therefore an effect on the validity and applicability of a principle as general principle of EU law.

This statement of principle is not without consequences, as it has at least two important concrete aftermaths. First of all, it allows us to avoid the difficult exercise of trying to provide a notion of general principle of EU law,[20] since, as a consequence of the above-stated premise, a principle can be considered to be a general principle of EU law only if and when the CJEU has qualified it as such. Secondly, the monopolistic role assigned to the CJEU in order to declare the existence of a principle as a general principle of EU law has, in turn, relevant implications with respect to the rank held by these principles in the system of sources of EU law.

As to this second point, the problem is that there is no specific provision in the EU Treaties, even after Lisbon, on the issue of the hierarchical position of general principles in the system of sources of EU law. On the contrary, Art. 6.3 TEU – as we have already recalled in Sect. 1.2 – states now that fundamental rights resulting from the ECHR and from the constitutional traditions of Member States constitute general principles of EU law,[21] without answering the underlying question of their hierarchical position. This second question must therefore be analysed in the wider context of the overall hierarchy of sources in EU law; this is a topic that has been thoroughly addressed in a recent paper,[22] so that we just need, here, to recall the paper and discuss its reasoning.

The central point of its reasoning is that, in as far as in the EU Treaties there is no provision similar to Art. 38 of the ICJ Statute (according to which case-law is one of the sources of international law, albeit of a secondary rank), in order to clarify the position of case-law in the hierarchy of sources of EU law one has to take into account the ways in which case-law can be overridden. In doing so the overall picture that emerges is that no other EU institution than the Court itself has the power to reform one of its own judgments. Only the Member States, in their capacity of "Masters of the treaties", have the power to amend primary law in order

[19] See in this regard the interesting remarks of Hofmann and Mihaescu 2013, p. 73.
[20] See Gaja 2007, p. 370, who provides a thorough overview as well as an extensive bibliography on the topic. See also the remarks of Albrecht Weber on this point, expressed in a paper translated by myself and published in an Italian Law Journal in 1992: Weber 1992, p. 397.
[21] As for the consequences of this see Tesauro 2013, p. 493.
[22] Ziller 2014, p. 334.

to counter the case-law of the CJEU, provided that the revision procedure of Art. 48 TEU is being followed. "Such a possibility of countering case-law by the 'pouvoir constituant' implies that, as a source of EU law, the CJEU's case law is ranked below primary law. Vice versa, the possibility for the CJEU to annul secondary law and the acts by which EU international agreements are concluded means that case-law is ranked above EU secondary law and EU international agreements."[23] This is true, of course, also for the case-law of the Court of Justice identifying general principles of EU law, regardless of the material source of the principles themselves.[24]

The ranking of the general principles of EU law above secondary EU law has two important consequences in practice. First, the incompatibility of a provision of secondary EU law with a general principle of law is one of the most important reasons for the annulment of acts of secondary legislation by the Court of Justice.

Secondly, as general principles of law are used by the CJEU also in order to interpret the provisions of primary law, such principles are binding to Member States in the same way as primary law.

The principle of proportionality is the typical example of a general principle of EU law, whose application by the EU Court of Justice led constantly to the two above-stated consequences. The infringement of this principle is one of the most frequent reasons for annulment of acts of secondary EU legislation,[25] and, at the same time, the Court of Justice has repeatedly stated that this principle should be applied as a criterion of interpretation by the authorities of the Member States when they implement EU law in their own national legal orders.[26]

1.4 A Further Consequence, Specific to the Italian Legal Order

To sum up, regardless of its material source of origin (the law of a Member State, international law, a provision of the Treaties, a provision of secondary legislation, etc.), once it is turned into a general principle of EU law by the Court of Justice, a principle prevails – as a case-law source of law and by virtue of the peculiar position of the Court of Justice in the system of the EU Treaties – both on secondary EU legislation, and on the national laws of the Member States, when they are acting within the scope of EU law. As the ECJ has expressly made clear already with the

[23] Ziller 2014, p. 345 et seq.

[24] Ziller 2014, p. 349.

[25] See most recently Joined Cases C-293/12 and C-594/12, *Digital Rights Ireland* (ECJ 8 April 2014), which states the invalidity of Parliament/Council Directive 2006/24/EC *on the retention of data generated or processed in connection with the provision of publicly available electronic communications services or of public communications networks*, O.J. L 105/54 (2006), because "by adopting Directive 2006/24, the EU legislature has exceeded the limits imposed by compliance with the principle of proportionality" (para 69).

[26] See for example, already more than 30 years ago, Case 258/78, *Nungesser v. Commission* (ECJ 8 June 1982).

judgment *Eridania* of 1979, "general principles of Community law [...] are binding on all authorities entrusted with the implementation of Community provisions".[27]

With specific regard to the Italian legal system there is, however, a further consequence arising from the fact that a principle was qualified by the EU Court of Justice as a general principle of EU law. By virtue of the provision contained in Art. 1.1 of Law 241/90 on Administrative Procedure,[28] as amended in 2005 by Law No. 15,[29] "Administrative activity pursues the goals determined by the law and is governed by criteria of economic feasibility, effectiveness, impartiality, publicity and transparency as provided for by this Law and by other provisions governing specific administrative procedures, as well as by the principles of Community law".[30]

So the fact that a principle has been identified and qualified by the EU Court of Justice as a general principle of EU law implies that this will apply in any case in our national system, irrespective of whether or not the administrative activity falls within the scope of EU law. EU principles are indeed identified as "governing principles" under the above-mentioned provision, with regard to all the administrative activities, within or without the scope of EU law.[31]

This interpretation of Art. 1 of Law 241/90 has been expressly confirmed in various decisions of our administrative Courts, which have stated that "the public administration is [...] required to give priority to the application of the general principles derived from EU law and consistently applied by the European Court of Justice", and that "such principles, in accordance with Article 1 of Law no. 241 of 1990, not only apply directly in our system [...], but must inform in any case the behaviour of the public administration".[32]

2 On the Principle of Proportionality

2.1 Introduction

The second part of this contribution will be devoted to the analysis of the principle of proportionality, and that for at least two reasons. The first reason is a personal one and concerns the jubilee, *Albrecht Weber*, to which this paper is of course dedicated. It is, in fact, during a short summer stay as a visiting researcher at the University

[27] Case 230/78, *Eridania* (ECJ 27 September 1979) para 31.

[28] Law No. 241 of 11 August 1990 setting new rules concerning administrative procedure and the right of access to documents, published in the Official Gazette of 18 August 1990, No. 192.

[29] Law No. 15 of 11 February 2005 that introduces Amendments to Law No. 241 of 7 August 1990, relating to general rules on administrative action, published in the Official Gazette of 21 February 2005, No. 42.

[30] Author's translation. Original wording: "L'attività amministrativa persegue i fini determinati dalla legge ed è retta da criteri di economicità, di efficacia, di imparzialità, di pubblicità e di trasparenza secondo le modalità previste dalla presente legge e dalle altre disposizioni che disciplinano singoli procedimenti, nonché dai princìpi dell'ordinamento comunitario."

[31] See Galetta 2010, p. 601.

[32] Italian Council of State (Consiglio di Stato), sec. V, 19 June 2009 n. 4035 (author's translation).

of Osnabrück – almost 25 years ago now – that I first got in touch with *A. Weber* and his chair. And it was already in 1992, during my LL.M. study at the University of Osnabrück (with *A. Weber* as my LL.M. tutor), that I started my research on the principle of proportionality, to which I devoted so many years at the beginning of my career as an academic.[33]

The second reason why I have chosen to focus now on the principle of proportionality is, conversely, a purely scientific one: the principle of proportionality is probably the best example of what happens when general principles are at first "extracted" by the Court of Justice from the national laws of the Member States,[34] and later on not only codified in primary EU law, but even incorporated (even though, in this case, only partially) into rules of the Treaties, moving this way from one material source to another (above Sect. 1.2).

2.2 A Quick Overview of the Original Material Source: The German Principle of Proportionality

To effectively summarise the intrinsic meaning of the principle of proportionality *Fritz Fleiner*, already in 1912, used the well-known and highly effective formula, according to which "[t]he police should not shoot sparrows with cannons",[35] meaning that all limitations on individual freedom must never exceed the measure of what appears absolutely necessary to achieve the goal of public interest pursued by the public authority. Later on, in 1955, *Rupprecht von Krauss* explained that we fall within the scope of the principle of proportionality only when the existence of a public interest is clear and when that public interest can be satisfied only by means of an invasive intervention in someone's private sphere.[36]

In German law the principle of proportionality is the union of three different elements which were brought together by the German Constitutional Court, already with the well-known *Apothekenurteil* of 1958,[37] within the principle of proportionality in the broad sense. The three elements are: suitability/appropriateness (*Geeignetheit*), necessity (*Erforderlichkeit*), and proportionality in the narrow sense (*Verhältnismäßigkeit im engeren Sinne*).

[33] My first publication on the topic was already in 1993 (Galetta 1993), but my book on the principle of proportionality was published only in 1998 (Galetta 1998a).

[34] Schwarze 2005, p. 694; Groussot 2006, passim.

[35] Author's translation. More precisely *Fleiner* stated: "Des Amtes der Polizei ist es, die 'nötigen Anstalten' zu treffen zur Erhaltung der öffentlichen Sicherheit und Ordnung. Die Beschränkung der individuellen Freiheit darf nie das absolut erforderliche Maß überschreiten. Die Polizei soll nicht mit Kanonen auf Spatzen schießen." See Fleiner 1912, p. 354.

[36] "Erst mit der Feststellung, daß ein Interesse der Allgemeinheit besteht, welches nur durch einen Eingriff in die private Sphäre befriedigt werden kann, gelangt man in den Anwendungsbereich des Grundsatzes." von Krauss 1955, p. 94.

[37] German Federal Constitutional Court (Bundesverfassungsgericht), 1 BvR 596/56 (judgment of 11 June 1958) in BVerfGE 7, 377.

As to the parameter of suitability/appropriateness, according to a well-known decision of the German Constitutional Court, a means used by the public authority appears suitable/appropriate to achieve a goal "when with its help the desired result can significantly be promoted ".[38] The prediction made must be justified and reasonable.[39] However, in this regard it suffices that there is an abstract possibility that the target is met.[40] The Federal Constitutional Court refers, as a matter of fact, to an *ex-ante* judgment, in relation to which the possibility of an error in the assessment of the possible future development of events is also recognised.

As for the second element of proportionality in the broad sense, which is identified as the "necessity" of the means used,[41] it must be understood in the sense that there is no other means that would be equally effective but less intrusive.[42]

Proportionality analysis is about means and end. So the third parameter, characteristic of the German model of the principle of proportionality, is proportionality in the narrow sense. Compliance with this third parameter implies, in brief, that the measure adopted by the public authorities must not be such as placing an excessive burden on the person concerned and to be, therefore, intolerable.[43] And it is no coincidence that proportionality in the narrow sense established itself as a criterion of evaluation only after 1945; it was in fact the experience of the totalitarian Nazi State that led to the idea among German lawyers that it is always necessary to compare the means used and its burdening effect and the objective pursued by a governmental measure, and weigh them in their respective importance.[44]

[38] German Federal Constitutional Court (Bundesverfassungsgericht), 1 BvR 52, 665, 667, 754/66 (judgment of 16 March 1971) in BVerfGE 30, 292, author's translation.

[39] Stein 1978, p. 279.

[40] "Die abstrakte Möglichkeit der Zweckerreichung genügt". German Federal Constitutional Court (Bundesverfassungsgericht), 1 BvR 52, 665, 667, 754/66 (judgment of 16 March 1971) in BVerfGE 30, 292.

[41] In German literature are used as synonyms, depending on the case: *Notwendigkeit; Subsidiarität; Grundsatz des schonendsten Mittels; Grundsatz des geringstmöglichen Eingriffs; Grundsatz des geringsten Mittels*. See Jakobs 1985, p. 102.

[42] See, among others, in the case-law of the German Federal Constitutional Court (Bundesverfassungsgericht): 2 BvR 326/69 et al. (judgment of 3 September 1971) in BVerfGE 30, 250; 1 BvL 5/64 (judgment of 18 December 1968) in BVerfGE 25, 1; 1 BvR 286/65 et al. (judgment of 10 May 1972) in BVerfGE 33, 171.

[43] See, among others, in the case-law of the German Federal Constitutional Court (Bundesverfassungsgericht): 1 BvR 596/56 (judgment of 11 June 1958) in BVerfGE 7, 377; 1 BvF 1/58 (judgment of 10 July 1958) in BVerfGE 8, 71; 1 BvR 71/57 (judgment of 16 June 1959) in BVerfGE 9, 338; 1 BvR 216/51 (judgment of 23 March 1960) in BVerfGE 11, 30; 1 BvL 44/55 (judgment of 17 July 1961) in BVerfGE 13, 97; 1 BvR 758/57 (judgment of 29 November 1961) in BVerfGE 13, 230; 1 BvR 760/57 (judgment of 29 November 1961) in BVerfGE 13, 237; 1 BvR 665/62 (judgment of 18 December 1962) in BVerfGE 15, 223; 1 BvL 15/62 (judgment of 16 February 1965) in BVerfGE 18, 353; 1 BvL 17/63 (judgment of 14 February 1967) in BVerfGE 21, 150; 1 BvR 175/66 (judgment of 29 November 1967) in BVerfGE 22, 380; 1 BvR 638/64 et al. (judgment 18 December 1968) in BVerfGE 24, 367; 1 BvL 3/66 (judgment of 15 January 1969) in BVerfGE 25, 112; 1 BvR 30/66 (judgment of 14 October 1969) in BVerfGE 27, 88; 1 BvR 307/68 (judgment of 14 October 1970) in BVerfGE 29, 221.

[44] See Stein 1978, p. 281; Lerche 1961, p. 129.

This assessment may lead to the conclusion that, at the end of the day, the public authorities have to refrain from adopting the decision at stake, whose content was involved in the comparative assessment between means and end, even if it has already passed the test concerning its suitability/appropriateness and its necessity.[45] The comparative assessment concerning the application of the parameter of proportionality in the strict sense is necessarily influenced, in its final outcome, by the burdening effect which the concrete measure would cause in the private sphere. As has long been stated in the case-law of the German Federal Constitutional Court, the more intense the burdening effect in the legal sphere of the individual, the more significant will have to be the general interest that with this intervention the State intends to pursue.[46]

As far as the scope of application of the principle in German law is concerned, it remains in close connection with fundamental rights: its origin – as already mentioned – does in fact go back to police law. Currently, however, its scope extends, more generally, to all measures implemented by the public administration in the exercise of its functions; therefore, to the entire sphere of action of administrative law.

In particular, within its scope fall, first of all, all administrative acts adopted in the context of the so-called *Eingriffsverwaltung*, i. e. those administrative acts that produce negative consequences for the addressee. The scope of the principle extends, however, even to those administrative acts that fall within the concept of *Leistungsverwaltung*, which consists essentially of administrative acts with a positive impact on the addressee and whose definition is to be found in § 48.1 of the German Law on Administrative Procedure (Verwaltungsverfahrensgezetz – VwVfG).

In German Law the principle of proportionality is applied also in criminal law[47] but not, vice versa, in the field of private law, except when it concerns the so-called *Drittwirkung*, the horizontal effect between individuals, of basic rights.[48]

2.3 The Principle of Proportionality in EU Law

As for EU law the principle of proportionality was first described by the well-known statement of *Lord Diplock*, according to which "[t]he principle of Proportionality prohibits the use of a steam hammer to crack a nut if a nutcracker would do it".[49] Like the already mentioned formula used by *Fleiner* (Sect. 2.2), even here the ref-

---

[45] See Ipsen 1995, p. 103, para 293.
[46] German Federal Constitutional Court (Bundesverfassungsgericht), 1 BvR 216/51 (judgment of 23 March 1960) in BVerfGE 11, 30.
[47] See Stern 1984, p. 863.
[48] German Federal Constitutional Court (Bundesverfassungsgericht), 1 BvR 435/68 (judgment of 24 February 1971) in BVerfGE 30, 173.
[49] Cited in: Weekly Law Reports, 1983, p. 155.

erence is only to the requirement of necessity that, in fact, played a central role in the evolution concerning the principle of proportionality within EU law.[50]

The Court of Justice made clear reference to this principle from the very beginning of its case-law[51] and gradually established it as an essential tool for judicial review, applied to almost all areas of EU law.[52] It is, as a matter of fact, the general principle "most frequently invoked before and examined by the Court".[53]

As is well known, with the Maastricht Treaty of 1992 the principle of proportionality – even if only in as far as the requirement of necessity is concerned – was placed directly inside the Treaty, in Art. 3b (later to become Art. 5 EC), which referred, however, solely to the activity of the Community institutions.

Later on, with the Treaty of Amsterdam of 1997, a Protocol on the application of the principles of subsidiarity and proportionality was adopted whose first provision repeats, essentially, the one contained in Art 3b, with the addition, however, that "each institution shall ensure that the principle of subsidiarity is complied with".[54] The mentioned Protocol was later incorporated, though with some modifications, into the Treaty of Lisbon (now Protocol No. 2), which has also replaced the old Art. 5 EC with Art. 5 TEU.[55]

Last but not least, a very relevant reference to the proportionality principle is found, now, in Art. 52.1 EUCFR, according to which "[a]ny limitation on the exercise of the rights and freedoms recognised by this Charter must be provided for by law and respect the essence of those rights and freedoms. Subject to the principle of proportionality, limitations may be made only if they are necessary and genuinely meet objectives of general interest recognised by the Union or the need to protect the rights and freedoms of others."

To sum up, there can therefore be no doubt that, in EU law, the principle of proportionality always has a binding effect. But, depending on the case, it imposes itself either in its capacity as a general principle of EU law, recognised as such by the Court of Justice, or it imposes itself because of its express mention in the Treaty or in the EU Charter of fundamental rights (which now, according to Art. 6.1 TEU, has the same legal value as the Treaties). The consequence is, in both cases, its hierarchical superiority with respect to the rules of secondary EU law.

Nevertheless, even when the principle of proportionality is expressly referred to in provisions of secondary EU law (regulations and sectorial directives that define each time its scope of application), this does not change its higher ranking, as a

[50] Further in Galetta 2012, para 4.

[51] Case 8/55, *Fédération Charbonnière* (ECJ 16 July 1956); Joined Cases 5-11, 13-15/62, *Società acciaierie San Michele* (ECJ 14 December 1962), p. 917; Case 18/63, *Schmitz* (ECJ 19 March 1964) p. 175.

[52] See among others, Case 11/70, *Internationale Handelsgesellschaft* (ECJ 17 December 1970) p. 1125; Case 5/73, *Balkan-Import-Export* (ECJ 24 October 1973) p. 1091.

[53] von Danwitz 2012, p. 367.

[54] Art. 1 of Protocol No. 2 on the application of the principles of subsidiarity and proportionality.

[55] Art. 5.4 TEU reads: "Under the principle of proportionality, the content and form of Union action shall not exceed what is necessary to achieve the objectives of the Treaties. The institutions of the Union shall apply the principle of proportionality as laid down in the Protocol on the application of the principles of subsidiarity and proportionality."

general law principle, with respect to the rules of secondary EU law. The central point to keep in mind in this regard is in fact – as I already explained at the end of Sect. 1.2 – that the moving of general principles from one material source to another does not change their intimate nature of being general principles of EU law. And it does not change, therefore, their position of hierarchical superiority with respect to the rules of secondary EU law.

2.4 From the German Model to a Model of Judicial Review of the Proportionality Characteristic of European Union Law

If there can be no doubt that the ECJ has, at first, extracted the principle of proportionality from German law,[56] it is equally certain that the "three steps" model of judicial review (suitability/appropriateness, necessity, and proportionality in the strict sense) proposed by the German doctrine[57] has never found full acceptance in the jurisprudence of the EU judges. The well-known *Schräder* judgment of 1989[58] – which was read by the German doctrine as the acceptance of the German model of a three-step review of proportionality, so well described in German literature, though seldom applied as such also by the German Courts – has not in fact been followed by a generalised application of a three-phase proportionality test (three-step analysis) by EU judges.

Indeed, in the context of EU law the three elements of suitability/appropriateness, necessity, and proportionality in the strict sense are rarely considered jointly by the judges of the European Union and the proportionality test performed by the EU judges is limited, in most cases, to the two elements of suitability/appropriateness and necessity.[59] Furthermore, the proportionality test is often performed by altering the sequence of application of its constituent elements.[60]

Beyond the (maybe) only formal differences, one condition that certainly contributes – and significantly, in my opinion – to reducing the possible "substantial" coincidence of the EU principle of proportionality with the German one is the well-known divergence of approaches between EU law and German public law, in as far as the system of judicial protection is concerned. The protection provided by the German Courts is subjectively oriented: it thus takes especially into account the intensity with which the measure exerted negative effects on the legal rights of the

[56] Galetta 1998a, p. 6; see also von Danwitz 2012, p. 367.

[57] Among many others see von Krauss 1955; Hirschberg 1981; Dechsling 1989.

[58] Case C-265/87, *Schräder* (ECJ 11 July 1989).

[59] See von Danwitz 2012, p. 373.

[60] See, for example, Case C-357/88, *Hopermann* (ECJ 2 May 1990). Although it must be said that, in this last respect, it is almost certainly a difference more apparent than real and due essentially to the differences in style and manner of drafting the judgments by the German Courts and by the EU Courts. While the first, in fact, have the habit of providing extensive and full reasons in judgments, the latter usually report only the essential steps of their legal reasoning. In this vein: Kischel 2000, p. 391.

appellant.[61] Conversely, the judicial protection accorded by EU judges takes essentially into account the interests actually at stake,[62] without giving a decisive weight to the extent of the sacrifice suffered by the individual.

The EU proportionality test consists, therefore, of operating a balance of the interests concretely at stake meaning the EU review of proportionality approaches the "bilan avantages-coûts" test applied in the case-law of the French *Conseil d'Etat*, which aims at allowing a rather comprehensive assessment and comparative evaluation of advantages and disadvantages produced by the measure adopted by a governmental authority, according to a multipolar conception of the interests involved.[63]

The last element I have highlighted provides, in my opinion, an explanation also for the fact – for which the doctrine often complains[64] – that it is difficult to identify, *a priori*, a stable rule concerning the intensity of the judicial review of proportionality operated by the EU judges. In fact, on the one hand, and despite the incredible amount of case-law where the possible infringement of the principle is evoked, cases in which EU judges have actually declared legislative or administrative measures taken by EU authorities unlawful for breach of the principle of proportionality are very rare.[65] On the other hand, there seems to be a rather different attitude of the EU judges with regard to the review of acts adopted by Member State authorities where, as a matter of fact, the review of proportionality is usually more intense and strict.[66]

Nevertheless, the differences in intensity of the judicial review of the principle of proportionality only in appearance depends on the fact that the measure to be reviewed is adopted, in one case by an EU authority, and in another case by a Member State authority. This is not the central point in the reasoning of the EU judges when reviewing proportionality, in my opinion. The differences in judicial review of proportionality seem to me to be rather related to the different weight attributed, from time to time, to the interests actually at stake. The concrete weight of the interests on the scale of the principle of proportionality depends also on the nature of the measure concerned. It is one thing when an EU judge has to review measures that aim to contribute "in the process of European integration undertaken with the establishment of the European Communities",[67] regardless of whether they are

[61] Kahl 2011, p. 42.

[62] As underlined already by Emiliou 1996, p. 171.

[63] Clearly in this vein Case 45/85, *Verband der Sachversicherer* (ECJ 27 January 1987) para 61. See also, more recently, Joined Cases T-37/07 and T-323/07, *Mohamed El Morabit* (CFI 2 September 2009), Case T-390/08, *Bank Melli Iran* (CFI 14 October 2009).

[64] See, for detailed references, von Danwitz 2012, p. 374, note 33.

[65] Nevertheless, see the recent (and noteworthy) decision in Joined Cases C-293/12 and C-594/12, *Digital Rights Ireland Ltd.* (ECJ 8 April 2014), declaring invalid Parliament/Council Directive 2006/24/EC on the retention of data on the ground that by adopting the Directive the EU legislature "has exceeded the limits imposed by compliance with the principle of proportionality" (para 69).

[66] This is reported, most recently, also by von Danwitz 2012, p. 378.

[67] Recital 1 of the Preamble to the TEU.

undertaken by an EU or by a Member State authority.[68] It is another case entirely, when the measure to be reviewed under the principle of proportionality is adopted in derogation to fundamental freedoms or to fundamental rights guaranteed by the EU Treaties. In such cases the principle of proportionality is reviewed, of course, more rigorously. The EU Court of Justice places strict requirements on the need for a national measure restricting fundamental freedoms,[69] as the need for the EU to guarantee the respect of such fundamental freedoms is the very reason of existence of the European Union itself.[70] Nevertheless, after the entry into force of the Lisbon Treaty, the Court of Justice places similar strict requirements and similar rigorousness on the proportionality test with regard to measures adopted by EU authorities in derogation to fundamental rights and freedoms recognised by the EU Charter.[71]

Finally, there is another factor that must be taken into account in assessing the case-law of the EU judges on the principle of proportionality, but that is rarely taken into account by the doctrine that criticises the Court of Luxembourg's jurisprudence. I am referring to the procedure in the context of which the review of proportionality is made, because it is one thing if the judicial review of proportionality is made in the context of an infringement procedure under Art. 258 TFEU (ex-Art. 226 EC) and another thing if it is made in the context of a preliminary reference procedure under Art. 267 TFEU (ex-Art. 234 EC). The different procedural context in either case will, in fact, deeply condition the Court's approach and the accuracy with which it will perform, in practice, its review of proportionality. It is because of the "division of labour between the ECJ and National Courts"[72] that in case of a preliminary reference procedure the ECJ will limit itself, in principle, to providing the national Court only with the benchmarks for its decision. In this second case it is in fact for the national Court to assess the concrete compatibility of national measures with the principle of proportionality as regards the individual case.[73]

[68] So clearly Case 29/77, *Roquette* (ECJ 20 October 1977) para 19 and 20; Joined Cases C-296/93 and C-307/93, *France and Ireland v. Commission* (ECJ 29 February 1996).

[69] See, for example, Case C-65/05, *Commission v. Greece* (ECJ 21 October 2006). Of the same opinion on this point von Danwitz 2012, p. 378.

[70] See Papadopoulou 1996, p. 252; von Danwitz 2003, p. 400.

[71] See the already quoted decision in Joined Cases C-293/12 and C-594/12, *Digital Rights Ireland Ltd.* (ECJ 8 April 2014), where the protection of the fundamental rights to privacy and to the protection of personal data were at stake.

[72] von Danwitz 2012, p. 379.

[73] See Case C-34–36/95, *De Agostini* (ECJ 9 July 1997) para 52; Joined Cases C-96/03 and C-97/03, *Tempelman* (ECJ 10 March 2005) para 49. More recently, Case C-182/08, *Glaxo Wellcome* (ECJ 17 September 2009) para 102.

2.5 *Feed-Back Effect and Spill-Over Effect of the EU Principle of Proportionality*

The development of an autonomous principle of proportionality in the context of EU law has not failed to have effects also on the German legal order, the one from which the principle had originally been extracted by the ECJ. This phenomenon has been described as the *feed-back effect* and it emerges clearly from an analysis of the case-law before German Courts from the beginning of 1990.[74]

A different phenomenon is the one described in academic literature as the *spill-over effect*.[75] This means, conversely, the legal systems of the Member States that, starting from a situation in which the principle of proportionality was unknown as such to their national legal tradition, then started to apply the EU principle of proportionality extensively, which means, also for cases without any direct relevance to EU law.[76]

A typical example of this phenomenon is what happened in the Italian legal order, as I will explain in detail in the next section. But Italy is not the only case. Another very relevant case of the spill-over effect of the principle of proportionality is the English legal order.[77] Gradually, the principle has made its own way into the case-law of the British domestic Courts, winning over initial resistance and favour for the national "blanket test" of Wednesbury.[78] To make a long story short, despite the influential exhortations of *Lord Diplock* to welcome the proportionality test,[79] in 1991 *Lord Ackner* still stated that there was no basis upon which the proportionality doctrine applied by the European Courts could be followed by the domestic Courts.[80] Nevertheless, after the incorporation of the ECHR into domestic law, with the adoption of the Human Rights Act of 1998,[81] the principle of proportionality has largely been employed by British domestic Courts, though perhaps not with the enthusiasm showed by *Lord Slynn*,[82] who suggested, in *Alconbury*, that proportionality should be a part of domestic law.[83]

---

[74] See for example German Federal Administrative Court (Bundesverwaltungsgericht), 11 C 35.92 (judgment of 27 January 1993) in *Deutsches Verwaltungsblatt* 1993, p. 613; 4 A 29.95 (judgment of 23 August 1996) in *Deutsches Verwaltungsblatt* 1997, p. 68; 7 VR 2.96 (judgment of 30 August 1996) in *Neue Zeitschrift für Verwaltungsrecht*, 1997 p. 496.

[75] See, among the most recent contributions, Groussot 2006.

[76] See Galetta 1998a, p. 5.

[77] See Galetta 2005, p. 554; Ligugnana 2011, p. 447.

[78] Birkinshaw 2014, para 8.02. See also Craig 1999, p. 95; Jowell and Birkinshaw 1996, p. 282; Hoffmann 1991, p. 114.

[79] See 1985 GCHQ decision of the House of Lords, *Council for Civil Service Unions v. Minister of State for the Civil Service*, Law Reports – *AC*, 1985, p. 374 (410).

[80] House of Lords, *Regina v. Secretary of State for the Home Department ex parte Brind* (7 February 1991).

[81] See Clayton 2001, p. 504.

[82] Birkinshaw 2014, p. 372.

[83] See House of Lords, *Alconbury* (9 May 2001). See also House of Lords, *Regina v. Shayler* (21 March 2002) para 75; House of Lords, *Wrexham County Borough Council v. Berry et al.* (22 May 2003); House of Lords, *Regina v. British Broadcasting Corporation ex parte Prolife*

2.6 The Principle of Proportionality in Italian Administrative Law

The phenomenon of spill-over of the EU principle of proportionality has manifested itself in Italian administrative law since the first half of the 1990s. More precisely, its first applications to domestic case-law without any direct relevance to EU law have manifested themselves in the jurisprudence of some Italian Administrative Courts of first instance.[84]

Before the introduction by case-law of the Italian Administrative Courts of first instance of the principle of proportionality, the only criterion for judicial review that conceptually approached the proportionality test applied in ECJ case-law was the test of reasonableness, used both by the Constitutional Court and by the Administrative Courts.[85] The vagueness that characterises the test of reasonableness[86] in its concrete applications[87] makes it however possible to state that, until the first half of the 1990s, there was within the Italian system of judicial review no test based on elements whose application could actually fulfil the requirements of judicial review on the action of the public authorities imposed by the application of the principle of proportionality of EU law.[88] In fact, the problems linked to the extreme "volatility" of the principle of reasonableness had crystallised over time, creating shortages in terms of legal protection afforded to the private holder of secondary interests conflicting with the primary interest pursued by the public administration with its administrative action. So it is also for this reason that, in the early 1990s, alongside the traditional test of reasonableness, a true test of proportionality has progressively been incorporated into the jurisprudence of Italian domestic administrative Courts.

To conclude, the gradual application of the principle of proportionality by the Italian domestic Courts (also for cases without any direct relevance to EU law) is, as a matter of fact, the result of two different factors: on the one hand it is the result (both direct and indirect) of its widespread application by the Courts of the European Union but, on the other hand, it is a consequence of the widespread dissatisfaction, often expressed by the administrative Courts themselves, with respect to the results to which the use of the traditional test of reasonableness led.

We must add to this that in the context of Italian administrative law, since the mid-1990s, the principle of proportionality has also been accepted in the language

---

Alliance (15 May 2003). For further references see Birkinshaw 2014, para 8.03; see further Brady 2012, p. 5.

[84] Regional Administrative Court of Lombardy (TAR Lombardia), sec. III (2 April 1997), n. 354; sec. III (16 April 1998), n. 752. See for further references Galetta 1998a, p. 231..

[85] See for details Galetta 1998b, p. 299.

[86] The principle of reasonableness is characterised by a large degree of uncertainty and its "evanescence" has been widely reported in the academic literature. See, for example, Ledda 1983, p. 438; more recently Astone 2012, p. 371.

[87] See, among many others, Italian Council of State (*Consiglio di Stato*), plenary (6 February 1993), n. 3; sec. V (18 February 1992), n. 132; sec. V (4 November 1992), n. 1168; sec. IV (1 July 1992), n. 654; sec. V (3 April 1990), n. 326; sec. V (3 April 1990), n. 332.

[88] See Galetta 1998a, p. 221.

of our national legislator. As a matter of fact we find pieces of legislation expressly referring to this principle not only, as is logical, when they are intended to transpose EU directives,[89] but also with regard to rules of national law without any direct relevance to EU law.[90]

In terms of the relevance of the principles of EU law for Italian domestic law the first five years of the millennium were crucial. First of all, in 2001 a constitutional revision allowed for the introduction of a specific reference to Community law in the Italian Constitution. With an amendment to the original provisions of Art. 117.1 of the Italian Constitution an important modification was in fact introduced, according to which "Legislative powers shall be vested in the State and the Regions in compliance with the Constitution and with the constraints deriving from EU legislation and international obligations".[91] Then – as mentioned in Sect. 1.4 – in 2005 a modification was introduced in Art. 1.1 of Law 241/90 on Administrative Procedure. According to this modification, Art. 1 now contains an express reference to "Community principles", identified as principles which shall govern all administrative activity.

Among these "Community principles" there is, without any doubt, the principle of proportionality, too. This means that all administrative activity must now be guided by the principle of proportionality, as it applies not only in as far as the judicial review on the misuse of administrative discretion is concerned. Rather, it is also a constant benchmark for public administration,[92] whose acts must, therefore, constantly be "proportionate" to the objective pursued. And this proportion can only be determined through the identification and comparison of all the competing inter-

---

[89] See, for example, Legislative Decree no. 163 of 12 April 2006 (Code of public contracts for works, services and supplies, transposing Directives 2004/17/EC and 2004/18/EC) which, in various provisions, makes specific reference to the principle of proportionality. See also Art. 1 of Legislative Decree no. 32 of 28 February 2008 (Amendments and additions to Legislative Decree no. 30 of 6 February 2007, implementing Directive 2004/38/EC on the right of EU citizens and their family members to move and reside freely within the territory of the Member States), which specifies how "removal orders shall be adopted in accordance with the principle of proportionality".

[90] Examples of the second type are, in particular: Legislative Decree No. 152 of 3 April 2006 (Environmental Regulations), whose Art. 178.3 expressly refers to the principle of proportionality among the principles to be fulfilled in the business of waste management. Law No. 448 of 4 August 2006 (Conversion into law, with amendments, of Decree-Law No. 223 of 4 July 2006, containing urgent measures for the economic and social recovery, containment and rationalisation of public expenditures and contrast of tax evasion), whose Art. 12.2, entitled "Provisions relating to the movement of vehicles and municipal and inter-municipal transport" expressly refers to the principle of proportionality among the principles to be fulfilled in order to protect the right to health, environmental health and safety of road users and the public interest to an adequate urban mobility. See also Law No. 262 of 28 December 2005 (Provisions for the protection of savings and regulation of financial markets), which makes express reference to the principle of proportionality in Art. 23 as a principle that the competent authorities must take into account when defining the content of acts of administrative rule making.

[91] See on this constitutional reform and its implications Galetta 2001, p. 293.

[92] In a recent and important Italian study on the principle of proportionality the reference was, as a matter of fact, to "the method of proportion as a general category of law". See Cognetti 2010, p. 15 (author's translation).

ests at stake (both public and private ones). This implies, concretely, a duty for the public administration to constantly investigate all possible alternatives to its action in order to always seek the most appropriate solution not only to pursue the goal of satisfying the primary public interest, but also in order to minimise the sacrifice imposed on conflicting private interests in view of the criterion of necessity.

As the criterion of proportionality in the narrow sense is then concerned, its application means, in my opinion, that the constant goal of public administration must be that of reaching an adequate balance of all interests at stake, through a balanced sacrifice of interests other than the primary public interest. Conversely, their sacrifice may not be justified, and the administrative action contrary to the principle of proportionality. This means that, before taking any decisions, the public authority shall investigate each case carefully and impartially, taking into consideration all the relevant factors. In view of a "proportionate" administrative action, such an investigation has therefore to be considered as a central step in each administrative procedure and the need of an adequate investigation related to the principle of proportionality contrasts, in my opinion, sharply with the pressure to adopt administrative acts as quickly and inexpensively as possible, which is so characteristic of the direction given by the Italian legislator to administrative activity over the past two decades.

3 Conclusions

In the opinion of eminent exponents of the French doctrine the EU judge – just like the French administrative judge – should continue referring to general principles of law beyond written sources, in so far as there are specific virtues in the flexibilities recognised in general principles of law when compared to written sources of law.[93] In my opinion there can be no doubt about this, as the reference to general principles of law allows EU judges to fill in the many gaps in the EU legal system which are inevitably related to the fact that the EU still follows the principle of conferral (Sect. 1.2). The reference to the laws of the Member States and, more generally, to rules "other" than the EU written sources is indeed a necessary part of the way of operating and even of "being" of the EU Courts.[94] This constant reference of the EU judge, in its judicial review activity, to rules "other" than those contained in EU written sources has transformed it into the most powerful vehicle of diffusion of principles and models of administrative action.[95]

[93] See Sauvé and Polge 2010, p. 743: "Les vertus reconnues aux principes généraux du droit, en particulier leur souplesse de consécration comme d' application et leur capacité à étendre la protection des individus au-delà des prévisions écrites, devraient conduire la Cour de justice des Communautés européenne a continué de recourir à cette technique."

[94] Tesauro 2013, p. 487.

[95] See on this point especially Schwarze 2010; see also Schwarze 2012, p. 117.

Proof of this is the principle of proportionality, which has rapidly extended its influence within national legal orders of the Member States, also for cases without any direct relevance to EU law. The best evidence of this phenomenon is, therefore, the domestic jurisprudence of the Italian Administrative Courts in the years after 2000, which is characterised by wide application of the principle of proportionality, both by the Regional Administrative Courts and by the Council of State.[96]

The principle of proportionality has substantially enriched the instruments of judicial review available to the administrative judge in order to operate his/her control on the legality of administrative action. It is, in fact, thanks to this tool that the administrative judge can now effectively review administrative measures with respect to whether the exercise of public power is revealed to be exuberant in relation to the minimum required for the public administration to pursue the public interest entrusted to its care.[97] Through its three-step test, the principle of proportionality allows the judge a closer consideration of the use made by the administration of its own power of appreciation. If compared to other tools traditionally used by the Italian administrative judges in order to ascertain a misuse of power on the part of the public administration (such as the principle of reasonableness), the principle of proportionally has proven itself a more powerful tool,[98] which therefore substantially enriches the instruments available to the administrative judge in order to verify a proper use of power by the public administration.[99]

References

Adinolfi, A. (1994). I principi generali nella giurisprudenza comunitaria e la loro influenza sugli ordinamenti degli Stati membri. *Rivista italiana di diritto pubblico comunitario*, *3*(4), 521–578.

Astone, F. (2012). Il principio di proporzionalità. In M. Renna, & F. Saitta (Eds.), *Studi sui principi del diritto amministrativo* (pp. 371–387). Milan: Giuffré.

[96] See Regional Administrative Court of Tuscany (TAR Toscana), Firenze, sec. I (6 March 2001), n. 381. See also, in the same vein, Regional Administrative Court of Puglia (TAR Puglia), Bari, sec. II (7 June 2001), n. 2405; Regional Administrative Court of Puglia (TAR Puglia), sec. II (24 October 2006), n. 3783; Regional Administrative Court of Lazio (TAR Lazio), sec. III (2 February 2007), n. 777; Regional Administrative Court of Trentino Alto Adige (TRGA), Trento (29 January 2009), n. 41; Regional Administrative Court of Lazio (TAR Lazio), sec. I (8 May 2009), n. 4994; Regional Administrative Court of Lazio (TAR Lazio), sec. I (8 May 2009), n. 5005; as well as Italian Council of State (Consiglio di Stato), sec. IV (1 October 2004), n. 6410; sec. VI (17 April 2007), n. 1746; sec. VI (8 February 2008), n. 424; sec. VI (10 March 2009), n. 1420; sec. VI (11 January 2010), n. 19.

[97] See especially Regional Administrative Court of Puglia (TAR Puglia), Bari, sec. II (24 October 2006), n. 3783; Italian Council of State (Consiglio di Stato), sec. V (29 December 2009), n. 8939.

[98] See already Galetta 1998a, p. 205.

[99] A very good example of what I mean is Italian Council of State (Consiglio di Stato), sec. VI (27 June 2007), n. 3704.

Brady, A. D. P. (2012). *Proportionality and Deference under the UK Human Rights Act*. Cambridge: Cambridge University Press.

Capotorti, F. (1983). Il diritto comunitario non scritto. *Diritto comunitario e degli scambi internazionali, 3*(4), 403–430.

Clayton, R. (2001). Regaining a Sense of Proportion: The Human Rights Act and the Proportionality Principle. *European Human Rights Law Review*, 504–525.

Cognetti, S. (2010). *Principio di proporzionalità. Profili di teoria generale e di analisi sistematica*. Torino: Giappichelli.

Craig, P. (1999). Unreasonableness and Proportionality in UK Law. In E. Ellis (Ed.), *The principle of proportionality in the Laws of Europe* (pp. 85–106). Oxford: Hart Publishing.

von Danwitz, T. (2003). Der Grundsatz der Verhältnismäßigkeit im Gemeinschaftsrecht. *Europäisches Wirtschafts- & Steuerrecht*, 393–402.

von Danwitz, T. (2012). Thoughts on Proportionality and Coherence in the Jurisprudence of the Court of Justice. In P. Cardonnell, & A. Rosas (Eds.), *Constitutionalising the EU Judicial System. Essays in Honour of Pernilla Lindh* (pp. 367–382). Oxford: Hart Publishing.

Dechsling, R. (1989). *Das Verhältnismäßigkeitsgebot. Eine Bestandsaufnahme der Literatur zur Verhältnismäßigkeit staatlichen Handelns*. Munich: Vahlen.

Emiliou, N. (1996). *The principle of Proportionality in European Law*. London: Kluwer Law.

Fleiner, F. (1912). *Institutionen des Deutschen Verwaltungsrechts*. Tübingen: Mohr.

Gaja, G. (2007). General Principles of Law. In R. Wolfrum (Ed.), *The Max Planck Encyclopedia of Public International Law* (pp. 370–378). Oxford: OUP.

Galetta, D.-U. (1993). Il principio di proporzionalità nella giurisprudenza comunitaria (nota a Corte di giustizia delle Comunità europee, Corte plenaria, sentenza 18.05.1993, in causa C-126/91). *Rivista italiana di diritto pubblico comunitario, 4*, 837–851.

Galetta, D. U. (1998a). *Principio di proporzionalità e sindacato giurisdizionale nel diritto amministrativo*. Milan: Giuffré.

Galetta, D. U. (1998b). El principio de proporcionalidad en el Derecho Público italiano. *Cuadernos de Derecho Publico, 5*, 299–329.

Galetta, D. U. (2001). La previsione di cui all'articolo 3, comma 1, cpv. 1, della legge di revisione del titolo V della costituzione come definitivo superamento della teoria dualista degli ordinamenti. In P. Bilancia, & E.De Marco (Eds.), *Problemi del federalismo* (pp. 293–310). Milan: Giuffré.

Galetta, D. U. (2005). Il principio di proporzionalità comunitario e il suo effetto di "spill over" negli ordinamenti nazionali. *Nuove autonomie*, 541–557.

Galetta, D. U. (2010). Diritto ad una buona amministrazione e ruolo del nostro giudice amministrativo dopo l'entrata in vigore del Trattato di Lisbona. *Diritto Amministrativo, 3*, 601–638.

Galetta, D. U. (2012). Il principio di proporzionalità. In M. Renna, & F. Saitta (Eds.), *Studi sui principi del diritto amministrativo* (pp. 389–412). Milan: Giuffré.

Galetta, D. U. (2013). Le fonti (del diritto amministrativo europeo). In M. P. Chiti (Ed.), *Diritto amministrativo europeo* (pp. 89–141). Milan: Giuffré.

Groussot, X. (2006). *Creation, Development and Impact of the General Principles of Community Law: Towards a jus commune europaeum?* The Netherlands: Europa Law Publishing.

Hirschberg, L. (1981). *Der Grundsatz der Verhältnismäßigkeit*. Göttingen: Schwartz.

Hoffmann, L. (1991). The Influence of the European Principle of Proportionality upon UK Law. In E. Ellis (Ed.), *The principle of proportionality in the Laws of Europe* (pp. 107–114). Oxford: Hart Publishing.

Hofmann, H. C. H., & Mihaescu, B. C. (2013). The Relation between the Charter's Fundamental Rights and the Unwritten General Principles of EU Law: Good Administration as the Test Case. *European Constitutional Law*, *9*, 73–101.

Hofmann, H. C. H., Rowe, G. C., & Türk, A. H. (2011). *Administrative Law and Policy of the European Union*. Oxford: OUP.

Ipsen, J. (1995). *Niedersächsisches Gefahrenabwehrrecht*. Stuttgart: Boorberg Verlag.

Jakobs, M. (1985). *Der Grundsatz der Verhältnismäßigkeit*. Cologne: Carl Heymanns Verlag.

Jowell, J., & Birkinshaw, P. (1996). English Report. In J. Schwarze (Ed.), *Das Verwaltungsrecht unter europäischem Einfluß* (pp. 723–737). Baden-Baden: Nomos.

Kahl, W. (2011). Die Europäisierung des subjektiven öffentlichen Rechts. *Juristische Arbeitsblätter*, 41–48.

Kischel, U. (2000). Die Kontrolle der Verhältnismäßigkeit durch den Europäischen Gerichtshof. *Europarecht*, 380–402.

von Krauss, R. (1955). *Der Grundsatz der Verhältnismäßigkeit in seiner Bedeutung für die Notwendigkeit des Mittels im Verwaltungsrecht*. Hamburg: Appell.

Ledda, F. (1983). Potere, tecnica e sindacato giurisdizionale sull'amministrazione pubblica. *Il diritto processuale amministrativo*, *4*, 371–445.

Lerche, P. (1961). *Übermaß und Verfassungsrecht. Zur Bindung des Gesetzgebers an die Grundsätze der Verhältnismäßigkeit und Erforderlichkeit*. Cologne: Carl Heymanns Verlag.

Ligugnana, G. (2011). Principio di proporzionalità e integrazione tra ordinamenti. Il caso inglese e italiano. *Rivista italiana di diritto pubblico comunitario*, 447–481.

Louis, J. V., & Ronse, Th. (2005). *L'ordre juridique de l'Union europeéne*. Basel: Helbing & Lichtenhahn.

Papadopoulou, R. E. (1996). *Principes Généraux du Droit et Droit Communautaire*. Brussels: Bruylant.

Prechal, S., & de Leeuw, M. (2008). Transparency: A General Principle of EU Law?. In U. Bernitz et al. (Ed.), *General Principles of EC Law in a Process of Development* (pp. 201–242). London: Kluwer Law International.

Sauvé, M., & Polge, N. (2010). Les principes généraux du droit en droit interne et en droit communautaire. Liens croisées pour un avenir commun. In J.-C. Masclet, H. Ruiz Fabri, C. Boutayeb, & S. Rodrigues (Eds.), *L'Union européenne: Union de droit, Union des Droits. Mélanges en l'honneur de Philippe Manin* (pp. 727–750). Paris: Pedone.

Schwarze, J. (2005). *Europäisches Verwaltungsrecht. Entstehung und Entwicklung im Rahmen der Europäischen Gemeinschaft* (2nd edn.). Baden-Baden: Nomos.

Schwarze, J. (2010). *Zukunftsaussichten für das Europäische Öffentliche Recht*. Baden-Baden: Nomos.

Schwarze, J. (2012). Zwischen Tradition und Zukunft: die Rolle allgemeiner Rechtsgrundsätze im Recht der Europäischen Union. In J. Schwarze (Ed.), *Europarecht. Strukturen, Dimensionen und Wandlungen des Rechts der Europäischen Union. Augewählte Beiträge* (pp. 114–127). Baden-Baden: Nomos.

Stein, T. (1978). *Der Grundsatz der Verhältnismäßigkeit*. Deutsche öffentlich-rechtliche Landesberichte zum X. internationalen Kongreß für Rechtsvergleichung in Budapest. (pp. 273–288). Tübingen: Mohr.

Stern, K. (1984). *Das Staatsrecht der Bundesrepublik Deutschland. Grundbegriffe und Grundlagen des Staatsrechts, Strukturprinzipien der Verfassung* (2nd edn.). Munich: Beck.

Tesauro, G. (2013). Alcune riflessioni sul ruolo della corte di giustizia nell'evoluzione dell'Unione europea. *Il Diritto dell'Unione Europea*, *3*, 483–498.

Weber, A. (1992). Il diritto amministrativo procedimentale nell'ordinamento della Comunità Europea. *Rivista italiana di diritto pubblico comunitario*, *2*, 393–412.

Ziller, J. (2014). Hierarchy of Sources and General Principles in European Union Law. In U. Becker et al. (Ed.), *Verfassung und Verwaltung in Europa. Festschrift für Jürgen Schwarze zum 70. Geburtstag* (pp. 334–352). Baden-Baden: Nomos.

The Democratic Deficit in the (Economic) Governance of the European Union

Hermann-Josef Blanke and Robert Böttner

Is a strengthening of legitimation at the national level, rather than the European Parliament, what we have to do to overcome the deficit? Or is there a continuous gap in that very legitimation? [. . .] In fact, the Union is on the path of progressive democratisation, but it is still a long way to go. (Massimo Vari)[1]

1 Democracy as a Guiding Principle of Reform for the European Union

Common European legal thinking reveals itself especially in the existence of a common European constitutional law (*Ius Publicum Europaeum Commune*[2]).[3] It denotes the ensemble of individual constitutional principles that are – written or unwritten – a common heritage of the various national constitutional states. With regard to the principle of democracy, the Jubilee, when conducting a comparative law study, found there to be a "relatively heterogeneous picture" among national constitutions, even though one can find "core elements of a 'common European democracy'". According to *Albrecht Weber*, these include periodic elections of State institutions, legally ensured responsibility of public decision making with the possibility for parliamentary minorities to gain power as well as representative party democracy.[4] Besides these elements, the equal participation of all governed in the exercise of public authority and constitutional freedoms is a mainstay of European "self-government".[5] The decision for parliamentary democracy in the European

[1] Vari 2013, p. 708, 719 (our translation).

[2] This Latin terminology, that connects *Hagemeier*'s traditional term of "Ius Publicum Europaeum" with the attribute "Commune", is traced back by von Bogdandy and Hinghofer-Szalkay 2013, p. 217, to *Ch. Starck*. In doing so, they refer to Martínez-Soria 2004.

[3] Cf. Weigand 2008; Häberle 1995.

[4] Weber 2010, Chap. 7, para 20. Well before the inclusion of the idea of a political union in the Treaties, the ECJ recognised the principle of democracy as a general legal principle; see Case 138/79, *Roquette Frères* (ECJ 29.10.1980) para 33.

[5] Calliess 2005a, p. 283.

H.-J. Blanke et al. (eds.), *Common European Legal Thinking*,
DOI 10.1007/978-3-319-19300-7_14

Union (Art. 10.1 TEU) is thus predetermined by the Member States' forms of government and therefore belongs to the fundamental laws (*Grundgesetze*), to the "essentials"[6] of the EU's constitutional compound.[7]

Common constitutional law is derived mainly from the national constitutions, from the London Treaty establishing the Council of Europe (1949) and the Convention for the Protection of Human Rights and Fundamental Freedoms (1950) as its most prestigious outcome, and from Community law (Union law), which is often spurred by the pioneering decisions of the European Court of Justice.[8] Constitutional and European law as well as their special disciplines play a crucial role in the development of a common European constitutional law. At the interface between national constitutional law and European law the mutual "permeability" of both orders (*entgrenzter Verfassungsstaat*)[9] calls for reflection particularly with regard to the principle of democracy. It contains a cultural juridical commonality that next to human rights is well anchored in the minds of Europeans. The constitutions of all Member States are based on the structural principle of democracy. The Union itself acknowledges the core concept of democracy as a general European constitutional tradition[10] (Art. 3.1 of the Additional Protocol to the ECHR[11]) by placing corresponding structural requirements on the Member States and declaring their factual continued existence to be a precondition for participating in the European integration (Art. 2 TEU). Nonetheless, it was only with the Treaty of Lisbon that the democratic principles of the Union (Art. 10–12 TEU) have been incorporated into primary law on the basis of Union citizenship (Art. 9 TEU).

In the Union's political reality, however, the question of the necessary level of democratic legitimation of supranational policy determines the debate in political science and in constitutional and European law. The crisis of the Union has given new impetus to this debate, especially in view of the dominance of the European Council and the marginal role of the European Parliament in crisis management.

This deficiency is based in the Union's current order of competence, i. e. the lack of competence on the part of the Union for economic policy, which is merely economic policy *coordination* (Art. 5.1 and 119.1 TFEU). This coordination remains in the realm of the Member States, namely their executive branches. This entails a lack of participation by the Union's legislative branch, including both the European Parliament and national Parliaments. A reform of the Union thus needs to tackle the substantive distribution of competences between the Union and the Member States, including the stronger involvement of parliamentary bodies in the legislative procedure. Moreover, the democratic foundation needs to be enhanced. Decisions which

---

[6] See the contribution by *Cruz Villalón* in this volume.

[7] Cf. also Sommermann 2005, p. 208 et seq.; with a critical view Nettesheim 2005, p. 188, who opinioned the EU's constitutional system "designed by an uninspired hand". Benz 2005, p. 261 holds that a presidential rather than a parliamentary system is more suitable for the EU.

[8] Häberle 1991, p. 262, 264.

[9] Sommermann 1998, p. 404 et seqq.; Sommermann 2005, p. 192 et seqq.; on the whole see Wendel 2011.

[10] Cf. BVerfG, 2 BvE 2/08 et al. (judgment of 30 June 2009) para 271 – Lisbon.

[11] BGBl 2002 II p. 1072.

are taken to consolidate EMU require democratic legitimacy and accountability. This contribution seeks to analyse the way in which democratic legitimation can be provided for the EU's economic and monetary governance.

From a long-term perspective, the involvement of the European Parliament is vital to convey democratic legitimation and to build a genuine EMU. This needs a fundamental reform of the Treaties including a uniform electoral system for EP elections or at least a uniform electoral procedure (cf. Art. 223.1 TFEU), although *equal* voting rights for all EU citizens do not seem to be an achievable aim.[12] Only such a system – by replacing the 1976 "Direct Elections Act"[13] – would lead to legitimation by the European Parliament that exceeds its current role of merely "complementing"[14] the democratic legitimation provided by national Parliaments and governments. Such a harmonised framework would lead to a politisation of negotiations in Parliament. Moreover, it would enhance public debate in the Union at large due to a genuine confrontation of government and an opposition at the European level with respect to the political preferences of national societies.[15]

Conversely, a uniform electoral procedure can be set up only when the peoples of the Union and their national political parties regard themselves as *one* political community.[16] In view of the obvious and manifest deficiency of the sense of a common European identity, the role of national Parliaments cannot be neglected. Their

[12] See Art. 14.3 TEU, which does not include the principle of *equality* of elections. Cf. Schorkopf, in Kahl et al. (2011), Art. 23 GG para 44; Hölscheidt, in Grabitz et al. (2011), Art. 223 AEUV para 47.

[13] Cf. Act Concerning the Election of the Members of the European Parliament by Direct Universal Suffrage, Council Decision of 20 September 1976 (Federal Law Gazette 1977 II p. 733); last amended by the Council Decision of 22 June 2002 and 23 September 2002 (Federal Law Gazette 2003 II p. 810; 2004 II p. 520).

[14] Cf. BVerfG 2 BvR 2134, 2159/92 (judgment of 12 October 1993), para 97 and 100: "At the same time, with the building-up of the functions and powers of the Community, it becomes increasingly necessary to allow the democratic legitimation and influence provided by way of the national parliaments to be accompanied by a representation of the peoples of the member-States through a European Parliament as the source of a supplementary democratic support for the policies of the European Union. [...] In the federation of States formed by the European Union, therefore, democratic legitimation necessarily comes about through the feed-back of the actions of the European institutions into the parliaments of the member-States; and within the institutional structure of the Union there is the additional factor (increasing to the extent that the European nations grow closer together) of the provision of democratic legitimation by way of the European Parliament elected by the citizens of the States."; BVerfG, 2 BvE 2/08 et al. (judgment of 30 June 2009) para 262 – Lisbon: "As long as, and in so far as, the principle of conferral is adhered to in an association of sovereign states with clear elements of executive and governmental cooperation, the legitimation provided by national parliaments and governments complemented and sustained by the directly elected European Parliament is sufficient in principle.".

[15] This has been the appropriate conclusion of the German Federal Constitutional Court (FCC) in its decision on the Treaty of Maastricht (BVerfGE 89, 155 [184 f.]). However, in its judgment on the Treaty of Lisbon as well as in its decisions of 9 November 2011 (BVerfGE 129, 300 – 5 % threshold for EP elections) and of 26 February 2014 (BVerfGE 2 BvE 2/13 et al. – 3 % threshold for EP elections), the FCC has erected high obstacles for the EP to evolve into a "full-fledged parliament". Calliess 2005a, p. 300, who already in 2005 concluded that with regard to the grown competences of the EP, the lack of a uniform and equal electoral procedure is no longer justified.

[16] Cf. Blanke and Pilz 2014, p. 557.

influence on the decisions taken in the European institutions can be strengthened by mechanisms which provide a vertical legitimation, endowing national Parliaments with the right to "define" the positions that the national government has to take over in its votes, especially in the European Council, the Council and the Euro Group. Moreover, a horizontal coordination of national Parliaments within a conference (e. g. COSAC – Sect. 5.4) or a second chamber (a "Congress" of national Parliaments – Sect. 5.3) is partially seen as a trigger to convey democratic legitimation to EU policy in EMU.

Consequently, in order to enhance democratic legitimation of decision making also in economic governance, national Parliaments should play a more vital role within the process of conferring democratic legitimation in those areas where the Union has a mere coordinating competence, namely employment and social policy (Art. 5.2 and 5.3 TFEU) and economic policy (Art. 5.1 TFEU). Secondly, it is the European Parliament we should focus our attention on (Sect. 5.1). We therefore propose a two-tiered approach: the introduction of new elements at European level by strengthening the national Parliaments in their current position (Sect. 5.2) and a Treaty reform (Sect. 6) that leads to enhanced economic coordination with the right of the European Parliament to be heard in the economic policies of the Member States. To reform the Union in a credible way means the results can be shared by the citizens. However, one should be aware that such a deep reform is neither feasible nor recommendable before the end of the crisis.

2 The Democratic Legitimation of the European Union

The preliminary question is the standard against which the level of democratic legitimacy of the Union is evaluated. To answer this, we will look at the theoretical foundations that democratic legitimation of a supranational polity requires as well as the requirements laid down by German constitutional law and jurisprudence.

2.1 Elements of a Democratic Theory for the European Union

Asking for democratic legitimation of an international organisation no longer comes as a surprise. Once international organisations can set binding rules without the need for transposition into national law at the national level (in general, the national Parliament), those decisions need to be backed democratically. A direct effect vis-à-vis the citizens of Member States, an element of supranationality, needs a legitimatory backup at the international level, i. e. at the source of the rulemaking.[17] This requires the consent of the governed, which means those who are affected and bound by these decisions. This includes first and foremost the citizens of the

[17] Cf. Ruffert and Walter 2015, para 100; cf. also Rawls 1993, p. 214.

Member States. With regard to the character of the Union as an international organisation, this, in some respect, also comprises the Member States themselves as legal entities, as rulemaking at the supranational level affects them in a way that they can no longer exercise some sovereign rights they have transferred to the supranational level. At the starting point of this analysis a supranational entity has to be understood as a constitutional compound of states and a union of citizens (*Staaten- und Bürgerunion*).[18] A highly integrated, supranational organisation is thus best interpreted as a federal-type organisation, an "institution of federalism",[19] or even a "Federation".[20]

Legitimation of an international organisation by citizens *and* by states in effect means that the legitimation of the organisation's action has to come from the citizens of the Member States, as they themselves – in a national context – form the democratic basis of the national polity that in turn would provide – as "State" – legitimation for the organisation. The question is how the electorate can be construed so as to be used as a foundation at both the national and supranational level. Most democratic polities are based on the principle of people's sovereignty, i. e. that all state authority is derived from the people.[21] However, this does not preclude the idea that the actual bearer of sovereign power is the individual. Historically, sovereign power in the sense of *J. Bodin*'s and *Th. Hobbe*'s *suprema potestas* was regarded as a unitarian concept of uniform and indivisible sovereignty of the State (i. e. the monarch) over the governed. The transfer of sovereign power to the people is not the mere transposition of this power as indivisible *suprema potestas*. The basis is not necessarily "the people" as subject of legitimation that is characterised by relative homogeneity or collective identity, but rather as a "pooling of legitimation" (*Legitimationszusammenschluss*).[22]

To grasp this idea, one has to depart from the traditional concept of people's sovereignty that can only be exercised by a pre-existing ethno-national or ethno-cultural community which is based on the idea of a "cultural nation" (*Kulturnation*).[23] Rather, one should go back to the original concept of state-nation (*Staatsnation*) as a constitutional summary of individual subjects of legitimation,[24] i. e. the term *demos* for the sum of the citizens that form the polity.[25] As *J. Habermas* puts it:

---

[18] Blanke, in Blanke and Mangiameli (2013), Art. 1 para 1, 4; see also Calliess 2014, Part 3, C, para 14.
[19] See the contribution by *Luther* in this volume.
[20] Cf. Schönberger 2004, p. 98 et seqq., 117 et seqq.; Schmidt 2005, p. 772.
[21] Cf. e. g. Art. 3.1 and 3.2 French Constitution; Art. 20.2 first sentence German Constitution; Art. 1.2 Italian Constitution; Art. 6.1 Irish Constitution.
[22] Schliesky 2004, p. 745; cf. also Oeter 2010, p. 67; Peters 2001, p. 657 et seqq.
[23] Thus apparently Isensee 1997; Isensee 2009; along the same line see also Franzius and Preuß 2012, p. 43 et seqq.
[24] Cf. Schliesky 2004, p. 745; cf. also Oeter 2010, p. 71, Calliess 2014, Part 3, C, para 16.
[25] Cf. Pernice 1993, p. 477 et seq.; Maurer 2013, p. 3 et seq.; in more detail Augustin 2000, especially p. 63 et seqq., 393 et seqq.; Peters 2001, p. 657 et seqq., 700 et seqq.; v. Komorowski 2010, p. 1014 et seqq., who from the perspective of the Basic Law reconstructs the model of dual legitimation as a model of off-centred, but also territorially uniform (*staatsgebietseinheitlich*) people's sovereignty.

"A nation of citizens must not be confused with a community of fate shaped by common descent, language and history. This confusion fails to capture the voluntaristic character of a civic nation, the collective identity of which exists neither independent of nor prior to the democratic process from which it springs."[26]

In a compound of states and citizens, democratic legitimation that stems from the individual can be constructed along two strands.[27] The first strand ties to the representation of the states in the organisation. The individuals, according to national (constitutional) law, elect the national Parliament, which in turn elects the national government, thereby forming a "chain of legitimation". The representatives of the states can thus base their legitimation on the national vote. They can convey democratic legitimation on the international organisation through government representatives meeting in a special body. This strand of legitimation has its normative anchor within the legal order of the Union in Art. 10.2 (2) TEU.

The second strand is the direct connection between the individual and the supranational level. This is done by an assembly of directly elected representatives. In a Union that is based on sovereign states, this can be done by way of an assembly of national MPs that come together with a sort of "double hat". The other possibility would be a directly elected assembly at the supranational level. In this respect, the individuals from the different Member States of the organisation can be perceived as a collective that exceeds the individual collectives at the domestic level. This direct conferral of democratic legitimation finds its normative expression in Art. 10.2 (1) TEU. However, the Treaty lacks a clear concept of how these two strands tie together and complement one another in the conferral of democratic legitimation.

These two pillars that have the potential to provide democratic legitimation can be examined along two dimensions (*F. Scharpf*) regarding the participation of the governed (input) and the effectiveness of the decisions taken (output).[28] As long as decision making of an organisation applies only to mere intergovernmental issues, i. e. binds the States in their international context, the principle of "one state, one vote" in the state chamber can suffice to live up to this requirement of equality.[29] However, as soon as the organisation can set binding rules with direct effect in the domestic legal order, equality can only be ensured if the population of the component states is duly taken into account, i. e. by realising the principle of "one citizen, one vote" in the parliamentary assembly.[30] Input legitimation in this regard aims at the inclusion of all citizens in the election of the representatives on the basis of common electoral rules. Those rules should apply equally to all citizens and ensure electoral equality. This comprises equality of the votes cast, but also equality in representation so that in essence the vote of every citizen has the same weight not only in the determination of the representatives, but also in the actual decision-mak-

[26] Habermas 2001, p. 15 et seq.; cf. also Oeter 2010, p. 70.
[27] Cf. Schorkopf, in Kahl et al. (2011), Art. 23 GG para 43, Calliess 2014, Part 3, C, para 14.
[28] Scharpf 1970; Scharpf 1999; see also Zürn 1996.
[29] See also the contribution by *Tomuschat* in this volume.
[30] Cf. Ruffert and Walter 2015, para 337–338.

ing process (i. e. that one elected representative represents more or less the same number of citizens).

If the Union is submitted to a state-analogous way of democratic legitimation, this requires public debate and the formation of a public opinion, channelled by political parties and organised interest groups, in the context and within the polity in which the respective elections take place. While identity of the governed in the sense of cultural identity and homogeneity is not a necessary prerequisite for input legitimation, legitimation will be stronger if there is a certain collective identity and identification with and acceptance of decisions.[31] As the constitutional development of an organisation is usually successive and gradual as compared to a state (usually in the context of a revolution), one needs to bear in mind the effect and feedback this development may have on the formation of a sort of collective identity of the sum of citizens gathered in this polity.[32] This includes elements of participatory democracy, i. e. the participation of the citizens in the democratic life of the polity by way of exchange of views among one another and the pooling of opinions but also an exchange of views with the governing institutions. This will eventually lead to the forming of what one could call a public opinion within the polity.[33] EU law approaches this element when in primary law it refers to citizens' participation – also through political parties at Union level (Art. 10.3 and 10.4 TEU) and the dialogue of the institutions with the citizens (Art. 11 TEU).[34]

Conversely, output legitimation refers to the outcomes of the decision-making process. Decisions are regarded and accepted as legitimate if they produce an effective outcome as an answer to the aims and requirements that the constitution of the polity postulates. Authority is reviewed with a view to concrete decisions regarding the rationality of the content and the effective orientation towards common interests.[35] Output legitimacy may be of special relevance in complex and technical areas, which are characterised by elements of rationality and inherent predictability and thus justify a certain independence from political evaluation,[36] for example financial and monetary policy (ECB, ESM). In this context, however, complex decision making should be designed in a way that enables the individual to attribute accountability for decisions. This includes transparency of deliberations and votes (and thus public control) and can take the form of parliamentary control of the bu-

[31] Cf. Höreth 1999, p. 88 et seq.

[32] Cf. in this sense also Maurer 2012 and Maurer 2013, p. 4; see also Franzius and Preuß 2012, p. 23.

[33] On this element see Eder and Trenz 2007.

[34] Cf. also Franzius and Preuß 2012, p. 24 et seqq.

[35] Cf. Schliesky 2004, p. 599 et seqq.

[36] Cf. Ipsen 1972, p. 1045. With regard to the US-American regulation commissions, *G. Majone* speaks of a "fourth branch of government". He holds that also the Community Treaties have established a "fourth branch of government", namely with the instrument of harmonisation (Art. 114 TFEU), which characterises the Union as a "regulatory State". See Majone 1994, p. 77 et seqq.; Majone 1996, passim; Majone 1998, p. 5 et seqq.; Majone 1999, p. 1 et seqq.; Majone 2001, p. 57 et seqq.; cf. in this respect also Case C-62/14, *OMT* (Opinion of AG Cruz Villalón of 14 January 2015) para 109 et seqq. with regard to the European Central Bank.

reaucracy/executive,[37] but also an unbundling of decision making. One needs to bear in mind that a potential enhancement of the problem-solving capacity and effectiveness of decision making (e. g. by qualified majority) does not necessarily enhance output *legitimation* but instead can tend to decrease legitimation by outvoting a minority.[38]

Input and output legitimation are not mutually exclusive, but instead can complement one another. Moreover, they must be viewed within the context and design of the polity. A certain level of output legitimation may suffice, as long as the organisation can be perceived in the words of *H. P. Ipsen,* as a mere "special-purpose compound of functional integration" (*Zweckverband funktionaler Integration*).[39] The more extensive competences become, especially with direct effect on the citizens, the more the need may arise for legitimation on the input level.[40] Technocratic governance and regulatory decision making end where conflicts on values and distribution cannot be solved or reconciled by experts, but rather need politically legitimised decisions. This becomes evident when legitimation by consensus or unanimity is compromised for the sake of effectiveness of the decision-making procedure and replaced by votes by a qualified majority (e. g. Art. 114.1 TFEU). This dynamic interpretation of the Treaties in light of the *effet utile*, which further distinguishes them from their origin in public international law, underlines once more the need for direct democratic legitimation by the citizens of the Member States. More and more this seems to collide with the procedure for the elections to the European Parliament, which is not based on the equality of votes by Union citizens. This can be – partially – compensated for if there is a broad consensus by the governed and thus the political system of complex organisations or polities is better constructed along the lines of consociationalism rather than the strict application of the majority rule.[41]

Taking all these elements together, legitimation of a polity can be summarised in the words of *Abraham Lincoln*[42] as government of the people (minimal consensus), by the people (input) and for the people (output).[43] These different paths for legitimising policy-making can, however, be pursued only in a credible way if people are not alienated from political decisions, but they are convinced that they are truly governing themselves and that they are *autonomous*, that is when they can reason self-consciously, be self-reflective, be self-determining and thus debate and deliberate different views and courses of action in private and public life.[44]

---

[37] Oeter 2010, p. 73, with reference to Max Weber 1918, p. 39–43, 99–105.

[38] Glaser 2013, p. 98; cf. also Scharpf 2006.

[39] Ipsen 1972, para 8, 24 et seqq. and 54, 124; Glaser 2013, p. 96; Nettesheim 2005, p. 166 et seq., holds that the Union is steadily on its way from functional integration to statehood.

[40] Cf. Nettesheim 2005, p. 154 et seq., who restates the views of authors from the late 1990s, holding that input and control should be given less attention in favour of expectations of results conducive to the common good (output) (p. 181 et seq.); Nettesheim 2014, para 14.

[41] Oeter 2010, p. 74; cf. also von Bogdandy 2012, p. 322.

[42] See also Art. 2 of the French Constitution: gouvernement du peuple, par le peuple et pour le peuple.

[43] Cf. Höreth 1999, p. 81 et seqq.; Schmidt 2005, p. 768.

[44] Kohler-Koch and Rittberger 2007, p. 13.

2.2 Requirements of German Constitutional Law

The starting point of this legal analysis is Art. 20 of the Basic Law (GG), which provides in paragraph 1 that the Federal Republic of Germany "is a democratic and social federal state" and in paragraph 2 that "[a]ll state authority is derived from the people [and] shall be exercised by the people through elections and other votes and through specific legislative, executive and judicial bodies". We find here the principle of popular sovereignty, which is the core element of the principle of democracy. The subject of legitimation for the ruling polity is thus the people – here the German people. Democracy and popular sovereignty as understood by the Basic Law is democratic popular sovereignty which is exercised by democratically legitimised institutions.[45] The decisive element is that all state authority can be traced back to the will of the people. In terms of this "theory of derivation" which was mainly spelt out in the German constitutional theory in order for this uninterrupted chain of legitimation *(ununterbrochene Legitimationskette)* to be valid, it needs to ensure that the people can exert effective influence on the exercise of state authority.[46] In the context of the Union this proves to be difficult as it seems impossible to trace the decisions made by its institutions back to the "will of a European people".[47]

Concerning European integration, one needs to take further into account the preamble to the Basic Law in which the German people states its determination to promote world peace "as an equal partner in a united Europe". This "openness towards European integration" is spelled out in Art. 23 GG which also refers to the democratic principle.[48] At first glance, this may seem circular and lead to the conclusion, that any polity that exercises sovereign rights transferred to it from the national (German) level needs to observe the same standards and requirements of popular sovereignty included in Art. 20 GG that apply to German state authority. However, this is not the case. Art. 23.1 GG is the constitutional *lex specialis* for European integration and needs to be a point of reference for legal

[45] Grzeszick, in Maunz and Dürig (2010), Art. 20 II GG, para 12.

[46] Böckenförde 2004, § 24, esp. para 11–25; Grzeszick, in Maunz and Dürig (2010), Art. 20 II GG, para 61; Sommermann 2005, p. 203 et seqq., proves that the doctrine of derivation is not the prevailing model in the constitutional law of the Member States of the Union. With a critical view Nettesheim 2005, p. 178, who rejects this model as "chain-of-legitimation fetishism" and who, not without irony, refers to Luhmann 2000, p. 36, when speaking of the inept idea of the people as a sort of overarching entity in which the miracle of the fusion of the individual wills to common will can happen.

[47] Nettesheim 2005, p. 178; Nettesheim 2014, para 11.

[48] Art. 23.1 GG reads as follows: "With a view to establishing a united Europe, the Federal Republic of Germany shall participate in the development of the European Union that is committed to democratic, social and federal principles, to the rule of law, and to the principle of subsidiarity, and that guarantees a level of protection of basic rights essentially comparable to that afforded by this Basic Law. To this end the Federation may transfer sovereign powers by a law [which] shall be subject to paragraphs (2) and (3) of Article 79". According to the aforementioned paragraph 3 of Art. 79 GG, amendments to the Basic Law "affecting [...] the principles laid down in Articles 1 and 20 shall be inadmissible". Art. 79.3 GG protects the so-called "inviolable core content of the Basic Law's constitutional identity" which is excluded from any transfer of sovereign rights.

analysis. As a constitutional reserve clause, it aims to safeguard the substantive requirements of Basic Law, i. e. the constitutional core principles, against essential amendments within Germany's participation in the building of a united Europe. In other words, this "structural safeguard clause" refers to the identity-securing clause (*Identitätssicherungsnorm*) of Art. 79.3 GG[49] which in turn refers to the *principles* laid down inter alia in Art. 20 GG and contains the outermost limits for the German *pouvoirs constitués*. Hence, from the point of view of constitutional law, the European Union can be said to be democratic, if its constitutional design observes the *fundamentals* of the principle of democracy laid down in and the sovereign statehood of Germany required by Art. 20 GG. What is required is a democratic elaboration commensurate with the status and the function of the Union.[50]

This includes, that in the end, the Federal Republic of Germany needs to retain substantial national scope of action for central areas of statutory regulation and areas of life.[51] The questionable statement which the German Federal Constitutional Court (FCC) delivered regarding the realms "which are not open to integration"[52] does not mean, as the FCC puts it, that the principle of democracy "may not be balanced against other legal interests" and that "it is inviolable".[53] Rather, the German constitution itself includes modifications of the democratic principle, e. g. for local self-government (Art. 28 GG), for functional self-government (Art. 86, 87.2 and 87.3, 130.3 GG) and – in the relevant case – for European integration (Art. 23 GG).[54] Sure, the FCC's approach is questionable with regard to the *specific* elements it lists as "not open to integration". The basic argument comes down to a question of whether certain legal matters, that usually fall within the competence

[49] Di Fabio 1993, 210.

[50] Cf. BVerfG, 2 BvE 2/08 et al. (judgment of 30 June 2009) para 228, 347, 266 et seq. – Lisbon. This view is shared by the European Commission in its letter in response to the Opinion of the House of Lords concerning the role of national Parliaments in the EU, C (2014) 4236 final of 23 June 2014. p. 3: "This general principle goes hand-in-hand with a second general principle, namely that 'in developing EMU, the level of democratic legitimacy always needs to remain commensurate with the degree of transfer of sovereignty from Member States to the European level'."

[51] BVerfG, 2 BvE 2/08 et al. (judgment of 30 June 2009) para 351 – Lisbon.

[52] BVerfG, 2 BvE 2/08 et al. (judgment of 30 June 2009) para 235, 239, 255 – Lisbon; see before BVerfG, 2 BvR 2134/92, 2 BvR 2159/92 (12 October 1993) para 101 – Maastricht. In the words of the FCC, in its judgment on the Treaty of Lisbon (para 249), these "essential areas of democratic formative action" include, among others, "citizenship, the civil and the military monopoly on the use of force, revenue and expenditure including external financing and all elements of encroachment that are decisive for the realisation of fundamental rights, above all in major encroachments on fundamental rights such as deprivation of liberty in the administration of criminal law or placement in an institution. These important areas also include cultural issues such as the disposition of language, the shaping of circumstances concerning the family and education, the ordering of the freedom of opinion, press and of association and the dealing with the profession of faith or ideology".

[53] BVerfG, 2 BvE 2/08 et al. (judgment of 30 June 2009) para 216 – Lisbon.

[54] Grzeszick, in Maunz and Dürig (2010), Art. 20 II GG, para 294.

of the national legislator, can be subject *in principle* to a supranational organisation with the applicability of qualified majority voting (Sect. 3.2.2).[55]

3 The Current Institutional Design of the Union for the Purpose of Democratic Legitimation

With the current level of integration, it can hardly be observed that there is either the political will or the legal (national constitutional) basis to transform the international organisation "European Union" into a federal state.[56] It is also true that the European Union does not comprise a single *demos* and can thus not rely on "an independent people's sovereignty for all Union citizens".[57] At the current stage of European integration, the democratic legitimation thus rests on "the continuing sovereignty of the people which is anchored in the Member States and from the circumstance that the states remain the masters of the Treaties".[58] The Union is partly considered as an "association of sovereign states" (*Staatenverbund*),[59] a "compound of Constitutions" (*Verfassungsverbund*),[60] partly as an "intensive alliance of states" (*intensive Staatenverbindung*)[61] or just as an entity *sui generis*.[62] All of these concepts are characterised by the assumption of "the precarious, the hovering, the intermediate" in the description of the constitutional and organisational design of the Union[63] and at the same time by the openness in its development.[64] Its constitutional categorisation and development prospects are indissolubly linked to the question of the suitable model of democratic legitimation of its sovereign power.

As long as this organisation is viewed as a mere "association of sovereign states", it may suffice to meet democratic standards that are below those required of a full-fledged nation state.[65] Accordingly, the German FCC in its decision on the Lisbon Treaty stated mainly with a view to the lacking democratic basic rule of equal

[55] Affirmatively Niedobitek 2009, p. 1271; Nettesheim 2013, p. 51 et seqq., holds that this can only be subject to a sector-specific evaluation. He criticises the FCC for being too undifferentiated when requiring plebiscitary legitimation in every case.
[56] BVerfG, 2 BvE 2/08 et al. (judgment of 30 June 2009) para 113, 277 et seq., 334 – Lisbon.
[57] BVerfG, 2 BvE 2/08 et al. (judgment of 30 June 2009) para 281 – Lisbon; cf. also see also Franzius and Preuß 2012, p. 30 et seq.
[58] BVerfG, 2 BvE 2/08 et al. (judgment of 30 June 2009) para 334 – Lisbon.
[59] Cf. the wording of the German FCC, BVerfG, 2 BvE 2/08 et al. (judgment of 30 June 2009) – Lisbon and BVerfG, 2 BvR 2134/92, 2 BvR 2159/92 (12 October 1993) – Maastricht.
[60] Pernice 1995, p. 261 et seqq. and Pernice 1996, Calliess 2014, Part 3, C, para 14: "Staaten- und Verfassungsbund".
[61] Cf. Schorkopf, in Kahl et al. (2011), Art. 23 GG para 42.
[62] Cf. Calliess 2010a, p. 167 et seq.; on the problems of developing a theory of European democracy in the light of the uncertainty of the Union's finality see Nettesheim 2005, p. 164 et seqq. (166) with reference from international literature.
[63] Cf. Schönberger 2004, p. 87; cf. already Ipsen 1972, Chap. 9 para 63, with reference to Schmitt 1928, p. 379; see also Blanke 1993, p. 420.
[64] Cf. Schorkopf, in Kahl et al. (2011), Art. 23 GG para 34.
[65] Scharpf 2007, p. 9; Schmidt 2005, p. 772.

opportunities of success ("one man, one vote") in the Union[66] that "democracy of the European Union cannot, and need not, be shaped in analogy to that of a state", but instead "the European Union is free to look for its own ways of reducing the democratic deficit[67] by means of additional, novel forms of transparent or participative political decision-making procedures". This holds true as long as "European competences are ordered according to the principle of conferral in cooperatively shaped decision-making procedures, and taking into account state responsibility for integration *(Integrationsverantwortung)*, and as long as an equal balance between the competences of the Union and the competences of the states is retained".[68]

In its rulings the FCC draws inspiration from the common model of legitimation of modern territorial states, i. e. of an electoral democracy (Art. 10.1 TEU).[69] This seems to be justified, since the Treaty of Lisbon codifies in primary law a state-analogous way of democratic legitimation of political power. This approach, however, is reaching limits, as becomes evident in the deviation from the territorially based democratic basic rule of equal opportunities of success. With the Treaty of Lisbon – notably with the consolidation of the principle of degressive proportionality (Art. 14.2 [1] sentence 3 TEU) – it has even become less probable that the Union will approach the ideal of an electoral democracy. As a consequence of this rule, the weight of the vote of a citizen from a small Member State may be about twelve times the weight of the vote of a citizen from a larger Member State.[70] At the same time, however, degressive proportionality is a viable compromise to reconcile the equality of states and the representation of the citizens and a concession to the current lack of responsiveness of the process of opinion making and policy forming due to the lack of a comprehensive political public.[71]

The question is whether the current design of the Union provides sufficient democratic foundation when measured against the criteria outlined above or whether it is still deficient.[72] The European Parliament and the Council are often seen as representatives of one and the same subject of legitimation[73] that occurs in two legal entities. As Union citizenship is accessory to national citizenship (Art. 9 TEU, 20 TFEU), the peoples of the Member States and the Union citizens comprise the same conglomerate of individuals. Authorship for the thesis of "transnationalisation of people's sovereignty", i. e. the "idea of people's sovereignty

[66] BVerfG, 2 BvE 2/08 et al. (judgment of 30 June 2009) para 279 – Lisbon; see also the contribution by *Tomuschat* in this volume.

[67] For the whole panorama of arguments about the democratic quality of the EU and on the question if there is a democratic deficit (G. Majone, R. Dahl, P. Graf Kielmansegg, A. Moravcsik, R.M. Lepsius, A. Follesdahl and S. Hix et al.) see Kohler-Koch and Rittberger 2007, p. 6 et seqq.

[68] BVerfG, 2 BvE 2/08 et al. (judgment of 30 June 2009) para 265 et seqq. (272) – Lisbon; see also di Fabio 2014, p. 13.

[69] Cf. Schorkopf, in Kahl et al. (2011), Art. 23 GG para 42.

[70] See BVerfG, 2 BvE 2/08 et al. (judgment of 30 June 2009) para 284 – Lisbon; von Achenbach 2014, p. 426; Arndt 2008, p. 258.

[71] Cf. Schorkopf, in Kahl et al. (2011), Art. 23 GG para 44.

[72] The claim of an "objective" democratic deficit, with regard to both public accountability and legitimacy, is rejected by Moravcsik 2008; cf. also Schmidt 2005, p. 767.

[73] Cf. von Bogdandy 2012, p. 322.

that is divided at the root" between the citizens of the European Union and the peoples of the Member States is claimed by *Habermas*.[74] This is closely connected to the approach that in the EU's "multilevel constitutionalism"[75] the same people are the point of reference for the different levels of action.[76] Union citizenship is an additional element that the peoples of the Member States have created themselves (through their governments by means of an international treaty).[77] Such a common citizenship can function as an overarching and connecting element of the otherwise unrelated national collectives without merging and melting them into one.[78]

This construction seems to be in accordance with the European Treaties (Art. 10.2 [1] TEU) concerning the *representation of citizens in the European Parliament*; with regard to the exercise of competences by other institutions and bodies of the Union, however, it may be contested (Sect. 2.2).[79] It is questionable also because in national law the texts of the constitutions do not directly refer to the individual citizen (voter) as a subject of legitimation.[80] While in Germany, public authority is exercised by the state organs, the French approach is based on *Rousseau*'s idea, articulated in Art. 3 of the Declaration of the Rights of Man and of the Citizen (1789)[81] and Art. 1 of Title III of the Constitution of 1791,[82] according to which the nation is the bearer of sovereignty.[83] The idea that only the individuals

---

[74] Habermas 2011, p. 62.

[75] Pernice 1998, p. 40 (43 et seqq.).

[76] Cf. Pernice 2005, p. 759 et seq.; Pernice 2002; Pernice 2009, p. 376; Peters 2001, p. 566; von Achenbach 2014, p. 416 et seq.; Uerpmann-Wittzack, in von Münch and Kunig (2012), Art. 23 para 14–16, 18; Härtel 2014, para 85; von Bogdandy 2010, p. 48. With a view on these two entities as separate and not coinciding see BVerfG, 2 BvE 2/08 et al. (judgment of 30 June 2009) para 346 et seqq. – Lisbon.

[77] Pernice 1999, p. 717, 720 et seqq.; von Achenbach 2014, p. 420; cf. also Pernice 2009, p. 374 et seqq.

[78] Cf. Franzius and Preuß 2012, p. 79; Joerges 2014, p. 37 et seq., with a sceptical view of the assumption of Habermas regarding a "convergence" of the European *demoi* and an "ever-more-Europe" option.

[79] See also BVerfG, 2 BvE 2/08 et al. (judgment of 30 June 2009) para 249, 251 et seqq. – Lisbon.

[80] Cf. Art. 3.1 and 3.2 of the French Constitution: "National sovereignty shall vest in the people, who shall exercise it through their representatives and by means of referendum. No section of the people nor any individual may arrogate to itself, or to himself, the exercise thereof." Art. 1.2 of the Italian Constitution: "Sovereignty belongs to the people and is exercised by the people in the forms and within the limits of the Constitution". Art. 6.1 of the Irish Constitution: "All powers of government, legislative, executive and judicial, derive, under God, from the people, whose right it is to designate the rulers of the State and, in final appeal, to decide all questions of national policy, according to the requirements of the common good".

[81] "Le principe de toute souveraineté réside essentiellement dans la nation. Nul corps, nul individu ne peut exercer d'autorité qui n'en émane expressément.".

[82] "La Souveraineté est une, indivisible, inaliénable et imprescriptible. Elle appartient à la Nation; aucune section du peuple, ni aucun individu, ne peut s'en attribuer l'exercice.".

[83] In the current Constitution of the Fifth Republic (1958) it says in the preamble: "Le peuple français proclame solennellement son attachement aux Droits de l'Homme et aux principes de la souveraineté nationale tels qu'ils ont été définis par la Déclaration de 1789, confirmée et complétée par le préambule de la Constitution de 1946 [. . .]". Art. 3 of the French Constitution: "La souveraineté nationale appartient au peuple qui l'exerce par ses représentants et par la voie du référendum. Aucune section du peuple ni aucun individu ne peut s'en attribuer l'exercice." On the

in their simultaneous status of national and Union citizens are the only subject of legitimation,[84] especially meets the concern that legitimation cannot be conferred by a political atomisation (of the citizens of each Member State towards the citizens of all the other Member States), but rather that it needs the inclusion of the citizens in an overarching – transnational – political context that is viewed by constitutional law in the *pouvoir constituant* of the people in the sense of Abbé *E. J. Sieyès*. The European Union lacks a linguistic community and thus a "pre-political, ethical communality";[85] in the consequence it (still) does not have a collective identity and it does not constitute a political community of solidarity which is oriented to a process of public opinion[86] and formed as a "voluntary nation" by means of communication on common challenges (Sect. 2.1).[87]

3.1 The Status of the European Parliament

There are a number of functions a parliament generally performs in order to generate democratic legitimacy or rather contributes to the legitimacy of the political system at large:[88] it represents the citizens, it takes part in legislation, including the national budget, and it elects the executive/government and controls it, thereby making it accountable to the citizens. Especially the role of the European Parliament – the genuine parliamentary law-making body of the Union – has increased steadily and significantly over time. Post Lisbon, the European Parliament meets a number of these criteria. It is the representation of the Union's citizens, the MEPs being elected in European elections (Art. 14.2 TEU), although, certainly, these are not (yet) genuine European elections as they follow the respective domestic electoral law. Moreover, even though seats are attributed to Member States in certain contingents, the EP does represent citizens rather than Member States. Most prominently, Art. 22.2 TFEU provides that Union citizens shall have the right to vote and to stand as a candidate in EP elections in the Member States in which they reside, regardless of their nationality. MEPs of one national contingent thus represent the Union citizens residing in one Member State, not the nationals.[89] The deficit in representation is that MEPs do not represent the citizens of "their" states according to electoral equality, but degressive proportionality (sentence 3 of Art. 14.2 [1] TEU). However, other (democratic) Member States know (significant) deviations from the

meaning of "nation" as subject of legitimation see Duguit 1921, § 48; Sommermann 1997, p. 86 et seq.

[84] von Bogdandy 2010, p. 48.

[85] Nettesheim 2005, p. 172.

[86] Heller 1963, 176.

[87] See Di Fabio 1993, 202 et seqq., who speaks of the European Parliament as a "State convention"; Nettesheim 2005, 170 et seqq. (172 et seq.), and others, see the chance for the formation of a political community in the Union, if it's action is based on universalistic principles such as freedom, equality, minority protection, neutrality or the commitment to *neminem laedere*.

[88] Cf. Hrbek 2012, p. 131 et seq.

[89] Halberstam and Möllers 2009, p. 1248 et seq.; von Achenbach 2014, p. 437.

principle of electoral equality as a necessary prerequisite of democracy, e. g. the United Kingdom or Spain.[90]

Secondly, the European Parliament shall, jointly with the Council, exercise legislative and budgetary functions (Art. 14.1 TEU). As the co-decision procedure has become the default legislative procedure ("ordinary legislative procedure", Art. 289.1, 294 TFEU), the European Parliament is now a full-fledged co-legislator in the Union's political system in most policy areas. However, within the legislative procedure the EP still lacks a core prerogative of a parliament, i. e. the right to legislative initiative. This is justified with a view to the special function of the Commission's right to initiative (Art. 17.2 TEU) in the institutional system of the Union, as it is concerned with the protection of outvoted parliamentary minorities and the Commission's obligation to guard the Union's interests.[91]

Thirdly, the European Parliament now has a decisive say in the Union's budgetary procedure but is still, however, sharing this right with the Council (argumentum Art. 314 TFEU). However, it is true that the Union currently does not dispose of the competence to raise taxes and thus the parliamentary body of the Union – the EP – does not have the power to effectively generate revenue. In parallel to the limited sovereign rights that the Union disposes of and relies on the transfer from its members, the EP does not have "budgetary sovereignty" in that it could pass a budget without the consent of the Member States of the Union.

Fourthly, the President of the European Commission now is elected by the European Parliament by absolute majority (Art. 17.7 [1] TEU) and, following that, the Commission as a body is subject to a vote of consent by the European Parliament (Art. 17.7 [3] TEU). In addition, the Commission as a body shall be responsible to the European Parliament. Accordingly, the European Parliament may vote on a motion of censure of the Commission (Art. 17.8 TEU, Art. 234 TFEU). Moreover, the European Parliament, because of the federal nature of the Union, resembles a sort of counterweight to the Commission and the Council and acts as an institutionalised opposition in the democratisation of the Union.[92]

This summary shows that, even though the European Parliament does not have the position a national Parliament has in the domestic sphere, it contributes strongly to the Union's democratic legitimation. Quite euphorically, the European Court of Human Rights has stated that the European Parliament, "which derives democratic legitimation from the direct elections by universal suffrage, must be seen as that part of the European Community structure which best reflects concerns as to 'effective political democracy'".[93]

From an overall consideration of the relevant decisions of the FCC, its rulings seem to play down the European Parliament's growing importance. Still in "Maastricht", the Court stated that "[a]lready at the present stage of development, the

---

[90] On this see Classen 2009, p. 883; cf. also Scharpf 2007, p. 6; Franzius and Preuß 2012, p. 53.

[91] Cf. Härtel 2006, § 18 para 12 et seq., who is in favour of a right of initiative for the EP; v. Komorowski 2010, p. 1080.

[92] Franzius and Preuß 2012, p. 56 et seq.

[93] Appl. No. 24833/94, *Matthews v. United Kingdom* (ECtHR 18 February 1999) para 52 with regard to Art. 3.1 of the Additional Protocol No. to the ECHR.

legitimation provided by the European Parliament has a supporting effect; this effect could become stronger if the European Parliament were elected by electoral rules consistent in all Member States [. . .], and if the Parliament's influence on the policies and legislation of the European Community were to increase".[94] Since then, Parliaments significance has grown, but the FCC does not seem to take notice of this fact in the Lisbon judgment. With this ruling, however, the FCC at the same time diminishes the EP's role in the conferral of democratic legitimation. In the Court's view, "the European Parliament is an additional independent source of democratic legitimation".[95]

Instead of positively describing the lines of legitimation the current set of EU constitutional law provides, the Court points out time and again, that the EU's democratic legitimation suffers from a deficit "when measured against requirements of democracy in states" while before the Court even admits that the EU "complies with democratic principles as a qualitative assessment of the organisation of its responsibilities and authority reveals that its structure is precisely not analogous to that of a state".[96] This deficit in the strand of direct democratic legitimation of the Union leads to the question of whether it can be compensated by indirect democratic legitimation, or, reversely, if an enhanced democratic legitimation that the European Parliament could provide when it would contribute as a co-legislator could compensate the "minus" of democratic legitimation by the Council (i. e. the Member States and thus the national Parliaments).[97]

3.2 Democratic Legitimation through the Council and the Involvement of National Parliaments

3.2.1 The Organisational-Personal Legitimation from the National Electorate to the Council Representative

The indirectness of democratic legitimation of Union (legislative) acts through the Council requires a different evaluation of its power due to the multistage electoral feedback and thus a longer "chain of legitimacy".[98] When looking at domestic

[94] BVerfG, 2 BvR 2134/92, 2 BvR 2159/92 (12 October 1993) para 100 – Maastricht.

[95] BVerfG, 2 BvE 2/08 et al. (judgment of 30 June 2009) para 265 et seqq. (271) – Lisbon. See before BVerfG, 2 BvR 2134/92, 2 BvR 2159/92 (12 October 1993) p. 18 et seq. – Maastricht. In the Maastricht judgment the judges have regarded the European Parliament's "complementary" function in providing "the basis for democratic support for the policies of the European Union" and thus they have made the national legislative bodies the relevant organs to convey democratic legitimacy in the context of Germany's participation in the process of European integration; see later on BVerfG, 2 BvR 2236/04 (judgment of 18 July 2005) para 81 – European Arrest Warrant.

[96] BVerfG, 2 BvE 2/08 et al. (judgment of 30 June 2009) para 289, 278 – Lisbon; see Schönberger 2009, p. 1213 et seq.

[97] Brosius-Gersdorf 1999, p. 167 et seq.; Huber 2002, p. 69, para 39; Calliess 2005b, p. 314 et seq.; Calliess 2014, Part 3, C, para 15.

[98] Cf. von Achenbach 2014, p. 19 et seq., 403.

peoples, the delegation of power is first made to the national Parliament and from those national MPs to the government and thirdly to the responsible government official voting in the Council.[99] This provides organisational-personal legitimation from the national electorate to the Council representative.[100] In that respect, it is only the individual Council representative, but never the Council as a whole, who is subject to democratic legitimation by the national peoples.[101]

Moreover, the concentration of democratic representation to one person means for the democratic subject a minimisation of pluralistic capacity in legislative decision making. This implies less institutional and procedural capacity to politically articulate a number of political preferences. Thus, in legislation the representation of the democratic subject by one person lacks an essential legitimising aspect, i. e. pluralistic capacity. Its legitimising capacity falls short of that of a parliamentary assembly.[102] This situation changes fundamentally if the decision of the European Council or Council representative – as foreseen by the German Responsibility for Integration Act (notably Sects. 4 to 9) – is bound to a previous formal act of parliament. However, the German standard is almost unique in that the national acts accompanying the ratification of the Treaty of Lisbon far exceed the European requirements for the participation of national Parliaments (Art. 12 TEU).

3.2.2 The Qualified Majority Voting Rule

In this context, the qualified majority as a default voting rule in the Council (Art. 16.3 TEU) has some specific democratic implications. Parts of the literature do not regard it as undemocratic, but rather as a core element of democratic exercise of power. Accordingly, at the European level the acceptance of majority decisions would not establish “heteronomy”.[103] In this regard, majority rule itself is not a limitation to democratic legitimation of decisions, but rather an inherent mode of democratic decision making.[104]

Undoubtedly, majority rule can lead to one or more Member States being outvoted. The mere possibility of being outvoted cannot be democratically deficient.[105] It can, however, infringe the principle of democracy, especially when the vote of the Council representative is based on a decision from its national Parliament.[106] This could be compensated by the requirement that the qualified majority comprises at least 55 % of the members of the Council (and at least 15) and representing Member States comprising at least 65 % of the population of the Union (Art. 16.4 TEU). This again is a sign of a balance between the “union of states” and the “union of

[99] von Achenbach 2014, p. 439 et seq.
[100] Böckenförde 2004, para 16.
[101] Rightly so Doehring 1997, p. 1133 et seq.
[102] von Achenbach, p. 405 et seq., 441.
[103] Mayer 2012, p. 69 et seq.
[104] von Achenbach 2014, p. 445.
[105] Ruffert 2004, p. 184.
[106] This is probably meant by Weber 2010, Chap. 7, para 54, and Nettesheim 2013, p. 49.

citizens" character of the EU. But here as well, one can imagine situations where the (narrow) majority supporting a Council decision does not necessarily reflect the majority of the Union's citizens.[107] Hence, the democratic legitimacy provided by national Parliaments when transposed through the Council is thus dissimilar to that at the national level. Thus far, the Council lacks democratic accountability with regard to content and subject matter.[108] However, it is recognised that such a weakness in legitimation can be compensated by the co-decision procedure and thus the equal participation of the European Parliament at Union level.[109]

3.2.3 The Role of National Parliaments in the European Union

Over the years, national Parliaments have acquired a more active role, namely in the scrutiny of EU legislation. An important step was the introduction in 2006 of the Political Dialogue with the Commission (the so-called Barroso procedure).[110] In its context, national Parliaments may submit to the Commission any comments on draft legislative acts. Most recently, the role of national Parliaments in the European Union has been reinforced by the Treaty of Lisbon (Art. 12 TEU and Protocols No. 1 and 2 TEU), confirming that national Parliaments "are an integral part of the institutional architecture of the EU".[111] This is due to the fact that they, too, are part of the democratic foundation of the Union. Especially the so-called early warning mechanism,[112] laid down in Art. 3 and 4 of Protocol No. 1 TEU in conjunction with Art. 6 of Protocol No. 2 TEU, has endowed national Parliaments with the right to submit to the Union – within a deadline of eight weeks – a reasoned opinion on EU law initiatives on whether they comply with the principle of subsidiarity or not. However, under the current early warning mechanism, a national Parliament only has the right to "reject" but not to amend a proposal. Moreover, national Parliaments or chambers may challenge an act before the European Court of Justice on grounds of infringement of the principle of subsidiarity (Art. 8 of Protocol No. 2 TEU). However, national Parliaments cannot – and should not – use the early warning mechanism to perform a *legal* review with regard to substance of draft EU legislation; this is not the task of a national Parliament, but of the (national or European) judiciary.[113]

Protocol No. 2 TEU outlines the objectives of subsidiarity and proportionality[114] in the form of a procedure that tries to make operational these principles as parame-

---

[107] In analogy to the criticism voiced by the German FCC with regard to the European Parliament; see BVerfG, 2 BvE 2/08 et al. (judgment of 30 June 2009) para 281, 292 – Lisbon.
[108] von Achenbach 2014, p. 443 et seq.
[109] Calliess 2014, Part 3, C, para 15.
[110] Cf. COM(2006) 211; Pierafita 2013, p. 6 et seqq.
[111] Hrbek 2012, p. 130; cf. also Baach 2008, p. 183 et seqq., 191 et seqq.
[112] See e. g. Pierafita 2013, p. 4 et seqq.; with a critical view De Wilde 2012.
[113] In this respect also De Wilde 2012, p. 12.
[114] On the relevance of these two parameters, see Blanke in Blanke and Mangiameli (2013), Protocol No. 2 TEU para 61 et seqq., 68 et seqq.; Kiiver 2006, p. 162: "and other criteria".

ters for the review of European draft legislation. It bestows national Parliaments and chambers with the right to initiate a scrutiny procedure. All in all, however, the direct role envisaged for the national Parliaments in the EU decision-making process turns out rather modest.[115] This is confirmed by the number of reasoned opinions issued under the Article 6 subsidiarity monitoring procedure by national Parliaments and chambers, notably the Swedish *Riksdag*, the Dutch *Eerste* and *Tweede Kamer* or the French *Sénat*.[116] Instruments of a *collective* role of the national Parliaments in the subsidiarity monitoring – beyond the toothless institution of the Conference of Parliamentary Committees for Union Affairs of Parliaments of the European Union (COSAC – sub V. 4) in Art. 9 and 10 of Protocol No. 1 TEU – cannot be identified in the Treaty.[117] Though, fostering subsidiarity monitoring runs the risk of bringing about "a re-nationalization and therefore particularization of European decision making to the detriment of Council efficiency".[118]

Moreover, a strengthening of the role of national Parliaments under the early warning mechanism would run the risk of introducing more "veto players" in the decision-making process and thus "multi-institutional rivalry" and increases the complexity of the EU's institutional design and law-making procedure.[119] However, justified by the will to retain or even regain national sovereignty, the British government has argued that giving greater weight to national parliaments in the EU's system of checks and balances "is one essential element in reconnecting Europe with ordinary citizens".[120] Therefore, they propose a "red card" mechanism, that would entitle a suffiencent number of national parliaments, not only for reasons of subsidiarity, but also proportionality and other factors, to actually block EU legislation in a given field.[121] The British proposal would be a clear opposition to the current attempt to establish cooperation between the EP and national parliaments,

[115] Kiiver 2006, p. 158 et seqq. who speaks in terms of a "COSAC subsidiarity experiment" and the "phantom collective".

[116] Since the entry into force of the Treaty of Lisbon, 318 reasoned opinions have been issued by national Parliaments/chambers under the Article 6 procedure. The Swedish parliament has issued a total of 51, the Dutch House of Representative 20, the Dutch Senate 17 and the French Senate 21. Germany accounts for 13 reasoned opinions, of which 10 originate from the *Bundesrat* and only 3 from the *Bundestag*. However, it is difficult to establish whether these reasoned opinions find there to be an infringement of the *principle of subsidiarity*, as foreseen by Art. 6 of Protocol No. 2 TEU, or if they claim there to be other shortcomings of the draft, such as the material scope, content etc. Conversely, since 2006 a total of 1,174 opinions have been issued under the (informal) "political dialogue" initiated by the Commission (data as of 18 February 2015).; on the latter see Casalena, in Blanke and Mangiameli (2013), Protocol No. 1 TEU para 18.

[117] Kiiver 2006, p. 158 et seqq. who speaks in terms of a "COSAC subsidiarity experiment" and the "phantom collective".

[118] Kiiver 2006, p. 168.

[119] Cf. Stratulat et al. 2014, p. 6 et seq.

[120] UK House of Lords, Evidence taken before the Select Committee on the European Union, Inquiry on "Renegotiation and Referendum on UK Membership of the EU", 30 June 2015, evidence by Mr David Lidington MP, p. 27.

[121] This is a crucial point within the approach by British Prime Minister D. Cameron for the reform of the EU: "...National parliaments able to work together to block unwanted European legislation..."; see The Telegraph (telegraph.co.uk) of 15 March 2014, "The EU is not working and we will change it". A similar idea had been voiced by then British Foreign Secretary W. Hague at a

since a red card system is rather confrontation between national parliaments and the EU.

Nonetheless, the weak forms of involvement of the national Parliaments in European decision making reveal a legal vacuum at the European level, which has caused national legislators to strengthen this indirect strand of democratic legitimation (especially in Denmark, Finland, Sweden, Great Britain, Austria and Lithuania).[122] This tendency of the national legislator to exceed the requirements of the Treaties to convey democratic legitimation for the legislation of the Union via the national Parliaments (*überschießende Binnentendenz*) is particularly strong in the German legal order, which takes on the requirements by the German FCC. The vocabulary for this "exceeding" need for legitimation according to German constitutional law includes "responsibility for integration" and "budgetary responsibility" in EU matters (Sect. 3.3).

3.3 The "Competition" between the European Parliament and the National Parliaments

Against this background, the key question is the relationship between the national Parliaments and the European Parliament as provider of democratic legitimation for the Union. The controversy essentially takes on the question of whether the European Parliament is the exclusive or at least primary source to provide democratic legitimation for the Union, or whether the democratic legitimacy of the Union is provided primarily by the national Parliaments (Sect. 3.1). This debate shows that the Treaty of Lisbon lacks a sophisticated concept on the relationship between these two parliamentary levels and that the Union does not (yet) have a mature form of government.

In the Lisbon judgment, the German FCC recognised the comprehensive right of the individual to participate in the democratic legitimation of German public authority – a "right to democracy". At the same time, with regard to the German Parliament's responsibility for integration in EU matters, the Karlsruhe Court affirmed the need that "the German Bundestag, which represents the people, and the Federal Government sustained by it, retain a formative influence on the political development in Germany". This is the case "if the German Bundestag retains its own responsibilities and competences of substantial political importance or if the

speech given on 31 March 2013 in Neuhardenberg near Berlin: "Maybe we should go ahead and think about a red card, granting national Parliaments the right to block EU legislation."

[122] Norton 1984, p. 201 distinguishes the types of parliaments (policy-making, policy-influencing and advisory). In recent literature cf. Buzogány and Stuchlik 2012, S. 359 et seq.; on the Danish model see Buche 2013, p. 367 et seqq. and Finke and Melzer 2012; cf. (without an analysis of the Baltic States) Mayer 2012, p. 177 et seqq., 210. Participation rights of the national Parliaments in Finland, Ireland, Malta, the Czech Republic and in some respect in Hungary, Poland and Slovenia are similar to those of the German *Bundestag* (Sect. 5.3); see Grabenwarter 2011, p. 112.

Federal Government, which is answerable to it politically, is in a position to exert a decisive influence on European decision-making procedures."[123]

These conclusions of the highest German court, however, seem to contrast with the Union Treaty of Lisbon regarding the role of the European Parliament and the Treaty's definition of the role of national Parliaments. According to the core provision of Art. 12 TEU "national Parliaments contribute actively to the good functioning of the Union". Also, as a consequence of the national judicial interpretations of the future competences and prerogatives of national Parliaments, on the one hand, and of the European Parliament's role in the process of legitimation of the Union (and in the inter-parliamentary cooperation) on the other hand, parliamentary participation will be structured in the Union mainly in a vertical dimension, between each executive and each Parliament, or in a horizontal dimension, that is, among national Parliaments. Solutions for this "multi-level parliamentary field" will depend on whether the enhanced involvement of national Parliaments, deriving from the Treaty of Lisbon, would result in an enrichment of the EU decision-making process or, on the contrary, would lead to a potential new brake in its functionality.[124] It is without any doubt that the participation of national Parliaments would make it more difficult for the citizens to establish accountability for and exercise democratic control over decisions.[125]

4 The Democratic Dilemma of the Union in the Crisis

Without prejudice to the analysed deficits, it can be concluded that, in general, at the current level of integration the Union provides for a reasonable basis for democratic legitimation. This is also true with regard to the regulations and the directive which the Union has adopted as a consequence of the economic, financial and budgetary crisis, to reform the Stability and Growth Pact and to strive for a greater macroeconomic surveillance. Thus, the double pack of European legislative measures, called "Six-pack" and "Two-pack", both based on Art. 121.6 TFEU and Art. 126.14 TFEU respectively (partly in conjunction with Art. 136.1 TFEU) have been adopted in the ordinary legislative procedure, i. e. with the participation of the EP. But deficits of this involvement are obvious when it comes to more political matters of the crisis management. This can be highlighted by two details of the reform package on issues of EMU.

---

[123] Cf. BVerfG – 2 BvE 2/08 (30 June 2009) para 246, referring to BVerfG – 2 BvR 2134/92 – Maastricht. As a result of this judgment the German *Bundestag* has enacted the "Act on the Exercise by the Bundestag and by the Bundesrat of their Responsibility for Integration in Matters concerning the European Union" of 22 September 2009 (BGBl. I, p. 3022), amended by Art. 1 of the law of 1 December 2009 (BGBl. I, p. 3822).

[124] Fasone and Lupo, in Blanke and Mangiameli (2013), Protocol No. 1 para 179; Kiiver 2005, p. 168, with a negative perspective.

[125] Benz and Auel 2007, p. 57; Benz 2005, p. 276, therefore prefers an ex post control by national Parliaments.

The European Semester establishes a new system of control and sanction with regard to the national budgets.[126] The rules imposed by the reform package are supposed to help avoid macroeconomic imbalances and budgetary deficits and in essence are the basis for the establishment of the financial solidarity instrument in the form of the European Stability Mechanism.[127] The political debate on the national budget is no longer a mere domestic one between a national government and its parliament. Rather, before government submits its draft budget to parliament, it has undergone coordination with the European Commission and within the Council. Thus, governments will have less room to manoeuvre and are most likely less willing to negotiate with parliament the issues that have already been discussed at European level regarding the national budget.[128] In the end, given its "budgetary responsibility" the formal vote on the domestic budget is taken by the national Parliament.[129] However, neither the national Parliaments nor the European Parliament have a say in the preliminary process of the European Semester.[130]

Even though the surveillance of the national budgetary draft by the European level is strict, there are no actual sanctions that could be imposed in case the national government disregards the Commission's recommendations. Sanctions only apply in case of an excessive deficit. But here as well there is no actual parliamentary involvement in case they should be imposed one day by the Commission. While the European Parliament could shape the legislative process of the reform (co-legislator for most of the legal acts), it did not end up with a decision-making power in the operative process. However, the European Parliament is well aware that economic governance in the Union needs to be backed by parliamentary decisions. In response to two Commission Communications[131] the EP reaffirms "that governance in the EU must not infringe on the prerogatives of the European Parliament and the national parliaments, especially whenever any transfer of sovereignty is envisaged" and stresses "that proper legitimacy and accountability require democratic decisions and must be ensured at national and EU levels by national parliaments and the European Parliament respectively".[132] It furthermore reiterates that "the Commission needs to take full account of Parliament's role as a co-legislator" since "Parliament is a legislative and budgetary authority on an equal footing with the Council".[133] As a consequence, it asks the Commission to be included in the new

[126] See Weber 2011, p. 936; Weber 2013, p. 378 et seq.
[127] Cf. Deubner 2014, p. 24.
[128] Deubner 2014, p. 25.
[129] Cf. most recently BVerfG, 2 BvR 1390/12 et al. (judgment of 18 March 2014) – ESM, for example para 163.
[130] Cf. Deubner 2014, p. 35: "serious gap in parliamentary attendance".
[131] European Commission, Ex ante coordination of plans for major economic policy reforms, COM(2013) 166 and European Commission, The introduction of a Convergence and Competitiveness Instrument, COM(2013) 165.
[132] European Parliament resolution of 23 May 2013 on future legislative proposals on EMU: response to the Commission communications, P7_TA(2013)0222, point 5.
[133] P7_TA(2013)0222, point 7.

ex ante coordination instrument in order "to be given a role in ensuring democratic accountability".[134]

As a consequence of this development, the Union citizenship and the European Economic Union do not seem to be in good shape. The loss of political influence of citizens through their representatives in the national Parliaments as a result of the dominance of the financial and economic governance of the heads of States and governments marks the weak position of the European *demoi*. This situation is only part of a general shift to the executive,[135] mainly in the form of a "de-parlamentarisation". This democratic deficit in a negative sense "unifies" the European peoples. There has been a downright loss of sovereignty by all Member States whose decisions in terms of budget policy have been "shifted" into the hands of the representatives of the national executives (convened in the European Council, in the Council and the Euro Group) and in favour of the European Commission ("Economic Government").[136] In terms of democracy these executive bodies are only indirectly legitimised and, therefore, not directly accountable to the citizens affected by the decisions taken in the area of economic and budgetary *governance*.[137] This leads to a new democratic deficit, as the European Parliament remains largely a passive observer while national Parliaments can only to some extent compensate this deficit since only some of them are able to exercise effective scrutiny over their national government.[138]

Recognising the strong demand for a "parliamentarisation" within the EU's multilevel system cannot ignore the fact that a stronger involvement of the European Parliament in the decisions on the EMU would boost democratic legitimacy only if the reform measures on the EMU and the decisions on bailout ("Financial Facilities") were to be taken within the institutional framework of the Union. If the debate on reforms in the EMU had taken place in the European Parliament and the Council, it would have led to provisions (under the Union's legislative procedure) that would have been embedded in the EU Treaties (*acquis*) so that no Member State could unilaterally draw them into question.[139] As is known, a number of Member States currently oppose these ideas. For various reasons, the Treaty on Stability, Coordination and Governance in Economic and Monetary Union (Fiscal Compact Treaty) as well as the Treaty Establishing the European Stability Mechanism have been

[134] P7_TA(2013)0222, point 16.

[135] Bauer 2005, p. 9; Sommermann 2005, p. 216 et seq., also sees parliamentary countermovements in some Member States; for the "increasingly compound and accumulated 'order' of executive power in Contemporary Europe"; see also Curtin 2014, p. 206 et seqq.; but in her opinion, "there is no single, comprehensive and unitary European executive institution or body that can in any meaningful way be described as an EU government…" ("fragmentation").

[136] See also Kadelbach 2013, p. 495 et seq.; Pinon 2013.

[137] Cf. Mangiameli 2013, sub 3 b, d, e.

[138] Cf. Maurer 2013, p. 5 et seqq.

[139] The institutional binding effect of a treaty revision would naturally be greater than the durability of a treaty under public international law, notwithstanding Art. 62 VCLT; with the same view apparently Kingreen 2015.

agreed on as international treaties outside the Union's legal framework.[140] Seen in this light, it seems logical that the European Parliament recommends to evolve the ESM "towards Community-method management and (to make it) accountable to the European Parliament" (Sect. 5.1).[141] The Commission shares this view in its Communication of 28 November 2012 "A blueprint for a deep and genuine economic and monetary union. Launching a European Debate" when it emphasises that democratic legitimacy and accountability are the "cornerstone of genuine EMU".[142] Any call for the enhancement of the role of the European Parliament leads to the question of what role national Parliaments should play in European integration and how their relationship to the European Parliament should be characterised (Sects. 3.2 and 3.3). In that respect, there is an undeniable tension with regard to the budgetary sovereignty and budgetary responsibility of the national Parliaments in the "polydimensional institutional order" (*A. Benz*) of the Union.

5 Options for a Deeper Democratisation of the European Monetary Union

In search of ways how the preponderant executives on national and Union level can be counterbalanced by enhanced parliamentary involvement, i. e. by the involvement of a parliamentary body with decision-making powers, several proposals have been put forward.

5.1 The European Parliament as the Institutional Point of Reference

A main group of proposals strives for improving parliamentary participation in the inter-governmental EMU in a horizontal setting which links the enhancement of democratic legitimation in economic governance to the European level. In this view the parliamentary decision-making centre of and for the Union is and should be the European Parliament. In this respect, the European Parliament points out "that the currency of the Union is the euro, that its parliament is the European Parliament

[140] Cf. Weber 2013, p. 381 et seqq.; Mangiameli 2013, sub 4 b, c, d; on the political development of the participation of national Parliaments in European policy-making up to the Constitutional Treaty cf. Maurer 2002.

[141] European Parliament resolution of 20 November 2012, P7-TA-2012-430, Recommendation 2.7 on ensuring democratic oversight of the ESM. The Parliament adds, that "key decisions, such as the granting of financial assistance to a Member State and the conclusion of memorandums, should be subject to proper scrutiny by the European Parliament." See also European Parliament resolution of 12 June 2013 on strengthening European democracy in the future EMU, P7_TA-PROV(2013)0269, point 11.

[142] European Commission, A blueprint for a deep and genuine economic and monetary union. Launching a European debate, COM(2012) 777 final/2, p. 36 et seq.

and that the future architecture of the EMU must recognise that Parliament is the seat of accountability at Union level; demands that whenever new competences are transferred to, or created at, Union level or new Union institutions established, a corresponding degree of democratic control by, and accountability to, Parliament be ensured".[143]

This is supported by the rationale and wording of the Treaties. According to Art. 3.4 TEU, the Union shall establish an economic and monetary union whose currency is the euro. In Title VIII of the TFEU on economic and monetary policy, Art. 139 ("transitional provisions") provides that "Member States in respect of which the Council has not decided that they fulfil the necessary conditions for the adoption of the Euro shall hereinafter be referred to as 'Member States with a derogation'". Hence, although the extension of the Euro to the whole of the EU appears illusory alone on account of the permanent opt-out of Denmark and Great Britain, it is foreseen by the treaty that in the end, all Member States of the Union adopt the Euro as currency. Thus, it seems natural that the parliament of the Union (the European Parliament) has to be included in the overall decision-making process on the coordination of the national economic policies, eventually having full co-decision rights on the new secondary law in the realm of EMU, once the Contracting States have adopted a treaty reform aiming at a "parliamentarisation" of the EMU. However, this step is intrinsically linked to an intrusion into the budgetary sovereignty of national Parliaments. The Treaty of Maastricht had left this untouched, as the Contracting States have decided that budgetary, fiscal and economic policies will all remain within the national competence – with EMU limited to a coordinating function (Art. 5 TFEU).[144] Moreover, these are important elements to influence the competitiveness of the Member States. This reveals also that the "horizontal dilemma" (*Ch. Deubner*) is two-fold: that not all Member States belong to the Eurozone – and yet the EU's institutions make decisions about Euro matters with all of its members as a matter of principle. As a result, although decisions on EMU's matters ever-deeper interfere in the national budgetary competence, only a limited number of Member States is directly affected by the decisions of the Council.

It may be characteristic of the legal and political constitution of the Union and namely of the decision-making culture of the European Parliament,[145] that the efforts of the academic literature to carve out elements of a theory of democracy for the European Union have so far not led to proposals for institutional reforms of the European Parliament. Instead, they build standards of "confidence-building practice", which can only to a limited extent be ensured institutionally.[146] The aim of this approach is to make the "existence of a European citizenship" the starting-point of a lively and credible democracy in the Union. In that context, the challenge of European politics is a form of parliamentarism that is rooted democratically

[143] European Parliament resolution of 12 June 2013 on strengthening European democracy in the future EMU, P7_TA-PROV(2013)0269, point 10; see most recently, European Commision, *5-Presidents-Report 'Completing Europe's Economic and Monetary Union'*, 2015, p. 17.
[144] Blanke 2011, p. 402 et seqq.
[145] Nettesheim 2013, p. 49.
[146] Nettesheim 2013, p. 41 et seq.

and substantially in the Union citizens through necessary provisions of control and participation.[147] Ideas of justice, morally founded preliminary decisions on the relationship of the Union towards its citizens and the exercise of power that is oriented towards the common good are thus determinants of European governance that is founded on trust[148] ("social legitimacy").

Deliberative discoursivity and decision making, transparency, free and equal participation in the procedures, reciprocal generality of all those affected by decisions, clear responsibilities and accountability as well as a decision-making ethos of supranational officials are indispensible provisions for this.[149] This concept, which is oriented towards the theory of supra-individual state purposes (*J. J. Rousseau, I. Kant, L. vom Stein, G. F. W. Hegel, Ch. Taylor*), classifies the decisions on the future of democracy of the Union into the overall context of the relationship of the individual and the societal side and thus is linked to the traditional idea of the human being as *zoon politicon*. The European Parliament only has a chance for stronger involvement in the economic governance of the Union in the medium term if such a reform can be thoroughly explained to the European electoral citizens. It is thus the task of the Strasbourg parliamentarians to explain to the citizens that the parliament of the Union is willing to exercise this competence expertly, close to the citizens and responsively and therefore also with the aim of reconciling the different interests of the Member States. At the same time this would change European integration into a citizens' project.[150]

5.2 *Strengthening the Role of National Parliaments*

As a consequence of the budgetary sovereignty of the Member States, national Parliaments must retain control of fundamental budgetary decisions even in a system of intergovernmental governing[151] and in a multilevel-governance system which becomes manifest in the EMU. Hence, an essential path could be the strengthening of parliamentary influence on their national governments and their position in EU decision making.[152] Putting too much emphasis on directly scrutinising EU legislation might distract national Parliaments from this parliamentary function and responsibility in the domestic context.[153] As outlined above, one major function of a parliament is controlling the executive/government (Sect. 3.1). Here, there is

[147] Nettesheim 2013, p. 47 et seqq.
[148] Nettesheim 2005, p. 172, 154; Nettesheim 2013, p. 44.
[149] Nettesheim 2005, p. 180 et seqq., p. 184; Nettesheim 2014, para 18; Sommermann 2005, p. 220 et seq.
[150] Cf. on the call for stronger participation of the citizens Huber 1999, p. 34, 55; Benz 2005, p. 274.
[151] Cf. in the case of Germany BVerfG, 2 BvR 1390/12 et al. (judgment of 18 March 2014) para 162 – ESM.
[152] Deubner 2014, p. 33 et seq.; Stratulat et al. 2014, p. 7 et seq.; Kreilinger 2013, p. 21.
[153] Similarly De Wilde 2012, p. 4, 8 et seq. and Franzius and Preuß 2012, p. 52.

room to alleviate the overall democratic shortcoming of the Union.[154] But this has to be done in a national context. As the Preamble to Protocol No. 1 TEU on the role of national Parliaments recalls, "the way in which national Parliaments scrutinise their governments in relation to the activities of the Union is a matter for the particular constitutional organisation and practice of each Member State". Therefore, scrutinising and shaping the national government's position (in the Council, the co-legislating body) may seem a viable way to proceed. In addition, this path could ensure national Parliaments' influence even in intergovernmental decision making. Mandating the national government can also give national Parliaments another form of "red card": a minimum of four negative votes in the Council is necessary to form a blocking minority [Art. 16.4 (2) TEU]. Moreover, objections of national Parliaments via a mandated government in the Council are not limited to subsidiarity aspects, as is the case in the early warning mechanism, but can comprise also questions of proportionality or even substance.[155]

Nonetheless, one should not disregard the fact that national Parliaments across Europe vary deeply in their capacity to control and influence the executive in EU decision making and within the conclusion of international agreements that supplement EU law or that have a specific close connection to it.[156] Their institutional strength is dependent on elements such as "access to information", "processing of information" and "oversight".[157]

The United Kingdom has adopted a regulation with its European Union Act 2011, which provides that a "Minister of the Crown may not vote in favour of or otherwise support a decision [regarding the passerelle clauses] unless [...] the draft decision is approved by Act of Parliament [and] the referendum condition is met" [Sects. 6 (1) and 7 (3)].[158] Similarly, Art. 23i of the Austrian Constitution, introduced by the "Lissabon-Begleitnovelle" (laws accompanying the Lisbon Treaty) of July 2010 provides that in the case of use of the passerelle clauses, the Austrian Council representative is obliged to require the authorisation of the two Chambers (two-thirds majority) before voting for it.[159]

A rather strong parliamentary scrutiny of the national government, i. e. a parliamentary mandate-based scrutiny of EU policy, exists also in other national Parliaments, among them the parliaments of the Baltic States, the Finnish *Eduskunta*

---

[154] Corbett 2013.

[155] Kiiver 2006, p. 162 who emphasises the right of the national Parliaments to scrutinise "proportionality and other criteria" notwithstanding the fact that in his opinion there is "no protocol or treaty provision authorizing [...] to do so".

[156] Cf. Sects. 5–9 EUZBBG on the broad range of matters that activate the *Bundestag*'s right to early notification and involvement by the federal government as well as to deliver opinions to the federal government. A sign of the mainly weak role of national Parliaments beyond matters concerning the European Union *stricto sensu* is the fact that only four national Parliaments (Finland, Estonia, Germany and The Netherlands) had to consent to the bilateral financial aid for Greece (international treaty).

[157] See the instructive study conducted by Auel and Tacea 2014.

[158] Cf. Denza, in Blanke and Mangiameli (2013), Art. 48 para 51; Casalena, in Blanke and Mangiameli (2013), Protocol No. 1 TEU para 96.

[159] Olivetti, in Blanke and Mangiameli (2013), Art. 12 para 72.

and the Danish *Folketing*.[160] In the case of Denmark, the parliament can issue instructions to the minister for the voting in the Council[161] for the most important proposals.[162] The consent of the Danish parliament is deemed granted as long as there is no majority *against* the position of the minister (negative parliamentarism).[163] At the end of their debate, the European Affairs Committee draws up a report on the agreed Danish position and a description of the minister's discretion to deviate from that. However, the mandate does not contain a *legal*, but merely a political obligation. Because of the lack of a legally binding character of the mandate, the most important instrument in the ex-post control is the possibility of the *Folketing* to issue a vote of no confidence against single minsters (Art. 15.1 of the Danish Constitution), which is an effective means of pressure in minority governments.[164]

It cannot be ignored that effective parliamentary control of the Council representative by national Parliaments collides with the organisational status and intergovernmental logic of decision making in the Council.[165] The parliamentarian positions can have an immense effect when unanimity is required, but mandatory voting remains also questionable in case of qualified majority in the Council of ministers,[166] as "tying the hands of the responsible minister" for the sake of strict scrutiny can hinder necessary flexibility and bargaining power in Council negotiations.[167] The political decision-making power of the Council as a constitutional institution of the Union, namely its ability to find a political compromise in controversial issues, should not be impaired by binding decisions of a parliamentary organ of a Member State towards the representative of the national executive in the Council. Otherwise this would lead to an encroachment of the domestic constitutional order on the institutional independence of the Council (Art. 13.2 in conjunction with Art. 16 TEU). This institutional independence is democratically moderated by Art. 10.2 (2) TEU in the sense of a responsibility of its members towards the national Parliament or the citizens of its country of origin. This does not include, however, a limitation by the right of national Parliaments to give the Council representative an imperative mandate. In that case, the Council would be downgraded to a mere body of coordination of votes that have been predetermined by the parliaments in the Member States. At the same time, this would be an infringement of the principle of sincere cooperation of the Member States in the Council [Art. 4.3 (2) and (3) TEU].

[160] Cf. Grabenwarter 2011, p. 110.

[161] Raunio 2005, p. 322 et seq.

[162] Cf. Mayer 2012, p. 191.

[163] Cf. Møller Sousa 2008, p. 432.

[164] Cf. Mayer 2012, p. 197 et seq.

[165] Cf. Baach 2008, p. 183 et seqq.; von Achenbach 2014, p. 442 et seq.; see also Dann 2004, p. 254 et seqq., who regards the collision of the logic of negotiation and decision making in the Council with effective parliamentary participation on the basis of the model of executive federalism (p. 269), which is founded on efficient, flexible negotiation and compromise (p. 95 et seqq.); on structural problems of control of international organisations or institutions by national Parliaments see Krajewski 2008, para 14.

[166] Finke and Melzer 2012, p. 10.

[167] Auel and Benz 2005, p. 373; cf. also Møller Sousa 2008, p. 434 et seq.; Mayer 2012, p. 207 et seqq.

Considering these integration policy aspects, the German legislator has provided an adequate instrument in the "Responsibility for Integration Act" (IntVG),[168] the core of the German legislation accompanying the ratification of the Treaty of Lisbon. Together with two supplementary Acts it governs the rights of the *Bundestag* and the *Bundesrat* in EU matters. With Art. 23.2 GG and 23.3 GG in conjunction with Sect. 8 of the supplementary Act on Cooperation between the Federal Government and the German *Bundestag* in matters concerning the European Union (EUZBBG)[169] on the one hand and Art. 23.2 GG and 23.4 GG in conjunction with Sect. 5 of the supplementary Act on Cooperation between the Federation and the *Länder* in matters concerning the European Union (EUZBLG)[170] on the other, the German constitutional order includes different sets of rights of the *Bundestag* and the *Bundesrat* to give their opinion to the federal government. They influence to different degrees the negotiations of the German federal government in the institutions and (preparatory) bodies of the Union (Sect. 4.2 EUZBBG and No. II.1 of the Annex to Sect. 9 EUZBLG). According to a general opinion, the federal government only has to "take into consideration" these opinions without being formally bound by them. The *Bundestag*'s right to submit opinions to the federal government for its deliberations in the Council is supposed to facilitate "the exercise of the responsibility for integration in a constructive and critical dialogue" [171] and thus to concretise the principle of democracy in the sense of the structural safeguard clause laid down in Art. 23.1 first sentence GG. However, the *Bundestag*'s opinion directly affects the government's deliberations in the Council "if the main interests expressed in the decision of the Bundestag cannot be asserted". In that case, the

[168] Act on the Exercise by the Bundestag and by the Bundesrat of their Responsibility for Integration in Matters concerning the European Union (*Integrationsverantwortungsgesetz* – BGBl. I p. 3022) as amended by Art. 1 of the Act of 1 December 2009 (BGBl. I p. 3822); cf. Casalena, in Blanke and Mangiameli (2013), Protocol No. 1 TEU para 100; on the whole see also Calliess 2014, Part 3, C, para 32 et seqq.

[169] Section 8 (4) EUZBBG (emphasis added): "If the Bundestag avails itself of the opportunity to deliver an opinion [...], the Federal Government shall invoke the requirement of prior parliamentary approval in the negotiations if the main interests expressed in the decision of the Bundestag cannot be asserted. The Federal Government shall notify the Bundestag thereof without delay in a special report. In its form and content, this report must lend itself to discussion by the bodies of the Bundestag. Before the final decision, the Federal Government shall endeavour to reach agreement with the Bundestag. [...] *The foregoing provisions shall not prejudice the right of the Federal Government, in awareness of the Bundestag's opinion, to take divergent decisions for good reasons of foreign or integration policy.*".

[170] Section 5 (2) EUZBLG (emphasis added): "To the extent that a project primarily affects the legislative powers of the Länder and the Federation has no legislative power, or a project primarily affects the structure of Land authorities, or the Land administrative procedures, the position of the Bundesrat shall be given the greatest possible respect in determining the Federation's position [...]. This is without prejudice to the responsibility of the Federation for the nation as a whole, including matters of foreign, defence and integration policy. [...] If agreement with the Federal Government is not reached and the Bundesrat confirms its opinion by a majority of two thirds, the Bundesrat's opinion is decisive. In matters that may result in increased expenditures or reduced revenues for the Federation, the consent of the Federal Government shall be required.".

[171] Cf. Saberzadeh, in von Arnauld and Hufeld (2011), Chap. 11 para 34 et seq.

federal government shall invoke the requirement of prior parliamentary approval in the negotiations (Sect. 8.4 EUZBBG).

Section 9 IntVG provides that in cases where the European Treaties foresee the possibility of an emergency brake procedure, the German representative in the Council must table a motion that the matter (e. g. legislation in the field of social security necessary to provide freedom of movement for workers or with regard to the national criminal justice system) be referred to the European Council if the *Bundestag* has adopted a decision instructing him or her to do so. A different approach is foreseen with regard to bridging and competence clauses (Sects. 4 through 7 IntVG) and the flexibility clause of Art. 352 TFEU (Sect. 8 IntVG). In this last case, the German representative in the Council or the European Council may take an affirmative vote or abstain from voting only after a law to that effect has been adopted. As a consequence, the German parliamentary assembly can exert a decisive influence on the European decision-making procedure.

Conversely, if a Union project primarily affects the legislative or administrative competencies of the *Länder*, the federal government must "duly take into account" the opinion delivered by the *Bundesrat*. This means that the *Bundesrat*'s opinion is binding *in that respect* and that the *Bundesrat* maintains the right to take final decisions in certain cases of national concurrent legislation (cf. Art. 72.2 GG).[172] With regard to the opinions by the *Bundestag* and the *Bundesrat*, German law recognises the primacy of the federal government in Council deliberations for matters of foreign and integration policy (Sect. 8.4 sentence 5 EUZBBG) or with regard to the *Bundesrat*'s opinions the "responsibility of the Federation for the nation as a whole" (Art. 23.6 second sentence GG in conjunction with Sect. 5.2 sentence 2 EUZBLG). Thus, the opinions of the German legislative bodies do not establish an imperative mandate, which frankly, would weaken instead of strengthening the position in the Council in case of majority votes.[173]

The "renationalisation" of decision-making in the Council that is linked to the participation of national Parliaments raises the question of how the stronger involvement of national Parliaments in enhanced coordination of economic policy will influence the interplay of Council and European Parliament. With a future involvement in European economic policy (Sect. 6), even in the form of the right to consultation, the European Parliament as a quasi-unitarian institution would enter into an even stronger institutional opposition to the Council as the federal institution of the Union. It would primarily be the responsibility of the European Parliament to lay down and voice the Union's interests in its opinion that would leave political positions of national Parliaments unconsidered or would even contradict them.

---

[172] Cf. Saberzadeh, in von Arnauld and Hufeld (2011), Chap. 11 para 42 with further reference.

[173] Calliess 2010b, p. 23.

5.3 Establishment of a New Parliamentary Body

A third option to strengthen the democratic legitimation on the EU level is the establishment of a genuine Eurozone parliament,[174] especially in connection with the idea of a genuine Eurozone budget.[175] It would be a new parliament with representatives elected by the citizens of the Eurozone countries. This assembly would be separate from the European Parliament, i. e. a second parliamentary institution solely for Eurozone matters as a sort of mirror for the Eurozone Council formation (Euro Group). However, this approach is hardly reconcilable with the principle of unity of the European Union. Moreover, this could lead to calls for separate parliamentary *fora* for other areas of variable geometry of Union law, such as the Schengen area.

One proposal aims to transpose the logic of the Euro Group to the European Parliament. According to this idea, a sort of intra-parliamentary "Euro chamber" would be established.[176] The underlying idea is that only those MEPs, who are elected from Eurozone countries, may take part in the votes on Eurozone issues. This idea however, practical as it may seem, contradicts the rationale of Art. 14 TEU according to which the "European Parliament shall be composed of representatives of the *Union's citizens*".[177] This view is shared by Parliament itself, e. g. in its latest attempt for European parliamentary election provisions when it called for the establishment of a "European" contingent in the Parliament, elected by all citizens alike.[178]

A second proposal puts the attention on the democratic legitimation of national Parliamentarians and calls for the establishment of a parliamentary assembly for the Euro area in the form of an assembly of delegations of national Parliaments of Eurozone Member States.[179] This proposal has to be seen in the broader context of a "third chamber" of national Parliaments in the EU legislative process.[180] It resembles the European Parliament of the early years when it had been a mere parliamentary assembly of national delegates. This assembly as well would be a parliamentary mirror of the executive Euro Group. However, doubts remain as to

[174] Cf. U. Guérot and R. Menasse, Es lebe die europäische Republik, F.A.Z. of 24 March 2013, p. 24; M. Roth, Der Euro braucht ein Parlament, 17 November 2011.

[175] Cf. See The Spinelli Group/Bertelsmann Stiftung, A Fundamental Law of the European Union, 2013; cf. also Andrew Duff (who was a member of the Federalists project group), A Fundamental Law of the European Union, Speech to the Federal Trust in London on 10 January 2012, http://www.fedtrust.co.uk/filepool/Andrew_Duff_Speech_10thJanuary2013.pdf

[176] See for example Future of Europe Group of the Foreign Ministers of Austria, Belgium, Denmark, France, Italy, Germany, Luxembourg, the Netherlands, Poland, Portugal and Spain, Final Report of 17 September 2012; cf. also Deubner 2014, p. 41.

[177] Emphasis added. Cf. also Maurer 2013, p. 6.

[178] See Parliamentary Resolution *on a proposal for a modification of the Act concerning the election of the members of the European Parliament by direct universal suffrage of 20 September 1976 (2009/2134(INI))*, A7-0027/2012. For genuine European (transnational) elections see Franzius and Preuß 2012, p. 118 et seqq.

[179] Cf. J. Fischer, Die ZEIT of 10 November 2011; see also Deubner 2014, p. 42.

[180] See with a similar idea Kadelbach 2013, p. 499 et seqq.

the added value of this parliamentary institution vis-à-vis the executive (Council). As national governments generally rest on the support of the majority in the national Parliament, national delegations to this Eurozone assembly would tend to be a mirror image of the national governments and hence the Euro Group.[181] Moreover, it is questionable whether this assembly of national delegates would come to genuine European debates. Such proposals want to give rise to a general overhaul of the European constitutional architecture that may lead to an actual representation of national Parliaments within the Union's system of government, going well beyond a *Network of national Parliament representatives.*[182] When debating on a Constitution for Europe these ideas have been presented by *Joschka Fischer* and *Tony Blair*[183] as well by *Lionel Jospin* who wished to set up a congress of national Parliaments.[184] All of them remained unheard[185] and have not found any repercussion in the present drafts on the future institutions of the Union.[186] Against the will of the national Parliaments and against the resistance of the European Parliament there will be no renaissance of this proposal.[187] A second (parliamentary) chamber with a real power to participate in the decision making of the Union would hinder the European Parliament's evolution towards a front-ranking body of democratic legitimation of Union decisions. Moreover, this would over-complicate the EU institutional framework, creating overlapping roles and functions, add to the complexity of the EU decision-making process and present a challenge to the activity of the EP.[188]

5.4 *Transnational Procedures of Democratic Accountability at EU Level as a Happy Medium – a Solution via COSAC?*

Considering the political and legal difficulty of a Treaty revision, it is worth considering changes below the threshold of a formal Treaty change that can help improve the Union's democratic foundation. The legislative procedures of the EU are a ver-

[181] This is the criticism with regard to the general idea of a national chamber at EU level voiced by Corbett 2013.

[182] Cf. Mangiameli 2013, sub 4 b, c, d.

[183] Cf. the speech delivered by J. Fischer 2000 and by T. Blair, Rede vor der Warschauer Börse v. 6.10.2000, http://www.europa-digital.de/aktuell/dossier/reden/blair.shtml

[184] L. Jospin, L'Avenir de l'Europe, 28.5.2001.

[185] Cf. Mayer 2012, p. 554 et seq.

[186] Cf. however the position of Valéry Giscard d'Estaing, who declared already in June 2011: "Or, le Parlement européen n'est pas directement en contact avec le milieu politique des Etats : c'est un milieu européen en fait. Il faudrait donc faire un congrès une fois par an – je crois que je suis raisonnable – avec les députés européens et deux fois plus de députés nationaux choisis selon les mêmes critères de représentation." (http://www.euractiv.fr/avenir-europe/valery-giscard-destaing-leurope-interview-506089).

[187] Cf. Blanke 2013, sub 4; already before the Constitutional Convention Blanke 2002; the idea of a Euro-Chamber is also rejected by Maurer 2013, p. 8.

[188] Cf. also Fasone, in Blanke and Mangiameli (2013), Protocol No. 1 TEU para 159.

tical point of reference for national Parliaments to present common positions after a horizontal coordination among them. This is clearly recognised by the Treaty of Lisbon, though it restricts these competences of national Parliaments to a mere right to information (Art. 12 lit. a TEU in conjunction with Art. 1 and 2 of Protocol No. 1 TEU). More powerful are only the competences of the national Parliaments within the scrutiny of legislative proposals of the Union under the aspects of subsidiarity and proportionality (Sect. 3.2.3). But also in these situations national Parliaments act as individual institutions without having to coordinate their positions within a network of parliaments. In this atomisation, it is hardly possible that the national Parliaments reach the quorum for triggering a subsidiarity complaint procedure (18 votes in favour of the so-called "yellow card"). This weakens their position, particularly in relation to the Commission.[189]

In providing democratic legitimation in EU affairs through an additional horizontal dimension, the Conference of Parliamentary Committees for Union Affairs of Parliaments of the European Union appears to be a possible institutional point of reference. The COSAC is an inter-parliamentary advisory body and composed as a forum of cooperation between the European Affairs Committees of the national Parliaments (Art. 10 of Protocol No. 2 TEU) and at the same time a facility in which the cooperation between national Parliaments and the EP shall be strengthened.[190] This ambiguous mandate for COSAC provides opportunities for an inter-parliamentary Union, but makes at once visible the limits of such cooperation. The chance of inter-parliamentary cooperation between national Parliaments and the European Parliament is to be seen in particular, in the exchange of information and in a network between the EP committees and the corresponding committees of the national Parliaments. The Lisbon Treaty permits with the explicit mention of the Common Foreign and Security Policy far more than just a cooperation between the European Affairs Committees of the national Parliaments and the EP (inter-parliamentary ad hoc conferences under Art. 10 sentence 2 of Protocol No. 2 TEU).[191]

Always, however, the role of COSAC is limited to an advisory body for a mere exchange of information (Art. 10.4 of Protocol No. 1 TEU). Despite their non-binding effect, resolutions of the COSAC need unanimity. In institutional terms, COSAC's biggest problem is that its tasks are not compatible with the EP's membership in COSAC. The objectives that the European Parliament pursues in the framework of COSAC often contrast with the interests of national deputies in safeguarding national sovereignty. Here again, the EP makes clear that it does not intend to withdraw from COSAC, but "to intensify the cooperation with national Parliaments on the basis of Protocol No. 1".[192] This, however, is to be interpreted as the EP's claim for leadership in the process of democratic legitimation of European policies. Proposals to develop COSAC institutionally – at least in terms of a transition to majority decisions when developing *mere standpoints* in the name of national

[189] Cf. Becker 2013.
[190] See Kreilinger 2013, p. 4 et seqq.
[191] Cf. Maurer 2013, p. 11 et seqq.; See Kreilinger 2013, p. 6 et seq.
[192] Decision 13.

Parliaments – have been predominantly rejected by the national Parliaments as they want COSAC to play only a minor role as a platform for the exchange of information and mutual inspiration.[193] On this point, most national Parliaments agree with the European Parliament. If this analysis is correct, increasing the democratic legitimation of European (crisis) policy through inter-parliamentary cooperation is "purely wishful thinking".[194]

In light of this sobering analysis the 25 Contracting Parties of the Fiscal Compact Treaty should ask whether the provision of Art. 13 of this Treaty will not have a mere placebo effect. According to this provision, the European Parliament and the national Parliaments will together determine the organisation and promotion of a conference of representatives of the relevant committees in order to discuss budgetary policies and other issues covered by the Treaty.[195] Hence, it is considered possible that not only the governments of the Member States, but also Parliaments discuss and agree on future European decisions regarding competitiveness and growth. Currently, the Conference meets twice a year to discuss sector-specific reform programmes (early summer) and debate national budget proposals (autumn). Ideally, the joint resolutions could serve as a reference for both the European Parliament and national Parliaments vis-à-vis the European or national executive, respectively.[196] But the success of such proposals taken within this inter-parliamentary budgetary conference depends on the European Parliament which has to enforce these standpoints in the European arena. To avoid another "impotent talking shop"[197] in the dialogue between the European Parliament and national Parliaments, the EP's competences in the area of budgetary governance would have to be strengthened. Hitherto the "budgetary" conference of representatives of the relevant committees of the EP and of national Parliaments reflects the powerlessness of the Union in the realm of domestic economic and financial policy. Nonetheless, enhanced inter-parliamentary cooperation, also in economic and financial matters, can help build "mutual understanding and common ownership for EMU as a multi-level governance system"[198] and could also be a point of reference for parliamentary participation in EU economic and financial matters, including in the future the European Semester and the ESM, via the European Parliament.[199] On a larger scale, one can even think about extending this inter-parliamentary Fiscal Compact Conference in a comprehensive way so as to include representatives of the relevant economic, financial, social and employment affairs committees and building on the structures of the existing EU Economic and Social Committee (Art. 301 et seqq. TFEU)[200] and the Employment Committee (Art. 150 TFEU).

[193] Cf. Mayer 2012, p. 170 with further reference in footnote 110.
[194] In that sense Mayer 2012, p. 173.
[195] Cf. Maurer 2013, p. 10 et seqq.; see also Kreilinger 2013, p. 8 et seqq.
[196] Maurer 2013, p. 11.
[197] Norman 2003, p. 98.
[198] European Commission, A blueprint for a deep and genuine economic and monetary union. Launching a European debate, COM(2012) 777 final/2, p. 36.
[199] Cf. Deubner 2014, p. 37 et seqq.
[200] With this proposal Maurer 2013, p. 13.

Thus, inter-parliamentary cooperation can be a starting point to better coordinate national Parliaments vis-à-vis the European level and counter-weight the decline of national parliamentary sovereignty.[201] It could promote truly European debates even in the domestic sphere and thus make a contribution to the Union's democratic foundation. Moreover, the exchange of information can help scrutinise the respective national government.[202] In addition, inter-parliamentary exchange of information and concerns may help to streamline arguments for and against certain legislative proposals that may result in consorted action of (chambers of) national Parliaments that more easily reaches the threshold of the yellow or orange card mechanism. As diverse as they may be throughout the Member States,[203] this would enable national Parliaments to speak with one voice instead of 28 (or around 40, when we take into account individual chambers). This could be done by annual or bi-annual meetings of national Parliaments or – even better – specialised parliamentary committees to discuss, for example, the Commission's annual work programme.

In this context, some national parliaments have proposed the introduction of a "green card" mechanism.[204] This proposal has been picked up by COSAC for further elaboration.[205] According to this idea, a certain number of national parliaments (similar to the yellow and orange card mechanism) could ask the European Commission to present proposals for new EU legislation or amendments to or withdrawal of existing EU legal acts, thereby granting national parliaments as an entirety the right to legislative initiative. However, *de constitutione lata* this could not be done in a way that would legally bind the Commission to either present a proposal or give reasons for not doing so. While this is the case with the EP (Art. 225 TFEU) and the Council (Art. 241 TFEU), granting such a right to national parliaments would disturb the institutional balance and legislative system of the existing Treaties. Consequently, the Commission rejects the "green card" as a binding instruments, but points out its readiness "to consider national Parliament's input on whether there is a need for new or modified rules in any policy field"[206] and suggests to integrate any new mechanism into an informal inter-institutional agreement. In contrast, the EP's Committee on Constitutional Affairs (AFCO) has welcomed the idea of a "green

[201] Cf. See Kreilinger 2013, p. 17.
[202] Peidrafita 2013, p. 8.
[203] Cf. Kiiver 2006, p. 185 et seqq.
[204] Danish *Folketing*, Twenty-three Recommendations – to strengthen the role of national parliaments in a changing European governance, January 2014, p. 2–3; UK House of Lords, European Union Committee, Report on "The Role of National Parliaments in the European Union" of 24 March 2014, para 55; Dutch *Tweede Kamer*, "Ahead in Europe. On the role of the Dutch House of Representatives and national parliaments in the European Union" see the final report on "democratic legitimacy" of 9 May 2014, p. 29; Lord Boswell of Aynho (Chairperson of the UK House of Lords European Union Committee), letter of 28 January 2015 to the national parliaments' European Affairs Committees, "Towards a 'green card'".
[205] COSAC, Twenty-second Bi-annual Report, 4 November 2014, p. 33 et seqq.; Twenty-third Bi-annual Report, 6 May 2015, p. 31 et seqq.
[206] European Commission, letter in response to the Opinion of the House of Lords concerning the role of national Parliaments in the EU, C(2014) 4236 final of 23 June 2014. p. 2.

card" as a positive suggestion to enhance the existing political dialogue as long as it does not amount to a real right of legislative initiative of national Parliaments on EU level. While according to the existing proposal the EP should not be formally involved, it nonetheless could be a valuable cooperation partner via its right of Art. 225 TFEU.

However, as outlined above (Sect. 5.3), it is not desirable to create a "chamber of national Parliaments" with actual decision-making powers in the legislative process at EU level (such as a "red card"), as they are each endowed with one national mandate "and not with [one twenty-eighth of] a European mandate".[207] Nonetheless, by better coordinating national Parliaments in the spirit of "deliberative supranationalism" one would establish a "virtual" third chamber, i. e. they do not meet together in the same physical space, but to some extent they fulfil the function of a parliamentary chamber at EU level.[208]

6 A Reform of the European Treaties as a Precondition for a Democratisation of Economic Governance in the Union?

Whatever institutional option will be chosen, a Treaty reform seems inevitable to strengthen the Union's democratic foundation with regard to economic governance. This reform needs to go hand in hand with a general reform of the EMU in order to achieve the aim of not only establishing a monetary, but also a genuine economic union. A reform of the European Treaties is thus twofold and comprises both a transfer of policy competences as well as a restructuring of the institutional design at Union level.

As a way out of the dilemma of democratic legitimacy deficit, a major reform of the European treaties has been proposed. Especially representatives of the southern European countries support the idea that EMU governance within the Union's institutional framework and an empowerment of the European Parliament as a body for democratic control are the necessary consequences of the loss of national sovereignty during the fiscal and financial crisis.[209] The European Parliament has pushed forward such demands.[210]

One element of a Treaty reform could be a shift of competences in the area of economic governance which is inseparably connected with other political items within the competence of the nation-state. At present, the Union's competence in employment (Art. 5.2, Art. 145 et seqq. TFEU) and social policy (Art. 5.3, Art. 151 et seqq. TFEU) is very limited. Member States shall, when coordinating their economic policies, regard these as a matter of common concern and conduct them with

[207] Kiiver 2006, p. 187.

[208] On the term see Cooper 2006, p. 283; Cooper 2012, p. 441 et seq.; Joerges 2014, p. 40 et seq., with a similar account.

[209] See for example the speech delivered by the Italian President Napolitano in October 2012: http://www.italianieuropei.it/italianieuropei-9-2012/item/2806-unione-politica-ed-europeizzazione-della-politica.html

[210] European Parliament resolution of 20 November 2012, P7-TA-2012-430, Decision 13.

a view to contributing to the achievement of the Union's objectives laid down in Art. 3 TEU (cf. Art. 121.1, 120 TFEU). However, these *political* commitments do not lead to any *legally binding* obligations for the Member States. The new macroeconomic imbalance procedure, the new surveillance and enforcement mechanism set up as part of the so-called "Six-Pack" legislation, can only be part of the solution. The corrective part, the Excessive Imbalance Procedure (EIP), can only respond to singular countries and responds only if excessive macroeconomic imbalances already occur.

However, national economic and social models are diverse.[211] The current Treaties bear evidence of this fact when they say that coordination of those polices shall have regard to national practices related to the responsibilities of management and labour (Art. 146.2 TFEU) and shall take account of the diverse forms of national practices, in particular in the field of contractual relations (Art. 151.2 TFEU). In employment policy, the EP is consulted when the Council draws up the national guidelines on employment policy (Art. 148.2 TFEU). In the realm of social policy, the EP and the Council can adopt directives in the ordinary legislative procedure for certain areas (Art. 153.2 [1] and [2] TFEU), while in others the EP is merely consulted (Art. 153.2 [3] TFEU), but a passerelle can be used to make most of these areas, too, subject to the ordinary legislative procedure (Art. 153.4 TFEU). For stronger democratic input, these passerelles should be made use of.[212] However, when adopting the broad guidelines of the economic policies according to Art. 121 TFEU, the EP is merely informed. As these broad economic policy guidelines form the basis for other measures in employment and social policy, we propose that the EP shall be at least consulted on these to have the possibility to give its input (and thus represent the Union's interests) as early as possible. This change could be achieved via a simplified revision procedure (Art. 48.6 TEU).

Secondly, it seems inevitable that in the long term the Fiscal Compact Treaty and the ESM-Treaty be incorporated into the EU's legal framework. For the former, this is expressly foreseen in its Art. 16. The same should apply to the ESM-Treaty, which would then have to be coordinated more closely with the rules on *no bail out*. An incorporation of the ESM into EU law would most likely entail dependence on the EU budget. When doing so, one should review how the European Parliament (as co-budgetary institution) could be incorporated into this framework, including a potential participation in a reformed European Semester.

7 Conclusions

This analysis seems to encourage those who consider that a competence of the European Parliament is essential to convey democratic legitimation to EMU governance. The European Parliament – in full consensus with the European Commission –

[211] Cf. Wagener and Eger 2014, Chap. 11.
[212] With the same result Maurer 2013, p. 6.

"considers it necessary to place the governance of the EMU within the institutional framework of the Union, which is a precondition for its effectiveness and for filling the current political gap between national politics and European policies." Therefore, it "stresses the full legitimacy of Parliament, as parliamentary body at the Union level for a reinforced and democratic EMU governance".[213] However, one should bear in mind that a strengthening of the rights of the EP can increase the risk of mutual blockades between the Council and the EP as the two law-making bodies, because in both institutions decisions along transparent lines of conflict would become less predictable and therefore coordination of policy-forming towards concerted decisions would become extremely difficult and complex.[214]

Without a doubt a stronger political role of the EP in the budgetary and fiscal policy of the Member States would mean running the risk of a collectivisation of sovereign debt. Among the Member States a more powerful role of European Parliament in budgetary and monetary governance is mainly supported by those debtor countries which are deprived in parts of their sovereignty as a consequence of the recommendations of the (former) "European Troika" consisting of IMF, European Commission and European Central Bank. Other countries, however, feel confirmed in their position that the fiscal policy has to be merely coordinated toughly and not smoothly at European level, though, the last word on decisions about expenditure must lie in their opinion in the hands of the national Parliaments. Both these approaches are variants of a common basic concept which is underpinned by the logic of strengthening the political institutions *together with* the civil society.

The conflicting political interests and constitutional positions of the Member States about the question of the extent to which national budgetary responsibility should be transferred to the European Union and the creation of a proper fiscal capacity for the EMU are highlighting one fact: In the medium term, the fiscal, financial and tax policy will remain in the responsibility of the Member States as "nation-states". Therefore, coordination at EU level with regard to economic and fiscal governance needs democratic legitimation and accountability which is rooted in the peoples of the nation-states. The European Parliament will only be able to attain a stronger position in this field – to the detriment of national Parliaments – if trust of the citizens of all Member States in the Union's institutions grows. This requires in particular both immediate responsivity in the decision-making processes in the European Parliament and the founding of transnational political parties.

Though, one cannot preclude that due to the complexity of decisions in financial, economic and monetary policy as well as concerning sustainable budgetary consolidation, a countermovement may form in the long run that considers that the significance of *government for the people* and thus the general welfare in those

---

[213] Cf. European Parliament resolution of 20 November 2012, P7-TA-2012-430, Decisions no. 1 and 13. Cf. also Decision no. 9: "The European Parliament [c]onsiders a substantial improvement of the democratic legitimacy and accountability at Union level of the EMU governance by an increased role of Parliament as an absolute necessity and a precondition for any further step toward a banking union, a fiscal union and an economic union" See most recently, European Commission, *5-Presidents-Report 'Completing Europe's Economic and Monetary Union'*, 2015, p. 17.

[214] Benz 2005, p. 276.

matters can only be ensured effectively by technocratic decisions. Admittedly, in these years of crisis another development seems to emerge, namely scepticism by a growing number of citizens towards all institutionalised forms of parliamentary democracy. It is characterised by protest ("Occupy" and "Blockupy") which strives to express the felt powerlessness against all forms of social and economic inequality and the refusal of "global capitalism" (embodied by "the banks"). As an alternative concept, they advocate "global justice". The fight against "TTIP" is one of the most significant ciphers of these protest movements and marks the shift towards an "autonomous and spontaneous sub-system of civil society"[215] which wants to keep open the political process and, therefore, rejects to set out its "results" in a legal framework.

References

von Achenbach, J. (2014). *Demokratische Gesetzgebung in der Europäischen Union*. Heidelberg: Springer.

von Arnauld, A., & Hufeld, U. (Eds.). (2011). *Systematischer Kommentar zu den Lissabon-Begleitgesetzen*. Baden-Baden: Nomos.

Arndt, F. (2008). Ausrechnen statt aushandeln: Rationalitätsgewinne durch ein formalisiertes Modell für die Bestimmung der Zusammensetzung des Europäischen Parlaments. *ZaöRV*, 247–279.

Augustin, A. (2000). *Das Volk der Europäischen Union*. Berlin: Duncker & Humblot.

Auel, K., & Tacea, A. (2014). Fighting Back? And if yes, how? Measuring Parliamentary Strength and Activity in EU Affairs. In C. Hefftler, C. Neuhold, O. Rozenberg, J. Smith, & W. Wessels (Eds.), *Palgrave handbook on national parliaments and the European Union*. London: Palgrave Macmillan.

Baach, F. (2008). *Parlamentarische Mitwirkung in Angelegenheiten der Europäischen Union*. Tübingen: Mohr Siebeck.

Bauer, H. (2005). Demokratie in Europa – Einführende Problemskizze. In H. Bauer, P. M. Huber, & K.-P. Sommermann (Eds.), *Demokratie in Europa* (pp. 1–20). Tübingen: Mohr Siebeck.

Becker, P. (2013). Die Subsidiaritätsprüfung in Bundestag und Bundesrat – ein rechtliches oder ein politisches Instrument? *ZPol*, 5–37.

Benz, A. (2005). Politikwissenschaftliche Diskurse über demokratisches Regieren. In H. Bauer, P. M. Huber, & K.-P. Sommermann (Eds.), *Demokratie in Europa* (pp. 253–280). Tübingen: Mohr Siebeck.

Benz, A., & Auel, K. (2007). Expanding National Parliamentary Control: Does it Enhance European Democracy?. In B. Kohler-Koch, & B. Rittberger (Eds.), *Debating the democratic legitimacy of the European Union* (pp. 57–74). Lanham: Rowman & Littlefield.

Blanke, H.-J. (1993). Der Unionsvertrag von Maastricht – Ein Schritt auf dem Weg zu einem europäischen Bundesstaat. *DÖV*, 412–423.

Blanke, H.-J. (2002). Essentialia einer europäischen Verfassungsurkunde. *ThürVBl*, 197–203, 224–232.

[215] Cf. Lord 2007, p. 150 who adds, that "the representative qualities of parliamentary policies can be achieved by filtering bottom-up initiatives".

Blanke, H.-J. (2011). The European Economic and Monetary Union – between vulnerability and reform. *International Journal of Public Law and Policy*, 402–433.

Blanke, H.-J. (2013). *The Role of national Parliaments in the European Union*, Evidence given to the House of Lords (September 2013).

Blanke, H.-J., & Mangiameli, S. (Eds.). (2013). *The Treaty on European Union (TEU) – A Commentary*. Heidelberg: Springer.

Blanke, H.-J., & Pilz, S. (2014). Solidarische Finanzhilfen als Lackmustest föderaler Balance in der Europäischen Union. *EuR* 541–566.

Böckenförde, E.-W. (2004). § 24, Demokratie als Verfassungsprinzip. In J. Isensee, & P. Kirchhof (Eds.), *Handbuch des Staatsrechts der Bundesrepublik Deutschland* 3rd edn. vol. II Heidelberg: Müller.

von Bogdandy, A. (2010). Founding Principles. In A.von Bogdandy, & J. Bast (Eds.), *Principles of European Constitutional Law* (2nd edn., pp. 11–54). Oxford, Munich, Baden-Baden: Hart, C.H.Beck, Nomos.

von Bogdandy, A. (2012). The European Lesson for International Democracy. *EJIL*, 315–334.

von Bogdandy, A., & Hinghofer-Szalkay, S. (2013). Das etwas unheimliche *Ius Publicum Europaeum*. *ZaöRV*, 209–248.

Brosius-Gersdorf, F. (1999). Die doppelte Legitimationsbasis der Europäischen Union. *EuR*, 133–169.

Buche, J. (2013). Europäisierung parlamentarischer Kontrolle im Norden Europas: Dänemark, Finnland und Schweden im Vergleich. In B. Eberbach-Born, S. Kropp, A. Stuchlik, & W. Zeh (Eds.), *Parlamentarische Kontrolle und Europäische Union* (pp. 367–395). Baden-Baden: Nomos.

Buzogány, A., & Stuchlik, A. (2012). Subsidiarität und Mitsprache. Nationale Parlamente nach Lissabon. *ZParl*, 356–377.

Calliess, C. (2005a). Optionen zur Demokratisierung der Europäischen Union. In H. Bauer, P. M. Huber, & K.-P. Sommermann (Eds.), *Demokratie in Europa* (pp. 281–318). Tübingen: Mohr Siebeck.

Calliess, C. (2005b). Das Demokratieprinzip im Europäischen Staaten- und Verfassungsverbund. In J. Bröhmer, & R. Bieber (Eds.), *Internationale Gemeinschaft und Menschenrechte. Festschrift für Georg Ress* (pp. 399–421). Cologne: Heymanns.

Calliess, C. (2010a). *Die neue Europäische Union nach dem Vertrag von Lissabon*. Tübingen: Mohr Siebeck.

Calliess, C. (2010b). Nach dem Lissabon-Urteil des Bundesverfassungsgerichts: Parlamentarische Integrationsverantwortung auf europäischer und nationaler Ebene. *ZG*, *25*(1), 1–34.

Calliess, C. (2014). *Staatsrecht III. Bezüge zum Völker- und Europarecht*. Munich: C.H.Beck.

Classen, C. D. (2009). Legitime Stärkung des Bundestages oder verfassungsrechtliches Prokrustesbett? *JZ*, 881–889.

Cooper, I. (2006). The Watchdogs of Subsidiarity: National Parliaments and the Logic of Arguing in the EU. *JCMS*, 281–304.

Cooper, I. (2012). A 'Virtual Third Chamber' for the European Union? National Parliaments after the Treaty of Lisbon. *West European Politics*, 441–465.

Corbett, R. (2013). *The Role of national Parliaments in the European Union*, Evidence given to the House of Lords (September 2013).

Curtin, D. (2014). Challenging Executive Dominance in European Democracy. In C. Joerges, & C. Glinski (Eds.). *The European Crisis and the Transformation of Transnational Governance. Authoritarian Managerialism versus Democratic Governance* (pp. 203–226). Oxford: Hart Publishing.

Dann, P. (2004). *Parlamente im Exekutivföderalismus*. Berlin: Springer.

Deubner, C. (2014). Stärkere Parlamente in der neuen WWU-Gouvernanz? *integration*, 21–44.

De Wilde, P. (2012). Why the Early Warning Mechanism does not Alleviate the Democratic Deficit. *OPAL Online Paper* (6/2012).

Di Fabio, U. (1993). Der neue Art. 23 des Grundgesetzes. *Der Staat*, 191–217.

Di Fabio, U. (2014). Entwicklungsperspektiven für das Europäische Parlament. *ZSE*, 9–17.

Doehring, K. (1997). Demokratiedefizit in der Europäischen Union? *DVBl*, 1133–1137.

Duguit, L. (1921). *Traité de droit constitutionnel* (2nd edn.). vol. I. Paris: Ancienne Libr. Fontemoing.

Eder, K., & Trenz, H.-J. (2007). Prerequisites of Transnational Democracy and Mechanisms for Sustaining it: The Case of the European Union. In B. Kohler-Koch, & B. Rittberger (Eds.), *Debating the democratic legitimacy of the European Union* (pp. 165–181). Lanham: Rowman & Littlefield.

Finke, D., & Melzer, M. (2012). *Parliamentary Scrutiny of EU Law Proposals in Denmark: Why do Governments request a Negotiation Mandate?* Reihe Politikwissenschaft, vol. 127. Vienna: Institut für Höhere Studien.

Fischer, J. (2000). Vom Staatenverbund zur Föderation – Gedanken über die Finalität der europäischen Integration. *integration*, 149–156.

Franzius, C., & Preuß, U. K. (2012). *Die Zukunft der europäischen Demokratie*. Baden-Baden: Nomos.

Glaser, K. (2013). *Über legitime Herrschaft. Grundlagen der Legitimitätstheorie*. Wiesbaden: Springer VS.

Grabenwarter, C. (2011). National Constitutional Law Relating to the European Union. In A. von Bogdandy, & J. Bast (Eds.), *Principles of European Constitutional Law* (2nd edn., pp. 11–54). Oxford, Munich, Baden-Baden: Hart, C.H.Beck, Nomos.

Häberle, P. (1991). Gemeineuropäisches Verfassungsrecht. *EuGRZ*, 261–274.

Häberle, P. (1995). Gemeineuropäisches Verfassungsrecht. In R. Bieber, & P. Widmer (Eds.), *L'espace constitutionnel européen* (pp. 361–389). Zurich: Schulthess.

Habermas, J. (2001). Why Europe needs a Constitution. *New Left Review*, 5–26.

Habermas, J. (2011). *Zur Verfassung Europas*. Berlin: Suhrkamp.

Halberstam, D., & Möllers, C. (2009). The German Constitutional Court says "Ja zu Deutschland!" *GLJ*, 1241–1258.

Härtel, I. (2006). *Handbuch Europäische Rechtsetzung*. Heidelberg: Springer.

Härtel, I. (2014). § 11, Gesetzgebungsordnung der Europäischen Union. In A. Hatje, & P.-C. Müller-Graff (Eds.), *Enzyklopädie Europarecht* vol. I Baden-Baden: Nomos.

Heller, H. (1963). *Staatslehre* (3rd edn.). Leiden: Sijthoff.

Höreth, M. (1999). *Die Europäische Union im Legitimitätstrilemma. Zur Rechtfertigung des Regierens jenseits der Staatlichkeit*. Baden-Baden: Nomos.

Hrbek, R. (2012). The Role of National Parliaments in the EU. In H.-J. Blanke, & S. Mangiameli (Eds.), *The European Union after Lisbon* (pp. 129–158). Heidelberg: Springer.

Huber, P. M. (1999). Demokratie ohne Volk oder Demokratie der Völker? Zur Demokratiefähigkeit der Europäischen Union. In J. Drexl, K. F. Kreuzer, D. H. Scheuing, & U. Sieber (Eds.), *Europäische Demokratie* (pp. 27–57). Baden Baden: Nomos.

Huber, P. M. (2002). *Recht der europäischen Integration*. Munich: Vahlen.

Ipsen, H. P. (1972). *Europäisches Gemeinschaftsrecht*. Tübingen: Mohr.

Isensee, J. (1997). Nationalstaat und Verfassungsstaat – wechselseitige Bedingtheit. In R. Stober (Ed.), *Recht und Recht. Festschrift für Gerd Roellecke* (pp. 137–163). Stuttgart et al.: Kohlhammer.

Isensee, J. (2009). Europa der Nationen oder europäische Nation – Von Grund und Ziel kontinentaler Organisation. In M. Herdegen, H.-H. Klein, H.-J. Papier, & R. Scholz (Eds.), *Staatsrecht und Politik. Festschrift für Roman Herzog* (pp. 131–153). Munich: Beck.

Joerges, C. (2014). Three Transformations of Europe and the Search for a Way Out of its crisis. In C. Joerges, & C. Glinski (Eds.), *The European Crisis and the Transformation of Transnational Governance. Authoritarian Managerialism versus Democratic Governance.* (pp. 25–46) Oxford: Hart Publishing.

Kadelbach, S. (2013). Lehren aus der Finanzkrise – Ein Vorschlag zur Reform der Politischen Institutionen der Europäischen Union. *EuR*, 489–503.

Kahl, W., Waldhoff, C., & Walter, C. (Eds.). (2011). *Bonner Kommentar zum Grundgesetz. Looseleaf*. Heidelberg: C.F. Müller.

Kiiver, P. (2006). *The National Parliaments in the European Union: A Critical View on EU Constitution-Building*. The Hague: Kluwer Law International.

Kingreen, T. (2015). Die Stunde der europäischen Legislative. *Legal Tribune Online* (19.2.2015).

Kohler-Koch, B., & Rittberger, B. (2007). Charting Crowded Territory: Debating the Democratic Legitimacy of the European Union. In B. Kohler-Koch, & B. Rittberger (Eds.), *Debating the democratic legitimacy of the European Union* (pp. 1–29). Lanham: Rowman & Littlefield.

von Komorowski, A. (2010). *Demokratieprinzip und Europäische Union*. Berlin: Duncker & Humblodt.

Krajewski, M. (2008). International Organizations or Institutions, Democratic Legitimacy. In R. Wolfrum (Ed.), *Max Planck Encyclopedia of Public International Law*. Oxford: OUP.

Kreilinger, V. (2013). The New Inter-Parliamentary Conference For Economic and Financial Governance. *Notre Europe Policy Paper* No. 100.

Lord, C. (2007). Parliamentary Representation in a Decentered Polity. In B. Kohler-Koch, & B. Rittberger (Eds.), *Debating the democratic legitimacy of the European Union* (pp. 139–156). Lanham: Rowman & Littlefield.

Luhmann, N. (2000). *Die Politik der Gesellschaft*. Frankfurt/Main: Suhrkamp.

Majone, G. (1994). The Rise of the Regulatory State in Europe. *West European Politics*, 77–101.

Majone, G. (Ed.). (1996). *Regulating Europe*. London: Routledge.

Majone, G. (1998). Europe's 'Democratic Deficit': The Question of Standards. *ELJ*, 5–28.

Majone, G. (1999). The Regulatory State and Its Legitimacy Problems. *West European Politics*, 1–24.

Majone, G. (2001). Non majoritarian Institutions and the Limits of Democratic Governance: A Political Transaction-Cost Approach. *Journal of Institutional and Theoretical Economics*, 57–78.

Mangiameli, S. (2013). *The role of National Parliaments in the European Union*. Evidence given to the House of Lords (September 2013).

Martínez-Soria, J. (2004). Die Neue Europäische Union – Erste Tagung der Societas Iuris Publici Europaei (SIPE). *JZ*, 1164–1165.

Maurer, A. (2002). Nationale Parlamente in der Europäischen Union – Herausforderung für den Konvent. *integration*, 20–34.

Maurer, A. (2012). *Parlamente in der EU*. Vienna: Facultas.

Maurer, A. (2013). *From EMU to DEMU: The Democratic Legitimacy of the EU and the European Parliament*. IAI Working Papers 13/11.

Mayer, M. (2012). *Die Europafunktion der nationalen Parlamente in der Europäischen Union*. Tübingen: Mohr Siebeck.

Møller Sousa, M. (2008). Learning in Denmark? The Case of Danish Parliamentary Control over European Union Policy. *Scandinavian Political Studies*, 428–447.

Moravcsik, A. (2008). The Myth of Europe's Democratic Deficit. *Intereconomics*, 331–340.

von Münch, & Kunig (Eds.). (2012). *Grundgesetz-Kommentar* (6th edn.). Munich: C.H.Beck.

Nettesheim, M. (2005). Demokratisierung der Europäischen Union und Europäisierung der Demokratietheorie – Wechselwirkungen bei der Herausbildung eines europäischen Demokratieprinzips. In H. Bauer, P. M. Huber, & K.-P. Sommermann (Eds.), *Demokratie in Europa* (pp. 143–190). Tübingen: Mohr Siebeck.

Nettesheim, M. (2013). Demokratische Legitimation und Vertrauenskultur: zu den Grenzen majoritären Entscheidens in der EU. In M. Niedobitek, & K.-P. Sommermann (Eds.), *Die Europäische Union als Wertegemeinschaft* (pp. 39–56). Berlin: Duncker & Humblodt.

Nettesheim, M. (2014). § 15. Rechtsstaatliche Demokratie in der EU. In T. Oppermann, C. D. Classen, & M. Nettesheim (Eds.), *Europarecht* 6th edn. Munich: Beck.

Niedobitek, M. (2009). The Lisbon Case of 30 June 2009 – A Comment from the European Law Perspective. *GLJ*, 1267–1276.

Norman, P. (2003). *The Accidental Constitution: The Story of the European Constitution*. Brussels: EuroComment.

Norton, P. (1984). Parliament and policy in Britain: the House of Commons as a policy influencer. *Teaching Politics*, *13*(2), 198–221.

Oeter, S. (2010). Federalism and Democracy. In A.von Bogdandy, & J. Bast (Eds.), *Principles of European Constitutional Law* (2nd edn., pp. 55–82). Oxford, Munich, Baden-Baden: Hart, C.H.Beck, Nomos.

Piedrafita, S. (2013). EU Democratic Legitimacy and National Parliaments. *CEPS Essay No. 7*.

Pernice, I. (1993). Maastricht, Staat und Demokratie. *Die Verwaltung*, 449–488.

Pernice, I. (1995). Bestandssicherung der Verfassungen: Verfassungsrechtliche Mechanismen zur Wahrung der Verfassungsordnung. In R. Bieber, & P. Widmer (Eds.), *L'espace constitutionnel européen* (pp. 225–264). Zurich: Schulthess.

Pernice, I. (1996). Die Dritte Gewalt im Europäischen Verfassungsverbund. *EuR*, 26–42.

Pernice, I. (1998). Constitutional Law Implications for a State Participating in a Process of Regional Integration. In E. Riedel (Ed.), *German Reports on Public Law Presented to the XV. International Congress on Comparative Law* (pp. 40–64). Baden-Baden: Nomos.

Pernice, I. (1999). Multilevel Constitutionalism and the Treaty of Amsterdam: European Constitution-Making Revisited? *CMLR*, 703–750.

Pernice, I. (2002). Multilevel Constitutionalism in the European Union. *ELRev*, 511–529.

Pernice, I. (2005). Zur Finalität Europas. In G. F. Schuppert, I. Pernice, & U. Haltern (Eds.), *Europawissenschaft* (pp. 743–792). Baden-Baden: Nomos.

Pernice, I. (2009). The Treaty of Lisbon: Multilevel Constitutionalism in Action. *Columbia Journal of European Law*, 349–407.

Peters, A. (2001). *Elemente einer Theorie der Verfassung Europas*. Berlin: Duncker & Humblot.

Pierafita, S. (2013). EU Democratic Legitimacy and National Parliaments. *CEPS Essay* 7/2013.

Pinon, S. (2013). Crise économique européenne et crise institutionelle à tous les étages. *Revue de l'Union Européenne*, 218–230.

Rawls, J. (1993). *Political Liberalism*. New York: Columbia University Press.

Ruffert, M. (2004). Schlüsselfragen der Europäischen Verfassung der Zukunft: Grundrechte Institutionen – Kompetenzen – Ratifizierung. *EuR*, 165–201.

Ruffert, M., & Walter, C. (2015). *Institutionalisiertes Völkerrecht* (2nd edn.). Munich: Beck.

Raunio, T. (2005). Holding Governments Accountable in European Affairs: Explaining Cross-national Variation. *The Journal of Legislative Studies*, 319–342.

Scharpf, F. W. (1970). *Demokratietheorie zwischen Utopie und Anpassung*. Konstanz: Univ. Verl.

Scharpf, F. W. (1999). *Regieren in Europa. Effektiv und demokratisch?* Frankfurt: Campus-Verl.

Scharpf, F. W. (2006). *Problem Solving Effectiveness and Democratic Accountability in the EU*. Reihe Politikwissenschaft, vol. 107. Vienna: Institut für Höhere Studien.

Scharpf, F. W. (2007). Reflections on Multilevel Legitimacy. *MPIfG* Working Paper No. 07/3.

Schliesky, U. (2004). *Souveränität und Legitimität von Herrschaftsgewalt*. Tübingen: Mohr Siebeck.

Schmidt, V. (2005). Democracy in Europe: The Impact of European Integration. *Perspectives on Politics*, *3*(4), 761–779.

Schmitt, C. (1928). *Verfassungslehre*. Munich: Duncker & Humblot.

Schmitz, T. (2012). § 84 Staatsvolk und Unionsvolk in der föderalen Supranationalen Union. In I. Härtel (Ed.), *Handbuch Föderalismus* (vol. IV, pp. 261–289). Heidelberg: Springer.

Schönberger, C. (2004). Die Europäische Union als Bund. *AöR*, 81–120.

Schönberger, C. (2009). Lisbon in Karlsruhe: Maastricht's Epigones At Sea. *GLJ*,1201–1218.

Sommermann, K.-P. (1997). *Staatsziele und Staatszielbestimmungen*. Tübingen: Mohr Siebeck.

Sommermann, K.-P. (1998). Der entgrenzte Verfassungsstaat. *Kritische Vierteljahresschrift für Gesetzgebung und Rechtswissenschaft*, *81*, 404–422.

Sommermann, K. P. (2005). Demokratiekonzepte im Vergleich. In H. Bauer, P. M. Huber, & K.-P. Sommermann (Eds.), *Demokratie in Europa* (pp. 191–221). Tübingen: Mohr Siebeck.

Stratulat, C., Emmanouilidis, J. A., Fischer, T., & Piedrafita, S. (2014). *Legitimising EU Policymaking: What Role for National Parliaments*. Brussels Thinks Tank Dialogue 2014. Discussion paper.

Streinz, R. (2012). *Europarecht* (9th edn.). Heidelberg: Müller.

Vari, M., & Istituto per la documentazione e gli studi legislativi (2012). *Presentazione del volume "The European Union after Lisbon. Constitutional Basis, Economic Order and External Action" di Hermann-Josef Blanke e Stelio Mangiameli* (pp. 703–728). Berlin Heidelberg: Springer-Verlag. Presented by G. Amato, P. De Ioanna & M. Vari.

Wagener, H.-J., & Eger, T. (2014). *Europäische Integration: Wirtschaft und Recht, Geschichte und Politik* (3rd edn.). Munich: Vahlen.

Weber, A. (2010). *Europäische Verfassungsvergleichung*. Munich: C.H. Beck.

Weber, A. (2011). Die Reform der Wirtschafts- und Währungsunion in der Finanzkrise. *EuZW*, 935–940.

Weber, A. (2013). Europa- und völkerrechtliche Elemente der Gewährleistung von Haushaltsdisziplin in der Währungsunion. *EuR*, 375–388.

Weber, M. (1918). *Parlament und Regierung im neugeordneten Deutschland*. Munich: Duncker & Humblot.

Weigand, E. (2008). Towards a common European legal thinking: a dialogic challenge. In H. Petersen, A. L. Kjær, H. Krunke, & M. Rask Madsen (Eds.), *Paradoxes of European Legal Integration* (pp. 235–251). Aldershot, Hampshire: Ashgate.

Wendel, M. (2011). *Permeabilität im europäischen Verfassungsrecht. Verfassungsrechtliche Integrationsnormen auf Staats- und Unionsebene im Vergleich*. Tübingen: Mohr Siebeck.

Zürn, M. (1996). Über den Staat und die Demokratie im europäischen Mehrebenensystem. *Politische Vierteljahresschrift*, *37*(1), 27–55.

The Role of Fundamental Rights in the EU Federal Community of Law

A Systematizing Essay

Peter-Christian Müller-Graff

The role of fundamental rights in the European Union's federal community of law alludes first to fundamental rights and second to the idea of a federal community of law.[1] Fundamental rights are collective promises of protection to any individual concerned. What is understood to be fundamental can vary. In a federal community of law, different promisors can compete. The question of the role of fundamental rights in a federal community of law cannot be appropriately addressed without first considering whether the federal category, elaborated by *Albrecht Weber* in his comprehensive book on European comparative constitutional law,[2] is adequate for the European community of law. Hence, the following observations are divided into three parts: (1) whether the comparative category of a federal community of law is fitting for the European Union; (2) which profiling characteristics of the protection of fundamental rights in the Union have to be discussed from such a comparative view; and (3) what is the prospective role of fundamental rights for the European community of law in relation to the classic transnational market freedoms of the internal market.

1 The Suitability of the Comparative Category of a Federal Community of Law

Using the comparative category of a federal community of law evokes the question of whether it is proper or misleading to use the word "federal" for the European Union in this specific context. One must tread with caution: It is difficult to even bring up the question of using the term "federal" in regards to the Union, even if only in an adjectival way, without being immediately torn apart by the gate keep-

---

[1] This contribution is based on the German text of a lecture held at the Austrian Constitutional Court in 2013; a German version is separately published.

[2] Weber 2010, p. 369 et seq.

H.-J. Blanke et al. (eds.), *Common European Legal Thinking*,
DOI 10.1007/978-3-319-19300-7_15

ers of the Holy Grail of sovereign statehood. This hostility is attributed to one's interpretation of the term "federalism".

1.1 If federalism is understood in the sense of a federal *state*, its marriage with the Union is immediately hit by the carnassial teeth of *Georg Jellinek's* three-element-dogmatics of statehood.[3] It is beyond serious doubt that in six decades of supranational European integration nothing has fundamentally changed in the central aspect that each Member State holds monopoly over legitimate physical power in its autonomously controlled territory and autonomously defines the criteria of its citizenship. Hence, it did not come as a surprise that the Bundesverfassungsgericht in its "*Lisbon*" judgment also drew this conclusion.[4] Conversely, nothing has changed in this respect in view of the Union. The Union does not dispose of the means of physical enforcement against reluctant natural or legal persons, nor is it entitled to autonomously define its territorial configuration, the criteria for Union citizenship, or its own competences.[5]

1.2 However, if the term "federalism" is separated from its origin as the fundamental source of legitimization of collective sovereignty, and related in a *functional* way only to the coexistence of public power of different public agents in the same territory as one model of the territorial partition of power ("Territoriale Herrschaftsteilung" in the comparative classification of *A. Weber*[6]), then parallel questions (although not similar answers) emerge regarding the order and relationship of these powers in a federal state and in the European Union. These questions can be called functional federal matters:[7] for example the questions of the partition and character of competences (such as exclusive or shared competences); the relation between conflicting provisions of the regional dimension and the overarching polity dimension; the issue of mutual loyalty. Since the Union is doubtlessly a community of law as described by the first President of the Commission of the EEC, *Walter Hallstein*,[8] a former professor for private law and economic law, it is reasonable to summarize the totality of answers of Union law to such parallel questions as a federal community of law.

[3] Jellinek 1900.
[4] German FCC, 2 BvE 2/08, 2 BvE 5/08, 2 BvR 1010/08, 2 BvR 1022/08, 2 BvR 1259/08, 2 BvR 182/09 (Judgment of 30 June 2009) para 299 – *Lissabon-Vertrag* (in BVerfGE 123, 267): sovereign power, para 344 et seq.: territory, para 346 et seq.: people.
[5] Müller-Graff 2012, A I, para 490 et seq.
[6] Weber 2010, p. 343 et seq., p. 369 et seq. (with a comprehensive comparison of the models of Germany, Austria, Switzerland and Belgium).
[7] Müller-Graff 2005, p. 105 et seq.
[8] Hallstein 1979, p. 51 et seq.

2 The Profiling Characteristics of the Fundamental Rights in the European Union in a Comparative Federal View

Moving on to the second question, namely to the profiling characteristics and the significance of fundamental rights in the European Union (after the ratification of the Charter of Fundamental Rights of the European Union together with the Reform Treaty of Lisbon) in a federal comparison – particularly in comparison with federal polities in European countries such as Germany, Austria and Switzerland – at least eight criteria deserve attention: (Sect. 2.1) the living federal promise of fundamental rights, (Sect. 2.2) the federal architecture of the sources of fundamental rights and in relation to the Union specifically, (Sect. 2.3) their federal scope of applicability, (Sect. 2.4) their direct applicability and character as subjective rights, (Sect. 2.5) their relation to national fundamental rights, (Sect. 2.6) their judicial enforceability, (Sect. 2.7) their scope of control relevance and (Sect. 2.8) their potential for judicial references and political guidelines.

2.1 *The Living Federal Promise of Fundamental Rights*

A federal community of law is not feasible without being founded upon the basis of a living mutual promise. This promise can vary. For example, Swiss citizens transmit from generation to generation the Rütli oath sworn by their forefathers on the meadows of the Alps (Schweizer Eidgenossenschaft). German citizens, after having overcome a most dire dictatorship, trust, in principle, in the federal Basic Law as conceived by the Herrenchiemsee Convention. The specific profile of the promise of the European Union and its community of law is established in the Treaties between the Member States which express the Union's aim to promote peace, its values and the wellbeing of its peoples (Art. 3.1 TEU)[9] and which guarantee in particular the individual transnational market freedoms as the prime vehicle of creating transnational contacts.

Under the specific aspect of fundamental rights, the mutual promise is laid down in the Lisbon Treaty's article on values, which binds the Union and its Member States to the values of respect for human dignity, freedom, democracy, equality, the rule of law and the respect for human rights (Art. 2 TEU). This is a rather highly abstract oath, with the article leaving open how it is implemented. For the Union – and in a limited way, for the Member States – the promise of respecting fundamental rights is entrusted by Art. 6 TEU to two sources: the Charter of Fundamental Rights of the European Union (EUCFR) and the fundamental rights as general principles of the Union's law as derived from the European Convention for the Protection of Human Rights and Fundamental Freedoms (ECHR) and the constitutional traditions common to the Member States.

[9] Müller-Graff 2012, A I, para 490 et seq.

2.2 The Federal Multipolarity of Sources of Fundamental Rights

The multipolarity of the federal architecture of the sources of fundamental rights in the Union is well known. Often called a "multi-level-system", this widely used wording should not evoke the idea of a simple hierarchy, which in reality does not match the normative complexity of the system. Normative declarations exist at many points in the federal legal cosmos of the Union: in subnational constitutions of federal states (e. g. Bavaria[10] or Vorarlberg[11]); in national constitutions;[12] in the codified primary law of the Union (this will be elaborated later on); and in the invisible energy of general principles of Union law.[13] By way of the latter ideas that have been developed in other normative universes, can serve as sources of inspiration, persuasive authorities and fortifiers of convincing authority for the development of Union law. These other normative universes are, in particular, international conventions or texts (such as the ECHR, the European Charter of Social Rights or the UN Declaration of Human Rights), but also national legal orders from both within and outside the Union. Against the background of the global spread of normative ideas and of the emergence of *transnational common legal thinking*, this multipolar situation offers fertile ground for inspiring thought about the abstract formulation of codified texts for the protection of fundamental rights and for the solution of concrete conflicts.

The multipolarity of sources of fundamental rights in a federal community of law is not particular to the Union. In addition to the examples of Germany and Austria already discussed, the same is true for Switzerland (e. g. the constitutions of the Canton of Zürich[14] and the Confederatio Helvetica[15]) and the United States (e. g. the constitution of Massachusetts[16] and the Federal Bill of Rights[17]). The specific characteristics of the role of the fundamental rights of the Union become apparent when comparing them to other criteria, such as, first of all, the federal scope of applicability.

2.3 The Restricted Federal Scope of Applicability

When using the German Grundgesetz standard for assessing the federal scope of applicability, the specific feature of fundamental rights in Union law becomes apparent. Art. 1.3 GG is worded (in translation): "The following basic rights shall

[10] Art. 98 et seq. of the Bavarian Constitution (1946).
[11] Art. 7 of the Constitution of Vorarlberg (1999/2014).
[12] See Die Verfassungen der EU-Mitgliedstaaten (6th edn., 2005).
[13] See Art. 6.3 TEU.
[14] Art. 9 to 18 of the Constitution of the Canton Zürich (2005).
[15] Art. 7 to 36 of the Swiss Constitution (1999/2013).
[16] Part the First (Art. I–CVI to XXX) of the Constitution of the Commonwealth of Massachusetts (1780).
[17] Bill of Rights (1789/1791).

bind the legislature, the executive, and the judiciary as directly applicable law." This applies to all public authorities within the federation: the federation itself, the states ("Länder"), the local communities and all other public agents.

2.3.1 Such a federal claim of universal applicability to all acts of all public authorities within the relevant territory is not inherent in the Charter of Fundamental Rights. Its scope of applicability is restricted by Art. 51.1 EUCFR, which says that "the provisions of this Charter are addressed to the institutions, bodies, offices and agencies of the Union ... and to the Member States only when they are implementing Union law."

A well-known dispute exists over whether the term "implementing" adopts the narrow implementation formula of the "*Wachauf*" judgment of the ECJ[18] or whether Art. 52.7 EUCFR activates the larger formula of the "*ERT*" judgment ("falling within the scope of Community law"[19]). According to that provision, "the explanations drawn up as a way of providing guidance in the interpretation of this Charter shall be given due regard by the courts of the Union and of the Member States." In addition, the formula, which the ECJ created in the "*Åkerberg Fransson*" decision,[20] has created concern[21] over whether the ECJ is beginning to transgress the limits intended by the Member States when they agreed on the term "implementing" (in the German version: "durchführen"). The Åkerberg formula stipulates that the Charter is applicable "in all situations governed by European law" and hence for "national legislation (which) falls within the scope of European Union law."[22] This formula is very abstract and could indeed open the way for encroaching upon the competences of the Member States. While further discussion of this point is not within the purview of this paper, it should be remembered that the ratified words of the Member States enjoy prime legitimate authority. Hence, the ECJ would be well advised to take a cautious view in defining the scope of applicability of the Charter in national measures.

Independently from the concrete definition of the demarcation line in Art. 51, it must be stated for a thorough comparison of federal communities of law that the Charter does not address national measures that are not implementing Union law. Additionally, implementing measures are not addressed in Britain and Poland to the degree stated in Protocol 30.[23] In particular, such laws, regulations or administrative provisions, practices or actions must not be found by the ECJ or any national court or tribunal as inconsistent with the rights, freedoms and principles of the Charter. Nevertheless, this does not preclude the national courts of these states from using the Charter as persuasive authority.

[18] Case 5/88, *Wachauf* (ECJ 13 July 1989) para 19.
[19] Case C-260/89, *ERT* (ECJ 18 June 1991) para 42.
[20] Case C-617/10, *Åkerberg Fransson* (ECJ 26 February 2013).
[21] See, e. g., Frenzel 2014, p. 1.
[22] Case C-617/10, *Åkerberg Fransson* (ECJ 26 February 2013).
[23] See Lindner 2008, 786.

2.3.2 Apart from that, all Member States are bound by fundamental rights as general principles of the Union's law, as stated in Art. 6.3 TEU, within the limits of the so-called extension jurisprudence of the ECJ to national measures ("Erstreckungsrechtsprechung") in accordance with "*Wachauf*"[24] and "*ERT*".[25] This would be different if the Charter were considered to be the exhaustive regulation of the protection of fundamental rights in the Union's law. But such an approach would clearly contradict Art. 6.3 TEU, and likely contradict the explicit safeguarding clause of the acquis in Art. 53 EUCFR. Conversely, an extension of the extension jurisprudence beyond the traditional limits would risk a circumvention of the idea of federal partition of protection.

2.4 Direct Applicability and Subjective Rights

In respect to direct applicability and subjective rights, the German Grundgesetz standard is clear; it rejects all theories, held, for example, under the Weimar constitution, which consider fundamental rights only as programmes for political action. The Charter lacks an equivalent statement. On the contrary a clear response to this question is made difficult to ascertain by the Charter's distinction between rights and principles in Art. 52.2 and 52.5 EUCFR. This indicates that not all provisions of the Charter contain rights, although the Charter does not precisely classify its provisions according to this demarcation line. Moreover, there might even be an overlap of both categories in certain provisions. Here, legal erudition is tasked with clarification. For example, one can hardly overcome the impression of a programme provision when Art. 38 EUCFR states, "Union policies shall ensure a high level of consumer protection." Different from the transnational freedoms, not every position mentioned in the Charter contains a subjective right (e. g. Art. 37 EUCFR which deals with environmental protection).

2.5 The Legal Question of Federal Primacy

In view of the legal question of federal primacy again the German Grundgesetz can serve as a federal standard against which to measure. It contains the short provision: "Bundesrecht bricht Landesrecht" ("Federal law shall take precedence over State law"; Art. 31 GG). This applies also to the relation between different rules on fundamental rights in the Federation and individual States. In Union law, conflicts concerning the scope and content of fundamental rights in relation to Member States should be solved, in principle, according to the "*Costa/E.N.E.L.*" jurisprudence,[26]

[24] Case 5/88, *Wachauf* (ECJ 13 July 1989) para 19.
[25] Case C-260/89, *ERT* (ECJ 18 June 1991) para 42.
[26] Case 6/64, *Costa/E.N.E.L.* (ECJ 15 July 1964).

which – as interpreted today – gives primacy to the Charter and the general principles over national laws. However, on this basis, a differentiated approach seems to be preferable.

2.5.1 As far as the compatibility of Union measures (in particular secondary law) with the Charter is concerned, its primacy should be beyond any doubt. National standards should play no autonomous role in this respect. This deviates from the conceptual approach of the Bundesverfassungsgericht in its "*Solange II*" decision[27] (as affirmed in its "*Lisbon*" decision[28]), but this approach is presently without practical consequences and also not persuasive in the system of German constitutional law (because of the openness of the national constitution towards European integration in Art. 23 GG and the competence attributed to the ECJ by the respective German consent Acts).

2.5.2 In relation to national implementing measures, which are *not completely* determined by Union law, the federal character of the Union commands a dual compatibility; meaning a national measure that is compatible with the Charter must also comply with the standards of national fundamental rights (as far as it is not completely determined by the directive), and vice versa. For example, a concrete national provision that implements a directive on data protection and satisfies the requirements of Art. 8 EUCFR must also fulfil the standards of a national fundamental right to privacy (as far as it is not completely determined by a directive). This approach also corresponds to the objective of Art. 53 EUCFR.

2.6 *The Judicial Enforceability of the Rights of the Charter*

A specific federal aspect is also inherent in the issue of judicial enforceability. In comparison to the German system, the peculiarity of the Union system is marked by a different partition of direct judicial protection and, at least until now, by a different context of consideration to the fundamental right argument. Different from German law, the Union's law does not offer individuals the direct procedural means to lodge a constitutional complaint based on the assertion of a violation of a fundamental right by a public authority ("Verfassungsbeschwerde") at the ECJ.

2.6.1 Consequently, an individual may only institute proceedings against certain *acts of the Union* before the ECJ on grounds of infringement of the Treaties (here the Charter included) or of any rule of law relating to their application under the restrictive conditions of Art. 263 TFEU. Otherwise, the complaint of an infringement

[27] German FCC, 2 BvR 197/83 (Order of 22 October 1986)–*Solange II* (in BVerfGE 73, 339 [387]).

[28] German FCC, 2 BvE 2/08, 2 BvE 5/08, 2 BvR 1010/08, 2 BvR 1022/08, 2 BvR 1259/08, 2 BvR 182/09 (Judgment of 30 June 2009) para 181 – *Lissabon-Vertrag* (in BVerfGE 123, 267 et seqq.); for the development of this jurisprudence see Müller-Graff 2011, p. 153 et. seq.

of a right of the Charter can only be treated by the ECJ in "indirect" procedures, such as a preliminary reference procedure (Article 267 TFEU) or an incident control (Art. 277 TFEU).

2.6.2 In view of *national implementing measures*, the competence for assessing claims that national measures contradict the Charter primarily rests with the national courts and requires the direct applicability of the invoked position. In such a case, the individual's complaint can only reach the ECJ by way of a preliminary reference procedure concerning the interpretation of the Charter, which can be initiated only by the decision of a national court. Regardless of this, the Commission can start an infringement procedure against a Member State (Art. 258 TFEU).

2.7 Factual Scope of Legal Conflicts and Judicial Control Relevance

Concerning the factual scope of legal conflicts and judicial control relevance, the role of the fundamental rights of Union law in the federal community of law depends on the volume of potential conflicts with public measures and their control. In comparison to the array of measures that are available to a state, several factors might lower the importance of fundamental rights concerning Union measures. This pertains in particular to Union legislation, where it takes place either in the form of directives (instead of regulations) and leaves the substantive implementing measures to the discretion of Member States or when texts are formulated in the open spirit of a "caractère diplomatique." Moreover, in the administrative area, the Union lacks physical enforcement power.[29] Union law offers only a restricted direct complaint procedure on the judicial level. Additionally, Union law looks to an array of many legal criteria other than fundamental rights when reviewing a measure or conduct of the Union. Therefore, it seems that serious friction areas with the Charter will most likely be confined to administrative acts and regulations of the Union and may more often arise in regards to national implementing measures.

2.8 Potential for Judicial References and Political Guidelines

Without prejudice to the foregoing considerations, the Charter offers an unlimited potential of arguments to be made by all public bodies in the federal community of law of the Union, including both Union institutions and national public agents. In particular, it can be expected that many policies of the Union will reference articles of the Charter as supporting the objectives pursued by a policy. However, caution must be taken; the more fundamental rights are referenced in daily life situations,

[29] See above Sect. 1.1.

the more their authority is endangered of being watered down. In light of the experience with the jurisprudence of the Bundesverfassungsgericht (in particular, the ability to file constitutional complaints against judgments of courts) it is possible to transform any social conflict into an issue of fundamental rights (e. g. even the issue of validity of the surety of a housewife given to a bank for the debt of her husband[30]). Such a development can transport regular legal arguments in a specific area of law into the rather abstract realm of discussions on fundamental rights and generate rather general assessments without additional concrete substance. Moreover, such a development may unduly restrict the discretion of the democratically elected legislator. Conversely, it provides an opportunity for strengthening the dominance of unbiased rationality (like in the "Unisex" decision of the ECJ[31]). This leads to the general issue of the proper mutual control and balance between political authorities and the judiciary.

In sum, the federal comparison demonstrates a specifically differentiated picture of the role of fundamental rights in the federal community of law of the Union. Moreover, an additional factor plays an important role – the guarantee of the transnational market freedoms.

3 The Prospective Role of Fundamental Rights for the European Community of Law in Relation to the Transnational Market Freedoms

In primary Union law the fundamental rights of Union law do not represent the full panoply of subjective rights. It is well known that the supranational integration of Europe was founded on the bedrock principles of transnational market access freedoms. Hence, the question arises as to how fundamental rights are to be understood in relation to these principles. In this respect, an analysis of several short test points is instructive: (Sect. 3.1) the normative-systematic functions, (Sect. 3.2) the dogmatic structure, (Sect. 3.3) the cooperative relationship, (Sect. 3.4) the conflict situation, and (Sect. 3.5) the relevance for the cohesion of European integration.

3.1 The Normative-Systematic Functions

Beyond the common function of granting subjective rights, the normative-systematic function of market freedoms and fundamental rights has to be distinguished. While market freedoms guarantee the free movement of productive factors and products within the internal market across state borders (Art. 3 TEU, Art. 26.2

[30] German FCC, 1 BvR 567/89, 1 BvR 1044/89 (Order of 19 October 1993)–*Bürgschaftsvertrag* (in BVerfGE 89, 214 et seqq.).
[31] Case C-236/09, *Test Achats* (ECJ 1 March 2011).

TFEU), the fundamental rights protect against public conduct in the context of Union law (in the sense of Art. 51 EUCFR).

3.1.1 If viewed under the aspect of subjective rights within the federal community of law, market freedoms horizontally open transnational opportunities and risks for natural and legal persons, while the fundamental rights vertically grant preventive or reactive protection in relation to public measures in the context of the Union. Hence, private dynamics are expected within market freedoms while public defence and promotion is expected within fundamental rights. Moreover, market freedoms are rooted in the institutional concept of a common economic area, originally conceived of by the *Jean Monnet* group, as an eo ipso functioning common market area.[32] In comparison, the objective of fundamental rights (as conceived in the 18th century) includes the protection of different individual positions against the collective public polity – notwithstanding the modern view, which ascribes them an additional objective content and the duty of proactive protection through the public polity.[33] An institutional function of the protection of fundamental rights for European integration can be conceived only on a rather highly abstract level as a community of values.[34]

3.1.2 Against the background of this model distinction, the question arises whether Art. 15.2 EUCFR blurs this distinction. According to that provision, a subset of market freedoms is inserted in the Charter, namely the free movement of workers, the right of establishment and the freedom to provide services. It is true that the scope of Art. 15 EUCFR is broader, because it defines the freedoms without limiting them to transnational projects; but it also comprises them. Insofar it generates the requirement of parallel interpretation in the Charter and the Treaty on the Functioning of the EU (Art. 52.2 EUCFR). In the judical practice the multitude of the first access to such problems can be expected to rest with the market freedoms; because, as outlined by the ECJ's President *Skouris*, usually the market freedoms open the competence of the Court.[35]

3.2 *The Dogmatic Structure*

In relation to the dogmatic structure of both sets of law, it has long been known that, despite all differences in the details, a parallel pattern of questions and criteria prevails: legal nature, entitled persons, addressees, substantive content, legitimate restrictions, and restrictions of restrictions. Examples of this parallelism include the "*Banana*" judgment of the ECJ (fundamental rights)[36] and the "*Schmidberger*"

[32] Monnet 1976, p. 186.
[33] See, e. g., Szczekalla 2002; see also Case C-368/95, *Familiapress* (ECJ 26 June 1997).
[34] In this direction Alston and Weiler 1998, p. 723.
[35] Skouris 2006, p. 93.
[36] Case C-280/93, *Germany v. Council* (ECJ 5 October 1994).

decision of the ECJ (free movement of goods).[37] In both groups of provisions, a powerful parallel in favour of the federal community of law can be seen in the requirement of proportionality, which tends to civilize politics and administration in detail. In each realm of sovereign power, a public measure is required to abstractly fulfil the same control criteria of the (potential) judicial review, namely suitability, necessity and a positive contribution to the common good ("Gemeinwohlgewinn"). According to a widely asserted impression, the judicial review of regulatory measures of the economy seems to be more rigid if market freedoms are restricted by Member states than if fundamental freedoms are restricted by the Union. However, without parallel constellations, such a comparison is methodologically unsustainable.

3.3 *The Cooperative Relationship*

The guarantee of transnational market freedoms and the protection of fundamental rights can enter into a cooperative relationship. In this respect, fundamental rights can reinforce market freedoms through an assessment of the proportionality of a restriction under the aspect of a contribution to the common good: for example, in the question of whether a prospective increase of health protection expected from a general national prohibition of alcopops advertising can be considered proportional in relation to the prohibition of marketing newspapers from other Member States, even in the case where the advertisement would be blackened out. Here, the freedom of expression and the pluralism of the media (Art. 11 EUCFR) can work as barriers to a legitimate restriction of the free movement of goods ("Schrankenschranken"). Besides, this line of reasoning presupposes the interpretation of "implementing" in Art. 51 EUCFR in the sense of the "*Åkerberg Fransson*" formula ("national legislation falls within the scope of Union law"[38]).

Conversely, a reinforcement of the fundamental rights by market freedoms can also occur: for example, if a national prohibition of marketing fruit liquors of low alcohol content does not serve health protection and is not necessary to protect the consumer against being misled,[39] then the assessment of an identical Union regulation cannot produce a different result in the light of the right to conduct a business (Art. 16 EUCFR).

[37] Case C-112/00, *Schmidberger* (ECJ 12 June 2003).
[38] Case C-617/10, *Åkerberg Fransson* (ECJ 26 February 2013) para 21.
[39] Case 120/78, *Cassis de Dijon* (ECJ 20 February 1979).

3.4 The Conflict Situation

The guarantee of market freedoms and the protection of fundamental rights not only have a potential for cooperation, but also for collision. In this regard, two areas of conflict have to be distinguished: (3.4.1) the area of the Union's policy to effectuate the market freedoms by adopting secondary law, in particular by approximating national provisions, and (3.4.2) the area of direct applicability of market freedoms.

3.4.1 For the first type of conflict, the potential control function of fundamental rights for relevant directives, regulations or decisions is evident. However, they are not the prime or sole measurement of primary law used in assessing whether secondary law complies with the federal community of law.

The first criterion to be met is the existence of Union competence in accordance with the principle of conferral (Art. 5.2 TEU). This means that, first of all, a secondary act which is supposed to effectuate transnational market freedoms has to be examined as to whether it is covered by the claimed competence of the Union to promote the establishment and the functioning of the internal market (e. g. Art. 114 TFEU). For example, the first tobacco advertising directive did not meet this criterion.[40] Serious doubts also exist as to the adequacy of the proposed Common European Sales Law as an approximation of national laws in the sense of Art. 114 TFEU[41] (without prejudice to the suitability of the competence of Art. 352 TFEU). If the competence for a concrete measure meets this first criterion, the next step in assessing compatibility with primary law is to examine whether a bundle of principles other than the fundamental rights is complied with. This bundle includes, in particular, subsidiarity (Art. 5.3 TEU), proportionality (Art. 5.4 TEU), sufficient reasoning (Art. 296.2 TFEU) and the market freedoms that bind the Union in its actions.[42] In the interest of keeping fundamental rights as a strong authority, they should come into play only if they can perform a genuine function which is not yet covered by other primary law requirements. And in terms of legal reasoning, the differentiated set of legal principles should not be swallowed by the sole idea of fundamental rights.

3.4.2 In the area of direct applicability of the market freedoms, the relation to fundamental rights is more complex. Here the question arises of whether a restriction of free transnational movement can be justified by the protection of national or European fundamental rights. Some efforts in scholarly literature to construe a simple hierarchical relation between the two general groups of norms (in the sense of a general primacy of one group over the other) do not match their equivalent rank in primary law, the difference of their functions, the variety of concrete collisions or the federal character of the Union's community of law. Concerning concrete colli-

[40] Case 376/98, *Germany/Parliament and Council* (ECJ 5 October 2000).

[41] Müller-Graff 2014a, p. 617 et seq.

[42] E. g. Case 15/83, *Denkavit Nederland* (ECJ 17 May 1984) para 15; Cases C-154/04 and C-155/04, *Alliance for Natural Health* (ECJ 12 July 2005) para 47.

sions, a distinction must be drawn between public or private actors as the originators of a restriction.

3.4.2.1 If a national public authority defends a restrictive measure (e. g. the prohibition of marketing virtual killing games[43] or the authorization of a demonstration for environmental protection on a motorway[44]) on the grounds that it is necessary for the protection of national fundamental rights, then the federal character of the Union's community of law requires that such an argument is treated in the same way as arguments that invoke other mandatory public interests, such as health protection in the sense of Art. 36 TFEU. As long as no exhaustive Union legal measure is adopted in the concrete matter concerned, a Member State enjoys the discretion to define its preferred level of protection. Hence, this approach in the reasoning of the ECJ decisions "*Omega*"[45] and "*Schmidberger*"[46] is convincing. However, in any case, the national measure has to comply with the general criteria of proportionality (i. e. suitability, necessity, proportionality in the sense of a gain for the common good of the Union) and the Member State concerned must justify invoking the protection of fundamental rights for the concrete measure.

3.4.2.2 If, however, a restriction originates from the conduct of a private actor, a different distinction must be drawn.

As far as restrictions flow from preference decisions of private market participants (e. g. the preference of a marble tradesman for Carrara marble thereby reducing his willingness to trade in other types of marble produced in other Member States), no justification is necessary. Preference decisions precisely fit the very purpose of transnational market freedoms, namely, promoting transnational competition.[47] Preference decisions are at the core of a market economy with free and undistorted competition.[48]

However, if the restriction to use a transnational market freedom is rooted in the conduct of a third party, which is not founded on a preference decision for a personal transaction (e. g., rules of international sport associations or boycotts by trade unions) and concerns a concrete project of transnational interaction of other market actors (e. g., the move of a football player from a Belgian soccer club to a French soccer club[49] or the registration of a Finnish ship in another Member State[50]), then such conduct is compatible with the relevant market freedom (e. g., the free movement of workers or services or the freedom of establishment) only if it can be justified by the guarantee of a national fundamental right. Art. 51 EUCFR

---

[43] Case C-36/02, *Omega* (ECJ 14 October 2004).
[44] Case C-112/00, *Schmidberger* (ECJ 12 June 2003).
[45] Case C-36/02, *Omega* (ECJ 14 October 2004).
[46] Case C-112/00, *Schmidberger* (ECJ 12 June 2003).
[47] Müller-Graff 2010, p. 329 et seq.
[48] Müller-Graff 2014b, p. 18.
[49] Case C-415/93, *Bosman* (ECJ 15 December 1995).
[50] Case C-438/05, *Viking* (ECJ 11 December 2007).

bars invocation of the Charter by the acting private party because it does not address private actions, statutes of private associations or collective bargaining agreements.

3.5 The Relevance for the Cohesion of European Integration

Eventually the role of fundamental rights in relation to market freedoms will also be determined by their contribution to the cohesion of the Union. Such a prognosis is difficult. On the one hand, there are good reasons for assuming that the permanent subtle orientation of people towards shared values, such as the permanent reliable realization of fundamental rights, can serve as an important factor of cohesion for the transnational federal polity of the Union. This concept is expressed by Art. 2 TEU which provides that the values of the Union (among them the respect for human rights) "are common to the Member States in a society in which pluralism, non-discrimination, tolerance, justice, solidarity and equality between women and men prevail". On the other hand, there are also good reasons to assume that the central factual cohesion generated by the multiple uses of the border-crossing market freedoms (which are also part of Art. 2 TEU) by multiple private actors can hardly be replaced by an orientation towards more abstract common values. Therefore, it seems safe to predict that the realization of both forms of subjective rights will contribute to the cohesion of the Union.

References

Alston, P., & Weiler, H. H. (1998). An "Ever Closer Union" in Need of a Human Rights Policy – The European Union and Human Rights. *European Journal of International Law*, *9*, 658–723.

Frenzel, E. M. (2014). Die Charta der Grundrechte als Maßstab für mitgliedstaatliches Handeln zwischen Effektivierung und Hyperintegration. *Der Staat*, *53*, 1–29.

Hallstein, W. (1979). *Die Europäische Gemeinschaft* (5th edn.). Düsseldorf, Wien: Econ.

Jellinek, G. (1900). *Allgemeine Staatslehre*. Berlin: Häring.

Lindner, J. F. (2008). Zur grundsätzlichen Bedeutung des Protokolls über die Anwendung der Grundrechtecharta auf Polen und das Vereinigte Königsreich – zugleich ein Beitrag zur Auslegung von Art. 51 EGC. *Europarecht*, *43*, 786–799.

Monnet, J. (1976). *Mémoires*. Paris: Fayard.

Müller-Graff, P.-C. (2005). The German Länder. Involvement in EC/EU Law and Policy Making. In S. Weatherill, & U. Bernitz (Eds.), *The Role of Regions and Sub-National Actors in Europe. Essays in European Law* (pp. 103–118). Oxford, Portland, Oregon: Hart Publishing.

Müller-Graff, P.-C. (2010). Die Marktfreiheiten als Herzstück der europäischen Wettbewerbsidee: Funktion und Wirkungen. In H.-J. Blanke, A. Scherzberg, & G. Wegner (Eds.), *Dimensionen des Wettbewerbs* (pp. 329–344). Tübingen: Mohr Siebeck.

Müller-Graff, P.-C. (2011). 60 Jahre Grundgesetz – aus der Sicht des Europarechts. *Jahrbuch des öffentlichen Rechts, Neue Folge 59*, 141–167.

Müller-Graff, P.-C. (2012). Verfassungsziele der EU. In M. Dauses (Ed.), *Handbuch des EU-Wirtschaftsrechts (loose leaf)*. Munich: C. H. Beck.

Müller-Graff, P.-C. (2014a). Der Begriff der Rechtsangleichung in Art. 114 AEUV im Licht eines gemeinsamen europäischen Kaufrechts. In U. Becker, A. Hatje, M. Potacs, & N. Wunderlich (Eds.), *Verfassung und Verwaltung in Europa. Festschrift für Jürgen Schwarze zum 70. Geburtstag* (pp. 617–640). Baden-Baden: Nomos.

Müller-Graff, P.-C. (2014b). Die horizontale Direktwirkung der Grundfreiheiten. *Europarecht*, *49*, 3–29.

Skouris, V. (2006). Das Verhältnis von Grundfreiheiten und Grundrechten im europäischen Gemeinschaftsrecht. *DÖV*, *59*, 89–97.

Szczekalla, P. (2002). *Die sogenannten grundrechtlichen Schutzpflichten im deutschen und Europäischen Recht*. Berlin: Duncker & Humblot.

Weber, A. (2010). *Europäische Verfassungsvergleichung. Ein Studienbuch*. Munich: Beck.

The Binding Force and Field of Application of the Fundamental Rights Enshrined in the Charter of Fundamental Rights of the European Union

Klaus Stern

With his book *Europäische Verfassungsvergleichung* (Comparative European Constitutional Law) published in 2010, *Albrecht Weber* made a seminal contribution to *ius commune europaeum*. It summed up in his view the quintessence of all his research and lecturing in the field of European public law. It is therefore fitting to celebrate his 70th birthday by compiling a special volume in his honour entitled "Common European Legal Thinking". As a long-time friend and colleague who has worked with him notably in an international context, it gives me great pleasure to contribute to the present work.

From the moment the Charter of Fundamental Rights of the European Union was proclaimed, *Albrecht Weber* took a close interest in how it had evolved and published subsequently on various aspects of its content. So on the occasion of his 70th birthday it is appropriate to pay tribute to his oeuvre by discussing a number of problems associated with the Charter.[1]

1 Binding Force for the Institutions and Bodies of the European Union

The Charter of Fundamental Rights of the European Union has binding force, according to Art. 51.1, first sentence EUCFR firstly, for the European Union as such, something that is self-evident given the Charter's primary law character and, secondly, also for the Member States when "they are implementing Union law". During the work of the Convention tasked with drawing up the Charter it quickly became apparent that many delegates wanted the provisions of the Charter to have binding force first and foremost for the Union and only secondarily for the Mem-

For his valuable assistance I would like to thank Dr. Andreas Hamacher.

[1] See Weber 2002, *Charta der Grundrechte der Europäischen Union,* (Charter of Fundamental Rights of the European Union, Introduction and Text in German, English and French); Weber 2000, *Die Europäische Grundrechtecharta auf dem Weg zu einer europäischen Verfassung* (The European Charter of Fundamental Rights on the road to a European constitution), NJW, p. 537 et seqq.; and Weber 2008, *Vom Verfassungsvertrag zum Vertrag von Lissabon* (From constitutional treaty to the Treaty of Lisbon), EuZW, p. 7 et seqq.

H.-J. Blanke et al. (eds.), *Common European Legal Thinking*,
DOI 10.1007/978-3-319-19300-7_16

ber States.[2] Art. 51.1, first sentence EUCFR seeks to provide further elucidation of this binding force by differentiating between "the institutions, bodies, offices and agencies of the Union" and including the provision "with due regard for the principle of subsidiarity". It is therefore necessary to examine precisely what European institutions and authorities this "quartet" is intended to cover.

The term "institutions" presumably means the European institutions on which the European Treaties have conferred specific sovereign powers and which functionwise correspond most closely to the supreme state organs of the Member States, although the functions these institutions perform, albeit generally comparable, may in certain respects differ considerably from those performed by state organs. The "institutions of the Union" are enshrined in the Union's primary law in Art. 13 TEU, which lists as follows: "– the European Parliament, – the European Council, – the Council, – the European Commission [...], – the Court of Justice of the European Union, – the European Central Bank, – the Court of Auditors". Art. 13.4 TEU further refers to the "Economic and Social Committee" and the "Committee of the Regions", which may rightly be characterised as "Nebenorgane" (subsidiary institutions).[3] Irrespective of whether these "Nebenorgane" belong also in a legal sense in the same category as the institutions specified in Art. 13 TEU or are deemed rather to be "bodies, offices and agencies" of the European Union, the Union has no "institutions" other than those specified in Art. 13 TEU. Art. 223 TFEU contains detailed provisions on the institutions of the Union but makes no reference to any increase in their number.

It is at present unclear whether any precise distinction can be made between "bodies" and "offices and agencies" of the Union or whether, as *A. Hatje* argues, this is merely a single "catch-all category" comprising "all bodies of the Union" which, "albeit not institutions, have the power to encroach on a person's fundamental rights".[4] The precise demarcation between "bodies" on the one hand and "offices and agencies" on the other is presumably a legal *non liquet*. It is therefore hardly surprising that in the literature there is little discussion of what distinguishes the two categories, the prevailing view being that this is a single collective term that refers to all four types of Union institution or authority.

The author shares the view put forward by *M. Borowsky* that "offices and agencies" is employed as a "somewhat nebulous general term for authorities obliged to respect fundamental rights", since there is no indication at all of how they differ from "bodies". If the term "bodies" is intended to denote "all other offices and agencies established by the founding Treaties or by secondary law",[5] the nebulous nature of the term is to be regretted and its inherent meaning must be seriously open

[2] On this and on the genesis of the norm see Borowsky, in Meyer (2014), Art. 51 para 2 et seqq. (also para 16 with citations).

[3] See e. g. Hatje, in Schwarze (2012), Art. 13 TEU para 23. Subsequently the author assigns these subsidiary institutions not to the "institutions" category but to the "bodies, offices and agencies" category, Hatje, in Schwarze (2012), Art. 51 EUCFR para 11. See, with the same basic tenor, the study by Streinz 2013.

[4] See Hatje, in Schwarze (2012), Art. 51 EUCFR para 11.

[5] See Borowsky, in Meyer (2014), Art. 51 para 18 et seq.

to doubt. Yet one thing at any rate is clear. The intention is for the European Union, whenever it acts in a sovereign capacity, to be bound by the obligations enshrined in the Charter. Hence the terms employed there are intended to be broadly interpreted, not least in order to prevent a situation in which the adoption of certain types of act or institutional procedure would enable the Union to evade its Charter obligations.

It follows therefore that the Charter also has binding force for juridical persons over whom the European Union has prime authority.[6]

2 Binding Force for the Member States of the European Union

The Charter has binding force for the Member States of the European Union only when they are specifically dealing with matters relating to Union law. The wording of Art. 51.1, first sentence EUCFR is designed to make clear that the Charter has binding force for the Member States only "when they are implementing Union law"; in this context binding force has a specific and defined content. It differs substantially from the comprehensive binding force which the fundamental freedoms stipulated in the TFEU have for the Member States. The prohibition of discrimination "on grounds of nationality" enshrined in Art. 18 TFEU is similarly binding and comprehensive.

In the literature there is considerable criticism of any narrow interpretation of the extent to which Member States are bound by Art. 51 EUCFR. The content and meaning of the provision per se is open to question both as regards any assumed enlargement[7] and further limitation[8] of its field of application. In this respect a number of stipulations relating to certain Charter guarantees are deemed to be of a *lex specialis* nature,[9] since these more specific stipulations are intended to take precedence over the provisions of Art. 51 EUCFR as *lex generalis*. While these guarantees of a *lex specialis* nature are not directly binding on the Member States unless they are implementing Union law, there exists nevertheless what might be called a "residual element of binding force", which requires the Member States to refrain from taking any measures or other actions that would hinder the exercise of fundamental rights enshrined in the Charter.

---

[6] See Jarass 2013, Art. 51 para 3 with citations; the author argues cogently that authorities obliged to respect fundamental rights must not be able to evade this obligation by delegating their tasks to private law entities. See also Borowsky, in Meyer (2014), Art. 51 para 16.

[7] Jarass 2013, Art. 51 para 3, argues that, by virtue of its specific provisions on fundamental rights, the Charter can acquire binding force for the Member States over and above that stipulated in Art. 51.1, first sentence EUCFR. The author makes explicit reference in this connection to Art. 21.2 and Art. 45 EUCFR.

[8] See Borowsky, in Meyer (2014), Art. 51 para 20; with reference to Art. 42–44 EUCFR also Jarass 2013, Art. 51 para 3.

[9] Hatje in Schwarze (2012), Art. 51 para 8, deems *leges speciales* to be primarily those guarantees that are addressed "explicitly only to the Union" in its capacity as fundamental rights guarantor.

To determine precisely how far the Charter is binding on the Member States, there is a need first of all to clarify the criteria for establishing whether, in a given situation, a Member State is in fact "implementing Union law".

The term "Union law" comprises all European primary and secondary law and includes also special types of action which the Union may take in particular circumstances.[10] Where the fundamental rights have binding force for the Member States, no distinction is made between the various levels of Union law. Although the wording of Art. 51.1 EUCFR might *prima facie* suggest otherwise, the fundamental rights have binding force not only for the Member States themselves but also for all state institutions and authorities that *eo ipso* exercise sovereign powers or are authorised by Member States to act on their behalf and in their interests. Hence it is appropriate to view the Charter as having binding force not only for the "institutions, bodies, offices and agencies" of the Union but also for those of the Member States.[11]

However, a Member State is not implementing Union law when it implements or adopts measures whose sole legal basis is its own domestic law. But if a given measure is "based" on Union law or the Member State measure is in some other respect at least partially "determined"[12] by Union law, it can generally be assumed that the Member State is implementing Union law.

Basically this covers two scenarios: firstly, when a Member State transposes Union law into domestic law and, secondly, when a Member State administers Union law on its own responsibility. The author shares the view put forward by *H. D. Jarass* and *S. Beljin* that measures taken by a Member State in this connection can be classified either as "normative" or "administrative" implementation. The way Member States administer justice and apply the law is further informed by "judicial implementation" aspects of Union law.[13]

As soon as a European Union directive is transposed by a Member State into domestic law, the conformity, firstly, of the directive itself with European fundamental rights and then of national action to implement it can be scrutinised. A process of twofold scrutiny is thus required to ensure that both are in conformity with the Charter itself as well as with general European norms on fundamental rights.[14]

---

[10] See Hatje, in Schwarze (2012), Art. 51 EUCFR para 14. For Union primary law Jarass 2013, Art. 51 para 15, adds the qualification "in so far as it is binding on Member States".

[11] See e. g. Jarass 2013, Art. 51 para 12, where the author refers to Rengeling and Szczekalla 2004, para 330 with citations. See also Case C-617/10, *Åkerberg Fransson* (ECJ 26 February 2013) para 19 et seqq.

[12] See Jarass 2013, Art. 51 para 16 et seq. with citations; in the first edition (2010), the author put it more clearly.

[13] For further explanation of these terms see Jarass and Beljin 2004, p. 6 et seqq.; also Jarass 2013, Art. 51 para 18 et seqq. On binding force in the context of judicial functions performed at Member State level see also Hoffmann and Rudolphi 2012, p. 598. In the context of Union law implementation Borowsky, in Meyer (2014), Art. 51 para 25 refers to the English term "agency situation".

[14] See also the apt comment by Jarass 2013, Art. 51 para 18 and Introduction para 54 with reference to Joined Cases C-465/00, C-138/01 and C-139/01, *Rechnungshof v. Österreichischer Rundfunk et al.* (ECJ 20 May 2003) para 68, 80.

However, the idea put forward by von Bogdandy et al. in this context is too far reaching. While basically recognising the limiting effect that Art. 51.1 EUCFR has on the scope of application of the Charter, they suggest that EU fundamental rights are nonetheless binding on Member States if the level of protection if fundamental rights drops beneath a certain level. Referring to the ECJ case law in van Gend en Loos, they argue that also the individual, i. e. Union citizens, is called upon to enforce European law. By linking Union citizenship to human rights, whose protection is a common value of the Union and the Member States according to Art. 2 TEU, they argue that the "core content" of the EU fundamental rights is enforceable in the Member States irrespective of whether Member States implement Union law according to Art. 51.1 EUCFR stricto sensu. They call it a "reverse Solange principle", thereby referencing to the case law of the German Federal Constitutional Court. Only as long as ("solange") Member States ensure the protection of the core content of thc fundamental rights of the Charter as protected by Art. 2 TEU, they remain autonomous outside the field of application of the EU Charter of Fundamental Rights.[15] This "Heidelberg proposal" disregards the legal situation of the Treaties, according to which the scope of application of the Charter is limited to those competences of the Member States that have their roots and basis in EU law (Art. 51.1 EUCFR), i. e. there has to be some kind of connection between the competences exercised by the Member States and EU law.[16] Furthermore, the proposal would extend the *status activus processualis* of the Union citizens before domestic courts via Art. 20 TFEU in a way that is irreconcilable with the Treaties, as a national impingement on fundamental rights, according to the authors, is subject to Union law and the "core content" of the fundamental rights of the Charter if it deprives Union citizenship of its practical effect or usefulness. Lastly, without wishing to ignore the worries concerning the political developments in Hungary, at present there is no deficit in the protection of fundamental rights in the legal orders of the Member States that would justify a "federal" interpretation of the Charter that extends well beyond the wording and *ratio legis* of Art. 51.1 EUCFR.

The binding force of the fundamental rights for the Member States does not, however, extend to any more far-reaching measures taken by Member States going beyond what is required to implement Union law. The Member States are required to implement Union law up to but not beyond this point.[17] Doubts may arise, however, as regards measures which, albeit not objectively required by Union law, may have been taken by a Member State in conscious or unconscious "over-fulfilment"[18] of its Union law obligations, perhaps with a view to exemplary national regulation of the matter in question. In such cases the precise extent to which the fundamental

[15] See in detail von Bogdandy et al. 2012, p. 65 et seqq.

[16] Cf. in this respect Case C-617/10, *Åkerberg Fransson* (Opinion of AG Cruz Villalón of 12 June 2012) para 51, 57.

[17] See Ladenburger, in Tettinger and Stern (2006), Art. 51 para 35; also Jarass 2013, Art. 51 para 16.

[18] Hain 2009, p. 18, e. g. argues that the Federal Republic of Germany tends towards "over-fulfilment" of the EU's state-aid rules.

rights are binding on the Member State is still unclear or has at any rate not been definitively clarified by European (fundamental rights) case law.[19]

Whether European fundamental rights have binding force for the executive and judicial branches of the Member States depends above all on whether the matter in question falls within the Union's legal sphere and hence European fundamental rights are fully or partially binding on the Member States, in other words, whether specifically Union law is being implemented or applied by the court ruling on the case. What counts here is whether the Union has availed itself of its competence to regulate a particular matter.[20] Certainly European fundamental rights cannot be invoked in a given matter unless the Union has actually exercised its regulatory competence in the matter, thus ensuring that this competence has not remained purely hypothetical.

Opinions differ as to whether European fundamental rights have binding force for the Member States also when they act within the parameters established by Union law, e. g. when they adopt measures whose existence and subsequent application entail legitimate limitations on European fundamental freedoms as provided for in the TFEU. Some authors regard Member States which take advantage of the scope for such legitimate limitations as no longer engaged in "implementing Union law" within the meaning of Art. 51.1, first sentence EUCFR.[21] Other authors[22] take a distinctly different view of the issue, aware that the ECJ[23] is of the same opinion. It is important to bear in mind that in adopting such measures the Member States are imposing limitations on grounds recognised as legitimate under Union law. Hence the imposition of legitimate limitations does not per se mean that European fundamental freedoms are no longer applicable and Union law is no longer being implemented.

Besides the aforementioned consideration, a further argument for a broad interpretation of the implementation concept is the fact that it is hard to see why Member States which for sound reasons have adopted national measures limiting European fundamental freedoms should also be allowed a rebate as regards the binding force of those freedoms. Only if this concept is interpreted as encompassing also national measures deemed legitimate in terms of European legal dogmatics on fundamental freedoms will it effectively contribute to a consistent interpretation of European fundamental rights,[24] something which is clearly vital given their importance as part

[19] See also the distinctions drawn by Ladenburger, in Tettinger and Stern (2006), Art. 51 para 35.

[20] See Jarass 2013, Art. 51 para 25.

[21] See inter alia Borowsky in Meyer (2014), Art. 51 para 29. For an analysis of the current discussion see Kingreen, in Calliess and Ruffert (2011), Art. 51 EUCFR para 13 et seqq. (16 et seq.).

[22] See inter alia Jarass 2013, Art. 51 para 21; also Hoffmann and Rudolphi 2012, p. 599; Blanke and Böttner 2014, para 337 et seq. Hatje, in Schwarze (2012), Art. 51 EUCFR para 18 et seq., argues for a broad interpretation of the "implementation concept".

[23] Hoffmann and Rudolphi 2012, p. 598 with footnote 15, with reference to Case 1-260/89, *Elliniki Radiophonia Tileorassi AE v. Dimotiki Etairia Pliroforisis and Sotirios Kouvelas ("ERT")* (ECJ 18 June 1991) para 42 et seqq.

[24] On grounds of the "uniform application and interpretation of Union law" Grewe 2012, p. 299, argues for a broad understanding of the binding force of the fundamental rights.

of European primary law. As *J. M. Hoffmann* and *V. Rudolphi* have rightly pointed out, a dogmatic-functional analysis reveals that in this context European fundamental rights do indeed serve to "limit the limitations that can legitimately be imposed on fundamental rights".[25]

It is important to distinguish between a situation where a Member State in its domestic law limits a European fundamental freedom and the situation where the Member States are *a priori* granted discretionary powers. In matters where Member States enjoy discretionary powers, the presumption also in the most recent ECJ case law is that they exercise such discretionary powers in the course of implementing Union law.[26] Only in cases and on matters that fall within the sole competence of the Member States and do not actually serve to fulfil Union law requirements can Member States acting in a sovereign capacity be assumed not to be bound by European fundamental rights. Whenever Member States adopt measures designed to fulfil Union law requirements or – depending on the scope of their discretionary powers – to achieve Union law objectives, Member States are implementing Union law and accordingly obliged to uphold both European and their own national guarantees of fundamental rights.[27] This twofold obligation[28] to uphold fundamental rights guarantees results in a particularly high degree of protection for the holders of those rights. European and Member State guarantees of fundamental rights, whether identical or different in scope, are assumed to have a cumulative effect,[29] at least when Member States are exercising their discretionary powers. In the latter case the more extensive guarantees provide a complementary form of protection. This complementary application is based notably on the hierarchy of protection principle ("Grundsatz der Meistbegünstigung"),[30] meaning that when various guarantees of protection are applicable, the guarantee that affords the higher degree of protection applies. European and Member State courts scrutinise first and foremost conformity with their own regimes to protect fundamental rights, although the latter especially are increasingly tending to scrutinise also conformity with European regimes.

---

[25] Hoffmann and Rudolphi 2012, p. 598, point out that following the Charter's incorporation into European primary law the ECJ has issued no (clear) ruling to date on the question of what binding force the fundamental rights have for Member States in the case of a legitimate limitation of European fundamental freedoms.

[26] See Hoffmann and Rudolphi 2012, p. 598, with reference to Joined Cases C-411/10 and C-493/10, *N.S. et al.* (ECJ 21 December 2011).

[27] See Jarass 2013, Art. 51 para 23 and Art. 53 para 10–13.

[28] See inter alia Borowsky, in Meyer (2014), Art. 53 para 22; also comments by Kirchhof 2013, p. 5, on overlapping competences of the European Court of Justice and Germany's Federal Constitutional Court in cases where a national and a European legislative act employ "identical wording".

[29] In such cases a cumulative effect is assumed also by Ladenburger, in Tettinger and Stern (2006), Art. 51 para 30 as well as Jarass 2013, Art. 53 para 11. See also Schmitz 2001, p. 836, where the author uses the metaphor of "layered nets" to describe how European fundamental rights function in practice.

[30] See Jarass 2013, Art. 53 para 11. Borowsky, in Meyer (2014), Art. 53 para 22 posits a "hierarchy of protection principle" (Grundsatz der Meistbegünstigung).

Even now there are growing indications that the limited binding force which the fundamental rights have for the Member States is likely to be a temporary phenomenon. As *C. Grewe* rightly points out, some "60–70 % of annual national regulatory output" is already "initiated" by the European Union.[31] With increasing advances in European integration, the relevance of European regulation for Member State legislation is in future more likely to increase than decrease. The originally intended constellation, whereby European fundamental rights would be binding on the Member States only in limited circumstances, has already been transformed into its opposite, with the exception now the rule.[32]

There is currently little evidence that the codification as primary law of the Charter's field of application as stipulated in Art. 51.1, first sentence EUCFR is likely to produce any fundamental change in ECJ case law to date on the extent to which European fundamental rights are binding on the Member States.

To what extent the fundamental rights enshrined in the Charter (may) be directly or indirectly binding also on private persons is an issue which still remains to be clarified.[33] They may be assumed to be directly binding certainly when private persons have been authorised to perform state functions and at least while performing those functions their character as private persons is therefore largely irrelevant. Incidentally, the constitutional law theory whereby fundamental rights which are binding on sovereign authorities also have an indirect or radiating effect in the private sphere applies likewise to European guarantees of fundamental rights.[34] Art. 51 EUCFR defines the field of application of the Charter but makes no mention of any indirect effect in the private sphere and contains no stipulations on this score. However, this does not *a priori* rule out the courts developing appropriate concepts in this connection.[35] In any event, especially the ECJ needs to pay close attention so as not to overstretch the scope of the Charter with regard to the horizontal effect. This is in particular true for a potential direct horizontal effect of the Charter provisions, as Art. 51.1 EUCFR is opposed to such effect as regards its wording, genesis and concept.[36]

[31] See Grewe 2012, p. 299.

[32] Grewe 2012, p. 299 rightly argues for the assumption that the fundamental rights are now generally binding on the Member States.

[33] Notably in ECJ judgments no clear line is apparent, see Jarass 2013, Art. 51 para 27. For further discussion of these issues see Borowsky, in Meyer (2014), Art. 51 para 31 with footnotes 177 and 178. For a general summary of the case for assuming the Charter fundamental rights are directly binding in the private sphere see Hatje, in Schwarze (2012), Art. 51 EUCFR para 22.

[34] See discussion by Jarass 2013, Art. 51 para 27; also Hatje, in Schwarze (2012), Art. 51 EUCFR para 22.

[35] See comments by Borowsky, in Meyer (2014), Art. 51 para 31. On an emerging direct effect in the private sphere see Hatje, in Schwarze (2012), Art. 51 EUCFR para 22, where the author argues that even when a direct effect in the private sphere cannot be assumed, this does not point to the existence of a "genuine gap in protection".

[36] See Müller-Graff 2014, p. 27 with further reference.

3 Functional Field of Application of European Fundamental Rights

Classical fundamental rights dogmatics recognises that fundamental rights guarantees serve different functions ("fundamental rights functions"). Basically the functions served by European fundamental rights guarantees are the same as or at any rate not significantly different from those served by the fundamental rights developed in Germany's Basic Law and whose value has been proven in practice.[37] Of course a number of differences do exist due to the specifically European character of the Charter. The relative importance of the various functions served by the Charter guarantees may differ from that found in other major international and national fundamental rights instruments. This can be explained not least by the fact that they were drawn up and adopted at different periods.

In addition to fundamental rights that guarantee what are essentially classical freedoms, the Charter also stipulates rights that require those bound by its provisions to afford protection to the individual holders of these rights.[38] The tableau of fundamental rights guarantees is complemented by various provisions requiring that, in the field of application of the Charter, those bound by its provisions at European and Member State level respect the equality of the holders of these rights and afford them equal treatment.[39] Although lacking any obvious uniform structure, the specific equal rights guaranteed by the Charter are grouped together in Title III under the heading "Equality".

Under this "Equality" heading the Charter specifies different types of equal rights. Art. 20, 21 and 23 EUCFR provide classical equal rights guarantees. These are namely "Equality before the law" (Art. 20), "Non-discrimination" (Art. 21) and, lastly, "Equality between women and men" (Art. 23). Women are cited first here not merely as an act of courtesy but in order to emphasise that, in the areas specified in the Charter, they should no longer suffer discrimination in relation to men. Title III contains further atypical equal rights guarantees which, albeit inspired by a comprehensive concept of equality, essentially denote freedoms or rights to participation for particular groups of persons. These guarantees relate to "The rights of the child" (Art. 24), "The rights of the elderly" (Art. 25) and, lastly, "Integration of persons with disabilities" (Art. 26). In addition, Art. 22 EUCFR requires the Union to respect "cultural, religious and linguistic diversity".

Also as regards scrutinising conformity with fundamental rights, the structure of the Charter allows an approach similar to that employed in this context in German legal dogmatics. The scope of protection afforded by a given fundamental rights guarantee is derived initially from the concrete wording of the guarantee in ques-

---

[37] For further discussion see Stern 1994, § 77 III.

[38] See Jarass 2013, Art. 51 para 39 et seqq.; Borowsky, in Meyer (2014), Art. 51 para 22; and Kingreen, in Calliess and Ruffert (2011), Art. 51 EUCFR para 23 et seqq.

[39] On fundamental rights serving an "equal treatment function" see Jarass 2013, Art. 51 para 44. For a systematic overview of equal rights in the Charter see Hölscheidt, in Meyer (2014), before Title III para 15 et seqq.

tion. Both in terms of fundamental rights dogmatics and in order to determine the precise scope of protection afforded by a given guarantee it is important to distinguish between the personal and the material scope of protection.[40]

It seems unclear to date how far the scope of protection can *a priori* be restricted[41] without invoking previously existing limitations on fundamental rights. An interesting approach to restricting the scope of protection is the idea put forward and immediately refuted by *W. Frenz* of extending the ECJ's "Keck ruling"[42] on European fundamental freedoms to the dogmatics of European fundamental rights, which would a priori exclude certain behaviours from the protection afforded by the rights enshrined in the Charter.[43]

One argument for greater unity in ECJ case law relating to European fundamental freedoms and European fundamental rights is that uniform parameters could certainly do much to make the two legal institutions more consistent with each other. Although they are indeed connected, European fundamental rights and European fundamental freedoms are nevertheless based on very different concepts, the latter being essentially prohibitions of discrimination in a specifically economic context. Given the continuing autonomy of the Member States and their legitimate desire to pursue their interests, some limitations on the scope of European fundamental freedoms may be required. European fundamental rights, however, are intended in their field of application to be guaranteed and realised as fully as possible,[44] even if some Member States – failing perhaps to recognise the basic conceptual difference between European fundamental rights and European fundamental freedoms – may introduce exceptions designed to ensure the contrary.

Since unlike Germany's Basic Law the Charter of Fundamental Rights does not stipulate any fundamental right guaranteeing general personal freedoms as defined in Art. 2.1 BL and which, given the far-reaching nature of this guarantee, could serve in a sense as a "catch-all fundamental right", the protection enjoyed by the holder of the Charter fundamental rights is limited to the protection afforded by the specific Charter right in question, unless in the particular case another Charter right can also be invoked.[45] This differs from the situation in Germany, where certain behaviours not entitled to protection by virtue of a specific basic right recognised in

[40] See inter alia Frenz 2009, para 460.

[41] See on this "immanent reduction" problem the discussion in Frenz 2009, para 466 et seqq. On how "human dignity" affects the freedom of the arts and sciences stipulated in Art. 13 see Bernsdorff, in Meyer (2014), Art. 13 para 13.

[42] Case 267/91 and 268/91, *Keck and Mithouard* (ECJ 24 November 1993). See comments on this ruling by inter alia Kingreen, in Calliess and Ruffert (2011), Art. 34–36 TFEU para 49 et seqq. On the evolution of case law following the ECJ's *Keck* ruling and the current validity of the formula then developed see Brigola 2012.

[43] See Frenz 2009, para 472 et seqq.

[44] See the perceptive analysis by Frenz 2009, para 473, where the author highlights also the qualitative differences that have emerged between European fundamental freedoms and European fundamental rights.

[45] See comments by Frenz 2009, para 476, where the author rightly points out that in the absence of a general catch-all fundamental right the European Charter of Fundamental Rights "does not encompass the whole spectrum of behaviours".

the Basic Law may nevertheless be entitled to protection if the relevant right derives from a more general "mother basic right"[46] enshrined therein.

The Charter of Fundamental Rights stipulates in Art. 52.1 EUCFR a general limitation that applies to (almost) all fundamental rights enshrined therein and is supplemented only by certain "special limitations" on the fundamental rights specified in Art. 8.2, first sentence EUCFR as well as Art. 17.1, second sentence EUCFR.

Art. 52.1 EUCFR makes clear in particular that "any limitation on the exercise of the rights and freedoms recognised by this Charter must be provided for by law and respect the essence of those rights and freedoms". The requirement that any limitation must be provided for by law is notable in the sense that, depending on to whom the obligation to respect fundamental rights is addressed, it may in some cases be fulfilled by a European norm and in other cases, where this obligation is addressed to a Member State, by a national legislative act.[47]

With regard to the requirement in Art. 52.1 EUCFR to respect the essence of the Charter guarantees, it is not *a priori* clear what legal significance should be attached to this requirement. To clarify what exactly respecting "the essence of [those] rights and freedoms" means in a given case, the relevant fundamental right guaranteed by the Charter must be precisely analysed and substantiated. It might be questioned whether the demands made on the limiting authority in this context are any less stringent than those stipulated in Art. 19.2 BL with regard to the basic rights enshrined in Germany's Basic Law.[48]

The wording of the relevant norms argues for such an assumption, however, since a requirement to respect the essence of the fundamental rights is less onerous than the absolute prohibition contained in Art. 19.2 BL, namely, that "in no case may the essence of a basic right be affected". It remains to be seen whether the requirement to respect the essence of rights develops in ECJ case law[49] into a genuine essence guarantee as defined in Art. 19.2 BL. Certainly the requirement to respect the essence of rights contained in Art. 52.1, first sentence EUCFR seems designed to prohibit any concrete measures that would completely disregard "essential aspects of a right".[50] However, in order to establish a comprehensive review concept

[46] See Frenz 2009, para 489, where the author argues that such protection can be assumed when otherwise "an unintended protection gap" would arise. See there also the concept of "mother fundamental right".

[47] See Becker, in Schwarze (2012), Art. 52 EUCFR para 4.

[48] Inter alia Becker, in Schwarze (2012), Art. 52 EUCFR para 7 sees in this stipulation in Art. 52.1 EUCFR only a "relative prohibition", arguing that where respect for the essence of rights is concerned the demands made on the limiting authority are less stringent than those laid down in Germany's Basic Law. For a general discussion of the essence guarantee in Germany's Basic Law see inter alia Brüning, in Stern and Becker (2015), Art. 19 para 10 et seq. On the genesis of the essence guarantee see Stern 1994, § 85 I. For a detailed overview of the reception of "the essence guarantee in case law and literature" see Nierhaus, in Kahl et al. (2008), Art. 19(2) para 11 et seqq.

[49] On the development of ECJ case law on the essence of certain rights see the discussion by Becker, in Schwarze (2012), Art. 52 EUCFR para 7 with citations.

[50] See Becker, in Schwarze (2012), Art. 52 EUCFR para 7 as well as Streinz and Michl, in Streinz (2012), Art. 52 EUCFR para 26 with reference to Case C-408/03, *Commission v. Belgium* (ECJ 23 March 2006) para 68.

that comprises both limits it is necessary that, in addition to the principle of proportionality, the "absolute limit" in the form of the essence of a right will receive a clearer substantial profile in the fundamental rights review of the Court.[51]

Art. 52.1, second sentence EUCFR cites as alternatives, moreover, two objectives which any measures limiting a fundamental right must not only serve but also, in the words of the Charter, "genuinely meet". The term "meet" presumably signifies something "more" that merely "serve".[52] The objectives cited in the norm are, firstly, "objectives of general interest recognised by the Union" and, secondly, "the need to protect the rights and freedoms of others". In the case of the first objective that may be served by measures limiting fundamental rights the close interconnections with the dogmatics of European fundamental freedoms are particularly evident. The "objectives of general interest" deemed to justify limitations on both fundamental rights and fundamental freedoms are seen as broadly identical, especially since recognition of European fundamental freedoms by the Union is taken as given.[53]

Lastly, Art. 52.1, second sentence EUCFR stipulates generally that limitations may be made only "subject to the principle of proportionality", a principle long recognised in ECJ case law.[54] This stipulation simply codifies something that is self-evident. Such a norm is needed, however, as a "core concept employed to balance competing legal interests".[55] How intensively proportionality is scrutinised may vary with the category of law applied, but the criteria employed – suitability, necessity and proportionality in the narrower sense[56] – are broadly similar. This familiar trio is employed also by the European Court of Justice when scrutinising the proportionality of a given measure, although in ECJ case law particular emphasis is placed on the two last-named criteria.[57] The final stage of scrutiny, when the proportionality or appropriateness of a given measure is determined, tends to be the most important, since it is at this stage that courts undertake a comprehensive evaluation and normative balancing of the competing interests at issue and decide

[51] Blanke 2015, p. 39 et seq., with regard to the freedom for entrepreneurs (Art. 16 EUCFR).

[52] von Danwitz, in Tettinger and Stern (2006), Art. 52 para 40 argues that the wording "genuinely meet" implies the need for "full scrutiny of suitability", since its prime purpose is to establish criteria for determining the proportionality of a given measure.

[53] See Becker, in Schwarze (2012), Art. 52 EUCFR para 5 with citations.

[54] See inter alia Case 116/82, *Commission v. Germany* (ECJ Judgments of 18 September 1986) para 19 et seqq. and Case C-331/88, *The Queen v. The Minister of Agriculture, Fisheries and Food and The Secretary of State for Health, ex parte Fedesa et al.* (ECJ 13 November 1990) para 13.

[55] See Becker, in Schwarze (2012), Art. 52 EUCFR para 6; also Borowsky, in Meyer (2014), Art. 52 para 22b.

[56] The last-named criterion is also termed "appropriateness". See also Borowsky, in Meyer (2014), Art. 52 para 22b. These criteria are discussed in depth by von Danwitz in Tettinger and Stern (2006), Art. 52 para 40 et seqq. and Becker in Schwarze (2012), Art. 52 EUCFR para 6. See also the contribution by Galetta in this volume.

[57] See Joined Cases C-96/03 and 97/03, *Tempelmann and Mr and Mrs T.H.J.M. van Schaijk v. Directeur van de Rijksdienst voor de keuring van Vee en Vlees* (ECJ 10 March 2005) para 47; also Borowsky, in Meyer (2014), Art. 52 para 22b. For an almost classical example of ECJ scrutiny dating from 1989 see Case 265/87, *Hermann Schräder HS Kraftfutter GmbH & Co. KG v. Hauptzollamt Gronau* (ECJ 11 July 1989) para 21.

whether "the ordered measure is appropriate to the intended objective".[58] This is clearly the material essence of the process of scrutinising whether a limitation on a particular Charter fundamental right is proportionate and therefore valid. Meanwhile, the Court's balancing of the freedom to conduct a business with the right of the public to access information has led to a new status of the principle of proportionality in the Court's argumentation.[59]

The stipulation in Art. 51.2 EUCFR that, among other things, "the Charter does not extend the field of application of Union law beyond the powers of the Union" may be seen as a response[60] to concerns emerging in some Member States even during the drafting process that the Charter might ultimately extend the powers of the Union.[61] These concerns were heightened by the perception that the Charter guarantees were liable to have what might be called a "power-sucking effect".[62] No modification of the respective powers of or division of powers "between the Union and the Member States"[63] is intended, however, as the wording of Art. 51.2 EUCFR makes clear.[64]

In the case of individual fundamental rights which are inherently freedoms, such fears of a possible extension of powers are clearly paradoxical, since sovereign power is on the whole more likely to be restricted than extended by respect for fundamental rights. In the case of fundamental rights that establish concrete protection and performance obligations, however, these concerns appear more understandable.[65] Nevertheless, the so-called "competence protection clause"[66] contained in Art. 51.2 EUCFR is of only declaratory, not constitutive significance.[67] In the fundamental rights context Art. 51.2 EUCFR would seem to place very narrow limits on or even completely rule out any application of the so-called "flexibility clause"

[58] See von Danwitz, in Tettinger and Stern (2006), Art. 52 para 42.

[59] See Case C-283/11, *Sky v. Österreichischer Rundfunk* (CJEU 2 January 2013) para 50–67; Blanke 2015, p. 38 et seqq.

[60] The basis for incorporating this stipulation in the Charter text was an ECJ judgment on the *Grant* case, see Case C-249/96, *Grant* (ECJ 17 February 1998) para 45; also explanatory comments by the Presidium of the Convention on Art. 51, reproduced inter alia by Geiger, Khan and Kotzur (2010), p. 1017. The key passage in the judgment is also cited and discussed by Borowsky in Meyer (2014), Art. 51 para 45 with footnote 222.

[61] Inter alia Borowsky, in Meyer (2014), Art. 51 para 14 and 37 regards the "fears" expressed as "probably not entirely groundless". See also Hatje, in Schwarze (2012), Art. 51 EUCFR para 28.

[62] See Borowsky, in Meyer (2014), Art. 51 para 14 and 37.

[63] See Hatje, in Schwarze (2012), Art. 51 EUCFR para 28.

[64] See Hatje, in Schwarze (2012), Art. 51 EUCFR para 28 et seq., where the author rightly points out that this norm serves not least "to protect the principle of conferral" (para 29).

[65] For an analysis of the substance of the fears giving rise to the stipulation contained in Art. 51.2 EUCFR see Borowsky, in Meyer (2014), Art. 51 para 37. Kingreen, in Calliess and Ruffert (2011), Art. 51 EUCFR para 22 rightly assumes, however, that performance obligations are meaningless "if they are addressed to entities that lack any relevant competence".

[66] This term is employed inter alia by Borowsky in Meyer (2014), Art. 51 para 37; also by Streinz, Ohler and Hermann 2010, § 14 V.3. Kingreen, in Calliess and Ruffert (2011), Art. 6 TEU para 13 argues that the second part of this clause corresponds to the "general competence protection clause" contained in Art. 6.1 (2) TEU.

[67] See Borowsky, in Meyer (2014), Art. 51 para 37 with reference to the "explanatory comments" on this norm; also Folz, in Vedder and Heintschel von Heinegg (2012), Art. 51 EUCFR para 8.

("Kompetenzergänzungsklausel") in Art. 352 TFEU allowing the Union's powers to be extended in certain circumstances, unless at any rate "objectives of the Treaties" other than those cited in the Charter can be invoked.[68]

The criticism voiced in some quarters concerning the lack of congruency between a number of the fundamental rights guaranteed by the Charter and the competences conferred *de lege lata* on the Union is ultimately not convincing. It is hardly possible to make any reliable predictions, after all, as to which fundamental rights guarantees are likely to be relevant to existing Union competences[69] and which can be deemed *a priori* irrelevant.[70] Particularly in this light it was a wise and far-sighted decision of the Convention to draft the Charter as a comprehensive bill of rights that gives the policies of the Union and the exercise of its sovereign power a modern, fundamental rights "look". The wording of the stipulation in Art. 51.2 EUCFR that the Charter does not establish any new tasks for the Union or modify any existing ones is justly criticised[71] by *C. Ladenberger* as "somewhat unfortunate".[72] The concept of "tasks" must rightly be viewed as a normative one, whereby it should be noted that the real purpose of this wording is to make clear that the Charter is not intended to establish any new "Union objectives" beyond those set out in the Treaties.

In this context there is a close connection between the wording employed in Art. 51.2 EUCFR and the wording of Art. 6 TEU. With reference to the guarantees enshrined in the Charter, Art. 6.2 (2) TEU stipulates that "[t]he provisions of the Charter shall not extend in any way the competences of the Union as defined in the Treaties".[73] The clause in Art. 6.2, first sentence TEU providing for the accession of the Union to the ECHR is followed, moreover, by a "competence protection clause"[74] in Art. 6.2, second sentence TEU: "Such accession shall not affect the Union's competences as defined in the Treaties." In that respect, one has to consider that, in fact, the Charter does not create any "new" rights. Rather, Art. 6.1 TEU only "recognises" and the Charter only "reaffirms" these rights, which result, in particular, from the constitutional traditions and international obligations common

[68] Both *A. Hatje* and *M. Borowsky* tend to this more restrictive view. See Hatje, in Schwarze (2012), Art. 51 EUCFR para 29. In support of *Hatje*'s view Borowsky, in Meyer (2014), Art. 51 para 39 cites examples of "Charter-external" circumstances that could justify the application of Art. 352 TFEU.

[69] See the in-depth analysis by Borowsky, in Meyer (2014), Art. 51 para 40 et seqq. The irrelevance of this lack of congruency for the "limited Union competences" is rightly pointed out by Ladenburger in Tettinger and Stern (2006), Art. 51 para 52 and the further discussion in para 54 et seqq.

[70] See also comments by Borowsky, in Meyer (2014), Art. 51 para 41.

[71] *C. Ladenburger* argues that the inclusion in the Charter of "a thematically complete catalogue of fundamental rights" is "right", see Ladenburger, in Tettinger and Stern (2006), Art. 51 para 64 with numerous citations.

[72] See Ladenburger, in Tettinger and Stern (2006), Art. 51 para 60.

[73] This clause is considered by Kingreen, in Calliess and Ruffert (2011), Art. 6 TEU para 13 – as already noted – to be a "general competence protection clause".

[74] Obwexer 2012, p. 118.

to the Member States, the ECHR, the Social Charters adopted by the Union and by the Council of Europe and the case-law of the CJEU and of the ECtHR.[75]

W. Obwexer interprets these provisions as intended to "preclude the Union from having any competence in its own right for fundamental rights".[76] To the extent that there is no intention to confer on the Union any competences based on the fundamental rights guaranteed in the Charter other than those already conferred on it under the Treaties, his analysis must be seen as correct. On the basis of ECJ case law as it relates at least to the sources of European fundamental rights protection specified in Art. 6 TEU,[77] the Union must nevertheless be conceded a "competence to protect fundamental rights" as well as to adapt, update and up to a point further develop European fundamental rights guarantees. Otherwise there is a danger that European fundamental rights may be hollowed out and thus no longer serve their purpose, which is to protect effectively the fundamental rights of people throughout the European Union in the light also of the pressures generated by major societal change as well as rapid technological innovation and the specific challenges that poses for fundamental rights.

On a critical note inter alia *H.-P. Folz* points out that currently it appears "uncertain, however,"[78] whether the European Court of Justice will let the stipulation contained in Art. 51.2 EUCFR (together with the stipulations in Art. 6.1 [2] TEU) hinder it from issuing rulings aimed at ensuring conformity with the guarantees enshrined in the Charter and which could in turn override the strict stipulations concerning the non-extension and non-modification of existing competences as well as the requirement that no existing tasks should be modified or new ones established. This is something which the Court's actual practice will clarify in due course. What can be safely said even now is that the Court has a difficult balance to strike if it seeks in its rulings, on the one hand, to ensure the fullest possible respect for the Charter guarantees as well as further fundamental rights deriving from other Union fundamental rights sources and, on the other hand, to observe treaty stipulations concerning the field of application of the Charter. It will therefore be very interesting to see whether and how the Court rises to the challenge.

---

[75] Fifth indent of the Preamble to the Charter; see Grabenwarter and Pabel, in Blanke and Mangiameli (2013), Art. 6 TEU para 27 and 34 et seqq.

[76] Obwexer 2012, p. 118.

[77] In recent years the scope of the ECJ's jurisdiction at least where fundamental rights are concerned has been steadily extended. The statement by *L. Scheeck* that the ECJ "is not a human rights court" might today more aptly read "not a purely human rights court". It is a court with extensive jurisdiction for EU law, an important part of which now concerns protection of European fundamental rights and human rights.

[78] See Folz, in Vedder and Heintschel von Heinegg (2012), Art. 51 EUCFR para 9.

References

Blanke, H.-J. (2015). Verfassungs- und unionsrechtliche Gewährleistung der Unternehmerfreiheit und ihre Schranken. In Gesellschaft für Rechtspolitik & Institut für Rechtspolitik an der Universität Trier (Eds.), *Die Unternehmerfreiheit im Würgegriff des Rechts?* (pp. 13–44). Tübingen: Mohr Siebeck.

Blanke, H.-J., & Böttner, R. (2014). § 2 Binnenmarkt, Rechtsangleichung, Grundfreiheiten. In M. Niedobitek (Ed.), *Politiken der Union* Europarecht, (vol. II, pp. 97–383). Berlin: De Gruyter.

Blanke, H.-J., & Mangiameli, S. (Eds.). (2013). *The Treaty on European Union (TEU) – A Commentary*. Heidelberg: Springer.

von Bogdandy, A., Kottmann, M., Antpöhler, C., Dickschen, J., Hentrei, S. & Smrkolj, M. (2012). Ein Rettungsschirm für europäische Grundrechte. Grundlagen einer unionsrechtlichen Solange-Doktrin gegenüber Mitgliedstaaten. ZaöRV, 45-78.

Brigola, A. (2012). Die Metamorphose der Keck-Formel in der Rechtsprechung des EuGH. Ein Eckpfeiler im System des freien Warenverkehrs in neuem Körper. *EuZW*, 248–253.

Calliess, C., & Ruffert, M. (Eds.). (2011). *EUV/AEUV* (4th edn.). Munich: C.H.Beck.

Frenz, W. (2009). *Europäische Grundrechte*. Handbuch Europarecht, vol. 4. Heidelberg: Springer.

Geiger, R., Khan, D.-E., & Kotzur, M. (Eds.). (2010). *EUV/AEUV* (5th edn.). Munich: C.H.Beck.

Grewe, C. (2012). Beitritt der EU zur EMRK und ZP 14: Wirksame Durchsetzung einer gesamteuropäischen Grundrechteverfassung? *EuR*, 285–309.

Hain, K.-E. (2009). *Die zeitlichen und inhaltlichen Einschränkungen der Telemedienangebote von ARD, ZDF und Deutschlandradio nach dem 12. RÄndStV*. Baden-Baden: Nomos.

Hoffmann, J. M., & Rudolphi, V. (2012). Die Durchführung des Unionsrechts durch die Mitgliedstaaten – Art. 51 Abs. 1 Satz 1 Alt. 2 Grundrechtecharta im Spiegel der Rechtsprechung des Europäischen Gerichtshofs. *DÖV*, 597–602.

Jarass, H. D. (2013). *Charta der Grundrechte der Europäischen Union* (2nd edn.). Munich: C.H.Beck.

Jarass, H. D., & Beljin, S. (2004). Die Bedeutung von Vorrang und Durchführung des EG-Rechts für die nationale Rechtsetzung und Rechtsanwendung. *NVwZ*, 1–10.

Kahl, W., Waldhoff, C., Walter, C., Dolzer, R. & Grasshof, K. (Eds.). *Bonner Kommentar zum Grundgesetz*. Heidelberg: C.F. Müller.

Kirchhof, P. (2013). Stabilität von Recht und Geldwert in der Europäischen Union. *NJW*, 1–6.

Meyer (Ed.). (2014). *Charta der Grundrechte der Europäischen Union* (4th edn.). Baden-Baden: Nomos.

Müller-Graff, P.-C. (2014). Die horizontale Drittwirkung der Grundfreiheiten. *EuR*, 3–29.

Obwexer, W. (2012). Der Beitritt der EU zur EMRK: Rechtsgrundlagen, Rechtsfragen und Rechtsfolgen. *EuR*, 115–149.

Rengeling, H.-W., & Szczekalla, P. (2004). *Grundrechte in der Europäischen Union*. Cologne: Heymanns.

Schmitz, T. (2001). Die EU-Grundrechtecharta aus grundrechtsdogmatischer und grundrechtstheoretischer Sicht. *JZ*, 833–843.

Schwarze, J. (Ed.). (2012). *EU-Kommentar* (3rd edn.). Baden-Baden: Nomos.

Stern, K. (1994). *Das Staatsrecht der Bundesrepublik Deutschland* vol. III. Munich: C.H.Beck.

Stern, K., & Becker, F. (Eds.). (2015). *Grundrechte-Kommentar* (2nd edn.). Cologne: Heymanns.

Streinz, R. (Ed.). (2012). *EUV/AEUV* (2nd edn.). Munich: C.H.Beck.

Streinz, R. (2013). Die verschiedenen unionalen Rechtsquellen in ihrem Zusammenspiel. *ZöR*, *68*, 663–683.

Streinz, R., Ohler, C., & Hermann, C. (2010). *Der Vertrag von Lissabon zur Reform der EU. Einführung mit Synopse* (3rd edn.). Munich: C.H.Beck.

Tettinger, P. J., & Stern, K. (Eds.). (2006). *Kölner Gemeinschaftskommentar, Europäische Grundrechte-Charta*. Munich: C.H.Beck.

Vedder, C., & Heintschel von Heinegg, W. (Eds.). (2012). *Europäisches Unionsrecht. EUV/AEUV/Grundrechte-Charta. Handkommentar*. Baden-Baden: Nomos.

Weber, A. (2000). Die Europäische Grundrechtecharta auf dem Weg zu einer europäischen Verfassung. *NJW*, 537–544.

Weber, A. (2002). *Charta der Grundrechte der Europäischen Union. Einführung und Text in deutscher, englischer und französischer Sprache*. Munich: Sellier.

Weber, A. (2008). Vom Verfassungsvertrag zum Vertrag von Lissabon. *EuZW*, 7–13.

The Strasbourg Court on Issues of Religion in the Public Schools System

Lech Garlicki

1 Religion and Education

1.1 Religions have always constituted an omnipresent phenomenon in all societies. Over the past almost 300 years, public schools have also emerged as a necessary component of a modern State. Since religious freedom assumes diversity and public schooling must maintain a certain degree of uniformity, a clash between conflicting approaches and demands becomes unavoidable. It is the function of the state to provide for a solution and, in the European legal space, it is the function of supra-national jurisdictions to watch over state action affecting individual rights.

The European Convention guarantees, on the one hand, the freedom of religion and conscience, understood i.a. as the freedom "either alone or in communication with others and public or private, to manifest religion or belief, in worship, teaching, practice and observance" (Art. 9 ECHR). Freedom of religion and conscience applies not only to adherents of religious denominations, "it is also a precious asset for atheists, agnostics, sceptics and unconcerned. The pluralism, indissociable from a democratic society, depends on it".[1]

On the other hand, Art. 2 of Protocol No. 1 establishes the right to education and provides that the State would "assume functions in relation to education and to teaching" but, in the exercise of those functions, should "respect the right of parents to ensure such education and teaching in conformity with their own religious and philosophical convictions".

Thus, the State has a right (or – rather – an obligation) to provide public schooling for all children whose parents are not ready to use private schools. At the same time, the State must respect both, the general freedom of religion and conscience and the specific guarantee of that freedom in respect to the operation of the public schools system.

This article is partly based on: Garlicki and Jankowska-Gilberg 2011.

[1] Appl. No. 14307/88, *Kokkinakis v. Greece* (ECtHR 25 May 1993) para 31.

H.-J. Blanke et al. (eds.), *Common European Legal Thinking*,
DOI 10.1007/978-3-319-19300-7_17

1.2 The very essence of the European Convention is to provide for general standards that must be uniformly respected by all 47 Member States. But acceptation of universal standards is not tantamount to acceptation of uniformity.

While contemporary Europe often emphasises the need for common standards and universal values, it has never been understood as the exclusion of national, regional and local differences. Each country of Europe has its own heritage that refers to tradition and history, religious and moral values, political and constitutional conventions and, simply, the way of living of the society. In other words, each country has, usually over centuries, elaborated its own identity that may be described as its own culture. The countries of Europe may uniformly adhere to general values like human rights and the rule of law, but pluralism occupies a prominent place among those values. Thus, the current process of European integration has a dialectic nature: the trend towards uniformisation collides sometimes with the quest for preservation of traditional values, relations and attitudes, in brief – distinct cultural identities of particular states. Needless to mention, religion and – in particular – religious structure of the society, constitutes one of the core elements of those cultural identities.

The European Convention acknowledges the predominant role of national authorities: "The machinery of protection established by the Convention is subsidiary to the national systems safeguarding human rights. The Convention leaves to each Contracting State, in the first place, the task of securing the rights and freedoms it enshrines [. . .] By reason of their direct and continuous contact with the vital forces of their countries, State authorities are in principle in better position than the international judge to give an opinion on the exact content of the [Convention] requirements."[2]

But, at the same time, the Convention sets standards that must be universally observed in all Member States.

This produces a certain tension between subsidiarity and universality which may be addressed only on a case-to-case basis. Therefore "some interpretational tool is needed to draw the line between what is properly a matter for each community to decide at local level and what is so fundamental that it entails the same requirement for all countries whatever the variations in traditions and culture. In the European system, that function is served by the doctrine of the margin of appreciation".[3] In a nutshell, this doctrine reserves for the Contracting States some room to decide how to implement the Convention standards in a way that corresponds best to the domestic conditions. While the very idea of margin of appreciation is based upon the respect for the subsidiarity principle,[4] it has never been stated in the written text of Convention. Rather, it emerged in the Strasbourg case-law as an entirely judge-

[2] Appl. No. 5493/72, *Handyside v. United Kingdom* (ECtHR 7 December 1976) para 48.
[3] Mahoney 1998, p. 1.
[4] "It is the essence of the national margin of appreciation that, when different opinions are possible and do exist, the international judge should only intervene if the national decision cannot be reasonably justified" (Appl. No. 17419/90, *Wingrove v. United Kingdom* (ECtHR 25 November 1996), the concurring opinion of Judge Bernhardt). See also Villiger 2007, p. 624–626.

made creation. Thus, it is the ECtHR who, in the final resort, delineates the scope of what shall be left for the States.

1.3 The application of the doctrine of the margin of appreciation is based upon three assumptions: (1) the Convention sets universal standards and within those standards allows the Member States a choice; (2) the Court should respect choices taken by the domestic authorities as long as they do not collide with any of the universal standards; (3) the scope of choice varies depending on several factors: in some situations domestic authorities are allowed a "wide" or (only) "certain" margin of appreciation, in others – the margin of appreciation remains very limited or does not exist at all. And, since it is the Court's function to decide what (if any) margin of appreciation is appropriate in respect to each particular type of case, the doctrine offers a considerable degree of flexibility in the application of general standards to individual situations.

Among the factors that determine the scope of the margin left for the State, the existence of a common cultural context (i. e. of a particular traditional combination of moral, religious, ideological, political and constitutional values and attitudes) in which particular rights operate within the society, is of a particular importance. It should not be, of course, forgotten that the Convention as such is based on a certain political philosophy, and that it also presupposes a universal acceptation of certain social, cultural and moral values. In particular, such values as tolerance, pluralism and democracy, constitute the core structure of the whole Convention system. Those values must be respected and protected by all Member States.

At the same time, however, there are, as there always have been, profound differences between societies (and – in consequence – between Member States) and – in the Convention process – those different identities of Member States must be accepted and respected.

The delimitation of the national margin of appreciation appears particularly difficult when there is a conflict involving important religious or/and philosophical values.[5] The Member States differ in their tradition and history, as well as in their religious structures, in the dominant moral values, and in the existing degree of tolerance. It must not be forgotten that over the last two decades those differences became more dramatic due to the geographical expansion of the Convention system and also due to the evolution of the role of Islam in some Member States. It may be very difficult to identify common ground to approach problems of religion and – in consequence – problems like family life, sexual orientation, abortion or euthanasia.

The underlying philosophy of the Convention assumes pluralism of views and judgments and requires tolerance. Tolerance means, on the one hand, that the very fact that others may have views and values that are not shared by a majority, cannot be called into question. But, it also means that those who represent less orthodox views and values must not disrespect feelings and reactions of other social groups. Those relations develop horizontally – among individuals and groups, and only indirectly may be controlled by the Convention standards. The State's role is focused

[5] Garlicki 2012, p. 727 et seqq.

primarily on securing a peaceful coexistence of different systems of values. Quite often it calls for elaboration of compromises (or, at least, for elaboration of a framework in which such compromises becomes feasible) and for the State acting as an arbiter. While such State action must respect all standards set out in the Convention (and in the case-law of the ECtHR), assessments of "necessity", "justifiability" or "public interest" cannot be taken in the Strasbourg ivory tower. The Strasbourg judges cannot ignore the local context of each and every case and are constantly faced with the contradiction between universalism and particularism. What may be perfectly acceptable in a Nordic society, may provoke shock and distaste in some other corners of Europe.

2 The Convention Framework of the Public Educational System

2.1 The State has a right as well as an obligation to establish a system of public schools and to see that each child be included into a decent system of public or private education. The right of access to public education refers, nowadays, to all levels of education. The Convention does not guarantee, in principle, a right to educate children at home.[6]

The State's obligation to provide for public education assumes that the State has a competence to organize the system. "The right to education guaranteed by the first sentence of Article 2 by its very nature calls for regulation by the State, but such regulation must never injure the substance of the right nor conflict with other rights enshrined in the Convention or its Protocols".[7] Under the case-law of the Strasbourg Court:

- the State has a wide discretion in determining its educational system: "the right to education [. . .] by its very nature calls for regulation by the State, regulation which may vary in time and place according to the needs and resources of community and individuals";[8] the right to education refers to the educational institutions actually existing in the material time; that right cannot be, in principle, understood, as enhancing the State's obligations to establish new schools of a particular type, e. g. schools with a particular language of instruction;
- the setting and planning of the curriculum fall in principle within the competence of the States;
- the State has the competence to organize the operation of public schools also in respect to the internal rules of behaviour (including common manifestations, dress codes, etc.) and to apply disciplinary sanctions to enforce those rules.

---

[6] See Appl. No. 10233/83, *Family H. v. United Kingdom* (ECommHR 6 March 1984); Appl. No. 17678/91, *B.N. and S.N. v. Sweden* (ECommHR 30 June 1993); Appl. No. 35504/03, *Konrad v. Germany* (ECtHR 11 September 2006).

[7] Joined Appl. No. 7511/76, 7743/76, *Campbell and Cosans v. United Kingdom* (ECtHR 25 February 1982) para 41.

[8] Appl. No. 2126/64, *Belgium Linguistic Case* (ECtHR 23 July 1968) para 32.

The State's powers must, however, remain consistent with the parents' rights to have their religious and philosophical convictions respected. In other words, the margin left for the organisational and regulatory activity of the State ends where the operation of a public school becomes incompatible with children's/parents' convictions.

One of the most important criterions in this respect is the prohibition of indoctrination: "the State, in fulfilling the functions assumed by it in regard to education and teaching, must take care that information or knowledge included in the curriculum is conveyed in an objective, critical and pluralistic manner. The State is forbidden to pursue an aim of indoctrination that might be considered as not respecting parents' religious and philosophical convictions. This is the limit that must not be exceeded. Such an interpretation is consistent at one and the same time with the first sentence of Article 2 of the Protocol no. 1, with Articles 8, 9 and 10 of the Convention and with the general spirit of the Convention itself, an instrument designated to maintain and promote the ideals and values of a democratic society."[9] Thus, neither the curriculum (as set in general regulations and as implemented in particular schools) nor the general operation and discipline within the public school system must transgress limits resulting from the prohibition of indoctrination.

The European standards are, by their nature, rather general and they call for compromise and good faith in the process of their national implementation. The very concept of indoctrination may vary according to different cultural and religious traditions of particular States and also – as was mentioned in the *Klejdsen* case – may vary according to the actual range of alternative educational possibilities that are made available to all students.[10]

2.2 The first of the "great decisions" of the Court concerning right to education were adopted already several decades ago: the 1968 *Belgium Linguistic* Case and the 1976 *Kjeldsen* Case set several principles that are still valid in the case-law of the Strasbourg Court. In the beginning of the current century, the Court – for the first time – was invited to take a closer look at the relationship between religious education and the mission of public schools; its findings were, in particular, summarized in Grand Chamber judgments in *Leyla Şahin* (2005), *Folgerø* (2007), *Lautsi* (2001) and, albeit indirectly, in *S.A.S.* (2014).

Two questions of this case-law seem to evoke a particular interest: (1) the place of religious instruction in public schools, first of all the content of instruction and its position within the school curriculum and (2) the manner and scope of expression of religious conviction in public schools, in respect to both, individual right of

[9] Appl. No. 5926/72, *Kjeldsen and Others* (ECtHR 7 December 1976) para 53.

[10] Appl. No. 5926/72, *Kjeldsen and Others* (ECtHR 7 December 1976) para 50: "In its investigation as to whether Article 2 of Protocol no 1 has been violated, the Court cannot forget, however, that the functions assumed by Denmark in relation to education and to teaching include the grant of substantial assistance to private schools. Although recourse to these schools involves parents in sacrifices [...] the alternative solution it provides constitutes a factor that should not be disregarded in this case".

students to express their individual convictions and the regulatory power of schools to promote/impose certain forms of religious expression.

3 Religious Instruction in Public Schools

3.1 Although the *Kjeldsen* Case did not deal directly with the problem of whether a public school is allowed to include religious instruction into its curriculum,[11] it was – and still is – the leading precedent also for that area.

The Court established four principal rules:

- the State's obligation to assure access to education enhances a power to decide what kind of public schools system should be established and a power to decide on the structure and content of the school curriculum;
- Art. 2 of Protocol No. 1 and, in particular, its "religious guarantee" applies to the entire educational program; it is not possible to draw distinction between religious instruction and other subjects;
- information transmitting religious, philosophical and moral messages constitute an indissociable part of many "nonreligious" subjects included into the school curricula; the Convention cannot be read as preventing States from imparting through teaching or education information or knowledge of a directly religious or philosophical kind; it does not even permit parents to object to the integration of such teaching or education in the school curriculum;
- however, every information that may have religious or philosophical connotations must be conveyed in an objective, critical and pluralistic manner; failure to observe this requirements transforms legitimate education into a process of indoctrination, be definition constitution violation of parents' rights.

These four rules are applicable to the regulation and content of the entire curriculum and are also determinative to the regulation and content of religious instruction understood as a separate subject offered to students.

3.2 In Europe, there is no uniform system of religious instruction in public schools, as – in a broader perspective – there is no uniform system of relations between the State and the religious communities. In consequence, the choice of one or another system clearly remains within the State's margin of appreciation. The Strasbourg Court is only allowed to examine whether a particular national system does not encroach upon parents'/student' rights as guaranteed by Art. 9 ECHR and Art. 2 of Protocol No. 1.

[11] It should be recalled that in *Kjeldsen*, the Court addressed the compatibility of the sex education with parents' rights under Art. 2 of Protocol No. 1. The applicants claimed that integrated and compulsory sex education, as introduced into State schools, was contrary to the beliefs they hold as Christian parents. The question, therefore, was not whether and how religion can be taught in public schools, but – rather – what are the limitations in teaching non-religious subjects that may offend religious convictions of the parents.

National regulations vary to a considerable degree, nevertheless it seems possible to organize them into three models:

- the secular model (based, in particular, on the French tradition of secularism) in which no religious instruction is offered in public schools or, at least, no religious instruction may constitute a part of the school curriculum;
- the model of integrated religious instruction, in which teaching of religion is provided as a separate subject, but this teaching is not based upon any particular religion and is constructed as a general, denominationally neutral instruction about problems of religion; this model exists in several European states and its compatibility with the Convention has been recently assessed in regard to regulations adopted in Norway, Turkey and Germany;
- the model of parallel (denominational) religious instruction, in which teaching of religion is not only provided as a separate subject but is also taught separately for each of the denominations represented among students of a particular school; in other words, each of the primary religions is invited to take care of instruction of its principles and beliefs; it is the responsibility of the school to arrange for parallel, denominationally oriented classes in religion; students (parents) must have a right to choose a religion class that corresponds with their convictions or, alternatively, a (religion-neutral) course on general ethics.

3.3 The secular model has never been examined by the Strasbourg Court in full. The existing case-law indicates only that there is no right to have religion courses taught in the public school system. As the Court observed in 2010, "the right to manifest religion in teaching does not [...] go so far as to entail an obligation on States to allow religious education in public schools or nurseries".[12] Furthermore, it indicates that religious problems can be addressed within – secularly oriented – courses on general ethics, providing the curriculum is not conceived as an atheistic

[12] Appl. No. 7798/08, *Savez Crkava "Riječ života" and Others v. Croatia* (ECtHR 9 March 2011) para 57. Nevertheless, in this case, the Court found a violation of Art. 14 (equality) as the Croatian regulations had been applied in a discriminatory manner.

or anti-religious indoctrination.[13] Thus, it could be assumed that, in principle, the decision to adopt a secular model falls under the state's margin of appreciation.

3.4 The integrated model has been assessed at length by the Court on several occasions; the leading case being *Folgerø v. Norway*.[14] In *Folgerø*, the Court established a violation of the Convention. Although the judgment was adopted by a narrow majority in the Grand Chamber (9:8), the split was not related to the proclamation of general principles, but rather to the manner in which those principles had been applied to the modalities of the Norwegian regulation.[15]

The Court summarised the "general principles" as to the interpretation of Art. 2 of Protocol No. 1 in the following manner:[16]

- the two sentences of Art. 2 of Protocol No. 1 must be interpreted not only in the light of each other but also, in particular, of Art. 8, 9 and 10 of the Convention;
- the guarantee of parents' rights (the second sentence of Art. 2 of Protocol No. 1) "aims at safeguarding the possibility of pluralism in education [...] In view of the power of the modern State, it is above all through State teaching that this aim must be realized";
- Art. 2 of Protocol No. 1 establishes an obligation of the State "to respect parents' convictions thorough the entire State education programme";
- the parents – in the discharge of a natural duty towards their children – may require from the State to respect their religious and philosophical convictions;

[13] In Appl. No. 45216/07, *Appel-Irrgang v. Germany* (ECtHR 20 October 2009), the Court upheld the system, adopted in Berlin, that provided for a compulsory course in ethics (religious instruction was also offered at the school premises but only as a supplementary option).
First, the Court disagreed with the applicants' argument that the ethics course constituted a non-neutral form of secular indoctrination. The Court analysed the content and structure of the program and arrived at the conclusion that both, the aims and the message of the course is conform with the requirements of pluralism and objectivity. The Court noted that the course "does not attach particular weight to any particular religion or denomination and its goal is to convey certain basis values common for all students".
Secondly, the Court rejected the argument that the course did not reserve sufficient space for information about Christian religion, contrary to the historical position of this religion in Germany. The Court confirmed the *Folgerø* approach that national tradition may justify more detailed presentation of the dominant religion. However, this principle cannot be interpreted as establishing an obligation of all states to do so. These decisions belong to the State's margin of appreciation.
Finally, the Court did not accept the argument that the very introduction of a mandatory course in ethics violated religious convictions of the applicants. The Court applied a twofold test: 1) whether the course was structured in a way that offered a priority to a particular religion; 2) whether it promoted a fight against the existing religions, in particular – Christianity. Negative response to both questions convinced the Court that there had not been any violation of the Convention.

[14] Appl. No. 15472/02, *Folgerø and Others v. Norway* (ECtHR 29 June 2007).

[15] The Norwegian regulation provided that all students of elementary and secondary schools have to take classes on Christianity, Religion and Philosophy (KRL) and allowed for partial exemptions from participation upon a reasoned request of parents.

[16] See Appl. No. 15472/02, *Folgerø and Others v. Norway* (ECtHR 29 June 2007) para 84.

- a balance between individual interest and that of a group must be achieved: it must "ensure the fair and proper treatment of minorities and avoid any abuse of dominant position";
- the setting and planning of the curriculum fall in principle within the States' competence: Art. 2 of Protocol No. 1 "does not prevent States from imparting through teaching or education information or knowledge of a directly or indirectly religious or philosophical kind"
- the State must "take care that information or knowledge included in the curriculum is conveyed in an objective, critical and pluralistic manner. The State is forbidden to pursue an aim of indoctrination";
- indoctrination means a situation in which "parents' religious and philosophical convictions are not respected".

The holding of *Folgerø* was threefold. In the general dimension, the Court accepted the model of integrated teaching as compatible with the Convention. Thus, the very fact that the subject "Christianity, Religion, and Philosophy" was included into the curriculum and, in principle, was compulsory for all students, did not constitute – in itself – a violation of the Convention. The violation resulted only from the – substantive and procedural – determination of this subject.

In the substantive dimension, the Court analysed, first, the structure of instruction. It accepted that Art. 2 of Protocol No. 1 provides for no right to isolation: it "does not embody any rights for the parents that their child be kept ignorant about religion and philosophy in their education". Furthermore – taking into account the religious context of Norway – the religious instruction may, quantitatively, focus on presentation of the Christian religion: "the fact that knowledge about Christianity represented a greater part of the curriculum [...] than knowledge about other religions and philosophies, cannot [...] of its own be viewed as a departure from the principles of pluralism and objectivity amounting to indoctrination".[17] However, the State's margin of appreciation becomes more limited as to the content of the instruction: since pupils were also invited to engage into different religious activities "which would in particular include prayers, psalms, the learning of religious texts by heart and the participation in plays of a religious nature", and since those activities offered some priority to the Christian religion, there emerged a situation of imbalance. This situation "would be capable of affecting pupils' minds in a manner giving rise to an issue under Article 2 of Protocol No. 1".[18]

In the procedural dimension, the Court placed a strong emphasis on the principle of exemption: parents (students) who regard the religious instruction, as provided by the school system, to be incompatible with their convictions must have a possibility to be exempted from instruction. The Court held that the system of (only) a partial exemption imposed too heavy a burden on the parents involved: parents were required regularly to analyse the content of upcoming lessons and exemption can be granted only if they were able to show that subjects to be taught are irreconcilable with their conviction. In addition, the requirement of written justification

[17] Appl. No. 15472/02, *Folgerø and Others v. Norway* (ECtHR 29 June 2007) para 89.
[18] Appl. No. 15472/02, *Folgerø and Others v. Norway* (ECtHR 29 June 2007) para 94.

of every exemption request could easily amount to parents' obligation to disclose their intimate convictions to the school authorities.[19] The lack of a proper exemption system combined with the actual programme of the KRL course, gave rise to a violation of Art. 2 of Protocol No. 1.

The *Folgerø* approach was followed in the *Zengin* judgment of 9 October 2007,[20] in which mandatory religious instruction in Turkish public schools was declared to violate the rights of parents guaranteed under Art. 2 of Protocol No. 1. While a possibility of exemption was provided for adherents of certain religions, it did not apply to some others, in particular to the Alevi faith that represented one of the Islamic denominations.

The Court recalled the general principles summarised in the *Folgerø* judgment. It reiterated that "in a pluralist democratic society, the State's duty of impartiality and neutrality towards various religions, faiths and beliefs is incompatible with any assessment by the State of the legitimacy of religious beliefs or the ways in which those beliefs are expressed".[21] The Court came to the conclusion that the Turkish regulation of the subject "Religious Culture and Ethics" cannot be considered to meet criteria of objectivity and pluralism and, more particularly in the applicant's particular case, "to respect the religious and philosophical convictions [of the] followers of the Alevi faith, on the subject of which the syllabus is clearly lacking".[22]

This substantive shortcoming was further strengthened by the lack of adequate procedural regulation. The procedure of exemption, being limited only to adherents of certain religions, does not provide sufficient protection for other religious minorities. This procedure was shaped in a manner that was "likely to subject them to a heavy burden and to necessity of disclosing their religious or philosophical convictions in order to have children exempted from the lessons in religion".[23]

The same approach was confirmed in *Mansur Yalçin and Others v. Turkey* in which the Court again was confronted with the lack of proper arrangements for the Alevi children. In addition the Court, in reference to Art. 46 of the Convention, noted the existence of a "structural problem" which requires the adoption of general measures. Apparently, the Turkish authorities did not implement the *Zengin* judgment in a correct manner, a reaction which, unfortunately, does happen also in other countries.[24]

This summary of the case-law dealing with the system of integrated religious instruction demonstrates certain general principles:

[19] See Appl. No. 15472/02, *Folgerø and Others v. Norway* (ECtHR 29 June 2007) para 95–100.
[20] Appl. No. 1448/04, *Hasan and Eylem Zengin v. Turkey* (ECtHR 9 October 2007).
[21] Appl. No. 1448/04, *Hasan and Eylem Zengin v. Turkey* (ECtHR 9 October 2007) para 54.
[22] Appl. No. 1448/04, *Hasan and Eylem Zengin v. Turkey* (ECtHR 9 October 2007) para 70.
[23] Appl. No. 1448/04, *Hasan and Eylem Zengin v. Turkey* (ECtHR 9 October 2007) para 76.
[24] Appl. No. 21163/11, *Mansur Yalçın and Others v. Turkey* (ECtHR 16 September 2014) para 84. The Court limited its judgment to Art. 2 of Protocol No. 1 and regarded it as "not necessary" to deal with the claim that also Art. 9 read in conjunction with Art. 14 had been violated (para 80). The latter holding provoked a (quite convincing) dissent of three judges (A. Sajó, N. Vucinić and E. Kūris).

- the decision to adopt such a system falls within the State's margin of appreciation;
- in the structure and content of such a course, quantitative distinctions, that offer certain priority for the "traditional religion of the State", are not prohibited per se; more problematic are qualitative distinctions, since they create a greater risk of (prohibited) indoctrination;
- there must be sufficiently effective procedural guarantees to be exempted from religious instruction; undue restriction of the exemption may constitute a violation of the Convention.

3.5 The third model of religious instruction is based on the principle of parallelism: every (important) denomination has the possibility to hold its "own" religious classes, each parent (student) has a right to choose one of those courses and, for those students who do not identify with any of those religions (that includes also agnostics and atheists) an alternative course of ethics must be provided.

This model has been, as yet, assessed only in respect to Polish regulation of religious instruction.[25] On the one hand, it was contested that the general model of religious instruction is incompatible with requirements of Art. 2 of Protocol No. 1. On the other hand, there were claims that the inclusion of grades (marks) for religion into school reports raises problems under Art. 9 and 14 of the Convention.

One of the possible approaches is that the general assessment of the Polish system should refer to the principles of interpretation of Art. 2 of Protocol No. 1 as recapitulated in the *Folgerø* case: the State is bound to respect parents' conviction throughout the entire public school education programme; the State must ensure the fair and proper treatment of minorities and avoid any abuse of dominant position of any particular group (religion); the curriculum – as set by the State – may include information of a religious/philosophical kind, but must assure that it is conveyed in an objective, critical and pluralistic manner; the State is forbidden to pursue an aim of indoctrination.

[25] Appl. No. 23380/94, *C.J., J.J. and E.J. v. Poland* (ECommHR 16 January 1996); Appl. No. 40319/98, *Saniewski v. Poland* (ECtHR 26 June 2001); Appl. No. 7710/02, *Grzelak v. Poland* (ECtHR 15 June 2010). Poland is a predominantly Roman-Catholic country. Under the Polish system, there are separate classes for each denomination represented by more than three pupils of a particular school. Pupils (parents) opt for one of the courses by submitting so-called "positive declarations". For pupils who do not wish to follow any of the religion courses, alternative course of ethics must be provided. A grade (mark) for those courses is included into the yearly school reports as well as into the final reports confirming the conclusion of a given level of schooling (i. e. elementary school, gymnasium and liceum). Grades (marks) obtained for religious instruction or ethics is counted towards the "average mark" obtained by a pupil in a given school year. It is provided that school reports contain a separate rubric "religion/ethics"; therefore it is not possible to determine whether a pupil followed one of the courses on religion or the course of ethics. The problem is that, in some schools, the course of ethics is not provided (because of a very limited number of interested pupils) and, in consequence, the yearly school report of pupils who did not attend the available course on Catholic religion may contain a straight line in the rubric "religion/ethics". This leaves a message that a pupil did not follow a course on the Catholic religion, and – most probably – was not a member of the Roman-Catholic Church.

It might be, however, observed that under the parallel system, each denomination holds classes on its "own" religion and, by definition, those classes must be oriented towards teaching and supporting the principles and belief of a particular religion. The requirement of objectivity and pluralism as well as the prohibition of indoctrination must also be present in that system, but must be interpreted accordingly. It is not impossible that the distinction between "bearing Christian witness and improper proselytism", adopted in the *Kokkinakis* case might be of some usefulness.[26] Therefore, while each separate Church may be allowed to convey the message on its doctrine and principles, the prohibition of "improper proselytism" would constitute an absolute limit. In other words, State tolerance of "improper proselytism" would be tantamount to indoctrination. Furthermore, the vulnerability of the school environment should also be taken into account. Thus, teaching religion (and, in particular – the dominant religion) can never result in discrimination of minorities or undue pressure on adherents of other religions as well as on atheists and agnostics.

In such a system, particular importance must be attached to the freedom of choice. Pupils (parents) should be free from any undue pressure or influence when opting for one of the courses on religion or ethics. As long as those courses remain optional and as long as the choice depends on the wish of parents and pupils, it may be assumed that such a system of teaching – in its model application – falls within the margin of appreciation as to the planning and setting of the curriculum accorded to States under Art. 2 of Protocol No. 1.

More problems may arise in practical implementation of this model. The Court seems to be clear on the matter of voluntariness: in both earlier decisions concerning (and upholding) the Polish regulation, it was emphasised that pupils were not obliged to attend religious instruction, as it was organized on a voluntary basis. An *a contrario* conclusion seems more than appropriate in this respect.

If no alternative course on ethics has been provided, it may – perhaps – be still maintained that the scope of the State's obligation depends on the number of pupils involved and that the State may not be absolutely required to provide such course for one pupil only. This problem has not yet been clearly addressed by the Court. What, however, the Court was invited to decide, was related to the "straight-line rule": if a student did not follow any of the available courses on religion and if no alternative course was provided, the school report contains a straight line in the rubric religion/ethic. In the *Grzelak* case, the Court arrived at the conclusion that this system creates discrimination of non-believers. It was argued that the fact of having no mark for religion/ethics inevitably has a specific connotation and distinguishes the persons concerned from those who have a mark for the subject. In a country, like Poland, it may amount to a form of stigmatisation of such persons.

[26] Appl. No. 14307/88, *Kokkinakis v. Greece* (ECtHR 25 May 1993) para 48.

4 Religion and Dress Codes at School

4.1 The school is a public institution and it goes without saying that the State must retain regulatory powers concerning not only the structure and content of the curriculum but also the rules governing the internal order and operation of the school. Those regulations may enter the religious sphere in two different ways:

- the school may establish prohibitions or requirements regulating individual behaviour of students that may interfere with their religious or philosophical convictions;
- the school may expose students to permanent contact with messages and/or symbols promoting a particular religion.

In practice, the former problem arises in respect to the prohibition of the Islamic scarf and the latter – in respect to the presence of a cross/crucifix in school classrooms. The Strasbourg Court has already had some opportunities to elaborate its position in both areas.

4.2 It is a valid principle that, in general, the establishment of dress codes remain within the school regulatory power.[27] Thus, only very oppressive (and clearly unreasonable) dress regulation would be regarded as undue interference with the personal autonomy of students and, henceforth, a violation of Art. 8 of the Convention. The standard of protection becomes, however, quite different when a dress code is applied to situations in which wearing a particular dress is motivated (required) by a particular religion. In such situations, recourse is made to Art. 9 of the Convention. This issue has arisen particularly in relation to the Islamic scarf and, as is well known, certain (but, by far, not all) European countries decided to prohibit the scarf to teachers and – sometimes – also to students. The problem evokes numerous controversies and is tackled from very different angles: for some, the prohibition exposes students to a grave moral dilemma and compels them to violate rules of their religion; for others – the very concept of the scarf symbolises inequality and sends a message incompatible with the basic values of the Convention.

The Court accepts that the problem of dress codes may affect freedom of religion.[28] It is clear that freedom of religion implies also freedom to manifest one's

[27] E. g. Appl. No. 11674/85, *Stevens v. United Kingdom* (ECommHR 3 March 1986): male students may be required to wear a tie at school.

[28] The problem has also been addressed in respect of non-educational environment. The general position of the Court is that restrictions must meet requirements of Art. 9.2 of the Convention.
Those restrictions may be, in the first place, justified by necessities of public safety. The Court accepted regulations requiring removal of a religious dress for a security check in an airport (Appl. No. 35753/03, *Phull v. France* ([ECtHR 11 January 2005]) or in a consulate (Appl. No. 15585/06, *El Morsli v. France* [ECtHR 4 March 2008]) as well as imposing obligation to appear bareheaded on identity photos for use on official documents (Appl. No. 24479/07, *Mann Singh v. France* [ECtHR 11 June 2007]).
Also requirements of public safety and protection of the rights of others may constitute valid grounds for restriction (see Appl. No. 48420/10, 59842/10, 51671/10 and 36516/10, *Eweida and Others v. United Kingdom* [ECtHR 15 January 2013]), where the Court, heavily relying on the

religion. "Bearing witness in words and deeds is bound with the existence of religious convictions."[29] However, since – under Art. 9.2 ECHR – freedom of religion may be subjected to limitations, it may be necessary to place restrictions on this freedom in order to reconcile the interests of the various groups and to protect a general public order. Thus, in assessing whether a particular dress code remains compatible with Art. 9, it is necessary to establish a reasonable balance between conflicting interests. In other words, once it is established that a prohibitive dress code interferes with the freedom of religion, the State must demonstrate that its establishment was "necessary in a democratic society". The basic norm of reference is here Art. 9 ECHR, a provision that leaves less room for the State's margin of appreciation than Art. 2 of Protocol No. 1.

4.3 Historically, the first question before the Strasbourg Court was raised by a teacher affected by the prohibition to wear the Islamic headscarf in the course of her teaching duties.

In the 2001 *Dahlab v. Switzerland* decision,[30] the Court upheld a dismissal of an elementary school teacher who had refused to stop wearing an Islamic headscarf. The Court, confirming the approach of the Swiss Federal Court, raised three principal arguments:

- the particular nature of the applicant's profession: a state school teacher represents the State educational authority (and the Swiss Constitution established the principle of denominational neutrality of public schools) and, in consequence enjoys a particular status involving both privileges and obligations: "State school teachers have to tolerate proportionate restrictions on their freedom of religion";
- the particular vulnerability of students/pupils affected: the applicant taught very young children and "it is very difficult to assess the impact that a powerful external symbol such as the wearing of a scarf may have on the freedom of conscience and religion of very young children [Such children] are more easily influenced

proportionality analysis, accepted a ban of wearing a Christian cross around the neck by nurses in geriatric hospitals, but rejected a similar ban imposed on British Airways personnel).

The most recent (albeit quite controversial) position was adopted by the Grand Chamber in Appl. No. 43835/11, *S.A.S. v. France* (ECtHR 1 July 2014). The Court considered the French ban on wearing burka and nijab in public places. The Court held that the ban served a legitimate aim, namely to ensure the observance of the minimum requirements of life in society as part of the "protection of the rights and freedoms of others" (para 140). As to the proportionality, the Court attached "some significance that the ban is not expressly based on the religious connotation of the clothing in question but solely on the fact that it conceals the face" (par.151). The Court accepted the Government's argument that the ban responded to a practice that the State deemed incompatible, in French society, with the ground rules of social communication and more broadly the requirements of "living together" (para 153). The legitimacy of such need to ensure "socialization" of every member of society, combined with the wide margin of appreciation in matters of general policy (para 154) justifies the restriction in question. See, however, quite convincing, dissenting opinion of Judges A. Nussberger and H. Jäderblom.

[29] See, generally, Appl. No. 14307/88, *Kokkinakis v. Greece* (ECtHR 25 May 1993) para 31.

[30] Appl. No. 42393/98, *Dahlab v. Switzerland* (ECtHR 15 February 2001).

than older pupils. In those circumstances, it cannot be denied outright that the wearing of a headscarf might have some kind of proselytizing effect";
- the particular nature of the Islamic scarf: wearing of the scarf results from a religious precept that "as the Federal Court noted, is hard to square with the principle of gender equality. It therefore appears difficult to reconcile the wearing of an Islamic headscarf with the message of tolerance, respect for others and, above all, equality and non-discrimination that all teachers in a democratic society must convey to their pupils".

Thus, the Court's position contained a double message. On the one hand, the Court focused on particularities of the assessed situation: a combination of the public status of the school and the very young age of the affected children, reserved more room for State interference with the freedom to manifest religious beliefs. Thus, the Court left open what its reaction would have been had a similar prohibition arisen in respect of another (higher) level of education. On the other hand, the Strasbourg Court recalled the position of the Swiss Federal Court containing a substantive, and general, condemnation of the very nature of the Islamic scarf. This might suggest that the Court would adopt a more restrictive approach also to other situations in which an Islamic scarf is displayed in public.[31]

4.4 There is still no clear answer which of these approaches would dominate the Court's case-law. The most prominent judgment was adopted in the 2005 *Leyla Şahin* case.[32] The Court examined upheld the Turkish university regulation prohibiting students to wear the Islamic headscarf.

The exact scope and authority of *Leyla Şahin* remains, however, not entirely clear. On the one hand, the Court accepted the application of the head-scarf ban on university students, i. e. considerably developed the *Dahlab*'s holding: it was extended from teachers to students (even, that students, unlike teachers, cannot be regarded as "agents of the State") and it was applied to universities (where, by definition, students are more mature and less prone to undue influence). On the other hand, the Court placed a lot of emphasis on the particular situation of Turkey as a country in which Islam represents a majority religion.

The Court recalled, firstly, the general principles as to the role of the State in the matters of religion. The State cannot be regarded as a passive observer only. On the

[31] The approach adopted by the ECtHR in the *Dahlab case* was de facto rejected in the recent judgment of the German Constitutional Court (27 January 2015, 1 BvR 471/10 and 1 BvR 1181/10). The German Court – amending the decision of 24 September 2003, 2 BvR 1436/02 – held that a blanket ban on the Islamic scarf collides with the guarantees provided in Article 4 of the German Basic Law. Such a ban can be introduced only in particular situations of conflict which would endanger "the inner peace at school" or the principle of State neutrality. It can apply to individual persons as well as to particular schools or school districts. As the ECHR establishes only "minimal standards" of protection, a higher standard adopted by the German Constitutional Court remains in perfect harmony with Article 53 of the Convention. But, at the same time, the German decision proposes a different intellectual approach to the problem and – in the framework of the "dialogue between courts" – it will be difficult for the Strasbourg Court simply to ignore the position of the Bundesverfassungsgericht.

[32] Appl. No. 44774/98, *Leyla Şahin v Turkey* (ECtHR 10 November 2005).

contrary, the State plays the role of "a neutral and impartial organizer of the exercise of various religions, faiths and beliefs; this role of the State is conducive to public order, religious harmony and tolerance in a democratic society". While tension between opposing religious groups form a part of reality, "the role of the authorities is not to remove the cause of tension by eliminating pluralism, but to ensure that the competing groups tolerate each other". Therefore, "a balance must be achieved which ensures the fair and proper treatment of people from minorities and avoids any abuse of a dominant position". This necessitates mutual compromises "entailing various concessions on the part of individuals and groups which are justified in order to maintain and promote the ideas and values of democratic society".[33]

Questions concerning the relationship between the State and religions are particularly complicated because, on the one hand – opinion in a democratic society may differ widely in respect to religion, and – on the other hand – it is not possible to discern throughout Europe a uniform conception of the significance of religion in society. It leaves more space for the role of national decision-making bodies, i. e. for the national margin of appreciation. "This will notably be the case when it comes to regulating the wearing of religious symbols in educational institutions". Consequently, "the institutions of higher education may regulate the manifestation of the rites and symbols of a religion by imposing restrictions as to the place and manner of such manifestation".[34]

The background for the reasoning in *Leyla Şahin* was offered by the 2003 *Refah Partisi* judgment.[35] In Refah Partisi the Court upheld the dissolution of a radical Islamic party. The Court noted that problems of religion and politics must be assessed upon the general system of values like pluralism, democracy and tolerance. The State has more room in controlling and banning actions that may represent a menace to those values.

In assessing the Turkish version of the scarf ban, the Court recalled its finding in *Dahlab* that "wearing the Islamic headscarf could not easily be reconciled with the message of tolerance, respect for others and, above all, equality and non-discrimination".[36] The Court took into account the particular situation in Turkey and, particularly "the impact which wearing such a symbol, which is presented or perceived as a compulsory religious duty, may have on those who choose not to wear it [. . .] In a country in which the majority of the population, while professing a strong attachment to the rights of women and a secular way of life, adhere to the Islamic faith, imposing limitations on freedom in this sphere may be regarded as meeting a pressing social need [. . .] especially since this religious symbol has taken on political significance in Turkey in recent years". In such a context, "where the values of pluralism, respect for the rights of others and, in particular, equality before the law of men and women are being taught and applied in practice, it is understandable

---

[33] Appl. No. 44774/98, *Leyla Şahin v. Turkey* (ECtHR 10 November 2005) para 107 et seq.

[34] Appl. No. 44774/98, *Leyla Şahin v. Turkey* (ECtHR 10 November 2005) para 109, 111.

[35] Appl. No. 41340/98, 41342/98, 41343/98 and 41344/98, *Refah Partisi (the Welfare Party) and Others v. Turkey* (ECtHR 13 February 2003).

[36] Appl. No. 41340/98, 41342/98, 41343/98 and 41344/98, *Refah Partisi (the Welfare Party) and Others v. Turkey* (ECtHR 13 February 2003) para 111.

that the relevant authorities should wish to preserve the secular nature of the institution concerned". The Court noted a particular significance that the Constitution of Turkey attaches to the principle of secularism: "this principle, which is undoubtedly one of the fundamental principles of the Turkish State which are in harmony with the rule of law and respect for human rights, may be considered necessary to protect the democratic system in Turkey. An attitude which fails to respect that principle will not necessarily be accepted as covered by the freedom to manifest religion".[37]

This led the Court to the conclusion that the ban on wearing religious symbols (i. e. – in reality – first of all, the scarf ban) satisfied the – quite stringent – requirements of Art. 9.2 of the Convention. Not surprisingly, it is also accepted under the – less restrictive – standards of Art. 2 of Protocol No. 1.

The holding of *Leyla Şahin* was easily applicable to other situations arising in Turkey,[38] but – at the same time – it was very much oriented towards the particular situation in this country. In the factual (social) dimension, the Court placed a strong emphasis on the dominant position of the Islamic faith in Turkey. In the legal (constitutional) dimension, the Court recalled the principle of secularism as one of the cornerstones of the Turkish democracy.

What was not clearly answered was the general scope of application of *Leyla Şahin*. The Court left open, at least to some extent, whether a similar ban would be upheld in a country in which – in the social dimension – Islam remains one of the minority religions (and, therefore, the impact of scarf wearing becomes less compulsory) and in which – in the constitutional dimension – the State decided not to adopt the principle of secularism.

4.5 Some answers were offered by the Court in the 2008 *Dogru v. France* judgment.[39] The Court accepted sanctions imposed, in 1999, on a student who refused to take off her head scarf in physical education and sport classes.[40]

The Court confirmed that "wearing the head scarf may be regarded as motivated or inspired by a religion or religious belief" and, therefore, enters into the ambit of Art. 9 and constitutes an interference with the freedom of religion.[41] Nevertheless, "having regard to the circumstances of the case, and taking account of the margin of appreciation that should be left to the States in this domain, the Court concludes that

---

[37] Appl. No. 41340/98, 41342/98, 41343/98 and 41344/98, *Refah Partisi (the Welfare Party) and Others v. Turkey* (ECtHR 13 February 2003) para 114–116.

[38] Appl. No. 61361/11, *Kurtulus v. Turkey* (ECtHR 24 January 2006) – head-scarf-ban can be imposed on teachers at public universities; Appl. No. 26625/02, *Köse and Others v. Turkey* (ECtHR 24 January 2006) – ban on religious symbols can be imposed on students of public schools of religious character.

[39] Appl. No. 27058/05, *Dogru v. France* (ECtHR 4 December 2008). Confirmed in a series of decisions on 30 June 2009 (Appl. No. 43563/08, *Aktas v. France*; Appl. No. 14308/08, *Bayrak v. France*; Appl. No. 18527/08, *Gamaleddyn v. France*; Appl. No. 29134/08, *Ghazal v. France*; Appl. No. 25463/08, *J. Singh v. France* and Appl. No. 27561/08, *R. Singh v. France*).

[40] Thus, the controversy preceded in date the 2004 amendments to the French Education Code that generally prohibited the wearing of signs or dress by which pupils overtly manifest a religious affiliation. The substance of the 2004 regulation has not been assessed by the Strasbourg Court.

[41] Appl. No. 27058/05, *Dogru v. France* (ECtHR 4 December 2008) para 47.

the interference in question was justified as a matter of principle and proportionate to the aim pursued".[42]

The Court raised three principal arguments:

- the lack of a common approach among the Member States: "where questions concerning the relationship between State and religions are at stake, on which opinion in a democratic society may reasonably differ widely, the role of the national decision-making body must be given special importance. This will notably be the case when it comes to regulating the wearing of religious symbols in educational institutions, in respect to which the approaches taken in Europe are diverse. Rules in this sphere will consequently vary from one country to another according to national traditions";[43]
- the necessity to place restrictions in order to reconcile the interests of the various groups: "the State may limit the freedom to manifest a religion, for example by wearing an Islamic headscarf, if the exercise of that freedom clashes with the aim of protecting the rights and freedoms of others, public order and public safety";[44]
- the secular nature of the French State: "in France, as in Turkey or Switzerland, secularism is a constitutional principle, and a founding principle of the Republic, to which the entire population adheres and the protection of which appears to be of prime importance, in particular in schools. The Court reiterates that an attitude that fails to respect that principle will not necessarily be accepted as being covered by the freedom to manifest one's religion and will not enjoy the protection of Article 9 of the Convention".[45]

A common assessment of *Dahlab*, *Leyla Şahin* and *Dogru* shows that the Court is ready to uphold reasonable restrictions on wearing religious symbols in public schools in respect to both, teachers and students. In all three cases, however, the Court attached certain significance to the fact that each of the three States adopted the principle of secularism as one of the cornerstones of the constitutional system.

More room for restrictions may result from the 2014 *S.A.S.* judgment[46] and its concept of (compulsory) "socialization". As it upheld a general ban on wearing "burkas" in public places, this clearly extends also to the educational environment. What remains unclear is how the concept of "living together" may justify other restrictive dress regulations adopted within the public school system.

4.6 All the above-mentioned cases dealt with prohibitions to wear particular religious symbols, i.e. with the traditional schemes in which the State imposes a restriction on individual action. An inverse situation emerges when an individual remains in a position of a passive addressee of actions taken by the State. The display of religious symbols by the authorities in public places represents one of

[42] Appl. No. 27058/05, *Dogru v. France* (ECtHR 4 December 2008) para 77.
[43] Appl. No. 27058/05, *Dogru v. France* (ECtHR 4 December 2008) para 63.
[44] Appl. No. 27058/05, *Dogru v. France* (ECtHR 4 December 2008) para 64.
[45] Appl. No. 27058/05, *Dogru v. France* (ECtHR 4 December 2008) para 72.
[46] Appl. No. 43835/11, *S.A.S. v. France* (ECtHR 1 July 2014).

the most prominent examples. It may raise problems particularly where individuals have no choice but to remain in a given place, in other words – in places where persons are dependent on it or in places where they are particularly vulnerable. It goes without saying that public schools belong to those places.

In the 2009 *Lautsi v. Italy* case, the Court addressed the question of mandatory display of a crucifix in classrooms in public schools and found that the Italian system had violated Art. 2 of Protocol No. 1 taken together with Art. 9 of the Convention. In 2011, however, the Grand Chamber overruled the Chamber's judgment and found no violation of the Convention.[47]

5 Concluding Observations

The case-law on issues of religion in public schools has considerably developed over the last decade; it followed trends visible in respect to other areas of religious freedoms[48] and, more generally, to almost all aspects of human rights protection. At the same time, however, matters of religious freedoms seem to raise particular difficulties and the Strasbourg jurisprudence is not always able to provide clear answers to all problems and controversies. The Court's task becomes especially complex as it faces a tri-dimensional difficulty: structural, methodological and politico-cultural.

The structural difficulty emerges from the very nature of the Strasbourg system. Problems of religion and of its place in the public sphere call for general solutions. The countries of Europe have not been, as yet, capable of agreeing on a common approach; there are still many different versions ranging from a secular State to a State-established Church. Some common rules can, of course, be elaborated by the judicial branch but it requires that courts act in a "constitutional capacity", i. e. that they are able (and willing) to establish general rules of a binding (quasi-constitutional) nature. The Strasbourg Court, however, was not conceived as a constitutional court. It deals with individual applications and, in consequence, its judgments and decisions are always strongly linked to the particular facts of a particular case. It is not always clear how the Court would react to another case arising from a slightly different set of facts. While it is true that the most important message of the Strasbourg judgments is contained in the motifs (in "The Law" part of judgments), those motifs are usually drafted rather in a form of persuasive arguments then of imperative commandments. It leaves some room for flexibility (for which, in particular, the technique of distinguishing is used), but it also creates a contradiction between the de facto constitutional role of the Strasbourg Court and its – individually oriented – ways of action.

The methodological difficulty results from the different nature and background of cases hitherto decided by the Strasbourg Court. It should not be forgotten that a good portion of the cases law, especially the case-law on the school dress codes

[47] Appl. No. 30814/06, *Lautsi and Others v. Italy* (ECtHR 3 November 2009; ECtHR GC 18 March 2011); see Blanke (2012), p. 1260 et seqq.
[48] See e. g. Sajó 2007.

(*Dahlab – Leyla Şahin – Dogru*), was created upon the scarf ban, i. e. in respect to a particular type of religious culture that (except Turkey) still remains a little foreign for the mainstream of approaches present within the European societies. Furthermore, it should not be forgotten that in the scarf cases the Court upheld the State-imposed ban on individual action, i. e. it confirmed the conventionality of the national legislation as remaining within the national margin of appreciation. Finally, those decisions of the Court should be assessed upon a more general problem, namely the obligation of the State to intervene when basic values of the Convention system are put in question. In other words, the scarf ban jurisprudence of the Court cannot be, at least intellectually, detached from its general position in respect to some radical interpretations of Islam. Thus, the scarf ban could have been seen upon the background of cases like the *Refah Partisi* judgment and it could prompt the Court to accept the national ban on wearing religious symbols in public schools. The question, however, remains to what extent this approach may find analogous application to situations in which – like in *Folgerø*, *Lautsi* or *Grzelak* – the Court is invited to reject general measures adopted by the State; those measures enjoy the support of the mainstream of public opinion in an affected country and – while those measures may interfere with certain rights of certain individual persons – there is no claim that they run counter to the very system of the Convention values.

The politico-cultural difficulty is the consequence of the lack of consensus as to the place of religion(s) in modern societies, and especially, as to its (their) place in the public sphere. The Court cannot and should not provide solutions of philosophical, sociological and political questions in a situation in which the European societies appeared unable to propose common approaches. The Court may provide certain framework (may establish certain limits) in this respect, but it cannot venture into areas that still remain uncharted. The scarf ban represents a very good example as it may be assessed from completely opposite perspectives. For some, the wearing of a scarf should be regarded as a "powerful external symbol" that may be regarded as hard to square with the principle of gender equality, i. e. with one of the basic values protected under the Convention. This approach is visible also in the Court's case-law on that matter. For others, however, the wearing of a scarf should be regarded as a manifestation of religious beliefs or, even, as an observation of an important religious obligation of every adherent to a particular religion. Therefore, any ban (understood as a State-imposed obligation to undress) may create grave moral conflicts for involved individuals (see in this respect the position of Judge *Tulkens*, the lone dissenter in *Leyla Şahin*). This argument appears in a stronger form in respect to the burka ban, as the Court was not ready to qualify the burka as a "powerful external symbol".

Since it is obvious that the width of the State margin of appreciation would become quite wide for the first approach and much more limited for the second approach, and since it is equally obvious that European states have not yet been able to adopt any common approach, the Strasbourg case-law would continue to "hang in the air" as long as European societies are unsure about their course of action. This makes the whole "religious jurisprudence" particularly open to flexibilities or – even – inconsistencies.

References

Blanke, H.-J. (2012). Religiöse Symbole im öffentlichen Raum. In M. Sachs, & H. Siekmann (Eds.), *Der grundrechtsgeprägte Verfassungsstaat. Festschrift für Klaus Stern zum 80. Geburtstag* (pp. 1249–1280). Berlin: Duncker & Humblot.

Garlicki, L. (2012). Cultural Values in Supranational Adjudication: Is there a "Cultural Margin of Appreciation" in Strasbourg?. In M. Sachs, & H. Siekmann (Eds.), *Der grundrechtsgeprägte Verfassungsstaat. Festschrift für Klaus Stern zum 80. Geburtstag* (pp. 727–744). Berlin: Duncker & Humblot.

Garlicki, L., & Jankowska-Gilberg, M. (2011). Religiöse Aspekte im öffentlichen Schulsystem vor dem Hintergrund der Rechtsprechung des EGMR. In B. Ehrenzeller (Ed.), *Religionsfreiheit im Verfassungsstaat. Zweites Kolloquium der Peter Häberle Stiftung* (pp. 121–134). Zürich: Dike.

Mahoney, P. (1998). Marvellous Richness of Diversity or Invidious Cultural Relativism? *Human Law Journal, 19*, 1–6.

Sajó, A. (Ed.). (2007). *Censorial Sensitivities: Free Speech and Religion in a Fundamentalist World*. Utrecht: Eleven International Publ.

Villiger, M. E. (2007). The Principle of Subsidiarity in the ECHR. In M. G. Kohen (Ed.), *Promoting Justice, Human Rights and Conflict Resolution through International Law: Liber Amicorum Lucius Caflish* (pp. 623–638). Leiden: Nijhoff.

Social Policy and Human Rights

Eberhard Eichenhofer

1 Introduction

1.1 Social Policy and Law

All *modern* societies are advanced *welfare* states. Therein social policy plays a pivotal role to further distributive justice. Modern welfare states dispose of a multi-layered, complicated and complex system of social legislation. It encompasses welfare = social assistance and social security law = social insurance. Further elements are social compensation for victims of crime and war, as well as social subsidies for families, education, migrants, handicapped people or other members of vulnerable groups.

Modern societies are built on the rule of law. Legal rules and institutions are created by a legislative body. Social policy assumes, hence, a legal character: The welfare state of today represents the transition from a needs- to a rights-based system. It represents the development from charity to entitlement.[1]

Social legislation brought about institutions administered by independent public or private agencies operating on the basis of highly technical legal provisions and in full respect of the rule of law. So, welfare and social security stand for a substantial part of the law of today. The rules and institutions of social policy are not only created and structured by the law, but they also lead to corresponding *individual rights*. Therefore, a further question can be raised, on whether these rights have any substance and origin in the idea of *human rights*. *Albrecht Weber* devoted much energy on interpreting the developments initiated by social policy on the international level.[2] So, it is an honour and pleasure to contribute to a *liber amicorum* for a good and "old" friend.

---

[1] Baldwin 1990, p. 32: "La justice d'aujourd'hui, c'est la charité d'hier!".
[2] Weber 1975, p. 229; Weber 2004.

H.-J. Blanke et al. (eds.), *Common European Legal Thinking*,
DOI 10.1007/978-3-319-19300-7_18

1.2 International and European Guarantees

Since the end of the Second World War the human rights to social security and social assistance have been widely acknowledged in international and European law as basic and fundamental human rights. Those rights are elaborated, acknowledged and figured out in various contexts, jurisdictions and legal frameworks.[3] They are established as rights to work, health care, social assistance, education and social security in the Universal Declaration of Human Rights and the International Covenant on Economic, Social and Cultural Rights. The Council of Europe stipulates in the European Social Charter a right to work, fair working conditions, social security and assistance.[4] Finally, the EU Charter of Fundamental Rights prescribes a right to work, social security and assistance as well as health care (Art. 15, 34 and 35). These rights are also stipulated by many national constitutions.[5]

Since the midst of the 20th century social security and social assistance have been established as fundamental human rights in international and European as well as national law. They are conceived as "human rights of the *second* generation".[6] In the language of "generations" of human rights, social rights are located between the civil and political rights (as human rights of the "first generation") and the ecological rights (as human rights of the "third generation"). This numbering unveils a historical perspective. Fundamental civil and political rights had been expressed in the late 18th century, whereas social rights had been envisaged in the 19th century and effectuated in the midst of the 20th century, while ecological rights had only been accepted in the late 20th xcentury.

1.3 Challenges

Despite the multiplicity of legal provisions in different frameworks and at various levels of law, neither the *content*, nor the *structure* of social human rights became so far *clear*. Even more, it is not ascertained whether the notion of social rights indicates more than a mere political programme – without any substance in law! There is, hence, a persisting challenge on whether social human rights are *genuine* human rights.

---

[3] van Langendonck 1998, p. 477; van Langendonck 2003, p. 613; van Langendonck 2008; Riedel 2007; Leisering (2008), p. 21 speaks of "welfare internationalism"; Eichenhofer 2012; Mikkola 2010.

[4] Council of Europe 1999.

[5] Iliopoulos-Strangas 2010; cf. § 75 of the Constitution of Denmark; Preamble of the French Constitution of the IV. Republic (1946); Art. 4, 31 of the Italian Constitution; Art. 45 II of the Constitution of Ireland; Art. 58 and the following Articles of the Constitution of Portugal; Westerhäll 2010, p. 563; cf. Becker et al. 2010; as far as the right to education is concerned: Weber 2004, p. 693.

[6] Gearty and Mantouvalou 2011.

The main arguments in the academic as well as the political discourse are the following: As social rights are addressed to the legislator in order to oblige and not to restrict it, social rights "mean resources, not immunities".[7] Can these entitlements ever become a content of a human right? If so, the Constitution limited the *sovereignty* of *Parliament*. Today, state deficits are high and public funds are scarce, the need to cut public expenditures prevails. Social rights might infringe the overall imperative of budget solidity and, thus, corrode the financial fundament of the state. Finally, a social right does not say much about its content as the concepts of welfare and social security are large, vague and open for competing interpretations and specifications. Under a guarantee of social policy institutions, it remains unclear, how they ever translate into specific social legislation.

In spite of all this criticism, one might legitimately ask in the defence of social rights: Can legal doctrine set aside the variety of provisions on social human rights at the various levels of human rights legislation, and, above all, can welfare and social security law be adequately understood at all without referring to individual social human rights?

Three items are controversial when discussing social human rights. These are the topics of natural law (2), parliamentary sovereignty (3), and justiciability (4). The answers to these questions can help to grant a deeper insight into the characteristics of both social rights and human rights. When analysing the subject matter, it is also necessary to observe the common features of the human rights of all generations (5).

2 Human Rights and Natural Freedom

2.1 Human Rights as Immunities?

Social rights are opposed to civil and political rights. This is based upon the assumption that human rights are expressions of *natural freedom*. In this regard, social human rights are said to mark a deep contrast to civil and political human rights – as the former neither limit, nor supersede the state's power. Social human rights are about resources and not about immunities. They are to create the "*positive freedom*" and not to protect the "*negative freedom*".[8] So indeed, social rights are not part of the "natural law".

In the political rhetoric as well as the academic doctrine "natural law" stems from a "natural" status of the human being, i. e. being free of any *state intervention*. Social rights, however, depend and rely on the state's ability to establish a framework which allows organising social life. So, if the overall purpose of human rights is conceived as being the protection of the personal sphere of freedom *against* any

[7] Plant 1998, p. 57.
[8] Berlin 1997.

state intrusions, social rights could never be protected as human rights as they only become *effective* within *social life*, which on its part is regulated by the state.

But is the underlying assumption of this argument correct? All civil and political rights assume their relevance in a societal context. The freedom of belief became a constitutional issue after the Reformation brought about different denominations and emerging religious conflicts among them. Thus, differences in belief became an issue for the individuals and the society at large. The freedom of belief has to solve conflicts in a society that is based on different confessions.

The freedom of expression lacks any importance in the absence of an audience. Hence, the freedom to express one's views is a means to enable individuals to take part in public debates. And the right to marry requires a partner. All civil and political rights are made for humankind, whereby the individuals are not to be understood as natural beings, but as members within a given society. "Human rights are not the rights of humans in a state of nature: they are rights of humans in society [...] they are rights of humans vis-à-vis each other."[9]

2.2 *Human Rights and State Intervention*

Human rights are made to hinder the state from intervening into the sphere of the individual.[10] This is an important, albeit an *instrumental* and *not* a *substantial good*.[11] In order to adequately determine the core of fundamental civil and political rights, one must also emphasise their salient influence on leading legislative actions of public authorities. Freedom does not characterise a status of natural independence, but is more appropriately explained "as effective power to achieve what one would choose is an important part of the general idea of freedom".[12] Thus, each kind of freedom is embedded in legal and social structures. The freedom of marriage does not imply the right to marry without state formalities, but that these formalities are adapted to the freedom of marriage. The freedom of association does not require that associations are not publicly registered, but that this registration does not depend on the composition, purpose or by-laws of the association. The freedom of belief is safeguarded, when practical life in accordance with one's religion is not publically or privately embarrassed. So, the human rights discourse is about the individual's role in a society based on rights. To determine this status by legal action means "a way of thinking about the *principles of human existence*, as well as a legal way of categorising recognition of and access to such principles".[13]

---

[9] Hunt 2007, p. 21.
[10] Tushnet 2008, p. 168.
[11] MacCormick 1982, p. 1, 10.
[12] Sen 1992, p. 69.
[13] de Búrca 2005, p. 3.

2.3 The Liberty-Ability Divide

The classical human rights are not adequately understood as immunities or negative freedoms. Each freedom is to be embedded into a legal framework in order to be effectuated. To protect negative rights, "a positive right to the protection of negative rights"[14] is required. A negative freedom is not to be epitomised as a sphere of *dispensing the individual* from the *prevailing world of law*, but as a guaranteed and limited sphere defined and determined within the law.

Therefore, it leads to paradoxical consequences to distinguish between *liberty* – guaranteed as a "negative freedom" – and *ability* – conceived as a "positive freedom" – as both concepts could never be separated in theory or reality: "If there is no possibility of performing an action, that is, we are clearly unable to do it [...], then the question of whether we are free to do it does not rise. If this is accepted then it cannot be true that liberty and the ability are categorically different. Rather the possibility of doing X is a necessary condition of whether we are free or unfree to do X."[15] So, the idea of immunities, liberties or the negative freedom as fundamental rights becomes only relevant to enable the human being to pursue her or his life in self-determination, to enjoy the "positive freedom". The negative freedom is an important means and not an end in itself.

2.4 The Naturalistic Component of Social Rights

Additionally, there is a component enshrined in all social rights which is only rarely sufficiently identified: All of them possess a genuinely *naturalistic component*, which civil and political rights lack! In the context of the right to social assistance and social security human beings are addressed as natural beings, who deserve food and shelter or who suffer from diseases and handicaps and, thus, are in urgent need of treatment and assistance. Social risks and social needs are to be jointly addressed as physical shortcomings. The right to work is addressed to give room for the activities of individuals, who are conceived as active by their nature and interested in taking part in social life. Again, human beings are conceptualised as natural beings that are in need of societal support. This is what the social right is all about. So, one can also emphasise a strong natural law component within the internationally acknowledged social rights. This also shows, why a theoretical split in a negative and a positive freedom cannot explain a social right, which has a factual basis in a status of personal suffering due to social shortcomings.

So, if *natural law* is supposed to be the conceptual basis of *human rights in general*, this feature is more to be found in social rather than civil rights. Their guarantees – belief, marriage, expression, collective action in corporations, associations and assemblies – are more related to an advanced and refined social culture

[14] Plant 1998, p. 57, 64.
[15] Plant 1998, p. 67 et seq.

than a natural status of humankind. In the end, one can define social human rights as means to empower the beneficiaries to overcome the shortcomings stemming from their existence as natural beings by social means.

3 Sovereignty

3.1 The State as Addressee of Social Rights

Social rights are *addressed towards the public*. But this addressee is *not* primarily the *state*, but other *individuals*, who are quite often organised in social intermediaries such as social insurances, local communities or members of the workforce of a country. This direction and determination of a social right becomes obvious by looking at the right to work. As the right to work entails a freedom of choice in regard to employer,[16] this requires that a worker can find an employer, who is willing to employ her or him and to collaborate. The rights to decent housing or good health care do not imply that the state owns houses or operates health-care facilities. These rights mean, however, that if these items are under the disposition of private owners due to property rights, private house-owners, hospitals or medical doctors are also bound to see that the guaranteed social rights become effective.

The right to social security depends on solidarity established within the corporation organised as a social security institution. This is constituted apart from the solidarity prevailing in a state. Those who are covered by social security are not identical with the citizens of a given state, as in the context of social security also non-nationals are covered due to their work or residence in the competent state. This difference is very important, because it unveils a profound lacuna in the prevailing theory on "social citizenship", which is very popular in the English-speaking world. Above all, this difference clarifies that social security does not coincide with the idea of national solidarity. It has much more to do with the solidarity among those who are working and living in the same country. This difference matters in an internationally open society.

Coverage in a national social security system creates and establishes a context and framework of distribution and redistribution among all the insured persons. Social rights are based on obligations and commitments imposed on the citizens of a given society: this commitment derives from existence as a member of society, embedded not in nationality but in residence and work within the boundaries of a national state. This integration not only provides for entitlements, but in doing so, it imposes at the same time commitments in relation to financing and facilitating the system so as to fulfil its protective function and make, thus, social life effective and productive.[17]

[16] Art. 23 of the Universal Declaration of Human Rights; Rittich 2007, p. 107; Craven 1995, p. 194.
[17] van Langendonck 2009, p. 311, 320.

As *social rights* are intended to give *entitlements* to be ensured by the state, it is to be observed: "The importance of rights to welfare [...] lies not only in the guarantee of a basic standard of living per se, but also, [...], in the fact that the fullest enjoyment of the civil rights of citizenship is dependent on welfare if these rights are to be more than formal and remote guarantees."[18]

In this respect, social rights are important to create the preconditions under which the civil society and democracy can flourish.[19] Social rights enable the human being to make use of civil rights and the idea of *social citizenship* gives *democracy* an "*added potency*".[20] "The idea of rights of welfare has also become linked with the idea of social justice" and, hence, "confer a social and economic state outside the market".[21] It "involves the idea of a just distribution of resources and, therefore, a correction of the market outcomes. It also entails that citizens have to cooperate and not only rely on mutual non-interference into individual rights".[22]

3.2 *Social Rights as Rights of Action and Recipience*

Social rights encompass *rights of action* and *rights of recipience*. Thus, giving benefits as well as imposing burdens implies questions of distributive justice. This is a common feature of all social protection systems. In the *Beveridge* Report the observation had already been made that "social security must be achieved by co-operation between the state and the individual".[23] "Rights of action are the absences of obligation. On the other hand, rights of recipience of a person are rights which correspond to the duties of another person or people [...] All moral rights of recipience can be expressed in terms of duties, not all duties are expressible in terms of rights."[24]

As a further characteristic social rights unveil the necessary interrelation between *rights* and *duties*. This context is pointed out by Art. 29.1 of the Universal Declaration of Human Rights: "Everyone has duties to the community in which alone the free and full development of his personality is possible." So, "all human rights of recipience correspond to duties of other human individuals".[25]

The right to social security precisely outlines this context. There, a *conditionality* of social rights is to be found in a *double sense*. Firstly, these rights depend on qualifying conditions elaborated by law and to be fulfilled by the beneficiary's living circumstances and assessed as being fulfilled by the administration. Secondly, the beneficiary is exposed to a series of actions in order to receive benefits, for example

[18] Harris 2000, p. 3, 23.
[19] Harris 2000, p. 23.
[20] Harris 2000, p. 31.
[21] Plant 1998, p. 57, 58.
[22] Plant 1998.
[23] McKeever 2009, p. 139, 141; William 2007, p. 333.
[24] McLachlan 2005, p. 30.
[25] McLachlan 2005, p. 53.

as an unemployed person to actively search for work, or as an injured person to be open to medical treatment, rehabilitation or vocational training. Benefits depend on administrations, which are capable of effectively charging insured persons through the payment of contributions. So, social rights are characterised by a societal and a collective component. More precisely, social rights go hand in hand with social responsibilities – "No rights without responsibilities!"[26]

In contrast to ecological rights social rights are the rights of individuals, whereas ecological rights are primarily addressed to certain groups of human beings. The intention of social rights is to safeguard the well-being of each individual. This is clearly illustrated by social security. In the case law of the European Court of Human Rights, the right to *social security assumes* the legal character of *property*.[27] This shows that social and civil rights are similar.

3.3 Social Rights and Social Legislation

The conditions for social rights are to be created by acts of *legislation*. The first and most fundamental prerequisite is to make social rights feasible; this requires the establishment by acts of legislation of *institutions* to *administer* social rights. From these circumstances stems a series of requirements, which are to be respected in order to ensure that the right be adapted to the needs of the beneficiaries. The *stakeholders* – trade unions, employers' associations and non-governmental organisations – should be integrated in the legislative process to give them a *voice*. The debate on social legislation should be profound and accompanied by a public discourse in order to raise awareness of the rights that are to be enacted amongst both the public and the beneficiaries.

Moreover, social rights depend on a multitude of social and institutional conditions. The right to work is bound to a whole range of potential *employers* and a *public* system of placement, a policy directed towards full employment with many instruments on training, assistance and – if necessary – public employment and labour legislation. The same is true for the rights to decent housing or health care. All these human rights are built on the organisational capacity of the state to regulate the labour market, housing and health care. The right to social security is built upon organisations. Establishing a relationship between a huge number of individuals confronted with the same social risk, borne by and the protection is based on *sol-*

[26] Giddens 1994, p. 65.

[27] European Court of Human Rights, Application no. 40892/98, *Koua Poirrez v. France* (ECtHR 30 September 2003); Application no. 17371/90, *Gaygusuz v. Austria* (ECtHR 16 September 1996); Application no. 65731/01 and 65900/01, *Stec and Others v. United Kingdom*, (ECtHR 6 July 2005), para 51, 41 E.H.R.R., 295 Stec: "in the modern, democratic state, many individuals are, for all or part of their lives, completely dependent for survival on social security and welfare benefits. Many domestic legal systems recognise that such individuals require a degree of certainty and security, and provide for benefits to be paid- subject to the fulfilment of the conditions of eligibility – as of right": Cousins 2009, p. 120.

idarity. "Solidarity is the child of interdependence, although not interdependence alone."[28]

A law that strengthens social solidarity constructs "a realm of social rights, of moral equality and identity among all citizens, created by modern society's interconnectedness".[29] Social rights thus give shape to this interdependence among the protected persons, working or living in a given state. Because of this they depend on institutions that have to be established by acts of state legislation; these are to be brought forward by the state and are accompanied by a bureaucracy, which attributes to the entitled a fair share of the outcome of the social product.[30] So, the welfare state cannot be adequately understood without *accepting bureaucracy* as its backbone. In this respect, fundamental social rights can be analysed as provisions to institute and establish institutional administrative frameworks, capable of making individual social rights effective.

These rights impose many commitments on the legislator. Insofar, the primary addressee of social rights is *Parliament*. It is *free to decide* on *how* the social goal is best achieved; but a guaranteed social right does not mean that one is *free to abstain from action*. Thus, it has to make sure, that individuals entitled to social rights can achieve a societal position in line with the given legal provision. If these commitments are based on international law, the implementation of specific measures is imposed on the state. This leads to the impression that international social rights might undermine both democracy and sovereignty. But this is a double misconception: firstly, as all human rights limit democracy, as they identify spheres of action beyond the discretion by the majority; and finally, in the post-World War II order of states, all states are deeply embedded in international and European law. Hence, all states have definitely lost their sovereignty.

The observation that all human rights are based on social circumstances and that they depend on legal provisions giving them shape and structure shows clearly that not only social human rights but all fundamental civil and political human rights have state power as their implicit precondition. Civil rights aim to create individual autonomy within a political community and political rights intend to give the individual a say in forming and executing the state power. The latter are not meant to establish a political order separate from the state, but to integrate the citizens into the making of state policy in the framework of a democratic government within a given state.

So again, civil and political rights cannot be conceived as the legal status of an isolated individual living apart from both state and society, but as a means to frame – shape, limit and legitimate – the execution of state power in relation to individuals living in a given society. In this context the state is not bound to abstain from action, but to take measures. Already in the 1793 French Version of the Declaration of Human and Civil Rights it was definitely expressed: "La Déclaration des

[28] Baldwin 1990, p. 32, 33.
[29] Baldwin 1990, p. 35.
[30] Habermas 1998, p. 104 et seq.

droits contient les obligations des législateurs" (The *declaration of rights implies* the obligation to *enact laws*!).

Parliament is, however, not bound by these rights as such, but it is bound to find the proper ways and means to make these rights become administratively and financially effective. So, the burden imposed by human rights on the state is not independent from political decisions – quite the contrary, *state policy* and *polity* is primarily based upon *how* to make human rights both *effective* and *protective*.

4 Justiciability

4.1 Prevailing Scepticism

What about the second topic? "Scepticism directed against the potential justiciability of economic, social and cultural rights is commonplace, not only in the international law sphere, but also in many domestic law systems."[31] "A standard objection to social rights is that they rest on the concept of needs, which is notoriously difficult to grasp, mostly because they are impossible to distinguish from preferences, so that one cannot determine with precision what really counts as needs."[32]

Do the various social rights give entitlements in *substance*? Could one ever imagine having a right to work in a *specific* workplace, or that the right to health means a right to have *good health for life*, or what about a right to welfare for the able-bodied: Are they entitled to live on the dole for life? So, one cannot only ask: "Do economic and social rights only exist on paper as part of treaties and constitutions to which governments often pay lip services at international fora?"[33] Are, at the same time, social rights in the last instance expressions of a *utopian thinking*, which is not appropriate to the brutish world of competition and markets – hence, in short, the world we are living in?

A characteristic of human rights is that they are abstract and therefore vague; this is quite common. "Human rights are difficult to define, but in general terms, they are regarded as fundamental and undeniable claims or entitlements which are essential for life as a human being."[34] It is true that when it comes to defining the *concept* of *welfare*, the latter assumed *different forms* in history and from a comparative perspective a plethora of legal organisations of welfare can be observed. The same is true, when it comes to social security, among which the conventional doctrine discerns an egalitarian Nordic, a conservative central European as well as a liberal, British approach.[35]

[31] Shany 2007, p. 77, 78.
[32] Fabre 2000, p. 33.
[33] Coomans 2006, p. 1.
[34] Ssenyonjo 2009, p. 9.
[35] Esping-Andersen 1990.

There is no doubt about the open and abstract character of human rights guarantees. This is not peculiar to social rights, but it characterises all the provisions on human rights. This feature is, however, not special to social rights, but identifies human rights legislation in general. What does belief, marriage, or art mean? Human rights are vague and consequently difficult to grasp indeed. This stems from the *legal character* of *all* human rights, which are both fundamental and abstract definitions of rights. As a further implication of what has been said, one can conclude that "all human rights are 'social' by nature".[36] The social nature of all human rights brings about that incrementalism of the implementation of human rights becomes a central topic in the context of social human rights.[37] Incrementalism is the reaction of the legal system to the distributive strand of social rights. This makes it necessary to counterbalance human rights of different human beings. In this process court rulings, legislative measures and a series of administrative initiatives are to be taken in order to further social rights in the context of human rights legislation.

4.2 Enforceability of Social Rights

Social rights are based upon state power, as they depend on the ability of the state to build legal institutions by political measures and legal action. Social rights need public support, as they create individual rights by imposing obligations on others. Paying social contributions has been made mandatory in order to allow social rights to become effective.

So, in the first place, it is up to state legislation to bring about and make *enforceable* the social human rights that are enshrined in international, European and national constitutional law. In a legal system based upon the rule of law each entitlement on social welfare or social security has to be submitted to a revision by independent tribunals, which have to assess whether an administrative decision has been taken in accordance with the legal provisions.

In an *interventionist state* role, social commitments are becoming leading *imperatives* for *legislative actions*. Hence, the state is also committed to protecting those people, who cannot take part in the market due to individual restraints or deficits. The *decommodification* of social services or goods and the payment of cash transfers is the sociological expression of delivering these items by means of law, instead of purchasing them on the market. The rationale behind the social strategy is to help those, who cannot help themselves.

This is very often done by virtue of utilising market forces to meet social ends. So, the state guarantee of social rights is possible in market economies under the assumption that each market economy is embedded in a publicly created legal order, determined to facilitate said market forces to cooperate and to protect the needy who cannot actively participate in the market process.

[36] Barak-Erez and Gross 2007, p. 7.
[37] King 2012, p. 289.

4.3 *Enforceability in the International and National Context*

As to the European or international guarantees of social human rights, specific enforcement procedures are developed in the context of the United Nations,[38] the Council of Europe[39] and the European Union (above all by the case law of the European Court of Justice).

Finally, it is a matter of the respective national Constitutions to safeguard that legislation keeps pace with human rights guarantees. For example, in Germany, the role of the Federal Constitutional Court is extremely strong. It sanctioned[40] a law on the determination of *social assistance* entitlements for *children*, which was taken as a percentage of the subsistence level for adults, as *inappropriate* and, hence, void under the Constitution, because, when doing this the legislator did not consider that the needs of children are not the same as those of adults.

There are many examples of judgments like this in many jurisdictions.[41] These examples clearly illustrate that social human rights are not only enforceable, but quite often have also been enforced! International and European provisions not only impose commitments due to their status in international or European law, but these guarantees also matter in the internal legislation of each Member State, as these guarantees are to be transformed and incorporated into national law as binding to whomever it may concern.

5 Social Rights as Human Rights

5.1 *Respect, Protection and Fulfilment of Social Human Rights – Three Dimensions of Human Rights*

Social rights, hence, are not fundamentally different to civil and political rights, and they cannot be opposed to ecological rights. Social rights have a collective component. It should be underlined "that the separation and division between the different sorts of rights should be rejected and that all rights are social".[42] Because of the lack of acknowledged social human rights, social rights are addressed in the context of civil rights.

[38] Langford 2008.
[39] Mikkola 2010.
[40] German Federal Constitutional Court (Bundesverfassungsgericht), 1 BvL 1/09, 1 BvL 3/09, 1 BvL 4/09 (9 February 2010).
[41] Langford 2008.
[42] Barak-Erez and Gross 2007, p. 8.

The German Constitution is an example of such an approach: it guarantees social rights in the framework of civil law guarantees such as property,[43] equality[44], or human dignity.[45] The most prominent example of this trend can be found in the case law of the European Court of Human Rights. It extends a series of provisions on civil human rights to social rights.[46]

The distinction between civil and political rights on the one side and social rights on the other reproduced the split in humankind during the *Cold War*. For decades this conflict embarrassed each debate on human rights.[47] "Today there is agreement that both sets of rights require abstention and intervention. Whether states need to commit resources for the realization of human rights does not depend on whether the right is civil, cultural, economic, political or social".[48] Since 1990 the "idea of the *interdependence* and *indivisibility* of the different kinds of rights has gained broad recognition".[49] So, in 1993 the Vienna World Conference on Human Rights laid down in its Final Declaration: "all human rights are universal, indivisible and interdependent and interrelated",[50] both social as well as civil rights.[51]

Social rights also concur with the *modern* understanding of *human rights*. *A. Sen* underlines that the right to development is justified to improve the substantive freedom of the individual[52]. In line with his[53] and *M. C. Nussbaum*'s argument[54], human rights are a legal expression to safeguard the capabilities of each person to acquire and play a substantive role under the conditions of the social division of labour and life as an individual being, whose position is based upon respect and human dignity. This position cannot be achieved as long as human rights are guaranteed in a restricted manner to only a partial guarantee of human rights and does not envisage them in the multiplicity of their various dimensions.

Human dignity is not safeguarded in a world, where *only political* and *civil rights* are upheld, while social and ecological rights are completely absent or neglected. Human rights cannot be separated from one another. Even more, civil and political rights are inhibited in their real effectiveness as long as social and economic rights

---

[43] German Federal Constitutional Court (Bundesverfassungsgericht), 1 BvL 17/77 et al. (28 February 1980); 1 BvR 995/95, 1 BvR 2288/95, 1 BvR 2711/95 (14 July 1999).

[44] German Federal Constitutional Court (Bundesverfassungsgericht), 1 BvR 323/51 et al. (17 December 1953); 1 BvL 97/78 (13 June 1979); 1 BvR 562/78 (27 January 1982); 1 BvR 35/82, 1 BvR 356/82, 1 BvR 794/82 (31 October 1984).

[45] German Federal Constitutional Court (Bundesverfassungsgericht), 1 BvL 1/09, 1 BvL 3/09, 1 BvL 4/09 (9 February 2010); 1 BvL 10/10, 1 BvL 2/11 (18 July 2012).

[46] Tomuschat 2007, p. 837, 840; Kapuy et al. 2007; Brems 2007, p. 135; Shany 2007, p. 77; Fredman 2008.

[47] Feyter 2005, p. 42 et seq.

[48] Feyter 2005, p. 43.

[49] Barak-Erez and Gross 2007, p. 5.

[50] Coomans 2006, p. 1, 2.

[51] Ssenyonjo 2009, p. 4.

[52] Sen 1999, p. 3: "Development can be seen as a process of expanding the real freedoms that people enjoy".

[53] Sen 1999; Sen 1992.

[54] Nussbaum 2000.

are not guaranteed. In *A. Margalit*'s[55] concept of a decent society a key target of all legal systems is to safeguard the respect of everyone. It refrains from discriminating against others and abstains from each humiliation. A decent society is built upon a political and social order based on the complete guarantee of all human rights for each individual. These rights cannot be guaranteed partially, but only entirely! A partial respect of human rights lacks the respect in substance!

As all human rights social rights are submitted and exposed to obligations to *respect*, to *protect* and to *fulfil* them.[56] The obligation to *respect* social rights "entails obligations not to interfere with the enjoyment of economic and social rights". The obligation to *protect* social rights "requires states to take measures that prevent non-state actors (third or private parties) [...] from interfering in any way with economic and social rights". The obligation to *fulfil* "requires states to adopt appropriate legislative, administrative, budgetary, promotional and other measures, including relevant politics to secure the goal of full realization of economic and social rights to those who cannot receive rights through their personal efforts". In accordance with these obligations, Art. 2 of the International Covenant on Economic, Social and Cultural Rights impose on states the commitment to "take steps [...] by all appropriate means"[57] in order to make economic, social and cultural rights effective.

5.2 Human Rights and Economic Resources

First, in order to make *human rights* effective one has to create individual rights by *legislation*. But this necessity is not restricted to social policy. The right to free assembly requires legislation in relation to the use of streets and squares for manifestations, because protesting as a human right means acquiring a privileged status as to the use of squares and streets. The right to association makes laws on the conditions and consequences of associating and the rights of the members of the association an urgent need. In order to give a corporation the status of a legal personality a register has to be installed. Marriage without legal forms and status is not different to the joint life in a non-marital relationship. "The right to a fair hearing is largely a positive right requiring significant expenditure of state resources on courts, prison systems and legal aid [...] All rights, and not only social rights, are public goods rendered possible by public institutions".[58]

As *social rights* are to be embedded in a system of *economic exchanges* they always and foremost have deep economic implications. As social rights are means of *decommodification*,[59] they are established beyond the market. They are excluded

[55] Margalit 1998.
[56] Ssenyonjo 2009, p. 25.
[57] Ssenyonjo 2009, p. 52.
[58] Langford 2008, p. 3, 30; Hepple 2011.
[59] Esping-Andersen 1990.

from the economic transaction, as they do not represent an object of economic acquisition – at least not for the entitled person. So, those persons that are entitled to social benefits are not required to buy the services or to acquire the means necessary to assume the part of beneficiary.

The rights, however, dispose of an enormous economic relevance, because the whole burden of financing is to be borne by the social security institutions. Social rights have – in other words – many financial and economic implications, as they give economic values free of charge to the beneficiary and impose the costs on the social security institutions. This explains their extraordinary financial and economic relevance.

Guaranteeing social rights does not imply that all workplaces, services and goods are owned by the state. Otherwise, only an orthodox communist society would be able to maintain fundamental social rights. This was the argument made by communist leaders, but there is no evidence that their position was correct, as equal distribution materialised on the basis of general scarcity and mass poverty. Social rights are to be *safeguarded* by the state; but the state is not addressed as the owner nor the organiser of workplaces, services and goods, but as the legislator and, therefore, as the organiser of societal life – a role it cannot abandon as long as the state is obliged to organise the market.

5.3 Social Rights and Social Justice

Thus, when analysing elementary assumptions on which social human rights are based, one can easily identify their function and structure, when conceiving social legislation as a legal means to give shape to *social rights*. Social rights are cornerstones to build *social justice*.[60] Social rights as rights "mean resources, not immunities",[61] "the idea of rights of welfare has also become linked with the idea of social justice",[62] they "confer a social and economic state outside the market".[63] "The importance of rights to welfare [...] lies not only in the guarantee of a basic standard of living per se, but also [...] in the fact that the fullest enjoyment of the civil rights of citizenship is dependent on welfare if these rights are to be more than formal and remote guarantees."[64]

Social justice is about *equality*. This is also a key dimension of human rights. So, in contrast to a wide-spread assumption[65] social justice does not mean emphasising equality to the detriment of liberty, but to safeguard the human rights of each individual in order to establish all the liberties of each one on the basis of equal-

[60] Plant 1998, p. 57.
[61] Plant 1998, p. 57.
[62] Plant 1998, p. 58.
[63] Plant 1998, p. 58; Harris 2000, p. 3.
[64] Harris 2000, p. 23.
[65] William 2007, p. 354: "taking liberty seriously thus provides good reason to restrict the extent of distributive principles".

ity. As social human rights deal with people in need, envisage individuals as sick, thirsty, hungry, workless or neglected, the nature of humankind becomes a leading dimension of legislation. Insofar, social rights are based upon a naturalistic vision of humankind, which explains their natural law background.

Social rights identify and demonstrate the target of *social policy* as they are based on the idea of common burden sharing and mutual help. Social rights and obligations, hence, go hand in hand. The beneficiary's right is embedded in the previous commitment to pay contributions; and the right to benefits can be made conditional on the willingness of the beneficiary to take part actively in measures to overcome the individuals' fate.

6 Conclusion

Thus, when social legislation creates individually enforceable social rights, these rights are human rights and, hence, to be respected, protected and fulfilled. These three commitments illustrate the target and destination of social legislation. In the context of respect, social legislation has to create institutions and single out legal social rights. In the context of protection, social legislation has to strengthen social rights and to defend them against interventions from third parties. In the context of fulfilment, social legislation is required to improve the status of beneficiaries in accordance with the progress of economy. In doing so, social policy substantially contributes to building a law, which is embedded in human rights principles and imperatives. But it is, however, "needless to say, human rights are still *easier* to *endorse* than *enforce*".[66]

Finally, social rights are relational and not substantial as they are meant to make people take part in the achievement of a given society. So, the content of social rights is defined by the cultural, economic and social level of a given society. All the *objections* against the concept and the idea of social human rights turned out to be "*extremely weak*".[67]

Social rights are integral parts of human rights. Today, social legislation is also an integral part of the law in general. As all branches of law are deeply interrelated[68], social rights are only one component of human rights in general as they are the fundament upon which the law of today is built. Welfare and social security represent a cornerstone in a world that has to prove that all the acknowledged human rights become a reality in society.

[66] Hunt 2007, p. 208.
[67] Plant 1998, p. 57, 63.
[68] Eichenhofer 2009, p. 181.

References

Baldwin, P. (1990). *The Politics of Social Solidarity. Class Basis of the European Welfare State 1875–1975*. Cambridge: Cambridge University Press.

Barak-Erez, D., & Gross, A. M. (2007). Introduction: Do we Need Social Rights?. In D. Barak-Erez, & A. M. Gross (Eds.), *Exploring social rights. Between Theory and Practice* (pp. 1–20). Oxford: Hart.

Becker, U., Pieters, D., Ross, F., & Schoukens, P. (2010). *Security: A General Principle of Social Security Law in Europe*. Groningen: Europa Law Publ.

Berlin, I. (1997). *Four essays on liberty*. Oxford: OUP.

Brems, E. (2007). Indirect Protection of Social Rights by the European Court of Human Rights. In D. Barak-Erez, & A. M. Gross (Eds.), *Exploring social rights. Between Theory and Practice* (pp. 135–171). Oxford: Hart.

de Búrca, G. (2005). The Future of Social Rights Protection in Europe. In G.de Búrca, & B.de Witte (Eds.), *Social Rights in Europe* (pp. 3–14). New York: OUP.

Coomans, F. (2006). Some Introductory Remarks on the Justiciability of Economic and Social Rights in a Comparative Context. In F. Coomans (Ed.), *Justiciability of Economic and Social Rights. Experiences from Domestic Systems* (pp. 1–16). Antwerp: Intersentia.

Council of Europe (1999). *Social Protection in the European Charter of Human Rights*. Strasbourg: Council of Europe Publ.

Cousins, M. (2009). The European Convention on Human Rights, Non-Discrimination and Social Security: Great Scope, Little Depth? *Journal of Social Security Law (J.S.S.L.)*, *16*, 120–138.

Craven, M. (1995). *The International Covenant on Economic, Social and Cultural Rights: a Perspective on its development*. Oxford: Clarendon.

Eichenhofer, E. (2009). Social security law and private law – divergent or convergent? In *Liber Amicorum prof. dr habil. Andrzej Marian Swiatkowski, Studies in Labour Law and Social Policy* (p. 181). Krakow.

Eichenhofer, E. (2012). *Soziale Menschenrechte im Völker-, europäischen und deutschen Recht*. Tübingen: Mohr.

Esping-Andersen, G. (1990). *The Three Worlds of Welfare Capitalism*. Cambridge: Polity Press.

Fabre, C. (2000). *Social Rights under the Constitution. Government and the decent life*. Oxford: Clarendon Press.

de Feyter, K. (2005). *Human rights: social justice in the age of the market*. Dhaka: University Press.

Fredman, S. (2008). *Human Rights Transformed*. Oxford: OUP.

Gearty, C., & Mantouvalou, V. (2011). *Debating Social Rights*. Oxford: Hart.

Giddens, A. (1994). *Beyond Left and Right*. Cambridge: Polity Press.

Habermas, J. (1998). *Faktizität und Geltung*. Frankfurt/Main: Suhrkamp.

Harris, N. (2000). The Welfare State, social security and social citizenship rights. In N. Harris (Ed.), *Social Security Law in Context* (pp. 3–38). Oxford: OUP.

Hepple, B. (2011). *Equality. The New Legal Framework*. Oxford/Portland: Hart.

Hunt, L. (2007). *Inventing Human Rights – A History*. New York, London: Norton.

Iliopoulos-Strangas, J. (Ed.). (2010). *Soziale Grundrechte in Europa nach Lissabon*. Baden-Baden: Nomos.

Kapuy, K., Pieters, D., & Zaglmayer, B. (Eds.). (2007). *Social security cases in Europe: The European Court of Human Rights*. Antwerpen: Intersentia.

King, J. (2012). *Judging Social Rights*. Cambridge: Cambridge University Press.

van Langendonck, J. (1998). The Right to Social Security and Allied Rights. In F. Ruland, B. v. Maydell, & H.-J. Papier (Eds.), *Verfassung, Theorie und Praxis des Sozialstaats, Festschrift für Hans F. Zacher zum 70. Geburtstag* (pp. 477–488). Heidelberg: Müller.

van Langendonck, J. (2003). Het recht op sociale zekerheid als mensenrecht. In Instituut voor Sociaal Recht. In K. U. Leuven (Ed.), *Sociale Bescherming op nieuwe paden: liber memorialis Béatrice Van Buggenhout* (pp. 613–622). Leuven: Univ. Pers Leuven.

van Langendonck, J. (2008). *The Right to Social Security*. Antwerpen: Intersentia.

van Langendonck, J. (2009). Freedom and Social Security. In *Liber Amicorum Prof. Dr. habil. Andrzej Marian Swiatkowski, Studies in Labour Law and Social Policy* (p. 311). Krakow.

Langford, M. (Ed.). (2008). *Social rights jurisprudence: emerging trends in international and comparative law*. Cambridge: Cambridge University Press.

Leisering, L. (2008). Soziale Globalisierung? Die Entstehung globaler Sozialpolitik. *Aus Politik und Zeitgeschichte (APuZ), 21*, 21–26.

MacCormick, N. (1982). Legal Right and Social Democracy. In N. MacCormick (Ed.), *Legal Right and Social Democracy, Essays in Legal and Political Philosophy* (pp. 1–17). Oxford: Clarendon Press.

Margalit, A. (1998). *The Decent Society*. Cambridge: Harvard University Press.

McKeever, G. (2009). Balancing Rights and Responsibilities: The Case of Social Security Fraud. *Journal of Social Security Law (J.S.S.L.), 16*, 139–168.

McLachlan, H. V. (2005). *Social Justice, Human Rights and Public Policy*. Glasgow: Humming Earth.

Mikkola, M. (2010). *Social Human Rights of Europe*. Helsinki: Karelactio.

Nussbaum, M. C. (2000). *Woman and human development, the capabilities approach*. Cambridge: Harvard University Press.

Plant, R. (1998). Citizenship, Rights, Welfare. In J. Franklin (Ed.), *Social Policy and Social Justice* (pp. 57–72). Cambridge: Polity Press.

Riedel, E. (2007). *Social Security as a Human Right*. Berlin: Springer.

Rittich, K. (2007). Social Rights and Social Policy. In D. Barak-Erez, & A. M. Gross (Eds.), *Exploring Social Rights: Between Theory and Practice* (pp. 107–134). Oxford: Hart.

Sen, A. (1992). *Inequality reexamined*. New York: OUP.

Sen, A. (1999). *Development as Freedom*. Oxford: OUP.

Shany, Y. (2007). Stuck in a Moment in Time: The International Justiciability of Economic, Social and Cultural Rights. In D. Barak-Erez, & A. M. Gross (Eds.), *Exploring Social Rights: Between Theory and Practice* (pp. 77–106). Oxford: Hart.

Ssenyonjo, M. (2009). *Economic, Social and Cultural Rights in International Law*. Oxford: Ashgate.

Tomuschat, C. (2007). Social rights under the European Charter on human rights. In S. Breitenmoser (Ed.), *Human rights, democracy and the rule of law: liber amicorum Luzius Wildhaber* (pp. 837–864). Zürich/St. Gallen: Dike-Verlag.

Tushnet, M. V. (2008). *Weak Courts, Strong Rights. Judicial Review and Social Welfare Rights in Comparative Constitutional Law*. Princeton: Princeton University Press.

Weber, A. (1975). Die Entwicklung des Mutterschutzes durch die internationalen Organisationen. *Recht der Arbeit (RdA), 28*(4), 229–232.

Weber, A. (2004). *Menschenrechte. Texte und Fallpraxis*. München: Sellier.

Westerhäll, L. V. (2010). Der Schutz der sozialen Grundrechte in der Rechtsordnung Schwedens. In J. Iliopoulos-Strangas (Ed.), *Soziale Grundrechte in Europa nach Lissabon* (pp. 563–596). Baden-Baden: Nomos.

William, L. (2007). *Philosophy of Private Law*. Oxford: OUP.

Human Rights and Counter-Terrorism: How to Reconcile the Irreconcilable?

The French Method

Thierry Renoux

The severe attacks in Madrid in 2004 and London in 2005 and Paris in 2015 have shown with horror the urgency of designing a common European strategy against terrorism supplementing the national normative system developed after the attacks of 11 September 2001 in the United States.

Confronted with the reality of terrorism, the EU has had to adopt a legal framework, tools and sufficient resources to effectively fight against terrorism, but – and this precision is of primary importance – with regard to respect for the rule of law and protection of human rights, "constitutional" principles of European law which *Albrecht Weber*, the dedicatee of this short paper has, better than anyone, shown the need for continuity in to ensure success.[1]

For its part, France has a long experience of terrorism as the word terrorism originates from the "Terreur" period, a totalitarian regime that took place after the French Revolution. So the first form of terrorism was a State one. However, in France human rights were confronted with Terrorism within the second half of the 20th century, in the historical context of decolonization. This period led to the development of legislation but also provoked deeper thinking on terrorism in a state governed by the rule of law. In cases of hostage taking by terrorist groups, France is also distinguished by the meticulous intelligence work which is very characteristic and most often ends up locating alive the kidnapped persons while refusing on principle to pay a ransom. This success led international observers to wonder whether a counter-terrorism model was about to take shape. But is there a French method of fighting terrorism? The answer is yes, without a doubt, whether it is to prevent (1), punish (2), or remedy terrorist acts (3).

This paper is a revised and improved version of a first draft presented at the Ninth World Congress of Constitutional Law, "Constitutional challenges: Global and Local", Oslo, June 16–20, 2014, Workshop # 1: "Constitutional Responses to Terrorism", chaired by David Cole (USA, Georgetown Law Center) and Lech Garlicki (Poland), Former Judge, ECtHR: http://www.jus.uio.no/english/research/news-and-events/events/conferences/2014/wccl-cmdc/wccl/papers/ws1/w1-renoux.pdf

[1] See, in particular, Weber 2004.

H.-J. Blanke et al. (eds.), *Common European Legal Thinking*,
DOI 10.1007/978-3-319-19300-7_19

1 Preventing Terrorist Acts

Unlike other countries, France never legally defined terrorism as an act of war. Its symbolic dimension and its purpose (taking down democratic constitutional institutions) allow differentiation between terrorism, serious criminality and armed conflict. This explains why the French method has always been based on police-related actions and human intelligence rather than military actions.

There are two ways to fight terrorism:

- Consider terrorism an act of war. Then the terrorist is an enemy and must be fought with military means. There is then no real place for the judiciary; only military authorities and courts have jurisdiction.
- Consider the terrorist a dangerous criminal. In this case, he must be fought using police forces with extended powers but always within the limits of legality and criminal proceedings; cases are brought before the regular courts. This is the approach chosen by French law, as it considers that a democracy does not declare war on a person but only on a State, and does not condemn groups of people *a priori* but only individuals committing criminal acts.

To prevent the spread of terrorism and in addition to intelligence actions led by the police, Act n° 1432 passed 21 December 2012 related to security and the fight against terrorism prohibits incitement and glorification of terrorism.

The French method is to determine the terrorist crime with the highest possible accuracy, both for the upstream where the aim is to prepare and plan an attack and for the downstream after the crime has already been committed.

In other words, any violent attack against the people, unlawful use of explosives, any expression of opinion, even one that is radical or fundamentalist, is not enough to constitute in itself a terrorist activity. The democracy is not totally defenceless, as these acts or activities are punished using other methods that share a common characteristic: they involve ordinary crime law and not counter-terrorism law.

The opposite attitude weakens the rule of law. In this struggle, with unequal arms, against terrorism, to abandon the rule of law and to embrace a security ideology is no more effective than allowing the use of torture "in exceptional circumstances".[2]

French legislation presents a series of possible options to bring to justice perpetrators of acts of terror, even when committed abroad, if the victims, or the terrorist, are French nationals or have their usual residence in France. Furthermore, French law allows, on the one hand, prosecution of people who trained in terrorist camps even if they have not committed any objectionable or criminal act, and on the other

[2] U.S. Senate Select Committee on Intelligence, Committee Study of the Central Intelligence Agency's Detention and Interrogation Program, Findings and Conclusions, Executive Summary approved December 13, 2012, updated for Release April 3, 2014; Declassification, Revisions, December 3, 2014, http://www.intelligence.senate.gov/study2014/sscistudy1.pdf, (accessed 10 December 2014).

hand, the freezing of financial assets of persons or entities that have a terrorist activity abroad, or who, by their actions, encourage anyone to acts of terrorism.

Efficiency relates mostly to the moment in a case where judges are referred to by intelligence services. The risk of excessive legalization of proceedings is either arriving too early or, conversely too late: too soon so that the intelligence services have not been able to collect enough evidence for the case; too late to prevent the terrorist act. The French system is therefore based on a specific approach to terrorism cases led by the police thus preventing an exceptional military-style legal regime.

But even within a police regime, it remains difficult to find a balance between the need for information and the protection of freedoms since the terrorist phenomenon hardly lends itself to legal analysis.

This protean character[3] is probably the origin of the lack of unitary definition of terrorism. The fight against terrorism expresses however, for each state, a prerogative of sovereignty. This explains why it made a very discreet and almost indirect entrance into the current French Constitution, i. e. on the occasion of the introduction of a provision on European judicial cooperation, regarded as effecting a transfer to the European Union of skills inherent in the national sovereignty, therefore requiring a prior revision of the Constitution.

France is a party to several Terrorism conventions such as the European Convention on the Suppression of Terrorism signed in Strasbourg on 27 January 1977[4] or the Convention for the Suppression of Nuclear Terrorism adopted in New York on 13 April 2005.

The difficulty is that these sectorial agreements on the fight against terrorism do not include a comprehensive definition of terrorism, but the listing of a series of acts that can be qualified as "terrorism". Thus, negotiations on an international convention generally defining the crime are in stalemate, due to differences in the application of the definition, for example, the states of the Organization of Islamic Cooperation that wishes to exclude from this definition acts committed against occupying armed forces and, in contrast, willing to include in this definition the actions of said armed forces.

The European Union has tried to adopt a common definition of terrorism. The Council Framework Decision of 13 June 2002 on the fight against terrorism[5] gives a broad outline of a definition of terrorism offences: In this respect, this text is one of the earliest international instruments to define a terrorist act by direct reference to the aim of destroying the foundations of democracy.

---

[3] Fletcher 2006, p. 894 et seqq.; Hennebel and Lewkowicz 2009, p. 17 et seqq.

[4] European Convention on the Suppression of Terrorism ETS n°90; Protocol amending the European Convention on the Suppression of Terrorism, 2003, ETS n°190.

[5] See also: Council of the European Union, 30 November 2005: The European Union Counter-Terrorism Strategy, 14469/4/05 REV 4, DG H2 and Council Decision 2007/124/EC of 12 February 2007 *establishing for the period 2007 to 2013, as part of the General Program "Security and Safeguarding Liberties", the Specific Program "Prevention, Preparedness and Consequence Management of Terrorism and other Security related risks"*, O.J. L 58/1 (2007).

But beyond this apparent diversity, in the French law method, three factors, constant and cumulative, are always taken into account when applying the legal qualification of acts of terrorism.

1st element: the exceptional severity o violence
Terrorism is usually considered to be a heinous crime endangering society.

All international instruments related to terrorism refer to its exceptional violence (e. g. "serious, particular gravity" or "cruel and treacherous means"). This violence is not only a mean but also an image, a feeling that terrorists want to disseminate. They play with emotions following their actions to divide society on the methods that should be used to respond to the terrorism threat. Therefore, terrorism is mostly a propaganda tool used to spread ideologies that are very often difficult to identify because they are heterogeneous, unstructured, and sometimes promoted by tiny, little-known terrorist groups. Of course, terrorism can also be used as a governance tool by dictatorial regimes (State terrorism) or by autonomous movements in localized conflicts. But the most famous form of terrorism is the international one. It results from tensions and conflicts within the international community claiming to serve the cause of ethnic, political or religious streams and can be seen as a modern substitute to ideological war.

2nd element: the purpose of the aggression
Targeted victims of terrorist acts are not chosen as individuals, with their specific characteristics, but solely because of the social function occupied or devastated areas: the "target" displays the subliminal message suggested by the attack. Therefore, both victims and terrorist strikes are only media used to disseminate the message. This explains why the press shows more interest in the claims and motives of the terrorists rather than in the future of the victims.

Moreover, this is also one of the grounds why terrorism benefits from a democratic constitutional framework where it can justify itself and find some legitimation. Under such a regime, it benefits from freedom of speech as the media and press becomes its involuntary and objective ally in spreading its propaganda. The difference of regime is crucial to differentiate terrorism from resistance. *M. Duverger* stressed that resistance is the use of violence against a violent and repressive regime, whereas terrorism is the use of violence against a democratic regime where peaceful forms of contestation are allowed.

Therefore, we consider that terrorism should be defined as being the pursuit of a political, philosophical or religious ideology, the purpose of which is to undermine the foundations of a pluralist democracy without using, as a matter of principle, its legal means of expression.

An assault may be committed without any ideological support. Instead, terrorism is still a vector of consciousness. In other words, terrorism is intended to replace the power of the state by another form of authority, political structure by another form of organization, denying the fundamental rights.

However, unlike organized crime, which can still serve its interests, terrorism is not primarily motivated by greed. Conversely, compared to targeted violence of any ordinary offences (e. g. the destruction of public property by dismissed employees or by disgruntled farmers), terrorism uses the same mode of expression: a symbol of media use. The aim is to destabilize a society, its infrastructure; the choice of the target has only one goal: amplify the scope of this event, vector an ideological message and exert pressure on the public using mainly images and symbols to communicate. And this symbol can be a public building, the daily presence of political authority, a person enjoying a public, religious or moral authority deemed illegal or undesirable. In each case, it is not an individual's vulnerability which is concerned, but it embodies the power challenged.

This is the content of the idea of "motive" or "purpose" of the terrorist act: seriously disturbing public order by intimidation or terror. This consideration of the motive of perpetrators is not to be confused with the intentional element of the offence. Although its consequences have been criticized, in particular as regards the requirements of the fight against international terrorism, the French law of 1986, which defines a terrorist offence taking into account mainly the purpose of violence, does not show an originality since this same approach is used to define the notion of crimes against humanity.

3rd element: the terrorist undertaking

It is in this third aspect that the fight against terrorism joined the fight against organized crime, which implies a strengthening of European and international judicial cooperation.

The legal characterization of terrorism requires that the act was prepared. To this end, the French Criminal Code provides that terrorist acts are parts of an undertaking ("une entreprise") and therefore it supposes some premeditation, preparation and organization to prevent any arbitrary factor: "Constitute acts of terrorism, when committed intentionally in connection with an individual or collective undertaking aimed at seriously disturbing public order by intimidation or terror, the following offences [. . .]."

The reference to the notion of "undertaking", in the light of the debates in Parliament and the circular application, implies that the infringement is committed (or planned) in a more general context. The terrorist agent may be, in theory, a "lone wolf". But reading websites dedicated to terrorism or having travelled to countries affected by terrorist groups, is not an element sufficient by itself to characterize a person as a "terrorist".

Upstream, at the stage of preparing an attack, the qualification of terrorism involves demonstrating:

1) an intentional element (e. g. the desire to cause destruction, death or serious injury to civilians),
2) a motive (the purpose of seriously disturbing public order by intimidation or terror),
3) finally, not one but two material elements of the offence, such as, for example, on one hand, the giving or receiving of terrorism training, and secondly, to possess,

> to seek, obtain or manufacture weapons, objects or substances likely to create a danger to others.[6]

In other words, in French law, the offence of terrorism is characterized on the one hand, *by belonging to or supporting a network of activists*, on the other hand, as *a preparation, a sufficient organization.* According to the circular application of the Criminal Code, "the concept of enterprise excludes any idea of improvisation", it implies "preparation and a minimum of organization, some premeditation [. . .], an organization where chance is excluded."[7]

In 1986, this formula was included in the Code of Criminal Procedure (Art. 706-16) before being introduced in the provisions of the new Criminal Code (1992, Art. 421-1), in the first chapter "Acts of terrorism", in Book IV. So in France, the legal classification of the offence of terrorism can only constitute a "Crime against the nation, the state and the public peace" within the meaning of Book IV.

One of the important advancements made by the French legislation was to consider terrorism as a separate and autonomous offence with its own legal basis. Thus, in France, to "punish without characterization" is unquestionable: the terrorist infraction under French law is in line with the constitutional principle of strict legality defined by Art. 8 of the Declaration of the Rights of Man and the Citizen of 26 August 1789.

2 To Punish People for Committing Acts of Terrorism

Solidarity and cooperation are the EU's response to the terrorist threat. Solidarity, because specialized European agencies are now responsible for coordinating investigations and preventing terrorist attacks (Europol and Eurojust) as well as establishment of rapid responses to attacks[8] and a European action plan to protect against chemical, biological and nuclear terrorism.

---

[6] The recent evolution of the terrorist threat leads to the fact that isolated individuals are committing or preparing, more and more frequently, violent acts of a terrorist nature. The French legal system (Act of 13 November 2014) allows prosecuting those who are preparing a terrorist act in a sufficiently concrete manner without being linked to a criminal association. But their preparations, even undertaken individually, must, like any offence of this nature, be related to a terrorist undertaking, which clearly distinguishes this model from the law of the UK. Law No. 2014-1353 of 13 November 2014 strengthened provisions on the fight against terrorism, Journal officiel de la République Française, n°263 of 14 November 2014, p. 19162.

[7] Thus, a simple endangering of the security of the State, even violent, is not in itself an act of terrorism: French Constitutional Council, Decision n°86-213 DC (3 September 1986) para 24. Similarly, the mere fact of helping an undocumented person to remain in the territory who commits an act of terrorism may not, without an act of participation in terrorist action, itself be considered an act of terrorism: French Constitutional Council, Decision n°96-377 DC (16 July 1996) para 7 et seqq.

[8] Of the 294 attacks recorded in Europe in 2009, only one is assigned by Europol to Islamist terrorism: http://www.consilium.europa.eu/uedocs/cmsUpload/TE-SAT%202010.pdf, accessed 10 December 2014.

Judicial cooperation, because the European Union not only promotes the use of the vital instrument named "the European arrest warrant", but also requires states to blacklist anyone suspected of terrorism (or business financing) activities; registration on these lists having the consequence of a freezing of assets.

In practice, if the Court of Justice of the European Union has seemed to want to give priority to protection of individual freedoms, namely by cancelling a European regulation implementing a special resolution of the UN Security Council[9], never could it be said that this choice, inspiring respect for fundamental rights, weakened the repression by the Member States.

And here again, the French law on terrorism is interesting in that it seeks to establish a balance between the fundamental principles of criminal law and the requirements of efficiency in the fight against terrorism. Whether it concerns prosecution rules (Sect. 2.1), judgment rules (Sect. 2.2) or the scale of penalties (Sect. 2.3), incrimination of being involved in terrorism shows derogation from the general rules, which at first glance, may raise doubts as to its constitutionality.

2.1 *Prosecution Rules*

Art. 706-17 of the French Criminal Procedure Code provides that for all terrorist investigations and judgments the prosecutor, an investigating judge, the criminal courts and the criminal courts of appeal of Paris have competence. This special competence applies to the whole French territory, but only when the prosecutor of the Parisian court decides to seize the case. In practice, this happens in almost every case. Thus, the Paris Tribunal has an anti-terrorist section, bringing together seven prosecutors, eight judges and several judges for enforcement of sentences.

Police custody can be extended up to a total length of 96 hours (4 days) instead of the 48 hours for ordinary criminal procedures, which may be applied by the prosecutor, by the liberties and detention judge or by the investigating judge. In exceptional cases, police custody can be extended up to 144 hours (6 days) if there is a serious risk of an imminent terrorist act or when it is necessary due to international cooperation. The first meeting with a lawyer can be postponed until the 72nd hour of police custody (Art. 706-88 Code of Criminal Procedure) but must be motivated by the imperious circumstances of the investigation, or to ensure evidence collection and conservation, or finally to prevent harm against individuals.

It must be kept in mind that in France those investigative measures initially used only to fight terrorism are now becoming more widespread and can be used in general criminal procedures against organized crime (e. g. infiltration operations, telephone tapping, geolocalization technologies etc.). The list keeps growing with-

[9] Joined Cases C-402/05 P and C-415/05 P, *Kadi and Al Barakaat v. Council and Commission* (ECJ GC 3 September 2008) p 461; Joined Cases C-584/10 P, C-593/10 P and C-595/10 P, *Commission et al. v. Yassin Abdullah Kadi* (ECJ GC 18 July 2013), p. 518. Comp. with Joined Cases T-208/11 and T-508/11, *Liberation Tigers of Tamil Eelam (LTTE) v. Council* (GC 16 October 2014), p. 885.

out criticism from the French Constitutional council despite the fact that a lot of those activities violate fundamental rights. In France, like in many other democracies, freedom is slowly being put aside under the pretext of security.

In its decision of 19 January 2006, the French Constitutional council, however, ruled that legislators must "ensure the balance between, on the one hand, the prevention of harm to public order necessary to safeguard the rights and principles of constitutional value and on the other hand, the exercise of constitutionally guaranteed freedoms, among which are respect for privacy and freedom of enterprise". Fortunately, the control made by an independent judge during the criminal procedure remains a constitutional requirement before any intrusive investigation.

Fortunately, the discretion of the legislator is not without limits: on the one hand and even for terrorism, control by an independent judge is a constitutional requirement prior to any measure of intrusive investigation, while on the other hand, the excessive administrative detention of a terrorist agent waiting to be expelled from the country undermines the individual freedoms of this criminal.

2.2 *Judgment Rules*

Judgment against an accused adult being prosecuted for terrorist acts follows the rules of composition and functioning of the criminal court ("Cour d'assises") in line with Art. 706-25 of the Criminal Procedure Code.

The reference to this provision shows, only from the procedural side, the consideration of terrorist violence as a war act in peacetime. Therefore, in terrorist-related cases, the rules derogate from the usual ones; the criminal court consists of one president and six professional assessors (without a jury) and for appeal procedures of eight professional assessors. The assessors are all professional judges chosen by the first president of the Court of Appeal for the duration of one quarter. Thus, unlike any other criminal court, the special criminal chamber for terrorist activities does not have a jury and the decision to condemn is not taken by a qualified majority (75 %) but by a simple one. Even if juries are a French tradition with regard to criminal law, it could be considered to be constitutional as there were always exceptions in French legal history. Moreover, the French Constitutional council has ruled in its decision of 3 September 1986 that the absence of a jury was beneficial for a proper administration of justice, with the motivation of this decision being the ground that pressures and threats could be made against jury members to alter their independence.

Security concerns have also led the legislator to allow the general prosecutor, after consulting the president of the "tribunal de grande instance" concerned, the representative of the bar of Paris, and when applicable the president of the criminal court of Paris, to decide that a court hearing will, exceptionally and for security reasons, take place in a location other than the usual one. Thus, in France, terrorists can be legally judged outside the confines of the courthouse and if necessary, without any public hearing.

Once taken, the decision of the criminal court can be appealed like any other court decision, which will follow the usual procedure.

2.3 *The Scale of Penalties*

The scale of penalties applicable to terrorist infractions is raised by one degree compared to ordinary law. This rule of increased penalties is part of a mechanism derogating the general principle of Art. 131-4 of the Criminal Code which states that there are no derogations to the scale of penalties provided there. However, the penalty for terrorism is in line with the principle of legality and the necessity of criminal offences and penalties formulated in Art. 8 of the 1789 Human Rights declaration.

Nevertheless, the law can, complying with the Constitution, create a system of exemption or penalty reduction for terrorists or accomplices who have prevented or mitigated an infraction by informing the public authorities. Also, the judge is always allowed to adapt the penalty to the personality of the offender.

Finally, a terrorist act can also be sanctioned by complementary and facultative penalties provided by the criminal code such as banning orders (not applicable to French citizens) or withdrawal of French nationality (applicable for individuals having acquired the French nationality and only if they have a second one).

3 Remedy

For a long time, the French State refused to allow terrorism's victims to benefit from a legal regime for damage compensation. Indeed, it was hardly understandable why the State should be required to compensate damage caused by terrorism. Terrorist actions are sudden and unpredictable, and thus no negligence from the police forces could lead to a liability of the State. Therefore, tribunals have refused all claims going in this direction.

Later, France adopted a special legal regime of compensation for victims of terrorism within the 9th of September 1986 Act on the fight against terrorism.[10] Since then, several texts have completed this special regime and the result was added to the insurance code so that finally, this compensation relies on ordinary mechanisms such as those that apply for car accidents. Thus, it does not matter whether the victim is a French citizen (only when a terrorist attack takes place in France) or whether the terrorist act was committed in France or abroad. Since 1990, the fund in charge

[10] Renoux 1988.

of those compensations has seen its mission evolve and is now the Guarantee Fund for victims of terrorist acts and other offences.[11]

Since its development, this system of compensation by the State has inspired a large number of international conventions, including in the Council of Europe.[12] These international compensation mechanisms are not contributions paid for national solidarity, but for the lack of solvency of the perpetrator of the terrorist act. In other words, these international conventions are limited to merely inviting signatory states to ensure on the one hand payment of a lump sum only for bodily injury caused by the attack, on the other hand to provide financial assistance for the victims of terrorism and their families.

However, in France the Guarantee Fund for victims of terrorist acts and other offences is only designed to establish a compensation amount for personal damages of victims from terrorist acts and cannot serve for any decisions regarding the amount of compensation for other offences. Indeed, for other offences the fund is just a payments entity and the decision to grant compensation or not is made by the board of compensations of victims of offences of the court. Thus, this does not prevent the parties from lodging a claim for damages before the relevant court.

It must also be noted that the compensation granted by the fund to terrorism's victims falls under the specific legislation for war damages, found to be consistent with the French Constitution. This means that the victims have a right to a civil pension similar to the one granted to veteran soldiers, a right to free health care and to specifically reserved employments. The fund is just an emergency measure to provide physical and mental comfort to the victims but also to help them manoeuvre administrative processes, engage with the court trial, provide individual assistance, social loans or financial aid.

Such an improvement in the compensation of victims of terrorism clearly reflects the French conception of the constitutional requirement of national solidarity, which has spread since to other areas in other fields such as disabled person's rights. The French method could be seen as defining terrorist acts as being a very serious form of organized criminality, thus a criminal matter regarding its prevention and punishment, but also to consider them as war acts requiring national solidarity with regard to victims' compensation.

References

Fletcher, G. (2006). The Indefinable Concept of Terrorism. *Journal of International Criminal Justice*, *4*(5), 894–912.

---

[11] A contribution (about 5 €) is thus levied on each insurance contract of goods in France. Revenues coming from this contribution largely feed the Guarantee Fund for victims of terrorist acts. See Articles L. 422-1 and R. 422.1 et seq. of the Insurance Code.

[12] European Convention on the Compensation of Victims of Violent Crimes, ETS n°116; Council of Europe Convention on the Prevention of Terrorism, CETS, n°196, entry into force 1 June 2007.

Hennebel, L., & Lewkowicz, G. (2009). Le problème de la définition du terrorisme. In L. Hennebel, & D. Vandermeersch (Eds.), *Juger le terrorisme dans l'Etat de droit* (pp. 17–59). Louvain-la-Neuve: Bruylant.

Renoux, T. (1988). *L'indemnisation publique des victimes d'attentats*. Paris: Economica.

Weber, A. (2004). *Menschenrechte. Texte und Fallpraxis*. Munich: Sellier.

Can Values Education Promote Cohesion in Europe?

Considerations on the Example of the EU Values of Freedom, Equality, Solidarity and Human Dignity

Reinhold Mokrosch and Arnim Regenbogen

"The European Union (EU) has been misunderstood for a long time as a purely economic community. Although the EU economy plays an important role, it should not be forgotten that the EU is a community of values in the first place." With these words the former president of the European Commission, *Jose Manuel Barroso*, inaugurated one of his speeches in the European Parliament, and he added (giving the gist of his words): "For both, the 'Treaty on European Union, 2009' and in, the 'EU Charter of Fundamental Rights, 2000' as well in the 'European Convention for the protection of Human Rights and fundamental Freedoms, 1950', values are laid down, which are applicable to all EU citizens and which impose on all of them equal rights and equal duties. These values often extend the significance of what is codified in the national constitutions of the 28 States of the EU."

Is it possible to promote a European identity based on shared values? Is Barroso right in seeing the EU primarily as a community of values? In case he is: What are the values? Furthermore, it must be asked, whether the EU is a community of values, or whether it should become such a community any time soon? And in what way, can the values given in the three EU Corpora be realised? By education? Or by economic prosperity? Or by meetings with members of different European nations? Or especially by the application to the democratic constitutions and by just policy? The realisation of freedom, equality, solidarity and human dignity, for example, depends in all individual cases in the particular states on social and political conditions. A pure awareness of freedom, equality, solidarity and human dignity is insufficient under any circumstances.

We would have had a better basis for European values, of course, if a common European *Constitution* had been concluded – a Constitution that would encourage the citizens of the Union to jointly confess the common values. But such efforts, as is known, have recently failed. With such a constitution, a common "*European Constitutional Patriotism*" (*J. Habermas*) could have been developed. Although the EU Charter of Fundamental Rights has been added in the Treaty of Lisbon, it is laid down that it is addressed to the Union and to the Member States only when they are implementing Union law (Art. 51.1 EUCFR), but the assumption of *direct*

H.-J. Blanke et al. (eds.), *Common European Legal Thinking*,
DOI 10.1007/978-3-319-19300-7_20

third-party effects of the EUCFR, i. e. direct third-party effects between private-law subjects, is controversial.[1]

A common "Constitutional Patriotism" is difficult to develop. Respect for the enforcement of European values is therefore dependent on the fact, that even the common basic standards are directly addressed to the constitutional systems of the particular states, and not immediately to the citizens of the Union. In what way are the decisions upon values in the EU taken and how are they implemented?

1 Values in the Codified Corpora of the EU

1.1 Values in the "Charter of Fundamental Rights", 2000[2]

We are inclined to assume that the list of values in the preamble of a treaty or a fundamental declaration of rights initially has declamatory character or that it is only declaimed as a possible target of the future. The text of the "EU Charter of Fundamental Rights" specifies the realisation of values, however, explicitly by normative broader obligations and prohibitions.

Some articles include implicit valuations, which go far beyond normative broader fundamental rights in the constitutions of particular states. So (human) "dignity" (Title I EUCFR) is not only, as otherwise frequently declared in documents, implemented by the "right to life" (Art. 2.1 EUCFR), but also by the right to physical integrity (Art. 2 and 3 EUCFR), the prohibition of torture, slavery and forced labour and inhumane treatment, finally by the prohibition of genetic selection and breeding of human beings as well as the prohibition of abuse of the human body for a profit-orientated trade in human organs (Art. 4 and 5 EUCFR).

Most of the rights under the heading "Freedoms" (Title II EUCFR) are specified as rights that are already set down in many European constitutions (freedom of thought, conscience, religious freedom, freedom of expression and information: Art. 10 and 11 EUCFR). In addition, the Charter (Art. 7 EUCFR) explicitly requires "respect for private and family life".

Among the professional freedoms (Art. 15 EUCFR) it is "everyone" to whom the "right to engage in work" is granted – as well as the right "to pursue a freely chosen and accepted occupation." (Art. 15.1. EUCFR). All EU citizens are free "to seek employment … and to provide services in any Member State" (Art. 15.2 EUCFR). Even "nationals of third countries … are entitled to working conditions equivalent to those of citizens of the Union" (Art. 15.3 EUCFR). This includes

[1] A general *direct* horizontal effect of the fundamental rights of the Charter is rejected by the prevailing view, but an indirect effect is supported; cf. recently Müller-Graff 2014, p. 5 (with footnote 28) and 29; for a direct horizontal effect, Sonnevend 2011 who refers to Case C-438/05, *Viking* (ECJ 11 December 2007) para 84.

[2] Regenbogen and Regenbogen 2001.

elsewhere the guaranteed titles to "protection in the event of unjustified dismissal" (Art. 30 EUCFR) and "fair and just working conditions" (Art. 31 EUCFR).

The principle of "Equality" (Title III EUCFR) is already applied in Art. 15.2 and 3 EUCFR, as has been shown above. The value of "Equality" is implemented especially in articles that go beyond the ones generally formulated in norms of equality of rights to all persons ("everyone" in Art. 20 EUCFR) – for example the prohibition of discrimination (Art. 21 EUCFR), especially for "reasons of nationality" (Art. 21.2 EUCFR). The granting of "specific advantages" to the right of equality of men and women does not preclude equality (Art. 23.2 EUCFR). Explicit priority has the legal rights of children (Art. 24 EUCFR), elderly people (Art. 25 EUCFR), and "persons with disabilities" (Art. 26 EUCFR).

Under the value "Solidarity" (Title IV EUCFR) rights under the employment agreement, which was already mentioned hitherto (Art. 15 EUCFR), are clarified once again: In addition to the multiple guaranteed rights in constitutions, as the right for the workers, the employees, and their organisations to defend their interests, including strike action (here: Art. 27 EUCFR), the EU Charter guarantees even the "right of access to a free placement service" (Art. 29 EUCFR) and the right to "health, safety and dignity" (Art. 31.1 EUCFR), which include as well a limitation of maximum working hours and the right to rest and to be paid during the annual leave of absence (Art. 31.2 EUCFR).

1.2 Values in the EU Treaty, Lisbon 2009

In the preamble to the Lisbon Treaty, to which all 28 EU Member States are committed, the EU contracting partners declare:

> Drawing inspiration from the cultural, religious and humanist inheritance of Europe, from which have developed the universal values of the inviolable and inalienable rights of the human person, freedom, democracy, equality and the rule of law, confirming their attachment to the principles of liberty, democracy and respect for human rights and fundamental freedoms and of the rule of law, desiring to deepen the solidarity between their peoples [...], resolved to establish a citizenship common to nationals of their countries, [...], to implement a common foreign and security policy including the progressive framing of a common defence policy, [...] (they) have decided to establish a European Union [...].

The basic value of freedom and the values of democracy are so named as special values. And the norms and values systems of human rights, the rule of law and fundamental freedoms are combined with the goals of a "common citizenship", a common foreign and defense policy.

"Citizenship" implies an obligation of the EU community for its citizens and a commitment of individual EU citizens to the EU Community. It complements national citizenship and is a prerequisite for the realisation not only of a common citizenship, but also for special union civil liberties. But who is an EU citizen? In the TFEU it is laid down that "Every person holding the nationality of a Member State shall be a citizen of the Union" (Art. 21.1 sentence 2 TFEU), i. e. whether he/she is a national citizen because of refugee, migrant, asylum seeker or resident status. For example: A certificate of naturalisation for a "foreigner" to become a "German" and at the same time an EU citizen in Germany can be acquired with respect to the *ius sanguinis*, in so far as the parents or a parent are German (practised for people of German descent from Russia or Romania), or under the ius soli, if anyone is born in Germany, irrespective of the citizenship of her or his parents.

With regard to this regulation the legal rights that are codified by the EU relate to all citizens in the Member States, where persons are nationals and EU citizens at the same time. In respect of this point of view only a community of all EU citizens is established, confirmed by the European Charter and EU treaties. But in particular EU countries' "civil" rights (not human rights in general) are introduced as privileges for genuine citizens ("nationals"), unlike the remaining specific human rights which apply also to the so-called foreigners as well. According to the EU Charter and EU treaties all European citizens should be entitled in the long run to total equality of rights. Native nationals then lose their preferential status when compared to the "foreigners". Thus, EU standards should be introduced uniformly in all Member States in the same way for all European citizens. This would require the complete equality of all EU citizens in each of the Member States.

In Art. 2 TEU, the scope of European values is explicitly extended to previously disadvantaged groups:

> The Union is founded on the values of respect for human dignity, freedom, democracy, equality, the rule of law and respect for human rights, including the rights of persons belonging to minorities. These values are common to the Member States in a society in which pluralism, non-discrimination, tolerance, justice, solidarity and equality between women and men prevail.

And Art. 2.5 supplements:

> [T]he Union shall [...] contribute to peace, security, the sustainable development of the Earth, solidarity and mutual respect among peoples, free and fair trade, eradication of poverty and the protection of human rights, in particular the rights of the child, as well as to the strict observance and the development of international law [...].

The three fundamental values of human dignity, freedom, and equality are mentioned, in reference to everyone, to each man and woman equally. Furthermore, the six standard values of solidarity, tolerance, justice, democracy, security and peace, and after these values nine standard catalogues are enumerated, which may be essential for the realisation of the nine values: human rights, children's rights, fundamental social rights, rule of law, pluralism, sustainable development, eradication of poverty, and (again) "citizenship". The respect of these values and value systems is not supervised, as we know, by an EU police, but for aggravating cases there is a European Court, which can be appealed to.

The transmission of European values through education and personal training was added in a "Memorandum on lifelong learning" of the European Commission in 2000, which clearly links lifelong learning to the basic values of the EU and the European peoples.[3] This is to be understood as a direct call for education in values as an "instrument" to implement said common values within the EU. Value education should promote the feeling of fellowship in the EU Community. Is this possible and is there a realistic expectation for it?

2 European Values – a Challenge for Education[4]

2.1 *Does Values Education at School Have Any Chance?*

Evidently, almost all countries of the EU show a strong demand for reliable values education at school. Parents, training managers, business managers, universities, and large parts of the public expect pedagogical teaching to be offered that educate children and adolescents in such a manner that they commit themselves to constructive value behaviour in Europe. The claim is justified. But is it also feasible? Can we educate and form children and adolescents at school by teaching them aesthetic, political, and religious values? Of course it is not possible for us to analyse this question for the whole of Europe. Therefore, we restrict ourselves to experiences in Germany.

Adolescents often discover a great discrepancy between the claim of values and their own social reality. Their confidence in existing legal practise is often destroyed when confronted with violations of human rights. Every day they hear and read in the media for example about Turkish girls, who are forced to get married by their parents, even in EU Member States; or about the inhumane treatment of refugees trying to reach "Fortress Europe". These permanently disadvantaged groups obviously are left without dignity as governmental policies do not sufficiently protect the dignity bestowed on them. Conditions of life set as a basis for legal principles to be applied at a general and not just regional level should actually be of universal validity.

In European school classes, moral, political and religious value standards should be tested. Whether they pass or fail, will depend mainly on the individual level of knowledge and morality of the students. Many of them are confused as far as their moral orientation is concerned; some are threatened by neglect. Media with socially destructive content, bad parenting, development injury, familial pressures that promote identification with negative peer groups, and negative public examples are responsible for a growing social immorality. It is difficult for moral educators to fight against factors that act in such a negative way.

Conversely, some students show an impressive moral and ethical behaviour. Illustrative teachers, good school conditions, reliable family constellations, positive peer groups, media design and the wide possibilities of political participation often

[3] European Commission, SEC (2000) 1832, http://tvu.acs.si/dokumenti/LLLmemorandum_Oct2000.pdf

[4] Mokrosch and Regenbogen 2009, esp. p. 32–40.

proved to be supportive in these cases. Of course it is a lot easier to discuss values with these children and adolescents and it is because of such positive experiences that one feels encouraged to continue with values education in schools.

2.2 *The First Step: To Promote a Legal Consciousness*

What could be the key in formal education to teaching the moral and political principles that define the peaceful coexistence of Europeans today? The disclosure of the currently valid European fundamental rights could encourage at least a respect for the observance of laws. But moral education is much more than merely guaranteeing the observance of legally binding laws and standards. It should promote active appreciation of the respective principles and values implied.

First of all, however, we shall turn to the question of how it is possible to convey legal consciousness to pupils at school.

During their school life, adolescents learn in very different school subjects all about laws, legal prescriptions and their respective applications, for example in history, politics, philosophy, religion, ethics, etc. Children, however, usually learn about general standards for regulated behaviour already at pre-school age, which helps them to develop an awareness of values at an early age. Later they learn such rules as components of a catalogue of standards: They develop a social horizon, for example, by acquiring knowledge on important provisions of the Road Traffic Act and information about the traffic criminal law. All of this knowledge already gained and tested is used for easier orientation in terms of their behaviour and assessing what is right or wrong. Children learn informal rules of behaviour and conduct, even before they start with the school curriculum. What counts is their willingness to try out the values they hold true for themselves within the larger context of values and norms of the society they live in. And it is obvious that adolescents are expected to respect the general norms of society and act accordingly even before they know the exact character of sanctions they would face in case they violated any even not strictly codified norm of action. Although all these skills are important for developing a proper sense of justice, they do not suffice to ensure the forming of a habit based on a respect for life, be it man or animal, nor do they give room for criteria that justify the appreciation of legal orders between rights and duties.

2.3 *The Second Step: Raising the Awareness of Values Which Constitute the Legal Norms*

If adolescents feel that the prescribed standards of behaviour are imposed on them by outside authorities, they may evade them in certain cases, deny them individually or discuss their rightfulness. Unreflected standards without any argumentation or fear of being punished are of no help when it comes to gaining insight into a value system that is generally considered to be reasonable and of high priority. Consequently, it is obvious to both, educators as well as parents that values education can by no means be restricted to the communication of norms and rules alone. What skills do young people need to be able to develop their own values during discussions that relate to competing opinions and values? Which values do young people need to develop a common respect or even a general appreciation of conventional norms and not just a mere obedience to a rule imposed on them? If rules and regulations and the claims of others are to be accepted quite naturally just as well as obligations that result from a peaceful coexistence with our fellow human beings, then it is indispensable for values education to be a part of education.

Despite the many difficulties that may arise from particular circumstances related to the structure of pupils or school facilities, the subject of values education will stand a good chance of being successful at schools, if it is organised in the form of dialogue, mentoring and from a relational perspective. In a direct or indirect manner, values education might be integrated into nearly all school subjects and topics and assume a major role. Education in general encourages pupils to take their own stand in situations of conflicts of values and norms and to give rational reasons for their opinions.

This holds particularly true for those value standards and their explanatory contexts that are generally accepted to be of universal validity in one's own cultural tradition. Thus, the members of our culture will mostly only accept an assertion of rights if the legal order referred to and justified in a convincing manner is of the same binding character for all addressees.

In the European key treaties and catalogues of fundamental rights, "values" are being employed as both, benchmarks for the adoption of legally binding norms across Europe as well as objectives of future political action. Therefore, European values education should primarily be oriented towards the core fundamental rights of the EU. These require namely the willingness of young people to adopt European values and beliefs not just for acknowledgement, but – as (future) EU citizens – to decide on the basis of their own values to adopt these values and to publicly advocate for them.

In the following I will present problems of values education in an exemplary manner when dealing with the fundamental values listed in the EUCFR: "Freedom" (Title II), "Equality" (Title III), "Solidarity" (Title IV), and human "Dignity" with a claim to universal human rights (Title I).

3 Values Education with Respect to the EU's Fundamental Values of Freedom, Equality, Solidarity, Human Dignity and Human Rights[5]

3.1 Digression: How are Values Formed in the Consciousness?[6]

Values education takes place in the form of a triangle:

(1) The *evaluated object* is usually a desired good, for example that all EU citizens should be free, equal, solidary and dignified. This is because they carry worthiness in themselves, which everybody likes to implement by means of the values of freedom, equality, solidarity and human dignity. Only when EU citizens are equal, free, solidary and dignified, will these four values – within the EU framework – become real.
(2) The *evaluating subject* only depicts these four values during the process of evaluation itself. For example, stating: Yes, this is where EU Citizens are free, equal, solidary and dignified, or where they are not free, unequal etc. The evaluating person helps to bring these values to life so that, on a basis of having been tested under EU conditions, they become real and vivid in people's consciousness, and the values do not exist independently of their evaluation (of course, the evaluating person has previous preconceptions of liberty, equality, etc.).
(3) It is this *Act of Evaluation* that enables the evaluating person to fill each value with life. Also, he/she objectifies these values, as others who witness this act of evaluation might agree by saying: Yes, this is where Union citizens are free, etc., and this where they are not … etc.

What does this imply for values education? It shows that values education is an act of self-assessment. Only if students evaluate themselves and make ratings, can they develop an awareness of values. Education in values is education in rating values. Individuals are verifying values only by rating them and filling them with life. Values education will remain unsuccessful if it remains on the outside and does not include self-education. It is the task of the teachers or trainers in values education to stimulate the act of rating in the hearts of their pupils. Norms, however, are instilled and set up externally although they also pass through the students' experience. Values in their semantics are borne in the consciousness of the individuals and not mediated by society.

In accordance with such values education as an education in rating, the following four values should be interpreted.

[5] With respect to the following analysis of the fundamental values of freedom, equality, solidarity and human dignity cf. Mokrosch and Regenbogen 2009, p. 52–60, 70–94.
[6] With respect to this digression cf. Mokrosch 2013, p. 43–64.

3.2 Freedom as a Political Benchmark and Educational Target

The main questions in a social, legal and political democracy are: Under what conditions may a European society be recognised as a free society? Under what conditions may EU citizens be recognised as free and equal citizens? What action should the EU take so that their citizens feel free under both, political and legal aspects? Perhaps it might help to take a look at the historical development of the socio-political understanding of freedom.

In 1651, shortly after the end of the 30-year war, the persecuted English philosopher *Th. Hobbes* (1588–1679) established the thesis that everyone would wage war on everyone, if the citizens did not come to an agreement to establish a national community.[7] This structure was to appoint a government or a sovereign, called Leviathan,[8] to which all citizens would have to transfer voluntarily their rights of self-preservation. No one should defend him/herself or should take revenge; everybody would have to wear artificial chains in the form of state laws. Only after this, would everybody be politically free. Political freedom consequently presupposed an act of voluntary submission to a political sovereign, who in turn guaranteed freedom. Hobbes was merely interested in negative political freedom which for him implied being free of political constraints. It would be then up to the citizens themselves for which purpose they would like to employ their freedom.

This idea of public order and of (negative) political freedom is still found today and it is represented by a state, which – neutral under religious and ideological criteria – intends to protect its citizens from hardship, poverty, violence, and disease, but does not give instructions on how to use their political freedom. In such a manner, negative political freedom may be turned into the opportunity to develop positive political freedom. It is recommended that one explain to students such a concept of political freedom under the condition of an ideologically neutral secular state.

Therefore, it is not only about justifying one's own claim to freedom, which is clearly stated in Title II of the EUCFR ("Freedoms"), for it often opts for the formulation: "everyone has the right to [...]" This refers to the claim to grant liberties not only to EU citizens; but to all persons, irrespective of their legal status as a national citizen, a Union citizen or a national citizen from outside the EU.

Nevertheless, education in terms of freedom will start off from the point that the addressees are initially dependents (children and adolescents). Therefore: Does education not always imply some accounted heteronomy and therefore rather entails dependency than freedom? Also: Does not the claim for individualisation and privatisation, in particular of young persons, compete with the concept of education for responsible freedom? Can education for freedom straighten out anything at all in view of stereotyped slogans such as "Free ride for free citizens!", "Freedom to choose for every free consumer!" and "Free choice of religion and belief

[7] Hobbes 1651, Part 1, Chap. 13 and 14; cf. also Hobbes 1642/51, Chap. 5.

[8] Ancient Near Eastern term for a mythological figure, in: Hobbes 1651, frontispiece: an emblematic of an artificial human form that is capable of acting the state manmade.

offered on the market of opportunities!", which reduce freedom to individualistic self-sufficiency.

Teachers are well advised to take such objections seriously and to deal with these questions in a very careful and responsible manner, thereby observing the following principles:

- The teacher must accept students as free individuals with an actual value consciousness. Students are not objects, but mature personalities with a right to be educated in freedom.
- Nevertheless, this also implies that any possible abuse of his right of freedom on part of the pupil should be sharply criticised by the teacher. Freedom can only be lived in a responsible manner if the limits of individual freedom are known and observed.
- Also, the teacher should criticise any given concept of freedom that is narrowed by egocentric and privatistic ideas. It should remain that individual claims can be associated with socio-political claims. Although students may submit a guarantee of freedom from state and society, they also have the duty to protect and promote the freedom of their classmates and other parts of the surrounding society. Facilitating social learning also serves the principle of continuous expansion of social behaviour and provides the basis for an understanding of the described positions of socio-political freedom.
- The teacher should rationally discuss the aspirations of children and adolescents for negative and/or positive freedom, as described above. But overall the teacher should motivate them not to be content with negative freedom, but should ask the pupils, what they want to do with their independence and negative freedom – in lively discussions with others. In this way, teachers support an inner drive for responsible use of freedom.
- Freedom should be taught as an emotion, as a right, and as a duty. Freedom as an *emotion* gives freedom a sense of liberation. This may happen in the conscious moments of falling in love or in the experience of becoming healthy again, or by looking back at the end of a stressful friendship or above all in the process of emancipation.
- Students need support for their personal development. Then they will be able to understand the meaning of freedom as a *right*: that every person is entitled to such feelings of personal and socio-political freedom, that it is a fundamental right and a human right. In this context, negative freedom as a freedom from something should be combined with positive freedom as a freedom to something, because the experience of a self-released freedom goes hand in hand with the idea of a social obligation in general. This relationship assumes that freedom arises only in community and can be confirmed only in community, if the desired effect is to promote the negative and possibly also positive freedom of others. Considering these principles, education for freedom could be possible at school.

3.3 Equality as a Benchmark in Education for Legality and in Value Development

The principle of equality in the EUCFR is, as shown above, guaranteed to all EU citizens and to all people from countries outside the EU (e. g. Art. 15.2 and 3 EU-CFR). It is, as shown above, specifically redeemed in articles, which exceed the mere norm of equality of rights of all persons (e. g. Art. 20 EUCFR). The value of equality is usually measured by the standard of "fair" treatment of all concerned. But what is justice, if you not only consider equal treatment with regard to the law, but also think of comparable opportunities in professional life and when claiming social benefits?

A social order is most likely to be called a just order, when the distribution of goods and burdens is settled between the parties in mutual agreement, largely irrespective of the question which of the popular principles of justice was enforced. In his treatise on the scales of justice,[9] *Aristotle* distinguished between the orientation towards material equality on the one hand and towards proportional distribution of achievements on the other. A further aspect to consider is that a scale may be called just, if previously disadvantaged persons are compensatorily preferred by the measure – an important idea of the modern welfare state.

But how can such a different understanding of justice lead to an allocation rule, which is accepted by all citizens despite their different individual value concepts? The principle of equitable distribution of goods according to the principle of equality or according to the benchmark of achievement or according to the needs of the previously disadvantaged is acceptable to the individual, if previously a consensus was reached in society.

In his study "About Justice",[10] the legal philosopher Chaim Perelman tried to find such a common formula, in which all these different criteria of justice were united. He formulated the high standard: Everyone should agree that justice implies to treat all persons in the same manner in case of individual decisions.

The imperative of equality before the law is precondition and part of most modern constitutions. Under moral, not only legal aspects, the respect for equal treatment of persons is also prescribed for those areas which have not introduced any respective provisions yet. The principle of gender equality, for instance, not only applies to the public sector, but also to education in the family and to private forms of employment. Until 1994, the principle of gender equality was merely expressed by the phrase "men and women are equal" as formulated in the German Basic Law (Art. 3.2 BL). But the EUCFR in addition allows the granting of "specific advantages in favour of the under-represented sex" (Art. 23.2 EUCFR). Since the reform of the German Constitutional Law after the reunification, the provision of legal gender equality was extended by a national objective which not only provides equal rights for woman, but also equality on a par with men: "The state shall promote the

[9] Aristotle (322 BC/1934), Vol. V.
[10] Perelman 1945/67.

actual implementation of equal rights for women and men and is working towards the elimination of existing disadvantages" (Art. 3.2 sentence 2 BL).

There is thus a difference in the principle of equality between equality of rights and equity with respect to the reduction of inequality. If this subject is to be treated in class as a lesson with a focus on legal education, it will require special treatment. A respective discussion could be opened with a dilemma that reveals different interests of adolescent boys and girls: equally qualified men and women apply for the same job, the employer decides in favour of a woman, in an attempt to rebalance the existing discrimination of women in higher positions. Boys – disadvantaged by this decision – will find it hard to accept this modern principle. It seems as if their generation now has to make up for something that privileged men of previous generations left behind.

The task, therefore, may not be solved by taking recourse to the quoted principle of parity in the German Constitution (Art. 3 BL) and the EUCFR (Art. 23). If autonomous legal awareness is to be promoted in legal education, different patterns of thought should be discussed that are not coded in civil rights. The question whether coded rights are always morally acceptable, must basically be admissible. Otherwise, it will hardly be possible to promote moral respect for a legal order. To discuss the problem of different criteria of values in the context of legal issues in the name of equality is therefore a fundamental prerequisite for the promotion of justice perception. Simple information about current legal decisions do not suffice, it would rather be worthwhile to have all legal principals checked according to the sense of justice of the young person. In addition, this could lead to the question, which moral, philosophical and ethical principles should form the basis for a just society.

3.4 Solidarity – a Long-Range Educational Goal

Solidarity is feasible at both individual and global level in relations between different societies. Education in solidarity, therefore, should consider both aspects. On one hand, children and adolescents should be educated to act in solidarity with their visible neighbour with the intention to help him, promote him, defend and support him, in short to act in solidarity with *him*. At the same time, they should be educated to act in solidarity with strangers (plural!) or even with the not-yet-born generation with the objective to provide for their life conditions and possibilities of survival – in short: to live in solidarity with *them*.

Besides this difference we should promote personal and structural solidarity. Human solidarity is a personal one, realised in relationships of "me" and "you" in ego-centred relations. These occur in relations between people – the relationship is usually asymmetric, because (with respect to *charity*, not to *friendship*!) it is the individual who takes care of others. Structural solidarity occurs, if an individual is related to the environment as a whole, for example in a relation between the self and the whole of nature, or with reference of the actually living to the not-yet-born, but as well between a specific individual and organisations or institutions as legal entities.

Both forms of solidarity are practised in an inter-individual radius of action, as well as in an inter-societal, therefore remote, area of action. For example, we can be jointly liable also in an area that demands structural solidarity, for example by sponsoring an African child over the long term and thus feel collectively responsible; and we can sponsor someone in a form of essentially human solidarity, if we wish to be collectively responsible for a structural solidarity within a structural context that is designed as "nature" as a whole, for example – for the preservation of living beings – or if we feel the need to feel responsible for the efficacy of social movements and institutions, or similar units.

This way of handling problems could help us:

- to eliminate prejudices and forms of hostility in relation to contexts which previously were experienced as "strange", and
- to respect others in their peculiarity and to get involved in social justice.

These are several educational objectives and competencies desirable in the long run that would include:

- to promote the ability to think globally and at the same time to act locally,
- to focus our attention on distress, poverty, and repression,
- to evolve an ability to proceed from a local area to a remote area of ethics,
- to encourage the open-mindedness to meet other cultures and religions.

In the first age-classes in secondary schools, these goals could be achieved by topics concerning social injustice and inter-religious conflicts in a society with immigration, as well as to such topics as terrorism and fanaticism, climate change, problems with the armament of legal and illegal forces and other forms of structural (and cultural) violence. And at college level, it is recommendable to study questions of war and peace and the problems of international military operations, of a worldwide economic order, and of international terrorism. In relation to these subjects, varieties of actions for peace in world religions could be discussed.

Therefore, when planning subjects of instruction it is necessary to differentiate between the two forms of solidarity: between inter-individual and inter-societal solidarity. Both are desirable goals of an education in solidarity.

This dual challenge is immensely difficult to deal with today. Children are often mature and socialised divisively. They often lack brothers and sisters, they are isolated from social groups, they are faced with patterns and role models on TV and in videogames that are examples of non-solidarity, and they are mainly focused on individual gratification in a consumerist world; this makes it difficult for teachers to provide an education in solidarity even in primary schools. Of course, children may come to know a community evolving solidarity and respect for common goods in schools, within groups of friends, even during one-time events like parties, festivals, and similar extraordinary meetings, but they often lack forms of lasting solidarity in their daily life. This makes it difficult for the teacher to respond with calls for solidarity in everyday life.

These experiences certainly do not correspond to the results of education of 6- to 12-year-old children with respect to solidarity from a global viewpoint. These children may feel more solidarity with impoverished, disenfranchised, and degraded children in the Sahara than with those in their own neighbourhood, as shown from experience. And they are more willing to offer small sacrifices to those from afar than to those nearby. Sponsorship of an African or Asian child can often be arranged easily. This is conceivable as the children do not worry about the distance to persons they do not even know; so they could not deny this sense of solidarity, as they do when face to face with comrades who are condemning them as "silly" or "foolish". With respect to these companions children feel they are being asked only to *think* in terms of solidarity but are not invited to *act voluntarily* according to this value. Therefore, it is obvious we need to connect education in solidarity with both the short- and long-range in terms of distance, so that children do not end up contradicting their own volition.

This is possible, because children have long practised a form of personal solidarity and not a structural one. They see only the individual cases of people suffering, but they do not even see through the social structures in foreign countries. It is all right that the previous mentioned point of view is able to intensify the awareness in the children's consciousness.

Young people are harder to win over to the valuation of solidarity on the one hand, because they already come from a childhood mostly free of feelings of fellowship, and on the other hand, because they are sceptical about the gossip in relation to solidarity. They seem to suffer from a negative view of social justice and the welfare state. Many of them do not believe – rightly or wrongly, as is to be seen – in the guarantee of job security, or of the redemption of pension rights and thus they have too little trust in a future based on social solidarity. And many of them do not know to whom they should demonstrate a claim of solidarity in our pluralistic society – and to whom it is not necessary. Therefore, values such as justice, equality, friendship and tolerance, are more important to them then the value of solidarity. In their narrow peer groups, however, they practise solidarity and friendship. But this seems to be not more than a form of clan solidarity; it does not include solidarity with strangers and foreigners, who have a deprived, dishonourable, and threatening status.

3.5 Human Dignity and Human Rights – Can Humanity be Generalised?

Parents and teachers again and again are confronted with an ethically important question with respect to the validity of present orders of right: Why do parts of our legal systems up to now only apply to Germans and EU-nationals, and not likewise for all people, without regard to their native country?

The ethical claim of respect for human dignity is laid down twice: in the EUCFR (Art. 1) as well as in the German Basic Law (Art. 1 BL) as one of the fundamental legal and policy-designing principles and rights. Examples of humiliation, or what young people understand by them, may be faced then with the importance of the right to dignity claimed for everybody, not only for persons with German and/or European citizenship, but also for aliens from outside the EU, albeit legally or illegally residing in Germany/the EU. The principle of generalisation (universality) of rights is expressed in catalogues of fundamental rights by the formulation: "Every person has the right to ...". This requires the formation of values and a discussion of the need to extend the scope of fundamental rights: These rights actually seem to be privileges of contemporaries. Why are they not in the same way also the rights of the not-yet-born? And how can the rights of plants and animals be taken into account? Some students call into question the legitimacy of traditional anthropocentric worldviews in a fundamental way. They combine their questions sometimes with demands for protection not only for humans but also for the whole of organic nature, a demand relating to the conservation of species, or even the preservation of the biosphere as a whole.

Another important aspect for the promotion of protection of human dignity has to do with the fact that young people almost on a daily basis experience serious violations of human rights in those States in which human rights are not implemented by applicable laws. Insights into the drama of this disregard of rights lead one to ask the fundamental question of the universality of all basic human rights.

Only if we assume that there are universally valid human rights (written or unwritten), can we distinguish between individual rights – which are granted because we are citizens of a country and at the same time citizens of the Union – and those that would have come to us as cosmopolites.

In this way we could promote an awareness of the dignity of all people, whether they live within or outside the EU, thus helping us to implement and to strengthen respect for human dignity in daily life. Therefore, education in values is to be introduced into or strengthened in families, kindergartens, schools, and institutes of the churches.

4 Can Values Education Promote Cohesion in Europe?[11]

In relation to the almost daily experienced violations of human rights by children, adolescents and adults, including denial of fundamental rights, perforation of the rule of law, dilution of democracy and economically, politically and socially caused danger to liberty, equality, solidarity and human dignity in Europe we should ask: What kind of answer to the question in the heading can be expected? First of all a clear "no" as an answer. Although the European Court of Justice tries to prevent the greatest injustices, the striving for solidarity among Union citizens is crumbling

[11] Mokrosch 2008, p. 164–166.

or has been rocked by populist "movements". Even if human rights are at least theoretically protected worldwide, resistance against international law violations is demanded. Our jubilee *Albrecht Weber* focuses continuously on them.

Those who try to implement values in families, kindergartens, schools, churches etc. should address local educational institutions where the possibilities of education in values are to be realised. Children and adolescents, despite socialisation difficulties, are open to European values – as described above – and develop an awareness of the realisation of values according to the principle "Think globally! Act locally!"

Is this sufficient for a growing cohesion in Europe? Not entirely; but as far as conscious valuations and goals really can influence factual circumstances, such base-oriented values, if taught in more than 300,000 schools, could lead to some results within the EU. But this is pure speculation. Up to now there have been no relevant empirical studies. This should be left to later research.

References

Aristotle (1934). *Nicomachean Ethics*. English version: Aristotle in 23 Volumes, vol. 19. Cambridge, MA: Harvard University Press. http://www.perseus.tufts.edu/hopper/text?doc=Aristot.+Nic.+Eth.+1094a+1&redirect=true.Translated by H. Rackham. London, William Heinemann Ltd.

Hobbes, T. (1642/51). *Elementorvm Philosophiæ: sectio tertia; de cive*. Paris 1642; English version: *De Cive. The Citizen Philosophical Rudiments concerning Government And Society*. London 1651.

Hobbes, T. (1651). *Leviathan. On the Matter, Form and Power of a Commonwealth, Ecclesiastical and Civil*. London: Andrew Crooke.

Mokrosch, R. (2008). Protestantische Werte-Erziehung und ihr Beitrag für das Zusammenwachsen Europas. In Evangelisch-Theologische Fakultät der Universität Wien (Ed.), *Wiener Jahrbuch für Theologie* (vol. 7, pp. 155–166). Münster: Lit.

Mokrosch, R. (2013). Religiöse Werte-Bildung im Pluralismus der Religionen. In E. Naurath et al. (Ed.), *Wie sich Werte bilden. Fachübergreifende und fachspezifische Werte-Bildung* (pp. 43–64). Göttingen: Vandenhoeck & Ruprecht.

Mokrosch, R., & Regenbogen, A. (Eds.). (2009). *Werte-Erziehung und Schule. Ein Handbuch für Unterrichtende*. Göttingen: Vandenhoeck & Ruprecht.

Müller-Graff, P.-C. (2014). Die horizontale Drittwirkung der Grundfreiheiten. *EuR, vol. 1*, 1–29.

Perelman, C. (1967). *Über die Gerechtigkeit*. Munich: C. H. Beck. *De la justice* (1945)

Regenbogen, A., & Regenbogen, A. (2001). *Menschenrechte*. Arbeitshefte Ethik Sek. II für den Ethik-, Religions- und Philosophie-Unterricht. Donauwörth: Auer.

Sonnevend, P. (2011). Der EuGH und die Drittwirkung der Unionsgrundrechte: Eine neue Grenze für die Privatautonomie. *Annales Universitatis scientiarum Budapestinensis de Rolando Eotvos, T. LII.*, 71–76.

The Legal Language of the Culture of Death in Europe

Manfred Spieker

1 The Culture of Death

The legal language of the "Culture of death" is full of ambivalences. By its central terms it sends signals which produce life-accepting associations and at the same time mask its intentions against life. But before we examine the language the "Culture of death" uses, we have to take a closer look at the term "Culture of death" itself. In the Pontificate of John Paul II, and especially in his Encyclical about the value and the inviolability of human life, "Evangelium Vitae", it plays a key role.[1] The term itself is a sort of hermaphrodite. It unites seemingly incompatible subjects. Everybody who uses the term must reckon with the objection, that it might better be called the "Unculture of death". The term culture, from the Latin term "colere" (cultivate, care for), means formed by man in contrast to the uncultivated nature which often is opposed to man. But the term goes far beyond the cultivation. It also means the humanization of the society, the refinement of social relationships. In Catholic Social Doctrine it includes all human activity in economy and politics, in science and arts. By this cultivation, the Second Vatican Council declares in "Gaudium et Spes", man unfolds the work of the Creator and not only pursues and develops things and society, but also himself.[2]

Death, in contrast, is the opposite of culture. It is part of nature which cannot be surmounted by human activity. So, "Culture of death" is a dense term. It combines incompatible things – culture, human activity and development, and death, the end of all activity. The term has nothing to do with *ars moriendi*, the art of dying undertaken by a mature person who faces death in a conscious and calm manner, or who even welcomes him as a sister as St. Francis of Assisi did. And it has nothing to do with murder or manslaughter, which have existed among people since Cain killed Abel, and which has always been cursed as a crime. "Culture of death" rather means certain behaviours on the one hand and social and legal structures on the other hand, which strive to make killing socially acceptable by camouflaging it as a medical

[1] John Paul II (1995), 24, 26, 28, 50, 64, 87, 95; cf. John Paul II (2003), 9, 95.

[2] II. Vaticanum (1965), 34–35, 53.

H.-J. Blanke et al. (eds.), *Common European Legal Thinking*,
DOI 10.1007/978-3-319-19300-7_21

service or a social assistance, or by justifying it as promising research. The Culture of death wants to liberate this killing from the curse of being a crime. Over the last 40 years it has emerged and grown in Western societies. It includes bioethical issues which have existed since man has existed, such as abortion and euthanasia, as well as newer problems which arose since the development of artificial insemination in the 1970s, such as embryonic stem cell research, cloning, Preimplantation Genetic Diagnosis and assisted reproduction itself. It uses an ambivalent language which has a sedating effect on society.

The examples of the ambivalence of this language illustrated in what follows are taken from the German language. But I am sure that the "Culture of death" acts in a similar way in other languages. It uses terms that produce positive associations at first sight; for example, terms like human rights, dignity, freedom, choice, assistance, solidarity, health, therapy and self-determination. The positive associations produced by these terms are used to make killing acceptable. Only at second sight does it become clear that these terms are sleights of hand hiding the opposite: the disregard of the right to life and the dignity of those who do not have a voice, the assertion of the will of the strong against the weak, the clinical removal of the unborn and the dying people who are a burden on society. Not only are activist groups like the abortion lobby using these sleights of hand but also the legislatures and the courts.

2 Abortion

The legalization of abortion in the free part of Europe began in 1967 in Great Britain, a few years after the introduction of contraceptive hormone preparations (1960). The German *Bundestag* has made four great reforms of the criminal law on abortion (in 1974, 1976, 1992 and 1995), with the expressed objective of strengthening the protection of life and reducing the number of abortions. The last two reforms were called the "Pregnancy and family assistance law" (1992) and the "Pregnancy and family assistance amendment law" (1995). Both laws did not offer any assistance, either to pregnant women or to families or unborn children. They only serve the purpose of de facto legalizing the priority of the "right" to abort over the right of the child to live. The titles of the laws were sleights of hand. The same applied in Ireland: The law passed in July 2013, which legalized abortion for the first time, was called "Protection of Life during Pregnancy Act". The fact that all the reforms in Germany failed to meet the expressed objective to improve the protection of life and to reduce the number of abortions, is shown by the abortion statistics, introduced in 1972 in the German Democratic Republic and in 1976 in the Federal Republic of Germany, and by the increasing social and judicial acceptance of abortion since the first reform 40 years ago.[3]

[3] Spieker 2011, p. 17 et seqq.

In German society, the abortion lobby includes an organization which calls itself "Pro Familia" and which is part of the worldwide pro-abortion organization Planned Parenthood. These names are sleights of hand too. The objective of these organisations is not helping families or supporting planned and responsible parenthood but the legalization of abortion. "Pro Familia" for example disseminates leaflets which describe the medical procedure of an abortion in language where every indication of the child (or respectively the embryo) is avoided. The procedure of the abortion is described as "suction of pregnancy tissue", as "removing the contents of the uterus" or, in relation to chemical abortion, as "expulsion of the pregnancy".[4] This language is stultification in the guise of information.

The German criminal law on abortion takes a special form in order to realize the "Culture of death". In Paragraph 218 of the German Penal Code (StGB) it prohibits abortion as a criminal offence, but in Paragraph 218a StGB it regulates the decriminalizing exceptions. The exceptions defeat the rule. A person who wants to have an abortion has no difficulties finding a physician willing to perform the procedure funded by taxes. At the centre of these exceptions is so-called pregnancy counselling. Abortion during the first 12 weeks after conception will not be punished if a woman provides the physician with a certificate that she has received advice at least three days before having the abortion. The dialectical cleverness of this counselling regulation consists in the fact that the advice certificate documents advice given in favour of protecting the life of the unborn child which at the same time is the necessary condition for an abortion which officially remains illegal, but is not liable to prosecution. The fact that the pregnant woman has a right to receive the advice certificate even without having manifested her reasons for considering abortion has been established by the German Federal Constitutional Court in a judgment of 27 October 1998.[5] The advice certificate converts the criminal act of killing an innocent person into a medical service. It is the basis of a contract under civil law between the abortionist and the pregnant woman for the purpose of killing her child. So, for the abortionist it is a license to kill. It grants the priority of the self-determination-right of the pregnant woman over the right of her unborn child to live. In society's perception the criminal law on abortion has become an abortion law. The abortion statistics, also a particularity of German criminal law, serve more to camouflage than provide information. They are published once a quarter and every March for the previous year, mostly with a reassuring undertone that the number of abortions has decreased again. The "Culture of death" knows how to avoid discussing the demographic reasons for the reduction and the abortions not included in the statistics on the one hand, and on the other hand the total number of abortions reported to the Federal Office for Statistics since statistics have been kept (up to 31 March 2015: 5,712,114).

[4] Familienplanungszentrum Pro Familia Hamburg (2004), p. 6, 13–15.

[5] German Federal Constitutional Court (Bundesverfassungsgericht), 1 BvR 2306/96 (judgment of 27 October 1998) para 218 et seqq. – *Bayerisches Schwangerenhilfeergänzungsgesetz, ambulanter Schwangerschaftsabbruch* (in BVerfGE 98, 324).

This dialectical regulation of pregnancy counselling also brought the Catholic Church in Germany into a state of deep conflict. The majority of the German bishops and Catholic lay people defended this regulation against the concerns of *Pope John Paul II* and the Prefect of the Congregation for the Doctrine of the Faith, *Joseph Cardinal Ratzinger*, with the argument that it offered the chance to convince a pregnant woman considering abortion to have her baby. The critics of the counselling regulation objected that by participating in this counselling system the Church was drawn into the "Culture of death". The Church must not provide counselling as a legal condition for abortion. After a four year struggle with the German bishops, in September 1999 *Pope John Paul II* ordered that the Church's counselling offices were no longer allowed to issue the certificate.[6] But the conflict and the continuing provision of pregnancy counselling with the certificate, offered by the association of Catholic lay persons "Donum Vitae", is paralyzing the Catholic church in Germany today, on the protection of unborn life, compared to the churches in many other countries, for example Poland, Ireland, Spain, Italy and the USA. There are neither pro-life-secretaries nor co-operation with the pro-life movement nor support for the yearly March for Life in Berlin. The "Week for life", celebrated every year together with the Lutheran Church in Germany, has degenerated to a simple invitation to "Be friendly to each other". Public support for the petition "One of us", organized all over the European Union in order to improve the legal protection of the embryo, which was given by *Pope Francis* on 12 May 2013[7], was not of interest to the German Bishops' Conference.

On the international level the legalization of abortion is propagated by several sub-organizations of the United Nations. Here, the sleight of hand the "Culture of death" uses is the right of reproductive health. This term was used for the first time in the Action Programme of the World Population Conference 1994 in Cairo. The 1995 World Conference on Women in Beijing also took it up. But it is also true that both conferences still retained the statement that abortion is not a method of family planning. The action programmes of these conferences do not have the character of binding international law but only of recommendations. But in the fight to legalize a right of reproductive health, including the right to abortion, in international law, several sub-organizations of the UNO and NGOs are active, like the Human Rights Council, the United Nations Population Fund (UNFPA), the World Health Organization (WHO), and the Committee on the Elimination of Discrimination against Women (CEDAW) which plays a central role in the fight to legalize abortion, and does as a new organization UN-Women, the "Entity for Gender Equality and the Empowerment of Women", founded on 2 July 2010. And like an engine behind these organizations stands the International Planned Parenthood Federation whose action programme gives absolute priority to that fight. The argumentation of these organizations uses another sleight of hand. It is called maternal mortality. They claim that maternal mortality is especially high if abortion is "unsafe". Unsafe

[6] Spieker 2008, p. 132 et seqq.

[7] Francis, speech at the Regina Coeli, 12 May 2003, L'Osservatore Romano (German), 17 May 2003, p. 1.

abortions are illegal abortions; that is why they say that the reduction of maternal mortality requires the legalization of abortion. At the UN General Assembly on 24 October 2011, these demands were controversially discussed and rejected, not least by the representative of the Holy See, Archbishop *Francis Assisi Chullikatt*.[8]

3 Euthanasia

Concerning euthanasia, the "Culture of death" has a few more problems in Germany than in some neighbouring states like the Benelux countries – at least with regard to the legislature. During the National Socialist Dictatorship euthanasia had been realized to a large extent. It aimed at the removal of the disabled, the incurably ill and weak people whose lives were considered to be unworthy of life and a burden for the people's community. Their killing was declared an act of love and compassion or, as *A. Hitler* himself described it in a decree of 1939, a mercy death. But German society has fewer problems with euthanasia, if it is not called euthanasia but "active assisted dying". In surveys this form of "assisted" dying is regularly supported by about two thirds of the population. At the beginning of 2013, the German *Bundestag* for the first time discussed draft legislation concerning assisted suicide. The liberal Minister of Justice only wanted to prohibit commercial assistance to suicide. Such a partial prohibition would *eo ipso* have legalized every non-commercial assistance to suicide – a typical strategy of the "Culture of death": under the guise of prohibiting killing, the legalization of killing is proposed and commercial organizations of assisted suicide quickly changed their legal status into charitable associations. Up to 2014, however, no law has been passed. But the German *Bundestag* started a new discussion in the autumn of 2014. The minister of health of the Christian Democratic Party intends to prohibit any businesslike assistance to suicide. *G. D. Borasio*, *R. J. Jox*, *J. Taupitz* and *U. Wiesing* presented a bill in August 2014 to legalise assisted suicide by medical doctors, close relatives and friends in a new § 217 StGB.[9]

The main argument the "Culture of death" is using to promote euthanasia is the right of self-determination. Everybody has the right to decide on his death himself. *H. Küng* and *W. Jens* call that "dying with dignity".[10] Nobody, as the liberal deputy *D. Marty* from Switzerland said at the Council of Europe, had "the right to impose the duty to continue life under unbearable suffering or agony on a terminally ill or dying person, if he himself had insistently expressed his wish to end it".[11] It becomes a "violation of human dignity" *P. Hintze* argues, if the protection of human life is changed into a state compulsion to suffering.[12] That is why assisted suicide should be legalized. Euthanasia is a logical consequence of

[8] Spieker 2014b, p. 111 et seqq.
[9] Borasio et al. 2014.
[10] Jens and Küng 1995.
[11] Council of Europe, Doc. 9898, para 61.
[12] Hintze et al. 2014, p. 2.

assisted suicide.[13] The Parliamentary Assembly of the Council of Europe has not followed this suggestion up to now. The "Culture of death" suggests that euthanasia serves the relief of suffering and the realization of the right of self-determination. It eliminates suffering by eliminating the suffering person. It ignores the prohibition of killing innocent persons and so undermines one of the conditions of legitimacy of constitutional democracy. In order to present euthanasia as an exercise of self-determination and even as a service to the common good, the "Culture of death" also uses some auxiliary arguments. A first additional argument has an anthropological character: the capacity to communicate is declared a constituting characteristic of human existence. If the ability to communicate has been extinguished or is no longer perceptible at first sight, as in the case of someone in a vegetative state or with certain forms of dementia, that person consequently is no longer considered to be a human being and his killing is no longer considered as the killing of a human being. That is why every adult, as a sociologist says, should deposit "a living will" in case of total or partial loss of his capacity to communicate, by which the persons responsible for his care are bound.[14] Another anthropological auxiliary argument is the definition of patients who are not able to communicate as "human Non-Persons" or "sentient property".[15] This allows "Non-Persons" to be dealt with as you deal with objects.

Finally, the "Culture of death" uses additional demographic and financial arguments when talking about euthanasia and assisted suicide. With a really brutal frankness they invite the vulnerable to commit an "altruistic suicide" and declare it a "last human act of solidarity". They say it is true that a person willing to commit suicide should take the negative consequences of self-killing on his social surrounding into consideration. But it could be expected from him that "in case of an incurable and highly care-intensive disease he senses the emotional burden, the utilization of time and financial burden of his existence for his family and friends. We are not only responsible for the negative social consequences when we depart this world but of course also for those of continuing our life."[16] Such invitations to commit socially beneficial suicide destroy the relationship between the physician and the patient. The patient turns from a suffering subject who receives compassion and solidarity from society into an object which is a burden for society. So, it is not the patient who can expect compassion from society but society which expects compassion from the patient."Who wants to continue life under those circumstances? That way, the right to self-killing inevitably becomes a duty to do it."[17] Where living-on is only one of two legal options everybody is forced to justify why he places the burden of his living-on on someone else's shoulders.[18]

The practice of euthanasia in the Netherlands and Belgium shows that the idea that euthanasia is available only in the case of a voluntary, informed and insistent

[13] Spieker 2014a.
[14] Feldmann 1990, p. 236.
[15] Smith 2005.
[16] Fenner 2007, p. 210; von Lewinski 2008, p. 186–204.
[17] Spaemann 1997, p. 20.
[18] Rau 2001, p. 27–28.

wish expressed by the patient is an illusion, as is the idea that the physicians would fulfil the legal duty to inform the regional controlling commissions about all euthanasia cases. Although the percentage of patients who have been killed without their consent, in 2001 still about 20 per cent, seems to have decreased according to the latest inquiry in 2010 by about half, it is a great problem.[19] And the fact that euthanasia also is administered without any consent can be proven by the Groningen Protocol from 2004, which allows the killing of severely disabled new-born and seriously ill children in their first year of life. Here, the "Culture of death" uses the term "after birth abortion". This example highlights two facts: On the one hand the term maintains the illusion that the killing of new-born children is not euthanasia because legal euthanasia requires consent which new-born babies are *eo ipso* not able to give, and on the other hand it relies on the acceptance of abortion. In 2012, *A. Giubilini* and *F. Minerva* argued the case for extending the "after birth abortion" to healthy new-born babies because they still do not have the moral status of a person. "Merely potential people cannot be harmed by not being brought into existence ... since non-persons have no moral rights to live, there are no reasons for banning after-birth abortions."[20] These experiences from the Netherlands show how euthanasia changes the self-conception of health professions and destroys the confidence of the patient in the physician. Physicians and nurses who become killing engineers – a new profession for which the Swiss Academy of Medical Sciences recommends separate professional training for the purpose of quality assurance – encounter distrust among the patients. Already in 2001, when the draft legislation was discussed in the Dutch Parliament, the Dutch Bishops had warned against this development.[21] The so-called "Credo-Card"[22] demonstrates this distrust. Instead of extending the radius of self-determination, the legalization of euthanasia increases the fear of heteronomy.

4 Embryonic Stem Cell Research, PGD and PND

In 2000, a wide bioethical debate started concerning problems of biomedicine arising from artificial insemination, after *J. Thomson* at the University of Wisconsin-Madison in 1998 for the first time succeeded in isolating embryonic stem cells. The aim of this research is to develop from embryonic stem cells, which are able to develop in an appropriate media into tissue and organs, therapies for up to now incurable diseases. But extracting a stem cell line means the destruction of the em-

[19] Onwuteaka-Philipsen et al. 2012, p. 4–5. Although the authors speak of 9 percent, almost 25 percent of the doctors who killed their patients via euthanasia did so without consulting neither the patients, nor their relatives, nor other doctors. For the figures in former years cf. Spieker 2011, p. 54–55.

[20] Giubilini and Minerva 2012, p. 3.

[21] Cf. Simonis 2002, p. 152.

[22] The Credo-Card is a document containing the owner's name and the inscription "Maak mij niet dood, Doktor" (don't kill me, doctor), thus expressing that in case of inability to express oneself, the owner does not want euthanasia.

bryo. Embryonic stem cell research uses the so-called spare or orphaned embryos produced during assisted reproduction. The objection of bioethics and constitutional law that no therapy, not even the most promising, may justify the killing of an embryo, even the one with little chance of being transferred into the uterus, encounters opposition. The "Culture of death" uses not only the promise of new therapies for until today incurable diseases but also some linguistic distinctions which give the impression that spare embryos are not legal subjects protected by the constitutional warranty of human dignity and the right to life, but objects that are available to serve society and research as a resource. The embryo *in vitro*, that is an embryo outside the uterus, is "human life", but still not a human, not even a "becoming human".[23] According to this view, it is not an embryo but a "pre-embryo". It has an "abstract", but no "concrete" possibility of becoming a human.[24] All these distinctions serve the purpose of denying to embryos the dignity of human life and protection of their right to live, and create from that basis property claims by society for research and therapeutic projects. As in the debate about euthanasia the "Culture of death" uses anthropological auxiliary arguments: the ability to communicate and to feel or develop personal interests are declared the constituting characteristics of human existence. The embryo *in vitro*, they say, does not live under communicative circumstances, is no "partner for discourse",[25] has no interests,[26] and has no feelings.[27] Consequently, it is not a person and has no rights. The result: it is allowed to consume embryos as a resource, which means to kill them. The European Court opposed a pioneering effort of the "Culture of death", in its judgment *Brüstle v. Greenpeace*. It denied an attempt to patent embryonic stem cells for scientific research because every fertilised human ovum is a human embryo. Therefore, a procedure which requires the destruction of a human embryo is not patentable.[28]

Preimplantation Genetic Diagnosis (PGD) allows embryos produced in the laboratory to be examined for certain dispositions to disease or disabilities and, in case of positive findings, to exclude them from being transferred into a uterus. PGD thus opens the door to a deadly selection of undesired embryos. It is permitted in many countries. When legalized in Germany on 7 July 2011, the "Culture of death" used especially many sleights of hand to hide the objective of the deadly selection. First of all they spoke of "Ethics of helping".[29] The definition which advocates of the legalization of PGD used already masks its core: the deadly selection. The PGD, they say, is "an instrument in the scope of artificial insemination which gives information about diseases of the fertilized ovum before it is implanted into the uterus".[30]

[23] Fischer 2001; Fischer 2002, p. 11 et seqq.; Kreß 2001, p. 230 et seqq.

[24] Zypries 2003, p. 6.

[25] Gerhardt, interview, Die Welt, 5 July 2001.

[26] Kersting 2001.

[27] Merkel 2001, p. 64.

[28] Case C-34/10, *Brüstle* (ECJ 18 October 2011), cf. Gärditz 2012, p. 87 et seqq.

[29] Hintze, parliamentary debate, 14 April 2011 (protocol n° 17/105, p. 11948–9) and 7 July 2001 (protocol n° 17/120, p. 13876).

[30] Flach, parliamentary debate, 14 April 2011 (protocol n° 17/105, p. 11945).

They claim it is a modern medical diagnosis to reduce severe health risks.[31] It gives parents with inherent genetic defects the opportunity to "have a healthy baby".[32] That is why the legislature does not have the right to refuse the couples in question from accessing PGD because we do not "just (tolerate) other forms of suffering but treat them and find therapies against them".[33] The ethics of helping or curing ignores the price we have to pay for this "diagnosis": the deadly selection of the embryos. It ignores the constitutional protection which grants every embryo after conception the protection of human dignity, the right to life and the prohibition of discrimination.

Since 1970 also developments in prenatal diagnostics (PND) full of linguistic sleights of hand have changed the experience of pregnancy for many women.[34] According to an inquiry of the German Centre of Health Information, about two thirds of pregnant women accept PND because they believe that the PND contributes to having a healthy baby.[35] They do not accept their child until the PND has certified that their child is medically normal. They suppress their natural tendency to be happy and to protect the child and are manœuvred into a hardly tolerable distance from their pregnancy and their own child. "A life under the delusion of optimization. From the beginning. At any cost. Especially parents feel this pressure. They shall be perfect parents of perfect children."[36] It is claimed that PND averts dangers for life and health of mother and child. Not uncommonly, it "serves a eugenic mentality".[37] Often, the only possibility of averting any dangers for the health of the child is an abortion. The "Culture of death" generally hides that fact behind terms like prevention, prophylactic measures, and avoidance of genetic anomalies or induced birth.[38] It is not permitted to speak about abortion. That is why an abortion after PND because of a severe disability of the embryo in the 23rd pregnancy week must be called a delivery, according to a judgment of the German Federal Labour Court of 15 December 2005. The court agreed with a mother who had brought a suit against the dismissal by her employer with the argument, inducing a premature labour was a "delivery".[39] That is why she had the right to receive maternal protection and, in consequence, protection against dismissal. The employer referred to the fact that an abortion was no delivery and so the dismissal was legal. The court forced him to revoke the dismissal.

---

[31] Leutheusser-Schnarrenberger, parliamentary debate, 14 April 2011 (protocol n° 17/105, p. 11970).

[32] Cf. the motives in the draft bill for legalisation, Bundestag, bulletin n° 17/5451, p. 8.

[33] Reimann, parliamentary debate, 7 July 2011 (protocol n° 17/120, p. 13879); von der Leyen, parliamentary debate, 7 July 2011 (protocol n° 17/120, p. 13909).

[34] Spieker 2012, p. 261 et seqq.

[35] Bundeszentrale für gesundheitliche Aufklärung 2006, p. 41.

[36] Hey 2012, p. 14.

[37] John Paul II (1995), 63.

[38] Beck-Gernsheim 1995, p. 124.

[39] German Federal Labour Court (Bundesarbeitsgericht), 2 AZR 462/04 (Judgment of 15 December 2005) (in NZA 2006, 994–997).

5 The Culture of Life

"Walk as children of light!" in order to create a cultural change. This invitation is the title of the final paragraph in the Encyclical *Evangelium Vitae* which is dedicated to the Culture of life. Of course, at the beginning of this process of renewal we have to expose the sleights of hand of the "Culture of death". But then further steps must follow. The fight between a "Culture of death" and the Culture of life must "develop a deep, critical sense". It is an illusion "to think that we can build a true culture of human life if we do not help the young to accept and experience sexuality and love and the whole of life according to their true meaning and in their close interconnection." [40] If the banalisation of sexuality, against which Paul VI in *Humanae Vitae* had already warned, is at the beginning of a disregard for unborn life and at the beginning of a "Culture of death", then the testimony of the beauty and richness of sexuality as a mutual complete gift, the observance of the biological laws which are inscribed in the human person, education in natural methods of regulating fertility and the discovery of the coherence between charity and truth stand at the beginning of the Culture of life. Self-giving, not self-determination is the key to achieving a fruitful life. This is valid not only for married couples. *Jesus Christ* lived that in exemplary manner 2000 years ago. In the Eucharist it becomes present every day. That is what the Council underlined in *Gaudium et Spes* 24. For *John Paul II* and *Benedict XVI* this truth guided their Pontificates; and also for *Pope Francis*, in his still young Pontificate. "Do not be afraid!" to proclaim that.

References

Beck-Gernsheim, E. (1995). Genetische Beratung im Spannungsfeld zwischen Klientenwünschen und gesellschaftlichem Erwartungsdruck. In E. Beck-Gernsheim (Ed.), *Welche Gesundheit wollen wir? Dilemmata des medizintechnischen Fortschritts* (pp. 118–138). Frankfurt/Main: Suhrkamp.

Borasio, G. D., Jox, R. J., Taupitz, J., & Wiesing, U. (2014). *Selbstbestimmung im Sterben – Fürsorge zum Leben, Ein Gesetzesvorschlag zur Regelung des assistierten Suizids*. Stuttgart: Kohlhammer.

Bundeszentrale für gesundheitliche Aufklärung (2006). Schwangerschaftserleben und Pränataldiagnostik. Repräsentative Befragung Schwangerer zum Thema Pränataldiagnostik. Cologne. English version: *Experience of Pregnancy and Prenatal Diagnosis 2006. Representative Survey of Pregnant Women on the Subject of Prenatal diagnosis*. http://www.bzga.de/infomaterialien/dokumentationen/experience-of-pregnancy-and-prenatal-diagnosis-2006/

Familienplanungszentrum Pro Familia Hamburg (Ed.). (2004). *Ich will noch kein Kind ... Infos zum Schwangerschaftsabbruch*. Hamburg: Familienplanungszentrum e. V.

Feldmann, K. (1990). *Tod und Gesellschaft. Eine soziologische Betrachtung von Sterben und Tod*. Frankfurt/Main: Peter Lang.

Fenner, D. (2007). Ist die Institutionalisierung und Legalisierung der Suizid-Beihilfe gefährlich? Eine kritische Analyse der Gegenargumente. *Ethik in der Medizin*, *19*, 200–214.

[40] John Paul II (1995), 97.

Fischer, J. (2001). Pflicht des Lebensschutzes nur für Menschen. Eine theologische Betrachtung der Embryonenforschung. *Neue Zürcher Zeitung*, *211* (12 September 2001), 16.

Fischer, J. (2002). Vom Etwas zum Jemand. Warum Embryonenforschung mit dem christlichen Menschenbild vereinbar ist. *Zeitzeichen*, *3*(1), 11–13.

Gärditz, K. F. (2012). Der Europäische Gerichtshof als Hüter der Menschenwürde: Embryonenschutz und Stammzellforschung. In M. Spieker, C. Hillgruber, & K. F. Gärditz (Eds.), *Die Würde des Embryos. Ethische und rechtliche Probleme der Präimplantationsdiagnostik und der embryonalen Stammzellforschung* (pp. 87–106). Paderborn: Schöningh.

Giubilini, A., & Minerva, F. (2012). After-birth abortion: why should the baby live? *Journal of Medical Ethics Online*, first published on 23 February 2012 doi:10.1136/medethics-2011-100411.

Hey, M. (2012). *Mein gläserner Bauch. Wie die Pränataldiagnostik unser Verhältnis zum Leben verändert*. Munich: DVA.

Hintze, P., Reimann, C., Lauterbach, K., Lischka, B., Reiche, K., & Wöhrl, D. (2014). *Sterben in Würde – Rechtssicherheit für Patienten und Ärzte, Eckpunktepapier vom 16.10.2014*. http://www.dagmar-woehrl.de/standpunkt/sterben-in-wuerde-positionspapier/

Jens, W., & Küng, H. (1995). *Menschenwürdig sterben. Ein Plädoyer für Selbstverantwortung*. Munich: Piper.

Johannes Paul II (1995). *Evangelium Vitae. Rome, 25 March 1995*. http://www.vatican.va/holy_father/john_paul_ii/encyclicals/documents/hf_jp-ii_enc_25031995_evangelium-vitae_en.html

Johannes Paul II (2003). Post-Synodal Apostolic Exhortation "*Ecclesia in Europa*". Rome, 28 June 2003. http://www.vatican.va/holy_father/john_paul_ii/apost_exhortations/documents/hf_jp-ii_exh_20030628_ecclesia-in-europa_en.html

Kersting, W. (2001). Hantiert, wenn es euch frei macht. *Frankfurter Allgemeine Zeitung*, *65*, (17 March 2001), I.

Kreß, H. (2001). PID, der Status von Embryonen und embryonale Stammzellen. Ein Plädoyer für Güterabwägungen. *Zeitschrift für evangelische Ethik*, *45*, 230–235.

von Lewinski, M. (2008). *Ausharren oder gehen? Für und wider die Freiheit zum Tode*. Munich: Olzog.

Merkel, R. (2001). Rechte für Embryonen?. In C. Geyer (Ed.), *Biopolitik. Die Positionen* (pp. 51–64). Frankfurt/Main: Suhrkamp.

Onwuteaka-Philipsen, B. D., et al. (2012). Trends in end-of-life practices before and after the enactment of the euthanasia law in the Netherlands from 1990 to 2010; a repeated cross-sectional survey. *The Lancet online* (11 July 2012).

Rau, J. (2001). *Wird alles gut? Für einen Fortschritt nach menschlichem Maß*. Frankfurt/Main: Suhrkamp.

Simonis, A. (2002). Care during Suffering and Dying, April 7th, 2000. In P. Kohnen, & G. Schumacher (Eds.), *Euthanasia and Human Dignity. A Collection of Contributions by the Dutch Catholic Bishop's Conference to the Legislative Procedure 1983–2001* (pp. 144–158). Utrecht: Leuven.

Smith, W. J. (2005). "Human Non-Person". Terri Schiavo, bioethics, and our future. In *National Review*, 29 March 2005. www.nationalreview.com/smithw/smith200503290755.asp.

Spaemann, R. (1997). Es gibt kein gutes Töten. In R. Spaemann, & T. Fuchs (Eds.), *Töten oder sterben lassen? Worum es in der Euthanasiedebatte geht* (pp. 12–30). Freiburg i. Br.: Herder.

Spieker, M. (2008). *Kirche und Abtreibung in Deutschland. Ursachen und Verlauf eines Konflikts* (2nd edn.). Paderborn: Schöningh.

Spieker, M. (2011). *Der verleugnete Rechtsstaat. Anmerkungen zur Kultur des Todes in Europa* (2nd edn.). Paderborn: Schöningh.

Spieker, M. (2012). Von der zertifizierten Geburt zur eugenischen Gesellschaft. *Imago Hominis, 19*, 261–270.

Spieker, M. (2014a). Die Logik des assistierten Suizids. *Zeitschrift für Lebensrecht (ZfL), 23*, 90–95.

Spieker, M. (2014b). Missbrauch der UNO – Der globale Kampf um die Legalisierung der Abtreibung. In B. Büchner, C. Kaminski, & M. Löhr (Eds.), *Abtreibung – ein neues Menschenrecht?* (2nd edn., pp. 83–103). Krefeld: Sinus.

Vatican Council, II. (1965). *Gaudium et Spes. Rome, 7 December 1965*. http://www.vatican.va/archive/hist_councils/ii_vatican_council/documents/vat-ii_cons_19651207_gaudium-et-spes_en.html

Zypries, B. (2003). *Vom Zeugen und Erzeugen. Verfassungsrechtliche und rechtspolitische Fragen der Bioethik.* Lecture at the Humboldt-Universität, Berlin, 29 October 2003, manuscript.

What do We Mean by Ethics in Finance?

Franz Zehetner

1 Dedication

If you were to try to describe the scientific community within the nomenclature of families, then *Albrecht Weber* would have been my brother for more than 40 years. We had with Professor *Hugo J. Hahn*[1] the same *spiritus rector*, who encouraged our interests in International and European Law. We became close friends and neighbours in the Austrian Salzkammergut. During common sailing trips on Lake Mondsee and when we visited the Salzburg Festival we developed a common understanding of approaching legal issues in an international context, which fits well with the title of this *liber amicorum*.

Albrecht Weber – we call him Peter – is a specialist in the field of comparative law. Therefore, I will try to continue my recent work in the context of MOCOMILA[2] to describe on a comparative basis some developments in the field of ethics in finance, which I assume is undergoing a transformation process from standards of ethics into binding norms.

2 Ethics in Finance?

The international banking crisis that began in 2008 and later developments have once again highlighted the problem that legally permissible behavior need not necessarily be ethical.[3] The United States pursued a strategy – allowed by US laws – to

[1] *Hugo J. Hahn* was in 1969 one of the founding members of the Faculty of Law at the Johannes Kepler University in Linz (Austria) and head of the Institute for International Law and International Relations; from 1974 he was full professor and director of the Institute of International Law, European Law und International Economic Law at the University of Würzburg.

[2] The Committee on International Monetary Law of the International Law Association (www.mocomila.org).

[3] Arrigunaga 2000, p. 323 referring to "Deposit Insurance Schemes" (DIS): "DISs erode market discipline. To the extent that depositors and other creditors are protected, DISs reduce their in-

H.-J. Blanke et al. (eds.), *Common European Legal Thinking*,
DOI 10.1007/978-3-319-19300-7_22

force non-US institutional investors to (partly) restructure some American Banks (e. g. Washington Mutual Inc.).[4] In the wake of the banking crisis a depletion of trust with negative effects for financial stability occurred.

A first proposal to deal in more detail with questions of ethics in finance came from *William Blair*, the Chairman of MOCOMILA, when he prepared the agenda for the MOCOMILA-Meeting in Madrid (September 2013). He stated in his remark "Is there a role for culture and ethics in financial regulation?"[5] that it is not always easy to pin down in the highly competitive commercial environment of international finance "what conduct is ethical". This question includes first the assumption that there is already a consensus concerning the vital role of ethics in finance and involves secondly doubts about whether ethics in finance is a "subset of general ethics".[6]

Some authors have argued that in the field of finance there is no ethics. Or in other words: "Finance and [...] ethics [...] do not belong together."[7] In fact, the recent financial crises may lead to the conclusion of a "disconnect between ethics and finance"[8] or – with view on the *Ponzi* scheme conceived by *Bernard Madoff* – "of a real divorce of ethics from finance".[9] But the concept of "divorce" contains the statement that ethics and finance were once "married". *Fernandéz* cites – referring to *Ferullo*[10] – "three stages in the modern history of economic thought: first, where finance and ethics were united; second, where they were rubbing shoulders; and third, where the separation was complete". But no one could be found who would have been happy with this development. And no one could be found who would not have argued for the importance of ethics in the field of finance. Overall, it may be assumed that there is a broad consensus that finance should not be conceivable without ethics.[11]

The second question concerns the very core of this topic: Is there a special ethics for the field of finance and if so, how many?[12] Reflecting the large number of existing different "codes of ethics" or "codes of conduct"[13] one might get – at a first glance – the impression that market participants tailor in a kind of do-it-yourself method their own specification of ethics in finance. Consequently, *William Blair* argues that "[f]urther analysis of the codes could usefully be done to identify what is

centive to monitor the financial condition and risk policies of banks. This behaviour allows bank owners and managers to engage in high-risk projects without having to pay a cost for doing so.".

[4] Zehetner 2009.

[5] Blair 2013, p. 10.

[6] Sifah 2012, p. 155.

[7] Ranaivoson 2012, p. 191.

[8] Fernandéz 2012, p. 297.

[9] Fernandéz 2012, p. 298.

[10] Ferullo 2010.

[11] Blair et al. 2014.

[12] This wording refers to the German title of the philosophy published 2007 by *Richard David Precht*: "Wer bin ich – und wenn ja wie viele?" ("Who I am – and if so how many").

[13] See the list prepared by Blair 2013, p. 8 and those ethical codes and codes of good conduct described by Sifah 2012, p. 159.

common ground, and where the differences are".[14] The notion of "difference" raises the further question whether codes of ethics in finance cannot only be different, but can also be in contradiction to each other. It must be assumed that a substantive difference in codes of ethics would – by definition – be *unethical.* But what could be used as a global benchmark for the ultimate decision on what is ethical and what is unethical in finance?

3 Global/General Ethics

On 4 September 1993 the Parliament of the World's Religions endorsed in Chicago a "Declaration Toward a Global Ethic".[15] The basic approach of this conference was to determine the common ethical principles of the world's religions and to publish these principles in many languages. This conference confirmed "that there is already a consensus among the religions which can be the basis for a global ethic – a minimal fundamental consensus concerning binding *values*, irrevocable *standards* and *fundamental moral attitudes*." The basic principle (in the German version: "the golden rule") which should be the irrevocable and unconditional norm for *all* areas of life, has the following wording: "What you do not wish done to yourself, do not do to others." This principle is also formulated in positive terms: "What you wish done to yourself, do to others!" This basic principle seems from the point of view of consequences very similar to *Kant*'s "Categorical Imperative": "Act only in accordance with that maxim through which you can at the same time will that it should become a universal law without contradiction."[16] These similarities led to the widespread view that these two principles are identical.

4 Ethics in Finance!

In order to prevent misunderstandings, it should be pointed out that it is not the intention of this contribution to distinguish between global ethics and ethics in finance. On the contrary: Ethics is not divisible, but you can distinguish different *layers* of ethics. In fact, some principles of ethics play a more important role in finance than in other areas of life. In this context, reference may be made again to the "Declaration Toward a Global Ethic", as mentioned above. Part III ("Irrevocable directives") subtitle 2 ("Commitment to a culture of solidarity and a just economic order") contains a directive, which was found by the Parliament of the World's Religions in "the great ancient religions and ethical traditions of human kind": "You shall not steal" or (in positive terms) "Deal honestly and fairly". The

[14] Blair 2013 p. 10.
[15] Cf. Global Ethic Foundation at http://www.weltethos.org/1-pdf/10-stiftung/declaration/declaration_english.pdf. Accessed 28 August 2013.
[16] Kant 1786/1993.

Parliament clarified this directive that "no one has the right to use her or his possessions without concern for the needs of society and Earth". This example shows that this clarification in the Declaration is only a lower layer of the basic principle of global/general ethics, the golden Rule or *Kant*'s "Categorical Imperative". The ethical directive "You shall not steal" is therefore only the more comprehensible expression of the basic principle of global/general ethics and there is also no contradiction.

Having this in mind you can start to analyze the existing "codes of ethics" or "codes of conduct" as further layers in this *holistic* approach to ethics: Look, for example, into the decision tree of the Code of Conduct of JPMorgan Chase & Co[17] with the questions "Would it be okay if everyone did it?" and "Am I sure I would not feel uncomfortable or embarrassed if I read about it on the front page of the newspaper?".[18] If you go into a more detailed analysis of the substantial rules of these codes, then you will find the above-mentioned basic principle of ethics but formulated in a more operative manner: The above-mentioned ethic directive "You shall not steal" (which is already a clarification of the basic principle "What you do not wish done to yourself, do not do to others") was translated in the Code of Conduct of JPMorgan with a short question and a clear answer: Q: "A co-worker asks me to share marketing strategies we used at my former company. Can I do that?" A: "You must not disclose that information. The marketing strategies of your former employer are likely to be proprietary and you have the obligation to protect them, even after leaving that company. Remember, you will have an obligation to protect the proprietary and confidential information of our Company, too, should you leave to work somewhere else." This seems to be an excellent example to show that ethics is indivisible and that the different aspects of ethics only reflect the basic principles of ethics.

We can summarize as an intermediate result: Ethics in finance means the specification of the general principles of ethics for the purpose of application and compliance in the field of finance. "Codes of ethics" or "codes of conduct" are only instruments to specify these general principles for this purpose, provided that they are consistent with the general principles of ethics.[19]

5 Ethics and Law

In describing the interactions between ethics and law even the lawyers have learned their lessons: *Bill Blair* explained us – referring to ethics in finance – that "it has to

[17] JPMorgan Chase & Co., Code of Conduct, June 2013, http://www.jpmorganchase.com/corporate/About-JPMC/document/229048_2013_CodeofConduct_05.31.13_ada.pdf
[18] JPMorgan Chase & Co., Code of Conduct, p. 4.
[19] Blair et al. 2014 p. 5: "Codes of conduct can play an important role in maintaining ethical standards if they are treated as part of the operation of the business. They can also contain a useful expression by those who actually run financial institutions of what they regard as ethical conduct.".

be recognized that there are the limits as to what further regulation can achieve".[20] And *John Plender*, a senior editorial writer and columnist at the Financial Times wrote that "[w]e have learned from experience that it is not possible to regulate people into good behaviour".[21] Although these observations seem to be correct, they reflect a certain contradiction with the legal reality: The extensive practice of "codes of ethics" or "codes of conduct", not only to define rules of ethics but to connect non-compliance with legal consequences, irritates. Are the rules of ethics (as defined in these "codes") changing their quality and are they becoming "binding rules"?

The following comparative analysis of some codes should provide a basic understanding of the phenomenon of transferring ethics into binding rules:

First, it should be emphasized that the terms "code of ethics" and "code of conduct" are merely descriptive, not normative. This means that with the use of these terms no information on their legal quality and their binding effects is connected. For this reason, many *definitions* of "code of ethics" contain – at a first glance – no express guidance relating to their possible binding effects:

"A guide of principles designed to help professionals conduct business honestly and with integrity. A code of ethics document may outline the mission and values of the business or organization, how professionals are supposed to approach problems, the ethical principles based on the organization's core values and their standards to which professionals will be held."[22]

"A written set of guidelines issued by an organization for its workers and management to help them to conduct their actions in accordance with its primary values and ethical standards."[23]

"A code of ethics is a formal document rather than merely an 'environment', an 'understanding', a 'consensus', 'unwritten rule', or just an aspect of 'corporate culture'. It is at minimum a published document."[24] "Codes of ethics are free-standing expressions of corporate will even when they are published as chapters or sections in a document which may contain a mission statement, a listing of corporate values, and general policies relating to operations."[25]

"Codes of ethics codify the values and principles of the company and define the responsibilities, duties and obligations organizational members have to the organization and its stakeholders."[26]

---

[20] Blair 2013, p. 4.

[21] Plender 2012, p. 16.

[22] Investopedia, Code of Ethics, http://www.investopedia.com/terms/c/code-of-ethics.asp. Accessed 22 December 2014.

[23] BusinessDictionary, Code of Ethics, http://www.businessdictionary.com/definition/code-of-ethics.html. Accessed 16 October 2014.

[24] Inc., Code of Ethics, http://www.inc.com/encyclopedia/code-of-ethics.html. Accessed 24 September 2014.

[25] Inc., Code of Ethics.

[26] Educational Portal, Code of Business Conduct: Ethics, Standards & Examples, http://education-portal.com/academy/lesson/code-of-business-conduct-ethics-standards-examples.html. Accessed 27 February 2015.

The finding that a code of ethics is – by definition – not necessarily binding must not be misunderstood to imply that it cannot be binding. On the contrary: Some argue, that "a code of ethics without sanctions [...] will be viewed by employees as merely a gesture without 'teeth'".[27] Consequently, it is postulated that a "properly framed code is, in effect, a form of legislation within the company binding on its employees, with specific sanctions for violation of the code".[28]

A detailed analysis of numerous codes of ethics shows that in many codes of ethics their binding effect is established by the code of ethics itself. Each norm addressee falling within the personal scope of the code has the obligation to comply with the code:

"Bank of America Corporation is committed to the highest standards of ethical and professional conduct. To help you understand how these standards apply to you and your teammates, this Code of Ethics provides basic guidelines for our daily conduct you are expected to adopt and uphold as a Bank of America *associate*."[29] The term "associate" is defined in a footnote and refers "to any Bank of America director, officer or employee".[30] These "associates" are the norm addressees of this code of ethics. The obligation to comply with this code of ethics is expressed with the "soft" wording that associates "are *expected* to follow the information in this code".[31] However, to avoid misunderstandings that this could be only a recommendation, the introduction to this Code of Ethics ends with a reference to the legal consequences of violations of this Code: "Violation of the Code of Ethics or these other policies, law or regulations constitutes grounds for disciplinary action, including termination of employment and possible legal action."[32] All substantive elements of a binding rule are given and all ethical principles, as defined in this Code of Ethics have become binding for the associates (as norm addressees).

A very short (two pages) Code of Ethics was published by the CFA Institute:[33] The enumeration of six principles of ethics is preceded by an introduction that firstly describes the norm addressees and secondly establishes the liability: "Members of CFA Institute (including CFA charterholders) and candidates for the CFA designation ('Members and Candidates') must: [...]".

The "sanctions" are described in the "Preamble": "Violations may result in disciplinary sanctions by CFA Institute. Sanctions can include revocation of membership, revocation of candidacy in the CFA Program, and revocation of the right to use the CFA designation." Again, all substantive elements of a binding rule are given.

---

[27] Inc., Code of Ethics.

[28] Inc., Code of Ethics.

[29] Bank of America Corporation, Code of Ethics, revised January 2009, http://www.media.corporate-ir.net/media_files/irol/71/71595/corpgov/CodeofEthics12908.pdf. Accessed 22 November 2014. p. 5 (emphasis added).

[30] Bank of America Corporation, Code of Ethics, revised January 2009, p. 6 footnote 3.

[31] Bank of America Corporation, Code of Ethics, revised January 2009, p. 6 (emphasis added).

[32] Bank of America Corporation, Code of Ethics, revised January 2009, p. 6.

[33] CFA Institute, Code of Ethics and Standards of Professional Conduct, http://www.cfapubs.org/doi/pdf/10.2469/ccb.v2014.n6.1. Accessed 15 September 2014.

The "Code of Ethics and Business Conduct" of U.S. Bank[34] contains all substantive elements of a binding rule in a blue coloured frame, which is part of the table of contents:[35] It is worth mentioning that this section starts with the sanctions: "*Anyone* who violates the U.S. Bank Code of Ethics and Business Conduct may face disciplinary action, up to and including termination."[36] But the term "anyone" is restricted in the very next sentence to the effect that the "U.S. Bank Code of Ethics and Business Conduct applies to all employees and directors of U.S. Bank and its affiliates". Again, all substantive elements of a binding rule are given.

The "Code of Business Conduct and Ethics of UBS"[37] contains two of the substantive elements of a binding norm in its "Preface" (concerning norm addressees and binding effects): According to the first paragraph of the preface this code "sets out the principles and practices that are *binding* for *all of the UBS's employees and Board members* to follow unreservedly both in letter and in spirit".[38] In the last paragraph of the preface, the binding nature of the UBS-Code is emphasized again: "Compliance with the principles set out in the Code is mandatory."

The chapter "Disciplinary measures"[39] contains the two subchapters "Violations" and "Appropriate action". In subchapter "Violations" is twice – that is redundant – very strikingly expressed that UBS will not tolerate violations of the Code. Subchapter "Appropriate action" refers to the appropriate actions of UBS to address violations: "Disciplinary measures may include reprimands, warnings, demotion and dismissal." Again, all substantive elements of a binding rule are given.

The substantive elements of a binding norm are formulated very clearly also in the RZB Group Code of Conduct ("RZB Group CoC"): [40]

The norm addressees, called "Target Group", are defined in Sect. 1.2 § 1 RZB Group CoC as follows: "The provisions of the RZB Group CoC apply to, and have to be observed by, all employees of the RZB Group globally." Section 1.2 § 2 RZB Group CoC refers to some details concerning the question of what is really meant by "globally": "Thus the RZB Group CoC applies to all employees in foreign branches, subsidiaries, whether directly or indirectly controlled by RZB, and companies in which a majority interest is held." Very interesting is the last sentence of Sect. 1.1 § 2 RZB Group CoC, which takes into account the fact that the RZB Group CoC cannot be binding on third parties without further act: "In addition, all third parties acting on behalf and/or in the name of RZB Group must commit themselves to comply with the provisions of the RZB Group CoC."

---

[34] US Bank, Code of Ethics and Business Conduct. Integrity * Respect * Responsibility* Good Citizenship, https://www.usbank.com/hr/docs/policies/coeHandbook.pdf. Accessed 5 December 2014.

[35] US Bank, Code of Ethics and Business Conduct, p. 4.

[36] Emphasis added.

[37] UBS, Code of Business Conduct and Ethics, download from https://www.ubs.com/global/en/about_ubs/about_us/code_of_conduct.html. Accessed 12 October 2014.

[38] Emphasis added.

[39] UBS-Code, p. 10.

[40] RZB group, Code of Conduct, http://www.rbinternational.com/eBusiness/services/resources/media/829189266947841370-829188968716049154_866477530159365956-829819009011584386-1-2-EN.pdf. Accessed 28 November 2014.

Furthermore, it is made perfectly clear in Sect. 1.3 § 1 RZB Group CoC that this Code is *binding*: "The RZB Group CoC is a binding set of rules governing everyday business dealings. The pursuit of profit does not justify any breaches of the law or the RZB Group CoC." This results in a de facto equality of the RZB Group CoC with the laws.

Finally, the RZB Group CoC also contains "Sanctions in Case of Violations of the RZB Group CoC":[41] "The RZB Group CoC forms an integral part of the general conditions of employment. Therefore, any breach of the RZB Group CoC has consequences under labour law and can be sanctioned by disciplinary measures, including termination of the employment without notice." Again, all substantive elements of a binding rule are given.

We can summarize as a further intermediate result: The codes of ethics as outlined above have in common that they *are* binding rules. The rules of ethics (as defined in these "codes") have changed their quality and become "binding rules". This also means that these specifications of general ethics have to be interpreted using the legal interpretation methods. The principles of general/global ethics (as mentioned above) will play an important role in the teleological interpretation of the individual codes of ethics.

From the viewpoint of their substance, the codes of ethics generally (i. e. not only in the field of finance) differ significantly: There are very short codes of ethics referring only to the principles of general/global ethics and there are also very extensive codes of ethics with very detailed and differentiated specifications of ethics, specially designed for the area in which the relevant company operates.

Furthermore, it was noticed that the title of the code ("of ethics", "of conduct" or "of ethics and conduct") refers to the main focus of the individual code: Codes of ethics focus on ethics and codes of conduct focus on conduct. Codes of conduct very often relate also to issues for which one cannot at first sight see the connection with the subject of ethics:

Take for example the RZB Group CoC, which also rules that the "RZB Group does not participate in the construction of nuclear power plants nor does it do business with nuclear power plants or their operators". This – binding – rule was therefore supplemented by an "ethical" reason: "Recent experiences show that the risks, associated with nuclear power plants both to the environment and human beings are currently not manageable."[42] The ethical justification of the rule concerning non-participation in business connected to war material weapons and other military equipment[43] is not apparent at first sight but can be found in the *argumentum e contrario*: "RZB Group does not participate in business connected to war material weapons and other military equipment (including equipment used for internal repression or aggression against foreign countries) with countries having ongoing or expected military conflicts or political unrest". *Argumentum e contrario*: Business connected to war material weapons with countries *not* having ongoing or expected

[41] Section 1.8 RZB Group CoC.

[42] Section 7.3 RZB Group CoC.

[43] Section 7.4 RZB Group CoC.

military conflicts or political unrest is *not* covered by this rule and seems therefore to be "ethical". Or not?

In any case, these two examples of a well-designed code of conduct show that the limits of what is ethical and what is not ethical seem very vague. It is therefore necessary to point out the duality of the global/general ethics to their specifications in the various codes of ethics in the field of finance. The latter *specify in binding form* the principles of global/general ethics, without thereby relieving the addressees of their moral obligation to comply with the principles of global/general ethics. "Even if the provisions of codes are followed to the letter, the ethical spirit which they are intended to embody may still not fully become part of a bank's culture in practice."[44]

6 Conclusions

- Ethics in finance means the specification of the general principles of ethics for the purpose of application and compliance in the field of finance.
- "Codes of ethics" or "codes of conduct" are instruments to specify these general principles of ethics for purposes of practical application.
- The majority of "codes of ethics" and "codes of conduct" are binding for the addressees listed in the relevant code.
- The majority of "codes of ethics" and "codes of conduct" contain sanctions.
- The rules of ethics (as defined in these "codes of ethics") have changed their quality and became "binding rules". These specifications of general ethics have to be interpreted using the legal interpretation methods. The principles of global/general ethics (as mentioned above) will play an important role in the teleological interpretation of the individual codes of ethics.
- "Codes of ethics" and "codes of conduct" do not relieve their addressees of their moral obligation to comply with the principles of global/general ethics.

References

Arrigunaga, J. (2000). Deposit Insurance Schemes: Reconciling Market Discipline with Financial Stability. In M. Giovanoli (Ed.), *International Monetary Law: Issues for the New Millenium* (pp. 323–354). Oxford: OUP.

Blair, W. (2013). *Is there a role for culture and ethics in the financial regulation? Functional or dysfunctional – the law as a cure. Risks and liability in the financial markets, International legal symposium, Stockholm, 30 August 2013, DRAFT*. http://papers.ssrn.com/sol3/papers.cfm?abstract_id=2313416

Blair, W., Cranston, R., Knowels, R., Russo, C., Kershaw, D., Fradd, E., Awrey, D., & Whittaker, A. (2014). *Law and Ethics in Finance Project. Response to the Banking Standards Review Consultation Paper 21 March 2014*. http://www.bankingstandardsreview.org.uk/assets/docs/

[44] Blair et al. 2014, p. 5.

responses/Law%20and%20Ethics%20in%20Finance%20Response.pdf. Accessed 27 February 2015

Fernandéz, B. F. (2012). Ethics vs. finance? An analysis of the origins, problems and future perspectives of this relationship. In C. Cosgrove-Sacks, & P. H. Dembinsky (Eds.), *Trust and Ethics in Finance: Innovative ideas from the Robin Cosgrove Prize* (pp. 297–314). Geneva: Globethics.net.

Ferullo, H. D. (2010). *La complejidad social del pensamiento económico, Ensayos*. Tucumán: Universidad del Norte Santo Tomás de Aquino.

Kant, I. (1786/1993). *Grounding for the Metaphysics of Morals* (translated by J.W. Elington). Cambridge: Hackett Publishing Company.

Plender, J. (2012). Preface. In C. Cosgrove-Sacks, & P. H. Dembinsky (Eds.), *Trust and Ethics in Finance: Innovative ideas from the Robin Cosgrove Prize* (pp. 11–16). Geneva: Globethics.net.

Ranaivoson, F. (2012). The reconciliation of finance an ethics: Integrating the interior and exterior dimensions of reality. In C. Cosgrove-Sacks, & P. H. Dembinsky (Eds.), *Trust and Ethics in Finance: Innovative ideas from the Robin Cosgrove Prize* (pp. 191–207). Geneva: Globethics.net.

Sifah, D. (2012). Ethics: An essential prerequisite of the financial system. In C. Cosgrove-Sacks, & P. H. Dembinsky (Eds.), *Trust and Ethics in Finance: Innovative ideas from the Robin Cosgrove Prize* (pp. 155–170). Geneva: Globethics.net.

Zehetner, F. (2009). Der kapitalverkehrsrechtliche Beitrag der USA zur internationalen Bankenkrise, Deregulation zum Zweck der Diskriminierung? In J. Aicher (Ed.), *Festschrift für Manfred Straube: Zum 65. Geburtstag* (pp. 427–443). Vienna: Manz.

The Importance and Impact of the Language Regime of the European Union on its Law

Margot Horspool

1 Introduction

I have known *Albrecht Weber* for about 15 years through our encounters at meetings of German and other European colleagues on subjects concerned with EU law. My knowledge of the German language and law has allowed me to participate in many such meetings which were not always accessible to those who do not master the language. *Albrecht* and I have recently embarked on an ambitious project on Comparing European Constitutions in English, based on his excellent work entitled *Europäische Verfassungsvergleichung*, which is in the process of being translated and adopted. We have identified a distinct gap in the legal publishing market concerning this subject and are aiming to follow the excellent example of *T. Weir* in his adaptation of Comparative European Law by *K. Zweigert* and *H. Kötz*.[1] I have also come to know *Albrecht* as a good friend and have recently shared our love of classical music in visiting several performances of the Salzburger Festspiele in July 2014.

European Legal thinking and scholarship is characterised by many common elements but equally by many differences which have had a greater or lesser effect on developments in the different legal systems and also within the same legal systems within the same country. This certainly applies to both Civil law and Common law systems, for example. Language has undoubtedly played a major role in such developments, although this is perhaps not always sufficiently recognised. To take just France and Germany as examples of the Civil law, the legal systems have, of course,

As *Albrecht Weber* has always shown a keen interest in the language question in the EU, which has been the subject of relatively little debate, particularly in the Anglophone part of the EU and outside it, I decided to base my contribution on an earlier article entitled: Over the Rainbow: Languages and Law in the European Union (In A. Arnull et al. [Eds.], A Constitutional Order of States? Essays in EU Law in Honour of Alan Dashwood [p. 99–122]. 2011. Oxford: Hart Publishing) in which, at the time of its publication, he showed great interest. The tenor of this contribution is, however, a different one, and attempts to show the extent to which the language arrangements have had an effect on common legal thinking in Europe, in particular through the case law of the CJEU of course, it has also been comprehensively reviewed and updated, in particular with new legislation.

[1] Zweigert and Kötz 1998.

H.-J. Blanke et al. (eds.), *Common European Legal Thinking*,
DOI 10.1007/978-3-319-19300-7_23

been shaped by historical developments, but also by their respective cultures, tightly bound up with their language. The Common law systems have developed individually too, although language has played a lesser role there, as many of the major systems share the same language. This in spite of the fact that, for example, the US and the case law have often been said to "be divided by a common language".[2]

Legal terminology, which evolved along with a particular legal culture, thus often does not have an exact equivalent in another language. For example, the civil law meaning of *delict* cannot entirely accurately be translated as *tort* in the common law. In the context of the European Union, this poses challenges in the implementation of regulations, as these laws may acquire subtle differences in meaning through the process of translation. This is less so the case with Directives, as they can be transposed more freely into national legislation, taking account of the special characteristics and drafting culture of the country. With the increasing mobility of European citizens, the number of cases with parties speaking different languages is likely to rise. Given the complexity of the demands of courtroom interpreting, legal interpretation requires extensive knowledge that goes beyond the translation of one language into another. Lack of proficient interpretation can give rise to errors which threaten the integrity of the justice process. Guaranteeing high-quality legal interpretation by rigorously trained professional interpreters should be entitled to generous assistance from public funds, as a requirement of the rule of law.

The use of many languages in a legal structure is well known in a national context, for example in the Russian Federation[3] or India[4], to name but a few. Closer to home there are examples of a multiple languages approach in countries inside and outside the European Union, such as Belgium (three languages: Dutch, French and German) and Switzerland (four languages: French, German, Italian, Romansh), but nothing on the scale of the European Union, which now boasts 24 languages (the latest being Croatian, when Croatia joined in 2013).[5]

It was not until 1958 that a first Regulation concerning the use and status of languages in the Community was adopted. It is clear from the text that the widening of the Community/Union in subsequent years was not in the mind of those who drafted the text, which is a relatively simple one. The distinction between "official" and "working" languages, although briefly mentioned in the Regulation, was not seriously put into practice until much later. This contribution looks at some of

[2] The Oxford Dictionary of Quotations attributes this rather hesitantly to *G. B. Shaw* but there seems to be a consensus that he probably never used these precise words, and that it is just a phrase polished up by many later.

[3] The Constitution of Russia allows the various Republics of Russia to establish official languages other than Russian (with the exception of Sewastopol, which was annexed by the Russian Federation along with the Republic of Crimea). Currently there are 35 languages which are official in certain parts of Russia.

[4] The official languages of the Republic of India are Hindi and English. However, the Eighth Schedule of the Indian Constitution refers to 22 *scheduled* languages, which have been given official status and recognition.

[5] Bulgarian, Croatian, Czech, Danish, Dutch, English, Estonian, Finnish, French, German, Greek, Hungarian, Irish, Italian, Latvian, Lithuanian, Maltese, Polish, Portuguese, Romanian, Slovak, Slovene, Spanish, Swedish.

the various ways in which the language regime, and the exponential growth of the number of languages, has contributed to shaping the nature of the development of the European Union and has undoubtedly had a profound effect on "Common European Legal Thinking".

The European Community and later the European Union did not, initially, concern itself to any great extent with problems which might be caused by language difficulties of any kind. The Member States in the 1950s and 1960s were still confident of a principal language such as French being sufficiently generally spoken and understood in the whole of the Community, not least by those actively involved in matters concerning the Community and its institutions, to feel the need (even if the political will had been present) to designate one or more "official" languages. In any event, the need for the presence of several languages was accepted as natural in such an entity which did not aspire to become a unitary state with the need for just one official language. The European Coal and Steel Community (ECSC) Treaty, the first Community treaty in 1952, does not even contain a provision concerning languages to be used in the Community.

The multitude of views as regards the exact legal and political nature of the European Union is rarely concerned with the contribution of the "language problem" created by the initial choice of more than one or two languages and the assumption that all languages were to be treated equally for all official purposes. This linguistic regime, together with the exponential growth in numbers of languages since, has shaped the development of the nature of the European Union to an extent perhaps not always apparent from official published sources. In fact, language and the language regime have in the past rarely been acknowledged as a major problem in the development of the Community.

This contribution attempts to shed some light on the difficulties and merits of the choices made by institutions and Member States as regards the use of languages in the European Union. Among the many problems that have grown over the years in the European Union, the linguistic regime is increasingly referred to. In the past, and until major enlargement of the Union occurred in 2004 and 2007, language did not play a major role in the public perception of the functioning of the European Union. It was not seen as a significant problem in the interpretation of Community law contained in the European Court of Justice rulings. In fact, the Court of Justice has, over time, developed methods of interpretation which so far have succeeded in coping successfully with multilingual texts, ranging from the development of "Community meanings" of words and expressions commonly used in the Member States (e. g. the term "workers"[6]) to the frequent use of purposive or teleological interpretation of Community legislation, moving beyond the wording of the legislation to examine its objectives. Even when the common law countries (the UK and Ireland) joined the Union in 1973 these methods used by the Court of Justice, which contrast with the favoured literal interpretation approach in the common law, continued to be used.

[6] See Case 53/81, *Levin v. Staatsscecretaris van Justitie* (ECJ 23 March 1982), as discussed below.

As a result, the use of these methods has increasingly filtered through into the statutory interpretation used by national common law courts. However, with the enlargement of the European Union by another 13 members since 2004, there has been the addition of another set of languages (from 11 pre-2004 to 24 in 2014). This number is bound to rise when more countries join. There is a growing awareness of the multilingual aspects of the Union and of the problems this may be causing. At the same time, as the Treaty of Lisbon evidences, there is a need to emphasise the advantages of linguistic diversity, as expressed, for example, in the fourth paragraph of Art. 3.3 TEU, which states that the Union "shall respect its rich cultural and linguistic diversity". However, the need to repeat this did not seem to arise in Title X Art. 167 TFEU, which does not mention languages or linguistic diversity, only diversity of cultures. The Charter of Fundamental Rights, which has become binding under the Lisbon Treaty, states (in Art. 22): "The Union shall respect cultural, religious and linguistic diversity." Perhaps the order of the words here is significant in terms of the desire to "play down" the linguistic element.

After the entry into force of the Lisbon Treaty, initially, there seemed to be a real impetus towards creating a greater awareness of the importance of language in the cultural development of the Union. In January 2007, the Commission developed a separate portfolio that included multilingualism in order to "reflect its political dimension in the EU given its importance for initial education, lifelong learning, economic competitiveness, employment, justice, liberty and security".[7] Quite a lot of activity was generated by the Commissioner in charge of the portfolio, with the organization of numerous events and initiatives. However, in a press release of 10 September 2014, the Commission announced that the unit currently dealing with multilingualism policy will be moved from DG Education and Culture to DG Employment.[8] While it remains to be seen how this organisational change will play out in practice, I share the concerns of the European Network to Promote Linguistic Diversity (NPLD) which fears that this "market-oriented approach to the languages of Europe" might subject the question of multilingualism in the European Union to "exclusively utilitarian" considerations.[9]

This contribution sets out firstly to explore the origins of the multilingual regime in the European Union, the efforts to come to grips with it and the attempts (none of which were wholly successful) to restrict the growing number of languages claiming official status with increasing membership. The multilingualism of EU Institutions is in stark contrast to the problem in the European Court of Justice, where the prevailing language is French, in particular in the deliberations of the Court. It is interesting to contrast developments in practical and ideological terms within the various Institutions of the Union and, more widely, within the Member

[7] European Commission (23 February 2007). A political agenda for multilingualism. Europa Memo/07/80 press release, http://europa.eu/rapid/press-release_MEMO-07-80_en.htm?locale=en

[8] European Commission (10 September 2014). The Juncker Commission: A strong and experienced team standing for change, http://europa.eu/rapid/press-release_IP-14-984_en.htm

[9] NPLD (September 2014). New European Commission: no place for multilingualism, http://www.npld.eu/news-and-events/latest-news/103/new-european-commission-no-place-for-multilingualism/

States, ultimately concentrating on the European Court of Justice. Looking to the future, I ask how it is possible to continue with the present regime at both ends of the spectrum. Finally, I include a section on rights to interpretation and translation in criminal proceedings, where I discuss the European Directive on Rights to Interpretation and Translation in Criminal Proceedings and the challenges of its implementation in the UK.[10] This appears to be a major step in the recognition of the importance of language in legal proceedings in national courts in the European Union.

2 Multilingualism in the European Union

The story is often told how the language regime in the European Communities was dictated by the interests of the original Member States. It is said that, although the original intention was to confine the languages to one (French) or at the most two (French and German), it was in fact the interests of Belgium, as much as those of the Netherlands, that made it necessary to have three, and then four, languages.[11] Belgium has three official languages, French, Dutch (Flemish) and German. German is spoken by a small minority in the east of the country, but Dutch is now spoken by a majority of Belgians and even at the time of the establishment of the European Coal and Steel Community, Dutch was one of the two major languages of Belgium and the Flemish part of the country was the less-developed and poorer part, with few people in the top echelons of politics and business, compared to the French-speaking Walloon part. This has led to a long period of conflict based on language between political parties and generally in society. The rise of the Flemish part of the country has now brought the two groups to a position of parity, with arguably a predominance of the Flemish part. During a political crisis which lasted from 2007 to 2011 Belgium, host to central European political institutions, threatened to split up into its component parts. While Belgium remains united, the country is divided along language lines, and the language problem was one of the main contributors to the crisis.[12]

When the European Communities were created, it was thought that it was Belgium which insisted on having Dutch as one of the languages. This inevitably meant that Italian had to be added as well. The first indication of the linguistic regime is after the establishment of the European Economic Community (EEC), when the Treaty of Rome entered into force in 1958.[13] The first regulation adopted in pur-

[10] See Sect. 3.

[11] French, German, Italian and Dutch, respectively.

[12] The "Belgian problem" is too complex to comment upon further here, and is beyond the remit of this article. See the contribution by *F. Delpérée* in this volume.

[13] Art. 217 of the EEC Treaty (now Art. 342 TFEU) provided as follows: "The rules governing the languages of the Institutions of the Community shall, without prejudice to the provisions contained in the rules of procedure of the Court of Justice, be determined by the Council, acting unanimously by means of regulations.".

suance to this Treaty sets out the "official languages and the working languages" of the EEC: Dutch, French, German and Italian.[14] However, this was not the first treaty setting up the European Communities. The Treaty of Paris establishing the ECSC in 1952 did not contain a provision regarding the official languages. Nevertheless, it had been clear from the start that the languages would be French, German, Italian and Dutch. During the arduous negotiations leading up to the eventual conclusion of the Treaty of Paris in 1952, the linguistic regime had been thought to be one of the thornier problems to resolve. In fact, it turned out to be easier to agree on the persons who were to become the members of the High Authority, with *J. Monnet* as its President, than on the language regime to be adopted.

R. Schuman, the French Foreign Minister, somewhat predictably, proposed that French should be the only official language. This was opposed in particular by *K. Adenauer*, the German Chancellor. Apparently a "Benelux Minister" proposed English as the only language. We can only speculate how different developments would have been if that eminently practical (if counterintuitive) proposal had been followed. It would have made an initial saving on the budget and would now make a considerable difference in the expenditure of the Union and hence in the individual contributions by Member States. It would speed up the procedures and publications within the Union, and accelerate the rendering of judgments by the European courts. It would have done away with the problems attached to translation, comprehension and interpretation of so many languages. Conversely, it would perhaps have made the entire enterprise even less democratic than it is accused of being already, as active participation would have been made dependent on knowledge of a second language, then, and even more now, the preserve of a certain elite. The discussion then returned to a level more along the lines of national interest. The pressure for Dutch came from the Dutch, supported by the Belgians (at least as regards the Flemish Dutch-speaking part). Eventually agreement was achieved concerning the four official languages.[15]

The negotiators were all versed in more than one language and it is interesting to note that, contrary to what one might expect, the negotiations between *K. Adenauer*, *A. De Gasperi*, *J. Monnet*, *R. Schuman*, *D. Stikker*, *P. van Zeeland* and *J. Bech* took place for the major part in German, which was their common language. Far from French being the obvious choice, therefore, if the selection had been based on a language spoken by most of the Member States, it would probably have been German. Of course, this would have been a clear political impossibility at that time. It should be pointed out that German is still the most widely spoken mother tongue in the Union, taking into account that Germany, Austria and Belgium have German speakers, as well as parts of Italy and Denmark. While English remains the most spoken foreign language, 12% of the European population speak French as their

[14] Council Regulation No 1 *determining the languages to be used by the EEC*, O.J. B 17, 385–86 (1958).
[15] Spierenburg & Poidevin (1993), p. 50.

second language, closely followed by German, with 11% of Europeans.[16] The predominance of French as a second foreign language in the Union is continuing to lose ground. In 2010, 72% of EU documents were published in English, 12% in French and just 3% in German.[17] Until the establishment of the two European Communities in 1957, the language question was not regarded as important enough to be enshrined in official texts, and the four languages were all used equally in meetings, although with the determination of the official seat of the ECSC in Luxembourg it became inevitable that French began to dominate. A particular influence in this respect was exercised by the situation in the European Court of Justice, where from the beginning it had been determined (albeit not in any public document) that the prevailing language would be French.[18]

What happened next is well known. First, in 1973, the UK, Ireland and Denmark were the first countries to accede to the Communities, adding English and Danish to the equation. At that stage it was no longer possible to avoid the addition of Danish, although in different circumstances, if Dutch and Italian had not already been there, it would have been unlikely that Denmark would have insisted on having Danish. In 1981 Greece joined, bringing in Greek, in 1986 Spain and Portugal followed, with Spanish and Portuguese respectively, and then in 1995 Austria, Sweden and Finland joined, bringing in Swedish and Finnish. Until May 2004, therefore, the European Union operated with 11 languages. The twelfth, Gaelic, was contributed by Ireland, but this language is not a working language and is practically never used, except on ceremonial occasions when Ireland has the Presidency of the Union. The Treaty texts, too, were drawn up in 12 languages. Since 1 January 2007 the texts of the Treaties have been available in 23 languages, with each being "equally authentic".[19] The Croatian version subsequently followed in accordance with Art. 55.2 TEU.

The only country's language missing is that of Cyprus. Although frantic efforts were made to bring about reunification of the island, only the Greek part of Cyprus has so far been included in the expansion, so this does not add another language to the EU range. At one time, it seemed possible that reunification would occur before the date for enlargement. Referenda were called for April 2004 in both the Greek and Turkish parts of the island, but only the Turkish referendum passed and reunification did not occur.[20] In spite of accession negotiations with Turkey having

[16] European Commission Report (June 2012). Europeans and their Languages. Special Eurobarometer 386, http://ec.europa.eu/public_opinion/archives/ebs/ebs_386_en.pdf

[17] Published on EurActiv (29 June 2010), http://www.euractiv.com

[18] See Sharpston, E. V. E. (29 March 2011). Appendix 5: Written Evidence of Advocate General Sharpston. The Workload of the Court of Justice of the European Union (House of Lords European Union Committee), http://www.publications.parliament.uk/pa/ld201011/ldselect/ldeucom/128/12816.htm. See below, Sect. 2.

[19] See Art. 55.1 TEU.

[20] The plan had been a quadrilateral meeting on 23 March 2004 to take forward the talks on reunification with a view to imminent accession to the EU on 1 May 2004. The success of these talks put forward a referendum on both the Greek and Cypriot parts of the island. This had been planned so as to enable Cyprus to enter the EU as a unified island on 1 May 2004. However, the referendum, although resulting in a positive vote by Turkish Cyprus, resulted in a negative vote by the Greek part.

been opened in October 2005, those talks are still ongoing and considering the concerns of some EU Member States, for example over Turkish police's use of force in the context of the Taksim Square demonstrations in 2013 Turkish accession in the near future seems very unlikely.[21] Popular support for accession in Turkey itself is also declining.[22] However, other States are much closer to accession, such as Montenegro, Serbia and Iceland, followed by Albania and Macedonia, and possibly also Bosnia and Herzegovina and Kosovo. This would add another set of languages to the total.

The concept of official languages and working languages was introduced in Art. 1 of Regulation 1/1958.[23] The Council, in determining the language regime – an indication of an awareness of the importance of the issue – based the Regulation on Art. 217 of the EEC Treaty, which provides for unanimous voting. It refers to "official" and "working" languages only in its first article. The rest of the Regulation only refers to official languages. Art. 4 states that regulations "and other documents of general application" shall be drafted in the official languages. Thus, this applies to a vast amount of Community documentation, including regulations, directives and decisions, as well as many types of non-binding documents "of general application". Art. 6 leaves it up to the various Institutions of the Community to decide in their rules of procedure which of the languages are to be used in specific cases. To take the example of the European Court of Justice, its rules of procedure stipulate the use of any of the official languages in cases before the Court; witnesses may be authorised to use a language other than one of the official languages.[24]

Although the concept of the difference between "working language" and "official language" has been developed further (not necessarily enshrined in any legal texts, but purely in procedural working rules), there will still be many instances where all the languages of the Union will have to be used. To begin with, high-level official documents must be translated into all the languages. This includes any texts with legal force. Apart from the text of the Treaties, the primary source of all Union law, all secondary legislation, in particular regulations and directives, has to undergo this process. The same applies in matters of interpretation. To take the example of the European Parliament, the most transparent of the Union institutions, which holds all its plenary sessions and most of its committee meetings in public, the plenary sessions will always have full interpretation from and into all the official languages.

A distinction has been drawn between "active" and "passive" languages. Thus, passive languages are those which may be spoken or written, but where there will be no interpretation or translation into those, as it will be assumed that the speakers of

[21] European Commission, *Enlargement Strategy and Main Challenges 2013–2014*, COM(2013) 700 final.

[22] See Chaturvedi, A (23 December 2013). Turkish Accession Prospects to the EU in the Current Scenario. A Policy Brief, http://www.ceu.hu/sites/default/files/attachment/event/9199/working-paper-archana-chaturvedi0_0.pdf

[23] Art. 1 of Council Regulation No 1 of 1958: "The official languages *and the working languages* of the Institutions of the Community shall be Dutch, French, German and Italian" (my emphasis).

[24] Art. 29.4 of the ECJ Rules of Procedure (1991) O.J. L 176/7; see Case T-120/99, *Kik v. Office for Harmonisation in the Internal Market* (CFI 12 July 2001) as discussed below.

those languages will have a sufficient understanding of one of the active languages. Active languages will be those which may be both written and spoken and into which other languages will be translated. It is usually assumed to be easier to read something in a foreign language than to write in the same language. It is generally also thought easier to understand a foreign language than to speak it. In both cases (the written and the spoken word), even this may sometimes be arguable. It is certainly easier to speak, say, standard English or German to a certain level, than necessarily to understand a Scottish, Irish, Cockney or Nigerian accent, or, for that matter, the upper-class mumble of the "educated classes" or "estuary English" for those who were not brought up in those regions. An Austrian or Bavarian accent certainly sometimes causes great difficulties for interpreters whose first language is not German and even for native speakers who are from a different part of the country.

Various solutions have been looked at in the past and are constantly being considered. Many working documents are now routinely produced in the "working languages". In 1994, the French Minister of Foreign Affairs, *A. Lamassoure*, citing the example of the European Trade Mark Office, which works in five languages – English, French, German, Italian and Spanish – proposed the same practice should be followed in the internal workings of the European Institutions.[25] The European Parliament, however, reacted to this by referring to Art. 6 of the EC Treaty (now Art. 18 TFEU), which prohibits any discrimination on grounds of nationality, and to Art. 128 of the Treaty (now Art. 167 TFEU), which refers to the Union's duty to "contribute to the flowering of cultures of the Member States" and, in particular to the Union's duty to "take cultural aspects into account in its action, in particular in order to respect and to promote the diversity of its cultures".[26] As referred to above, linguistic diversity is now even contained in the Lisbon Treaty.[27]

In practice, however, many meetings of working groups and committees in the Commission or the Council, political groups in the European Parliament and cases heard by Chambers in the European Court of Justice will use a reduced number of languages, depending on the circumstances and practical requirements. This more or less informal practice is set to grow. In respect of the spoken word, there are additional physical difficulties. Any meeting which has an "official" character, such as Council of Ministers' sessions, and plenary sessions of the European Parliament and of the European Court of Justice of the European Union and its Grand Chamber currently employ the full panoply of languages, using simultaneous interpretation. This means that 24 interpretation booths have to be used, with considerable dimensions. This rules out many conference venues, leaving purpose-built ones in the usual venues of these meetings. One solution would be obvious here. It is often mistakenly thought that all the languages are interpreted directly from one into another, for example Greek into Danish. In fact, those who can interpret (or translate) one into the other are very few and far between. The usual practice, which has ex-

[25] Agence Europe, 22 December 1994.
[26] Art. 167.4 TFEU.
[27] See Art. 3.3 TFEU.

isted since the very beginning of the Communities, is that of "relay". A "minor" language, such as Dutch or Danish, will be understood by a minimum of two interpreters translating into one of the "major" languages, such as French, English or German, which is the working language of a majority of interpreters and translators. All will master at least one, and often more, of these.

Interpretation, say from Danish into English, will then be picked up by all the others and translated into their respective Greek, Czech and so on. There are two dangers inherent in this system. First, it means that, say, a Greek delegate will not only receive an interpretation with a greater delay than a French delegate, but also that his or her interpreter has to rely on a colleague, rather than on the original speaker, for what is being said. The danger of "glitches" is readily apparent and there are myriad stories of misunderstandings that have arisen through this method. In the European Parliament, where speaking time is often restricted to seconds rather than minutes, a delegate will usually beware of saying anything remotely colloquial or ambiguous, not to mention anecdotes, in making his or her point. An idealistic but inexperienced British MEP, speaking about the European Community "shooting the rapids of European integration", found himself confronted by puzzled Germans and others demanding what the shooting of *Kaninchen* (rabbits) could possibly have to do with the debate. And what of the German chairman, trying desperately to get a discussion going, whose question was rendered by the slightly bored interpreter as: "Gentlemen, who will open the bowling?", only to be faced by the sudden response from the British delegate: "Mr Chairman, it is the football season"? It is, in fact, surprising how few these incidents are, much of which, in my view, is undoubtedly largely attributable to the great conscientiousness and professionalism of the interpreters.

It has more and more become the practice to restrict the use of active languages in the Institutions, so that many meetings will use a greater number of passive than active languages. For example six or seven, up to 11, languages will be allowed to be spoken by delegates, but will only be interpreted into four or five, typically English, French, German, Spanish and Italian. Nevertheless, by law, all plenary sessions of the European Parliament, meetings of Councils of Ministers and many others still have to use the full array of official languages. The same applies, mutatis mutandis, to the translation of documents. Art. 24 TFEU provides that "every citizen of the Union may write to any of the institutions, bodies, offices or agencies referred to in this article or in Art. 13 TEU" in one of the languages of the Member States. Documents are now often translated at one remove, for example from Greek into English and from there into Danish or Hungarian. Most documents will always exist in the major "working languages". However, what is now occurring is that if a piece of legislation has been drafted in French and English, some of the translations will take the English text as its base (probably mostly those into the languages of the more recent Member States) and others will use the French as a base (certainly Italy and Spain, and possibly Romania). Many people are being trained as translators and interpreters in the "newer" languages.

However, there are fears that the EU will face a serious shortage of interpreters. Apparently, the knowledge of a foreign language by native English speakers has taken a rapid dive in the last decade and the European Parliament struggles to recruit English-language interpreters.[28] One of the causes was undoubtedly the decision by the British government to abolish the compulsory teaching of a foreign language at schools after the age of fourteen. The so-called "Paris Declaration" adopted at the International Annual Meeting on Language Arrangements, Documentation and Publications (IAMLADP) at the OECD in June 2010 warns that a "global shortage of qualified linguists" means that without a new generation of trained language professionals "international organisations will be unable to perform their vital tasks".[29] Various efforts are now being made to counter this threat. EU institutions are running joint awareness campaigns to encourage young people to consider language careers in Brussels. For example in November 2014, several events were organised in the context of a "Conference on translation and interpretation", which sought to "promote and raise the profile of language professionals" and to "shed some light on the challenges of this sector, the need for qualified linguists and the utmost importance of appropriate, high-level training".[30] Despite these efforts, one cannot help but fear that there will be great difficulties in the future unless the many already existing informal arrangements could be agreed officially and, ideally, at least the number of active languages could be reduced to a minimum. Allowing all Union languages to be used as passive languages where necessary could preserve the democratic element. However, an official arrangement regarding this would undoubtedly require unanimous agreement by all the Member States, probably by way of Treaty amendment. This does not seem likely at the present time.

A number of Union Agencies and other bodies have adopted different language regimes. An example is the language regime of the Trade Mark Office, which has not been without its problems. This is illustrated in the case of *Christina Kik*, a Dutch trademark agent in the Netherlands.[31] When the Office for Harmonisation in the Internal Market (Trade Marks and Designs) was set up, provision was made for it to operate in just five languages: English, French, German, Italian and Spanish. These languages were given official status, but other EU languages could be used in an application.[32] However, in such a case the applicant was required to indicate a "second language" on their application that would be the language of any proceedings, and this "second language" had to be one of the "official" languages. Ms *Kik* made her application to register the trademark KIK in Dutch and indicated Dutch also as the "second language". This application was dismissed as it was "vitiated

[28] EurActiv.com (6 April 2012). Parliament struggles to recruit English-language interpreters, http://www.euractiv.com/culture/parliament-struggles-recruit-english-interpreters-news-512000

[29] European Commission. Language Open Doors – Vassiliou backs international declaration supporting multilingualism, http://ec.europa.eu/commission_2010-2014/vassiliou/headlines/news/2010/06/20100628_en.htm

[30] European Commission (2014). Conference on translation and interpretation: Cultural and linguistic diversity – a challenge for democracy, http://ec.europa.eu/languages/events/2014/2811-tsd2014_en.htm

[31] Case T-120/99, *Kik v. Office for Harmonisation in the Internal Market* (CFI 12 July 2001).

[32] Art. 115 of the Council Regulation (EC) No 40/94 *on the Community trade mark*, O.J. L 11/1 (1994), provides for the language regime of the Office.

by a procedural irregularity". The Court of First Instance and the ECJ considered whether there was a Community law principle of non-discrimination as between the official languages of the European Community as alleged by the applicant, based on the wording of Regulation 1/58. The applicant argued that, therefore, the entire language regime established by Art. 115.2–6 of Regulation 40/94 was unlawful. This was rejected by both courts as Regulation 1/58, being a secondary instrument of Community law, could not be held to have laid down such a general principle. The ECJ stated:

> 84. Moreover, Article 217 of the Treaty [now Article 342 TFEU] authorises the Council to determine the rules governing the languages of the institutions of the Community, acting unanimously. It was in application of that provision that it adopted Regulation No 1, Article 1 of which lays down the official languages and working languages of the Community institutions. Those official languages are not, it will be observed, exactly the same as those identified in Articles 8d and 248 of the Treaty.
>
> 85. Further, Regulation No 1, in particular Article 4, requires that regulations and other documents of general application be drafted in the eleven official languages of the Union. It follows from that provision, and from Article 191 of the EC Treaty [now Article 294 TFEU] requiring publication in the Official Journal of the European Union of regulations, directives, and decisions adopted in accordance with the procedure referred to in Article 189b of the EC Treaty [now, after amendment, Article 294 TFEU], read in conjunction with Article 5 of Regulation No 1, which provides for the publication of the Official Journal in the official languages, that an individual decision need not necessarily be drawn up in all the official languages, even though it may affect the rights of a citizen of the Union other than the person to whom it is addressed, for example a competing economic operator.

3 The Special Linguistic Status of the Court of Justice of the European Union

The linguistic issues with regard to the Court are somewhat different from those of the other institutions. First, there is the issue of the language of the proceedings before the Court. The Rules of Procedure provide here that it is even possible to use a language which is not one of the official languages of the European Union in the oral proceedings in the examination of witnesses or experts if the Court's permission is granted.[33] To take an example: some of the Baltic states (e. g. Latvia) have a substantial minority population that speaks Russian. Although Latvian is the only official language, Russian can be used in court proceedings there. It is therefore wholly conceivable that an Art. 267 reference from a Latvian court to the Court of Justice would require the proceedings to be conducted partially in Russian. Secondly, although not specifically stated in the Court's Statute or Rules of Procedure (which do not refer to the language used in the judges' deliberations, whilst providing for everything else in respect of the use of language – even those which are not Community languages), it is known and accepted that officially the only language used in the Court's deliberations is French.

---

[33] Art. 38.7 of the CJEU Rules of Procedure of 25 September 2012, O.J. L 265 (2012).

When the Court was created in 1953 the reasons for this seemed self-evident. French was still regarded as the language spoken by the elite in the Member States, it was the language most used in international discussions and debates between European jurists, and it was the language in which most legal texts and articles intended for an international audience were written. Comparative law, as understood and studied at the time in Continental Europe, concerned principally the comparison between different civil law systems, particularly those of France and Germany. The International Court of Justice (ICJ) in The Hague and the European Court of Human Rights (ECtHR) in Strasbourg both use only French and English in their deliberations. It is quite likely, therefore, that the same practice would have been followed by the Court of Justice if the UK had been one of the founder members of the Community. As it was, the Court ended up with one language only in respect of its deliberations. This led quite naturally to French being used as the general working language of the Court as the procedural rules and the grounds for judicial review in the Treaties were closely aligned on the rules in French administrative law. This was perfectly acceptable with the six founder members, where jurists generally had a mastery of French.

When Denmark, Ireland and the UK joined in 1973, this became less obviously the case. However, by then the practice was entrenched and, on the whole, care was taken to appoint judges and advocates general to the Court who had a mastery of French. This was becoming more difficult, however, with the first accessions, and with the advent of Greece, Spain and Portugal the problem was somewhat aggravated though still manageable. The addition of the two Nordic countries and Austria compounded the problem. Now, however, with 13 new members, 11 of whom are Central or Eastern European, where French is not widely spoken and English (and sometimes even German) is the more prevalent second language, the difficulties have become more serious. The judges rarely deliberate in a plenary composition as a full Court, and chambers consisting of three or five judges hear most cases. They sit as a Grand Chamber of 13 judges when this is requested by an institution or a Member State which is party to the proceedings.[34] It would seem that, at least in the case of the normal hearings in chambers, there could be a choice of either an additional language (possibly English in most cases) for the deliberations or another language as the single language for the Chamber, in order to avoid having to have interpretation. It is possible that in practice the latter is already happening to some extent.

It is interesting to speculate how influential the French filtering effect has been in practice, both in the selection of judges and advocates general and that of other Court officials, such as registrars and, in particular, judges' clerks. As the choice of the language of deliberation is in law a matter for the Court to decide, in theory a change could be made in the near future. This, however, would require unanimous agreement by the members of the Court, just as the judgments do. This may prove difficult, not least as the retention of French as the sole language of deliberation for

[34] Art. 16 of the Protocol on the Statute of the ECJ added by the Treaty of Nice.

so long may be attributed to some extent to judicial conservatism or, very likely, to a combination of French cultural hubris and others' cultural cringe.

It should be pointed out, however, that neither the ICJ nor the ECtHR seem to experience any great difficulty from the fact that their deliberations are in both French and English, with bilingual documents and simultaneous interpretation. Even in the Vatican, admittedly not a court but surely one of the most conservative establishments in existence, Latin, while retaining its official status, has been in decline as the sole language of debate ever since the Second Vatican Council, for example in meetings of the College of Cardinals. Thirdly, there has been abundant case law dealing with the problems of interpretation of Union law in different languages when the language versions were not entirely equal or open to misinterpretation. It is inevitable that such instances will multiply with the advent of a large number of new languages. Conversely, it is true that the Court has become extremely adept at coping with the difficulties inherent in multilingualism, and has in a number of cases set out its view of how any discrepancies between statutory texts should be dealt with. In the well-known case of *CILFIT*,[35] which instructs national courts in the concept of "Acte Clair", the Court stated that a matter does not have to be referred to the ECJ for a preliminary ruling in the following circumstance:

> The correct application of Community law may be so obvious as to leave no scope for any reasonable doubt as to the matter in which the questions raised is to be resolved. However, before coming to this conclusion the national court must be convinced that the matter is equally obvious to the courts of the other member states and to the ECJ.

The ECJ adds more caveats:

> This possibility must be assessed on the basis of the characteristic features of Community law, as Community legislation is "drafted in several languages" (only seven in 1982), all equally authentic and that, even if the different language versions are "completely in accord with one another". Community law first of all uses terminology which is peculiar to it, secondly legal concepts do not necessarily have the same meaning in Community law and in national law,[36] and thirdly "every provision of Community law must be placed in its context and interpreted in the light of the provisions of Community law as a whole, regard being had to the objectives thereof and to its state of evolution at the date on which the provision in question is to be applied".[37]

In the early case of *Stauder v. City of Ulm*,[38] when the Community only had four languages, the Court had to deal with a decision regulating the sale of "Christmas butter" to poor pensioners. It stipulated that Member States had to take all necessary measures to ensure that the butter reached the right recipients, and to this end the German version stated that beneficiaries had to produce a coupon bearing their name, whereas in the other (French and Italian) versions the coupon simply had to

[35] Case 283/81, *CILFIT et al v. Ministry of Health* (ECJ 6 October 1982).
[36] For example in Case 53/81, *Levin v. Staatsscecretaris van Justitie* (ECJ 23 March 1982), the ECJ defined the concept of "worker" as a Community concept, different from that in Member States; Art. 17 EC introduces "Citizenship of the Union" which "shall complement and not replace national citizenship".
[37] Case 283/81, *CILFIT et al v. Ministry of Health* (ECJ 6 October 1982) para 20.
[38] Case 29/69, *Stauder v. City of Ulm* (ECJ 12 November 1969).

"refer to the person concerned", thus leaving other possibilities open. Mr *Stauder* felt his human rights had been infringed by the divulging of his name to retailers. The Court pointed out that, for the sake of uniform interpretation of Community law, in such a case one could not look at one version in isolation but the real intention of the draftsman could only be gleaned from looking at all four language versions. In the view of the Court, not surprisingly, the most liberal interpretation had to prevail, provided that it achieved sufficiently the objective pursued by the decision. It could not be accepted that the authors' intention was to impose a stricter obligation on one Member State than on another.

Case C-72/95 *Kraaijeveld v. Gedeputeerde Staten van Zuid-Holland* concerned the Dutch interpretation of the text of a directive which provided for environmental protection consisting of "canalization and flood relief works". The Dutch government, which maintained that the Dutch version for its purposes was the only authentic one, contended that its implementation of the Directive excluding dykes below a certain size from this category (5 km in length) should be accepted. This would mean no environmental impact assessment would be necessary for such a dyke. Flood relief and canalisation work is carried out to regulate water flow or for the benefit of river navigation. This changes the character of the watercourse itself and the flora and fauna in and around the river. Dyke reinforcement work does not have any such effect. The Court answered these arguments by pointing out that, as it had said in *CILFIT*, interpretation of a provision of Community law involved a comparison of the language versions. In case of divergence between these, the provision should be interpreted by reference to "the purpose and the general scheme of the rules of which it forms part".[39] There then follows an examination of all the language versions in the annex to the directive concerned. The English and Finnish are similar ("canalization and flood relief works"), whereas the German, Greek, Spanish, French, Italian, Dutch and Portuguese versions refer to canalisation and regulation of watercourses. The Danish and Swedish versions contain one single expression reflecting the idea of regulating watercourses. The Court then wisely points out that the purpose and general scheme of the directive indicate that it has a broad objective and that, therefore, the annex must be interpreted to encompass all works for retaining water and preventing floods, and therefore dykeworks, "even if not all the linguistic versions are so precise".[40]

The Court's method of interpreting Union law according to the "purpose and the general scheme" of the provisions in question is one it uses very generally, whether there is a linguistic diversion or not, as we can see in one of the earliest, and probably the best known, of its cases, Case 26/62 *van Gend & Loos v. Nederlandsche Administratie der Belastingen*,[41] where it interprets a Treaty article "in the light of the spirit and the general scheme of the Treaty" in order to define the doctrine of

[39] Case C-72/95, *Kraaijeveld v. Gedeputeerde Staten van Zuid-Holland* (ECJ 24 October 1996) para 28.

[40] Case C-72/95, *Kraaijeveld v. Gedeputeerde Staten van Zuid-Holland* (ECJ 24 October 1996) para 31.

[41] Case 26/62, *van Gend and Loos* (ECJ 5 February 1963).

direct effect of Community law, entitling individuals to rely on Community law before their national courts. A further method used by the Court for overcoming the difficulty of different meanings of the same word is to give a "Community definition" (now, presumably, to be referred to as a "Union" definition) of such a word, as it did, for example, in Case 53/81 *Levin v. Staatssecretaris van Justitie*[42] to forge a Community meaning for the word "worker" (in German "Arbeitnehmer"). Over the years, the ECJ has developed not just its own style, but undoubtedly a unique way of looking at and interpreting Union law. Although many of the features and workings of the Court have grown to resemble common law methods, and much of the Court's reasoning, not to mention its straying beyond the confines of interpretation into the realms of lawmaking and setting precedent, is often regarded by civil lawyers as resembling that of the common law judge, the principal method of statutory interpretation in the common law, to look at the literal meaning, cannot be generally used by the Court.

I have mentioned only some examples of the difficulties such interpretation would cause. Nor is the interpretation necessarily that of a civil law court, which would use "travaux préparatoires" and teleological or contextual interpretation. It borrows from all these methods, but mostly prefers its own approach, accentuating the need to balance the interests of institutions against those of Member States and/or individuals, and interpreting Union law accordingly both in respect of the place of provisions in the Treaties, their "spirit and general scheme", weighing them with a view to balancing those interests, and giving the maximum possible effect to those legal provisions in terms of Union interests. In the interests of legal certainty, as the Court emphasised in *CILFIT*, it is concerned particularly with the uniform interpretation of Union law. This was apparent in Joined Cases C-261/08 and C-348/08 *Zurita García and Choque Cabrera*,[43] referred to the Court of Justice by the Spanish *Tribunal Superior de Justicia de Murcia*. These cases concerned the issue whether the Convention implementing the Schengen Agreement (the CISA) and the Schengen Borders Code require the competent authorities in the Member States to adopt a decision to expel any third-country national who has been determined to be unlawfully present on the territory of a Member State. Two expulsion orders were adopted against two Bolivian nationals, Mrs *Garcia* and Mr *Cabrera*, because they were unlawfully present on Spanish territory. Art. 6b of the CISA, which has now been replaced with the same wording by Art. 11.3 of Regulation 562/2006, provides:

1. If the travel document of a third-country national does not bear an entry stamp, the competent national authorities may presume that the holder does not fulfill, or no longer fulfills, the conditions of duration of stay applicable within the Member State concerned.
2. This presumption may be rebutted where the third-country national provides, by any means, credible evidence such as transport tickets or proof of his or her

[42] Case 53/81, *Levin v. Staatsscecretaris van Justitie* (ECJ 23 March 1982).
[43] Joined Cases C-261/08 and C-348/08, *María Julia Zurita García and Aurelio Choque Cabrera v. Delegado del Gobierno en la Región de Murcia* (ECJ 22 October 2009).

presence outside the territory of the Member States, which shows that he or she has respected the conditions relating to the duration of a short stay.

3. Should the presumption referred to in paragraph 1 not be rebutted, the third-country national may be expelled by the competent authorities from the territory of the Member States concerned.

Art. 23 of the CISA states:

1. Aliens who do not fulfill or who no longer fulfill the short-stay conditions applicable within the territory of a Contracting Party shall normally be required to leave the territories of the Contracting Parties immediately. [...]
3. Where such aliens have not left voluntarily or where it may be assumed that they will not do so or where their immediate departure is required for reasons of national security or public policy, they must be expelled from the territory of the Contracting Party in which they were apprehended, in accordance with the national law of that Contracting Party. If under that law expulsion is not authorized, the Contracting Party concerned may allow the persons concerned to remain within its territory.

According to Spanish law and the interpretation thereof, the penalty imposed in such an instance is to be restricted to a fine, except where there is an additional factor which would justify replacing the fine with expulsion. The Court stated that it was clear from the interpretation of the provision by the Spanish Supreme Court (*Tribunal Supremo*) that any decision must be specifically reasoned and must comply with the principle of proportionality.[44] Spanish law provides for a fine to be paid unless there are additional factors which would justify expulsion. The third-country national may, however, provide credible evidence to rebut the presumption of unlawful stay and show to have compliance with the conditions relating to the duration of a short stay. Pursuant to Art. 6b.3 of the CISA (now Art. 11.3 of Regulation No 562/2006[45]), should the presumption not be rebutted, the third-country national *may* (my italics) be expelled by the competent authorities from the territory of the Member States concerned. It was correct, as the Commission pointed out, that there is a discrepancy between the wording of the Spanish-language version of Art. 11.3 of Regulation No 562/2006 and that of the other language versions. The Spanish language stated that the competent authorities "shall expel" the third-country national if the presumption is not rebutted, whereas in all the other language versions expulsion is an option, not an obligation for those authorities.[46]

According to its settled case law, the Court emphasised the need for uniform application and interpretation of Community law,[47] which therefore made it im-

[44] Joined Cases C-261/08 and C-348/08, *María Julia Zurita García and Aurelio Choque Cabrera v. Delegado del Gobierno en la Región de Murcia* (ECJ 22 October 2009) para 22.

[45] O.J. L 105/11 (2006).

[46] Joined Cases C-261/08 and C-348/08, *María Julia Zurita García and Aurelio Choque Cabrera v. Delegado del Gobierno en la Región de Murcia* (ECJ 22 October 2009) para 52 et seq.

[47] E. g. in Case 29/69, *Stauder v. City of Ulm* (ECJ 12 November 1969) para 3; Case 55/87, *Moksel Import und Export* (ECJ 7 July 1988) para 15; Case C-268/99, *Jany and Others* (ECJ 20 November 2001) para 47; and Case C-188/03, *Junk* (ECJ 27 January 2005) para 33.

possible to consider one version of the text in isolation, but requires that "it be interpreted on the basis of both the real intention of its author and the aim he seeks to achieve, in the light, in particular, of the versions in all languages".[48] Thus, it came to the logical conclusion that wording used in one language version of a Community provision could not serve as the sole basis for the interpretation of that provision, or be made to override the other language versions in that regard. The discretionary nature of the power of expulsion was also confirmed by the Advocate General as appearing in the Spanish language version of the Art. 6b of the CISA. The Court stated that:

> In the present cases, as the Spanish-language version of Article 11(3) of Regulation No 562/2006 is the only one which diverges from the wording of the other language versions, it must be concluded that the real intention of the legislature was not to impose an obligation on the Member States concerned to expel, from their territory, third-country nationals in the event that they have not succeeded in rebutting the presumption referred to in Article 11(1), but to grant those Member States the option of so doing.[49]

It was up to the national law to lay down the basic rules, but it was clear from the information provided to the Court in the course of the written procedure that, under national law, a decision imposing a fine was not a permit for a third-country national unlawfully present in Spain to remain legally on Spanish territory. It was also apparent that in case of failure to comply with any decision to leave, irrespective of whether the fine had been paid, a third-country national may be prosecuted under Art. 53 (a) of the Law on Aliens and risks being expelled with immediate effect. The Court therefore concluded that:

> Consequently, the reply to the question referred is that Articles 6b and 23 of the CISA and Article 11 of Regulation No 562/2006 must be interpreted as meaning that, where a third-country national is unlawfully present on the territory of a Member State because he or she does not fulfil, or no longer fulfils, the conditions of duration of stay applicable there, that Member State is not obliged to adopt a decision to expel that person.[50]

This is a striking example of the difficulty which may arise with a difference in translation which is considerably more than a nuance. In this case, there was, perhaps, an advantage in having many language versions. If there is only one version that is different from all the others, this may constitute a stronger argument in favour of coming down on the side of all those other language versions. This is true, in particular, when the Court wishes to give the widest possible interpretation favouring the individual to the language in EU legislation. However, what if a number of the other language versions also contained an obligation rather than an option?[51] Examples of such language problems are still relatively rare, but are

[48] Joined Cases C-261/08 and C-348/08, *María Julia Zurita García and Aurelio Choque Cabrera v. Delegado del Gobierno en la Región de Murcia* (ECJ 22 October 2009) para 55.
[49] Joined Cases C-261/08 and C-348/08, *María Julia Zurita García and Aurelio Choque Cabrera v. Delegado del Gobierno en la Región de Murcia* (ECJ 22 October 2009) para 56.
[50] Joined Cases C-261/08 and C-348/08, *María Julia Zurita García and Aurelio Choque Cabrera v. Delegado del Gobierno en la Región de Murcia* (ECJ 22 October 2009) para 66.
[51] European Commission, *Proposal for a council framework decision on certain procedural rights in criminal proceedings throughout the EU*, COM(2004) 328, O.J. C 295/1 (2009).

bound to increase with the rise in the number of languages in the Union. There are many other factors which will play a role in this respect. It is not just the number of languages which will contribute, there is also an increasing danger connected with educational factors. The teaching of languages in the Union has been steadily deteriorating, and not just in the UK, although it is being felt acutely there.[52]

4 Interpretation and Translation in Criminal Proceedings

The growing awareness of linguistic problems is shown in the adoption of a directive concerned with interpretation and translation in criminal proceedings. On 30 November 2009, the Justice Council adopted a roadmap for strengthening the procedural rights of suspected or accused persons in criminal proceedings. The roadmap called for the adoption of five measures covering some important procedural rights, based on a "step-by-step" approach and invited the Commission to present the necessary proposals to this end. Directive 2010/64/EU on the right to interpretation and translation in criminal proceedings, which entered into force on 20 October 2010 addresses the objectives of measure A of the EU's roadmap.[53] The Stockholm Programme,[54] adopted by the European Council of 10–11 December 2009, refers to the roadmap and reaffirms the importance of the rights of the individual in criminal proceedings as a fundamental value of the Union and an essential component of mutual trust between Member States and of public confidence in the EU. The explanatory memorandum to the Directive refers to rights to translation and interpretation under the ECHR and the EU Charter. Art. 5.2 ECHR, the right to liberty and security, states: "Everyone who is arrested shall be informed promptly, in a language which he understands, of the reasons for his arrest and of any charge against him ...".

Art. 6 ECHR, the right to a fair trial, states:

(3) Everyone charged with a criminal offence has the following minimum rights:

  (a) to be informed promptly, in a language which he understands and in detail, of the nature and cause of the accusation against him; ...
  (e) to have the free assistance of an interpreter if he cannot understand or speak the language used in court.

These rights are also enshrined in the Charter of Fundamental Rights of the European Union in its Art. 6 and 47–50. In particular, Art. 47 EUCFR guarantees the right to a fair trial, including the right to legal advice and representation; Art. 48 guarantees respect for the presumption of innocence and the rights of the defence.

---

[52] See European Commission (July 2012). Key Data on Teaching Languages at School in Europe 2012, http://eacea.ec.europa.eu/Education/eurydice/documents/key_data_series/143EN.pdf

[53] European Council of 30 November 2009, *Resolution on a Roadmap for Strengthening Procedural Rights of Suspected or Accused Persons in Criminal Proceedings*, O.J. C 295/1 (2009).

[54] European Council of 10/11 December 2009, *The Stockholm Programme – An open and Secure Europe Serving and Protecting Citizens*, O.J. C 115/1 (2010).

There are a few cases concerning the use of interpretation in the ECtHR, based on Art. 6. In *Luedicke, Belkacem and Koç v. Germany*,[55] the ECtHR stated that the accused has the right to interpretation free of charge, even in the event of his conviction. Interpretation should be of a high enough standard to enable the defendant to have knowledge of the case against him and to defend himself.[56] The right applies to documentary material and the pre-trial proceedings. In *Brozicek v. Italy* the ECtHR held that the standard of interpretation must be "adequate" and that details of the charge must be given to the person in a language that he understands. It is for the judicial authorities to prove that the defendant speaks the language of the court adequately and not for the defendant to prove he does not.[57]

Cuscani v. UK[58] is a case where the trial judge at Newcastle Crown Court, confronted with an Italian-speaking defendant who had asked for an interpreter and whose command of English was clearly totally inadequate, asked whether anyone in court who knew the applicant was fluent in both English and Italian and could act as an interpreter for the applicant. The applicant's counsel, without consulting his client, pointed out that the applicant's brother was present, and the court agreed to make use of him, if need be. The applicant's brother was never requested to translate any statement during the course of the proceedings. It subsequently transpired that the brother had a lesser command of the English language than the defendant. The interpreter must be competent and the judge must safeguard the fairness of the proceedings.

Directive 2010/64/EU sets out practical measures required for its linguistic provisions to avoid a repetition of a *Cuscani* situation. It thereby provides useful procedural flesh on the bones of Art. 5 and 6 ECHR. It specifically refers to cases brought under the European Arrest Warrant, which has shown the need for such a measure. The legal basis for the directive is Art. 82.2 TFEU, which provides for the ordinary legislative procedure to be used. The Article calls for minimum rules to be drawn up, of which this Directive is the first. Its provisions cover such matters as offering training to judges, lawyers and prosecutors, police and other relevant court

[55] Appl. nos. 6210/73, 6877/75, 7132/75, *Luedicke, Belkacem and Koç* (ECtHR 28 November 1978). The Court thus finds that the ordinary meaning of the term "free" in Art. 6.3 (e) is confirmed by the object and purpose of Art. 6. The Court concludes that the right protected by Art. 6.3 (e) entails, for anyone who cannot speak or understand the language used in court, the right to receive the free assistance of an interpreter, without subsequently having claimed back from him payment of the costs thereby incurred.

[56] Appl. no. 783/82, *Kamasinski v. Austria* (ECtHR 19 December 1989).

[57] Appl. no. 10964/84, *Brozicek v. Italy* (ECtHR 19 December 1989) para 41: "the Italian judicial authorities should have taken steps to comply with it so as to ensure observance of the requirements of Art. 6 § 3 (a) (art 6-3-a), unless they were in a position to establish that the applicant in fact had sufficient knowledge of Italian to understand from the notification the purport of the letter notifying him of the charges brought against him. No such evidence appears from the documents in the file or the statements of the witnesses heard on 23 April 1989. On this point there has therefore been a violation of Art. 6 § 3 (a) (Art 6-3-a).".

[58] Appl. no. 3277/96, *Cuscani v. UK* (ECtHR 24 September 2002).

staff,[59] and allows for a higher level of protection as these are only minimum rules. On the face of it, this measure provides for something which should be greatly welcomed, as some of the cases referred to above show. It builds on some initiatives taken by the Commission, such as a report with recommendations on the quality of interpretation and translation published in 2008 which include a curriculum in legal interpreting and a system of accreditation, certification and registration for legal interpreters, as well as the launch of an initiative for a master's degree in translation (EMT), using a network of existing programmes in legal translation at master's level throughout the EU.[60]

The UK has opted-in to the directive and has revised Code C. 13 of the Police and Criminal Evidence Act (PACE) accordingly. The urgency of this reform was recently put into perspective by the Minister of State for Justice, *Lord McNally*, who explained that there are about "800 requests a day for such interpretation. In the first quarter of its operation there were 26,000 requests in 142 languages."[61] While PACE seems to cover the requirements of the directive, there remain considerable practical challenges with regard to the quality of interpreters and the costs of the services.

The Ministry of Justice's Framework Agreement contract for the provision of public service interpreting came into effect on 30 January 2012. The Ministry's decision to contract out interpretation services has been subject to a welter of criticism. It appears it was taken largely out of cost-cutting considerations, with the main contract having been awarded to one company, which has imposed new terms and conditions under which interpreters are required to operate and has led to incidents, for example because of the use of unqualified or inexperienced interpreters, considered to be capable of undermining British justice and the right to a fair trial.[62] The decision of the Ministry of Justice has been termed "shambolic" by Members of Parliament[63] and was the subject of two parliamentary select committee inquiries, with the Justice Select Committee (JSC) publishing its report in 2013.[64] The Ministry's efforts to balance cost efficiency and the need to satisfy the considerable

[59] Art. 6 of Parliament/Council Directive 2010/64/EU *on the right to interpretation and translation in criminal proceedings*, O.J. L 280/1 (2010).

[60] See points 17 and 18 of the Explanatory Memorandum.

[61] House of Lords (9 July 2012). Parliamentary Debates – House of Lords' Official Report of Proceedings Hansard, HL col. 908, http://www.publications.parliament.uk/pa/ld201213/ldhansrd/text/120709-0001.htm

[62] Linguist Lounge (24 January 2013). Letter from Professional Interpreters for Justice to Helen Grant, http://www.linguistlounge.org/all-articles/the-letters-page/724-letter-from-professional-interpreters-for-justice-to-helen-grant

[63] The Law Society Gazette (4 February 2013). MPs condemn "shambolic" court interpreter deal, http://www.lawgazette.co.uk/news/mps-condemn-shambolic-court-interpreter-deal/69322.fullarticle; see also Institute of Race Relations (14 February 2014). Shambolic and Unworkable: Outsourcing of Court Interpreting Services, http://www.irr.org.uk/news/shambolic-and-unworkable-outsourcing-of-court-interpreting-services/

[64] See Commons Select Committee (2013). Interpreting and Translation services and the Applied Language Solutions contract, http://www.parliament.uk/business/committees/committees-a-z/commons-select/justice-committee/inquiries/parliament-2010/interpretation-and-translation-services/

demand for qualified interpreters in a period where major cuts in legal aid have been made and are taking effect are likely to lead to even greater difficulties in the future.

One may contrast this with the situation in Germany: Sect. 185.1 of the Courts Constitution Act states: "If persons are participating in the hearing who do not have a command of the German language, an interpreter shall be called in."[65] The costs are covered by the state.[66] Court interpreters are chosen from a database which is administered by the federal-state administration of justice department.[67] The right to a fair trial includes the need to recognise interpreters as an integral part of the justice system. The statement by *Baroness Jean E. Coussins* in the parliamentary hearings, for example, highlights this: "... the complaints we hear daily from judges and others about the failure to supply interpreters, or the sending of unqualified people with no experience of simultaneous interpreting and some people who were simply incompetent – in one case not understanding the difference between murder and manslaughter."[68] This statement makes clear that excessive cost considerations will have a clear impact on the right to a fair trial. High standards of interpretation and translation are essential to secure that right and it is clear that the excessive economy in interpreting and translation services will have a detrimental effect on the rule of law and thereby on the core of the justice system.

The privatisation of language services seem to indicate that policy makers do not see the provision of interpretation and translation as an integral part of the justice system, but as mere provision of a service. This is evident in cases like *Mihaly Ungvari*[69], where the Court of Appeal held that if the appellant had access to the free assistance of a "competent interpreter", he was not entitled to the assistance of an interpreter drawn from National Register of Public Service Interpreters, from which court interpreters had always been drawn in the past. However, this approach by the UK government could be considered to be in line with the "utilitarian" approach towards languages demonstrated by the EU Commission, for example in the recent decision of the EU to move the unit of multilingualism to DG Employment referred to above.

5 What of the Future?

Can a sensible solution be found for the problems described above? There is a need to strike a balance between democratic and cultural needs for multilingualism and practical and realistic considerations of language in a world which is increasingly

[65] German Courts Constitution Act (9 May 1975). Federal Law Gazette [*Bundesgesetzblatt*] Part I p. 1077, http://www.gesetze-im-internet.de/englisch_gvg/englisch_gvg.html

[66] See Sect. 187 German Courts Constitution Act.

[67] See Dolmetscher- und Übersetzerdatenbank, http://www.justiz-dolmetscher.de/

[68] Justice Committee (September 2012). Written evidence from Involvis Ltd., http://www.publications.parliament.uk/pa/cm201213/cmselect/cmjust/645/645vw50.htm

[69] Court of Appeal, *R v Ungvari* (18 July 2003), [2003] EWCA Crim 2346.

"globalised" and where the general language of communication is often inevitably English, in the use of computers, email and much else. This would call for concessions on the part of Member States which may be politically difficult to make, but should not be impossible if a realistic attitude prevails over outdated procedures and if, in particular, economic considerations are sensibly balanced against the basic human rights of individuals. With the continuing expansion of the European Union, who knows how many languages will be "official" languages in, say, 20 or 30 years' time? A number of 30, or even 35, languages would not appear to be fanciful. It is true to say that in the nearly 60 years which have elapsed since the first Community (ECSC) was established, when just four languages were used, the steady growth in numbers has been accommodated in various ways and by various methods without causing quite the enormous problems which one could have imagined.

At first, the distinct impression was for a long time that the issue was simply being ignored, or at least dismissed as not important. Regulation 1/1958 only appeared after the establishment of the EEC, albeit as the first regulation. More recently, with the promotion of "linguistic diversity" and the inclusion of language as part of a Commissioner's portfolio, the emphasis has been more on the protection of minority languages in the European Union than on facing the issue of the official languages. However, much of the practical side of the problem has been tackled by internal arrangements within the institutions without any binding rules ever being drawn up. It should not be forgotten that the EU has only ever been able to function as well as it has through the mutual co-operation and consensus between the Member States and institutions. Much of the legislation of the EU has been, and still is, passed by consent of all the Member States, something which is not always immediately realised by students studying the law of the European Union. It is not in the interest of institutions or Member States to propose, or try to pass, laws which Member States will simply try to avoid implementing, or even applying when they are implemented. It is, perhaps, a manifestation of the existence of a spirit of consensus in a constitutional order of states which transcends the character of a loose conglomerate of countries or even just a customs union concluded with purely national economic interests in mind, even if their interests still tend to converge based on national considerations. The Union's reactions to shocks such as the credit crisis in 2009 and the sudden realisation of the immigration issues arising from additional membership of what may be like-minded countries, but not countries with sometimes even approximately the same level of economic development, not to mention the very recent agonizing events in respect of the Greek debt crisis which led to a complete breakdown in trust between Member States, tend to show up the fault lines in the existing order.

Up to the present a consensus often tends to emerge, often at the very last minute, not necessarily in every detailed action, but in a broader spectrum. The same kind of consensus may be able to persist as to the use of languages, determining numbers as and when convenient and according to the varying needs of institutions and agencies. Nevertheless, such informal arrangements must reach their limits somewhere. The number of translators and interpreters inside the EU institutions rises exponentially with each addition of a new language. Buildings to contain ever larger numbers of translators (or can it all be done online eventually?) and, even more ludicrously, ever larger numbers of interpreters in ever larger interpreters' booths would add an intolerable burden to the Union's building budget. It would appear that the dilemma will have to be faced sooner rather than later. Major incidents concerning different translation or interpretation in a political or legal context appear to be waiting to happen.

References

Spierenburg, D., & Poidevin, R. (1993). *Histoire de la Haute Autorité de la Communauté Européenne du Charbon et de l'Acier*. Brussels: Bruylant.

Zweigert, K., & Kötz, H. (1998). *An Introduction to Comparative Law*. Oxford: Clarendon Press. Translated by Tony Weir

Multilingualism and its Consequences in European Union Law

Jacques Ziller

1 Multilingualism as a Fundamental Feature of EU Law

When discussing the nature of EU law it is common usage to highlight the principles of direct applicability and of primacy as the two fundamental features that distinguish EU law both from classic international treaty law and, to a certain extent, from domestic law. Increasingly reference is also being made to the consequences of the principle of sincere cooperation, which, contrary to direct applicability and primacy, is being expressly mentioned in the EU Treaties, i. e. in Art. 4.3 TEU. Strangely enough most of the EU law literature does not dwell on a fourth principle, which to my view is of fundamental importance to the nature of EU law, namely the principle of multilingualism. This is the reason why I thought it necessary to dedicate a whole section to multilingualism in my own handbook of EU law, in the chapter on Fundamental Features of EU Law.[1] Interestingly most colleagues, albeit acknowledging the originality of my approach, told me that you could not put multilingualism at the same level as direct effect or supremacy. *Albrecht Weber*, this book's addressee, is not one of the latter colleagues; on the contrary, throughout his major work on *European Comparative Constitutional Law*,[2] *Weber* clearly shows his consciousness of the importance of language differences, including the fact that "the signification of a concept may break away from its etymological sources and bring forward a different content; even concepts such as *Constitution, Verfassung, Grundgesetz, Grondwet* (the Netherlands) show differences in their significations."[3]

One issue is more important than the theoretical question of where to put the principle of multilingualism: the multilingual nature of the EU is only too often ignored by scholars who refer to only one language version of EU primary and secondary law, and – maybe worse – of CJEU case law. This is more and more common to the authors who use only the English language version for references, albeit writing in another language. Such an attitude sometimes leads to important

[1] Ziller 2013, p. 212–223.
[2] Weber 2010, p. 11.
[3] Weber 2010, p. 11.

H.-J. Blanke et al. (eds.), *Common European Legal Thinking*,
DOI 10.1007/978-3-319-19300-7_24

misunderstandings of the concepts used in EU law. Furthermore, due both to its multilingual nature and to the multiplicity of concepts to be dealt with in view of the growing number of EU Member States, scholars who are excellent specialists of domestic law very often encounter problems with EU law, due to the fact that the same words do not have the same meaning when used in EU law and in domestic law. This chapter will recall and develop the legal notion of multilingualism of EU law and its consequence, before discussing the autonomy of EU law concepts with regard to concepts that are being used with the same wording in the domestic law of EU Member States.

In way of introduction, it is worthwhile to give a few illustrations of misunderstandings generated by multilingualism. The first of those misunderstandings relates to a somewhat strange line of literature, which developed at the end of the 1990s in the framework of the discussion of a European civil code: some scholars started to explain that there could be no harmonization of property law because the EC had no competence in that field (which is true), in quoting Art. 295 EC,[4] according to which "[t]he Treaties shall in no way prejudice the rules in Member States governing the system of property ownership"; such a reasoning was implying that on the other side the EC had a competence for the harmonization of contract law or torts law (which is wrong), as there was no provision comparable to Art. 295 EC with respect to contracts or liability law.

Such a discussion seemed totally out of place to French or Italian native-speaking EU law specialists, but not too many others. A comparison between the four language versions of 1957 reveals the source of the misunderstanding. Art. 345 TFEU (ex-Art. 295 EC, wording unchanged since 1957) says "[l]es traités ne préjugent en rien le régime de la propriété dans les États membres" and "[i] trattati lasciano del tutto impregiudicato il regime di proprietà esistente negli Stati membri", making it obvious that the underlying issue was that of public enterprises and nationalizations, which existed in different forms in all the founding Member States, a hot issue of home political debate in all the Parliaments that would eventually have to give their authorization for ratification. The German version "[die] Verträge lassen die Eigentumsordnung in den verschiedenen Mitgliedstaaten unberührt" undoubtedly reflected the same idea. However the Dutch version said "[d]e Verdragen laten de regeling van het eigendomsrecht in de lidstaten onverlet", a wording that might be read in literal terms as *the Treaties shall not prejudice the regulation of property law in the Member States*. I submit that any EU lawyer accustomed to the methods of interpretation of EU law would come to the conclusion that the English version – which was produced in 1972 – did its best to reflect the idea of the French, German and Italian versions, which as a matter of fact was in no way contradicted by the Dutch version, and hence deduct that Art. 345 TFEU has nothing to do with the issues of conferral. On the contrary, as happens for contract law or torts law, if a legal issue arises that falls into the scope of EU law, there is no impediment for harmonization in order to solve that specific issue. This being said, the misunder-

[4] See Losada Fraga et al. 2012.

standings I am referring to with this example have not spilled over from academia to practice, to my knowledge.

A second example shows how multilingualism can raise political problems. The Constitutional Treaty of 2004 contained a provision that has been sacrificed in the Lisbon Treaty in order to save the reforms on which there had been agreement during the IGC of 2003–2004, and which had been proposed by the European Convention 2002–2003: Art. I-6 of the Treaty establishing a Constitution for Europe stated: "The Constitution and law adopted by the institutions of the Union in exercising competences conferred on it *shall have primacy* over the law of the Member States", "Die Verfassung und das von den Organen der Union in Ausübung der der Union übertragenen Zuständigkeiten gesetzte Recht *haben Vorrang* vor dem Recht der Mitgliedstaaten", "La Constitution et le droit adopté par les institutions de l'Union, dans l'exercice des compétences qui sont attribuées à celle-ci, *priment* le droit des États membres", "La Costituzione e il diritto adottato dalle istituzioni dell'Unione nell'esercizio delle competenze a questa attribuite *prevalgono sul* diritto degli Stati membri". It is worthwhile noting that the French text of the European Convention's draft Treaty (Art. 10) was saying "La Constitution et le droit [...] *ont la primauté sur* le droit des Etats membres", which was identical to the English version – knowing that the European Convention was discussed on drafts that were presented in English and French. Whereas the General Secretariat of the Council, which prepared the text that was submitted to the representatives of Member States during the 2003–2004 IGC, preferred to submit a French version that it deemed more elegant – a position that I do not share – the English version remained unchanged; that is probably not by chance. Indeed, discussion in Member States in the framework of the preparation and adoption of the Constitutional Treaty[5] showed that – at least for non-English native speakers – the word *supremacy*, which had been hitherto used by English language literature for the concept of *primauté/Vorrang* raised a lot of political opposition, while the word *primacy* raised less opposition, maybe because it was not used in US or UK law, contrary to what was happening with the wording of Article Six of the United States Constitution: "This Constitution, and the Laws of the United States which shall be made in Pursuance thereof; and all Treaties made, or which shall be made, under the Authority of the United States, *shall be the supreme Law of the Land*; and the Judges in every State shall be bound thereby, any Thing in the Constitution or Laws of any State to the Contrary notwithstanding".[6] As a matter of fact, the Spanish Constitutional Court constructed an entire reasoning upon the difference between *supremacía* and *primacía* in its Ruling of 13 December 2004 on the Constitutional

[5] See Albi and Ziller 2007.

[6] Emphasis added. On the whole discussion around *primacy* and *supremacy* see Amato and Ziller 2007, p. 89–113.

Treaty,[7] in order to reconcile as much as possible the supremacy of the Constitution in the domestic order with the primacy of EU law.

A third example shows how scholarship can be abused by non-existing conceptual differences in case law, due to varying translations. For some reason, the case law of the CJEU – at least before the adoption of the Charter of Fundamental Rights – contained variations in the translation of the words *bonne administration*: whereas the French version of the relevant rulings (which are always drafted in the French language) invariably said *bonne administration,* in other languages different terms are being used. For instance, in the German version of the *Burban* ruling[8] (a case where the language of the proceedings was also French, hence the only with authentic value), the translators preferred *ordnungsgemäße Verwaltung* instead of *gute Verwaltung*, *proper administration* instead *good administration*, *sana amministrazione* instead of *buona amministrazione.* The English translators sometimes used *sound administration* or even *good governance* for the same *bonne administration*, the Italian translators *buon andamento dell'amministrazione*, etc.[9] Much ado for nothing? The point is that there is a temptation for scholars who do not work on the French version to elaborate absurd typologies on the basis of non-existing differences. In order to offend nobody, I prefer not to give any references, but I can testify that I had to deal with doctoral students' works in the European University Institute, which showed the reality of such a risk.

Last but not least one such difference in wording is certainly at the root of some of the divergences between on the one side the CJEU and most of the non-German speaking scholars and on the other side the *Bundesverfassungsgericht* and a significant number of German *Staatsrechtslehrer*. The issue is the wording of Art. 51.1, first sentence EUCFR on the scope of application of the Charter. The English version says "[t]he provisions of this Charter are addressed to the institutions, bodies, offices and agencies of the Union with due regard for the principle of subsidiarity and to the Member States only when they are *implementing* Union law", the French "[l]es dispositions de la présente Charte s'adressent aux institutions, organes et organismes de l'Union dans le respect du principe de subsidiarité, ainsi qu'aux États membres uniquement lorsqu'ils *mettent en œuvre* le droit de l'Union"; but the German says "Diese Charta gilt für die Organe, Einrichtungen und sonstigen Stellen der Union unter Wahrung des Subsidiaritätsprinzips und für die Mitgliedstaaten ausschließlich bei der *Durchführung* des Rechts der Union". It is well known to specialists that the German wording was personally chosen by *Roman Herzog*, Chairman of the Convention which drafted the Charter, that it was one of the rare cases where the texts discussed in the Praesidium were not drafted only in the French and English versions, and furthermore that the English word *implementing* as well as the French *mettent en oeuvre* were chosen on purpose because

[7] Spanish Constitutional Court (Tribunal Constitucional de España), Declaration 26/2014, Case 6603/2004, Treaty establishing a Constitution for Europe (13 December 2004) – unofficial translation on http://www.tribunalconstitucional.es/es/jurisprudencia/restrad/Paginas/DTC122004en.aspx; see Perez-Tremps and Saiz Arnaiz 2007, p. 49.

[8] Case C-255/90 P, *Jean-Louis Burban v. European Parliament* (ECJ 31 March 1992).

[9] See Galetta and Ziller 2007.

they admit a broader interpretation than *executing* and *exécutent*. As a matter of fact the "Explanations" in the Charter[10] state that "as regards the Member States, it follows unambiguously from the case law of the Court of Justice that the requirement to respect fundamental rights defined in the context of the Union is only binding on the Member States when they act in the scope of Union law [*wenn sie im Anwendungsbereich des Unionsrechts handeln*] [...] The Court of Justice confirmed this case-law in the following terms: 'In addition, it should be remembered that the requirements flowing from the protection of fundamental rights in the Community legal order are also binding on Member States when they implement Community rules [*müssen bei der Durchführung der gemeinschaftsrechtlichen Regelungen aber auch*] [...]'". Those Explanations perfectly reflect the differences in positions in the Praesidium and can be used in order to support either interpretation: the restrictive one preferred in Germany and by the *Bundesverfassungsgericht*[11] or the broad one preferred by the CJEU in *Åkerberg-Fransson*[12] but also by most of the commentators in other languages.

2 The Multilingual Nature of EU Law

The multilingual nature of EU law cannot be compared with the experience of any other international organization and even less to that of most multi-lingual States, as a result not only of the number of languages involved, but also the fact that no language has a legal status superior to others.

Art. 3 TEU on the objectives of the Union provides that "[the Union] shall respect its rich cultural and linguistic diversity" and Art. 4 TEU that "[t]he Union shall respect the equality of Member States before the Treaties as well as their national identities". There is quite some discussion about the meaning of "national identities", but there are no divergences on the fact that language is a fundamental part of national identity. As a consequence, it not admissible to give preference to one of the official languages, whether English, French or any other language.

2.1 The Origins of EU Linguistic Regime

The ECSC Treaty of 1951 was drawn up in French only. It did not contain any provision on the use of languages of the Community institutions. However, the subsequent recognition of Dutch, French, Italian, and German as official languages and working languages of the ECSC was an easy decision for the Foreign Ministers of the Member States in the light of the practical necessities encountered in manag-

[10] O.J. C 303/32 (2007).

[11] German Federal Constitutional Court (Bundesverfassungsgericht), 1 BvR 1215/07 (24 April 2013).

[12] Case C-617/10, *Åklagaren v. Hans Åkerberg Fransson* (ECJ 7 May 2013).

ing the ECSC that foreshadowed the language regime of the two Communities that would be born a few years later.

Within the framework of the Treaties of Rome of 1957 the language issue was addressed and solved right at the start. Both Treaties were signed in the official languages of the Contracting States: Dutch, French, Italian and German. Art. 248 EEC (now Art. 55 TEU) as well as Art. 225 Euratom, listed the official languages of the Treaties (nowadays 24, since the accession of Croatia) and further provided that "the *texts in each of these languages being equally authentic*, shall be deposited in the archives of the Government of the Italian Republic, which will transmit a certified copy to each of the governments of the other signatory States".[13] Art. 217 EEC (now Art. 342 TFEU) provided furthermore that "by means of regulations the languages of the institutions of the Community [now Union] shall, without prejudice to the provisions laid down in the rules of the Court of Justice, the Council, acting unanimously."

The first Regulation ever adopted by the Council of the EEC is Regulation No. 1/58 *determining the languages to be used by the European Economic Community*,[14] which laid the foundations for full multilingualism. Art. 1 of Regulation 1/58 provided that "[t]he official languages and the working languages of the institutions of the Community shall be Dutch, French, German and Italian". Those were the four official languages of the Member States of the Communities until 1972. Dutch was the official language not only of the Netherlands but also one of the official languages of Belgium; French was the official language not only of France but also one of the official languages of Belgium and Luxembourg, and an official language in the Valle d'Aosta in Italy; German was not only the official language of the Federal Republic of Germany but also one of the official languages of Belgium and Luxembourg, and an official language in the Trentino-Alto Adige autonomous provinces in Italy.

On the occasion of the successive enlargements of the Communities and EU, the principle of multilingualism has always been maintained, and EEC Regulation 1/58 has been updated from time to time to take account of new accessions, and therefore the number of treaty languages has grown from four to seven in 1973, eight in 1981, ten in 1986, twelve in 1995, twenty one in 2004, twenty three in 2007 and twenty four in 2013. With future enlargements the same technique will be used as was used so far, i. e. adding a new paragraph specifying "by virtue of the accession treaties, are equally authentic versions of this Treaty language [. . .]", and correspondingly amending Regulation 1/58.

In 2005, the Council amended Regulation 1/58.[15] A special characteristic of this latest change was that it was not needed due to a new enlargement, but it only intended to "regularize" the position of the Irish language, which had until then a

[13] Emphasis added.
[14] O.J. L 17/385 (1958).
[15] Council Regulation (EC) No 920/2005 *amending Regulation No 1 of 15 April 1958 determining the language to be used by the European Economic Community [. . .] and introducing temporary derogation measures from those Regulations*, O.J. L 156/3 (2005).

somewhat special status, as Irish has been mentioned as one of the authentic treaty languages since 1973 but was not established as a fully fledged official/working language in Regulation 1/58. Ireland requested that Irish be added in Regulation 1/58 as a consequence of the acknowledgment of Maltese as a treaty and official/working language, with the revision of Regulation 1/58 that occurred as a result of the 2004 enlargement. In Malta, as in Ireland, there are two official languages: Irish or Maltese, and English. Albeit having requested and obtained the relevant amendment to Regulation 1/58, the Irish government has so far favoured maintaining the exemption – established since 1973 – of an Irish language translation for all the acts of the Union.

Art. 41.4 EUCFR provides for the right – also embedded in Art. 20.2 lit. d TFEU – to address the institutions offices, bodies and agencies of the Union in the language of one's choice and to obtain a reply in the same language. Provided it is one of the official languages of the Union. Art. 2 of Regulation 1/58 already provided in its first version that "[d]ocuments which a Member State or a person subject to the jurisdiction of a Member State sends to institutions of the Community may be drafted in any one of the official languages selected by the sender" and that "[t]he reply shall be drafted in the same language." The Regulation provided moreover in Art. 3 that "[d]ocuments which an institution of a the Community sends to a Member State or to a person subject to the jurisdiction of a Member State shall be drafted in the language of that State." The Treaty of Amsterdam in 1997 introduced into primary EU law the rule of Art. 20.2 lit. d TFEU according to which EU citizens enjoy "the right to petition the European Parliament, to apply to the European Ombudsman, and to address the institutions and advisory bodies of the Union in any of the Treaty languages and to obtain a reply in the same language."

To summarize the language regime of EU institutions, bodies, offices and agencies[16] in a nutshell, the principle is that all 24 languages are official and working languages, according to the provisions of Regulation 1/58. That Regulation applies in the absence of more specific provisions established by the regulation establishing an office or agency – as is the case for OHIM, the EU's agency for trademarks, whose working languages are only five.[17] It has to be stressed that the Commission's Rules of Procedure[18] do not establish what its working languages are, but Art. 25 empowers the Commission to establish rules of application of the Rules of Procedure; as a consequence the working languages of the Commission are identical to the official languages, albeit the main *de facto* working language is English (for about 65 % of non-binding documents which the Commission produces), followed by French (less than 20 %), German, Spanish and Italian (less than 15 % on the whole). The CJEU has a language regime of its own, established in Protocol No 3 on the Statute of the CJEU: the authentic language of Court rulings is the language of procedure of the case, i. e. normally the treaty language chosen by the

[16] For more details see Galetta and Ziller 2007.

[17] Council Regulation (EC) No 207/2009 *on the Community trade mark (codified version)*, O.J. L 78/1 (2009).

[18] Rules of Procedure of the Commission of 8.12.2000, O.J. L 308/1 (2001).

referring party or the language of the addressed Member State in case of a procedure for failure to fulfil its obligations. The provisions of Protocol No. 3 on the language regime are amongst those that can only be amended by the treaty amending procedure of Art. 48 TEU, while most of the procedural provisions of the Protocol can be amended through the ordinary legislative procedure (Art. 281 TFEU).

The issue of the cost of multilingualism is often being used instrumentally in order to request a reduction of the working languages or even of the official languages of the EU. As for costs, no precise figures are available; anyway the costs in time devoted to translation should be added to the financial costs. Complaining about these costs is rather sterile, especially in the light of more important values such as the rule of law and citizenship; after all, also democracy has important financial costs. At any rate, the principles of direct applicability and of uniform application of EU law have a necessary consequence, i. e. the availability of binding EU law texts in all the official languages of the Member States. If EU institutions were not to carry the costs of the work that is needed to establish all language versions of EU law, the relevant costs would have to be borne by citizens and legal persons of the countries whose language would not be an official language of the Union. Those budgets would have to bear not only the direct cost of translation, but also the costs arising from the absence of authentic value of the translated versions of EU acts. Indeed the absence of an authentic value of home-made translations would presumably lead to a multiplication of ill-founded court actions by individuals and businesses, and to a multiplication of infringement actions against Member States. It is better therefore to consider multilingualism as a fact the costs of which one can only work on marginally. It would be in any way wrong to think that the language problems in the EU may be reduced in the future with greater integration of Member States: in the United States of America the growth of multilingualism is becoming a novel issue in the discussion on democratic institutions and amongst others for participation rights.[19]

2.2 The Principle of Equal Value of all Linguistic Versions of EU Legal Texts

The principle of equal legal value of all language versions of EU acts is the central feature of the language regime of the EU. Multilingualism, as guaranteed by the Treaties and the Charter and by Regulation 1/58, is deeply rooted in the very nature of EU law.

As indicated by the CJEU in its *Skoma-Lux* ruling, the Court "has held that the *principle of legal certainty* requires that Community legislation must allow those concerned to acquaint themselves with the precise extent of the obligations it imposes upon them, which may be *guaranteed only by the proper publication of that*

[19] See for instance amongst many others Chen et al. 2007.

legislation in the official language of those to whom it applies [. . .].[20] In addition, it would be *contrary to the principle of equal treatment* to apply obligations imposed by Community legislation in the same way in the old Member States, where individuals have the opportunity to acquaint themselves with those obligations in the Official Journal of the European Union in the languages of those States, and in the new Member States, where it was impossible to learn of those obligations because of late publication. Observing fundamental principles of that kind is *not contrary to the principle of effectiveness of Community law* since the latter principle cannot apply to rules which are not yet enforceable against individuals."[21] The quoted judgement implicitly refers also to its jurisprudence in *Kik*, where the Court, contrary to the Court of First Instance held that "the Treaty contains several references to the use of languages in the European Union. None the less, those references *cannot be regarded as evidencing a general principle of Community law* that confers a *right* on every citizen to have *a version* of anything that might affect his interests *drawn up in his language in all circumstances.*"[22]

In case of divergence between the various language versions of the EU Treaties or Acts, the Court has clearly established that none of the versions prevails over the other; and this is true even if a version could be identified as an "original" text in which the document was drafted before being translated. Since the entry into force of the Treaty of Accession of Denmark, Ireland and the UK Danish and English versions of the previously existing law, including treaties, are also in force, which have the same value as those in French, Italian, Dutch and German versions, in spite of the fact that it is easy to show that the Rome Treaties were negotiated primarily in French, Italian and German and afterwards translated into Dutch in view of the signature that took place on March 27th 1957.

The ruling of the ECJ in *Stauder* is very interesting and very illustrative of language issues in the interpretation of EU law. The issue that was raised before the Court of Justice stemmed from a difference between versions of a Commission decision that restricted the supply of butter at reduced prices to beneficiaries of certain forms of social assistance. In the German and Dutch versions of Art. 4 of that decision, it was stated that "the Member States must take all necessary measures to ensure that beneficiaries can only purchase the surplus butter on presentation of a coupon indicting their names (auf ihren Namen ausgestellt)", whilst in the other versions it was only stated that a "coupon referring to the person concerned" had to be shown. The Court stated in this regard that "when a single decision is addressed to all the member states the necessity for uniform application and accordingly for uniform interpretation makes it impossible to consider one version of the text in isolation but requires that it be interpreted on the basis of both the real intention of its author and the aim he seeks to achieve, in the light in particular of the versions in all

[20] The judgement refers to Case C-370/96, *Covita* (ECJ 26 November 1998) para 27, Case C-228/99, *Silos* (ECJ 8 November 2001) para 15 and Case C-108/01, *Consorzio del Prosciutto di Parma and Salumificio S. Rita* (ECJ 20 May 2003) para 95.

[21] Case C-161/06, *Skoma-Lux* (ECJ 11 December 2007) para 38–40 (emphasis added).

[22] Case C-361/01 P, *Christina Kick v. OHIM* (ECJ 9 September 2003) para 82 (emphasis added).

four languages. In a case like the present one, the most liberal interpretation must prevail, provided that it is sufficient to achieve the objectives pursued by the decision in question. It cannot, moreover, be accepted that the authors of the decision intended to impose stricter obligations in some member states than in others."[23]

There is thus an abundant case law on the interpretation of treaties and secondary legislation in case of divergence between the various language versions. The consequences of the principle may be summarized as follows. Since all language versions have the same authentic value, including those which are a translation subsequent to the adoption of the rule – as happens usually as a result of enlargement to new Member States – interpretation requires a comparison of all language versions. All versions have the same weight, irrespective of the statistical significance of the population that uses the language. In case of discrepancies, the norm must be interpreted in the light of the purpose and logic of the general rules of which it forms part. The ambiguity of a language version can be solved by resorting to other versions if they are clear and if the comparison can reveal errors in the formulation of one of the languages. These principles apply to the interpretation of legal acts, which are, in principle, published in all official languages, unlike decisions addressed to single subjects: the latter are translated into other than the original authentic languages only when published for the information of possible interested parties. As regards the judgments of the Court of Justice only the language version in the language of the case will prevail in case of divergence, even though, in practice, the use of the French version can be of great help to the interpreter, since French is the working language of the Court, and especially the language in which the judge rapporteur draws up the text of the judgment.

A special procedure ensures that the drafting of any legislative proposal by the Commission has been set up within its legal service in order to guarantee the possibility of finding an equivalent for each legal concept that is understandable in all official languages.[24] The Council Legal Service has established a procedure that leads to the same result for the final version of the texts approved by it. Differently, it should be noted that the amendments of the Treaties have always been negotiated in one or two languages (usually in French, and to a lesser extent also in English). After their political approval – usually during a meeting of the European Council – the other language versions are prepared before the formal signature of the Treaty, work which explains why usually one to two months are needed between approval of a new Treaty in principle and its signature. The Constitutional Treaty of 2004 and the Treaty of Lisbon of 2007 have been occasions of wide ranging checks of the correspondence between the different versions of the Treaties; for this purpose some changes of primary legislation were only made in some versions.

Even in the absence of obvious differences between the language versions of the Treaties or EU acts, as well as of the judgments of the Court of Justice, the multilingual character of EU law has an important impact on the interpretation of EU law. It is worth mentioning the role of the principle of equal legal value of linguis-

[23] Case 29–69, *Erich Stauder v. City of Ulm – Sozialamt* (ECJ 12 November 1969) para 3, 4.
[24] Piris 2005.

tic versions in the application of the *acte clair* theory. In the 1982 *CILFIT* Case, regarding an issue raised by an Italian importer of wool who had to pay fees for health inspections of wool imported from non-EU countries, the Court has established the conditions under which the national courts may refrain from submitting to the Court of Justice a question for interpretation of Community law. As the Court explained "the correct application of community law may be so obvious as to leave no scope for any reasonable doubt as to the manner in which the question raised is to be resolved. Before it comes to the conclusion that such is the case, the national court or tribunal must be convinced that the matter is equally obvious to the courts of the other member states and to the court of justice. Only if those conditions are satisfied, may the national court or tribunal refrain from submitting the question to the court of justice and take upon itself the responsibility for resolving it. However, the existence of such a possibility must be assessed on the basis of the characteristic features of community law and the particular difficulties to which its interpretation gives rise. To begin with, it must be borne in mind that community *legislation is drafted in several languages and that the different language versions are all equally authentic. An interpretation of a provision of community law thus involves a comparison of the different language versions*."[25]

As already indicated, the national courts refer usually only to the version in their own language. However, there are exceptions. For example, the *Finanzgericht* Hamburg, in connection with a request for a preliminary ruling in the proceedings in *Stolle*, compared different language versions of a note attached to a Regulation[26] and pointed out that "the German version of that note differs from the French and English version of it as regards the definition of the concept of 'drawn'. In particular, although the French and English versions state that, in order for a poultry carcass to be classified under subheading 0207 12 90, the carcass must be 'completely drawn', the German version states that all of the giblets must be removed ('sämtliche Innereien entfernt sind'). Consequently, the referring court wonders whether the German version of those notes correctly reproduces the intention of the European legislature." The CJEU answered that "although the expression 'sämtliche Innereien entfernt sind' in German does not constitute a literal translation of the words 'complètement vidés' in French and 'completely drawn' in English, the specification in the German version that all the organs of a carcass coming under subheading 0207 12 90 must be removed is not really different in meaning from that of the French and English versions specifying that the carcass must be completely drawn"[27] Ergo, multilingualism is a difficult issue to solve for a national judge, and a reference for preliminary ruling is usually the only way to deal with linguistic differences, in order to understand whether or not they represent an issue.

[25] Case 283/81, *CILFIT* (ECJ 6 October 1982) para 16–18 (emphasis added).

[26] Commission Regulation (EEC) No 3846/87 *establishing an agricultural product nomenclature for export refunds*, O.J. L 366/1 (1987).

[27] Joined Cases C-323/10 to C-326/10, *Gebr. Stolle GmbH & Co. KG and Doux Geflügel GmbH v. Hauptzollamt Hamburg-Jonas* (ECJ 24 November 2011) para 47.

2.3 Multilingualism as an Issue for EU Law and Policies

Next to the language regime of the EU institutions, bodies and agencies, the issue of multilingualism is also of relevance in relation to the law and policies of European integration. One important issue is the need to mediate possible conflicts between, on the one hand, Member States' law concerning the use of languages and, on the other hand, the fundamental freedoms of movement of persons, goods, services and capital, and the prohibition of discrimination on grounds of nationality.

Three cases are of particular interest as illustrations of this issue. In its ruling of 1989 in *Groener*, the Court stated that "the EEC Treaty does not prohibit the adoption of a policy for the protection and promotion of a language of a Member State which is both the national language and the first official language. However, the implementation of such a policy must not encroach upon a fundamental freedom such as that of the free movement of workers. Therefore, the requirements deriving from measures intended to implement such a policy must not in any circumstances be disproportionate in relation to the aim pursued and the manner in which they are applied must not bring about discrimination against nationals of other Member States" and concluded that "it is not unreasonable to require [the teachers] to have some knowledge of the first national language", even if it is not being used in daily life by most of the population, as is the case for the Irish.[28]

Conversely, the issue of labelling, presentation and advertising of foodstuffs generated important case law already in the 1980s, on the basis of Art. 14 of Directive 79/112/EEC.[29] In *Piageme*, the ECJ held that the Community rules "preclude a national law from requiring the exclusive use of a specific language for the labelling of foodstuffs, without allowing for the possibility of using another language easily understood by purchasers or of ensuring that the purchaser is informed by other measures".[30] This abundant case law pushed the Commission to issue an *Interpretative Commission communication concerning the use of languages in the marketing of foodstuffs in the light of the judgment in the Peeters case.*[31]

There are also significant rulings in relation to the use of language and the freedom of movement of persons. Two cases relating to the free movement of persons are of particular relevance to the German language. In *Angonese*[32] an Italian citizen who was a German native speaker and resided in the province of Bolzano had been a candidate in a competition for a job at the *Cassa di Risparmio*. He did not possess the required certificate of bilingualism that was required in the Province. The Court held that "where an employer makes a person's admission to a recruitment

[28] Case C-379/87, *Anita Groener v. Minister for Education and the City of Dublin Vocational Educational Committee* (ECJ 28 November 1989) para 19, 20.

[29] Council Directive 79/112/EEC *on the approximation of the laws of the Member States relating to the labelling, presentation and advertising of foodstuffs for sale to the ultimate consumer*, O.J. L 33/1 (1979).

[30] Case C-369/89, *Piageme and others v. BVBA Peeters* (ECJ 18 June 1991) para 19.

[31] COM(93) 532 final, O.J. C 345/3 (1993).

[32] Case C-281/98, *Roman Angonese v. Cassa di Risparmio di Bolzano SpA* (ECJ 6 June 2000) para 45.

competition subject to a requirement to provide evidence of his linguistic knowledge exclusively by means of one particular diploma, such as the Certificate, issued only in one particular province of a Member State, that requirement constitutes discrimination on grounds of nationality contrary to Article 48 of the EC Treaty". In *Bickel and Franz*,[33] a German and an Austrian citizen had problems with the police authorities and justice in the province of Bolzano. The Court held that "the exercise of the right to move and reside freely in another Member State is enhanced if the citizens of the Union are able to use a given language to communicate with the administrative and judicial authorities of a State on the same footing as its nationals. Consequently, persons such as Mr Bickel and Mr Franz, in exercising that right in another Member State, are in principle entitled, pursuant to Article 6 of the Treaty, to treatment no less favourable than that accorded to nationals of the host State so far as concerns the use of languages which are spoken there." Albeit a criminal trial was at stake in that case, it is undisputed that the same reasoning applies to administrative proceedings involving European citizens in the German-speaking Trentino-Alto Adige, as well as European citizens of the French language in the Valle d'Aosta or tongue Slovenian in Friuli-Venezia Giulia – to take just the case of bi- or multilingual Italian regions. The same reasoning applies obviously in any other bi- or multilingual region of an EU Member state where the relevant languages are EU official languages. It is clear that there is no obligation to allow the use of these languages beyond the boundaries of the regions in which there is a specific bi- or plurilingual status in national law, nor to allow the use of other EU languages that do not enjoy a particular status according to the relevant member State Law.

3 The Autonomy of EU Law Concepts in Relation to Concepts of Domestic Law

3.1 Interpretation of EU Law and the Diversity of National Legal Systems

The diversity of national legal systems of the Member States affects in a major way the interpretation of EU law, as well as its multilingual character. In the aforementioned *CILFIT* ruling, the Court of Justice pointed out in para 19 that "it must also be borne in mind, even where the different language versions are entirely in accord with one another, that community law uses terminology which is peculiar to it. Furthermore, it must be emphasized that legal concepts do not necessarily have the same meaning in community law and in the law of the various member states." The *CILFIT* ruling notwithstanding, a substantial number of scholars – and also quite some number of judges – only too often make the mistake of assessing the

[33] Case C-274/96, *Criminal proceedings against Horst Otto Bickel and Ulrich Franz* (ECJ 24 November 1998) para 16.

interpretation of EU law given by the CJEU according to the parameters of their own national law, forgetting that these parameters change from one EU country to the other.

Even among countries that share the same language, there are important differences between legal systems. For example, the concepts of German law are often quite different from those of Austrian law; civil law was codified in different periods and with different tools: the relevant codifications came into force in 1794 for Prussia, in 1811 for Austria, and in 1901 for united Germany. Administrative procedure was already codified in 1925 in Austria, but only in 1975 in Germany; Austria has had a system of judicial review of the constitutionality of laws since 1920, Germany since 1949, and so on. As a result the intuitive approach to EU law is different for a lawyer who has been educated in Austria and for a lawyer who has been educated Germany, also because the Austrian tradition of hermeneutics have been marked by formalism much more than the German tradition. Similar considerations also apply to the countries that have French in common as the official national language; while also having in common the Civil Code of 1804, the civil law of Belgium and that of Luxembourg often differ from French civil law. In addition, there are also many differences between Belgium and the Netherlands who share the Dutch language; these two countries also shared the same Civil Code as France and Luxembourg until 1987, at which point the Netherlands replaced the Code Napoléon of 1804 with an entirely new one. Last but not least, it may be mentioned for example, that in France the law of contracts and torts of public authorities is generally subject to a specific discipline developed independently by administrative courts, while in Belgium civil courts apply the Civil Code to such matters.

The concepts used in EU law, while they often find their origin in the legal systems of the Member States have to be interpreted autonomously, since their original meaning is different from one Member State to another. A typical example is that of the concept of "subjective right". Such a concept is in use in most of the EU Member States in order to identify a right belonging to a person (natural or legal). The scope of the concept is however quite different from one legal system to another and the term is hardly used in the UK and Ireland as the notion of "subjective right" has hardly any relevance in common law. In Italy and Germany, the concept of subjective right is crucial in order to determine which courts – ordinary courts or administrative courts – are competent to deal with a case; or what type of judicial review can be undertaken, and in order to know what rules and principles apply to a case. In France the concept of subjective right is not useful at all in order to establish the competence of ordinary or administrative courts, or the available remedies; and that concept has a very limited impact on the content of the applicable rules of law, differently from – again – German and Italian law. This being said the concept of "subjective rights" is certainly not identical in German and Italian law.

Differences in the understanding of concepts are reflected, for instance, in the famous *Van Gend en Loos* ruling,[34] as far as the determination of the rights guaranteed by the EEC Treaty is concerned. When reading the opinion of AG *Karl*

[34] Case 26/62, *van Gend & Loos* (ECJ 5 February 1963).

Roemer[35] – who had been a practicing attorney in Germany until 1953 and was AG of the ECJ from 1954 until 1973 – it appears that his reasoning derives from the notion of German subjective right, and that such a reasoning quite logically leads him to deny the existence of a right based upon Art. 12 of the EEC Treaty, which contained a stand still clause on customs duties in the Member States. On the contrary, in reading the ruling, it appears that the majority of the Court was in favour of a much broader conception of the notion of right, which almost coincides with that of a protected interest. There are also interesting differences between the language versions of the *Van Gend en Loos* ruling. For instance, the Italian translation uses the expression *diritto soggettivo* whereas the French version says *droits individuels*. The reason was that judge *Trabucchi* wanted to make it clear to Italian lawyers that the rights that were referred to in the ruling were not mere *interessi leggittimi* – that enjoyed a lower degree of protection in the Italian legal system as far as liability was concerned. Furthermore, the Dutch and German versions of the ruling easily show that the Court took over the vocabulary of the reference of the Amsterdam duties court, whereas for the French or Italian doctrine, the vocabulary of the ruling departs from that of the reference: it is therefore not astonishing that French and Italian speaking scholarship – and later on also the English speaking one – have seen far more judicial activism in the *Van Gend en Loos* ruling than the Dutch or German scholarship.[36]

This being said Community law included from the outset – i. e. in the Treaties themselves – a series of concepts that were autonomous with respect to the legal system of each Member State. A typical example is that of the competition rules contained in the Treaties. These rules relating to private companies, now contained in Art. 101 and 102 TFEU, had no equivalent in 1957 in national law of five out of six founding states. Only Western Germany had adopted antitrust legislation at the request of the Allies. That legislation was clearly inspired by US American legislation that had already a long tradition that began with the Sherman Antitrust Act of 1890. Apart from Germany, there were at that time hardly any other European countries with similar legislation – even outside of the Community Member States; competition law consisted almost only in protecting traders against "unfair competition" with the prohibition of sale at a loss, and so on. The ECSC Treaty already contained competition rules that were also inspired by American antitrust law.[37] It is therefore logical that the ECSC High Authority and the Commission, as well as the Court of Justice, have developed a legal framework in an autonomous way with respect to the law of Member States, which turned out as a series of new concepts for almost everyone in Western Europe.

In the EEC Treaty itself, there is a quite striking example, namely that of *service of general economic interest*. The concept is contained in Art. 106.2 first sentence TFEU (unchanged since 1957) according to which: "Undertakings entrusted with the operation of services of general economic interest or having the character of a

---

[35] Case 26/62, *van Gend & Loos* (Opinion of AG Roemer of 12 December 1962).

[36] For further details see Ziller 2012.

[37] Reuter 1953, p. 202–214.

revenue producing monopoly shall be subject to the rules contained in the Treaties, in particular to the rules on competition, in so far as the application of such rules does not obstruct the performance, in law or in fact, of the particular tasks assigned to them". French scholarship has for a long time criticized this wording, i. e. the use of the terms *service d'intérêt (économique) général* instead of *service public (économique)*, unlike under Art. 93 TFEU in relation to transport policy (also unchanged since 1957), according to which "Aids shall be compatible with the Treaties if they meet the needs of coordination of transport or if they represent reimbursement for the discharge of certain obligations inherent in the concept of a public service". The problem is that in France *service public* is a central concept of administrative law. In addition, the concept of *service public économique et commercial* has been clearly defined in the case law since 1921.[38] However, whereas this concept of public service was utmost clear to a French lawyer and commonly used in everyday language (albeit with a different and somewhat ideological connotation as opposed to its legal meaning), it was and remains unknown in the law of the majority of other Member States, even those such as Italy, which use the same expression of *servizio pubblico*. In the Dutch version of the Treaty it says "*openbare dienst*" with quotation marks within Art. 93 TFEU: that was the way the Dutch lawyers chose to indicate that a literal translation of public service does not match with Dutch law, as *openbare dienst* means really *civil service*, in French *fonction publique* as does by the way the German "öffentlicher Dienst": the German version of the Treaties should probably also use inverted commas for *Begriff des öffentlichen Dienstes* or put it into the plural *öffentliche Dienste* in order to make it correspond to *service public* at least in daily language.

3.2 EU Law and the Diversity of Legal Families

With the growth in the number of Member States and in the extension of the material scope of EU law, differences between national legal systems that are relevant to the interpretation of EU law have increased, while in the same time there has been an increasing impact of EU law on the Member States' legal systems, which led to their approximation in many fields.

The impact of enlargement on the issue of differences between national legal systems tends to be overestimated, both as regards the enlargement of 1973 with the accession of two common law countries, and that of 2004/2007 with the accession of ten countries that have had for forty years a "communist" regime. Enlargements have led to problems, yet I submit that those problems are not due to differences between legal systems of the Member States.

[38] The concept has been established case law known to French lawyers as the "Bac d'Eloka" case: Tribunal des conflits, *Société commerciale de l'Ouest africain* (22 January 1921), Rec. Lebon p. 91.

There is as widespread but mistaken idea according to which there would be a *summa divisio* between legal systems (even at global level) opposing the so-called common law systems and civil law systems, and that this opposition would be a problem for the coherence of EU law. As is well known, the expression *common law* refers to the legal systems of Great Britain and Ireland, of the United States of America and Commonwealth countries – including Australia, Canada and New Zealand – as well as other former British colonies. Those legal systems have in common their origin, i. e. in the law of English Crown Courts before independence of the United States of America in 1776. The concept of *civil law* is usually being used with the *Code Civil* of 1804 in mind, in order to refer to the legal systems of continental European countries and their former colonies, countries in which the law has been to a large extent codified, especially since the beginning of the nineteenth century. For a long time already has the age-old Anglo-French opposition assumed the form of an ideological opposition between lawyers, as demonstrated by the famous statements of *Dicey* according to which *droit administratif* would be the contrary of the rule of law. Nowadays there is, a mythical view of the common law as the law best adapted to a free market economy, as demonstrated in the field of "law and economics"; there is also a no less mythical view of civil law as the law of State interventionism. Both views ignore the fact that the first "modern" codifications had been adopted significantly prior to the French Civil Code of 1804, as soon as 1687 in Denmark, 1734 in Sweden and 1794 in Prussia.

In a nutshell we can say that if it is true that there are some important differences between the legal systems of the common law family and legal systems of the civil law family, there is often more in common between a common law country and a civil law country – e. g. England and France – than between two countries of the same family – e. g. France and Germany – when it comes to certain concepts or ways of reasoning. A basic mistake that is often made is to think that the system of sources of law is dramatically different between common law countries, where law would be essentially jurisprudential, and civil law countries where it would be essentially based upon statutory law. This error is leading part of the scholarship to write that the importance of judge-made law in the development of Community law would be due to the influence of common law thinking, disregarding the evidence, i. e. that the landmark decisions in *van Gend en Loos* (1963) and *Costa v. ENEL* (1964) were adopted about ten years before accession of Ireland and the UK to the European Communities, and furthermore in a time in which the prospects for UK accession had been frozen by *de Gaulle*'s refusal in 1962 to continue negotiation on the matter.

With regard to the legal systems of the countries of Central and Eastern Europe, it has to be remembered that previous legal traditions are probably far more important than the legal system of the communist period. The traditional influence of Austrian law in Czechoslovakia, Poland, Hungary and part of Yugoslavia (Slovenia, Croatia and Bosnia-Herzegovina today) as well as that of German law in the Baltic countries (Estonia, Latvia and Lithuania) and in a large part of Poland, and even that of French law in Bulgaria and Romania, has been reinvigorated after the end of the communist regimc in 1989 and has probably more importance in terms of legal concepts and methods than the fact that those countries have experienced a communist regime.

The administrative law systems of the Member States have been of particular relevance to the development of EU law since the beginning, since the drafting of the ECSC Treaty, the adoption of the first pieces of ECSC secondary rules and decisions, and since the first rulings of the Luxembourg court. The problems to be addressed by the Court and other Community institutions were very similar to those which Member State courts had to deal with when judging cases derived from the relations between public administration and private parties. Such a starting point is reflected in the wording of Art. 215 EEC, now Art. 340 TFEU: "In the case of non-contractual liability, the Union shall, in accordance with the general principles common to the laws of the Member States, make good any damage caused by its institutions or by its servants in the performance of their duties." This wording recalls that – beyond differences between systems, such as the fact that administrative courts adjudicated on State liability in some countries and civil courts in other – what matters is the fact that courts are faced with the same problems, and often come to the same solutions.

The first AG to the Community Court was *Maurice Lagrange* – soon joined by *Karl Roemer*. *Lagrange* was a member of the French *Conseil d'Etat* and had already drafted the ECSC Treaty Articles dedicated to Court proceedings. *Lagrange* had authored conclusions in more than 60 cases from 1953 to 1964, including in the leading case *Costa v. ENEL* in 1964. There is no doubt that he has brought to the Luxembourg Court the traditional pragmatism and traditional functionalist and teleological reasoning of the *commissaires du gouvernement* of the French Conseil d'Etat, thus compensating for the influence of legal tradition of civil courts and civil law scholarship of the Romano-Germanic legal system. In this context it may be useful to recall for instance the judgment of 7 February 1947 in *d'Aillières*[39] (*Lagrange* was a member of the Conseil d'Etat from 1923) where the French Supreme administrative court did not hesitate to contradict the wording of a statutory provision, by stating that it could have neither the purpose nor the effect to exclude the possibility of a remedy for annulment of an administrative decision, while the relevant statute, an *ordonnance* adopted by the provisional government after the liberation of France from German occupation had expressly provided that the decisions of committees having to adjudicate on acts of collaboration with occupying forces "shall not be subject to any appeal." Typically many of the solutions developed in the second half of the twentieth century by the UK Courts – where there is no institutional separation between ordinary courts and administrative courts – are close to those made by the Conseil d'Etat. This influence is clearly due to a large extent to the regular meetings between the justices of the House of Lords and those of the French Conseil d'Etat, which have taken place since the 1970s. French administrative law had developed since the 19th century, not on the basis of the Civil

[39] French Administrative Court (Conseil d'État), *D'Aillières* (7 February 1947), Rec. Lebon p. 289.

Code but mainly by way of pragmatic judge-made law, a situation that was familiar to the British courts.

By way of conclusion I submit, with all due respect, that differently from Latin until the end of the 17th century the time has not yet come where the English language might be considered as the *lingua franca* of EU law. If any, the German language is probably more appropriate for legal science, due to its properties as an agglutinative language, with the proviso that whereas it is usually not too difficult to translate from another language (like English, French, Italian or Spanish for instance) into German – the reverse is not true: German is a difficult language for foreigners and for legal translators. The study of EU multilingualism[40] should therefore be more developed and would certainly also benefit the consolidation of common European legal thinking.

References

Ajani, G., Peruginelli, G., Sartor, G., & Tiscornia, D. (2007). *The Multilanguage Complexity of European Law – Methodologies in Comparison*. Florence: European Academic Press Publication.

Albi, A., & Ziller, J. (2007). *The European Constitution and National Constitutions: Ratifications and Beyond*. Alphen aan den Rijn: Kluwer Law International.

Amato, G., & Ziller, J. (2007). *The European Constitutions – Cases and Materials in EU and Member States' Law*. Cheltenham: Edward-Elgar.

Chen, A. H., Youdelman, M. K., & Brooks, J. (2007). The Legal Framework for Language Access in Healthcare Settings: Title VI and Beyond. *J Gen Intern Med, 2007 Nov; 22(Suppl 2)*, 362. doi:10.1007/s11606-007-0366-2

Galetta, D.-U., & Ziller, J. (2007). Il regime linguistico della comunità. In M. P. Chiti, & G. Greco (Eds.), *Trattato Di Diritto Amministrativo Europeo* (2nd edn., pp. 1067–1113). Milan: Giuffré.

Losada Fraga, F., Juutilainen, T., Havu, K., & Vesala, J. (2012). Property and European Integration: Dimensions of Article 345 TFEU.*Helsinki Legal Studies Research Paper No. 17*. http://ssrn.com/abstract=2012983

Olsen, F., Lorz, A., & Stein, D. (2009). *Translation Issues in Language and Law*. Basingstoke: Palgrave Macmillan.

Perez-Tremps, P., & Saiz Arnaiz, A. (2007). Ratification of the Treaty Establishing a Constitution for Europe: Prior Constitutional Review, Referendum and Parliamentary approval. In A. Albi, & J. Ziller (Eds.), *The European Constitution and National Constitutions: Ratifications and Beyond* (pp. 45–56). Alphen aan den Rijn: Kluwer Law International.

Piris, J. C. (2005). The Legal Orders of the European Community and of the Member States: Peculiarities and Influences in Drafting. *Amicus Curiae, Issue March/April 2005*, 21. doi:DOI: http://dx.doi.org/10.1234/ac.v2005i58.1090.

Reuter, P. (1953). *La Communauté européenne du charbon et de l'acier*. Paris: LGDJ.

Weber, A. (2010). *Europäische Verfassungsvergleichung*. Munich: Beck.

[40] To mention only two good publications: Ajani et al. 2007; Olsen et al. 2009.

Ziller, J. (2012). Das Verhältnis von nationalem Recht und Europarecht im Wandel der Zeit: "Relire Van Gend en Loos – Van Gend en Loos wiederlesen". In J. Schwarze (Ed.), *Das Verhältnis von nationalem Recht und Europarecht im Wandel der Zeit* (pp. 37–46). Baden-Baden: Nomos.

Ziller, J. (2013). *Diritto delle politiche e delle istituzioni dell'Unione europea*. Bologna: Il Mulino.

Salvador de Madariaga's Federalism: A Two-Part Look at the European Integration and Spain's Decentralization

Jaime Nicolás Muñiz

Europe must become federated . . . , but as little as possible (Salvador de Madariaga, 1952).

In the 1920s and early 1930s of the last century, *Salvador de Madariaga* (1886–1978), as a result of his cosmopolitan nature and internationalism, to use two concepts from his era, was one of the most enthusiastic Europeans in favour of the *Briand* Initiative and the League of Nations, which he formed part of from the time it was created, as one of the still few but great Spaniards who served that institution. Moreover, *Madariaga* always remained loyal to the seminal supra-national experiment that the League represented. This can be seen in his radical understanding and even an exculpation which he rightly expressed about what has been considered that organisation's failure: "No, it is not the League of Nations that has failed. It is the nations in the League that have."

In fact, *Madariaga*'s thinking always reached above and beyond just sovereign States. His philosophies, which, despite everything, always include some sort of "nationalistic" dimension in which one can sense a "national" and even "pro-Spanish" (españolista – a rather pejorative label, because of its extremism) sentiment, never ended with the nation or the State.

International society was always present in his approaches. In his organically based, naturalist viewpoint of social affairs, which focuses on the family more than the individual, understood as a self-contained unit that leads into the national State, *Madariaga* verified the necessary and healthy "intrusion" of other collective entities – social institutions with a greater or lesser natural substrate – such as municipalities, local communes and regions, or in other words the intra-national realm. However, at the same time, he also highlighted the essential nature of what he referred to as the *super*-national realm, above and beyond nations and not simply *inter*-national. Whereas internationality can be seen, in his judgement, as a mere piece of physical, mechanical and relational data, and does not necessarily imply the acceptance of an order beyond nations; the idea of supernationality bears with it the notion of a higher, integrating realm, a sphere which *Madariaga* realizes has not yet been defined and is not easy to organize. However, despite that fact, it is

H.-J. Blanke et al. (eds.), *Common European Legal Thinking*,
DOI 10.1007/978-3-319-19300-7_25

no less necessary than other internal, institutionally related and even corporative mediations of the national State.

Madariaga has given a name of its own to this realm, which is brilliant and highly descriptive: the "Co-World" (*Co-Mundo*). This "Co-world" is not a universal State, or even a universal nation, which would not be or evoke anything more than a reduction of the rich diversity of nations and States to a political or cultural hegemony, but rather something more "natural": a world belonging to all for all.

When thinking of a united Europe, which he began to design and dream at the same time as developing his universalist calling in the League of Nations, *Madariaga*, who never abandoned that calling – in fact, moved by the horror of World War II, all he did was change the order of his immediate concerns for pragmatic reasons, while adding intensity and placing a higher priority on the European project – conceives Europe in "federal" terms, as an alliance (because none other is the clear meaning of *foedus*).

Basically, *Madariaga* began thinking of Europe as a "Europe of homelands" (patrias). This concept, which later, due to its appropriation by De Gaulle, was considered very French and to a certain extent became sidelined as a result, always had a distinct meaning of its own for *Madariaga*, involving the need to preserve the vital substrate of federated nations in that alliance. To him, integration was a union that would not artificially break up the natural, organic entities that comprise the various homelands, or their national character, cultures, languages and lifestyles.

At the same time as referring to these homelands, *Madariaga*, in any case, drew attention to the limits of the national chauvinism of the *über alles, au-dessus de tout* and *right or wrong* of some nations. He brilliantly criticized the semi-religious cult of patriotism and warned about the dire consequences of nationalism. He loved homelands, all of them, but he did not go so far as to worship them, not even his own. He praised the specific nature of each homeland (England, France, Spain), but his choice was in favour of an integrating fusion of these characters and lifestyles. *Madariaga* preferred to be European – an option which he made clear in *Englishmen, Frenchmen, Spaniards*, his 1928 work which dazzled Europeans. He finished off the work by extending it to include all the other peoples of Europe in his no less compelling *Sketch of Europe,* in 1952.

It is therefore no surprise that, immediately after the end of the war, *Madariaga* was one of the spearheads in the fight for European unity. In fact, although he lacked the important support of a State, with all of its authority, because of his status as an exile, and only because of this, at the decisive congress of the European Movement in The Hague in 1948, he was asked to preside over the cultural commission, the third of this congress' commissions, and in principle also the least important, but he was capable of showing off its value to the fullest. Later, when he held a position on the executive board of the European Movement and held the first presidency of the recently created International Liberal Movement, in 1949 he founded the College of Europe, through which he attempted to draw attention to the essential nature of understanding Europe as a cultural endeavour (compared with the limited nationalism of European post-war universities), and the European Centre of Culture in Geneva. By doing so, he became the "ideologue" (or perhaps better stated, the intellectual inspiration) of the European Movement), above all thanks to his *Spirit of Europe*, a text written in 1952 at the request of the Movement and so well executed that he saved the organization from having to commission two other manifestos initially planned from the Catholic and Protestant confessional perspectives. Including them as complementary works was now practically unnecessary in light of the all-encompassing work by *Madariaga*.

Not because of any Florentine political wizardry, but rather because of the depth of his European faith and his profound knowledge of the transcendence of the idea of Europe, *Madariaga* is one of the few who got it right by not getting tied up in the frequent internal quarrels of the European movement, proclaiming himself neither a federalist nor a confederalist, and neither functionalist nor institutionalist.

Always racing to the heart of the matter, to *Madariaga* the problem lay elsewhere, in knowing whether Europeans truly existed, a question the discussion of which he devoted his essay on *The Human Sciences and European Integration* (Leyden, 1960) to, after being the focal point of his interventions in The Hague. The important thing was to ascertain and reveal the essence of Europe and to unveil its historical reality. In fact, after the war, *Madariaga* became even more European, though at the cost of being less supernational, less global. It was not in vain, however, that, beyond his comprehension and exculpation, the League of Nations had failed. This "European" turn can be seen even in the title of his great essays on nationalism and internationalism. He no longer speaks of nationalities, of Spaniards, Frenchmen or Englishmen, but rather of Europe.

And he then becomes more optimistic about Europe, about Europeans and what we can call the European. In a certain way, he lets us see that the Europeans' great difficulty in viewing themselves as Europeans, to cease fixating mainly on their differences and distinct features and instead focusing on what they have in common, is precisely because of the fact that Europeans are so close to one another: we lack the perspective required to see our natural unity.

In his "Sketch of Europe", *Madariaga* gives an artistic form to this perspective by turning to one of Hollywood's "European" films, *The Ghost Goes West*, by *René Clair*. In it, like extravagant American millionaires have done so many times in actuality and can be seen in many places all around America, for instance, in Manhattan's Cloisters, made as if it were a sort of thematic amusement park, a Texan tycoon acquires a Scottish castle and dismantles it piece by piece, including the ghost, to take it to the United States, where he rebuilds it in the middle of a landscape which one can easily imagine bears absolutely no resemblance to the castle's original Scottish location. As if this were not enough, the rich American uses heavy machinery to have it placed in the middle of a moat, where he has no less than a gondola put in place along with its gondolier. Even without the ghost, the image of this musty castle already seems ghastly within the Texan landscape, but with the presence of the gondola, what interests us most here, the sensation of perplexity and strangeness rises even more amongst the movie's viewers. There is no doubt that neither a Scot nor an Italian, nor a Spaniard, German, Pole or Russian, could explain what this fine Venetian vessel and its presumptuous gondolier are doing there, transplanted in what would constitute a daring exercise for one's imagination on the

Spanish plateau, the hills of the Rhine, the icy steppes of Eastern Europe or foggy Scotland, as it floats around the dark, bulky fortress and its ghost. The American owner does not find this odd at all, though. To him it is completely natural, and, since Clair was not oblivious to any of this, in his film he has the business magnate explain that it was all done "*in order to make it look more European.*"

Nothing is clearer to *Madariaga* either, who tells us that, "after all, particularly when viewed from another continent, or in other words with proper perspective, the Venetian gondola and the Scottish castle seem like perfect colleagues and natural neighbours in a painting drawn by history and the psychology of a known internal unity." In any case, however, *Madariaga*'s Europe is a complex Europe, as contradictory as that image of the gondola and fortress, a Europe in tension that reclaims a dialectical, integrating vision with the intra-European tensions and conflicts to which those tensions give shape.

In this document, he proclaims his federal vision of Europe, and it could be no other way, because his project for a United Europe in no way renounces the acknowledgement of a set of national and irremovable differences, but also declares that they themselves are enriching within the ideas of Europe. What is more, they bear the vital European substance, without the recognition of which Europe would surely be no more than a cold, inert design. *Madariaga* wants a united Europe, but one which is complex and multi-faceted: a Europe with many centres, a federal, decentralized Europe.

In any case, because he does not intend to eliminate diversity or these tensions, he also claims that "Europe ... must be federated as little as possible." At the same time, he calls for the birth of a new solidarity so that "the men of Europe [can] feel even freer in this new Europe than in the anarchic, divided Europe of the past" (*ibid.*). Moreover, it is upon these tensions – bipolar tensions amongst all the great European peoples (Germans versus Frenchmen, Spaniards versus Portuguese, Austrians versus Germans, Englishmen versus Continentals, Southerners versus Northerners, Westerners against Easterners and so forth) that *Madariaga* draws his sketch of Europe.

Furthermore, to *Madariaga* "Europe is not and will never be a nation. It is a bunch of nations", – a bunch, a word which expresses a multi-faceted nature and cohesion all at once. And we must not forget that bunches of grapes are only beautiful when they are complete, but no longer when someone begins to pick off their fruit. By the way, because of this lack of "national unity" (and surely more so because they were well-aware of their notable organic corporative anti-democratism in the 1930s), he is opposed to the election of the European parliament by direct suffrage amongst Europeans. Definitively, he sees Europe as a "variety-unit," in which the variety produces wonderment, but the unit wins out *(Sketch of Europe).* He is, after all, a great, definitive pro-European. Meanwhile, *Madariaga*'s European federalism is eminently practical. This is what lies behind his somewhat disconcerting words, stated above, forming what is nearly a motto: "Europe must be federated, but as little as possible": *ma non troppo.* It is too valuable a project to ruin it by excess, ambition or haste.

Moreover, along these same practical lines, nationalism disgusts him because of its fake mysticism, which is why he does not propose a new European mysticism in opposition to it. *Madariaga* is content with carefully demonstrating that the European community is a historical reality ("Europe is already a fact, though some may not have realized it yet"), which is exactly why he demands new forms of organizational policies, placing little importance on articulating specific proposals, and not having left behind many well-grounded specific ideas in this respect either:

> Europe has one single body and one single soul, but a dozen heads and hearts. It can be compared with a monster whose body is ripped to pieces by the effort and beating of its twenty hearts. Approximately twenty governments in Europe do not acknowledge (or do not wish to acknowledge) that those decrees which aim only at their own countries are at the same time ineffective within and inoperative abroad, that, starting right now, no European government will ever be in the proper condition to manage its own country, though it may not abstain from taking part directly in directing the affairs of other people in Europe, while in each country that makes up Europe there is a whole sphere of public life that has become European and requires an equally European government (*The Spirit of Europe*).

We can also complete this picture with a few exact words by *Madariaga*, which reflect the depth of his vision for Europe and his European feeling, taken from his vibrant interventions in The Hague, in 1948:

> [Europe] will have been born when Spaniards say "our Chartres", the English talk about "our Krakow", the Italians "our Copenhagen"; when the Germans say "our Bruges"; and all of them reel back in horror before the idea of placing any of these places in criminal or destructive hands. Then Europe will be a living thing, because it is then that the Spirit which leads the course of History will have pronounced the words of creation: FIAT EUROPA!

Eloquent words in the mouth of someone whose ideas, in all else, were based on what amounted to the awaited pre-existence of a Europe whose unity could not be conceived by *Madariaga* as anything other than, in the way of the Italians, a continental *Risorgimento*, the unification of one single spirit that was already a reality, but which still lacked a set of common political institutions, though it did have one thing: a promising Renaissance.

Now let us look back into the past, to shift from the supranational realm to the internal, to nationalities and regions. When analysing *Madariaga*'s thought on the regional question – in essence the same as what we call today in Spain the autonomous regional problem, territorial articulation of the State or political decentralization – here, too, we may begin by remembering his same words which we placed at the forefront of reflections upon Europe and supranational communities. Becoming federated, but only as much as necessary, that is our author's motto. Inward and outward, both in Europe and within Spain.

We have already seen this formula with respect to Europe. It is not a half-hearted idea of eclecticism, but rather is complex, Galician, as one might say of a man from Galicia with the universal standing of *Don Salvador*. And while it was complex in its "European version," it was even more so, if possible, in his projection into its "Spanish version."

It could be no other way, because few people besides *Madariaga* are so knowledgeable of the profound history of Spain. In his thorough historical knowledge, as well-grounded and assimilated as his philological wisdom, which are both so closely related, lies the key to *Don Salvador*'s pro-Spain (españolista) stance, which would perhaps have been more appropriately defined as "Hispanism" by the no less intelligent *Claudio Sánchez Albornoz*, President-in-exile of the Spanish Republic. In effect, *Madariaga* is profoundly regionalist, and at the same time a steadfast Spanish nationalist, though never a Castilian nationalist, a category that at least today – and, to some extent, in History too – is rather an ideological construction of its supposed opposites than a tangible entity.

It should be no surprise then that *Madariaga*'s "regionalist" proposal is so similar, perhaps without wanting to be, to what the reality of the Spanish autonomous regional State is today. In other words, it is a strong, decisive commitment to a form of regionalism integrated into a higher unit, in the same way that *Don Salvador*'s sovereignism can only be explained within the higher framework of his idea of Europe and, within his broad conception thereof, the Co-world, or if you prefer, in the same way that his internationalism could only be fully explained from the perspective of his deep sense of the State and his no less complete Hispanism.

Of course, this is not the place for reproducing the brilliant and surprisingly dense historical analysis carried out by *Madariaga* in his monumental *Spain*, a mature work which modestly and contradictorily subtitles *Essay of Contemporary History* – here the note of contradiction, or better stated, of complexity to which we have just alluded –, or the reflections he makes in his *Memories of a Federalist*, or in *From Anguish to Freedom*, or in his controversial – not at all liberal, yet dazzling and anti-Republican – *Anarchy or Hierarchy*, works which mark his deep national commitment. In any case, though, nothing seems less opportune to me than "revealing" the keys of such a powerful and, at the same time, current way of thinking as is that of *Salvador de Madariaga* regarding this decisive topic.

Madariaga, as great a liberal as he was reticent as a democrat, is a fervent regionalist, whose regionalism knows only one limit, separatism, which provokes him no less than his decisive autonomous regionalism does. Upon first glance, in *Madariaga* there is an elementary, organically oriented, almost landscapist approach to regionalism. It could appear that he approaches regionalism in a somewhat folkloristic way, by adaptation to the landscape. What matters is the recognition of the personality – rather than the singularity, as we hear today, with more strong accents and purposes, in the contemporary Spain's political debate – of the different natural communities, a roundabout expression taken on in order to avoid more direct, politically charged labels such as nations, nationalities or "mere" regions. But this is not so. It is not that simple. To *Madariaga* it certainly seems that "the more the social landscape adapts to the natural landscape, the easier it will be for men and their nature to adapt, in turn, to what nature expects of them." And he has no doubt that the region is an essential element in social geography.

After all, however, his reference to the landscape is above all metaphoric, because while *Madariaga* advocates federalism and regionalism, he does so not for a simple natural reason, but rather one which is institutional and administrative: because ultimately decentralization means bringing responsibility closer to the places where it must actually be exercised. What is more, *Madariaga*'s regionalism does not simply involve the landscape; it is neither naturalist, nor merely administrative either, but rather notably political. He has a political conception of the region that is no less intense than today's autonomous regionalism. In fact, it may be even stronger, as when he writes (and not casually), "No more one only minister of the government who issue all kinds of orders from Madrid; instead, ten or twelve politically decentralised agents ruling from La Coruña to Seville and from Barcelona to Las Palmas; forget the single parliament in Madrid, but rather have as many Parliaments as there are kingdoms, countries or regions."

What this truly means for *Madariaga* is the idea of "making regions be born again, as the fourth part of the political building that we aspire to erect – to construct living political entities capable of dealing with the governance of their affairs without the national government's intervention." Because "regions must have complete freedom to govern themselves; and their parliaments must, as well, to legislate within the borders of their territory of their natural area of competence. They will vote their budget and direct contributions which, through meetings by local government and councils, will collect taxes and distribute funds to taxpaying families; however, they would also directly collect and distribute the contributions by those families or entities whose importance is higher up than the competence of the municipality and the local area where they reside. Likewise, they would legislate in order to equitably offset the tax burdens of rich and poor areas. They would also create their own judiciary and police." Can one imagine any greater autonomous regionalism than that described in this plan?

It is no less true (and, for the same reason, is shocking) that the greatest development in *Madariaga*'s autonomous regional plan coincides with his least "democratic" stage, when he was politically involved in the ministries of the two conservative "Dark Years" of Spain's Second Republic. However, that is not of specific interest to us here, nor does it lessen his true autonomous regional claims which, beyond the politically articulated conception of the State's territorial organization, are approached parallel to the anti-separatist obsession – as we may rightly describe it – of our thinker. This antiseparatism is not visceral, however, or capricious; it is a unitarianism that is not only based on a knowledge of Spanish history beyond compare – of both Spain and the plural peoples of Spain – but also of the republican virtue of solidarity. And also of grandeur, because he never loses sight, not even when he focuses on the smallest of territorial realms, of his open-minded thinking, of wide-open spaces and communities, that of his universal federalism. After all, to *Madariaga* the ultimate meaning of the State, and of regions and countries (he leaves out the term nationalities, surely due to conviction and an awareness of its problems), does not lie in themselves, but rather in the worldwide community, the Co-world he worked so hard on.

With a bit of humour and somewhat of a contradiction, but great eloquence, he explained that complex intersection of planes, in well-spoken words taken down in an interview from 1931:"Catalonia strives to be Europe and Asturias wants to remain Asturias; doing the latter, Asturias is much more European than the former." Today we can switch Catalonia's and Asturias' names for those of any other Spanish region, nationality or country in Spain, and even Europe, that we want.

Madariaga's words continue to brim over with all the depth and currentness that we have attempted to express succinctly herein. There is no doubt that his ideas could be used to acquire a certain level of complexity that is often missing when examining the serious problems and tensions in the territorial organization of the Spanish State, and to surmount the troublesome *impasse* which its constitutional framework has reached. Anyway, Catalonia, which often stresses too emphatically its European calling and which often tends to "forget" Spain in its relations to Europe, should not forget *Madariaga*'s words.

European Belgium

Francis Delpérée

1 For more than 50 years, Belgium has lived in harmony with Europe – in its various configurations.

Belgium has contributed to the emergence of strong legal thinking in several ways. This thinking cannot ignore national borders, but seeks to transcend them. It aims especially to bridge the barriers typically created between the disciplines of constitutional law, which are national by definition, and institutional law, now emerging at European level and distinct from classical international law.

Albrecht Weber's work, which is based on a comparative knowledge of our continent's political and social realities, perfectly illustrates this approach. It helps to break down old conceptual frameworks. At the same time, it paves the way for the establishment of an institutional "new world".

This transdisciplinary exercise is not always as simple as one might imagine or hope.[1] There are methodological difficulties, linked in particular to the use of various idioms. There are misunderstandings that arise from the development of stories and from cultures that are distinctive and sometimes conflicting. There is also political resistance – frankly speaking, nationalist and sub-nationalist resistance – which has resulted in unfinished business or obvious failures.

Now it is more important than ever to follow the advice of the poet *Boileau*: "Vingt fois sur le métier remettez votre ouvrage" (Your work must be polished and honed to perfection). Moreover, in the words of another writer, *L. Aragon*, we must be realistic and accept the idea that "Rien n'est jamais acquis à l'homme/Ni sa force, ni sa faiblesse, ni son coeur" (Nothing is man's forever, neither his strength, nor his weakness, nor his heart). The same can be said for the life of institutions. *Sisyphus* and his boulder spring to mind here.

In that context, one question needs to be asked. Why did Belgium, this small State in Western Europe, want and why did it manage to make its own contribution to the building of Europe? Why did it devise this contribution in both theoretical and practical terms? Why does it continue to invest so much energy in doing this?

[1] Delpérée 2013, p. 197 et seq.

H.-J. Blanke et al. (eds.), *Common European Legal Thinking*,
DOI 10.1007/978-3-319-19300-7_26

And why, in a world awash with Euro-scepticism, does it demonstrate so much faith in Europe? A faith that is said to be capable of moving mountains.

One explanation has been put forward. Belgium has faced institutional problems for half a century and done its best to deal with them. Despite making steady progress, it keeps an open mind as to future options. So it could be said that Belgium is better prepared than others to deal with the challenges – sometimes the very same ones – now faced by the European Union. These challenges stimulate Belgium to develop, so tenaciously and enthusiastically, a range of solutions. The country may one day call upon solutions like these in such circumstances, however troubled or confused the latter prove to be.

Belgium has Europe in its DNA, embedded in its traditions and political initiatives. Why then should it not at times humbly point the way forward for its European partners?

Though Belgium's citizens may struggle to imagine how their country will evolve, the country also believes that its future and maybe its very existence are closely tied up with those of the European Union. Could the EU provide some of the walls to prop up the nation's federal structure? Here, too, Belgium believes that this is a risk (or challenge) worth taking.

2 I always compare a State to a house. When I visit a house – to rent it, to buy it, or to live there, when I wonder which plan it was built on, when I want to understand how the inhabitants lived or worked there – it can be helpful to have one – or several – keys to enter that house.[2]

I offer the use of three keys to enter the Belgian house. The first one is the federal key, the second one is the parliamentary key and the third one is the European key. I would like to use these keys to explain, in broad terms, how the Belgian State is organised and how it functions in the heart of the European Union.

2.1 In most States worldwide, State structures are unitary structures. The law – known as national law – is the same for everyone. It applies everywhere on the State's territory, to all people, in all situations. "The Republic is one and indivisible", as it says in the French Constitution.

Belgium was born in 1830. For 150 years, it existed under a unitary system. The Constitution underlined this in Art. 10: "Belgians" are "equal before the law". They were obviously equal before the *same* law, in other words before the national law. In a unitary State, the law is "the same for every-one", in the words of the French *Déclaration* of 1789.

A simple system of public institutions took shape under this unitary perspective. "One" King, "one" government, "one" Parliament, "one" Supreme Court (*Cour de cassation*). Nothing could be simpler. Naturally, in this unitary State, there were – and there still are today – local authorities that we call municipalities (589 in number) and provinces (10 in number). But these authorities were subject to the rules established by national law. A rule established by the City of Antwerp or a

[2] Delpérée 2006.

rule established by the Province of Namur could, for example, be repealed by the Minister of the Interior if it did not comply with the national law or if it was not in the public's interest as defined by the unitary State.

Since 1970, however, this simple and practical situation has gradually been changed. Step by step (1970, 1984, 1988, 1991, 1994, 2014), Belgium has been developing into a federal State.

This is a major change. In a federal State, the law is no longer the same for everyone. It is based on what is known in the United States, Canada, Australia or India as the 'sharing of powers'. There are different legislative bodies at work at the same time. There are several laws, rather than just one. Various different laws apply to citizens, depending on where they live in the territory of Belgium.[3] The recurrent question is: "Who does what, who may do that, who has the power to do what?"

To take just one example, the rules on erecting, demolishing or renovating a building now vary, depending on whether you live in Flanders, Brussels or Wallonia. The rules on organising or providing education are no longer the same in the North and the South of the country. In addition to the federal law, there are now community laws and regional laws.

The federal law, and community or regional law (which we will call decrees), have identical value. Perfectly identical, to be precise. A law is the same as a decree. A decree is the same as a law. In theory, the federal law cannot intervene in the fields of competence of community or regional law. Competences are considered exclusive. As in other federal States, there are no concurrent competences.

[3] Delpérée and Verdussen 2005, p. 193–208: "The principle of equality, which is at the very heart of our political society, ordinarily serves as a backdrop against which the state of legal relations between individuals is assessed. This same principle is often used to measure the progress of democratic society. But what if it were also used to measure the state of legal relations between the various political entities comprising the federal State? It follows that the question of federal equality would have to be approached from a dual perspective, one that considers both functional and institutional dimensions. With respect to the functional perspective, we tend to consider the federal entity, on the one hand, and the federated units, on the other hand, as having equal footing in exercising their functions and powers. Sovereignty is shared; each partner being master of its domain of activity. However, if inequality is organised to the benefit or detriment of either of the partners, one should wonder whether institutional realities are properly reflected in formal arrangements and whether an authentic federal system can develop under these conditions. From an institutional perspective, we tend to think that a federal system of government, which rests on the functional equality of the constituent entities, does not necessarily require their institutional equality. For instance, the federated units can enjoy institutional arrangements differing with respect to the organisation of public authorities or the distribution of powers among them. In other words, equality does not signify identity. Certain institutional differences can be tolerated, accepted, and even encouraged. Admittedly these should not lead to a situation where one federated unit is placed in a subordinate position in relation to the other units or the federal entity. However, these differences can also serve to distinguish, in a very clear manner, the status of the political entities comprising the federal system. Thus, a federalism premised on the principle of equality produces a regime of shared sovereignty, and does not exclude the development of differentiated sovereignties".

Conversely, the community or regional law cannot intervene in the field of federal law. The exclusivity operates in both directions.

So we have a Belgium that is now part of the group of 30 federal States that are to be found around the world. However, federal Belgium has a number of unique features, which set it apart from the other federal States. Quite simply, it is engaged in "Belgian-style" federalism.

2.1.1 Federal States tend to be created by association – a method expressed by the motto *E pluribus unum*. The founding peoples come together, they meet, they associate to found a State.

Conversely, federal Belgium is being created by disassociation. It is a unitary State that is gradually turning itself into a federal State. This means that this State is transferring more and more competences and means to the communities and regions.[4] In brief, it is stripping and impoverishing itself.

This raises a rather worrying question. Just where will the process of disassociation end? Is not the disassociation paving the way for disunion or division? Is federalism just an intermediate step on the path towards the emergence of three new States? I do not have a definite answer to this question. We shall see.[5]

2.1.2 The other federal States are multipolar States: the United States (50 in number), Switzerland (26), Germany (16), Canada (10, not including the Northwest Territories), Mexico, Brazil, Austria, India, and so on.

As for federal Belgium, it is bipolar. What we are engaged in is two-sided federalism. I know that we have Brussels and we have the German-speaking Community, which cannot be reduced to two blocs. But the institutional arrangements are organised around two major political communities: Flanders and Wallonia.

We are two. Still two. The North and the South. The Council of Ministers: seven French-speaking ministers, seven Dutch-speaking ministers; the Constitutional Court: six French-speaking judges, six Dutch-speaking judges; the parliamentarians: two language groups. Not three, not four, not five.

This situation has serious consequences. Bipolar federalism is not a federalism of cooperation. It is more a federalism of confrontation, of competition and even of conflict. Belgians spend a great deal of time solving (or trying to solve) a number of political conflicts, at the end of which no political authority wants to be a loser. It can be hard to find "win-win" solutions.

2.1.3 The other federal States are, in general, organised around a simple structure. There is a first stage, that of the federal State. There is a second stage, comprising the federated authorities. They are called "States" (in inverted commas), *Länder*,

[4] In Belgium, the federated entities have jurisdiction only by devolution. Residual powers belong to the federal State. Certainly, the Constitution contemplates the future transfer of the residual powers to the federated entities. However, in order for that to happen, there would have to be a constitutional accord, and this is not foreseeable at present. As the Constitutional Court has said, this provision is therefore of no effect (n° 76/98).

[5] Delpérée 2007; Hasquin 2014.

cantons, regions, and so on. Yet these federated authorities are all of the same kind. They have identical competences. They have similar means.

However, federal Belgium practises a layered federalism. At the federated level, there is no single type of authority. There are two of them. There are communities – which match linguistic and cultural concerns. There are regions – which match economic and social concerns.

This may seem surprising. But, when all is said and done, we experience the same realities at European level: the Europe of 28 is not the Europe of the Euro, nor is it the Europe of Schengen. There are European policies with a variable geometry.[6]

To further complicate this presentation of the institutions, the two authorities that are present in the North of the country, the Flemish Community and the Flemish Region, decided to merge their institutions, administrations and budgets. The same movement has not yet happened in the South of the country.

Within each community and each region, there is a government, a parliament, and an administration – but there is no real network of justice institutions. This institutional system is, broadly speaking, modelled on the one that exists at the federal level.[7]

2.2 Parliamentarianism is a political system in which a parliament can control a government (and its administration) and possibly vote it out of office. It is also a political system in which a government can dissolve a parliament. In short, it is a system of mutual revocability.

Belgium fits well into this perspective.

Here is a recent example. In April 2010, the parliamentary majority was divided on an issue of major political significance: the definition of electoral constituencies in and around Brussels. At that time, the French-speakers made use of the so-called alarm bell. What could the *Y. Leterme* government do? *Leterme* had only one solution. He resigned on 26 April. A few weeks later, on 7 May 2010, efforts to put together a new government with the same majority came to nothing. The government brought about the dissolution of the houses, in the hope that the election would offer results that would lead to a solution to this political conflict. Just the opposite happened. The legislative elections were held on 13 June in the same year. The government of *E. Di Rupo* came into being on 5 December 2011, one and a half years later, at the end of an interminable political crisis.

Belgium therefore has a parliamentary system just like Westminster. But the country has three special features that should be highlighted.

2.2.1 Belgium's Parliament has two houses, two parliamentary assemblies. We use the same terms as the United States: the House of Representatives and the Senate.

---

[6] This illustrated a major concern in Belgian federalism. Let's solve problems one at a time, one after another. Let's build institutions in response to specific needs, and not according to an abstract political scheme.

[7] Delpérée and Depré 1998; Lejeune 2010; Uyttendaele 2014.

The bicameral system, as practised in Belgium, is not egalitarian. This will always be the case.

The House has most of the political control over the government. If necessary, it can vote the government out of office.

The House has exclusive control of the budgetary function.

The House plays a key role in the legislative function. Notably, the government presents all bills that it wants to become law to the House.

What about the Senate? It no longer has control over most of the legislative function, it no longer has political control, and it has lost its budgetary function. The Senate has turned into a think tank.

If it is able, if it has the means, the Senate can compile, for the government or the first house, a number of dossiers, including legislative ones, which these authorities will have to see through to completion.[8] I pick out just one example. A senatorial commission looked carefully at the way in which the King and members of the royal family carried out their activities. This commission drafted a report on this subject, which was used as a platform for an important discussion in this field, including in the House of Representatives.

2.2.2 The Parliament can vote out the government. The government can dissolve the assemblies. However, it should never be forgotten that the government and Parliament are allies, not opponents. In political science, this is called "majority rule" and also applies in Belgium. It can be found within a party in the Parliament as well as in the whole government.

The difficulty lies in the fact that this majority is automatically a composite majority. Neither do we have homogeneous governments, nor do we have minority governments. There is a simple explanation for that. For more than a century, we have practised proportional representation. Given that the main party in the government is the Dutch-speaking New Flemish Alliance, which represents 20.3 % of the electoral body, one might assume that the governments are always governments with a broad coalition: four (as is the case today), five or six partners.

Another reason for the difficulty is that the Belgian government must have equal representation on both sides. That means, from a mathematical viewpoint, that it must include seven French-speaking ministers and seven Dutch-speaking ministers. Above all, from a political viewpoint, this means that the government benefits from having a majority in both the North and the South of the country.[9]

The length of the crisis – one and a half years in 2010–2011 – highlights the difficulty of putting together governments like this.

The division within the governmental majority, which is also the parliamentary majority, is the main cause of political crises that may arise in Belgium.

[8] Sägesser and Istasse 2014; Delpérée 2014a.

[9] Delpérée 2014b.

2.2.3 Given this context, it is tricky to define the King's role.

Belgium adopted its Constitution on 7 February 1831. At that time, the nation lacked a king. A delegation travelled to London. It met with Prince *Leopold of Saxe-Coburg*. He was the widower of *Charlotte*, the aunt of the woman who would become Queen *Victoria*. He was hesitant about accepting the Belgian crown. He said he wanted to read the text of the new Constitution. He was allowed to do so, and then announced to the delegation members: "Gentlemen, you have rudely treated the monarchy, which was not there to defend itself."

Which provisions of the Constitution did the future King find so shocking? More than likely it was Art. 105 ("The King has no powers other than those formally attributed to him by the Constitution") as well as Art. 106 ("No act of the King can take effect without the countersignature of a minister, who, in doing so, assumes responsibility for it").

So the monarchy's power was limited and shared.

There can be no doubt that the King has official duties. He signs laws. He concludes treaties. He appoints ministers. He appoints judges and civil servants. All this is done with the consent of a minister.

There can also be no doubt that he has an unofficial duty. To take but one example, the King of the Belgians makes a speech on 21 July, for the national holiday. This is not a speech from the throne, as is delivered in Westminster. The King drafts this speech himself, with the assistance of his immediate staff. The text is then sent to the Prime Minister, who is allowed to make one or two comments, on style and content. The King then makes his speech, which really is his "own" but which is agreed with the Prime Minister.

2.3 As already highlighted, Belgium clearly has a European vocation. It is not just the city or Region of Brussels that aspires to become the seat, or one of the seats, of the European Union. The entire country and its citizens fall into this category.[10]

This option is not really debatable. Belgium sometimes does have reservations about European initiatives. It discusses their merits, it questions the terms of their implementation, and it balks at the adoption of measures which, especially in terms of the budget, significantly limit the country's sovereignty. In all circumstances

---

[10] Delpérée 2001: "In 1970, i. e. fifteen years after the appearance of the first steps towards European integration, Belgium modified its Constitution and introduced a 'general clause of integration'. It states that the 'execution of specified powers' could be entrusted by a treaty or a law 'with institutions of public international law'. This constitutional clause allows important transfers of competence – especially with the treaties of Maastricht and Amsterdam – in fields of economic or financial policy. However, it raises major constitutional problems. For example, constitutional problems arise when Community treaties not only consider the transfer of a national matter to the European order, but also turn their attention to solving questions of internal organisation of the Belgian state or of its political collectivities, notably by defining the conditions of the municipal electorate. It is also the case when Community treaties do not only consider the transfer of a national matter to the European order but also turn their attention to handling questions of federal competence. In order to avoid conflicts within the internal order, it is made clear that the communities and the regions have to approve such treaties."

though, it seeks to show how favourably it is disposed towards action at European level. This choice is significant in itself.

Belgium contributes to the gradual development of a common culture and constitutional practice, within which the country finds the foundation of its political organisation. It is irresistibly drawn to positioning itself firmly in favour of "multi-level government".

2.3.1 A common constitutional culture has been developed for more than 60 years in the heart of Europe. A pioneering culture that is based on the three States which make up Benelux. This culture also draws on the institutional experience of Belgium's two large neighbour States, France and the Federal Republic of Germany.

This culture is that of a Romano-Germanic legal system. It is statutory law. A law developed by parliamentary and governmental authorities, working together on the same political tasks. This constitutional culture is not that of other European States. *A fortiori*, it is not yet that of the Union.

Belgium has no hesitation in explaining its impatience with the Union's tardy embrace of constitutional culture. When necessary, it points out European law's lack of coherence, certainty and stability, including in the field of institutional law.

The coherence of EU law is problematic. There are too many texts. At the same time, there are too few that include proper legal rules. Certainly, there are legal rules in due form. These are, for example, rules found in the Treaties or in secondary legislation. They stand alongside a set of proposals, statements, recommendations, roadmaps, and so on. They coexist with various political, economic and financial instruments whose status is unclear – which is a euphemism[11]. This coexistence is damaging. The time is right for making law, real law. In Europe, bad law typically prevails over good law. Now is the time to restore a better balance.

There is also a lack of legal certainty. In theory, the law establishes a hierarchy of rules. It links the different standards to each other. In Europe, there are legal rules. Some are part of Community law, while others belong to international law.[12] Their provisions overlay one another and are sometimes contradictory. To take just one example, the famous Treaty on Stability, Coordination and Governance

[11] In September 2010, the European Council launched the first European Semester. To that end, it modified the "Code of Conduct on the implementation of the Stability and Growth Pact". This document was the basis for the European Semester of 2011. The Semester only became binding after another year had passed, following pressure from the European Parliament. Today, it is integrated as one of the rules that make up the *Six-Pack*. Another example can be seen in the "Euro Plus Pact". Signed in March 2011 by the Heads of State or government of the Member States of the Eurozone and six other Member States, it includes a number of commitments on competitiveness, employment, public finance and financial stability. However, it is not a treaty or a Community act. It is still no more than a political commitment. All the same, it is included in the European Semester and is being assessed by the Union's institutions. What value should be attached to the recommendations that are based on non-compliance with this pact?

[12] The Treaties establishing the European Financial Stability Facility (EFSF) and the European Stability Mechanism (ESM), just like the "Fiscal Compact Treaty" (TSCG), are not a matter for Community law. They are international treaties, respectively linking 27 Member States (EFSF), 17 Member States (those of the Eurozone – ESM) and 25 Member States (TSCG).

in the Economic and Monetary Union modifies the provisions of the *Six-Pack* by tightening them. This means that an international treaty, signed by 25 Member States, corrects an act of Community law adopted by 27 Member States.[13] It is high time to build an ordered and structured legal system. There is still a distinct lack of legal stability in Europe. In principle, law is long-lasting and sustainable. Yet this is an area where impermanence dominates. The ink on the treaty had barely dried before some were calling for a new institutional negotiation, sometimes on the key points. The *Six-Pack* was just coming into effect when the *Two-Pack* was added. Is this a good way to proceed at a time when economic and social behaviour must be controlled? Empiricism, not to mention institutional tinkering, is not the best way to work. We need to give time to the rules and institutions to acclimatise before reviewing provisions or modifying the key elements.

2.3.2 A common constitutional practice grows through the courts, which still operate within separate institutional groups. These are constitutional courts (with the exception of the Netherlands), Councils of State or administrative courts, Supreme Courts or Superior courts of justice, the Court of Justice of the European Union, the European Court of Human Rights, and so on.

It is important to align their concerns and interventions. Formal or informal modes of operation are implemented to this end. For example, the constitutional standard may expressly refer to a conventional standard or the constitutional court may always return to the same international standard. *R. Arnold* notably quotes the decision of the German Federal Constitutional Court of 14 October 2004: "The European Convention on Human Rights is in force in the German legal system [...] It has the value of a federal law. It must be taken into account in the interpretation of national law, including human rights and the rule of law." To quote that other decision of 30 June 2009 on the Lisbon Treaty: "The State is open [...] domestic standards should be interpreted in accordance with international law."

The conventional standard may refer, even if only through national traditions, to constitutional texts. But the reference is mainly to the institutional structures of the States, or at least the way they view the protection of fundamental rights. It is still possible for the judge to use catalogues that are not applicable strictly speaking, but which he will use for the purpose of comparison or as an integral element of an internationally recognised *opinio juris*.

2.3.3 Belgium's future cannot be separated from that of the European Union. It is no coincidence that Belgium's capital aspires to be one of the most effective seats for the Union's institutions. This aspiration is not supposed to antagonise any other city in Europe. The Belgians have understood the strategic importance of Europe for the existence of their small nation.

---

[13] A further example is the separation of competences between the Union and the States, which is not made with reference to a clear dividing line. A number of competences are concurrent rather than exclusive. Under these conditions, the principle of subsidiarity must be used to allow either the Union or the States, depending on the situation, to assert their authority and exercise their responsibilities.

If divided, how could the Belgians possibly lay claim to the title of being 'Europe's star pupil'? If separated, how could they recommend that their own motto, "L'union fait la force" (strength through unity), be applied on a wider scale?

Belgium's best chances are to be found in Europe, which obliges the Belgians to look further ahead and to keep their eyes on the horizon. If Europe struggles, that is bad for Belgium. If federal Europe moves forward, that is good for federal Belgium.

The opposite is also true. If Belgium were not to make a success of its institutional restructuring,[14] the country would be living proof that two peoples cannot live together within the same State. How then could 27 other Member States reconcile themselves with that? However, if Belgium were to find itself on a path to a new balance, albeit at the cost of arrangements that are sometimes conceptually complex and tricky to implement,[15] it would demonstrate to everyone through example that it only takes a little imagination and knowhow to build and live in a new structure. It would also show that living in such a structure is not always wonderful, but at least the experience can be orderly and comfortable.

3 The fusion between Belgium and Europe is complete. Nobody would dare to suggest that Europe's future belongs solely to the Belgians. Yet it is tempting to think that Belgium's future largely belongs to its European partners.

The European partners should think carefully about their responsibilities! They must not get side-tracked by the financial disputes that EU citizens struggle to comprehend, even though these disputes can sometimes affect them so hard! It would be better for the partners to help citizens by offering innovative and dynamic policies that encourage them to be supportive! For instance, citizens should also be invited to collaborate with their counterparts from other continents! Lastly, the partners should strive to resolve political and social issues, instead of focusing on economic and financial difficulties!

Europe needs more soul, something that does not fall under the law – be it treaties, directives or case law. This extra soul will ultimately be forged from the mindset of the Union's leaders and citizens. Ideally, it will one day be incorporated into the legal sphere – in our thoughts and actions!

[14] Many Belgians hope that the consolidation will be successful one day. A small minority believes it is the first step towards even greater "detachment", or even secession, within the Belgian State.

[15] The explanation of the institutional system – European Belgium – may seem clear. But the system is complicated. It gives rise to a number of difficulties and conflicts. Conflicts over competences, conflicts of interest, political conflicts, and so on. Most importantly, conflicts over the vision of Belgium's immediate future or definitive future. Belgium is not at ease. I doubt that it will be in the short term.

References

Delpérée, F. (2000). *Le droit constitutionnel de la Belgique*. Brussels: Bruylant.

Delpérée, F. (2001). Constitutional law. In H. Bocken, & W.De Bondt (Eds.), *Introduction to Belgian Law*. Brussels: Bruylant.

Delpérée, F. (2006). *La Constitution de 1830 à nos jours, et même au-delà*. Brussels: Ed. Racine.

Delpérée, F. (2007). *La Belgique, un projet d'avenir?* Brussels: Ed. Luc Pire.

Delpérée, F. (2013). La protection des droits fondamentaux en Europe: à quand un cours d'harmonie?. In A. Alen, V. Joosten, R. Leysen, & W. Verrijdt (Eds.), *Liberae Cogitationes. Liber amicorum Marc Bossuyt* (pp. 197–210). Cambridge: Intersentia.

Delpérée, F. (2014a). Le nouveau Sénat. Quelles réalités, quelles perspectives? *La Revue générale*, *9*(10), 9–11.

Delpérée, F. (2014b). *Aux urnes, citoyens!* Hamme-Mille: Les Claines.

Delpérée, F., & Depré, S. (1998). *Le système constitutionnel de la Belgique*. Larcier: Brussels.

Delpérée, F., & Verdussen, M. (2005). L'égalité, mesure du fédéralisme. In F. Gélinas, & J.-F. Gaudreault-DesBiens (Eds.), *Le fédéralisme dans tous ses états: Gouvernance, identité et méthodologie/The states and moods of federalism: Governance, identity and methodology* (pp. 193–208). Brussels: Bruylant.

Hasquin, H. (2014). *Déconstruire la Belgique? Pour lui assurer un avenir?* Brussels: Académie royale de Belgique.

Lejeune, Y. (2010). *Droit constitutionnel belge. Fondements et institutions*. Brussels: Larcier.

Pâques, M. (2005). *Droit public élémentaire en quinze leçons*. Brussels: Larcier.

Sägesser, C., & Istasse, C. (2014). *Le Sénat et ses réformes successives. Courrier hebdomadaire n° 2219–2220*. Brussels: CRISP.

Uyttendaele, M. (2005). *Précis de droit constitutionnel belge – Regards sur un système institutionnel paradoxal* (3rd edn.). Brussels: Bruylant.

Uyttendaele, M. (2014). *Les institutions de la Belgique*. Brussels: Bruylant.

Vande Lanotte, J., & Goedertier, G. (2007). *Handboek Belgisch publiekrecht* (5th edn.). Bruges: Die Keure.

The Italian Senate under Reform: Sacrifice or Self-Reflection?

Jörg Luther

1 Introduction

Albrecht Weber's "Europäische Verfassungsvergleichung" (2010) is a wonderful "late work" that applies to the constitutional framework of public powers a method first developed for the analysis of the "Fundamental Rights in Europe and North America". This method looks at the historical context, at the gradual development of textures and at the functions of fundamental principles and organisational structures, including a multilevel approach and moments of evaluation and assessment (*Wertung*) based more on fundamental principles and rights than on organisation and powers. There is a personal colour and also a national style in this comparative law methodology mostly based on a philosophy of legal positivism. The European comparison of constitutions aims to be helpful for practices of constitutional reform, constitutional adjudication and international law and for the systemic construction of an *ius constitutionale europaeum*.

The question is whether the knowledge of comparative law always promotes cultural and economic development or sometimes endangers a specific constitutional heritage and identity. Comparative constitutional law has always been influenced by comparative private law know-how on legal transplants and circulation of legal models that even in "public" law often happen in silence: "ça va sans dire". The empirical research on the real use of comparative arguments and foreign materials in constitutional law-making and judgments is still in the earliest stages.

It might be useful to reflect more on the normative basis and on the impact of comparative arguments and non-national ideas in constitutional law-making procedures. Especially in the European Union and in the Council of Europe, there could be an interest and perhaps even more than a duty of good neighbourhood to observe the constitutional law developments in all Member States and to establish a sort of transnational "constitutional dialogue". This dialogue can be promoted by conferences of constitutional judges, academic meetings and blogs on the internet, but it needs to be deepened through scientific research. A good way to start this dialogue could be a tale of experiences of the use of comparative law in constitu-

H.-J. Blanke et al. (eds.), *Common European Legal Thinking*,
DOI 10.1007/978-3-319-19300-7_27

tional reforms. From an Italian, German and European point of view, the ongoing reform of bicameralism could offer an argument and example for a reflection on the conditions and outcomes of comparative constitutional reasoning.

2 European Inputs for a Reform of the Italian Senate?

Bicameralism was first officially compared by the Venice Commission. An excellent report by *Patrice Gélard* in 2006 concluded:

> 43. Europe's second chambers, which are too often the butt of criticism and frequently misunderstood, merit more consideration. Of course it is perfectly understandable if small countries and ones that are still establishing their democratic system feel that second chambers are not essential. However they are necessary, and will become increasingly so, in federal states and ones that are constitutionally regionalised or heavily decentralised, where second chambers represent geographical areas whereas first chambers represent peoples.
>
> 44. Unlike lower houses, second chambers should not necessarily be elected by direct universal suffrage, thus enabling the former – other than in exceptional circumstances – to have the final word in the adoption of legislation and sole power to overturn governments.[1]

The report criticised the "ambiguities of selection by direct universal suffrage": "Outside of federal states, direct universal suffrage to select members of both chambers of bicameral parliaments, even with different voting systems, creates a constitutional peculiarity that either necessitates equality between the two or, if the second chamber has fewer powers than the first, infringes the principle of popular sovereignty. [...] In the former case, one may question the value of a system where the selection of both chambers by direct universal suffrage creates constitutional clones. Both then represent the population at large, which may impede the efficient conduct of parliamentary business. Italy falls into this category, with the collapse of the constitutional initiative designed to turn the Senate into the representative of the regions."

This strange call for popular sovereignty was made by an international advisory body that could be perceived itself as an outcome of the senatorial tradition of the *Consiglio dei Pregadi* in Venice. Of course, the Italian Senate is not just a clone, nor an identical twin brother of the first Chamber, but why should people not wish to elect a bicameral parliament? The constitutional initiative of the Italian Government of that time did not just "collapse" but was rejected by an act of popular sovereignty. So why should populations finally accept uniform second chambers? The criticisms are well known: second chambers are expensive and they impose excessive delays on the work of the first – elected – chambers. We will see that these criticisms have become nowadays a key argument of constitutional politics: the debt crisis needs sacrifices, needs political cost cutting and needs quicker decisions.

[1] European Commission for Democracy Through Law (Venice Commission). Report on Second Chambers in Europe: "Parliamentary complexity or democratic necessity?" by Mr Patrice Gélard, Council of Europe, CDL(2006)059rev, http://www.venice.coe.int/webforms/documents/?pdf=CDL(2006)059-e

The Council of Europe itself is facing similar criticism being an organisation based on a spirit of federalism, with a Parliamentary Assembly, a Committee of Ministers and a Congress of Local and Regional Authorities, all non-directly elected bodies that could be considered virtually as a bi- or even tricameral system with federal roots. The report acknowledges that "federal states in Europe and elsewhere in the world all have bicameral systems", but it has to be added that outside Europe even federal states with unicameral systems exist[2], that second chambers in federal states can be replaced or bypassed by conferences and other mechanisms of cooperative federalism and that in multiparty democracy they never stand just for the representation of geographical areas.

Even the European Union is an institution of federalism, not a federal State. If we look at the role of the directly elected Parliament and the Council of Ministers and at the new indirectly elected Presidency of the Commission, we can find in the institutional pluralism elements of a more or less symmetric bi- or tricameralism. If we look furthermore at the consultative organs of the Committee of Regions (CoR) and the Economic and Social Committee, we can find other elements of a partially equal, partially unequal pluri- or even multicameralism. From a constitutional economics perspective, the rationality of all forms of institutional pluralism in a common market is always questionable.[3] If the economists hold that bicameralism has negative effects on government spending, on the one hand inhibiting government interference in economy and welfare action, on the other hand increasing budget deficits,[4] the public finance policies of the Eurozone could push for less powerful second chambers.

A recent study carried out for the Committee of the Regions (CoR) tried to obtain inspiration for its own role in the (future) EU decision-making process looking at the following second chambers:

1 Austria: Federal Council (Bundesrat), 2 Belgium: Senate (Sénat/Senaat), 3 Czech Republic: Senate (Senát), 4 France: Senate (Sénat), 5 Germany: Federal Council (Bundesrat), 6 Ireland: Senate (Seanad Éireann), 7 Italy: Senate (Senato), 8 The Netherlands: Upper Chamber or Senate (Eerste Kamer), 9 Poland: Senate (Senat), 10 Romania: Senate (Senatul), 11 Slovenia: National Council (Državni Svet), 12 Spain: Senate (Senade), 13 United Kingdom: House of Lords.[5]

---

[2] Watts 2006, p. 2: United Arab Emirates, Venezuela, and the small island federations of Comoros in the Indian Ocean, Micronesia in the Pacific, and St. Kitts and Nevis in the Caribbean.

[3] Leen 2013, p. 3.

[4] Neiva 2009, p. 4.

[5] Other special cases should be added: 1) The old State Council of Luxembourg has an observer status in the European Association of Senates, being a body of experts, including academics, that delivers opinions on drafts and amendments and approves the request for not re-examining legislation after a first debate. 2) The legislative power in Cyprus "shall be exercised by the House of Representatives in all matters except those expressly reserved for the Communal Chambers" (Art. 61), two regional legislatures without a higher second chamber. 3) The Norwegian Storting, established in 1814, split itself in the Odelsting and Lagting, but a constitutional reform ended this unique case of semi-bicameralism in 2009, and all Scandinavian and Baltic States were now unicameral countries.

The study made an evaluation: "In order to guarantee a solid degree of legitimacy to second chambers and to avoid continuous debates on reforms, a clear differentiation between second chambers and first chambers has to be assured, both with regard to their composition and to their legislative competences." But why and how does differentiation matter with reference to legitimacy? The answer is to a certain extent self-interested:

> As far as their composition is concerned, the differentiation may be expressed through a second chamber representing sub-national entities, as provinces, regions, departments, municipalities, etc. while the first chamber represents the people on a population basis. Territorial representation constitutes a common feature between most second chambers in European Member States and the CoR at the European level and should be maintained for the latter since it constitutes its core mandate.[6]

The report observes that most second chambers have differentiated legislative competences and exercise different types of oversight over executive actions "other than a no confidence vote strictu sensu." That statistical approach has some normative impact. The final recommendations can not only be directed to the CoR, but even redirected to national constitution makers, including the Italian Senators. One could even try a constructive dialogue: 1) Increase the quality and the impact of opinions in the legislative process! Yes, but if quality depends mainly upon knowledge and time, the greatest attention should be paid to rationality and simplification of bicameral procedures. 2) Build a second chamber enjoying strong legitimacy! And if the strongest legitimacy remains popular election, would it be wise to stop popular election? 3) Include experts! Is not the greater age of Senators, the former Presidents of the Republic and the lifelong senators already the best guarantee of expertise? 4) Strive for a suspensive veto power upon draft legislation involving regional and local interests! Does not all state legislation potentially involve regional and local interests and all regional legislation potentially involve national interests? 5) Develop a constructive dialogue with the government! How could the second chamber be involved in the existing direct dialogue through conferences? 6) Seek to achieve a consensus on territorial considerations! How could the second chamber offer a service of arbitration for conflicts between state, regions and local governments? 7) Strive to be acknowledged as a "constitutional" watchdog! So shouldn't the Senate have direct access to the Constitutional court?

The rationalisation of the institutional architecture of the European Union needs of course to be distinguished and separated from the reform of "fundamental structures, political and constitutional, inclusive of regional and local government" of the Member states (Art. 4.2 TEU). But this treaty provision has acknowledged that homologation of national identities is a concrete risk and the report shows how statistics can push for "normalisation". From a normative point of view one has to remember that each national case of bicameralism is a specific one and comparative law should not forget that the world of second chambers is still the most differentiated, heterogeneous and exceptional one. For second chambers are not shaped by geography, but by history. From that point of view the Italian Senate is a very

[6] Schmitt 2014, p. 2.

special case that has always been suspected of being an anachronism or "historical hangover".[7]

3 The Italian Senate as an "Institutional Memory" for the State

The official website of the Italian Senate tells one that it was set up in 1848 under the Statute established by *King Albert* for the Kingdom of Sardinia and Piedmont during the European revolutions. The monarchical Senate was composed of the royal family and an unlimited number of lifelong, at least 40-year-old members pertaining to specific categories of elites from the Church, parliament, government, diplomacy, judiciary, administrative divisions, military, academia, as well as cultural heroes such as *Manzoni*, *Carducci* or *Verdi* and industrial elites such as *Agnelli* (Art. 33). The Senate participated in legislative power and could be brought to the High Court of Justice for impeachment, being in this case "not a political body" (Art. 36), but it did not decide on tax and budget matters and on motions for a vote of confidence in the government. It was an elitist project, not an elected body similar to the Belgian Senate of 1831, nor an aristocratic one like the still unreformed UK House of Lords or the Sicilian *Camera de Pari'* kept by the Constitution of 1812, but very close to the French *Chambre des Pairs* of 1830 as integrated by the electoral law of 29 December 1831.

If we look at the history of written constitutions, the prototype was the Chamber of Senators in the Polish constitution of 1791. But it is worth noting that there was already a strong Republican tradition in the first Italian constitutions written at the end of the eighteenth century under French hegemony, with adaptations of the Council of Elders (1795) and the *Sénat Conservateur* (1799). The Constitution of Bologna divided the legislative power into a Major and a Minor Council (1795). The *Repubblica Ligure* created a Council of Sixty and a Council of (30) Seniors (1797), the Cisalpine Republic the *Consiglio de' Juniori* and the *Consiglio degli Anziani* (1798), the Roman Republic a Tribunato and a Senate (1798) and the Republic of Naples (1799) a Senate for the proposal and a Council for the approval of laws.

These precedents show that there was a more idealistic than real continuity with older institutions of the *Ancien Régime* such as, for example, the Senate of Bologna vested by *Napoleon* with powers of the transitory period. A similar continuity can be found in the distinction between "assemblies" and "councils" of the American colonies, renamed "Senate" since the Virginia Constitution of 1776 provided for direct election on a district basis.[8] The states' support of bicameralism tipped the scales in favour of the federal compromise of a state-based Senate and against a unicameral Congress of the Confederation. As *J. Madison* argued in Federalist Pa-

[7] Luther 2006, p. 8.
[8] Bicameral governments existed also in larger cities such as Philadelphia, Baltimore, Boston, St. Louis, Detroit, Pittsburgh, New York and New Orleans.

per No. 62, the purposes of republican bicameralism were greater political stability, better laws and even less corruption: "It [i. e. a senate] doubles the security to the people by requiring the concurrence of two distinct bodies in schemes of usurpation, of perfidy, where the ambition or corruption of one would otherwise be sufficient."[9] That idea was already rooted in the ideas of mixed constitution of *J. Harrington*'s "Political Aphorisms" of 1659: "The reason for a senate is that a popular assembly, rightly constituted, is not capable of any prudent debate" and "the reason of the popular assembly is that a senate, rightly constituted for debate, must consist of so few and eminent persons that, if they have the result too, they will not resolve unto the interest of the people, but according to the interest of themselves. A popular assembly without a senate cannot be wise", but "a senate without a popular assembly will not be honest".[10]

The denomination *Senato* chosen in 1848 was not only ambiguous in a monarchical and republican sense, it included still further institutional memory. In the tradition of Savoy, the Senates of Turin and Chambery which date back to the beginning of the sixteenth century were similar to French parliaments with jurisdiction and the power to examine acts of the sovereign (*interinazione*). The Italian republican tradition of the Minor Councils in Venice, Pisa, Florence and Genova since Renaissance was anticipated by the re-establishment of a Senate in Rome in the context of the medieval Pontifical State.

It might be a myth that senators or senates always existed in Italian history, but the Senate was known as the most stable institution of ancient Rome. The Eurasian roots dated back to Greek and Indian assemblies of tribal elders and clan leaders that elected kings, but *T. Livius* assigned to *Romulus* the invention of an institution based on the representation of "patres familiarum vel gentium". The Senate ratified by its authority the deliberations of the popular assemblies[11] or voted a decree or a "senatus consultus" requested by the magistrate.[12] As *M. Tullius Cicero* anticipated, constitutional bicameralism was based on mixed government: "if there exists not in the state a just distribution and subordination of rights, offices, and prerogatives, so as to give sufficient domination to the chiefs, sufficient authority to the counsel of the senators, and sufficient liberty to the people, the form of the government cannot be durable."[13]

History was needed for the legitimacy of the new Kingdom of Italy and the new laws needed a chamber of historical reflection on the State, with a symbolic starting point in the Roman heritage. The creation of the "Senate" in 1848 was therefore a programme of stability and continuity rooted in history, a typical idea of the *Risorgimento*. The historical roots of the new Italian State were impressed in the architecture of Palazzo Madama (*Christine of France*) in Turin, the first seat of the

[9] Madison 1788, http://www.constitution.org/fed/federa62.htm
[10] Harrington 1977, p. 771 et seq.
[11] Cicero (about 50 BC), III, 28: "Cum potestas in populo auctoritas in senatu sit.".
[12] Gaius (about 160), D. 4: "Senatus consultum est quod senatus iubet atque constituit; idque legis vicem optinet, quamvis fuerit quaesitum.".
[13] Cicero (45 BC/1877/2005), On the Commonwealth, Book II, XXXIII, http://www.gutenberg.org/files/14988/14988-h/14988-h.htm

Italian Senate in 1848 – today a museum of ancient art – that incorporated roman basements and the "porta romana" of the old town, some renaissance windows, a medieval castle of the regional gentry of Acaja, a modern baroque façade designed by *F. Juvarra* and an imitation of the neo-gothic hall of the House of Lords of 1847 (later demolished).

4 The Imperfect Doctrine of "Perfect Bicameralism"

The life of the Senate under the constitutional monarchy was characterised by a weakening of its power through the dynamics of parliamentarisation of the government. Nominations being proposed by prime ministers for reform purposes and abused even for batches of peers, the number of senators rose from 58 up to 464 in 1892 and up to 600 under fascism. Long debates over elected senators had been opened already by *Cavour*[14] and were stimulated by comparative search under *L. Palma* and *G. Mosca*[15] and ended during fascism when *S. Pannunzio* considered the "Senato politico" a representation of the State opposed to the new more technical first Chamber, the *Camera dei fasci e delle Corporazioni*, as a corporative representation of Society.[16]

The Constituent Assembly was elected simultaneously through a referendum that decided for the abolition of the monarchy. There was no majority for an abolition of the Senate, being still a place for dissenting voices of senators such as *L. Albertini*, *F. Ruffini*, *L. Einaudi* and *B. Croce* notwithstanding strong mass-batches decided in 1929 and 1939. The Institution has been suspended in 1943.

The Constituent Assembly was dominated by political parties such as the *Democrazia Cristiana* opting for a representation of local autonomies and professional categories as living forces of the national society. This model was promoted by Roman Catholic social teaching (*Quadragesimo Anno*, 1931) and implemented by the Irish Senate (1937), the *Felsöház* of Hungary (1926), the Romanian Senate (1923) and, even under stronger conditions of corporatism, by the constitutions of Portugal (1933: Art. 102), Austria (1934: Art. 44: Council of State, Council of Culture, Council of Economy, Council of Regions preparing legislation), Estonia (1937) etc. Republican and liberal ideas were more open to privileged forms of territorial representation, less influenced by federalism (US prior to 1919) and more inspired by the Senate model of the third French Republic (1875), partially adopted even in Belgium and Poland (1921) and slightly modified in the fourth French Republic (1946). The leftist parties sympathised rather with Jacobine unicameralism, German revolutionary models of a workers' council or the congress of the Soviet (1924), divided under *J. Stalin* into a Soviet of the Union and a Soviet of Nationalities (1936). Meanwhile, the first draft of the Italian constitution provided still that

[14] Cavour 1848. See Aimo 1977.

[15] Palma 1882 proposed an election by provinces, Mosca 1910 an election at provincial level in constituencies formed by social forces. Critically Ugo 1881, p. 140.

[16] Tupini 1946, p. 125.

a third of Senators should be elected by regional councils, the final compromise opted for a more elastic formula that aimed at excluding any element of federalism: "Art. 57. The Senate of the Republic is elected on a regional basis [. . .]." The number of Senators was determined by a formula 1:200,000. Candidates were elected for five years by direct and universal suffrage and had to have attained the age of forty to be eligible (Art. 58, 60), but the former Presidents of the Republic and "citizens who have honoured the Nation through their outstanding achievements in the social, scientific, artistic and literary fields" chosen by the President were life Senators (Art. 59).

The new Constitution opted for equal powers for both chambers, not for equal legitimacy because it left open the choice of the electoral system. The Constituent Assembly itself adopted furthermore a specific transitory norm: "III. For the first composition of the Senate of the Republic, Deputies to the Constituent Assembly who possess all the requirements to be Senators and who: – had been Presidents of the Council of Ministers or of legislative Assemblies; – had been members of the dissolved Senate; – had been elected at least three times including to the Constituent Assembly; – had been dismissed at the sitting of the Chamber of Deputies of 9 November 1926; – had been imprisoned for not less than five years by a sentence of the special Fascist tribunal for the defence of the State; shall be appointed Senators" (transitional provision III).

Another transitory norm provided elections for the new Regional Councils within one year, but the ordinary regions were established only a quarter of a century later. The Constituent Assembly itself adopted the electoral law for the second Senate in 1948, offering an authentic interpretation of "regional basis" as a simple constituency. The idea to frame a territorial representation through a majority system with uninominal voting was frustrated by a rule that subordinated uninominalism to the achievement of 65 % of the votes of the constituency, providing proportionality for all other seats. The plan of *A. De Gasperi* to apply the transitory norm even to the second legislature failed as well as the attempt to frame a majority bonus at the Chamber of Deputies' elections of 1953. The constitutional reform of 1963 finally fixed the number of elected senators at one half of deputies (315–630) and synchronised the initially differentiated duration of the legislatures.

So what are the remaining normative differences between the two Chambers? (1) The Senators are older and can be presumed to be more experienced in politics. (2) The presence of life Senators can promote quality of debates and representation of public opinion. (3) The functions of the President of the Republic, in all cases in which the President cannot perform them, shall be performed by the President of the Senate. (4) In cases of election of the President of the Republic, Constitutional judges and members of the High Council of the Judiciary, both Chambers vote together and the votes of the first chamber's members have nearly double weight. (5) Both chambers have their own sometimes diverging standing rules. (6) They could differentiate the rules on incompatibility. (7) They might be framed by different electoral laws. (8) The Constitution fixes the number of seats of the smallest regions. (9) The "regional basis" clause allows regional parties to be represented at least in the second chamber.

The debates on reformation of bicameralism started immediately and have never ended. When the French Constitution of 1958 re-established a principle of functional equality of the two chambers in which the first could prevail, the Italian doctrine started to distinguish perfect and imperfect forms of bicameralism.[17] Defenders and deniers of the final arrangement agreed to call the Italian bicameralism "perfect".

The reform debate focussed mainly on three topics of that "perfect" bicameralism at different times: (i) the rationalisation of procedures since the 1970s; (ii) the need for representation of regional and local autonomies since the 1980s; (iii) the rationalisation of the parliamentary form of government since the 1990s. The topics were focussed using comparative research on political pressures for unicameralism, federalism and presidentialism.

(i) Starting from the suppression of the second chamber in Greece (1952) and Denmark (1953), unicameralism was perceived in the 1970s as a European trend (Sweden 1970, Portugal 1976). The main objection to bicameralism was that duplication of procedures should be restricted, a second chamber being expensive and producing an excessive slowdown in the legislative process with the risk of a never-ending *navette*. This argument has never been verified empirically,[18] but the parliamentary practice and procedures have clearly strengthened the cooperation between both chambers. From a technical point of view, duplication causes loss of time especially when a new government is formed and two votes of confidence need to be expressed. Conversely, the division of the law-making process does not necessarily cost time as the Italian Parliament normally undertakes just two readings of a law whereas other parliaments could have more readings. Duplication is irrational for technical administrative procedures, but it could be a means for the rationalisation of political procedures. Italian bicameralism works already under a system of *de facto* unicameralism, in which the second chamber simply can give formal ratification to the decisions of the first chamber. Since the 1980s, further constitutional reform proposals were discussed by three bicameral commissions. The first, headed by *A. Bozzi*, proposed leaving the law-making to the first chamber and assigning a governmental oversight role to the second. In 1990, the Senate adopted a reform that authorised both Chambers to adopt a law without the other chamber's express approval if no re-examination is demanded within 15 days and if a second examination is not prescribed by the Constitution. But this so-called "procedural bicameralism" was not approved by the first chamber and thus did not become law.

(ii) The second objection was outlined when the constitutional project of regionalism was finally realised over the entire national territory. The "regional basis" clause was reconsidered as an unfulfilled promise and a new Senate of Regions as a good support for real regionalisation.[19] The Spanish constitution of 1978 offered a new interpretation of this clause in a context of a more asymmetric regionalism.

[17] Bon Valsassina 1959, Weber 1972, Paladin 1984.

[18] For constitutional economics: Tsebelis and Money 1997.

[19] For the first time: Occhiocupo 1975.

In 1980, G. *Amato* proposed taking the German Bundesrat as a model, a proposal that stimulated intensive comparative law research.[20] The Government launched in 1983 a State-Regions Conference. In 1987, the leader of the Lega Nord, *U. Bossi*, was elected Senator. In the 1990s the demand for federalism increased, the reforms of *F. Bassanini* devolved further competences to regional and local governments and a governmental committee headed by *F. Speroni* proposed transforming the Senate into a representation of regional and local governments. The Reform Commission headed by *M. D'Alema* reached in 1997 a temporary bipartisan consensus on a smaller size for both chambers, the exclusion of the Senate from a vote of confidence and differentiated law-making procedures with the last word belonging to the Chamber of Deputies except for laws affecting the system of autonomies decided in an *ad hoc* Senate composed of 200 municipal, provincial or regional representatives elected by special constituencies in each Region. In 2001, the centre-left majority under the government of *G. Amato* finally adopted a constitutional reform ratified by referendum that extended regional legislative powers and created a bicameral commission in Parliament for all regional affairs. A transitory norm that allows the participation of representatives of Regions and local authorities in that commission was not implemented. In 2005, a referendum rejected a constitutional reform of the centre-right majority under the government of *S. Berlusconi* for a "federal Senate" elected with a restriction of eligibility to former representatives of local autonomies, excluded from the vote of confidence and provided with asymmetrically reduced legislative powers.[21]

(iii) The third objection was raised when the electoral system changed and a more stable form of government was required in the European context. In 1991, a referendum abolished the 65 % quorum requested for direct election of members of the Senate and created in this way a mixed system, majoritarian for 2/3 and proportional for 1/3 of the seats of the Senate, later extended even to the other chamber. In a context of public prosecutors fighting strongly against party corruption ("tangentopoli"), the electoral reform seemed to increase the stability of governments and marked a trend from a multi-party-system and a "consociativist democracy" to an imperfect bipolarism under "majoritarian democracy". The direct election of mayors since 1993 and of presidents of regional governments since 1995 favoured a bipartisan consensus even for semi-presidentialism in 1997, but that part of the bicameral constitution reform project failed. In 2005, a new reform provided a proportional system altered by both "barring" clauses and by a "majority bonus" (*premio di maggioranza:* 340 of 630 seats in the Chamber of Deputies and 55 % of the seats in each regional constituency of the Senate) for the list or coalition that obtains the highest number of valid votes. Political parties are obliged to present a candidate for the Presidency of the Council of ministers, but that is not binding for

[20] Amato 1980, p. 182; Mattarella 1983; Paladin 1984; Violini 1989; Pezzini 1990; Palermo 1997.

[21] For further Italian comparative search see Provincia di Roma (2003); Luther et al. 2006; Bonfiglio 2006; Baldini 2007; Ciolli 2010; Sgrò 2012. For foreign research see Mastias and Grangé 1987; Tsebelis and Money 1997; Gross 2003. For the reform debate see Mangiameli 2014, p. 23 et seqq.

the President's later nomination. This electoral reform produced definitely more stable majorities in the first than in the second chamber. The unwritten rule that assigned to the opposition the presidency of the first chamber and to the majority the presidency of the Senate was no longer respected. The second government of *R. Prodi* was defeated in 2008 in a no-confidence vote of the Senate which was suspected to have been influenced by corruption. The last government of *Berlusconi* had a full majority in both chambers but resigned due to the financial crisis. *M. Monti*, a former EU-commissioner, formed a new technocratic government with bipartisan support after having been nominated a life Senator by the President of the Republic. The powers of the President of the Republic have been strengthened, re-election accepted and even direct election of the President is no longer generally excluded. After the failure of the parliamentary approach to constitutional reforms, bicameralism is today suspected to have weakened the parliamentary form of government.

5 How Comparative Constitutional Experiences Become Constitutional Policies

The elections of 2012 produced an absolute majority in the first chamber, but not in the second.

When the new Parliament failed in 2013 to elect a new President, *G. Napolitano* accepted to be the first re-elected, under the condition that a new political government of "broad agreements" among left- and right-wing parties would make a special commitment to constitutional reform: "Recent years have seen a failure to provide satisfactory solutions for well-founded needs and urgent calls for institutional reform and a renewal of politics and of the parties, in a situation that became interwoven with an acute financial crisis, a grave recession, and growing social malaise. [...] Unforgivable was the failure to reform the electoral law of 2005. (...) No less unforgivable is the failure to make any headway on the reforms – limited and targeted as they were – pertaining to the second part of the Constitution, reforms that took such effort to agree on and yet which never managed to break the taboo of 'equal bicameralism'."[22]

The mission had been prepared by a small group of experts nominated immediately before the re-election. The new left-right Government of *E. Letta* created an enlarged committee of constitutional lawyers and politicians and tabled a bill in parliament for a new constitutional law providing another special revision procedure with a mandatory referendum to be completed at the end of 2014. The commission recommended a reform of regionalism and of bicameralism, designing various transformation or abolition options on the basis of the following introductory observations:

[22] Discourse in Parliament, 22 April 2013, http://www.quirinale.it/elementi/Continua.aspx?tipo=Discorso&key=2700

> Comparative constitutional experiences allow to establish some link between the form of government and the bicameral structure of parliament. States with unicameral parliaments are normally parliamentary democracies. When parliamentary democracies have bicameralism, they provide normally for significant differences in powers, functions and criteria of composition of the two chambers; especially the vote of confidence will only be assigned to one chamber. Forms of equal or quasi equal bicameralism exist under presidential governments or under other non-parliamentary governments. Our model of parliament is ... characterized in an absolutely symmetric way by two chambers that have totally identical functions and powers. Italy presents thus the unique case of a democracy where confidence powers and legislative functions are conferred equally and symmetrically to both chambers.

Comparative law offered in fact the first justification for homologation, preventing any idea of a sort of Italian exceptionalism.[23] One could specify that the Italian constitution already allows differentiation, that a quasi-symmetrical bicameralism still exists in other parliamentary democracies (e. g. the Netherlands) and that bicameralism could at least prevent a trend towards more presidentialism, but the Italian Senate was said to have no further rationality, being nowadays abnormal and anachronistic from the comparative perspective.

In 2014 the reform quandaries were further complicated by the Constitutional Court. The first decision of 2014 struck down two rules of the electoral laws of both chambers, namely the rule that provides fixed party lists for elections excluding personal preferences and the aforesaid "majority bonus", because no minimum share of votes was fixed and no stable and homogeneous majorities in both chambers were ensured. The decision has been criticised because it (1) was held contrary to prior decisions declaring similar questions inadmissible, (2) manipulated existing electoral laws leaving the parliament only with the further revision of the current electoral system and the choice of an entirely new one, (3) made explicit reference to German constitutional jurisprudence.

Conversely, the New Year speech delivered by the President of the Constitutional Court endorsed the presidential inputs for constitutional reform: "By force of experience of a long and tortuous constitutional jurisprudence – prior and subsequent to the reform of 2001 –, we have to point out two needs which are complementary: on the one hand a strong simplification of the criteria of distribution of competences is unavoidable, on the other hand institutional opportunities for a confrontation need to be strengthened in order to give back to politics more appropriate means for governing conflicts between the centre and the periphery, without expecting adjustments and repairs from the judiciary."[24] The "institutional opportunities" were offered by the reform of bicameralism.

We do not know whether the constitutional reform makes unofficially part of the structural reforms prospected to and expected by the European Union and the so-called Troika. A document of the Minister of Finance of February 2014 stated: "In June 2013, the Government inaugurated a programme of constitutional reforms to streamline governance. The proposals under discussion aim at modernising

[23] Della Cananea 2014, p. 6.
[24] Relazione del Presidente Gaetano Silvestri sulla giurisprudenza costituzionale del 2013, http://www.cortecostituzionale.it/documenti/relazioni_annuali/Silvestri_20140227.pdf (my translation).

the electoral law, the form of Government and Parliament."[25] In fact, the new government of *M. Renzi* immediately made proposals for both an electoral and constitutional reform – under the existing revision procedures (Art. 138) – in order to change a third of the provisions of the Constitution including bicameralism. Both reform proposals were approved, the constitutional one with some significant amendments by a first vote of the Senate on 8 August 2014. The central States' competences should be extended, mixed legislation of the State and the Region – following the German reform example – mostly abolished. The new "Senate of the Republic" shall "represent the territorial institutions". The Senate still has full legislative power on constitutional amendments and laws, laws regarding local government, referendums and the protection of linguistic minorities and in matters related to the rights of families and health care. In addition, it may propose amendments or other kinds of bills, but the Chamber of Deputies has the final decision. In a few cases (including budget matters) this final decision has to be taken by absolute majority. The Senate "has the concurrent legislative power in matters of Art. 29 and 32.2[26] and in such cases and with such modalities as established by the Constitution". It no longer has power to hold a vote of confidence and exercises no control over the government, but has substantial competences in EU and public administration matters. For that purpose it has "functions of coordination (*raccordo*) between the European Union, the State and the constituencies of the Republic" and it "participates in the decisions regarding the elaboration and implementation of normative acts and policies of the European Union and evaluating their impact. It carries out the evaluation of the activities of public administrations, the implementation of state legislation, control and evaluation of public policies."

The Senate modified the rules of its own composition proposed by the government, reducing the presidential power of nomination from 21 to 5 senators (for a seven-year term)[27] and providing that the remaining 95 senators are distributed among the regions in proportion to their population, being elected on a proportionality basis by the regional council among the mayors of the region (21) and among its own members (74). The new formula of "territorial representation" and of election without direct universal suffrage is most similar to the Austrian model of *Bundesrat*, but as the Regional councils are elected under a majority system and as membership in a regional council is not incompatible with positions in the regional government, the new second chamber could have some similarity to the German *Bundesrat*. If a political career goes from the lower to the higher level, "Senators" could become "Juniors". They would be out of the sphere of control of the regional council. An informal control could be realised by Senators representatives of the opposition and, last but not least, by the presidents of the regional councils. In the end, political parties will bring the new Senate under their control, but "territorial

[25] http://www.dt.tesoro.it/export/sites/sitodt/modules/documenti_it/analisi_progammazione/analisi_programmazione_economico/Nota_riforme_in_inglese_febbraio_2014-final.pdf

[26] Fundamental rights related to the family and to health care.

[27] In December 2014, the Committee of constitutional affairs of the first chamber voted for the abolition of the senators nominated by the President of the Republic.

representation" could strengthen their internal federalism and the regional level of government could become a laboratory for legislative and political alternatives.

6 Concluding Doubts

The outcome of the controversial reform process shall not be prophesied, but for the scientific dialogue at least some general doubts need to be outlined.

First quandary: Is self-reform the best reform? A directly elected chamber that decides through constitutional amendment to be changed into a body with less democratic legitimacy sacrifices its authority and risks losing its identity.[28] Conversely, self-restraint could be a virtue of political "regeneration" and "self-reflection" a therapy of post-democratic traumata. The conflict of interests of the deciding Senators could be a moment of moral self-coercion and should not be resolved through a delay of the entry into force of the reform as provided by the rejected reform proposal of 2005.

Second quandary: Should a non-federal second chamber share constitution-making power? As long as the State is not of a federal type, a second chamber representing mostly regional and local autonomies should not be necessarily part of the *pouvoir constituant constitué.* If constitutional laws need the highest form of democratic legitimacy, there could be a lack of coherence if a non-directly elected chamber on the one hand is excluded from ordinary legislation, on the other hand entrusted with a full veto power on constitution-making. Constitutional reforms could be better entrusted to qualified majorities in parliament and to a referendum than to a veto power of a Senate that represents "territorial institutions" and defends few social rights.

Third quandary: How much democratic legitimacy does a second chamber need? If all political powers need to have democratic legitimacy, the shift from symmetric to asymmetric forms of bicameralism should avoid unreasonable losses of legitimacy. The choice to exclude the second chamber from the vote of confidence in the government would make it not unreasonable to conserve direct election of senators, with the principle "no equal legitimacy without equal powers" being a dogma not commanded by popular sovereignty.[29] Almost identical functions can require almost identical legitimacy: that happened to the Italian Senate in the past. And the people can be sovereign even when electing both, representatives that decide and representatives that control. The people of course can decide to prefer the referendum to a second chamber, unlike the Danish people preferred, it would not lose sovereignty when delegating the choice of the watchmen to other elected authorities.

Fourth quandary: In a parliamentary democracy can bicameralism be combined with any voting system? Should the form of bicameralism depend upon the form

[28] Fusaro 2013, p. 12.
[29] In that sense Luciani 2014, p. 10.

of government and the form of government upon the electoral system, all choices are inextricably linked even if made by different sources of law. The Italian case shows that a difference in the voting systems of the two chambers became incompatible with symmetric powers. The Australian case shows that different voting systems justify different functions, being the Government not bound by confidence od State. The US case shows that if both chambers had a majoritarian voting system, the second chamber is less stimulated to be a "chambre de réflexion". The territorialisation of representation in the second chamber could weaken the principle of political equality of citizens: if mountains and islands are less populated, the vote of citizens residing in such areas should not be privileged to an unreasonable measure.

Fifth quandary: How much does economy have to do with bicameralism? Comparative constitutional law can learn from constitutional economics, but not without considering history. As *Jeremy Waldron* pointed out reading the classics, *Bentham*'s perfection thesis that all advantages of a second chamber could be obtained in the first one was confuted already by Mill and Bagehot.[30] The concurrence of a second chamber helps to prevent representatives from "the consciousness to have only themselves to consult", this being no perfect representation of the people. The contemporary debates on "post-democracy" and "populism" give further plausibility to the argument that the imperfect character of democracy derives from the fact that all people(s) are imperfect themselves. The need for a "chambre de réflexion" being more perceived in bigger states, the yet unanswered question is how to make bigger democracies more reflexive without corporatism. In the current debate on a new reform of the House of Lords[31], the Italian idea for the people to be represented as a union of territorial pluralism has influenced at least the Labour Party's project of an elected Senate of Nations and Regions. Meanwhile, the Irish people rejected the abolition of the *Seanad Eireann*, the Canadian Supreme Court decided that a similar reform of the Canadian Senate needed to be ratified by the provinces.[32]

Sixth quandary: Let the people decide? The Italian Senate is expected to be reformed, but the political consensus on the reform details is fragile. The first word has been given to the Senators, but they know that the last word is reserved for the people. The more the reform expectations grow, the more the legitimacy of the institution itself is at stake. The people can decide to honour such self-reflection, but in the long run they could even prefer to sacrifice the institution in order to save finances and to punish political parties, following the Bavarian precedent of 1999. The chances provided by good reformation are that people learn with new senators how to keep their law-makers under democratic control and to maintain a sufficiently idealistic and realistic political self-understanding of society. The risk is that bad reformation could be the last one before abolition.

[30] Waldron 2012, p. 7 et seqq.

[31] See Russell 2013.

[32] Supreme Court of Canada, Reference re Senate Reform (25 April 2014), 2014 SCC 32.

Nevertheless, the real value of reformation will depend not only on general ideas and consensus, as the devil is well known to dwell in the details of more complicated law-making procedures.

References

Aimo, P. (1977). *Bicameralismo e regioni*. Milan: Edizioni di Comunità.

Amato, G. (1980). *Una Repubblica da riforma*. Bologna: Il Mulino.

Baldini, V. (Ed.). (2007). *La camera degli interessi territoriali nello stato composto*. Napoli: Satura.

Bonfiglio, S. (2006). *Il Senato in Italia*. Roma: Laterza.

Bon Valsassina, M. (1959). *Il bicameralismo imperfetto o limitato nelle Costituzioni contemporanee*. Napoli: Jovene.

Conte di Cavour, C. B. (1848). La riforma del Senato. *Il Risorgimento, 27 May*(130), 1.

Cicero, M. T. (about 50 BC). *De Legibus*, http://www.thelatinlibrary.com/cicero/leg.shtml. Accessed 31 November 2014.

Cicero, M. T. (45 BC/1877/2005). Tusculan Disputations. Translated by C. D. Yonge. New York: Harper & Brothers (1877), eBook Project Gutenberg (2005), http://www.gutenberg.org/files/14988/14988-h/14988-h.htm. Accessed 31 November 2014.

Ciolli, I. (2010). *Il territorio rappresentato*. Napoli: Jovene.

Della Cananea, G. (2014). The End of (Symmetric) Bicameralism or a Novus Ordo? *Italian Journal of Public Law*, *6*, 1–8.

Fusaro, C. (2013). *Bicameralism in Italy. 150 Years of Poor Design, Disappointing Performances, Aborted Reforms*. http://www.carlofusaro.it/in_english/Bicameralism_in_ITA_2013.pdf. Accessed 31 November 2014

Gaius (about 160). Gai Institutiones, http://www.thelatinlibrary.com/gaius1.html. Accessed 31 November 2014.

Gross, T. (2003). Zwei-Kammer-Parlamente in der Europäischen Union. *Zeitschrift für ausländisches öffentliches Recht und Ausländerrecht*, *63*, 29–57.

Harrington, J. (1977). *The Political Works of J. Harrington*. Cambridge: University Press.

Leen, A. (2013). *Fiscal Bicameralism: The Core of a EU Constitution (24 March)*. http://ssrn.com/abstract=2238647 or http://dx.doi.org/10.2139/ssrn.2238647. Accessed 31 November 2014

Luciani, M. (2014). *Il bicameralismo, oggi. Rivista Associazione Italiana dei Costituzionalisti, 2*. http://www.rivistaaic.it/la-riforma-del-bicameralismo-oggi.html. Accessed 31 November 2014

Luther, J. (2014). Il bicameralismo si supera se si reinventa (ma anche se si rottama). *Il Piemonte delle autonomie*, 1(2). http://piemonteautonomie.cr.piemonte.it/cms/index.php/il-bicameralismo-si-supera-se-non-si-reinventa. Accessed 31 November 2014

Luther, J., Passaglia, P., & Tarchi, R. (Eds.). (2006). *A World of Second Chambers*. Milan: Giuffré.

Madison, J. (1788). The Senate. *The Federalist*, 62, 27 February 1788, http://www.constitution.org/fed/federa62.htm. Accessed 31 November 2014

Mangiameli, S. (2014). The Regions and the Reforms. In S. Mangiameli (Ed.), *Italian Regionalism: Between Unitary Traditions and Federal Processes* (pp. 1–34). Berlin: Springer.

Mastias, J., & Grangé, J. (1987). *Les secondes chambres du parlément en Europe occidentale*. Paris: Economica.

Mattarella, S. (1983). Das Zweikammersystem in Italien. *Archiv des öffentlichen Rechts, 108*, 370–391.

Mosca, G. (1910). La riforma del Senato italiano. *Rivista di diritto pubblico e della pubblica amministrazione in Italia, 2*(1), 564–570.

Neiva, P. (2009). *Presidentialism, Bicameralism, Federalism and Budget Deficits: The Effects of Political Institutions on Government Spending*. http://paperroom.ipsa.org/papers/paper_257.pdf. Accessed 31 November 2014

Occhiocupo, N. (1975). *La "Camera delle regioni"*. Milan: Giuffre.

Paladin, L. (1984). Tipologia e fondamenti giustificativi del bicameralismo. *Quaderni costituzionali, 4*, 219–242.

Palermo, F. (1997). *Germania ed Austria: modelli federali e bicamerali a confronto*. Trento: Università degli Studi.

Palma, L. (1882). La riforma del Senato in Italia. *Nuova antologia, 61*, 193–223.

Pezzini, B. (1990). *Il Bundesrat della Germania federale*. Milan: Giuffré.

Provincia di Roma (Ed.). (2003). *Un Senato delle autonomie per l'Italia federale*. Napoli: Edizioni Scientifiche Italiane.

Russell, M. (2013). *The Contemporary House of Lords: Westminster Bicameralism Revived*. Oxford: University Press.

Schmitt, P. (2014). *Comparative overview of consultative practices within the second chambers of EU national legislatures. European Union*. http://cor.europa.eu/en/documentation/studies/Documents/comparative-overview-of-consultative-practices-within-the-second-chambers-of-eu-national-legislatures.pdf. Accessed 31 November 2014

Sgrò, F. (2012). *Il Senato e il principio della divisione dei poteri*. Milan: Giuffré.

Tsebelis, G., & Money, I. (1997). *Bicameralism*. Cambridge: University Press.

Tupini, G. (1946). *Il Senato*. Bologna: Zanichelli.

Ugo, G. B. (1881). *Il Senato nel Governo Costituzionale*. Torino: Loescher.

Violini, L. (1989). *Bundesrat e Camera delle Regioni*. Milan: Giuffré.

Waldron, J. (2012). *Bicameralism. New York University School of Law, Public Law & Legal Theory Research Paper Series. Working Paper No. 12–19*. http://ssrn.com/abstract=2045646. Accessed 31 November 2014

Watts, R. (2006). *Federal Second Chambers Compared, federalism.it, 15*. http://www.federalismi.it/ApplOpenFilePDF.cfm?dpath=document&dfile=27072006094033.pdf&content=Federal+second+chambers+compared+-+stato+-+dottrina+-+. Accessed 31 November 2014

Weber, A. (2010). *Europäische Verfassungsvergleichung. Ein Studienbuch*. Munich: C. H. Beck.

Weber, Y. (1972). La crise du bicamérisme. *Revue du droit public et de la science politique, 5*, 573–606.

Romania's Accession to the European Union: The Rule of Law Dilemma

Reimer von Borries

1 The Challenge of the Rule of Law

1.1 How can the EU ensure respect for the Rule of Law, enshrined in Art. 2 TEU, by its Member States and by Accession Candidates? How far do the monitoring and supervisory competences of the EU reach in this regard? How effective could such a monitoring be? These questions moved more and more into focus after the 2004/2007 enlargement of the EU. As Romania shifted from the collapse of the Ceausescu régime in December 1989 to EU membership in January 2007, the question of how respect for the Rule of Law could be effectively ensured was an issue of permanent debate, and so it continues to be. The numerous Regular and Monitoring Reports of the Commission on the accession negotiations 1998–2006, its Strategy Papers during this period and its frequent Regular Reports in the framework of the Cooperation and Verification Mechanism (CVM) after 2007 provide a rich source of information about this unique debate, at least from the perspective of the EU.[1]

1.2 This paper seeks to analyse the efforts of the EU to promote respect for the Rule of Law in Romania during the pre-accession period and thereafter and to highlight the main issues at stake, in particular its efforts to strengthen the *independence of the judiciary* which is central to the Rule of Law concept.[2] For a complete account of the role of the Rule of Law principle during the accession negotiations, one would have to take into account the disputes within the Romanian government and within Romanian society. However, this would exceed the scope of this study. As the result of the overview given in this paper, the author suggests that certain lessons for future enlargements should be learned from the experience of Romania's accession to the EU.

[1] Wennerström 2007, p. 197 et seq.

[2] Wennerström 2007, p. 205. A discussion of these basic concepts in EU law, German law and the ECHR is beyond the scope of this paper. See Schmidt-Aßmann 2004; Kuijer 2004; Ullerich 2011.

H.-J. Blanke et al. (eds.), *Common European Legal Thinking*,
DOI 10.1007/978-3-319-19300-7_28

1.3 In December 2006, almost two weeks before accession, the European Commission established a "mechanism" designed to promote judicial reform and the fight against corruption in Romania (below, Sect. 4).[3] However, seven years later – in its report of 22 January 2014 "*On Progress in Romania under the Cooperation and Verification Mechanism*" – the Commission still registered important deficits in these areas.[4] Thus, the struggle to enforce respect for the Rule of Law continues today to be an issue in Romania and indeed has developed into an "endless story".[5] Therefore, one could ask the question whether the EU should consider developing and applying more precise criteria for scrutiny of the Rule of Law, and whether it should create more effective tools for their enforcement, in acceding countries as well as in the existing Member States (below, Sect. 5).

2 The Road to the Accession Negotiations (1991–1999)

2.1 First Steps Towards the Respect for the Rule of Law

2.1.1 After the breakdown of the Ceausescu regime, Romania undertook a number of steps with the aim of ensuring respect for the Rule of Law in the country. In particular, a new Constitution[6] was adopted that defined Romania as "a democratic and social state governed by the rule of law" (Art. 1.3).[7] The revised Constitution of 2003 explicitly added to this declaration of good intentions that "(t)he State shall be organized based on the principle of the separation and balance of powers" (Art. 1.4), but this principle already implicitly underlay the constitutional structure of 1991.[8] According to the jurisprudence of the Constitutional Court, it is the most important principle of the Romanian constitutional order.[9] The Constitution also provides that "judges shall be independent and subject only to the law" (Art. 123.2, since 2003: Art. 124.3) and that they "shall be irremovable according to the law" (Art. 124.1; since 2003: Art. 125.1).[10]

---

[3] Decision 2006/928/EC of 13 December 2006, O.J. L 354/56 (2006).

[4] Progress Report of 22 January 2014, COM(2014) 37.

[5] Roos 2011, p. 7 et seq.

[6] Constitution of Romania of 21 November 1991; English version www.cdep.ro/pls/dic/site.page?id=256&idl=2. For the genesis of the Constitution of 1991 see Slavu 2008, p. 156; Hein 2013, p. 285 et seq.

[7] Kerek 2010, p. 479, observes that according to the Constitutional Court practice, the Rule of Law is a structural principle which does not have the quality of a legal norm.

[8] Hein 2013, p. 309.

[9] Kerek 2010, p. 481.

[10] Detailed rules for the judicial system were adopted by Law no. 92/1992, Monitorul Oficial no. 197/1992.

2.1.2 As a safeguard for the independence of the judiciary, the Constitution foresees an independent institution, the Superior Council of Magistracy (SCM).[11] Its members were originally elected by Parliament (Art. 132 Constitution of 1991), since 2003 they are elected in general meetings of the magistrates (Art. 133.2). The principal task of the SCM is "to nominate judges and public prosecutors for appointment by the President of Romania" (Art. 133.1; since 2003: Art. 134.1)[12] and to make decisions in relation to their career (promotion and transfer of and sanctions against judges "in accordance with the law": Art. 124.1 sentence 3; since 2003: Art. 125.2).[13] Prosecutors were placed under the authority of the Ministry of Justice but obliged to observe the principles of legality and impartiality (Art. 131.1; since 2003: Art. 132.1).[14]

2.1.3 The Constitution contains a catalogue of fundamental rights (Art. 22–49, since 2003: Art. 22–53)[15] and a Constitutional Court (Art. 140 et seq.; since 2003: Art. 142 et seq.).[16] It includes procedures for challenging the constitutionality of legal provisions before and after their coming into force (Art. 144 a] and c]; since 2003: Art. 146 a] and d]).[17] Constitutional issues arising in individual cases before the ordinary courts are subject to an incidental procedure before the Romanian Constitutional Court ("concrete judicial review");[18] such issues can also be submitted to the Court by the Ombudsman.[19] However, it has been observed that in spite of these comprehensive legal safeguards, the judiciary largely remained *de facto* dependent on the executive branch[20], at least until the sweeping reforms in 2003–2005 (below, Sect. 3.3), and that judicial independence therefore was "a myth rather than reality"[21] in Romania.

---

[11] The SCM was already foreseen in the Constitution of 1909 and existed until 1949; Hein 2013, p. 300.

[12] See Ionescu 2008, p. II/75 et seq. For a critical assessment of the provisions on the judiciary see Hein 2013, p. 309 et seq., a survey of the development of Romanian constitutional law is given by Blokker 2012a, p. 187 et seq.

[13] Ionescu 2008, p II/71.

[14] On the role of the *prosecutors* in Romania between the executive and the judiciary see Carausan 2009, p. 112.

[15] Since 2003: Art. 22–53. See Ionescu 2008, p. II/28 et seq. For an overview of the jurisprudence of the Romanian (and the Hungarian) Constitutional Court on fundamental rights see Kerek 2010, p. 279–498.

[16] Law no. 47/1992 on the organisation and functioning of the Constitutional Court, Monitorul Oficial no. 643/2004; a comprehensive account is given by Kerek 2010, p. 148. In the following: RCC.

[17] Kerek 2010, p. 186 et seq.

[18] Kerek 2010, p. 209; Ionescu 2008, p. II/82.

[19] See Ionescu 2008, p. II/30 et seq. and II/88 et seq.; Gionea and Tontsch 2007, p. 117 et seq.; Kerek 2010, p. 209 et seq. The Constitution provides for the possibility of a direct action of the Ombudsman, but does not provide for a constitutional complaint ("Verfassungsbeschwerde") by individuals.

[20] Hein 2013, p. 313; Regular Report of 13 November 2001, SEC(2001) 1753, p. 20.

[21] Coman and Dallara 2012, p. 835; Hein 2013, p. 311; OSI Report 2002, p. 171 et seq. See also the critical observations by Rothacher 2002, p. 423 et seq., 438, and by Gallagher 2005, p. 285.

2.1.4 After becoming a Member State of the Council of Europe in 1993 (CoE), Romania ratified the European Convention of Human Rights (ECHR) which obliged it to ensure the independence and impartiality of justice by guaranteeing a fair trial (Art. 6.1).[22] According to Art. 20.2 in combination with Art. 11.2 of the Romanian Constitution, the provisions of the ECHR take precedence over national law. Romania also ratified step by step the relevant Conventions of the CoE, the UN and the OECD.[23] According to Art. 3 of the CoE Statute, respect for the Rule of Law is the main criterion for membership.[24] At the time of the accession to the CoE, Romania did not fulfil all requirements regarding the Rule of Law, but the CoE applied a "lax" admission policy, expecting later improvements[25], therefore it was a so-called "*therapeutic accession*".[26] Corresponding to the rules of the CoE, Romania was by its accession obliged to adapt its judicial system accordingly if necessary.[27] The following monitoring by the CoE ended in 1997 with a Resolution of the Parliamentary Assembly of the CoE on honouring Romania's obligations and commitments.[28]

2.2 *Accession Preparations*

2.2.1 On 8 February 1993 Romania signed the Association Agreement (Europe Agreement) which created a free trade area with the (then) European Community[29] and which entered into force on 1 February 1995.[30] It stipulated in the Preamble as its objective the creation of "a new political and economic system which respects the rule of law and human rights". The Europe Agreement functioned *de facto* as a pre-accession instrument.[31] On 22 June 1995 Romania submitted an applica-

[22] Rengeling and Szczekalla 2004, § 44 para 1155–1188; Kuijer 2004, p. 9 et seq., 79 et seq.; Müller 2009, p. 461 et seq.; Tschirky 2011, p. 87 et seq.; Meyer-Ladewig 2011, para 90–100; Grabenwarter and Pabel, in Dörr et al. (2013), p. 742–838; Grabenwarter 2014, para 66 et seq.

[23] Agenda 2000, p. 41; Regular Report of 5 November 2003, SEC(2003) 1211, p. 22.

[24] As to the approach of the CoE to the Rule of Law see Kuijer 2004, p. 79 et seq.; Trechsel 2005, p. 81 et seq.; Grabenwarter and Pabel, in Dörr et al. (2013), p. 742–838; Seibert-Fohr 2012, p. 1334.

[25] Cremona 2003, p. 229; Sticht 2006, p. 360 et seq.; Sannerholm 2012, p. 63.

[26] Tschirky 2011, p. 327; De Witte 2003, p. 229; Sannerholm 2012, p. 62 et seq.

[27] Tschirky 2011, p. 30; Sannerholm 2012, p. 63. See also the Recommendation no. CM/REC (2010) on judges: independence, efficiency and responsibilities. The ECtHR issued numerous judgments against Romania for violation of Art. 6.1 ECHR due to excessive judicial delays; see Tschirky 2011, p. 30; Progress Report of 18 July 2012, COM(2012) 410, p. 8, footnote 23; Regular Report of 5 November 2003, SEC(2003) 1211, p. 27 et seq.

[28] Sticht 2006, p. 362.

[29] From 1993 until 2007, Romania was also a member of the Central European Free Trade Agreement (CEFTA).

[30] O.J. L 357 (1994).

[31] Commission Communication, *The Europe Agreements and Beyond: A Strategy to prepare the Countries of Central and Eastern Europe for accession*, COM(94) 320; Maresceau 1997, p. 16 et seq.

tion for membership of the EU in accordance with Art. O TEU of the Treaty of Maastricht (which had entered into force on 1 November 1993). Since this article did not contain a reference to the Rule of Law as a precondition for accession[32], the European Council undertook to fill the gap at its meeting in Copenhagen on 21/22 June 1993 by a declaration according to which "the associated countries in Central and Eastern Europe that so desire shall become members of the European Union ... as soon as an associated country is able to assume the obligations of membership by satisfying the economic and political conditions required" (iii.1), among them "stability of institutions guaranteeing democracy, the rule of law, human rights and the respect and protection of minorities ... " (iii.2).[33] The European Council of 15/16 December 1995 in Madrid added to these criteria the requirement that the Candidate Countries must also adapt their administrative and judicial structures correspondingly.[34]

2.2.2 The Treaty of Amsterdam (which entered into force on 1 May 1999) constitutionalised the political Copenhagen criteria by providing in Art. 49.1 TEU that an applicant state must respect the principles set out in Art. 6.1 according to which "the Union is founded on [...] the rule of law". Conversely, the Treaty of Lisbon (which entered into force on 1 December 2009) referred in Art. 49.1 TEU to the values enshrined in Art. 2 TEU (formerly Art. 6.1) and stipulated that "the conditions of eligibility agreed upon by the European Council" (i. e. the Copenhagen criteria) "shall be taken into account".[35] Thus, the Rule of Law was attributed the quality of a guiding value both for the EU and for the Member States[36] but was not further spelled out in the TEU in view of the differing traditions of the Member States. Its legal significance remains therefore the subject of legal disputes to this day. According to the prevailing opinion, Art. 2 TEU has not the quality of a legal norm[37] but constitutes a cipher or shorthand formula for a broad range of specific rights guaranteed by the TEU.[38] However, acceding countries need to adapt themselves in time to membership in the EU as a community of law.[39] Correspondingly, when implementing and applying EU law, they must take into account the fundamental rights recognised by the ECJ as "general principles of Community law" and the pro-

[32] Art. O TEU-Maastricht took over the wording of the accession clause of Art. 237 EC.

[33] Doc. SN 180/1/93 REV 1; Bull. EC 6-1993, p. 12; Tatham 2009, p. 206 et seq.; Fierro 2003, p. 138 et seq.; Hillion 2004, p. 13 et seq.; Inglis 2010, p. 36 et seq.

[34] Doc. SN 00400/95EN.

[35] And not as a *legal norm*: Hilf and Schorkopf, in Grabitz et al. (2013), Art. 2 TEU, para 46; Ohler, in Grabitz et al. (2013), Art. 49 TEU, para 15–17.

[36] Schorkopf 2000, p. 69 et seq. and 234 with regard to the values "recognised" by Art. 2 TEU; Scheuing 2005, p. 162 et seq.; Nusser 2011, p. 147 et seq.; Yowell 2012, p. 107 et seq.

[37] Hilf and Schorkopf, in Grabitz et al. (2013), Art. 2 TEU, para 34; Ohler, in Grabitz et al. (2013), Art. 49 para 17; Ullerich 2011, calls the Rule of Law concept in Art. 2 TEU a "Strukturprinzip" (p. 118) and "Argumentationsfigur" (p. 174).

[38] Schmidt-Aßmann 2004, para 7; Hilf and Schorkopf, in Grabitz et al. (2013), Art. 2 TEU, para 46.

[39] For the meaning of this concept see Kochenov 2008, p. 100; Ullerich 2011, p. 144 et seq., 184; Hilf and Schorkopf, in Grabitz et al. (2013), Art. 2 TEU, para 34 et seq.

visions of the Charter of Fundamental Rights of the European Union (binding since 1 December 2009).[40] In the present context this concerns in particular the right to a fair trial provided for in Art. 6.1 ECHR[41] and Art. 47 EUCFR with the independence of the judiciary at its core.[42] EU fundamental rights can even have an impact outside the scope of EU competence, given the fact that in practice the EU and the autonomous national "sphere" are closely interwoven.[43] In addition, the Member States are obliged to offer a degree of judicial protection for EU law in their courts which is equivalent to the protection granted for national law and is "effective".[44] Conversely, the EU does not have the competence to impose on Member States and Candidate Countries a particular model for the organisation of the judiciary.

2.2.3 In the Agenda 2000[45] and in its Opinion on Romania's Application for Membership of the European Union[46] the Commission delivered a mixed picture of Romania's compliance with the political accession conditions. It concluded that "Romania's institutions are democratic ..." but "need to be anchored by greater respect for the primacy of law at all levels of the apparatus of state".[47] It noted "shortcomings with regard to respect for fundamental rights" and observed that the Romanian judicial system was not working satisfactorily, but it arrived at the conclusion that "Romania is on the way to meeting the political conditions laid down by the Copenhagen European Council". At its meeting in Luxembourg on 12/13 December 1997, the European Council made the fulfilment of the political Copenhagen criteria a prerequisite for opening the accession negotiations with the CEECs.[48] However, despite the shortcomings observed by the Commission, the European Council decided at its meeting in Helsinki on 10/11 December 1999 to start negotiations with Romania.[49] According to a widespread opinion this decision

[40] For the scope of their application see inter alia Große Wentrup 2003, p. 49 and 64 et seq.; Brosius-Gersdorf 2005, p. 17; Scheuing 2005, p. 162–164; Kokott and Sobotta 2010, p. 2 et seq.; Nusser 2011, p. 9, 40, 119 et seq. and 126 (to the right to a fair trial); Ullerich 2011, p. 117; Yowell 2012, p. 107 et seq.; Azoulai 2012, p. 207 et seq.; Blanke 2012, p. 161 et seq. See also Case C-617/10, *Aklagaren v. Fransson* (ECJ 26 February 2013) para 17–19.

[41] Meyer-Ladewig 2012, p. 233 et seq.

[42] Rengeling and Szczekalla 2004, § 44 para 1158–1188 (wirksamer Rechtsbehelf, unparteiisches Gericht); Grabenwarter and Pabel, in Dörr et al. (2013), p. 742–838 (in particular para 48 et seq. on the independence of the courts); Meyer-Ladewig 2011, para 67 et seq.

[43] Rengeling and Szczekalla 2004, § 4 para 327 et seq., underlining the difficulty of delimiting clearly the two "spheres" of competences. A special case of a supervisory EU competence in the area of Member State's competences is the procedure provided by Art. 7 TEU (see below Sect. 5.2).

[44] Bobek 2012, p. 315 et seq.; Adinolfi 2012, p. 299.

[45] Agenda 2000 for a stronger and wider Union, Bull. EU Supplement 5/97. In the section "Political criteria – Human Rights", the Agenda 2000 briefly referred to the ECHR without going into details.

[46] Bull. EU Supplement 8/97; Regular Report of 15 July 1997, COM (97) 2003.

[47] Point 1.3. of the "General Evaluation".

[48] See de Witte 2003, p. 230; Kochenov 2008, p. 65.

[49] and with Bulgaria. They actually started on 15 February 2000 and ended on 14 December 2004.

was not based on Romania's achievements in the accession process but on political (foreign and security policy) considerations.[50]

2.3 The Pre-Accession Strategy of the EU

2.3.1 The Pre-accession strategy, launched by the European Council in Essen on 9/10 December 1994[51] and further developed by the European Council in Luxembourg on 12/13 December 1997 into an "enhanced pre-accession strategy" for all Central and Eastern European countries including Romania[52], established the so-called Accession Partnerships between the EU and the individual Candidate Countries. These Partnerships which served to bring together the various forms of support by the EU in a single framework[53] included direct contacts between these countries and the Commission, the submission of annual reports on the progress of the negotiations by the Commission and increased pre-accession assistance (mainly through the PHARE programme). The Candidate Countries were obliged to adapt their national action programmes and to implement legislation correspondingly. Romania submitted in 2001 a National Programme for Accession to the European Union, which included a reform of the judicial system.[54] The Accession Partnerships, introduced by Council Regulation (EC) No. 622/98 of 16 March 1998[55], made the political accession criteria de facto legally binding and the pre-accession financial assistance directly dependent on progress towards meeting the accession criteria.[56]

2.3.2 The Partnership with Romania began in 1998[57] and was extended in 1999, 2002 and 2003.[58] It obliged Romania to elaborate a strategy for the reform of the judiciary, providing a transparent system and objective criteria for recruiting and selecting magistrates as well as for removing them from office and for sanctioning them for misconduct, improving the administration of the courts by modern case management, developing clear criteria for case assignment and extending access to free legal aid. For the implementation of the Accession Partnerships, a series of "Action Plans for reinforcing administrative and judicial capacity" were elaborated

[50] Gabanyi 1999/2000, p. 421.
[51] Doc. SN 00300/94EN.
[52] Doc. SN 400/97; Maresceau 2003, p. 9 et seq.
[53] Maresceau 1997, p. 52; Inglis 2010, p. 119 et seq.
[54] Maresceau 1997, p 30; see www.infoeuropa.ro/insidePage.php?webPageld=77&id=18146
[55] O.J. L 85/1 (1998), based on former Art. 238 EC.
[56] Maresceau 1997, p. 3; Kochenov 2008, p. 34 et seq.
[57] Council Decision (EC) No. 98/261/EC, O.J. L 121/11 (1998).
[58] Council Decisions (EC) No. 1999/852/EC, O.J. L 335/15 (1999); (EC) No. 2002/92/EC, O.J. L 44/82 (2002); and (EC) No. 2003/397/EC, O.J. L 145/21 (2003).

by the Commission in cooperation with the candidate countries[59], in particular for the purpose of strengthening the independence of the judiciary.[60]

3 The Rule of Law in the Accession Negotiations (2000–2007)

3.1 Procedural Aspects

3.1.1 The European Commission played a leading role in the accession process by acting as the principal interlocutor with the Candidate Countries[61] and by virtue of its task to prepare the common (negotiation) positions of the EU Member States for the COREPER and the meetings of the Member States with the Candidate Countries in the Accession Conferences.[62] Thus, its assessment of the progress made by the Candidate Countries "was the basis for the decisions of the Council and the EC Member States to move on along the lines of pre-accession".[63] The Commission apparently did not start the monitoring on the basis of a comprehensive conception of the Rule of Law but proceeded rather pragmatically.[64] Following the request by the European Council on 12/13 December 1997 in Luxembourg[65], the Commission submitted between 1998 and 2006 seven annual Regular Reports, four Strategy Papers (2001–2004) and three Composite Monitoring Reports (2005, 2006[1] and 2006[2]) which provided a wider perspective of the accession process including proposals for the next negotiation rounds.[66] These reports are a fascinating source of information about the developments in Romania at that time, drafted from the EU point of view.[67]

3.1.2 The reports comprised three main sections corresponding to the three Copenhagen criteria:[68] a first section dedicated to the political criteria, a second section focussing on the economic criteria (divided into 29 chapters of the acquis, each covering a specific policy area) and a third section concerning the capacity to implement the acquis communautaire. The first section was split into three sub-sections: (1) Democracy and the Rule of Law, (2) Human and Civil Rights and the Protection of Minorities and (3) Others (e. g. civil and political rights, economic, social

[59] Regular Report of 9 October 2002, SEC(2002) 1409, p. 133; Tatham 2009, p. 362 et seq.
[60] Regular Report of 5 June 2002, COM(2002) 256.
[61] Maresceau 1997, p. 75; O'Brennan 2006, p. 74–94; Kochenov 2008, p. 59; Coman 2007, p. 184.
[62] Kochenov 2008, p 59; Tatham 2009, p. 247 et seq.; Hillion 2004, p. 13.
[63] Maresceau 1997, p. 3 and 59.
[64] Wennerström 2007, p. 197, 212 and 296, maintains that the Reports "reveal the conception of the Commission on the Rule of Law". According to Seibert-Fohr 2009, p. 419, the Commission was "influenced" in the negotiations by "the essential parameters of the ECHR".
[65] Conclusions of the European Council, Doc. SN 400/97, para 10 and 29; Hillion 2004, p. 14.
[66] "an incredible amount of documents": Kochenov 2008, p. 7 and 67–78.
[67] Wennerström 2007, p. 197 et seq., 212 et seq.; Maresceau 2003, p. 32 et seq. The Progress Reports 1998–2006 have been closely analysed, inter alia, by Kochenov 2008.
[68] Kochenov 2008, p. 86 et seq.

and cultural rights, minority rights, combating organised crime, drugs, and the fight against corruption in general). The following observations focus on the subjects discussed by the Commission under sub-section (1) "Democracy and the Rule of Law", which in turn is subdivided into three parts corresponding to the "separation of powers" principle (Parliament/Executive/Judiciary), plus a part on Anti-corruption measures.

3.1.3 From the very start of the reporting, the Commission asserted that Romania fulfilled the political criteria for accession,[69] but at the same time the Commission realised that Romania had great difficulties in this regard.[70] Therefore, since 2003, it increasingly expressed "serious concern" about the effectiveness of Romania's efforts to fulfil the political criteria and urged it more and more firmly to make further progress on the reform of the judicial system.[71] Because of these shortcomings, Romania had to experience a setback on the road to accession when the European Council decided in 1997 not to start the negotiations with Romania (and Bulgaria) at the same time as with the other Candidate Countries but to postpone them until a later date.[72] The European Council in Copenhagen on 12/13 December 2002 set January 2007 as the "objective" for Romania's (and Bulgaria's) accession whereas it determined May 2004 as the date of accession for the ten other Candidate Countries.[73]

3.2 *Observations of the Commission Regarding the Rule of Law*

3.2.1 The principal aim of the Commission in sub-section (1) was the protection of the independence of the judiciary from political influence.[74] The Commission frequently denounced the continuing involvement of the Romanian Ministry of Justice in judicial affairs and in particular about political appointments of judges.[75] Indeed, public officials and politicians could, under certain conditions, be appointed as judges and prosecutors without having to pass the competition principally prescribed by the law for entry into the judicial career.[76] The Commission took note of the work on judicial reform (draft law of November 1999) and recognised "impor-

[69] Regular Report of 8 November 2000, COM(2000) 710, p. 25 and 87, of 13 November 2001, SEC(2001) 1753, p. 30, and of 9 October 2002, SEC(2002) 1409, p. 129.
[70] Emmert 2003, p. 306.
[71] Emmert 2003, p. 306; Coman 2007, p. 184.
[72] They actually started on 15 February 2000 and ended on 14 December 2004.
[73] Doc. 15917/02 of 29 January 2003.
[74] The Commission further discusses in section (1) ("political criteria") several other points such as fundamental freedoms and Human Rights, the fight against corruption (outside the judiciary), combating organised crime, and money laundering; this paper concentrates on the issue of the independence of the judiciary.
[75] Regular Report of 9 October 2002, SEC(2002) 1409, p. 25.
[76] In 1999/2000: 70 out of 70 appointments, in 2000/2001: 45 out of 53 appointments: OSI Report 2002, p. 176.

tant progress in improving the functioning of the judiciary". But it deplored at the same time that the reform process had only reached "an early stage" and insisted that it "need(ed) to be continued and consolidated". It therefore demanded that the judicial reform should become a political priority and that the independence of the judiciary should be ensured more effectively.

3.2.2 The Commission also criticised the limited administrative capacity of the judicial system and noted the extremely heavy workload of individual judges, an insufficient management of cases, a lack of technical equipment and insufficient human and financial resources. It therefore urged Romania to develop a comprehensive strategy for a better functioning of the judicial system. The Romanian Government thereupon drafted an Action Plan for strengthening Romania's administrative and judicial capacity.[77] Later during the negotiations, the Commission acknowledged however that the administrative capacity of the courts and their working conditions had considerably improved but demanded further human and financial resources to improve the management of the court system and to fill the considerable number of vacancies.[78]

3.2.3 The Commission firmly advocated the strengthening of the SCM,[79] an institution first established in Romania in 1909, abolished in 1952 and then re-established by the Constitution of 1991 as an independent institution for the purpose of safeguarding the independence of justice.[80] But it criticised the lack of transparency in the selection of the Council members and, in particular, the continuing strong influence of the Ministry of Justice over the Council.[81] An additional problem for the effectiveness of the SCM was the fact that it did not act as a full time body since its members continued to exercise their functions as judges and prosecutors. The Commission also regularly noted in its reports that *corruption* "continues to be a widespread and systemic problem" and "that it is largely unresolved and affects all aspects of society", in spite of the anti-corruption measures adopted and international conventions ratified by Romania and of the establishment of various Governmental institutions charged with fighting corruption. The Commission also observed that the "effective implementation of the existing laws is limited" and demanded that the efforts for this purpose should be continued.

[77] Regular Report of 9 October 2002, SEC(2002) 1409, p. 11.
[78] Regular Report of 5 November 2003, SEC(2003) 1211.
[79] Also designated as "High Judicial Council".
[80] Ionescu 2008, p. II/78; Coman and Dallara 2012, p. 838; Kochenov 2008, p. 261; Seibert-Fohr 2009, p. 425; Hein 2013, p. 300.
[81] Regular Report of 9 October 2002, SEC(2002) 1409, p. 25.

3.3 Constitutional and Judicial Reform

3.3.1 Following increasing disputes within Romania on constitutional issues and pressure by the Commission in the run-up to the closure of the accession negotiations[82], the Government initiated a fundamental revision of the Romanian Constitution in 2003, aiming (among others) at excluding as far as possible a political influence on the judiciary.[83] For this purpose, this goal found its expression by enshrining explicitly the separation of powers principle in the Constitution (Art. 1.4) and by a further strengthening of the SCM as the guarantor of the independence of justice, particularly through a modified method for the selection of magistrates.[84] The proposals for the appointment, promotion and transfer of judges, and for sanctions against them, were made the exclusive competence of the SCM (Art. 125.2 of the revised Constitution). The SCM also received the competence to nominate public prosecutors for appointment by the President of Romania (Art. 134.1) and to nominate the Prosecutor General upon a proposal by the Minister of Justice.[85] The judges of the High Court of Justice and Cassation (Art. 126 of the Constitution) are now nominated by the SCM and appointed by the Romanian President for life. The members of the SCM are elected for six years without the possibility of re-election (Art. 133.4).[86] The prosecutors continued to be formally under the authority of the Minister of Justice but are independent in their opinions[87], in accordance with the Recommendation 2000/19 of the CoE on the role of Public Prosecutors in the Criminal Justice System.

3.3.2 A new competence of the Romanian Constitutional Court (RCC) to settle constitutional disputes among state institutions ("Organstreitigkeiten") was created (Art. 146 e),[88] and the power of the Romanian Parliament to supersede decisions of the RCC by a two-thirds majority was abolished. Also the erga omnes effect of the decisions of the RCC was now explicitly anchored in the text of the Constitution (Art. 147.4). The objections raised by a group of Members of Parliament against the constitutional changes were rejected by the RCC.[89] The Commission praised the revision of the Constitution as a big step towards a more effective separation be-

[82] Tatham 2009, p. 491; Coman and Dallara 2012, p. 837; Hein 2013, p. 359; Blokker 2012a, p. 6 and footnote 18.
[83] Monitorul Oficial no. 643/2004; Text in English: www.cdep.ro/pls/dic/site/page?id=371. See Carp 2007, p. 200; Bormann 2004, p. 207–267; Hein 2013, p. 359 et seq., p. 375 et seq. The draft revision had been checked by the Venice Commission 2002; see its Opinion CDL-AD(2002) 17 of 9 July 2002.
[84] Ionescu 2008, p. II/78; Kerek 2010, p. 481.
[85] Ionescu 2008, p. II/79; Carp 2007, p. 878.
[86] Decision of the RCC no. 148/2003 of 16 April 2003 on the Draft Constitution, Monitorul Oficial no. 317/2003 www.ccr.ro/decisions/pdf/en/2003/D148_03.pdf; Hein 2013, p. 367 and 371. The RCC made numerous reservations to the draft.
[87] Decision of the RCC no. 375/2005 of 6 July 2005, Monitorul Oficial no. 591/2005, p. 19.
[88] See Valea 2010, p. 95 et seq.; Kerek 2010, p. 239–241; Roth 2006, p. 141; Hein 2013, p. 369.
[89] Decision of the RCC no 356/2003 of 22 September 2003, Monitorul Oficial no. 686/2003.

tween politics and law, in particular preserving the independence of the judiciary.[90] The constitutional reform also included a new European integration clause according to which the provisions of the EU Treaties and of EU regulations "shall take precedence over the opposite provisions of the national laws, in compliance with the provisions of the accession act" (Art. 145.2).

3.3.3 The implementation of the constitutional reform of 2003 led to a follow-up by implementing legal provisions. Against the background of urgent demands by the Commission and the European Parliament[91] for further improvements of the judicial system, a sweeping legislative reform occurred in 2004–2005:[92] The Parliament adopted three important laws designed to ensure the proper functioning of the judiciary: (1) Law no. 303/2004 on the Status of Judges and Prosecutors, as amended by Law no. 247/2005 concerning the reform of property and justice, subsequently amended by Emergency Ordinance no. 100/2007 and Law no. 97/2008,[93] (2) Law no. 304/2004 on the Organisation of the Judiciary, as amended by Law no. 247/2005, and (3) Law no. 317/2004 on the Superior Council of Magistracy, as amended by Law no. 247/2005.[94] The constitutionality of Law no. 247/2005 was challenged before the RCC by a group of Members of the Romanian Parliament and by the High Court of Cassation and Justice. With its judgment of 6 July 2005, the RCC rejected most of the complaints but declared a few provisions unconstitutional, among them the provision that the elected members of the SCM could not hold a position as judge or prosecutor.[95] Conversely, the Court accepted the retirement age as a limitation of the activity of a judge or prosecutor as compatible with the constitutional principle of the immovability of judges.[96]

3.3.4 Following the decision of the RCC, the Parliament adopted on 13 July 2005 as a compromise a law providing that "the elected members of the SCM shall suspend their activity as judge or prosecutor". Thus, they would *pro forma* be in the position to remain members of their original panels during their term. The exclusive power of the SCM plenum of nominating judges and prosecutors for appointment by the President of Romania was retained.[97] Following the approval of the compromise by the RCC[98], the reform law entered into force on 2 August 2005. Thereby

[90] Regular Report of 5 November 2003, SEC(2003) 1211, p. 20; Hein 2013, p. 378.
[91] Resolution 2004 P5_A(2004)0103.
[92] Hein 2013, p. 404.
[93] Between 2000 and 2005, this law had been amended no less than nineteen times; Coman 2007, p. 195.
[94] Carp 2007, p. 202; Coman and Dallara 2012, p. 844.
[95] Decision of the RCC no. 375/2005 of 6 July 2005, Monitorul Oficial no. 591/2005; Coman 2007, p. 212 et seq.; Carp 2007, p. 204 et seq.; Hein 2013, p. 396 et seq.
[96] Carp 2007, p. 224 et seq.
[97] With regard to public prosecutors upon a proposal by the Minister of Justice: Hein 2013, p. 392 et seq.; for details on the status, independence and impartiality of the public prosecutors see Carausan 2009, p. 104–128. In the decision no. 375/2005 the RCC emphasised the functional independence of the prosecutors from the Ministry of Justice (see footnote 85).
[98] Decision of the RCC no. 419/2005 of 18 July 2005, Monitorul Oficial no. 653/2005.

the constitutional dispute was solved[99] and an important step towards the conclusion of the accession negotiations made.[100]

3.3.5 The principal aim of the comprehensive reform of the Romanian judicial system in 2003–2005, which was strongly influenced by pressure from the side of the Commission, was to improve the independence of the judiciary through an effective separation of powers in order to exclude in the future any political influence from the side of the Government over judges.[101]

- The SCM is now composed of nine judges and five prosecutors from various career levels, two representatives of the civil society, elected by the Senate, and three *ex officio* members: the President of the High Court, the General Prosecutor attached to the High Court and the Minister of Justice (as an ordinary member, according to Art. 133.2 of the Constitution).[102] The President and the Vice-President of the SCM are elected by the SCM plenum. The representatives of the judges and prosecutors in the SCM are elected in general assemblies of the magistrates and appointed by the Romanian President for a term of six years without the possibility of re-election (Art. 133.4). They are obliged to exercise their function full-time but remain *pro forma* members of their panels.[103]
- The High Court was granted budgetary autonomy. A public tender was made a prerequisite for the appointment to high-level judicial positions. The National Anti-Corruption Prosecutor was attached to the High Court and thereby obtained administrative autonomy.[104] The General Prosecutor's right to introduce extraordinary appeals against judicial decisions (a violation of the principle of legal certainty, repeatedly criticised by the Commission) was abolished.[105]
- The evaluation of the magistrates is made by the Judicial Inspection Service which reports to the SCM plenum; its tasks were more closely regulated in order to avoid an undue influence on the decisions of the courts.[106]
- Disciplinary matters concerning magistrates are decided by the SCM (in separate panels for judges and prosecutors).
- The National Institute of Magistracy, formerly dependent on the Ministry of Justice and responsible for organising the selection and training of magistrates, was subordinated to the SCM.

---

[99] Other constitutional conflicts occurred between 2006 and 2009 concerning the prosecution of high-level corruption, a subject which is outside the scope of this paper. See Smilov and Toplek 2007.
[100] An overview of the modified provisions on the Judicial Power is given by Ionescu 2008, p. II/75 et seq.; for an evaluation see Hein 2013, p. 403 et seq.
[101] Hein 2013, p. 378.
[102] Ionescu 2008, p. II/78 et seq.
[103] Carp 2007, p. 203; Coman and Dallara 2012, p. 845.
[104] Ionescu 2008, p. II/78.
[105] "*recurs in anulare*". Hein 2013, p. 381; see Regular Reports 2000/2002/2003 and Monitoring Report 2006.
[106] Coman and Dallara 2012, p. 863; see also Geissler and Rebegea 2011, p. 2–4.

3.3.6 In its 2005 Monitoring Report, the Commission welcomed the reform and noted that "the legal framework now offers sufficient guarantees for magistrates' personal and institutional independence".[107] A German author observed that a substantial part of the problems related to the Rule of Law has been solved within the period of monitoring.[108] The Commission also found progress in practice since the SCM "has started to address fundamental challenges" but suggested that the role of the SCM should be further strengthened, in particular by ensuring the observance of objective criteria for recruiting magistrates and SCM staff. The SCM was made responsible for clearing up corruption cases among the judiciary and initiating disciplinary actions against judges which could lead to sanctions or removal from office. The Commission also stressed that further efforts regarding the proper functioning of the judiciary are needed and that the implementation of the action plan on justice reform should continue.[109]

3.3.7 In 2005, the Romanian Government adopted a new National Strategy and Action Plan on Justice Reform for 2006–2007 which the Commission appreciated as a sign of the "overall progress of the reform efforts".[110] In 2006 the Commission found that the implementation of the strategy and of the action plan on justice reform was continuing and that "significant progress" was being made in this respect, inter alia by providing the random allocation of cases to judges in order to strengthen impartiality and exclude corruption. However, it warned that "further progress is still necessary in the area of judicial reform and the fight against organised crime and corruption" (point 3.3.1) and set as a benchmark, inter alia, that Romania should "(e)nsure a more transparent and efficient judicial process notably by enhancing the capacity and accountability of the Superior Council of Magistracy".[111] In the annexed Country Report, the Commission explained in detail its assessment of the shortcomings regarding the justice system in Romania.

3.3.8 The 2004–2005 legislation had the aim to ensure the formal and institutional independence of the judiciary and thereby to improve the impartiality of judicial decisions. It was by many observers seen as a turning point in the judicial reform efforts since it made the SCM "virtually autonomous". The SCM established a more transparent recruitment and promotion system for magistrates and amended several

[107] Comprehensive Monitoring Report of 25 October 2005, COM(2005) 534, p. 10; Coman and Dallara 2012, p. 840.
[108] Hein 2013, p. 469 with reference to the period 2003 to 2009 ("ein wesentlicher Teil der rechtsstaatlich prekären Probleme ist im Verlauf des Untersuchungszeitraumes gelöst worden"). This was accomplished with the assistance of the German IRZ-Foundation which was between 2000 and 2010 the most important "Twinning"-partner of the Romanian Ministry of Justice; see Trappe 2012, p. 345; Olaru 2012, p. 435 et seq.; critical to the EC method applied in the Romanian Justice Sector: Rem and Gasper 2008, p. 15 et seq.
[109] Monitoring Reports of 2005 and 2006.
[110] Monitoring Report of 26 September 2006, COM(2006) 549, p. 6.
[111] Monitoring Report of 26 September 2006, COM(2006) 549, p. 10.

regulations.[112] Also, the accountability of the judges was reinforced[113] by a Code of Ethics adopted by the SCM on 26 April 2005.[114] However, in spite of the far-reaching constitutional and legal reforms, many observers remained sceptical of the results. Scholars criticised the "excessively strong role" attributed to the SCM[115] by the law of 2004 and registered severe deficits in its actual functioning[116] and a lack of a pro-active approach and questioned the ability of the SCM to effectively accomplish its mission.[117] Conversely, external observers recently praised the presence of "a new generation of reform oriented judges" in the SCM, due to a change in its composition since 2010.[118]

3.3.9 The Commission principally supported the establishment of judicial councils in the Candidate Countries[119] but increasingly criticised the inactivity of the Romanian SCM and noted a series of unresolved problems in the judicial system, among them the length of proceedings, the excessive workload, the deficient consistency of the jurisprudence and widespread corruption.[120] In spite of the continuous reformative efforts, the SCM remained therefore "a fairly highly disputed institution".[121] The question of whether a judicial council as established in several EU Member States[122] is an appropriate instrument for guaranteeing judicial independence at all is the subject of controversial discussions in the literature and cannot be discussed here.[123]

3.3.10 The *European Council* regularly endorsed the assessment of and the recommendations made by the Commission regarding the Rule of Law in Romania without going into many details and urged the country to continue domestic reforms.[124] On 12/13 December 2002 in Copenhagen it set for Romania and Bulgaria

---

112 Denis-Smith 2009, p. 65 et seq.
113 Ionescu 2008, p. II/80.
114 Coman and Dallara 2012, p. 876.
115 Seibert-Fohr 2012, p. 1342 et seq.; Parau 2012, p. 643.
116 Parau 2012, p. 619 et seq.
117 Coman and Dallara 2012, p. 879 et seq.; Mendelski 2011a, p. 155 et seq.; Hein 2013, p. 403, footnote 1; Tanasescu and Popescu 2012, 166 et seq.; see also Garoupa and Ginsburg 2009, p. 201–232.
118 Geissler and Rebegea 2011, p. 5.
119 Coman 2007, p. 186; Seibert-Fohr 2009, p. 425; Seibert-Fohr 2012, p. 1342.
120 Comprehensive Monitoring Report of 25 October 2005, COM(2005) 534, p. 4; a critical view is also taken by Rem and Gasper 2008, p. 16–23 who analyse the Twinning Projects at the SCM.
121 See for example Coman and Dallara 2012, p. 880; Seibert-Fohr 2012, p. 1295.
122 See for examples Weber 2010, p. 314–317.
123 For the "Pro" and "Contra" see Hein 2013, p. 439 et seq.; Tanasescu and Popescu 2013, p. 306 et seq. Wittreck 2006, p. 617, 641 et seq. and 660 et seq., calls self-administration of the judiciary "a wrong track" ("Irrweg"); critical also Bobek 2007, p. 110, regarding judicial councils in the new East European Member States, and Parau 2012, p. 619–665. Conversely, see Rieger 2011, p. 126 et seq. on the reform discussion in Germany which seems to favour a stronger role of judicial self-administration.
124 Conclusions of 13 December 2002, of 13 December 2003 and of 17 December 2004. See O'Brennan 2006, p. 55–73.

the *objective* of an accession on 1 January 2007 whereas it decided at the same time that the other ten Candidate Countries could already join on 1 May 2004.[125] In April 2005 the Council of the EU gave its formal assent to the Accession Treaty with reference to the Commission's Opinion of 22 February 2005.[126] The European Parliament welcomed the Commission's conclusions and recommendations in various reports and resolutions and repeatedly noted "significant improvements" but regularly criticised the deficits regarding the Rule of Law and urged Romania to continue and reinforce its efforts to implement judicial reforms.[127] With the Legislative Resolution of 13 April 2005, the European Parliament gave its assent to the Accession Treaty of Romania.[128] In the Legislative Resolution of 13 June 2006, it noted the "considerable progress made by Romania in the past months to meet the European Union's political and economic criteria" and supported the envisaged accession date of 1 January 2007.[129] At the same time, it again urged Romania "to consolidate the ongoing reform of its judicial system, by further enhancing the transparency, efficiency, and impartiality of the judiciary ...".

3.4 The Rule of Law in the Accession Treaty

3.4.1 In its Opinion on the application for accession to the European Union by the Republic of Bulgaria and Romania of 22 February 2005, the Commission once again confirmed, with reference to its Strategy Paper of 6 October 2004,[130] that Romania fulfils the political criteria and is ready for membership by 1 January 2007.[131] At the same time, it called on Romania "to pursue vigorously the improvements that still need to be made in the context of the political and economic criteria for membership" and announced that it "will continue to closely monitor the implementation of the commitments and obligations taken on" by Romania.[132] Therefore, in the view of the Commission the Rule of Law problems in Romania were not yet solved at this time.

---

[125] Conclusions of 13 December 2002, Doc. 15917/02 of 29 January 2003, para 3 and 14.

[126] OJ L 157/9 of 21 June 2005.

[127] In particular Resolutions P5_TA(2002)0317 and P5_TA(2002)0536. See O'Brennan 2006, p. 95–112.

[128] O.J. L 157/7 (2005).

[129] Resolution P6-TA(2005)0531 of 15 December 2005 points 5 and 6; see further Resolution P6_TA(2006)0512 of 30 November 2006 commenting on the Monitoring Report of 26 September 2006, COM(2006) 549.

[130] COM(2004) 657.

[131] O.J. L 157/3 (2005), point 5. With reference to the Opinion of the Commission, the Council formally accepted Romania's application for admission: Decision of 25 April 2005, O.J. L 157/9 (2005).

[132] O.J. L 157/4 (2005), recital 9.

3.4.2 Under these circumstances, the Commission proposed a special postponement clause for the Accession Treaty with Romania,[133] providing the possibility of postponing the accession by one year in case the problems regarding the political criteria were not solved by 2007.[134] In its Progress Reports of 25 October 2005 and of 16 May 2006, the Commission was not yet ready to give "green light" for the date of accession.[135] Only in its last report of 26 October 2006 did it finally accept the envisaged accession date,[136] in spite of the still-existing shortcomings regarding the Rule of Law.[137] By that means, the Commission presumably took into account the sweeping legal reform of the years 2003–2005[138] but also the prevailing view of the European Council and among the Member States. They obviously attached more weight to the long-term political and strategic advantages of Romania's membership for the EU than to the current Rule of Law deficits.[139] In this regard, it was assumed that Romania would make better progress as a Member State than if it remained outside the Union.[140]

3.4.3 At the conclusion of the accession negotiations on 14 December 2004, Romania accepted the specific commitments and requirements regarding the judiciary (Annex IX of the Act of Accession referred to in Article 39 of the Protocol).[141] According to Point I. (3) of Annex IX, Romania obliged itself "to develop and implement an updated and integrated Action Plan and Strategy for the Reform of the Judiciary including the main measures for implementing the Law on the Organisation of the Judiciary, the Law on the Status of Magistrates and the Law on the Superior Council of Magistracy". Romania had to submit these documents no later than March 2005 and to ensure adequate financial and human resources.[142]

---

[133] Signed on 25 April 2005 in Luxembourg.
[134] Tatham 2009, p. 114.
[135] Slavu 2008, p. 144.
[136] Germany ratified the Accession Treaty just one week before it entered into force (on 24 November 2006).
[137] Slavu 2008, p. 149.
[138] Coman and Dallara 2012, p. 10.
[139] Thus political considerations had priority according to external observers; see e. g. Smith 2003, p. 130, and Slavu 2008, p. 236 and 257.
[140] Carey 2011, p. 333.
[141] Inglis 2010, p. 210.
[142] O.J. L 157/174 and L 157/374 (2005).

4 Post-Accession Promotion of the Rule of Law in Romania (2007–2014)

4.1 The Co-Operation and Verification Mechanism (CVM)

4.1.1 During the accession negotiations, the Commission apparently became more and more aware of the fundamental character of Romania's problems of respecting the Rule of Law in practice. Therefore, in its reports since 2003, the Commission more firmly insisted on the compliance with the political criteria, made more concrete suggestions and demanded the enforcement, not only the implementation of the measures promised by the Romanian Government. According to many observers, this manner of action considerably contributed to the adoption of the judicial reform package 2003–2005.[143] The Commission recognised the "good will" and "determination" of the Romanian Government toward implementing the new constitutional and legal framework, but it nevertheless observed a clear weakness in translating these intentions into results. In other words, the permanent progress reported since 1997 was from the Commission's viewpoint still insufficient at the time of accession.

4.1.2 As a consequence, the Commission decided to continue the monitoring process after accession[144] and for this purpose on 13 December 2006 adopted a Decision establishing "a mechanism for cooperation and verification of progress in Romania to address specific benchmarks in the areas of judicial reform and the fight against corruption", based upon Art. 4.3 of the Treaty of Accession and Art. 37 and 39 of the Act of Accession ("CVM Decision").[145] In the view of the EU, the continuation of the monitoring was a "more 'cooperative' approach" compared to a postponement of the accession.[146] The decision recalls that "(t)he European Union is founded on the rule of law, a principle common to all Member States" (recital 1), and "on the mutual confidence that the administrative and judicial decisions and practices of all member states fully respect the rule of law" (recital 2) and that "(t)his implies for all Member States the existence of an impartial, independent and effective judicial and administrative system" (recital 3). It therefore obliged Romania, in essence, to respect "(t)he strict separation of the executive, legislative and judicial power" and warned that without irreversible progress in reforming the legislative, administrative and judicial system and in fighting corruption, Romania would risk being unable to correctly apply EU law. Meeting these objectives was

[143] See footnote 83, part 3.3.

[144] Originally it was only conceived for a period of "up to three years": Monitoring Report of 16 May 2006, COM(2006) 214, p. 9; Monitoring Report of 26 September 2006, COM(2006) 549, p. 9.

[145] Decision 2006/928/EC, O.J. L 354 (2006), p. 56; see Alegre 2009, p. 5–7; Inglis 2010, p. 204 et seq.; Szarek-Mason 2010, p. 227–233; Carrera, Guild and Hernanz 2013a, p. 15–17; Carp 2014, p. 1–16.

[146] Inglis 2010, p. 7.

regarded as a long-term task, and therefore the decision was to remain effective until the benchmarks set for the application of the CVM were satisfactorily fulfilled (recital 9).[147]

4.1.3 The benchmarks provided, inter alia, that Romania was under an obligation (1) to "ensure a more transparent and efficient judicial process notably by enhancing the capacity and accountability of the Superior Council of Magistracy", (2) to establish an "integrity agency [...]. for verifying assets, incompatibilities and potential conflicts of interests [...].", (3) "to continue investigations into high-level corruption" and (4) to "take further measures to prevent and fight against corruption".[148] Should Romania fail to address these benchmarks adequately, safeguard measures could be applied as foreseen in Art. 38 and 39 of the Act of Accession. The following observations concentrate on the first two benchmarks: the reform of the judicial system and the integrity agency. Pursuant to Art. 2.2 of the Decision, the Commission has to submit at least every six months a report to the European Parliament and the Council regarding the progress made by Romania in addressing the benchmarks. Accordingly the Commission submitted between February 2007 and June 2014 altogether 20 CVM reports on Romania: 8 regular progress reports, 5 interim reports and 7 "update" or "technical" reports. This paper concentrates on the most recent reports covering the years 2012,[149] 2013[150] and 2014.[151] The accompanying "Technical Reports" which provide useful additional material cannot be analysed here due to lack of space.[152]

4.1.4 In its first CVM Report of 27 June 2007 the Commission requested that the Romanian Government drafts a new Plan providing a time schedule for the implementation of the reform measures to be taken for compliance with the CVM benchmarks. The Government accordingly elaborated a comprehensive Action Plan for Meeting the Benchmarks established within the CVM[153] which served as the basis for monitoring the implementation of the Judicial Reform Strategy 2005–2007 and of the National Anti-Corruption Strategy 2005–2007. The Plan mainly addressed the strengthening of the administrative capacity of the SCM, increasing the accountability of its members, increasing the efficiency of the judiciary by improving court infrastructure and management, consistency of the jurisprudence and adoption of new procedural codes. Subsequently the Government adopted a de-

[147] Objections by the Romanian Government against the extended duration of the monitoring are not known.
[148] The issue of corruption in the justice system is beyond the scope of this paper in spite of its high relevance for the independence of the judiciary; see the Progress Reports 2009–2014 and the Commission Communication on Fighting Corruption of 3 February 2014, COM(2014) 38, Annex 23 on Romania; Smilov and Toplek 2007; Roos and Rebegea 2009; Bormann 2009, p. 125 et seq.; Szarek-Mason 2010, p. 182, 221–238 (on Romania and Bulgaria).
[149] Progress Report of 18 July 2012, COM(2012) 410.
[150] Progress Report of 30 January 2013, COM(2013) 47.
[151] Progress Report of 22 January 2014, COM(2014) 37.
[152] Technical Report of 22 January 2014, SWD(2014) 37.
[153] www.just.ro/Portals/0/Right_Panel/Plandeactiune/plan_actiune_en-21122007(1).pdf

tailed Strategy for the Development of the Judiciary as a Public Service for the years 2010–2014.

4.1.5 In its Progress Reports, the Commission observed that Romania had put in place the basic legal framework in all areas covered by the CVM, but that the implementation and enforcement of this framework were not satisfactory.[154] The Commission also criticised that Romania had not fully taken account of the objections and recommendations made in the Monitoring Reports and that the judicial reform process moved too slowly. The Commission recognised that the independence of the judiciary had gradually increased between 2007 and 2012[155] but noted continuing structural and technical problems (organisation and efficiency of the judicial system, inconsistency of jurisprudence, lack of publicity).[156] In particular, the Commission condemned the politically motivated attacks and personal threats made by politicians and in the media against members of the High Court, the SCM and the RCC[157] which had led the members of the RCC to address on 3 July 2012 a letter to the ECtHR, the Venice Commission and other international institutions expressing serious concerns.[158] Summing up, the Commission came to the opinion that Romania had not sufficiently implemented its commitments yet and therefore insisted again on Romania's full respect for fundamental values such as the Rule of Law and the separation of powers.[159]

4.1.6 Conversely, the Commission strongly appreciated the role of the SCM in supporting judicial reform and the fight against high-level corruption.[160] It paid tribute to the SCM as "the main defender of the independence of justice" which had "pursued this task in a systematic and professional way" and praised the performance of the National Anti-Corruption Directorate (DNA) and of the National Integrity Agency (ANI) in prosecuting high-level corruption.[161] The ANI was established in 2007[162] with the aim to promote integrity within the public administration and the judiciary by verifying conflicts of interest and incompatibility and identifying potentially unjustified wealth among public officials and elected politicians. However, in 2010 the RCC decided that parts of the law regarding the ANI were unconsti-

[154] Hein 2013, p. 463.
[155] Also a new framework for judicial inspections was adopted; Progress Report of 30 January 2013, COM(2013) 47, p. 8.
[156] Progress Report of 18 July 2012, COM(2012) 410, p. 6.
[157] Progress Report of 18 July 2012, COM(2012) 410, p. 3 and 19; Technical Report of 22 January 2014, SWD(2014) 37, p. 5.
[158] Urgent Communication of the Romanian Constitutional Court of 3 July 2012; see Venice Commission 2012, p. 14 et seq.
[159] Progress Report of 18 July 2012, COM(2012) 410, p. 19.
[160] The Council and the European Parliament regularly endorsed the Commission's evaluation of the functioning of the SCM.
[161] For details on the ANI see Progress Report of 18 July 2012, COM(2012) 410, p. 14–16.
[162] Law no. 144/2007 regarding the setting up, organisation and functioning of the National Integrity Agency.

tutional.[163] In reaction to the judgment, the Parliament adopted a revised version of the law limiting the competences of the ANI – it now could only refer cases to prosecutors – and exempting Members of Parliament from the scope of application of the law.[164]

4.1.7 In order to meet the concerns of the EU, the Ministry of Justice drafted a new Strategy for the Development of the Judiciary 2014–2018.[165] In the legislative field, several new codes – a new Criminal Code, Criminal Procedure Code, Civil Code and Civil Procedure Code – were elaborated and already partly adopted.[166] In spite of these achievements, the Commission found that the political commitment of the Government and the Parliament to the Rule of Law was lacking in recent decisions, particularly in appointments to key positions in the judicial institutions, the General Prosecutor and the Chief DNA Prosecutor among them. The Government also continued to rely to a wide extent on Emergency Ordinances.[167] External observers got the impression that after accession the political will for judicial reforms had decreased.[168] In its most recent Progress Report,[169] the Commission concluded that the independence of the judiciary and the respect for the Rule of Law continued to be a disputed issue in Romania, in particular since certain decisions of the Parliament had put in question the core principles and objectives of the judicial reform.

4.1.8 In view of these problems, the Commission submitted again in the 2012 and 2014 reports numerous recommendations for restoring the Rule of Law. The most important points were (1) that the Code of Conduct for Members of Parliament should oblige the Members of Parliament to respect the independence of the judiciary and judicial decisions, (2) that the integrity rules should not provide exceptions to the applicability of the rules on incompatibilities, conflict of interest and unjustified wealth and (3) that, in the case of a revision of the Constitution, the principles of the separation of powers and of the independence of the judiciary be respected.

[163] Technical Report of 20 July 2010, SEC(2010) 949, p. 8 et seq., and of 20 July 2011, SEC(2011) 968, p. 8 et seq.
[164] Progress Report of 20 July 2010, COM(2010) 949, p. 9. For details on the constitutional conflict over the parliamentary immunity see Hipper 2014, p. 15.
[165] Progress Report of 22 January 2014, COM(2014) 37, p. 6; Technical Report of 22 January 2014, COM(2014) 37, p. 14.
[166] Technical Report of 30 January 2013, COM(2013) 47, p. 7/8, and of 22 January 2014, COM(2014) 37, p. 7–10. The new *Civil Procedure Code* entered into force on 15 February 2013.
[167] In 2011, no less than 140 Emergency Ordinances had been issued by the Government (see Venice Commission 2012, p. 5 et seq.), in 2013 the Government issued no less than 96.
[168] Coman and Dallara 2012, p. 840; Carey 2011, p. 351.
[169] Progress Report of 22 January 2014, COM(2014) 37.

4.2 Constitutional Conflicts

4.2.1 A matter of particular concern for the Commission was the stability of the Constitutional order in Romania and the respect for the decisions of the RCC in the light of the numerous constitutional conflicts that arose between 2007 and 2013.[170] These conflicts which mainly concerned the functions and competences of the President of Romania and of the Romanian Parliament cannot be discussed here in detail.[171] It seems that the RCC acted in this period by and large successfully as the defender of the Rule of Law protecting the balance of powers and the Supremacy of Law against intrusions by the Government and Parliament.[172] The constitutional turmoil reached its peak in July 2012 when the Government and Parliament adopted a number of measures aiming at the removal of the President of Romania:[173] The Parliament prematurely terminated the mandate of the Ombudsman who had the power to investigate alleged illegal acts of the administration, such as serious cases of corruption and to challenge Government Ordinances and laws before the RCC, and limited the scope of its mandate.[174] The appeal of the Ombudsman at the RCC was not successful due to the lack of competence of the Court for reviewing internal acts of Parliament.[175] The Government also modified the Law on the RCC by an Emergency Ordinance, removing the competence of the Court to adjudicate on the constitutionality of internal parliamentary decisions.[176] However, the RCC later declared the Emergency Ordinance and the Law approving it a violation of the Rule of Law and of the principle of equality of the citizen before the law.[177]

4.2.2 The Romanian Parliament further adopted amendments to the Criminal Code exempting Members of Parliament from provisions on certain corruption offences. A wide range of categories of persons were removed from liability for criminal offences, and the prescription period was substantially reduced. In January 2014 the RCC in an advisory opinion held that these amendments were unconstitutional.[178] Further Parliament decided that the President of Romania had violated the Constitution and should be removed from office, but the Court found that the allegations did not warrant an impeachment. Parliament then initiated an impeachment referendum. The RCC found that the Emergency Ordinance of the Government reducing

[170] Progress Report of 30 January 2013, COM(2013) 47, p. 2 et seq.; Progress Report of 22 January 2014, COM(2014) 37, p. 3–5; see the chronology of the events in the Opinion of the Venice Commission 2012, p. 3 and Blokker 2012b, p. 8 et seq.
[171] Therefore they are largely outside the scope of this paper and cannot be discussed here in detail.
[172] Technical Report of 28 January 2014, SWD(2014) 37, p. 4. See the detailed survey on the jurisprudence of the Constitutional Court in Kerek 2010, p. 279–498.
[173] See Venice Commission 2012, p. 18.
[174] Progress Report of 18 July 2012, COM(2012) 410, p. 18; Carp 2014, p 8 et seq.
[175] Decision no. 732/2012 of 9 July 2012, Monitorul Oficial no. 477/2012.
[176] Emergency Ordinance no. 38/2012; see Carp 2014, p. 8 and 11.
[177] Decision No. 727/2012 of 9 July 2012, Monitorul Oficial no. 477/2012; Decision no. 738/2012 of 19 September 2012. See Venice Commission 2012, p. 8; Carp 2014, p. 8–10.
[178] Technical Report of 22 January 2014, SWD(2014) 37.

the quorum of votes for a success of the referendum on the matter[179] was constitutional and the referendum valid,[180] but the lowering of the participation threshold from 50 to 30 % of the electorate could only apply one year after the entering-into-force of the law. However, because the turnout was too low the referendum on the suspension of the President was invalid.[181]

4.2.3 The Venice Commission criticised the "event-driven changes of electoral legislation" as a violation of the Rule of Law and an abuse of the instrument of the Emergency Ordinance.[182] In order to cope with the constitutional conflicts (at least until the end of the former President's tenure in November 2014), the President and the Prime Minister concluded in 2013 a so-called Institutional Collaboration Agreement on the respect of the independence of the judiciary and the supremacy of the Rule of Law.[183] The Government further committed itself to a restrictive use of Emergency Ordinances. Consequently, the Commission concluded that the rules of the Constitution were no longer put in question and that the Constitutional Court had consolidated its role as an important arbiter and defender of constitutional key principles such as the separation of powers.[184]

4.2.4 Recently, a discussion on far-reaching amendments of the Romanian Constitution began,[185] in particular regarding the question of limiting the competences of the President of Romania (against the background of the various conflicts between the current President and the Government) and of abolishing the second chamber of Parliament. In early February 2014, the Romanian Parliament submitted a revised draft to the Venice Commission for comments;[186] the draft provided inter alia an amendment of Art. 21 of the Constitution according to which "Parties are entitled to a fair trial and the solution of their cases within an optimal and predictable time", further a change of the composition of the SCM by increasing the number of SCM members by two extra representatives of the civil society. The Venice Commission appreciated this proposal but recommended creating "a clear and improved basis" for the SCM and a better regulation of the status of the prosecutors.[187] The nomination of judges and prosecutors should in the future be entrusted to the respective

[179] Emergency Ordinance No. 41/2012; see Venice Commission 2012, p. 9; Carp 2014, p. 9 and 11.
[180] Decision no. 6 of 21 August 2012; Progress Report of 30 January 2013, COM(2013) 47, p. 3, footnote 4.
[181] Venice Commission 2012, p. 12 point 47.
[182] Venice Commission 2012, p. 10 point 33.
[183] Progress Report of 30 January 2013, COM(2013) 47, p. 6; Gabanyi 2013, p. 442.
[184] Progress Report of 22 January 2014, COM(2014) 37.
[185] See Venice Commission 2014, passim; Technical Report of 22 January 2014, SWD(2014) 37, p. 5–6. A first proposal had been published in 2011 by the (then) Prime Minister Emil Boc (available under www.rcis.ro).
[186] Venice Commission 2014, p. 5 point 23. For a detailed survey of the proposed provisions see Venice Commission 2014, passim; Blokker 2012a, p. 7 et seq.; Carp 2014, p. 8–13. See also www.gov.ro/programme-for-government-2013-2016_12a105576.html
[187] Venice Commission 2014, p. 33 and 28.

sections of the SCM instead of to the plenum[188] and the term of the SCM members should not be reduced from six to four years.[189]

4.2.5 On 17 February 2014, the RCC delivered an advisory opinion on the draft Constitution assessing 25 of the proposed provisions, among them the extension of the SCM, as unconstitutional.[190] The Commission, too, was concerned about the tendency of the envisaged modifications of the Constitution and reminded the Government to make sure that the reform would fully respect the basic requirements of the Rule of Law, the principle of the separation of powers and the independence of the judiciary.[191] The discussion on the constitutional reform was then temporarily interrupted but the subject will presumably be resumed after the presidential elections of November 2014.

5 Lessons for the Future

5.1 The New EU "Framework"

5.1.1 The CVM focused on Rule of Law problems in two new Member States, Romania and Bulgaria, and was only conceived for a limited time (though without a fixed time limit) but is still applied.[192] Considering the problems experienced after the 2004–2007 accessions, the European Parliament,[193] the Council of the EU[194] and the European Commission[195] called for a new procedure to ensure the compliance of all Member States with the fundamental values of the Union enshrined in Art. 2 TEU on a permanent basis. Following these calls, the Commission adopted in March 2014 a Communication entitled "A new EU Framework to strengthen the Rule of Law". It would in principle apply to all member states on an equal footing but would allow particular problems to be addressed in individual cases[196], "to

[188] Venice Commission 2014, p. 29.
[189] The Venice Commission also recommended a special clause for the transfer of competences to the EU.
[190] Venice Commission 2014, p. 4.
[191] Progress Report of 30 January 2013, COM(2013) 47, p. 6; Progress Report of 22 January 2014, COM(20143) 37, p. 3.
[192] Roos 2011.
[193] Resolution P7_TA(2013) 0315 16 February 2013 (with reference to the Resolution of 12 December 2012); see also the Fundamental Rights Reports of the EP 2012, 2013 and 2014.
[194] Council Conclusions of 11 March 2013, referring to Doc. 6269/13 of 12 February 2013 and to the resolution of the European Parliament of 3 July 2013.
[195] Speech 12/596 by President Barroso: www.europa.eu/rapid/press_release_SPEECH-12-596_en.htm; Speech 13/677 of 4 September 2013 by Vice-President Reding (with reference to the Romanian rule of law crisis in 2012).
[196] Commission Communication of 11 March 2014, COM(2014) 158; Press release of the Commission of 11 March 2014 IP/14/237. See also Carrera, Guild and Hernanz 2013a, p. 50.

resolve future threats to the rule of law in Member States before the conditions for activating the mechanisms foreseen in Article 7 TEU would be met".[197]

5.1.2 The Framework is conceived as a preventive instrument in cases where national safeguards are not sufficient, for measures of the Member States outside the scope of EU law, which are likely to systematically and adversely affect the respect for the Rule of Law in a Member State.[198] The procedure is not intended to replace the infringement procedure under Art. 258 TFEU or the special supervisory procedure of Art. 7 TEU, but it would be applicable as a complement to these (and also to the procedures applied by the CoE). Essentially, the Commission provides for a "structured exchange" with the Member State concerned which in the first instance may lead to a "rule of law opinion" (not to be published) and afterwards, if necessary, to a "rule of law recommendation" (to be published), with a follow-up likely to lead, in the end, to the application of the Art. 7 TEU procedure.[199] According to the Commission, these measures should be based on information from various sources, inter alia from the European Agency for Fundamental Rights.[200] It remains to be seen whether the initiative of the Commission will turn out to be effective or whether a new legal basis in the TEU is required, to be created on the occasion of the next Treaty amendment.

5.1.3 The initiative of the Commission was appreciated by various observers because it is targeted to fill a serious gap of the EU legal system[201] but it also leads to a number of delicate questions: Does the TEU provide a sufficient legal basis for "an enhanced or new monitoring, supervision and enforcement role" of the Commission for the protection of the common values enshrined in Art. 2 TEU below the threshold of Art. 7 TEU?[202] How is a "systemic threat" defined?[203] Would the EU be in the position to supervise the compliance of the Member States with the Rule of Law at all?[204] In its Communication, the Commission does not indicate a legal basis for the proposed procedure. Vice-President Reding insisted that the Framework is based on existing TEU competences but at the same time admitted

[197] About this procedure see the Commission Communication, *Respect for and promotion of the values on which the Union is based*, COM(2003) 606; Schorkopf, in Grabitz et al. (2013), Art. 7 TEU para 62; Carrera, Guild and Hernanz 2013a, p. 50 (for a new "Copenhagen mechanism"). An earlier proposal had already been made by the EP in its Draft Treaty establishing the European Union of 19 March 1984, O.J. C 77/33 (1984), Art. 4.4 and 44.

[198] For a critical appraisal of the Commission's proposals see Bieber and Maiani 2013, p. 1085 et seq.

[199] See Schorkopf, in Grabitz et al. (2013), Art. 7 para 29 et seq.; on the Communication of the Commission see para 62. On former Art. 6.1 see Alegre 2009, p. 18 et seq.; Carrera, Guild and Hernanz 2013a, p. 38.

[200] Council Regulation (EC) No. 168/2007, O.J. L 53/1 (2007).

[201] Carrera, Guild and Hernanz 2013a, p. 5.

[202] For the scope of Art. 7 TEU see Schorkopf, in Grabitz et al. (2013), para 22 and 29; Grote 1999, p. 284 et seq.; Ullerich 2011, p. 74 et seq.; Mangiameli 2012, p. 37–39.

[203] Carrera, Guild and Hernanz 2013a, p. 1, voice doubts whether the Communication had added anything new.

[204] De Witte 2003, p. 234.

that future changes of the TEU could be taken into consideration.[205] Principally, the EU is only entitled to act if a Member State violates the fundamental rights included in the general principles of union law or of the Charter of Fundamental Rights in connection with the implementation and application of specific provisions of EU law, according to the "principle of conferral" (Art. 5.1 TEU). The Communication therefore triggered a controversial legal debate in the Council.[206]

5.2 *Considerations for Future Enlargements*

5.2.1 According to the European Commission and the Council, the Copenhagen criteria continue to be relevant for the ongoing and future accession negotiations with several South-East European states and with Turkey.[207] In its most recent Communication on the negotiations the Commission promised emphatically that "[t]he rule of law is now at the heart of the enlargement process".[208] Given the strongly different political and social structures and cultural traditions of the current candidate and applicant countries,[209] one may wonder how the European Union will be able to keep its identity, and in particular effectively ensure the respect for the Rule of Law and of human rights, after further enlargements.[210] This concerns on the one hand the Rule of Law standard applied at accession (the political accession criteria), and on the other hand the tools available after accession for the effective enforcement of this standard. Some observers fear that a future European Union would possibly comprise a considerable number of new Member States which for a long time period do not fulfil the political accession criteria, and where interests and corruption undermine rule implementation in practice despite rule adoption on paper.[211] Such a situation would obviously put in question *the value-oriented homogeneity strived for and therefore the credibility and the success of the* EU.[212]

---

[205] In case of a lack of an EU competence such a mechanism could possibly be created by an agreement between the Member States outside the framework of the TEU; see Case C-370/12, *Pringle* (ECJ 27 November 2012); see the comments to the case by Bieber and Maiani 2013, p. 1081 et seq.

[206] Opinion of the Legal Service, Doc. 10296 of 27 May 2014 (partly confidential). Sceptical Hipper 2014, p. 3. An overview of possible Rule of Law "supervision mechanisms" is given by Alegre 2009, p. 4 et seq.

[207] See the annual Communications from the Commission on "Enlargement Strategy and Main Challenges", in particular the most recent Communications of 16 October 2013, COM(2013) 700, and of 8 October 2014, COM(2014) 700; on the negotiations with Turkey see Fierro 2003, p. 148 et seq.

[208] Communication of 16 October 2013, COM(2013) 700, p. 2, 6 and 14.

[209] Wennerström 2007, p. 35; Ullerich 2011, p. 165; Hilf and Schorkopf, in Grabitz et al. (2013), p. 26–28.

[210] Hatje 2005, p. 149, sees the danger of an overstretching of the EU in the case of further enlargements; in this sense apparently also Oppermann 2005, p. 72 et seq.

[211] Mendelski 2011a, p. 177 et seq.

[212] Schorkopf 2000, p. 69 et seq., 99; Ullerich 2011, p. 73 et seq.; Mangiameli 2012, p. 21–46.

5.2.2 The situation is easier during the course of the accession negotiations: Already at its meeting in Brussels on 16/17 December 2004, the European Council had asked the Commission to propose a procedure for the case of "a serious and persistent breach in a candidate State of the principles of liberty, democracy, respect for human rights and fundamental freedoms and the rule of law". According to the European Council, in such situations the Commission should be in the position to recommend, on its own initiative or on the request of one third of the Member States, the *suspension* of the negotiations and propose the conditions for their eventual resumption.[213] A decision of the European Council on such a recommendation would require a qualified majority and would be binding for the Member States acting in the Accession Conference. For future accessions, the Copenhagen criteria remain *pro forma* valid[214], but there is a general consensus that they do not provide a sufficient base for ensuring a sufficient Rule of Law standard.[215] Various institutions and scholars have therefore drafted catalogues of the requirements for the respect for the Rule of Law, supplementing and concretising the existing rules of the EU and of the relevant recommendations of the CoE.

5.2.3 More recently, the Commission announced that it is following a so-called new approach for the current and future accession negotiations aimed at giving priority to strengthening the Rule of Law.[216] It called the issue "a continuing major challenge" and maintained that it was already given greater attention in recent years than in the past, for example during the negotiations with Croatia and ahead of the negotiations with Albania and Montenegro. The Commission underlined that there is a need for "inclusive, transparent, and ambitious judicial reforms" and that therefore in the future the issues of the independence of the judiciary and of fundamental rights would be tackled earlier in the accession process on the basis of precise action plans and track records, aiming at building up truly independent and efficient judiciaries.[217] Therefore, in a recent enlargement paper, endorsed by the Council in December 2011, the Commission urged that Candidate Countries should tackle issues like judicial reform and the fight against organised crime and corruption early in accession negotiations and that the reforms should be deeply rooted and irreversible.[218]

---

[213] Council Doc. 16238/1/04 REV 1 of 1 February 2005, para 23 "Framework for Negotiations".

[214] Conclusions of 13 December 2002, Doc. 15917/02 of 29 January 2003 (point 18 on Turkey, point 23 on the countries of the Western Balkan) and of 16 June 2006, Doc. 10633/1/06 REV 1 of 17 July 2006, para 56; Communication "Enlargement Strategy and Main Challenges 2013–2014" of 16 October 2013, COM(2013) 700, p. 1; Wennerström 2007, p. 167.

[215] See the view of numerous authors cited above under Sect. 5.1.2.

[216] Communication of 16 October 2013, COM(2013) 700, p. 7; Inglis 2010, p. 411–425.

[217] Communication of 6 November 2007, COM(2007) 663, p. 2; Communication of 16 October 2013, COM(2013) 700, p. 7.

[218] Communication of 12 October 2011, COM(2011) 666, p. 5; also, further financial assistance will be required for improving the justice sector, the independence of the judiciary and the fight against corruption and organised crime. For the period 2007–2013, the EU put over 800 Mio. Euro pre-accession assistance at the disposal of the new Candidate Countries for these purposes; see Communication of 16 October 2013, COM(2013) 700, p. 7.

5.2.4 In its recent Communication on the enlargement process of 16 October 2013,[219] the Commission conceded that the problems of the Rule of Law enforcement were not taken seriously enough in the past and promised that in the next negotiation rounds they will be given more space and time, because "[t]he rule of law is now at the heart of the enlargement process". However, the experience of the 2004–2007 enlargement demonstrated that adoption of a comprehensive constitutional and legal framework is not by itself sufficient to ensure the respect for the Rule of Law but that effective instruments are required to secure its correct application and enforcement. The chances for successfully changing and reorganising a national legal system by an "intervention" from outside may be limited as comparative law studies have demonstrated, and the "transformation" of a society needs time.[220] Obviously, all efforts to ensure the respect for the Rule of Law are in vain without the existence of an appropriate cultural "climate".[221] However, there seems now to be a broad consensus that the relevant criteria for the Rule of Law should not be "watered down" but must be applied rigorously,[222] and that political goals and expected economic advantages should not supersede the Rule of Law requirements.[223] How this could effectively be accomplished still remains an open question, considering the experience of the recent enlargements.[224] Looking back to the enlargement process in the last decade, it had been observed that "[t]he political criteria have proved to be the most crucial part of conditionality",[225] and it is safe to foresee that they will continue to be the most crucial criteria in future enlargements, in particular regarding the respect for the Rule of Law.

References

Adinolfi, A. (2012). The "Procedural Autonomy" of Member States and the Constraints Stemming from the ECJ's Case Law: Is Judicial Activism still necessary? In H.-W. Micklitz & B. de Witte (Eds.), *The European Court of Justice and the Autonomy of the Member States*. Cambridge, Antwerp, Portland: Intersentia.

At the same time, the European Council concluded that Turkey fulfils the political criteria (including the Rule of Law): Conclusions of 16/17 December 2004, Doc. 16238/1/04 of 1 February 2005, p. 4 et seq.

[219] Communication of 16 October 2013 "Enlargement Strategy and Main Challenges 2013–2014", COM(2013) 700, p. 6, and 2014–2015 of 8 October 2014, COM(2014) 700 (see in particular Annex "Summary of findings" p. 30–48).

[220] Wagener 2011, p. 210 et seq., on the conditions of transformation and re-integration; sceptically Hatje 2005, p. 149 ("overstretching the EU"); Hipper 2014, p. 3.

[221] Howard 2001, p. 101–103; Slavu 2008, p. 233; Tatham 2009, p. 483; Coman and Dallara 2012, p. 880.

[222] House of Lords Report 2013, para 24 and 46.

[223] Rem and Gasper 2008, p. 5.

[224] A systematic strengthening of the monitoring on the basis of Art. 7 and 17 TEU and Art. 352 TFEU is considered possible from the legal point of view by Bieber and Maiani 2013, p. 1091.

[225] This view of Nicolaidis and Kleinfeld 2012, p. 16, appears to be a widely held opinion.

Alegre, S. (2009). Safeguarding the Rule of Law in the EU: Synthesis Report. In S. Alegre, I. Ivanov, & D. Denis-Smith (Eds.), *Safeguarding the Rule of Law in an Enlarged EU: The Cases of Bulgaria and Romania* CEPS Special Report (pp. 1–19). Sofia: Open Society Institute. www.ceps.eu/system/files/book/1833.pdf

Azoulai, L. (2012). The Case of Fundamental Rights: A State of Ambivalence. In H.-W. Micklitz & B. de Witte (Eds.), *The European Court of Justice and the Autonomy of the Member States* (pp. 207–217). Cambridge, Antwerp, Portland: Intersentia.

Bieber, R., & Maiani, F. (2013). Enhancing centralized enforcement of EU law: Pandora's Toolbox? *CMLRev.*, *51*, 1057–1092.

Blanke, H.-J. (2012). The Protection of Fundamental Rights in Europe. In H.-J. Blanke, & S. Mangiameli (Eds.), *The European Union after Lisbon. Constitutional Basis, Economic Order and External Action* (pp. 159–232). Berlin, Heidelberg: Springer.

Blokker, P. (2012a). Constitution-Making in Romania: From Reiterative Crises to Constitutional Moment? *Romanian Journal of Comparative Law*, *3*(2), 187–204.

Blokker, P. (2012b). Romanian Constitutionalism: Form without Content?www.academia.edu/1937927/Romanian_Constitutionalism_Form_Without_Content

Bobek, M. (2007). Iudex ex machina: Institutional and Mental Transistions of Central European Judiciaries. In R. Coman & J.-M. De Waele (Eds.), *Judicial Reforms in Central and Eastern European Countries* (pp. 107-134). Brugge: Vanden Broele.

Bobek, M. (2012). Why there is no principle of "Procedural Autonomy" of the Member States. In H.-W. Micklitz, & B.de Witte (Eds.), *The European Court of Justice and the Autonomy of the Member States* (pp. 305–323). Cambridge, Antwerp, Portland: Intersentia.

Bormann, A. (2004). Die rumänische Verfassungsreform 2003. *Jahrbuch für Ostrecht*, *45*, 207–267.

Bormann, A. (2009). Rumänien: Rechtsrahmen und Institutionen. In H. Küpper (Ed.), *Korruptionsbekämpfung in Osteuropa* (pp. 185–242). München: forost.

Brosius-Gersdorf, F. (2005). *Bindung der Mitgliedstaaten an die Gemeinschaftsgrundrechte*. Berlin: Duncker & Humblot.

Carausan, M. (2009). Institutional Uncertainties of the Rule of Law – the Public Prosecutor's Office between the Executive and the Judiciary. *Transylvanian Review of Administrative Sciences*, *28*, 104–128.

Carey, H. F. (2011). European Promotion of Democracy, Human Rights and the Rule of Law in Romania. In R. F. King, & P. E. Sum (Eds.), *Romania under Basescu. Aspirations, Achievements, and Frustrations during His First Presidential Term* (pp. 313–345). Lanham, Plymouth: Lexington Books.

Carp, R. (2007). A constitutional principle under scrutiny: the immovability of judges – Romanian regulations in a comparative law perspective. In R. Coman, & J.-M.De Waele (Eds.), *Judicial Reforms in Central and Eastern European Countries* (pp. 199–225). Brugge: Vanden Broele.

Carp, R. (2014). The Struggle for the Rule of Law in Romania as an EU Member State: The Role of the Cooperation and Verification Mechanism. *Utrecht Law Review*, *10*(1), 1–16.

Carrera, S., Guild, E., & Hernanz, N. (2013a). *Rule of law or rule of thumb? A New Copenhagen Mechanism for the EU. CEPS Policy Brief No. 303. Brussels: Center for European Policy Studies*. www.ceps.eu/book/rule-law-or-rule-thumb-new-copenhagen-mechanism-eu

Carrera, S., Guild, E., & Hernanz, N. (2013b). *The Triangular Relationship between Fundamental Rights, Democracy and the Rule of Law in the EU. Towards an EU Copenhagen Mechanism*. www.europarl.europa.eu/studies

Coman, R. (2007). Media, Justice and Politics or How the Independence of the Judiciary became an Issue in Romania. In R. Coman, & J.-M.De Waele (Eds.), *Judicial Reforms in Central and Eastern European Countries* (pp. 157–198). Brugge: Vanden Broele.

Coman, R., & Dallara, C. (2012). Judicial Independence in Romania. In A. Seibert-Fohr (Ed.), *Judicial Independence in Transition*. Beiträge zum ausländischen öffentlichen Recht und Völkerrecht, (vol. 233, pp. 835–881). Heidelberg, New York, Dordrecht, London: Springer.

Cremona, M. (2003). *The enlargement of the European Union*. Oxford, New York: Oxford University Press.

Dallara, Cr. (2014). The Successful Laggard in Judicial Reform: Romania Before and After Accession. In Cr. Dallara (Ed.), *Democracy and Judicial Reforms in South-East Europe* (pp. 57-80). Zurich: Springer International Publishing.

De Witte, B. (2003). The Impact of Enlargement on the Construction of the European Union. In M. Cremona (Ed.), *The Enlargement of the European Union* (pp. 209–252). Oxford, New York: Oxford University Press.

Denis-Smith, D. (2009). The case of Romania. In S. Alegre, I. Ivanova, & D. Denis-Smith (Eds.), *Safeguarding the Rule of Law in an Enlarged EU. The cases of Bulgaria and Romania*. CEPS Special Report. (pp. 52–84). Sofia: Open Society Institute.

Dörr, O., Grote, R., & Marauhn, T. (Eds.). (2013). *EMRK/GG Konkordanzkommentar zum europäischen und deutschen Grundrechtsschutz* (2nd edn.). vol. II. Tübingen: Mohr Siebeck.

Emmert, F. (2003). Administrative and Court Reform in Central and Eastern Europe. *Eastern European Law Journal, 9(3)*, 288-315.

Fierro, E. (2003). *The EU's Approach to Human Rights Conditionality in Practice*. London, New York: Martinus Nijhoff Publishers.

Gabanyi, A. U. (1999–2000). Rumänien. In W. Weidenfeld & W. Wessels (Eds.). *Jahrbuch der europäischen Integration* (p. 421–424). Baden-Baden: Nomos.

Gabanyi, A. U. (2013). Rumänien. In W. Weidenfeld, & W. Wessels (Eds.), *Jahrbuch der europäischen Integration* (pp. 441–444). Baden-Baden: Nomos.

Gallagher, Tom (2005). *Modern Romania*. New York: New York University Press.

Garoupa, N., & Ginsburg, T. (2009). Guarding the Guardians. Judicial Councils and Judicial Independence. *American Journal of Comparative Law*, *57*, 201–232.

Geissler, T., & Rebegea, C. (2011). *The Old and the New Romanian Superior Council of Magistracy. Country Report. Rule of Law Program, South East Europe*. Berlin: Konrad-Adenauer-Stiftung e. V.

Gionea, V., & Tontsch, G. H. (2007). Die Verfassungsgerichtsbarkeit in Rumänien. In O. Luchterhandt, Chr. Starck, & A. Weber (Eds.), *Berichte* Verfassungsgerichtsbarkeit in Mittel- und Osteuropa, (Teilband I, pp. 105–127). Baden-Baden: Nomos.

Grabenwarter, C. (2014). *European Convention on Human Rights – Commentary*. München, Oxford, Baden-Baden, Basel, Portland: C. H. Beck, Hart Publishing, Nomos, Helbing Lichtenhahn.

Grabitz, E., Hilf, M., & Nettesheim, M. (Eds.). (2013). *Das Recht der Europäischen Union. Kommentar* vol. I. Munich: C. H. Beck. Loose leaf.

Große Wentrup, A. (2003). *Die Europäische Grundrechtscharta im Spannungsfeld der Kompetenzverteilung zwischen Europäischer Union und Mitgliedstaaten*. Berlin: Duncker & Humblot.

Grote, R. (1999). Rule of Law, Rechtsstaat and "Etat de droit". In C. Starck (Ed.), *Constitutionalism, Universalism and Democracy – a comparative analysis* (pp. 269–306). Baden-Baden: Nomos.

Hatje, A. (2005). Grenzen der Flexibilität einer erweiterten Europäischen Union. *Europarecht*, *vol. 2*, 148–161.

Hein, M. (2013). *Verfassungskonflikte zwischen Politik und Recht in Südosturopa. Bulgarien und Rumänien nach 1989 im Vergleich*. Baden-Baden: Nomos.

Hillion, C. (2004). The Copenhagen Criteria and their Progeny. In C. Hillion (Ed.), *EU Enlargement. A Legal Approach* (pp. 1–22). Oxford, Portland: Hart Publ.

Hipper, A. M. (2014). *Political Judicialization – The Quest for the Romanian Constitutional Court*. www.bgss.hu_berlin.de/bgssonlinepublications/workshopDocu/advocatesnotariesofdemocracyfolder/paper1

House of Lords (2013). *The future of EU enlargement. European Union Committee. 10th Report of Session 2012–13*. London: The Stationary Office Limited.

Howard, A.E.D. (2001). Judicial Independence in Post-Communist Europe. In P.H. Russell & D.M. O'Brian (Eds.), *Judicial Independence in the Age of Democracy. Critical Perspectives from around the World* (pp. 89–110). Charlottesville, London: University of Virginia Press.

Inglis, K. (2010). Evolving Practice in EU Enlargement. *Studies in EU External Relations* vol. 4. Leiden, Boston: Martinus Nijhoff Publishers.

Ionescu, C. (2008). Romania. In C. Kortmann, J. Fleuren, & W. Voermans (Eds.), *Constitutional Law of 2 EU Member States: Bulgaria and Romania. The 2007 Enlargement* (pp. II/1–II/104). Deventer: Kluwer.

Kerek, A. (2010). *Verfassungsgerichtsbarkeit in Ungarn und Rumänien*. Berlin: Berliner Wissenschafts-Verlag.

Kochenov, D. (2008). *EU Enlargement and the Failure of Conditionality. Pre-accession Conditionality in the Fields of Democracy and the Rule of Law*. Alphen aan de Rijn: Kluwer Law International.

Kokott, J. & Sobotta, Chr. (2010). *The Charter of Fundamental Rights after Lisbon*. AEL Working Papers 2010/6. Florence: Academy of European Law.

Kuijer, M. (2004). *The Blindfold Lady Justice – Judicial Independence and Impartiality in Light of the Requirements of Article 6 ECHR*. Leiden: Wolf Legal Publishers.

Mangiameli, S. (2012). The Union's Homogeneity and its Common Values in the Treaty on European Union. In H.-J. Blanke, & S. Mangiameli (Eds.), *The Treaty on European Union. The European Union after Lisbon. Constitutional Basis, Economic Order and External Action* (pp. 21–46). Berlin, Heidelberg: Springer.

Maresceau, M. (1997). *Enlarging the European Union – Relations between the EU and Central and Eastern Europe*. London, New York: Longman.

Maresceau, M. (2003). Pre-accession. In M. Cremona (Ed.), *The Enlargement of the European Union* (pp. 9–42). Oxford: Oxford University Press.

Mendelski, M. (2011a). Romanian Rule of Law Reform: A Two-Dimensional Approach. In R.F. King, & P.E. Sum (Eds.), *Romania under Basescu* (pp. 155–179). Lanham/New York/Toronto/Plymouth: Lexington Books. http://www.coe.int/t/dghl/cooperation/cepej/profiles/Romanian_Rule_of_Law_Reform_%20Mendelski_2011.pdf

Mendelski, M. (2011b). Rule of Law Reform in the Shadow of Clientelism: The Limits of the EU's Transformative Power in Romania. *Polish Sociological Review*, *2*, 235–253.

Meyer-Ladewig, J. (2011). *EMRK. Europäische Menschenrechtskonvention. Commentary* (3rd edn.). Baden-Baden: Nomos.

Meyer-Ladewig, J. (2012). The Rule of Law in the Case Law of the Strasburg Court. In H.-J. Blanke, & S. Mangiameli (Eds.), *The European Union after Lisbon: constitutional basis, economic order, and external action* (pp. 233–250). Berlin, Heidelberg: Springer.

Müller, L. F. (2009). Judicial Independence as a Council of Europe Standard. *German Yearbook of International Law*, *52*, 461–486.

Nicolaidis, K., & Kleinfeld, R. (2012). *Rethinking Europe's „Rule of Law" and Enlargement Agenda: The Fundamental Dilemma*. OECD/EU. SIGMA Paper No. 49. http://dx.dol.org/10.1787/5k4c42jmn5zp-en

Nusser, J. (2011). *Die Bindung der Mitgliedstaaten an die Unionsgrundrechte: Vorgaben für die Auslegung von Art. 51 Abs. 1 S. 1 EuGrCh*. Tübingen: Mohr Siebeck.

O'Brennan, J. (2006). *The Eastern Enlargement of the European Union*. New York, London: Routledge.

OSI Report (2001). *Monitoring the EU Accession Process. Judicial Independence*. Budapest: Open Society Institute.

OSI Report (2002). Monitoring the EU Accession Process.*Judicial Capacity in Romania*. Budapest: Open Society Institute.

Olaru, A. (2012). Activities of the Ministry of Justice in Collaboration with the German Foundation for International Legal Cooperation – IRZ. In S. Hülshörster, & D. Mirow (Eds.), *Deutsche Beratung bei Rechts- und Justizreformen im Ausland: 20 Jahre Deutsche Stiftung für Internationale Rechtliche Zusammenarbeit* (pp. 435–438). Berlin: Berliner Wissenschafts-Verlag.

Oppermann, T. (2005). Die Grenzen der Europäischen Union oder Das Vierte Kopenhagener Kriterium. In C. Gaitanides (Ed.), *Europa und seine Verfassung. Festschrift für Manfred Zuleeg zum siebzigsten Geburtstag* (pp. 72–79). Baden-Baden: Nomos.

Parau, C. E. (2012). The Drive for Judicial Supremacy. In A. Seibert-Fohr (Ed.), *Judicial Independence in Transition* (pp. 619–666). Heidelberg, New York, Dordrecht, London: Springer.

Reding, V. (2013). *The EU and the Rule of Law – What next? Speech/13/677*. Brussels: Centre for European Policy Studies.

Rem, D., & Gasper, D. (2008). *Romania's accession process into the European Union*. ISS Working Paper, vol. 463. The Hague: Institute of Social Studies.

Rengeling, H.-W., & Szczekalla, P. (2004). *Grundrechte in der Europäischen Union. Charta der Grundrechte und Allgemeine Rechtsgrundsätze*. Köln, Berlin, München: Carl Heymanns.

Rieger, A. (2011). *Verfassungsrechtliche Legitimationsgrundlagen richterlicher Unabhängigkeit*. Frankfurt/Main: Peter Lang.

Roos, S. R. (2011). Die (un)endliche Geschichte der bulgarischen und rumänischen Justizreform. *Konrad-Adenauer-Stiftung Auslandsnachrichten*, *1*, 7–24.

Roos, S. R., & Rebegea, C. (2009). *Anticorruption Policies in the Justice System. Debate and Book Launch*. Berlin: Konrad-Adenauer-Stiftung. www.kas.de/rspsoe

Roth, A. (2006). Verfassungstext und Verfassungswirklichkeit in Rumänien. In D. Fischer (Ed.), *Transformation des Rechts in Ost und West. Festschrift für Prof. Dr. Herwig Roggemann zum 70. Geburtstag* (pp. 137–150). Berlin: Berliner Wissenschafts-Verlag.

Rothacher, A. (2002). *Im Wilden Osten. Hinter den Kulissen des Umbaus in Osteuropa*. Hamburg: Krämer.

Sannerholm, R.Z. (2012). *Rule of Law after war and crisis: ideologies, norms and methods*. Cambridge: Intersentia.

Scheuing, D. H. (2005). Zur Grundrechtsbindung der EU-Mitgliedstaaten. *Europarecht*, 162–191.

Schmidt-Aßmann, E. (2004). Der Rechtsstaat. In J. Isensee, & P. Kirchhof (Eds.), *Handbuch des Staatsrechts der Bundesrepubik Deutschland* 3rd edn. (vol. II, pp. 541–611). Heidelberg: C.F. Müller.

Schorkopf, F. (2000). *Homogenität in der Europäischen Union. Ausgestaltung und Gewährleistung durch Art. 6 Abs. 1 und Art. 7 EUV*. Berlin: Duncker & Humblot.

Seibert-Fohr, A. (2009). Judicial Independence in European Union Accessions: The Emergence of a European Basic Principle. *German Yearbook of International Law*, *52*, 405–436.

Seibert-Fohr, A. (2012). Judicial Independence – The Normativity of an Evolving Transnational Principle. In A. Seibert-Fohr (Ed.), *Judicial Independence in Transition* (pp. 1279–1360). Heidelberg, New York, Dordrecht, London: Springer.

Slavu, S. (2008). *Die Osterweiterung der Europäischen Union. Eine Analyse des EU-Beitritts Rumäniens*. Frankfurt/Main: Peter Lang.

Smilov, D., & Toplek, J. (2007). *Political Finance and Corruption in Eastern Europe: the transition period*. Farnham: Ashgate.

Smith, K. E. (2003). The Evolution and Application of EU Membership Conditionality. In M. Cremona (Ed.), *The Enlargement of the European Union* (pp. 105–139). Oxford, New York: OUP.

Sticht, M. (2006). *Der Beitrag des Europarats zur demokratischen Transformation in Mittel- und Osteuropa seit 1989 am Beispiel von Ungarn, Rumänien und Aserbeidschan*. Berlin: Berliner Wissenschafts-Verlag.

Szarek-Mason, P. (2010). *The European Union's Fight Against Corruption. The Evolving Policy Towards Member States and Candidate Countries*. New York: Cambridge University Press.

Tatham, A. F. (2009). *Enlargement of the European Union*. Alphen/Netherlands: Kluwer Law International.

Tanasescu, S. E., & Popescu, R. D. (2012). Romanian High Judicial Council – Between Analogy of Law and Ethical Trifles. *Transylvanian Review of Administrative Sciences, 36*, 165–176.

Tomescu, C., & Levai, M. C. (2012). The Principle of Equilibrium and Separation of Powers under the Romanian Constitution. *The USV Annals of Economics and Public Administration*, 12(1), 284–293. http://www.seap.usv.ro/annals/ojs/index.php/annals/article/viewFile/483/483

Trappe, J. (2012). EU-Twinning-Projekte als Chance der internationalen rechtlichen Zusammenarbeit. In S. Hülshörster, & D. Mirow (Eds.), *Deutsche Beratung bei Rechts- und Justizreformen im Ausland: 20 Jahre Deutsche Stiftung für Internationale Rechtliche Zusammenarbeit* (pp. 341–348). Berlin: Berliner Wissenschafts-Verlag.

Trechsel, St. (2005). *Human Rights in Criminal Proceedings*. Oxford, New York: Oxford University Press.

Tschirky, A. (2011). *The Council of Europe's activities in the judicial field*. Zürich/Basel/Genf: Schulthess Juristische Medien.

Ullerich, R. (2011). *Rechtsstaat und Rechtsgemeinschaft im Europarecht*. Baden-Baden: Nomos.

Valea, D. C. (2010). The Competence of the Constitutional Court of Romania to settle the Constitutional Conflicts between the Public Authorities. *Curentul Juridic, 42*, 95–102. www.ideas.repec.org/s/pmu/cjurid1.html

Venice Commission (2002). Opinion of 5–6 July 2002 on the Draft Revision of the Constitution of Romania. *CDL-AD, 012*.

Venice Commission (2003). Opinion of 14–15 July 2003 on the Draft Revision of the Constitution of Romania. *CDL-AD, 004*.

Venice Commission (2010). Report on the Independence of the Judicial System, Part I: The Independence of Judges. *CDL-AD, 004*.

Venice Commission (2012). Opinion no. 685/2012 of 14–15 December 2012 on the Compatibility with Constitutional Principles and the Rule of Law of Actions taken by the Government and the Parliament of Romania in respect of Other State Institutions. *CDL-AD, 026*.

Venice Commission (2014). Opinion no. 731/2013 of 21–22 March 2014 on the Draft Law on the Review of the Constitution of Romania. *CDL-AD, 010*.

Wagener, H.-J. (2011). *Wirtschaftsordnung im Wandel. Zur Transformation 1985–2010*. Marburg: Metropolis.

Weber, A. (2010). *Europäische Verfassungsvergleichung. Ein Studienbuch*. München: C. H. Beck.

Wennerström, E. O. (2007). *The Rule of Law and the European Union*. Uppsala: Iustus Förlag.

Wittreck, F. (2006). *Die Verwaltung der Dritten Gewalt*. Tübingen: Mohr Siebeck.

Yowell, P. (2012). The Justiciability of the EU Charter of Fundamental Rights in the Domestic Law of the Member States. In P. M. Huber (Ed.), *The EU and National Constitutional Law* (pp. 107–123). Stuttgart: Richard Boorberg.

Dealing with Data – Legislative Challenges and Opportunities for the Digital Single Market from the Perspective of Research

Rudolf W. Strohmeier and Daniel Spichtinger

Abstract
Data is becoming increasingly important for all aspects of the European economy and this ubiquity of data presents a conundrum for the legislator, who is under pressure from different stakeholders which often have divergent understandings of what actually constitutes "data". It is therefore all the more surprising, that so few studies, reports and press articles actually address the variety of data in different contexts. This paper provides several classification systems for data and then provides two case studies – at the time of writing still ongoing in the legislative process – about the implications of data in (i) the revision of the copyright review (text and data mining) and (ii) data protection legislation, with emphasis on the perspective of the research community. Both legislative proposals have a potentially significant impact on the ongoing efforts to eliminate barriers in order to realise economic benefits of the digital economy. The authors assert that a flexible framework, which takes the variability of data into account, is needed in order to square the potential tension between accessibility of research data on the one side and IPR and data protection on the other side. They point to the Horizon 2020 open access to research data pilot as a potential example of how such a practical solution could be achieved. The article concludes by pointing to the changes in the scientific system, which are likely to give rise to further opportunities but also challenges for legislators and policy makers alike.

1 Everything is Data . . .

Policy and legal issues related to data seem to be everywhere nowadays: earlier in 2014 Europeans were shocked by revelations on widespread spying on supposedly private data by the US National Security Agency. This has led to a heightened sensitivity on the part of European citizens on how their personal data is being collected and used, for instance by commercial services such as Facebook or Google.

All views expressed herein are entirely of the authors, do not reflect the position of the European Institutions or bodies and do not, in any way, engage any of them.

H.-J. Blanke et al. (eds.), *Common European Legal Thinking*,
DOI 10.1007/978-3-319-19300-7_29

The magazine "Wired" has even warned on its cover page that "the data industry is selling your life".[1]

At the same time, data is becoming increasingly important for all aspects of the European economy. More and more data is being generated and it has been estimated that big and open data can potentially add 1.9 % to the EU's GDP by 2020.[2] These gains can be derived from productivity increases, the opening up of public sector data and better decision making thanks to data-driven processes. The digital economy is therefore considered a key potential source of growth, innovation and ultimately employment[3], a fact that is reflected in the agenda of the new *Juncker* Commission, which has made completing the digital single market a priority.[4] The European Commission has recognised the particular importance of data for the digital economy[5] and has *inter alia* launched a Public Private Partnership on the value of big data. This Public Private Partnership links up European industry (large players and SMEs), researchers, academia and the European Commission to cooperate in data research and innovation.[6]

It is important to point out that the trend of "datafication" does not only affect sectors traditionally associated with the digital economy – such as IT – but that all parts of the economy are becoming digitised. Big and Open Data have been estimated to have an impact on sectors as diverse as agriculture, public administration, health, retail, transportation and the work place. Data are a core asset that can create a significant competitive advantage and drive innovation, sustainable growth and development in all these sectors. In business, the exploitation of data promises to create added value in a variety of operations, ranging from optimising the value chain and manufacturing production to more efficient use of labour and better customer relationships.[7]

The importance of data for industrial processes is captured by the term "industry 4.0". The first three industrial revolutions came about as a result of mechanisation, electricity and IT. Now, digitisation (also called "the internet of things") is considered by some[8] to be ushering in a fourth industrial revolution: smart machines, storage systems and production facilities will be capable of autonomously exchanging information, triggering actions and controlling each other independently. This facilitates fundamental improvements to the industrial processes involved in manufacturing, engineering, material usage and supply chain and life cycle management, resulting in smart factories and smart products. However, if industry 4.0 is to be successfully implemented, research and development activities will need to be

[1] Wired of 14 November 2014, title page, p. 98–105.

[2] Buchholtz et al. 2014.p. 6–7.

[3] European Policy Centre 2010, p. 4.

[4] Juncker 2014, p. 5; European Commission (2015), *Digital Single Market Strategy*, COM(2015)192 final, 6.5.2015.

[5] European Commission, *Towards a thriving data-driven economy*, COM(2014) 442 final.

[6] European Commission, *European Commission and data industry launch € 2.5 billion partnership to master big data*, Press release IP-14-1129.

[7] Kounatze 2013, p. 4.

[8] In particular Forschungsunion/acatech 2013.

accompanied by the appropriate industrial and industrial policy decisions. In a 2013 report the German Industry 4.0 Working Group[9] identified not only technical and social but also legal issues that need to be addressed in connection with data, namely:

(i) adequate protection of company data and access to the data of third parties, which may necessitate the adaptation of existing business models,
(ii) liability as concerns the use of data across companies, in particular as concerns unauthorised use of such data,
(iii) use of personal data and data protection issues (see also discussion below).

In order to address these issues, the working group recommends not primarily legal action but a mix of instruments, which includes legal expertise at an early stage.

Another characteristic of data in the 21st century is the sheer volume of it. In 1836, *Charles Darwin*'s voyage of scientific discovery on the HMS Beagle delivered home to England 770 pages of diary, 1,383 pages of geological notes, 1,529 specimens preserved in spirits and another 3,907 dried. In 2011, by comparison, the US GenBank database stored DNA sequence information from scientists around the world on more than 380,000 species – growing at 3,800 species a month.[10] With institutions such as the European Bioinformatics Institute doubling its data storage every year it is no surprise that the Scandinavian research organisation SINTEF reported in 2013 that 90 % of all the data in the world had been generated over the previous two years.[11] The European Commission's High Level Expert Group report on Scientific Data is therefore aptly entitled "Riding the Wave".[12] The group suggested the importance of developing appropriate infrastructure to cope with what has been variously (and with slightly different emphasis) referred to as "data tsunami", "data deluge" or "big data" and its use in research as "data intensive science".

Big Data thus has the potential to become a new general-purpose technology, with the information and knowledge embedded in Big Data increasingly becoming the key to economic and scientific competitiveness. In other words, Big Data has revolutionary potential, changing everything from the way businesses work to the way products and services are produced, delivered, received and consumed as well as science and research are being conducted. However, it is still worth pointing out that data itself is worthless. It is how data is used – for instance as the "raw material" in smart phone apps – that creates value.

---

9 Forschungsunion/acatech 2013, p. 62.
10 Hudson (w.d.), p. 4.
11 Dragland 2013.
12 European Commission 2010.

2 ... but all Data are Different

The ubiquity and pervasiveness (see Sect. 1) but at the same time the variety of what is considered "data" present important challenges in legislating on data-related issues. It is all the more surprising, then, that so few studies, reports and press articles actually define what they mean when they discuss "data". When, for instance, a data protection activist talks about usage "data" from a social network this is something very different from what a particle physicist at CERN has in mind.

On the most general level the Cambridge Dictionary defines data as "information, especially facts or numbers, collected to be examined and considered and used to help decision-making or information in an electronic form that can be stored and processed by a computer".[13] In a research context, examples of data include statistics, results of experiments, measurements, observations resulting from fieldwork, survey results, interview recordings and images. Nowadays, the focus is on research data that is available in digital form. A further useful definition is provided by the United States Government's Office of Science and Technology Policy in its Memorandum on Increasing Access to the Results of Federally Funded Scientific Research where data is defined "as the digital recorded factual material commonly accepted in the scientific community as necessary to validate research findings including data sets used to support scholarly publications".[14] In a research context, a further distinction can be made between:

- Data generated primarily for research purposes – this is already an extremely broad field covering different definitions of data. What is considered data varies enormously, for instance in archaeology (e. g. pictures of a dig site), medicine (e. g. clinical trial data) or particle physics (e. g. CERN data).
- Data not primarily generated for research purposes, which can, however, be used for research:
  - So-called "Public Sector Information", that is data collected by public authorities, such as statistics (e. g. census data, demographic and economic indicators), geospatial data (e. g. maps), transport data (e. g. traffic information) or company and business registers.
  - Data that is "out there", that is on the internet – for instance on social networks such as twitter or Facebook, including but not limited to usage data of these sites. The Twitter DataGrants pilot program, for instance, aims at giving a handful of research institutions access to Twitter's public and historical data.[15]

For the research sector a further proposed classification of data is as follows:

a) Metadata/bibliographic data that describe data: metadata is found in online catalogues, archives, repositories, etc.

---

[13] Cambridge Dictionaries Online 2014.
[14] OSTP 2013, p. 5.
[15] Twitter 2014.

b) Data underlying publications (i. e. the data needed to validate the findings presented in scientific publications), often presented as part of publications ("enriched publications", with links to data).
c) Curated data, for example data collections, structured databases (held in repositories and data centres, both institutional and discipline-based), including relevant workflows and protocols.
d) Raw data and data sets: these are not curated and typically held on institute hard drives and in drawers. The amounts of un-curated raw data are probably enormous.

Another configuration yet, distinguishes between open data, enterprise data and personal data.[16] While research data cannot be neatly fitted into this categorisation – it could sit in each of the three proposed sections – the category of personal data is certainly an important one, although here again, a distinction between Facebook or Twitter usage statistics and (for instance) patient data used in medical research is needed. Personal data and data protection issues will be further explored below.

3 Legislative and Policy Challenges as Concerns Research Data on the European Scale: Two Case Studies

As for data generated primarily for research purposes, the EU's multiannual framework programme for Research and Innovation, Horizon 2020, has funding of nearly 80 billion € and is therefore expected to generate a significant amount of such data. It is therefore in the interest of the EU to ensure that best use of this data is made. On the one hand this includes technical challenges – making sure that the data generated is findable, accessible, interoperable and re-usable (FAIR) – but, on the other hand, legislative issues also play a major role, such as:

i. To what extent does copyright legislation affect the ability of researchers to re-use data?
ii. To what extent does data protection and privacy legislation affect the ability of researchers to conduct and (re)use research?

Question (i) establishes a clear link with one of the priorities of the *Juncker* Commission, namely completing the digital single market. It is worth remembering that in digital matters the EU is still composed of 28 individual single markets, each with its own legal framework. As a result not all economic benefits of the digital economy are realised. The so-called "Digital Single Market" (DSM) therefore extends the concept of the common market – the *raison d'être* for the European Union – into the digital sphere and intends to eliminate key barriers. Of course, this goes far beyond research data and includes issues such as online consumer access to music, movies and sports events.[17]

[16] Filippov 2014, p. 13.
[17] For the wider context see for instance European Parliament 2013.

However, copyright is certainly relevant for text and data mining (TDM, also called content-mining), an automated technique with which researchers can analyse patterns and trends of millions of articles or data at the same time. Because they cannot identify all interesting publications, researchers have to rely on machines that "mine" content and identify pertinent scholarly publications. In order to mine text and data, it is necessary to access, copy and analyse material and relate it to existing information. This can be illegal under current copyright law, even if the user already has access to, and paid for, the material. An economic analysis suggests long-term GDP gains with TDM in an order of magnitude of € 30 billion per year, when limited to the narrowest TDM definition. However, at present, the use of TDM tools by researchers in Europe appears to be lower than their main competitors.[18] In the international context the US asserts a "fair use" doctrine for TDM activity which allows snippets of text to be freely copied. Countries like Canada, Israel, Singapore, Japan and South Korea have adopted a similar "fair use" approach.

In 2012, an orientation debate on copyright led to a Commission Communication on content in the digital market,[19] which included a structured dialogue with stakeholders called "Licences for Europe" (LfE). While there is some consensus among different stakeholders that the EU's copyright system in general needs to be upgraded to adequately reflect the realities of the 21st century (current legislation stems from 2001[20]), opinions diverge sharply on how exactly TDM should be treated in the future copyright system. In the Licences for Europe context, traditional scientific publishers clearly favoured the use of licences to copyrighted material while researchers[21] strongly favoured a copyright exception to TDM, free of charge, for research content. Their position was also strongly supported by research libraries, universities, research centres and open access publishers. This division of opinions is also reflected in the responses to the 2014 public consultation on the review of the EU copyright *acquis*, which included several questions on text and data mining.[22]

Copyright reform in the context of completing the digital single market will remain high on the agenda in the coming months and the issue of text and data mining is certain to be re-examined in this light. A Commission proposal for the modernization of the EU copyright rules is foreseen in the Commission work programme for end 2015.

---

[18] European Commission, *Standardisation in the area of innovation and technological development, notably in the field of Text and Data Mining. Report from the Expert Group*, 2014, p. 3, http://ec.europa.eu/research/innovation-union/pdf/TDM-report_from_the_expert_group-042014.pdf (accessed 11 November 2014).

[19] European Commission, *On content in the Digital Single Market*, COM(2012) 789.

[20] Parliament/Council Directive 2001/29/EC *on the harmonisation of certain aspects of copyright and related rights in the information society*, O.J. L 167/10 (2001).

[21] LIBER/LERU 2014.

[22] European Commission 2014, p. 63–67.

Question (ii) has direct relevance to the currently ongoing revision of the European Data Protection Directive (95/46/EC),[23] which covers the use of personal data across a wide range of sectors. Here, again, how personal data is defined has broad ramifications for the applicability of the directive in a variety of sectors, including research. The definition contained in Art. 2a of Directive 95/46/EC reads as follows: "personal data shall mean any information relating to an identified or identifiable natural person ('data subject'); an identifiable person is one who can be identified, directly or indirectly, in particular by reference to an identification number or to one or more factors specific to his physical, physiological, mental, economic, cultural or social identity". This reflects a wide notion of "personal data", which has been maintained throughout the legislative process.[24] In fact, a revised definition proposed in context of the 2012 review (see below) broadens the definition even more and in article 3 defines as a "data subject" "an identified natural person or a natural person who can be identified, directly or indirectly, by means *reasonably likely* to be used by the controller or by any other natural or legal person, in particular by reference to an identification number, location data, online identifiers or to one or more factors specific to the physical, physiological, genetic, mental, economic, cultural or social identity of that person" (emphasis added).[25]

In effect, this means that data are "personal data" when someone is able to link the information to a person, even if the person holding the data cannot make this link. The definition illustrates the high importance that European legislation asserts for data protection and privacy, as compared to the United States, where the government has largely refrained from such regulation, instead allowing companies and associations to regulate themselves, save for a small number of narrowly drawn regulations targeting specific industries.[26]

On 25 January 2012 the European Commission proposed a comprehensive reform of the 1995 data protection rules to strengthen online privacy rights and boost Europe's digital economy since technological progress and globalisation have profoundly changed the way our data is collected, accessed and used. In addition, the EU Member States implemented the 1995 rules differently, resulting in divergences in enforcement. The Commission argued that a single law will do away with fragmentation and administrative burdens, leading to savings for businesses of around € 2.3 billion a year and that the reform will help reinforce consumer confidence in online services, providing a much needed boost to growth, jobs and innovation in Europe.[27] The Commission sees this as reinforcing the view that data protection

---

[23] Parliament/Council Directive 95/46/EC *on the protection of individuals with regard to the processing of personal data and on the free movement of such data*, O.J. L 281/31 (1995).

[24] Data Protection Working Party 2007, p. 4.

[25] Commission Proposal for a Directive of the European Parliament and of the Council *on the protection of individuals with regard to the processing of personal data by competent authorities for the purposes of prevention, investigation, detection or prosecution of criminal offences or the execution of criminal penalties, and the free movement of such data,* COM(2012) 10 final.

[26] Fromholz 2000.

[27] European Commission, *Commission proposes a comprehensive reform of data protection rules to increase users' control of their data and to cut costs for businesses*, Press release IP12–46.

can be a European asset – not a barrier – when dealing with personal data in the context of the digital single market. The Boston Consulting Group estimates that the value created through personal data can reach € 1 trillion in Europe by 2020, or roughly 8 % of the combined GDP of the EU-27.[28] The proposed data protection reform would help the digital single market realise this potential, notably through three main innovations:

- One continent, one law: The regulation will establish a pan-European law for data protection.
- One-stop-shop: companies will only have to deal with one single supervisory authority.
- The same rules for all companies – regardless of their establishment: companies based outside of Europe will have to apply the same rules.

In March 2014 the European Parliament passed an amended version of the proposed regulation (report *Jan-Philipp Albrecht* and *Dimitrios Droutsas*) with strong support in the plenary.[29] However, from a research perspective the Welcome Trust and other scientific stakeholders have raised severe concerns with two of the amendments introduced by the European Parliament, namely on Art. 81 and 83. They argue that the changes introduced would prohibit or make practically impossible the use of personal data in research without specific consent. They uphold that the requirement for specific consent fails to take account of the fact that this research is already subject to ethical approval and strict confidentiality safeguards. The Trust and the large number of scientific organisations co-signing the position paper maintain that the amendments would put at risk significant European investments in genetics, cohort studies, biobanks, disease registries and the use of routinely collected data, and associated progress towards understanding society, health, and disease research.[30] In the meantime negotiations between the Council of Ministers and the European Parliament in the political trilogue have started with the aim to reach agreement till end 2015.

4 The Horizon 2020 Research Data Pilot: A Differentiated Approach

So, how can the potential tension between accessibility of research data and issues, such as IPR or data protection be squared? What is needed is a flexible framework, which takes the variability of data into account. A suitable example may be the European Commission's open access to research data pilot for the research it funds under the Horizon 2020 framework programme for research and innovation.

---

[28] Boston Consulting Group 2012.

[29] European Commission, *Progress on EU data protection reform now irreversible following European Parliament vote*, MEMO-14-186-EN.

[30] Welcome Trust et al. 2014.

The Regulation establishing Horizon 2020[31] states in recital 28 that "to increase the circulation and exploitation of knowledge, open access to scientific publications should be ensured. Furthermore, open access to research data resulting from publicly funded research under Horizon 2020 should be promoted, taking into account constraints pertaining to privacy, national security and intellectual property rights." As for the provisions regarding open access to publications, this was integrated as an obligatory clause in the grant agreement that beneficiaries have to sign with the Commission (Art. 29.2). In order to "promote" open access to data, as stipulated by the legislator, the European Commission set up a limited pilot scheme, which is anchored in the Horizon 2020 work programme.[32]

Horizon 2020 contains both large-scale calls for consortia of research organisations and industrial companies as well as actions supporting individual researchers, SMEs, public private partnership and many more. These varying so-called "beneficiaries" of Horizon 2020 in principle own the results of the research conducted and are free to exploit it. However, the Commission has repeatedly highlighted the importance of optimising the circulation, access to and transfer of scientific knowledge and stressed that *research and innovation benefit from scientists, research institutions, businesses and citizens accessing, sharing and using existing scientific knowledge and the possibility to express timely expectations or concerns on such activities.*[33] This recognises that all research builds on former work and depends on scientists' possibilities to access and share scientific information. Fuller and wider access to scientific publications and data can therefore help to accelerate innovation, foster collaboration and avoid duplication of effort by building on previous research results as well as making research more accessible for companies (in particular SMEs) and not-for-profit organisations. This is particularly valuable if exploitation is not undertaken by the primary beneficiary; added value can also be created through the re-use of data already generated. This has the potential to further enhance the research funded by the European taxpayer and to support Horizon 2020 in its contribution to economic growth and job creation.

The Commission considered it important that any pilot action on open research data would be designed in a way that is acceptable to the main stakeholders in the research ecosystem. Issues and challenges of access to research data were therefore extensively discussed with individual researchers, industry, research funders, libraries, publishers, infrastructure developers and others in the form of (i) a one day event where individual presentations and discussion could be heard and (ii) a written consultation period.[34] It quickly became apparent that any pilot scheme

[31] Parliament/Council Regulation (EU) No 1291/2013 *establishing Horizon 2020 – the Framework Programme for Research and Innovation (2014–2020)*, O.J. L 347/104 (2013).

[32] European Commission Decision C (2014)4995 of 22 July 2014, *Horizon 2020 Work Programme 2014–2015*, p. 19.

[33] European Commission, *Reinforced European Research Area Partnership for Excellence and Growth,* COM(2012) 392 final.

[34] European Commission, *Report of the European Commission Public consultation on open research data,* https://ec.europa.eu/digital-agenda/sites/digital-agenda/files/Report_2013-07-OpenResearchData-Consultation-FINAL1.pdf (accessed 12 November 2014).

would need to balance openness with IPR and commercialisation issues, privacy concerns, security as well as data management and preservation questions. Considerable efforts were therefore undertaken in 2013 in designing a pilot scheme that would be ambitious, pragmatic and flexible at the same time. The results led to a system which is very clear on (i) which thematic areas of Horizon 2020 are included in the pilot, (ii) what kind of data is expected to be made open access, and (iii) the implications for data management.

Horizon 2020 is grouped into three pillars: (i) excellent science, (ii) industrial leadership, and (iii) societal challenges as well as cross-cutting issues on widening participation in the framework programme, actions on science, with and for society, the European Institute of Technology (EIT) and Euratom. Within these pillars, the thematic areas that are covered by the pilot – that is those areas where EU-funded projects would by default be expected to participate – are listed in the bi-annual work programmes. For the 2014–2015 Work Programme these are:

- Excellent Science – Future and Emerging Technologies,
- Excellent Science – Research infrastructures – part e-Infrastructures,
- Leadership in enabling and industrial technologies – Information and Communication Technologies,
- Societal Challenge: Secure, Clean and Efficient Energy – part Smart cities and communities,
- Societal Challenge: Climate Action, Environment, Resource Efficiency and Raw materials – with the exception of raw materials topics,
- Societal Challenge: Europe in a changing world – inclusive, innovative and reflective Societies,
- Science with and for Society.

On the basis of this initial structuring, two additional factors were then taken on board: firstly it was recognised that there are also good reasons for *not* making data available in open access (see above), and projects were therefore given several options to "opt out" of the pilot, namely in cases which would create conflicts a) with the project's obligation to protect results (in case of commercialisation), b) conflicts with confidentiality obligations, c) conflicts with security obligations, or d) with rules on protection of personal data. Finally, projects can also opt out if achieving the action's main aim is jeopardised by making specific parts of the research data openly accessible. Secondly, due account was taken of the fact that project applicants might like to participate in the pilot even when their project is *not* part of the so-called "core areas" listed above. In that case they will be given an opt-in possibility on a voluntary project by project basis. The options to "opt-out" or to "opt-in" are implemented as part of the electronic proposal submission process, through an easily clickable form.

The second issue to be resolved concerned the kind of data that was to be made available. An initial scoping exercise showed the enormous amount and variety of objects which have been classified as "data" (see Sect. 2 above). It was therefore decided that the pilot action would primarily apply to data underlying scientific publications because (i) this data is presumed to be cleaned and structured since it has been used to create a publication, (ii) there is a need to increase the reproducibility of the results reported in scientific articles. Projects can of course go beyond this initial requirement and also publish curated data not connected to a publication, or raw data; but they are not obliged to do so. Projects participating in the pilot are obliged to outline which data they want to make open as part of a data management plan, which is a document outlining how the research data collected or generated will be handled during a research project, and after it is completed. It should be noted that both the decision on whether to participate in the pilot or not is not part of the evaluation for funding. In other words, proposals are not evaluated more favourably because they are part of the Pilot and will not be penalised for opting out of the Pilot. The Commission will carefully monitor the further uptake of the pilot and its implementation in all stages of Horizon 2020 projects with a view to further contribute to the development of European data policies.

5 Conclusion: A Further Challenge on the Horizon: Data in a Broader Scientific Context

This contribution has looked at several legislative issues concerned with "data" from a research perspective. However, it should not be forgotten that systemic changes are currently taking place in the way the science and research system functions. These changes include a shift towards a more open, collaborative and networked way of doing research, employing "big data" and using multi-actor input. This phenomenon, sometimes called "Open Science" or "Science 2.0" is enabled by digital technologies and driven by the globalisation and growth of the scientific community, as well as by the increasing need to address the Grand Challenges of our times. Open Science impacts the entire research cycle, from the inception of research to its publication, as well as the way this cycle is organised. This is why the European Commission is at the time of writing (autumn 2014) conducting a stakeholder consultation process on the issue, including an online public consultation followed up by multi-stakeholder workshops. In the online consultation 498 contributions as well as 28 voluntary position papers were received. While the preliminary results are currently being analysed it is already clear that there are links between the changing scientific system, promoting the international excellence of the EU's research and science, ensuring the effective use and dissemination of project results as well as the digital single market. Open science trends are therefore likely to give rise to further opportunities but also challenges to legislators and policy makers alike.

References

Boston Consulting Group (2012). *The Value of Our Digital Identity*. https://www.bcgperspectives.com/content/articles/digital_economy_consumer_insight_value_of_our_digital_identity/. Accessed 12 November 2014

Buchholtz, S., Bukowski, M., & Śniegocki, A. (2014). *Big and open data in Europe: A growth engine or a missed opportunity? Warsaw Institute of Economic Studies/Demos Europe*. http://www.bigopendata.eu/wp-content/uploads/2014/01/bod_europe_2020_full_report_singlepage.pdf. Accessed 14 November 2014

Cambridge Dictionaries Online (2014). *English definition of data*. http://dictionary.cambridge.org/dictionary/british/data. Accessed 14 November 2014

Data Protection Working Party (2007). *Opinion 4/2007 on the concept of personal data. 01248/07/EN. WP 136*. http://ec.europa.eu/justice/policies/privacy/docs/wpdocs/2007/wp136_en.pdf. Accessed 12 November 2014

Dragland, A. (2013). *Big Data – for better or worse. SINTEF News Room*. http://www.sintef.no/home/Press-Room/Research-News/Big-Data--for-better-or-worse/. Accessed 11 November 2014

European Commission High level Expert Group on Scientific Data (2010). Riding the wave. *How Europe can gain from the rising tide of scientific data. Final report. A submission to the European Commission*. http://cordis.europa.eu/fp7/ict/e-infrastructure/docs/hlg-sdi-report.pdf. Accessed 11 November 2014

European Commission (2014). *Report on the responses to the Public Consultation on the Review of the EU Copyright Rules. Directorate General Internal Market and Services Directorate D – Intellectual property*. http://ec.europa.eu/internal_market/consultations/2013/copyright-rules/docs/contributions/consultation-report_en.pdf. Accessed 12 November 2014

European Commission (2015). *Communication on A Digital Single Market Straegy for Europe*, COM(2015)192 final. http://ec.europa.eu/priorities/digital-single-market/docs/dsm-communication_en.pdf

European Parliament (2013). *Public and Commercial Models of Access in the Digital Era. Directorate-General for Internal Policies. Policy Department B. Structural and Cohesion Policies*. http://www.europarl.europa.eu/RegData/etudes/etudes/join/2013/495858/IPOL-CULT_ET%282013%29495858_EN.pdf. Accessed 12 November 2014

European Policy Centre (2010). *The Economic Impact of a European Digital Single Market. Copenhagen Economics. Final Report*. http://www.epc.eu/dsm/2/Study_by_Copenhagen.pdf

Filippov, S. (2014). *Data Driven Business Models. Powering Startups in the Digital Age. Digital Insights. European Digital Forum*. http://www.europeandigitalforum.eu/component/attachments/attachments.html?id=234

Forschungsunion Wirtschaft – Wissenschaft/acatech – Deutsche Akademie der Technikwissenschaften (2013). *Deutschlands Zukunft als Produktionsstandort sichern. Umsetzungsempfehlungen für das Zukunftsprojekt Industrie 4.0. Abschlussbericht des Arbeitskreises Industrie 4.0*. http://www.bmbf.de/pubRD/Umsetzungsempfehlungen_Industrie4 0.pdf

Fromholz, J. (2000). The European Union Data Privacy Directive. *Berkeley Technology Law Journal*, 15 (1), Article 23. http://scholarship.law.berkeley.edu/cgi/viewcontent.cgi?article=1281&context=btlj

Hudson, R.L. (w.d.). *Open Infrastructures for Open Science. Horizon 2020 consultation report*. http://cordis.europa.eu/fp7/ict/e-infrastructure/docs/open-infrastructure-for-open-science.pdf. Accessed 12 November 2014

Juncker, J. C. (2014). *New Start for Europe: My Agenda for Jobs, Growth, Fairness and Democratic Change. Political Guidelines for the next European Commission. Opening Statement in the European Parliament Plenary Session. Strasbourg, 15 July 2014.* http://ec.europa.eu/about/juncker-commission/docs/pg_en.pdf

Ligue des Bibliothèques Européennes de Recherche (LIBER), League of European Research Universities (LERU) (2014). *Letter on EPC Copyright Vision Paper 2014: Copyright enabled on the network.*. http://libereurope.eu/wp-content/uploads/2014/06/LIBER-EPC-letter.pdf. Accessed 11 November 2014

Office of Science and Technology Policy (OSTP) (2013). *Increasing Access to the Results of Federally Funded Scientific Research Memorandum for the Heads of Executive Departments and Agencies.*. http://www.whitehouse.gov/sites/default/files/microsites/ostp/ostp_public_access_memo_2013.pdf. Accessed 14 November 2014

Reimsbach-Kounatze, C. (2013). *Exploring data-driven innovation as a new source of growth. Mapping the Policy Issues Raised by "Big Data". OECD.* http://www.oecd.org/officialdocuments/publicdisplaydocumentpdf/?cote=DSTI/ICCP%282012%299/FINAL&docLanguage=En

Twitter (2014). *Twitter #DataGrants selections.* https://blog.twitter.com/2014/twitter-datagrants-selections. Accessed 13 November 2014

Welcome Trust et al. (2014). *Protecting health and scientific research in the Data Protection Regulation (2012/0011(COD)). Position of non-commercial research organisations and academics – July 2014.* http://www.wellcome.ac.uk/stellent/groups/corporatesite/@policy_communications/documents/web_document/WTP055584.pdf. Accessed 12 November 2014

Objectives and Methods of a Transnational Science of Administrative Law

Karl-Peter Sommermann

Looking through the publications of the past decades in the field of Public law, an increasing number of books and articles dealing with subjects and analytical questions that transcend the national legal sphere can be observed.[1] Often, it is obvious that the steadily expanding European law gave rise to such studies. However, the range of analysed issues reaches further: Legal studies and not least the science of public law begin to rise above the restrictions of national legal thinking. Among the scholars, who in this sense have broken ground for a more open understanding of legal research, *Albrecht Weber* has played a prominent role. It suffices to mention his project on the fundamental rights in Europe and North America and his book on European comparative constitutional law.[2] Scholars like *Rudolf von Ihering* who, at the end of the nineteenth century, called upon his colleagues to overcome the danger that legal science might sink into parochialism, would have very much welcomed this development.[3]

Starting from the findings that the legal discourse has increasingly gained a transnational character, the following reflections will focus on administrative law. They will discuss, first, the national origins of administrative law and early international exchange processes (Sect. 1 and 2), then turn to the progressive development of a European and international administrative law (Sect. 3) and finally discuss the

An essentially similar version in German language will be published in the book "Öffentliche Angelegenheiten – interdisziplinär betrachtet", edited by the author.

[1] Among the most visible publications are the comprehensive collective works *Ius Publicum Europaeum* (edited by Armin von Bogdandy and Peter M. Huber, so far five volumes, 2007 et seqq.) and *Handbuch der Grundrechte in Deutschland und Europa* (edited by Detlef Merten and Hans-Jürgen Papier, so far nine volumes, 2004 et seqq.). An overview of national administrative law systems with a focus on transversal topics of administrative law is offered, for instance, by Michel Fromont (2006), *Droit administratif des États européens*, Paris: puf. For constitutional law, see Constance Grewe and Hélène Ruiz Fabri (1995), *Droits constitutionnels européens*, Paris: puf. Comparative texts on particular topics are contained in Giandomenico Falcon (Ed.) (2005), *Il diritto amministrativo die paesi europei tra omogeneizzazione e diversità culturali*, Padova: CEDAM. For further references see footnotes 2 and 25–31.

[2] Albrecht Weber (Ed.) (2001 et seq.), *Fundamental Rights in Europe and North America, Part A*, The Hague: Kluver; Albrecht Weber (2010), *Europäische Verfassungsvergleichung*, Munich: Beck.

[3] von Ihering 1907, p. 14–15.

H.-J. Blanke et al. (eds.), *Common European Legal Thinking*,
DOI 10.1007/978-3-319-19300-7_30

objectives and methods of an emerging transnational legal science that accompanies this evolution (Sect. 4 and 5).

1 Administrative Law as an Autochthonous Law?

Administrative law is commonly said to belong to those fields of law, "in which the national character of a people or State is most pronounced".[4] While the diversification of government structures in Europe can be traced back far into the past, the private law systems remained interconnected by an overarching "common law" (*ius commune*) that was based on Roman law,[5] whose basic elements did not get completely lost when legislators attempted to reconstruct and concretise the general principles of law in a rational way[6] by national codifications[7]. In his book "Geschichte und Literatur der Staatswissenschaften" (History and writings of Political Sciences), published in the middle of the 19th century, *Robert von Mohl* analysed constitutional literature in Switzerland, the United States of America, England, Germany and, in particular, France. He described therein indirectly the different paths that political systems had followed since the middle ages, using models of the evolving political theory.[8] At the time the book was published, administrative law science was starting to become autonomous from the so-called "political law" (*Staatsrecht*).[9] However, this distinction could not yet be a topic of analysis, and even less so the evolution of national systems of administrative law in which, in the second half of the 19th century, the combination of nation-state thinking with legal positivism fostered the emphasis on the individuality of national law.

However, it would be misleading to assume that the national political and administrative systems existed isolated from each other in the 19th century. It goes without saying that the constitutionalist movement brought about a transnational discussion on fundamental concepts of State organisation, and that the flow of political and constitutional ideas between the States never dried up completely. *Mohl* and other authors of the first half of the 19th century used their reflections on for-

[4] Scheuner 1963, p. 714. See, from a comparative perspective, already: von Stein 1870, p. 13 (in the new edition by U. Schliesky from 2010, p. 11). According to Stein, the individual differences of the States reflect "the true, unexhaustable wealth of life in the world [...] which is nowhere greater than in the field of public administration and its law".

[5] See Eisenhardt 1995, p. 165 et seq. (para 243 et seq.).

[6] In Germany, the rationalistic approach was specifically directed against romantic legal thinking which considered law as an evolving expression of national culture and therefore uncodifiable. This line of reasoning was prominently represented by Friedrich Carl von Savigny, 1814.

[7] See here Cabrillac 2002, p. 68 et seq.

[8] Mohl 1855/56/58 (re-printed 1960); particularly intense comparative approach in Vol. 3, p. 3 et seq.

[9] For a short overview of the origins of administrative law in Europe since the 18th century cf. Sordi 2010, p. 23–36. For the development in Germany cf. Stolleis 1992, p. 229–265, in particular p. 258 et seqq.

eign political systems, in particular on the American system of government,[10] also as background for considerations on political reforms in their own countries.[11] And somewhat later, even bold concepts for a European and international administrative law emerged precisely in the period of national isolationism.[12] Overall, despite the strong divergences, it cannot be said that national administrative law evolved in an autochthonous way.

2 The Science of Administrative Law Between National Self-Reference and International Openness

In the course of the 19th century, the creation of an independent science of administrative law became manifest in works, that did not content themselves with a mere collection, compilation and ordering of relevant legal sources, but instead showed the endeavour to contribute to a systemic approach to administrative law by identifying and outlining the principles that underlie the administrative regulations in different policy fields. In Germany and Italy, where the coherence of the law was of special importance for the stabilisation of the national unity that was attained only late, but also in France where the development of an independent administrative law had started already in Napoleonic times, the leading textbooks reflected the new approach in their titles, such as the works "Grundsätze des Verwaltungsrechts" (Principles of Administrative Law) by *Friedrich Franz Mayer*[13], "Principii di diritto amministrativo" (Principles of Administrative Law) by *Vittorio Emanuele Orlando*[14] or "Les principes généraux du droit administratif" (General Principles of Administrative Law) by *Gaston Jèze*[15]. Although these titles do not make any reference to the particular national legal systems, the books dealt with the foundations of their own legal order. However, the study of the basic elements of administrative law suggested that valuable inspiration could come from neighbouring legal orders. *Otto Mayer*, who is deemed to be the founding father of modern German administrative law and who, during his professorship at the University of Strasbourg, had written a theory of French administrative law,[16] used French concepts for the systemisation and dogmatic comprehension of the German administrative law. However, he transformed the French concepts into specific German

[10] See especially Mohl 1824; Mohl 1836; Mohl 1844. In his article of 1836 he already discussed Alexis de Tocqueville's *De la démocratie en Amérique*, 1835.

[11] See Lerg 2011.

[12] Cf., in particular, von Stein 1882. For an analysis see Sommermann 2007a, p. 860 et seq. with further references.

[13] F.F. Mayer 1862. The main objective of the work was to connect "particularities to general aspects" and to infer the "supreme, guiding principles" (p. V).

[14] Orlando 1891. See as well Romano 1901.

[15] Jèze 1904. See also the preface of the second edition of 1914. p. VII: "J'ai l'ambition de dégager, des lois, règlements, pratiques administratives et arrêts des tribunaux, les principes juridiques qui dominent l'ensemble des institutions du Droit administratif français.".

[16] O. Mayer 1886.

notions. A well-known example is the adoption of the term "acte administrative" (administrative act), which in French law includes general regulations by the administration, while it was limited in Germany from the very beginning to decisions in individual cases.[17] *Otto Mayer* clearly shows the ambivalence between the concern to safeguard and further develop a specific national administrative law, on the one hand, and to maintain a productive transnational discourse, on the other hand. In France, a similar attitude can be observed in the late phase of the Third Republic. While the 19th century authors had still been aware of their leading role attained during the Napoleonic era and therefore had predominantly and nearly exclusively concentrated on the development of their own legal order, which they perceived as superior, a new perspective opened with the turn of the new century. The legal theory and doctrine in the neighbouring countries, in particular Germany, were brought under the focus of scientific debate again. This new academic orientation is represented by the eminent scholars of the so-called "theoretical era" of the Third Republic, notably *Léon Duguit*[18], *Maurice Hauriou*[19] and *Raymond Carré de Malberg*[20].[21] Despite their attention to German authors like *Friedrich Gerber*, *Otto von Gierke*, *Paul Laband*, *Rudolf von Gneist* and *Georg Jellinek*, their texts aimed at the delimitation of French and German conceptual foundations.

3 The Consolidation of a European and International Administrative Law

The interest in constitutional and administrative law of foreign countries continued until the 1920s, i. e. particularly in the period of nationalist thinking[22] Thereafter, it took half a century, before comparable fundamental discourses took place again in the transnational arena. Although comparative law was well established and in search of its methodological foundations,[23] a new field of transnational research only opened up with the progress of European integration.

[17] O. Mayer 1914, p. 61 et seq., 95 et seq.
[18] Duguit 1913; Duguit 1921–1925.
[19] Hauriou 1892; Hauriou 1923.
[20] Carré de Malberg 1920/22.
[21] For a discussion of German conceptions and doctrines by the cited authors cf. Sommermann 1997, p. 85–89.
[22] Cf. the years in which the aforementioned books were published. Heuschling 2008, p. 502 et seq., speaks of the "golden era" of public law theory in France.
[23] See the balance drawn 50 years ago on the state of comparative public law and its methods by Kaiser 1964, Strebel 1964, Bernhardt 1964 and Zemanek 1964.

3.1 Stock-Taking of European Administrative Law

The transnational dialogue was significantly stimulated by the increasing conditioning of the procedure of the administrative authorities through secondary EC law in the 1980s. In the 1990s, secondary law instruments increasingly comprised the steering of organisational arrangements in the Member States.[24] It had long become clear that an equally effective implementation of the substantive European law could only be attained if national administrations worked at a functionally comparable level. This was and is still not the case and therefore has prompted the European legislator again and again to intervene in the procedural and organisational arrangements of Member States.

In Germany, it was *Jürgen Schwarze* who first outlined the "European administrative law" as an independent area of law in his book "Europäisches Verwaltungsrecht im Werden" (European administrative law in progress), published in 1982. During his professorship at the European University Institute in Florence, he conceived his work on "European Administrative Law", which was published in 1988 in two volumes. Aimed at showing, "as a kind of handbook, the state of development currently reached in European administrative law", it was intended not only to highlight "the influences of national principles of administrative law on European Community law" but also to reveal "the repercussions of the newly elaborated European law on the national systems of administrative law".[25] The objective of the book was not to give a comprehensive presentation of the matter. After a basic chapter on European administration, its legal sources and on the role of comparative law, a second chapter is dedicated to an outline of the administrative law systems of the (then) 12 Member States of the Community, in form of country reports. Subsequently, the manual gives a deeper analysis of the relevant principles and subject areas.

Admittedly, the technique to create a basis for comparison through equally structured reports was not new. In the meantime, numerous country reports on central fields of public law have been published and they are generally combined with more or less comprehensive comparative analyses.[26] There is not yet a clear-cut

[24] Cf. Sommermann 2008a, p. 188–190.

[25] Schwarze, 1988, p. I; English version 1992, p.V. New edition of the German original released in 2005, with an introductory discussion of the new developments in European administrative law, 2005.

[26] Examples (beyond those in footnote 1) for corresponding comparative overviews in the field of administrative law: Carl Hermann Ule, Franz Becker and Klaus König (Eds.) (1967), *Verwaltungsverfahrensgesetze des Auslandes*, 2 Volumes, Berlin; Javier Barnes (Ed.) (1993a), *El procedimiento administrativo en el Derecho comparado*, Madrid; Hermann Hill and Rainer Pitschas (Eds.) (2004), *Europäisches Verwaltungsverfahrensrecht*, Berlin; Jean-Bernard Auby (Ed.) (2014), *Codification of Administrative Procedure*, Brussels. In the field of civil service: Siegfried Magiera and Heinrich Siedentopf (Eds.) (1994), *Das Recht des öffentlichen Dienstes in den Mitgliedstaaten der Europäischen Gemeinschaft*, Berlin; Christoph Demmke (2004), *European Civil Services between Tradition and Reform*, Maastricht. For procedural administrative law see: Javier Barnes (Ed.) (1993b), *La justicia administrativa en el Derecho comparado*, Madrid; Yann Aguila, Yves Kreins and Adam Warren (2007), *La justice administrative en Eu-*

answer to the question of what European administrative law exactly means, be it the sum of all European legal norms that determine the action of the EU organs and of the national public authorities when they implement the law of the Union, be it furthermore all common standards as well as the different phenomena of mutual influence.[27] In all of the larger Member States, works have been published that start from a broad understanding of European administrative law. Examples include the "Tratatto di diritto amministrativo europeo", edited by *Mario P. Chiti* und *Guido Greco*[28] and first published in 1997, and the "Droit administratif européen", edited by *Jean Bernard Auby* und *Jacqueline Dutheil de la Rochère*, published ten years later.[29] In turn, the book by *Paul Craig*, titled "EU Administrative Law" and published in 2006,[30] is essentially limited to an analysis of EU law and of the respective case law of the European Court of Justice. A last example constitutes the book "Europäisches Verwaltungsrecht", written by the public law professor and judge of the European Court of Justice *Thomas von Danwitz* and published in 2008.[31] It offers country analyses and a comparative approach that combines national and Union law.

It is difficult to maintain an overview of the huge number of publications that have been published on European administrative law in the meantime. Nevertheless, they allow reliable conclusions about the scope of common European standards. While previously emphasis was primarily put on the divergences,[32] today, rather than discrepancies, convergences are highlighted.[33] These result, on the one hand, from an ever more densely knitted network of Union provisions, for instance in the field of regulatory law,[34] and on the other hand, from a horizontal exchange of concepts of public management that have to be captured in the respective legal framework, an example being the public-private partnerships.[35] It can be seen that the concepts of modernisation that have been discussed internationally have had a

rope/Administrative justice in Europe, Paris. Country reports on various administrative law and constitutional law topics can be found, respectively, in the "Annuaire Européen d'Administration Publique" published by the Centre de Recherches Administratives of Law School of the University of Aix-en-Provence (Volume 36 (2013) was recently published) and in the "Annuaire International de Justice Constitutionnelle" of the Gropue d'Études et de Recherches sur la Justice Constitutionnelle of the same University (Vol. 29 (2013) published recently). Albrecht Weber has cooperated in this yearbook, see, for instance Weber 2003.

[27] On the terminological question see Sommermann 1991, p. 891; Sommermann 2008a, p. 182; Siegel 2012, p. 70 et seq. (para 68 et seq.).

[28] Chiti and Greco 2007.

[29] Auby and Dutheil de la Rochère 2007 and second edition 2014.

[30] Craig 2006.

[31] von Danwitz 2008.

[32] Cf. Scheuner 1963, p. 714; Kahn-Freund 1974, p. 17; Ipsen 1982, p. 123; critical of the thesis of convergence also Siedentopf and Speer 2002, p. 756.

[33] Cf. already Fromont 1992, p. 197; cf. also the articles in Marcou 1995; Sommermann 2002.

[34] See Britz 2006, p. 46 et seq., and the corresponding chapters in Fehling and Ruffert 2010; from a comparative approach, particularly on Germany and France, Masing and Marcou 2010.

[35] See Hodge et. al. 2010; on the European law dimension, see Mörth 2008; Ferraro 2010.

strong impact also in the legal sphere and take the role of a convergence accelerator.[36]

Not only for this reason, there is an interdisciplinary need for research. The convergences in administrative law did not automatically lead to an equally reliable and effective implementation of Union law in the Member States. The attention of legal scholars and practitioners therefore turns increasingly towards the substructures of the law, in particular to the different legal and administrative cultures.[37] Art. 41 EU-CFR represents an important starting point, which might become an "instrument of convergence".[38] This provision comprises, alongside "hard" legal rules and principles, also "soft" standards, which refer to ethics in Public Administration. In this line of reasoning, the European Ombudsman has concretised the right to good administration, as one can conclude from the European Code of good administrative behaviour.[39] However, a further analysis of the cultural dimension of public administration would need the application of methods provided by social sciences which could also lead to the creation of typologies.[40]

3.2 *The "Discovery" of International Administrative Law*

If European administrative law, as a field of research, is still in a phase of discovery, this is even truer for international administrative law, at least as far as the subject area and the methodology are concerned. The internationalisation of administrative law has been a growing concern of legal science since the turn of this century. Numerous multilateral treaties like the Convention on Nuclear Safety of 1994,[41] for instance, contain provisions referring to organisational or procedural arrangements of the national public administration. A treaty like the Aarhus-Convention of 1998,[42] which had been elaborated in the frame of the United Nations Economic Commission for Europe, impressively illustrates how EU law can be pre-shaped by international law too, so that the national legal systems are being steered simultaneously by international treaties and secondary Union law.[43] Hence, the analysis of the effects of international influence on European and national administrative law has become an essential task of legal research. On the occasion of becoming Professor emeritus, *Eberhard Schmidt-Aßmann*, in his lecture at the University of

[36] See Chevalier 2014, p. 58, 85 et seq. However, cf. also Kuhlmann and Wollmann 2013, p. 244 et seqq. who differentiate between "discursive convergence" and "practice convergence" and hint at the fact that the latter often remains far behind the former.

[37] Cf. Sommermann 2014a.

[38] Chevalier 2014, p. 311 et seq.

[39] European Ombudsman 2005.

[40] See König 2003. Approaches in this sense can be found in the contributions to König et al. 2014.

[41] Convention on Nuclear Safety of 20.9.1994, UNTS 1963, p. 293; ILM 33 (1994), p. 1518.

[42] Convention on Access to Information, Public Participation in Decision-making and Access to Justice in Environmental Matters of 25.6.1998, O.J. L 124/4 (2005); ILM 38 (1999), p. 517.

[43] Cf. Wiesinger 2013, in particular p. 134 et seq., 322 et seq.

Heidelberg in 2006, advocated the establishment of international administrative law as a new and promising field of research.[44] He proposes a definition of international administrative law that does not draw a parallel to international private law, which would mean to conceive it as law concerning conflicts of law,[45] but understands it as the sum of international norms that determine the administrative action of international bodies and national public authorities. This understanding of the term can nowadays be deemed as consolidated.[46]

3.3 Overcoming the Divide Between National, European and International Law

Already today, it is becoming evident that national, European and international administrative law cannot be divided in practice. The manifold interrelations between the different levels are too dense. This statement not only applies to concrete legal requirements that have been established by the higher level and have to be complied with by national authorities, but also to the interpretation of national administrative law in the light of EU law or international law and EU law in the light of international law.

The identification of common values constitutes an important factor for the merging of legal horizons of the Member States. European administrative law has developed on the basis of a Community law (later Union law), which, over the years, increasingly placed more emphasis on common values.[47] And for an even larger group of States, the ECHR and the case law of the ECtHR have contributed to preparing the ground for common-value-based legal reasoning.[48] As is well known, the Court has deduced from the Convention rights also guarantees for ad-

[44] Schmidt-Aßmann 2006, p. 317 et seq.

[45] It is in this sense that Engel 1992, p. 451 et seq., and Breining-Kaufmann 2006, p. 75–136, use the concept, following the tradition of Karl Neumeyer, 1910–1936. For Neumeyer, it is "the task of international administrative law [...] to draw the limits of public power in administrative issues against the jurisdiction of other communities, in the same way, as it is the task of international private law to establish the corresponding limits of private law" (Vol. 1, p. IV). For a recent analysis of the conflict-of-law rules regarding public law cf. Kment 2010, p. 202–265.

[46] In this sense already Tietje 2001, passim; cf. also Schmidt-Aßmann 2006, p. 335 et seq. (p. 336: "International administrative law means administrative law founded on international law"). Similarly, Cassese 2006, p. 38–67, when recognizing the emergence of a "global administrative law", puts the focus on networks with national and international actors. In French language one can differentiate between the "droit administratif international", which refers to the conflicts of law regime, i. e. the territorial scope of norms, and the "droit international administratif" which relates to the international law as a legal source. See Nguyen, 2006 p. 75, 80, 88 et seq.

[47] See nowadays Art. 2 TEU; on the evolution cf. Mangiameli, in Blanke and Mangiameli (2013), Article 2 para 1 et seq.; Sommermann 2014b, p. 287, 288 et seq., on the common basis of values in the European Union see also König 2008, p. 845; Chevalier 2014, p. 57 et seq.

[48] Cf. Nußberger 2012, p. 148 et seq.

ministrative procedures.[49] Regarding international administrative law, the common axiological basis does not play the same role yet. In this context, references to common values can be found, for instance, in the international human rights treaties and in international environmental law, especially in the legal instruments of the Rio process.[50]

4 Objectives of a Transnational Science of Administrative Law

It is an essential task of the science of administrative law today to make visible and to analyse the interrelations that exist between national, European and international law and result from an intensified international cooperation and increasing networking of the national administrations among each other, and to contribute to the conceptual development of the law. The discussion on generalisable concepts and methods has to be held in close exchange with researchers of other countries.[51] In this double sense, we can speak of a transnational science of administrative law.[52] Three objectives or tasks are of primary importance: First, the systematic attention to/concern for the trans- and international discourse about the concepts of administrative law; second, the analysis and conceptualisation of the interoperability of the different legal orders; and third, cooperation in the systemic development of European and international administrative law.

4.1 Opening the Discourse Space

An extensive administrative cooperation between Nation States in technical matters started quite early. Well known is the creation of so-called administrative unions in the 19th century, such as the International Telegraph Union, founded in 1865, and

[49] See Application No. 21151/04, Megadat.com *SRL v. Moldavia* (ECtHR of 8 April 2008) para 72: "The Court notes in this connection that where an issue in the general interest is at stake it is incumbent on the public authorities to act in good time, in an appropriate manner and with utmost consistency [. . .]."; in para 73 the Chamber criticises the absence of a hearing. See Application No. 33202/96, *Beyeler v. Italy* (ECtHR GC of 5 January 2000) para 120, and the later judgments in Application No. 22279/04, *Plechanow v. Poland* (ECtHR of 7 July2009) para 102, and Application No. 10373/05, *Moskal v. Poland* (ECtHR of 15 September 2009) para 51; para 72 of the latter reads: "in the context of property rights, particular importance must be attached to the principle of good governance. It is desirable that public authorities act with the utmost scrupulousness, in particular when dealing with matters of vital importance to individuals.".

[50] Cf., in particular, the Rio Declaration on Environment and Development of June 1992, A/CONF. 151/26/Rev. 1, Vol. 1, p. 3; ILM 31 (1992), p. 876.

[51] On these foundations of a methodological Europeanization and a transnational science of law cf. von Bogdandy 2011, p. 4, and Duve 2013, p. 7 et seq.

[52] For "transnational law" as an analytical framework see Calliess and Maurer 2014, p. 12. Different concepts of "transnational law" are discussed in Viellechner 2014, p. 58–75.

the World Postal Union, which was established in 1878.[53] Since then, the cooperation has been extended to policy fields that include promotional and protective obligations of the States in their internal sphere, for example in the field of social policy or environmental protection. In the European Union, acting in the framework of a dynamically evolving legal community or legal union is prevailing. However, not only Union law, but also international law can determine procedures and organisation of the national administrations. It goes without saying that a transnational science of law must not limit itself to the analysis of legal structures, but has to contribute, in transnational cooperation, to the shaping of fundamental concepts of an overarching administrative law. For the functioning of the Union, it is indispensable to find a common understanding on principles like the rule of law/Rechtsstaat[54] and its sub-principles such as legal certainty, protection of legitimate expectations and proportionality or – to give a topical example of a principle where the scope is debated – solidarity.[55] In this context, it is not enough to wait for the case law of the European Court of Justice to clarify specific aspects of those principles. The search for coherent conceptual foundations must be underpinned by a broad academic discourse. Although the key concepts that are laid down in the fundamental articles of the treaties seem to reflect a consensus, their concretisation in the individual case often remains strongly disputed, because of different cultural connotations and historical backgrounds.[56]

The further process of European integration depends in the legal as well as in the political sphere on sustainable common ideas regarding the fundamental concepts of the Union. Thanks to their terminological openness, the key principles, such as rule of law/Rechtsstaat, democracy and solidarity, can adopt the function of sluice mechanisms:[57] The inflowing concepts and ideas will gradually be lifted to a common conceptual level.

4.2 Achieving Intercommunicability and Interoperability of the Legal Systems

The law of the European Union provides for numerous obligations of cooperation between the national administrations.[58] Alongside this legally institutionalised cooperation, informal networks have long been created. These networks often precede a legal institutionalisation of cooperative procedures. This happened, for instance,

[53] For an analysis of the administrative unions see von Liszt 1902, p. 139 et seq., 227 et seq.; Tietje 2001, p. 124 et seq.

[54] For an analysis of the *Rechtsstaat* as a common European principle and its merger with the concept of the rule of law cf. Weber 2010, p. 144 et seq.; Sommermann 2007b.

[55] Cf. Sommermann 2014c.

[56] Cf. Nicolaidis and Kleinfeld 2012.

[57] The term "Schleusenbegriffe" (sluice-concepts) has been coined by Böckenförde 1969/91, p. 144 et seq. On the "sluice-function" of European principles see von Bogdandy 2009, p. 22.

[58] Cf. Schmidt-Aßmann 2004, p. 36 et seq., 383 et seq., 388 et seq., 404 et seq.

regarding the external relations of the German Federal Financial Supervisory Authority with the corresponding institutions of other European States.[59]

Duties to cooperate which are induced by Union law become manifest, for example, in the law of product authorisation. In terms of sensitive products, such as genetically modified food, all Member States participate in most procedures of authorisation by mediation of the European Commission or of a European agency, to the extent that no central authorisation procedure is provided for.[60] A further example of a matter where cooperation has been institutionalised is food safety. In this case, however, the creation of isomorphic administrative structures at national level and a corresponding establishment of authorities at Union level were finally triggered by the BSE crisis and the creation of the European Food Safety Authority.[61] In the field of services, it was the directive of 2006 which imposed substantial duties of cooperation[62] and which entailed in Germany the insertion of a special chapter on European administrative cooperation into the Law of administrative procedure.[63] Quite apart from linguistic difficulties in the transnational communication, the competences of the national authorities and their procedures need to be coordinated and adjusted.

Overall, it becomes ever more necessary to improve the interoperability of the administrative systems, and this necessity favours tendencies of convergence in the administrative systems. This observation can be combined with studies of political and administrative science which have long dealt with the reasons for the transformation of administrative systems.[64] The science of administrative law can contribute to finding solutions for a better coordination by looking at the legal and institutional preconditions for cooperation as well as at the legal modalities and strategies of the States, when they comply with their duties of implementation or with functional requirements.

---

[59] See Möllers 2005, p. 359. On international law aspects concerning transnational administrative activities cf. Kment 2010.

[60] For an analysis of the respective authorisation procedures cf. Sydow 2004, p. 168 et seq.; Siegel 2009, p. 232 et seq.

[61] Established by Regulation (EC) No 178/2002, O.J. L 31/1 (2002), which led to the creation of corresponding national authorities, thus ensuring a high degree of interoperability between the Member States and the EU. Among the early created national authorities are the *Agencia Española de Seguridad Alimentaria y Nutrición* in Spain (2001), the *Bundesamt für Verbraucherschutz und Lebensmittelsicherheit* in Germany (2002) and the *Autorità nazionale per la sicurezza alimentare* (soon renamed *Agenzia nazionale per la sicurezza alimentare*) in Italy.

[62] See Art. 28 of Pariament/Council Directive 2006/123/EC *on services in the internal market (Services Directive)*, O.J. L 376/36 (2006).

[63] See Part I Chap. 3 (§§ 8a–8e) of the Administrative Procedure Act, inserted by Law of 17.7.2009, BGBl. 2009 I, p. 2091.

[64] Cf. Kuhlmann and Wollmann 2013, p. 51 et seqq. (with further bibliographical references). For an examination of convergence factors regarding a specific principle of administrative law see Knill and Becker 2003, p. 447–481.

4.3 *System Building*

There is a close link between the value- and principle-orientation of the transnational approach[65] and the objective to identify system-building elements of European and international administrative law. Like in national law systems, these elements can be found by using inductive or deductive methods.[66] Every legal order can only attain coherence by the legal recognition of general guiding principles. In this process, system building will occur, as a rule, going down from a high level of abstraction to a middle level of abstraction. The consolidation of coherence in the legal order remains a permanent task. As far as international administrative law is concerned, the necessary unity has still to be attained and become visible.

5 Methods of a Transnational Science of Administrative Law

The methodology of an administrative law science which can be qualified as "transnational" necessarily has to include a comparative approach,[67] which in turn also extends to the methodological foundations of the jurisprudence of the compared countries,[68] in particular the principles of interpretation. On this basis, questions concerning the further development of legal methodology and the elaboration of common legal standards can be answered more precisely.

5.1 *Comparison as a Starting Point*

The comparative method initially follows the general rules of comparative law,[69] i. e. it aims at the identification of differences and similarities,[70] divergences and convergences,[71] universalisation and particularisation.[72] Generally, the search for functional equivalents prevails.[73] The extent of the contextualisation of the relevant

---

[65] See above Sect. 4.1.

[66] Cf. Sommermann 2014d, p. 871 et seq.

[67] Cf. also the title of the book "Comparative Law as Transnational Law", Miller and Zumbansen 2012.

[68] Cf. Ruffert 2007, p. 7 et seqq.

[69] Cf. Weber 2010, p. 10 et seq.; Sommermann 2004, p. 660 et seq.

[70] Cf. the distinction of the "method of agreement" and the "method of difference" developed by John Stuart Mill: Mill 1881, Book II Chap. 8.

[71] Cf., for instance, Bell 1992; Weber 2003.

[72] Cf. Miller and Zumbansem 2012, p. 7: "Comparative law's enduring problem is the question of whether comparison serves universalizing or particularizing ends; whether function's abstraction or context's embeddedness should preoccupy and guide the compartist." The contrasting classification made by the authors corresponds to the distinction between universalist and culturalist approaches which is used by other authors, cf. Sommermann 2013, p. 205 et seq.

[73] Zweigert and Kötz 1996, § 3 II (p. 33 et seq.); Weber 2010, p. 11; Sommermann 1999, p. 1923.

legal elements depends on the envisaged findings.[74] If, for instance, the comparison shall provide information about specific regulatory techniques, the contextualisation will rather be limited to a look into the legal context. If, however, questions concerning the dogmatic classification of types of administrative action are raised or if, to put an even more complex case, the role of an institution within the governmental structure is questioned, a far more extensive contextualisation will be needed. In the latter case, the comparative analysis will transcend the legal sphere and meet with approaches and findings of political and administrative science.

5.2 The Further Development of Legal Methodology

A further development of legal methodology by a transnational approach can first and foremost be expected in the field of methods of interpretation. Alongside the refinement of the recognised principle to interpret national law in conformity with Union law and international law,[75] it has to be considered if and to what extent the comparison can be used to make the interpretation of national law more rational. Higher knowledge of foreign administrative systems allows for more persuasive arguments when referring to regulations or interpretations of other countries in order to complete the legal reasoning. Even if legal comparison must not necessarily be recognised as a "fifth method of interpretation"[76], it can serve, at any rate, as an auxiliary instrument of interpretation.[77]

5.3 Approaches of Synthesis

Under the expression "approaches of synthesis", we understand the methodological instruments that serve the identification of common legal standards and the elaboration of new standards. The identification of existing standards in a community of States is generally effected by an evaluative legal comparison (*wertende Rechtsvergleichung*), which does not aim at the lowest common denominator, but inquires if a rule exists in a majority of Member States, if this rule does not contravene fundamental principles of one of the States where it is not yet recognised and if it fits well in the common legal framework.[78]

[74] Cf. Sommermann 2004, p. 665, 670 et seq.; Hirschl 2014, p. 231 et seq.
[75] On the interpretation of national law in conformity with Union law see Weiß 2014, p. 489 et seq., on the interpretation in accordance with international law, in particular international human rights cf. Sommermann 2008b, p. 28 et seq. and 31 et seq.; Knop 2013, p. 209 et seq.
[76] Häberle 1989, p. 916.
[77] Cf. Sommermann 1997, p. 409 et seq.; Sommermann 2004, p. 654 et seq.
[78] Cf. Grosche 2011, p. 287 et seqq.; see already Fuss 1964, p. 946 note 11; Zweigert 1964, p. 611; Bleckmann 1992, p. 29 et seq.

When developing new legal standards, several dimensions have to be considered. If the favoured solution already exists in one legal order, it has to be examined to what extent it can be decontextualised and therefore be transferred into other legal orders. Furthermore, the effects of the application of the new regulations in practice should be taken into account from the very beginning; that is why practitioners should be involved in the discussions or deliberations at an early stage.[79]

6 Conclusions

The precedent considerations lead to the following conclusions:

1. The transboundary exchange of concepts of constitutional and administrative law is not a new phenomenon. Already in the 19th century, the then emerging science of administrative law showed transnational characteristics.
2. What is new is the ever more densely woven legal integration of the national administrative law in the supranational and international legal regimes. This embeddedness entails the necessity to develop a systematic transnational science of administrative law, which takes into account in its analyses and dogmatic understanding of the law the interrelations between the different levels and the expanded possibilities and duties of the States to cooperate among each other.
3. In order to attain inter-culturally sustainable results, a close cooperation among the administrative lawyers of the different States is indispensable.
4. The convergence and merger of the legal horizons can form the basis for the development of a transnational administrative law and of conceptions for a better interoperability of the national systems of public administration as part of an overarching order.
5. The comparison is central for the methodology of the transnational science of law. The requirements of the comparison differ according to the goal of the study. The comparative approach is not limited to basic research, but rather an essential instrument for the further development of the juridical hermeneutics and for the rational development of new common legal standards.

References

Aguila, Y., Kreins, Y., & Warren, A. (2007). *La justice administrative en Europe/Administrative justice in Europe*. Paris: puf.

Auby, J.-B. (Ed.). (2014). *Codification of Administrative Procedure*. Brussels: Bruylant.

Auby, J.-B., & Dutheil de la Rochère, J. (Eds.). (2007). *Droit administratif européen*. Brussels: Bruylant.

Auby, J.B., & Dutheil de la Rochère, J. (Eds.). (2014). *Droit administratif européen* (2nd edn.). Brussels: Bruylant.

[79] Cf. Sommermann 2013, p. 208 et seq.

Barnes, J. (Ed.). (1993a). *El procedimiento administrativo en el Derecho comparado*. Madrid: Civitas.

Barnes, J. (Ed.). (1993b). *La justicia administrativa en el Derecho comparado*. Madrid: Civitas.

Bell, J. S. (1992). Convergences and divergences in European Administrative Law. *Rivista italiana di diritto pubblico comunitario, II*(1), 3–22.

Bernhardt, R. (1964). Eigenheiten und Ziele der Rechtsvergleichung im öffentlichen Recht. *ZaöRV, 24*(3), 431–452.

Blanke, H.-J., & Mangiameli, S. (Eds.). (2013). *The Treaty on European Union (TEU) – A Commentary*. Berlin, Heidelberg: Springer.

Bleckmann, A. (1992). Die wertende Rechtsvergleichung bei der Entwicklung europäischer Grundrechte. In J. F. Baur (Ed.), *Europarecht, Energierecht, Wirtschaftsrecht. Festschrift für Bodo Börner* (pp. 29–37). Cologne: Heymanns.

Böckenförde, E.-W. (1969). Entstehung und Wandel des Rechtsstaatsbegriffs. In H. Ehmke, C. Schmid, & H. Scharoun (Eds.), *Festschrift für Adolf Arndt* (pp. 53–76). Frankfurt a.M.: Europäische Verlagsanstalt. Contained also in E.-W. Böckenförde, Recht, Staat, Freiheit (143–169), Frankfurt a.M.: Suhrkamp, 1991.

von Bogdandy, A. (2011). Deutsche Rechtswissenschaft im europäischen Rechtsraum. *Juristenzeitung, 66*(1), 1–6.

von Bogdandy, A., & Huber, P. M. (2007). *Ius Publicum Europaeum*. 5 volumes so far. Heidelberg: C.F. Müller.

von Bogdandy, A., & Bast, J. (2009). *Europäisches Verfassungsrecht* (2nd edn.). Berlin, Heidelberg: Springer.

Breining-Kaufmann, C. (2006). Internationales Verwaltungsrecht. *Zeitschrift für Schweizerisches Recht, 125*(II), 75–136.

Britz, G. (2006). Vom Europäischen Verwaltungsverbund zum Regulierungsverbund. *Europarecht, 41*, 46–77.

Cabrillac, R. (2002). *Les codifications*. Paris: puf.

Calliess, G.-P., & Maurer, A. (2014). Transnationales Recht – eine Einleitung. In G.-P. Calliess (Ed.), *Transnationales Recht* (pp. 1–36). Tübingen: Mohr Siebeck.

Carré de Malberg, R. (1920). *Contribution à la théorie générale de l'État, spécialement d'après les données fournies par le droit constitutionnel français*. 2 volumes. Paris: Recueil Sirey.

Cassese, S. (2006). *Oltre lo Stato*. Roma-Bari: Editori Laterza.

Chevalier, E. (2014). *Bonne administration et Union européenne*. Brussels: Bruylant.

Chiti, M. P., & Greco, G. (Eds.). (2007). *Trattato di diritto amministrativo europeo* (2nd edn.). vol. 2 volumes. Milan: Giuffrè.

Craig, P. (2006). *EU Administrative Law*. Oxford: OUP.

von Danwitz, T. (2008). *Europäisches Verwaltungsrecht*. Berlin: Springer.

Demmke, C. (2004). *European Civil Services between Tradition and Reform*. Maastricht: EIPA Publications.

Duguit, L. (1913). *Les transformations du droit public*. Paris: Armand Colin.

Duguit, L. (1921–25). *Traité de droit constitutionnel*. 5 volumes. 2nd edn. Paris: Fontemoing.

Duve, T. (2013). Internationalisierung und Transnationalisierung der Rechtswissenschaft – aus deutscher Perspektive. *LOEWE Research Focus "Extrajudicial and judicial Conflict Resolution"*, Working Paper No. 6.

Eisenhardt, U. (1995). *Deutsche Rechtsgeschichte* (2nd edn.). Munich: C.H. Beck.

Engel, C. (1992). Die Einwirkungen des europäischen Gemeinschaftsrechts auf das deutsche Verwaltungsrecht. *Die Verwaltung*, *25*, 437–476.

European Ombudsman (2005). *The European Code of Good Administrative Behaviour*. Luxembourg: Office for Official Publications of the European Communities.

Falcon, G. (Ed.). *Il diritto amministrativo die paesi europei tra omogeneizzazione e diversità culturali*. Padova: CEDAM.

Fehling, M., & Ruffert, M. (Eds.). (2010). *Regulierungsrecht*. Tübingen: Mohr Siebeck.

Ferraro, V. (2010). *I partenariati pubblico – privati nella prospettiva del diritto europeo*. London: Esperia Publications.

Fromont, M. (1992). La justice administrative en Europe: convergences. In M. Long (Ed.), *Mélanges René Chapus* (pp. 197–208). Paris: Montchestien.

Fromont, M. (2006). *Droit administratif des États européens*. Paris: puf.

Fuss, E.-W. (1964). Rechtssatz und Einzelakt im Europäischen Gemeinschaftsrecht. *NJW*, *17*, 1600–1604, 327–331, 945–951

Grewe, C., & Ruiz Fabri, H. (1995). *Droits constitutionnels européens*. Paris: puf.

Grosche, N. (2011). *Rechtsfortbildung im Unionsrecht*. Tübingen: Mohr Siebeck.

Häberle, P. (1989). Grundrechtsgeltung und Grundrechtsinterpretation im Verfassungsstaat. *Juristenzeitung*, *44*, 913–919.

Hauriou, M. (1892). *Précis de droit administratif et de droit public*. Paris: L. Larose & Forcel.

Hauriou, M. (1923). *Précis de droit constitutionnel*. Paris: L. Larose & Forcel.

Heuschling, L. (2008). Wissenschaft vom Verfassungsrecht: Frankreich. In A.von Bogdandy, P. Cruz Villalón, & P. M. Huber (Eds.), *Handbuch Ius Publicum Europaeum* 2. Heidelberg: C.F. Müller.

Hill, H., & Pitschas, R. (Eds.). (2004). *Europäisches Verwaltungsverfahrensrecht*. Berlin: Duncker & Humblot.

Hirsch, R. (2014). *Comparative Matters – The Renaissance of Comparative Constitutional Law*. Oxford: OUP.

Hodge, G. A., Greve, C., & Boardman, A. E. (Eds.). (2010). *International Handbook on Public-Private Partnerships*. Cheltenham: Edward Elgar Publishing.

von Ihering, R. (1907). *Geist des römischen Rechts auf den verschiedenen Stufen seiner Entwicklung* (6th edn.). vol. Part I. Leipzig: Breitkopf & Härtel. 1st edn. 1854.

Ipsen, H.-P. (1982). Contribution to the discussion. In J. Schwarze (Ed.), *Europäisches Verwaltungsrecht im Werden* (p. 123). Baden-Baden: Nomos.

Jèze, G. (1904). *Les principes généraux du droit administrative*. Paris: Berger-Levrault.

Jèze, G. (1914). *Les principes généraux du droit administrative* (2nd edn.). Paris: Berger-Levrault.

Kahn-Freund, O. (1974). On Uses and Misuses of Comparative Law. *The Modern Law Review*, *37*(1), 1–27.

Kaiser, J. H. (1964). Vergleichung im Öffentlichen Recht. Einleitung. *ZaöRV*, *24*(3), 391–404.

Kment, M. (2010). *Grenzüberschreitendes Verwaltungshandeln*. Tübingen: Mohr Siebeck.

Knill, C., & Becker, F. (2003). Divergenz trotz Diffusion: Rechtsvergleichende Aspekte des Verhältnismäßigkeitsprinzips in Deutschland, Großbritannien und der Europäischen Union. *Die Verwaltung*, *36*, 447–481.

Knop, D. (2013). *Völker- und Europarechtsfreundlichkeit als Verfassungsgrundsätze*. Tübingen: Mohr Siebeck.

König, K. (2003). *On the Typology of Public Administration. Second Braibant Lecture*. Brussels: International Institute of Administrative Sciences.

König, K. (2008). *Moderne Öffentliche Verwaltung*. Berlin: Duncker & Humblot.

König, K., Kropp, S., Kuhlmann, S., Reichard, C., Sommermann, K.-P., & Ziekow, J. (Eds.). (2014). *Grundmuster der Verwaltungskultur*. Baden-Baden: Nomos.

Kuhlmann, S., & Wollmann, H. (2013). *Verwaltung und Verwaltungsreformen in Europa*. Wiesbaden: Springer.

Lerg, C. A. (2011). *Amerika als Argument. Die deutsche Amerika-Forschung im Vormärz und ihre politische Deutung in der Revolution von 1848/49*. Bielefeld: transcript Verlag.

von Liszt, F. (1902). *Das Völkerrecht* (2nd edn.). Berlin: Haering.

Magiera, S., & Siedentopf, H. (Eds.). (1994). *Das Recht des öffentlichen Dienstes in den Mitgliedstaaten der Europäischen Gemeinschaft*. Berlin: Duncker & Humblot.

Marcou, G. (Ed.). (1995). *Les mutations du droit de l'administration en Europe – pluralisme et convergence*. Paris: l'Harmattan.

Masing, J. & Marcou, G. (Eds.). *Unabhängige Regulierungsbehörden*. Tübingen: Mohr Siebeck.

Mayer, F. F. (1862). *Grundsätze des Verwaltungs-Rechts mit besonderer Rücksicht auf gemeinsames deutsches Recht, sowie auf neuere Gesetzgebung und bemerkenswerte Entscheidungen der Obersten Behörden zunächst der Königreiche Preußen, Baiern und Württemberg*. Tübingen: Laupp.

Mayer, O. (1886). *Theorie des französischen Verwaltungsrechts*. Strassburg: Karl J. Trübner.

Mayer, O. (1914). *Deutsches Verwaltungsrecht*, vol. 1 (2nd. edn.). München/Leipzig: Duncker & Humblot.

Merten, D., & Papier, H. J. (Eds.). (2004). *Handbuch der Grundrechte in Deutschland und Europa* vol. 7 volumes so far. Heidelberg: C.F. Müller.

Mill, J. S. (1881). *A System of Logic* (8th edn.). New York: Harper & Brothers.

Miller, R. A., & Zumbansen, P. C. (Eds.). (2012). *Comparative Law as Transnational Law*. Oxford: OUP.

Möllers, C. (2005). Transnationale Behördenkooperation – Verfassungs- und völkerrechtliche Probleme transnationaler administrativer Standardsetzung. *ZaöRV*, *65*, 351–389.

Mörth, U. (2008). *European Public-private Collaboration: A Choice between Efficiency and Democratic Accountability?* Cheltenham: Edward Elgar Publishing.

Mohl, R. (1824). *Das Bundes-Staatsrecht der Vereinigten Staaten von Nordamerika*. Stuttgart: Cotta.

Mohl, R. (1836). Amerikanisches Staatsrecht. *Kritische Zeitschrift für Rechtswissenschaft und Gesetzgebung des Auslandes*, *8*, 359–386.

Mohl, R. (1844). Entwickelung der Demokratie in Nordamerika und in der Schweiz. *Kritische Zeitschrift für Rechtswissenschaft und Gesetzgebung des Auslandes*, *16*, 275–310.

Mohl, R. (1855–56–58). *Die Geschichte und Literatur der Staatswissenschaften*. 3 volumes, Erlangen: Ferdinand Enke (Reprint Graz: Akademische Druck- und Verlagsanstalt, 1960).

Neumeyer, K. (1910, 1922, 1926/30, 1936). *Internationales Verwaltungsrecht*, 4 volumes, München: Verlag für Recht und Gesellschaft.

Nguyen, M. S. (2006). Droit administratif international. *Zeitschrift für Schweizerisches Recht (ZSR)*, *125*(II), 75–136.

Nicolaidis, K., & Kleinfeld, R. (2012). *Rethinking Europe's "Rule of Law" and Enlargement Agenda: The Fundamental Dilemma*. SIGMA Paper, vol. No. 49. Paris: OECD.

Nußberger, A. (2012). Europäische Menschenrechtskonvention. In J. Isensee, & P. Kirchhof (Eds.), *Handbuch des Staatsrechts der Bundesrepublik Deutschland* 3rd edn. (vol. X, pp. 135–171). Heidelberg: C.F. Müller.

Orlando, V. E. (1891). *Principii di diritto amministrativo*. Florence: Barbèra.

Romano, S. (1901). *Principii di diritto amministrativo italiano*. Milan: Società editrice libraria.

Ruffert, M. (2007). The Transformation of Administrative Law as a Transnational Methodological Project. In M. Ruffert (Ed.), *The Transformation of Administrative Law in Europe/La mutation du droit administrative en Europe* (pp. 3–52). Munich: Sellier.

von Savigny, F.C. (1814). *Vom Beruf unserer Zeit für Gesetzgebung und Rechtswissenschaft*. Heidelberg: Mohr und Zimmer.

Scheuner, U. (1963). Der Einfluss des französischen Verwaltungsrechts auf die deutsche Rechtsentwicklung. *DÖV*, *16*(19–20), 714–719.

Schmidt-Aßmann, E. (2004). *Das Allgemeine Verwaltungsrecht als Ordnungsidee* (2nd edn.). Berlin et al.: Springer.

Schmidt-Aßmann, E. (2006). Die Herausforderung der Verwaltungsrechtswissenschaft durch die Internationalisierung der Verwaltungsbeziehungen. *Der Staat*, *45*, 317–348.

Schwarze, J. (Ed.). (1982). *Europäisches Verwaltungsrecht im Werden*. Baden-Baden: Nomos.

Schwarze, J. (1988). *Europäisches Verwaltungsrecht. 2 volumes*. Baden-Baden: Nomos.

Schwarze, J. (1992). *European Administrative Law*. London: Sweet and Maxwell.

Schwarze, J. (2005). *Europäisches Verwaltungsrecht. 2 volumes* (2nd edn.). Baden-Baden: Nomos.

Siedentopf, H., & Speer, B. (2002). Europäischer Verwaltungsraum oder Europäische Verwaltungsgemeinschaft? – Gemeinschaftsrechtliche und funktionelle Anforderungen an die öffentlichen Verwaltungen in den EU-Mitgliedstaaten. *DÖV*, *28*, 753–763.

Siegel, T. (2009). *Entscheidungsfindung im Verwaltungsverbund*. Tübingen: Mohr Siebeck.

Siegel, T. (2012). *Europäisierung des Öffentlichen Rechts*. Tübingen: Mohr Siebeck.

Sommermann, K.-P. (1991). Europäisches Verwaltungsrecht oder Europäisierung des Verwaltungsrechts? *DVBl.*, *111*(16), 889–898.

Sommermann, K.-P. (1997). *Staatsziele und Staatszielbestimmungen*. Tübingen: Mohr Siebeck.

Sommermann, K.-P. (1999). Die Bedeutung der Rechtsvergleichung für die Fortentwicklung des Staats- und Verwaltungsrechts in Europa. *DÖV*, *52*(24), 1017–1029.

Sommermann, K.-P. (2002). Konvergenzen im Verwaltungsverfahrens- und Verwaltungsprozessrecht europäischer Staaten. *DÖV*, *55*(4), 133–143.

Sommermann, K.-P. (2004). Funktionen und Methoden der Grundrechtsvergleichung. In D. Merten, & H.-J. Papier (Eds.), *Handbuch der Grundrechte* (vol. 1, pp. 631–678). Heidelberg: C.F. Müller.

Sommermann, K.-P. (2007a). Europäisches Verwaltungsrecht als „die großartigste Rechtsbildung der Weltgeschichte"? – Die Vision von Lorenz von Stein aus heutiger Perspektive. *DÖV*, *60*(20), 859–867.

Sommermann, K.-P. (2007b). Entwicklungsperspektiven des Rechtsstaates: Europäisierung und Internationalisierung eines staatsrechtlichen Leitbegriffs. In S. Magiera, & K.-P. Sommermann (Eds.), *Freiheit, Rechtsstaat und Sozialstaat in Europa* (pp. 75–90). Berlin: Duncker & Humblot.

Sommermann, K.-P. (2008a). Veränderungen des nationalen Verwaltungsrechtes unter europäischem Einfluss. In J. Schwarze (Ed.), *Bestand und Perspektiven des Europäischen Verwaltungsrechts* (pp. 181–199). Baden-Baden: Nomos.

Sommermann, K.-P. (2008b). Offene Staatlichkeit: Deutschland. In A.von Bogdandy, P. Cruz Villalón, & P. M. Huber (Eds.), *Handbuch Ius Publicum Europaeum* (vol. II, pp. 3–35). Heidelberg: C.F. Müller.

Sommermann, K.-P. (2013). Erkenntnisinteressen der Rechtsvergleichung im Verwaltungsrecht. In A. Gamper, & B. Verschraegen (Eds.), *Rechtsvergleichung als juristische Auslegungsmethode* (pp. 195–210). Vienna: Jan Sramek Verlag.

Sommermann, K.-P. (2014a). Towards a Common European Administrative Culture?. In K. König, S. Kropp, C. Reichard, K.-P. Sommermann, & J. Ziekow (Eds.), *Grundmuster der Verwaltungskultur* (pp. 605–630). Baden-Baden: Nomos.

Sommermann, K.-P. (2014b). Die gemeinsamen Werte der Union und der Mitgliedstaaten. In M. Niedobitek (Ed.), *Europarecht – Grundlagen der Union* (pp. 287–320). Berlin/Boston: De Gruyter.

Sommermann, K.-P. (2014c). Some Reflections on the Concept of Solidarity and its Transformation into a Legal Principle. *Archiv des Völkerrechts*, *52*, 10–24.

Sommermann, K.-P. (2014d). Prinzipien des Verwaltungsrechts. In A.von Bogdandy, S. Cassese, & P. M. Huber (Eds.), *Handbuch Ius Publicum Europaeum* (vol. V, pp. 863–892). Heidelberg: C.F. Müller.

Sordi, B. (2010). Rechtsstaat and the Rule of law: Historical reflections on the emergence of administrative law in Europe. In S. Rose-Ackerman, & P. L. Lindseth (Eds.), *Comparative Administrative Law* (pp. 23–36). Cheltenham, UK: Edward Elgar.

von Stein, L. (1870). *Handbuch der Verwaltungslehre und des Verwaltungsrechts*. Stuttgart: Cotta. newly edited by U. Schliesky, Tübingen: Mohr, 2010

von Stein, L. (1882). Einige Bemerkungen über das internationale Verwaltungsrecht. *Jahrbuch für Gesetzgebung Verwaltung und Volkswirthschaft*, *6*, 396–442.

Stolleis, M. (1992). *Geschichte des öffentlichen Rechts in Deutschland* vol. 2. Munich: C.H. Beck.

Strebel, H. (1964). Vergleichung und vergleichende Methode im öffentlichen Recht. *ZaöRV*, *24*(3), 405–430.

Sydow, G. (2004). *Verwaltungskooperation in der Europäischen Union*. Tübingen: Mohr Siebeck.

Tietje, C. (2001). *Internationalisiertes Verwaltungshandeln*. Berlin: Duncker & Humblot.

Ule, C., Becker, F., & König, K. (Eds.). (1967). *Verwaltungsverfahrensgesetze des Auslandes. 2 volumes*. Berlin: Duncker & Humblot.

Viellechner, L. (2014). Was heißt Transnationalität im Recht?. In G.-P. Calliess (Ed.), *Transnationales Recht* (pp. 57–76). Tübingen: Mohr Siebeck.

Weber, A. (Ed.). (2001). *Fundamental Rights in Europe and North America (Leaflet)*. The Hague: Kluwer.

Weber, A. (2003). Notes sur la justice constitutionnelle comparée: convergences et divergences. *Annuaire international de justice constitutionnelle*, *19*, 29–41.

Weber, A. (2010). *Europäische Verfassungsvergleichung*. Munich: Beck.

Weiß, W. (2014). Unionsrecht und nationales Recht. In M. Niedobitek (Ed.), *Europarecht – Grundlagen der Union* (pp. 393–501). Berlin/Boston: De Gruyter.

Wiesinger, N. (2013). *Innovation im Verwaltungsrecht durch Internationalisierung*. Tübingen: Mohr Siebeck.

Zemanek, K. (1964). Was kann die Vergleichung staatlichen öffentlichen Rechts für das Recht der internationalen Organisationen leisten? *ZaöRV*, *24*(3), 453–471.

Zweigert, K. (1964). Der Einfluss des europäischen Gemeinschaftsrechts auf die Rechtsordnungen der Mitgliedstaaten. *Rabels Zeitschrift*, *28*, 601–643.

Zweigert, K., & Kötz, H. (1996). *Einführung in die Rechtsvergleichung* (3rd edn.). Tübingen: Mohr Siebeck.

New Frontiers of Administrative Law: A Functional and Multi-Disciplinary Approach

Private Life of Administration - Public Life of Private Actors

Javier Barnes

> (People) seldom realise at the time how deeply dynamic changes are cutting. Old pictures of a political and legal scene remain current long after it has been drastically altered.[1]

One important issue that today's *common European legal thinking* must deal with regards the dualism present in contemporary legal systems: the distinction between public and private law. For an administrative lawyer this is a critical question, because administrative law was conceived as "règles dérogatoires au droit commun". From the original perspective, administrative law lies beyond private law. Public and private law were located on two sides of a well-delineated border. The application of private law by the administration has been seen, not without reason, in a negative light, as an avoidance of administrative law and the guarantees it affords. In any case, the traditional approach has been a zero-sum game: the science of administrative law remained well beyond the rule of private law.

With the passage of time, however, this perspective has been broadened with new outlooks, whilst keeping in mind that the relationship between the two branches of law is quite complex and not one of mere opposition, in cadence with the ever-changing dividing line between what is public and what is private. The impact of the European Union has contributed in many ways to this constant state of flux and interaction between the spheres of public and private responsibility. In short, today we recognise a complementary function between the two branches of law. Indeed, public and private law constantly interact and find new ways of combining, exchanging tools and adapting solutions. That is the reason why the science of administrative law can concern itself with private law matters, when the actions of the Administration are subject to private law. Administrative law, therefore, is the legal branch that encompasses the application of the executive powers of the administration, as well as those actions of the administration subject to private law.

This article takes a step even farther, and proposes that administrative law not only concerns the actions of the administration subject to private law (the "private life" of the administration), but also when the actions of private agents can be classified as "administrative" (the "public life" of private actors). This chapter

[1] Frankfurter 1941, p. 585, cited by Taggart 1997, p. 2.

H.-J. Blanke et al. (eds.), *Common European Legal Thinking*,
DOI 10.1007/978-3-319-19300-7_31

specifically focuses on those areas that are dominated by non-governmental entities (the "public life" of private actors).

Employment law, for instance, is one well-known and consolidated area where the influence of public law values can be seen. Indeed, it is a branch of the law strongly infused with public law values, but it is just an example from an extensive field of examples. This chapter, however, will confine itself to only *new* areas of interaction between private and public law, and, in these areas, mainly to the (analogous and flexible) application of "administrative life principles" to *services of general interest* and *regulatory activities* carried out by non-state actors under private law. It is the nature of the activity being exercised, not the actor that matters here – a *functional approach*, as it is also the "public life" of the activity itself – where there is no exercise of public power involved – that defines it.

In other words, this article will focus on those private bodies, without position of formal executive power, that are being and must be increasingly subjected to higher levels of responsibilities, in that they affect members of the public to a significant degree; private bodies which in addition work closely with administration, that is, in a collaborative and networked environment.

When I refer to private bodies or to non-state actors in this chapter, I mean certain, specific non-governmental entities, such as professional associations with self-regulatory regimes, standard-setting bodies, credit rating agencies, unions, or companies in regulated sectors that provide services of general interest.

1 Rethinking the Boundaries of Administrative Law: Old and New Questions

1.1 Preliminary Remarks About the Scope and Meaning of "Administrative" Action. The Eternal Question Concerning its Conceptual Frontiers

I shall start with two critical questions:

Firstly, what makes the executive power and the administration *unique* in comparison to the legislature and to the judiciary? This is a very well-known and longstanding problem; one that is, in fact, impossible to solve, given that an administrative action might be judicial or legislative in nature. However, this classical problem at least assumes that these administrative actions, be they difficult to define, are carried out by an administration or by a governmental agency. In short, administrative law is centred in, and applicable by, an actor: a public administration (exercising power). This is a *subject-centred* administrative law.

Secondly, what makes an action "*administrative*" or not, regardless of the actor? The classification of activities as "administrative" by virtue of their character is very difficult, if they are not previously so defined by legal provisions or by case law. This question assumes a functional approach: administrative law can be applicable when a certain kind of activity is performed (i. e. public procurement regulations), whether by public or private entities and whether domestically or extraterritorially. This is a *function-centred* administrative law.

Two problems, one common denominator: what is "administrative action"? If the definition of *administration* based on the principle of division of power has been problematic from the very beginning of the administrative law (a), an emergent issue even more complex regards the *boundaries* of this branch of the law, that is, if it can be at times applicable to private actors as well, and if so, under what conditions (b).

Can this conceptual change cause a new crisis? "The literature of the last ten years contains numerous references to two opposite trends: on one hand, 'the end of administrative law', on the other, the 'new administrative law'."[2]

In any case, from our point-of-view, we can appreciate two tendencies, or challenges, for the traditional perspective, both clearly evident in the European Union. The first, the proliferation of private entities that without true executive powers nonetheless carry out functions that can be considered socially relevant, and therefore, "administrative"; the other, an increase of powerful administrations whose actions reach far beyond the enforcement of preceding statutes enacted by parliaments.

a) In effect, on the one hand, at present there is a flourishing interest in administrative law around the world. In an age in which many formerly state-provided services are being contracted out, administrative law is increasingly expanding its ambit beyond its historical limits.
   The profound changes brought about by globalisation or privatisation coincide with an upsurge in theoretical interest and research in administrative law, and, curiously, more so in common law countries since the 1980s.[3] And also just as curiously, when an expanding administration downsizes to a contracting one, the growth of administrative law paradoxically becomes greater.[4] At the same time that many regard the deregulation and the contracting out of formerly state-provided services or regulatory functions as a threat to the very core of public law values, others believe that the new, parallel mission of administrative law should be to inoculate private law with public law values rather than to replace existing private law with rival legal norms.[5] In fact, the response of many administrative lawyers to these reforms is "to distil the essence of administrative law for trans-

[2] Cassese 2012, p. 603.

[3] See Taggart 1997, p. 2. From a civil law view, one might say that common law countries have been very familiar with extensions of common law doctrines (principle of "business affected with a public interest", and "prime necessity") to newly developing public utilities, that is, companies providing the public with gas, water, transportation, telephone, telecommunications, and the like at reasonable prices and without discrimination. "Early on in America a coherent body of law developed under this rubric of public utilities" (Taggart 1997, p. 7).

[4] Taggart 1997, p. 3, and note 10. It might be no coincidence that the self-conscious identification of public law values dates back to the early 1980s in Britain and was a response to deregulation, privatisation and the underlying theoretical attacks on the "public-regarding" starting point of administrative law.

[5] Harlow 2009, p. 75–97; McLean 2009, p. 23; Freeman 2003.

porting to the newly 'deregulated' and 'privatized' areas".[6] Furthermore, new collaborative ways of global governance contribute to promote this growth, as the newly designated "global administrative law" shows.[7]

b) At the same time, powerful, networked administrations (super-agencies) are emerging in areas such as markets regulation, environmental protection, energy, public health, food safety, public security, and aviation safety, among others. Albeit that administrative law was mainly born as an implementation tool, these administrations now play leading roles, in that they establish substantive primary legislation by themselves and implement it. In addition to this, the domain of public administration has grown in general over the past century, threatening the primacy of legislatures as the policy-making organ of government.
   It is this first trend that interests us here. Nevertheless, we will explore first the context of change and transformation that exists in contemporary administrative law (Sect. 1.2 to 1.4).

1.2 The "Porousness" and Openness of Old Premises. The Emergence of New Spaces

a) To begin with, *private institutions* increasingly apply administrative law principles not only at the domestic or the European level, but also in the global arena. An example of the former are the private companies working in water, energy, transport, and postal services,[8] or many private companies owned by governments,[9] in that they are subject to public procurement law when acting as contracting entities or authorities.[10] The latter is exemplified by the Internet Corporation for Assigned Names and Numbers (ICANN) bylaws,[11] which in themselves are a sort of administrative procedure act.[12]
   At the same time, *public bodies* making non-mandatory decisions are more and more expected to act as if they were enacting formal regulations. For instance, in many legal systems the administration has to observe procedural rules to enact

[6] Taggart 1997, p. 3.
[7] See Casini 2014.
[8] For instance, these firms are treated in Europe as contracting entities. Public contracts which are awarded by the contracting authorities operating in the water, energy, transport and postal services sectors are covered by Parliament/Council Directive 2004/17/EC *coordinating the procurement procedures of entities operating in the water, energy, transport and postal services sectors*, O.J. L 134/1 (2004). The current list of contracting authorities and entities can be found in the Annexes to Commission Decision 2008/963/EC, O.J. L 349/1 (2008).
A general view at http://ec.europa.eu/internal_market/publicprocurement/index_en.htm
[9] See Art. 1.9 of Parliament/Council Directive 2004/18/EC *on the coordination of procedures for the award of public works contracts, public supply contracts and public service contracts*, O.J. L 134/114 (2004).
[10] See note 1 and 2.
[11] See Art. I–IV (http://www.icann.org/en/about/governance/bylaws/bylaws-08apr05-en.htm).
[12] Cassese 2012, p. 607.

voluntary codes of practice, such as recommended best practices for fisheries management.[13] A central bank attending the *Basel Committee* on Banking Supervision (BCBS)[14] should apply some procedural mechanisms, such as notice and comment procedures and common understanding, before making recommendations.

As we will see, all these different activities historically have in common that they, at least in part, did not have to comply with traditional administrative law requirements.

b) Indeed, traditional administrative law systems were constructed according to three main premises: the first, administrative law is inherently national, that is to say, a state-centred "product"; the second, it is a law designed for the executive branch and its administration, when they discharge administrative authority; and finally, administrative law has a definite executive and subordinate character: the administration puts into action what ordinary statutes have previously established.

Nevertheless, in recent decades, administrative lawyers have begun to rethink these traditional frontiers. Administrative law is no longer strictly a *national* law, no longer exclusively a law for exercising executive *power*, and is no longer a law that merely *implements* primary and preordained legislation. Globalisation, privatisation, and the rising era of "super-agencies" are well-known phenomena that speak for themselves. These are three trends in clear opposition to the classical definition of administrative law.[15]

The porousness of these premises opens new fields of interest to this evolving administrative law. We are not talking about a *quantitative* expansion of the scope of administrative law. Rather, we propose a *qualitative* redefinition of this scope, and, given that the pillars of administrative law are in a process of transformation, rethinking its boundaries is required.

[13] US APA, Japanese APA, EU Soft-Law.

[14] Article I, 3 Basel Committee on Banking Supervision (BCBS) Charter: "The BCBS does not possess any formal supranational authority. Its decisions do not have legal force."

[15] To give a few cases to illustrate:

– Administrative law now extends beyond the scope of the state: for example, the meetings of various central banks at the Basil Committee of Banking Supervision, or the indirect application by national administrations of regulations enacted by the WTO or the EU.

– Administrative law no longer just rationalises the exercise of power by the state and authorities, it also concerns itself with: (i) the private actions of the administration (i. e. the management of urban transport by a municipal enterprise); (ii) actions carried out by private parties (regulated sectors, such as energy, for example); (iii) the making of soft law (such as best practice guidelines).

– Administrative law not only controls solely the administration's implementation of regulations; it has to deal, as well, with the various aspects of an increasingly more powerful administrative authority: town and regional planning, environmental policies, food safety, financial markets regulation, etc.

1.3 A Brief Exploration of the New "Lives" of Interest to Contemporary Administrative Law

New fields of interest could be described as follows:

1.3.1 *The Private Life of Administration:* When Administration Performs Activities Required by its Public Life that are Regulated *under Private Law*

To give an example, according to the European law, government-owned private-law companies are considered a "contracting authority" in regards to public procurement law. Therefore, they are required to award private contracts in accordance to the principles of equality, publicity and free competition enshrined in administrative law. Another example: if public services are carried out by private-law companies owned by an administration, they must allow other companies to compete unhindered in the marketplace. These government-owned private companies are subject to state aid laws and, consequently, they cannot enjoy an unlimited guarantee from the state, such as immunity from private law procedures in cases of insolvency and bankruptcy.[16] In both cases – notwithstanding administrative acts that fall under private law – these companies are not exempt from administrative law: in the former example, they must observe principles of public procurement; in the latter, they must comply with state aid rules.

Questions here are not limited to answering what administrative actions may be performed by a private law regime (whether or not they are permissible), but also under which conditions they should be carried out, and by which means.

1.3.2 *The Public Life of Private Actors:* When Private Actors are Involved in Services of General Interest (Energy, Transport, Telecommunication etc.) or Participate in a Regulatory Process (Standard-Setting Process, Assessments, Monitoring and the Like).

In the recently "deregulated" and "privatised" areas, the state and the administration have by no means disappeared. If we take a look at financial market regulation, public health, energy, transport, food safety, product and management standards, environmental issues, and economic services, among others, it is not difficult to discern the labyrinth in which the multitude of public and private actors interact in each area, both inside and beyond national boundaries. The European Union repeatedly illustrates this phenomenon, which is appropriately described by metaphors of network, cascade or composite organisation and composite procedure.

[16] Case C-559/12 P, *France v. Commission* (ECJ 3 April 2014).

For our purposes, the general outcome is that no private actor involved in these areas acts in isolation. On the contrary, private organisations have become integral parts of a joint plan, and as pieces of this complex plan, the private actors must meet some of the similar requirements as the public agents.

Which principles or criteria should rule the public-interest activities of these private actors? In this case we refer to the denominated "regulated sectors" such as telecommunications, energy or the post, whose services are guaranteed, but not directly provided, by the state.

Moreover, when private actors are involved in a regulatory cascade: how should professional associations proceed to establish codes of conduct when they act under self-regulatory regimes? How should companies assessing and certifying private or public activities proceed in such cases? Which principles should govern the ICANN and ISO decision-making procedures or the assessments of credit rating agencies?

Again, one issue here is to analyse which public values or administrative principles should be applied in a situation that is governed by private law, and with what tools.

1.3.3 *The Public Life of the Administration Beyond Command and Control Regulations*: The Administration's Non-Mandatory Decisions and Other Administrative Actions that are Not Properly Decisions

Soft law created by the administration and other activities carried out by the administration, like information gathering, are much more numerous and important than before. In these instances, what procedural principles should the administration follow in order to establish soft law mechanisms, such as guidelines or recommendations? And what procedural guidelines should be observed when the administration negotiates, is involved in consensus-building, reports on the state of public health or of the economy, or assesses the environment? In the case of soft law, neither binding nor enforceable means are used; in the latter instances, substantial activities are realised, but no decisions made.

Traditional administrative procedure acts regulate mandatory decisions made by the administration. New procedural mechanisms are being developed to deal with these non-binding "products", and also with those administrative activities, such as information gathering and sharing, when no formal decision is made.

1.3.4 *The Iinternational and Global Life of the Administration*: The Administration's Actions in "Outer Space", i. e. Beyond the Confines of the State

For example, taking into account that a central bank is not answerable to the electorate, how should a central bank make decisions in the regional or global arena, such as in the realm of the Basel Committee? Whom does that central bank represent, and to whom is it accountable? Which decision-making process ought to be followed by the central bank acting beyond the state? Important dilemmas and legitimacy questions concerning the administrative process are arising in this area. As *S. Cassese* states, new developments, such as a growth of a global space, "require administrative law scholarship to be denationalized".[17]

1.3.5 The *Influential Life and Political Leadership of the Administration*: The Administration's Actions in a Steering Role, Beyond the Mere Implementation of a Prior Primary Legislation

Taking into account that the administration does not only implement a well-defined public policy, and that it must also define and develop relevant political goals, means and tools in significant domains by itself (Sect. 1.1), what principles should be complied with by European food safety or drug agencies, for example, so that their actions are effective, accountable, verifiable and motivated?

One problem here is that the binary classification "legislation (by parliament) – implementation (by the administration)" can no longer claim to be representative of the whole regulatory process.

Most of the historical administrative law tools designed to steer and to control a well-defined administration through detailed ordinary statutes have become ambiguous or even obsolete. For instance, in these scenarios, judicial review may not be a simple decision made by a single national agency, but one made by various administrations working together. In such a case, composite procedures from administrations of different jurisdictions must be structured to allow accountability and review. Administrative procedure plays here a leading political role. A reconsideration of the parliament's leading role in the process is required as well.

1.3.6 Interaction between Public and Private Law

These "lives" are not separate in the real life. To give an example, globalisation and privatisation may work together. "In the global polity, hybrid and private bodies are as numerous as public bodies."[18]

Public-private divide, state and beyond the state lines, or legislation and implementation division, are in many ways blurred. The panorama has become more complex, and as a result, there are new territories and perspectives emerging for administrative law. Accordingly, it is becoming clear that traditional "administrative law" is itself an overly constraining rubric and that we need to construct an expanded framework. As *S. Cassese* states, the crisis of administrative law refers most precisely to the adjective, not the noun: the so-called "administrative" law, more than just the law of the administration, is the genuine law of society.[19]

---

[17] Cassese 2012, p. 603.
[18] Cassese 2012, p. 607.
[19] Cassese 2014, p. 397.

1.4 The Exercise of Administrative Power by Administrations as a Central and Traditional Criterion of Administrative Law

The "exercise of administrative power" has been, from the very beginning, the central concept of administrative law. Consequently, delegation and attribution of powers to the administration, on the one hand, and accountability and judicial review of administrative action, on the other, remain since the outset core principles underpinning the limits and scope of the administrative law field. Accordingly, administrative law is a branch of the law that comes into play when two basic requirements are met: subject (an administration in action), and action (a vested power). In short, administrative law is born linked to an administration "in uniform", in the exercise of authority.

Such limiting criteria were soon undermined: administrative law also became applicable to other actors outside the administration itself (a), as well as to other activities different from the exercise of authority (b).

a) This subjective conception (the exercise of power *by* the administration) was expanded in two main ways. Firstly, administrative law also applies to private actors exercising administrative authority. When private actors exercise governmental power (*ejercicio privado de funciones públicas* in Spain or in France, *Beleihung* in Germany, etc.), they are required to comply with rules of administrative law, even though they are not a public administration. Thus, for example, the Council of Europe Convention on Access to Official Documents of 18 June 2009 establishes that "public authorities" are also "natural or legal persons insofar as they exercise administrative authority".[20] The rationale here is still consistent: it refers to the exercise of administrative authority.
Secondly, administrative law is applicable to other public powers which do not form part of the administration in many jurisdictions, such as the parliament, the judiciary, the ombudsman, or the European Court of Auditors, but do exercise administrative authority in the case of personnel selection and management or of public contracting, among other issues. This is also the case of the administrative functions of public powers regarding their employees and assets.
This double-fold expansion to actors other than public administrations requires the relaxation of a subjective criterion in favour of an objective one. Namely, that the exercise of administrative authority entails the use of administrative law, regardless of whether the subject exercising such power is a public administration or not. *As long as administrative authority is exercised, administrative law necessarily comes into play.*
b) An administration does not exercise authority when it is subject to private law (e. g. to provide a service through a corporation or foundation). The traditional approach when this occurs seems to be a zero-sum game: either the administration exercises administrative powers and therefore acts under administrative law,

[20] Article 1, 2) a, in French: *les personnes physiques ou morales, dans la mesure où elles exercent une autorité administrative.*

or it does not – and therefore acts under private law. For this reason, in continental Europe, since the early twentieth century, the phenomenon of the application of private law by or to an administration had been considered something negative ("an escape from administrative law", "*huida al Derecho Privado*", "*Flucht ins Privatrecht*") because when dressed as a "civilian", leaving behind the "uniform", the administration was considered to have tacitly dissociated itself from the controls and guarantees of administrative law.

c) Increasingly, however, this view is changing. Administrative law does not disappear when the administration is subject to private law. Moreover, the administrative law system has entered into the realm of private law in different ways in order "to fill the accountability vacuum left by the retreating state":[21]
Many administrative law authors hold that, even when the administration is subject to private law, it still has to observe certain criteria of public law. For example, a public-capital corporation, created to provide the public service of urban transportation or electric power, must respect fundamental rights, equality and antidiscrimination principles, and the principle of proportionality.[22]
Lawmakers have started to create more direct routes of application. Sometimes statutes dictate that an administration wearing "civilian clothes" should still be governed by certain principles of administrative law. This is the case, for example, of the requirement to comply with the principles of public procurement law of public-capital corporations when acting as a contracting authority. Increasingly, the "private life" of administration,[23] and the "public life of private actor" as well, are regulated by statues that oblige the application of public norms. Public law values are being gradually included into legislation and administrative schemes.
Case law extends these public law values into the newly "deregulated" and "privatised" environment. There are, of course, other strategies and approaches;[24] however, this article is focused on the need to infuse public law values to interactions with private law.

For examples of the above-mentioned ideas see Table 1.

---

[21] This expression comes from Taggart 1997, p. 2.

[22] For example, the German doctrine on "Verwaltungsprivatrecht". It applies when an administration carries out important activities related to public service (gas, oil, water etc.) by means of private law, such as through a company.

[23] For example, the Italian Administrative Procedure Act ("Legge sul procedimento amministrativo") establishes: "1-bis. La pubblica amministrazione, nell'adozione di atti di natura non autoritativa, agisce secondo le norme di diritto privato salvo che la legge disponga diversamente.".

[24] See Hoffmann-Riem and Schmidt-Aßmann 1996.

Table 1 Illustration of New Open Space for Administrative Law

Traditional Adm. Law	Present (in Addition)	New Frontiers	Examples
Law within state boundaries (Inherently national law)	Law beyond the state	Permeability of the border between the state and "outer space" Supranational administrative space (e. g. the European Union and the global arena)	Presently, there is an international life of the administration in active development: – Financial markets – Public procurement – International trade/Lex Mercatoria – Internet (ICANN) – ISO/GLOBALG.A.P. – Lex Sportiva – Environmental Law – Aviation or Food safety
"Command and control" law (exercise of public authority on a "hard law" basis)	Law that applies, beyond administrative powers, to both administrations and certain private actors (regardless of whether or not they actually wield power).	Permeability of the border between the state and society: from public-private divide to public-private co-responsibility and collaboration. Public actors, subject to private law, are required to comply with certain public principles, values and rules (contracting authority, transparency and accountability). Similarly, the public actor is subject to public law even when not exercising authority (soft law recommendations). Private actors are recognised to have relevant regulatory functions (self- or co-regulation) and, consequently, they are required to comply with certain public values, principles and rules.	Today, there is an actively evolving private life of public administrations (governed by private law but also influenced by administrative law): A clear example is when the administration acts as a "civilian" – removing its public "uniform" (as is the case of an enterprise that provides public transport services or airport management). There is a growing public life of private actors. Two examples: – When a private organisation is involved in the regulatory process (ISO, GLOBALG.A.P., professional associations, etc.). – When a private, regulated sector company provides services of general interest and is therefore required to comply with the principles of public procurement, etc. Currently, an ever-increasing public life of administrations beyond command and control regulations (under administrative law) exists: – When an administration acts in a non-coercive way or carries out activities that do not require decision-making (Soft Law).
Branch of the Law for implementation and application of the substantive rules made by parliament	Substantive primary legislation to be made by "super-agencies"	From a binary regulatory scheme (legislation-implementation) towards a circular regulatory cycle (agenda and priority setting-draft-rules and regulations-implementation-monitoring-review) and greater leeway given to agencies	Urban planning, environmental issues, financial markets regulation etc Regulatory impact assessments

2 Private Life of Administration and Public Life of Private Actors

2.1 *Principles of Public Life*

Some of the public law norms that we are interested in are openness and transparency, honesty and fairness, objectivity and impartiality, participation and representativeness, rationality and the duty to give reasons, equality or antidiscrimination principles, accountability and review, and so on. Of course, these values are not the only ones underlying the legal system.

We understand "principles of public law" to be those principles that must be accomplished by administrations and private bodies not exercising executive authority, mainly in services of general interest and in regulatory activities subject to private law.

2.2 *"The Public Life of Private Actors" (Services of General Interest and Regulatory Activities)*

For the purposes of this chapter, we are mostly interested in those private actors that do not exercise administrative authority, but do participate in *regulatory activities* (a) or in *services* of *general interest* (b). This is what we refer to as the "public life of private actors". In our view, the key point in those situations is that *administrative authority is not exercised* by the involved private entities. In spite of this, new pathways may be opened to administrative law.

On the one hand, private actors working in regulated sectors (such as telecommunications, water, energy, post and the like) are subject not only to common private law, but also to some principles, rules, and guarantees of administrative law (i. e. public procurement in water, energy, transport and postal services sectors must to be followed by private companies in some cases).[25] *Public service activities* are a concern of administrative law whether they are carried out by the administration or by non-governmental actors.

On the other, non-governmental actors collaborate in a variety of ways in all stages of the regulatory process, from standard-setting to implementation and enforcement[26] (i. e. voluntary standards, certification, labelling systems etc.). A regulatory space occupied by a variety of public and private actors, each with different resources, contrasts with the traditional state-centred concept of regulation,

[25] Parliament/Council Directive 2004/17/EC *coordinating the procurement procedures of entities operating in the water, energy, transport and postal services sectors*, O.J. L 134/1 (2004). In Spain, in application of this Directive, a statute was enacted by Ley 31/2007 of 30 October 2007, sobre procedimientos de contratación en los sectores del agua, la energía, los transportes y los servicios postales.

[26] Freeman 2000a, p. 816.

in which the public agency has formal top-down control over standard-setting, implementation, and enforcement. Indeed, private actors participating in a regulatory cascade (standardisation, evaluation, certification, monitoring, and so forth) are, or should be, subject to public values and guarantees of administrative law as well. For example, the Italian Administrative Procedure Act (*Legge sul procedimento amministrativo*) establishes that private actors must apply administrative principles when they participate in some regulatory activities:

> Art. 1-ter: "I soggetti privati preposti all'esercizio di attività amministrative assicurano il rispetto dei criteri e dei princìpi di cui al comma 1, con un livello di garanzia non inferiore a quello cui sono tenute le pubbliche amministrazioni in forza delle disposizioni di cui alla presente legge."

These principles must be observed by private actors in the same way administrations do:

> Art. 1.1: "L'attività amministrativa [...] è retta da criteri di economicità, di efficacia, di imparzialità, di pubblicità e di trasparenza secondo le modalità previste dalla presente legge e dalle altre disposizioni che disciplinano singoli procedimenti, nonché dai princìpi dell'ordinamento comunitario."

In a broad sense, if a regulatory function can be described as an enactment of requirements, restrictions or conditions, or setting standards or giving guidance, in relation to any activity,[27] and these functions can be carried out not only by public regulators, but also by non-governmental actors, one can conclude that the principles of good regulation must be applied to all of them (proportionality, accountability, consistency, transparency or targeting, for instance).

Similar cases also happen in the global arena. The ICANN Bylaws[28] are a good example. They provide the "core values" concerning the performance of its

[27] See UK Legislative and Regulatory Reform Act, Part 2.
[28] http://www.icann.org/en/about/governance/bylaws#I

mission,[29] as well as the principles such as non-discriminatory treatment,[30] transparency,[31] accountability, review,[32] and the like. In another example, the European Regulation on Credit Rating Agencies[33] establishes various principles that must be observed by the affected private agencies: transparency, independency, expertise, and rules on conflict of interest, and so forth.[34] In short, regulatory activities are

[29] Article I, Sect. 2:.

"In performing its mission, the following core values should guide the decisions and actions of ICANN:.

1. Preserving and enhancing the operational stability, reliability, security, and global interoperability of the Internet.
2. Respecting the creativity, innovation, and flow of information made possible by the Internet by limiting ICANN's activities to those matters within ICANN's mission requiring or significantly benefiting from global coordination.
3. To the extent feasible and appropriate, delegating coordination functions to or recognising the policy role of other responsible entities that reflect the interests of affected parties.
4. Seeking and supporting broad, informed participation reflecting the functional, geographic, and cultural diversity of the Internet at all levels of policy development and decision-making.
5. Where feasible and appropriate, depending on market mechanisms to promote and sustain a competitive environment.
6. Introducing and promoting competition in the registration of domain names where practicable and beneficial in the public interest.
7. Employing open and transparent policy development mechanisms that (i) promote well-informed decisions based on expert advice, and (ii) ensure that those entities most affected can assist in the policy development process.
8. Making decisions by applying documented policies neutrally and objectively, with integrity and fairness.
9. Acting with a speed that is responsive to the needs of the Internet while, as part of the decision-making process, obtaining informed input from those entities most affected.
10. Remaining accountable to the Internet community through mechanisms that enhance ICANN's effectiveness.
11. While remaining rooted in the private sector, recognising that governments and public authorities are responsible for public policy and duly taking into account governments 'or public authorities' recommendations.

These core values are deliberately expressed in very general terms, so that they may provide useful and relevant guidance in the broadest possible range of circumstances. Because they are not narrowly prescriptive, the specific way in which they apply, individually and collectively, to each new situation will necessarily depend on many factors that cannot be fully anticipated or enumerated; and because they are statements of principle rather than practice, situations will inevitably arise in which perfect fidelity to all eleven core values simultaneously is not possible. Any ICANN body making a recommendation or decision shall exercise its judgment to determine which core values are most relevant and how they apply to the specific circumstances of the case at hand, and to determine, if necessary, an appropriate and defensible balance among competing values."

[30] Article II, Sect. 3:.

"ICANN shall not apply its standards, policies, procedures, or practices inequitably or single out any particular party for disparate treatment unless justified by substantial and reasonable cause, such as the promotion of effective competition.".

[31] Article III.

[32] Article IV.

[33] Parliament/Council Regulation (EU) No 462/2013 *amending Regulation (EC) No 1060/2009 on credit rating agencies*, O.J. L 146/1 (2013).

[34] See Sect. 6–12.

also of importance to administrative law, whether they are performed by administrations or by private actors, inside or beyond the state.

2.3 Why Are Public Values Expanding Into Private Law?

Sometimes the transfer of public values to private law is simply due to a lawmaker's decision based on heterogeneous reasons, as in the above-mentioned examples (European public procurement law, Italian law on administrative procedure, etc.). In other cases, the incorporation of administrative law values or principles is achieved through soft law (codes of practice, guidelines, recommendations, etc.), or through self-regulation. This is the case of ISO, ICANN and of many other private organisations. Practical reasons may also come into play, or coincide. In any event administrative law is the most experienced branch of the law regarding not only the control and legitimacy of power, but also the provision of *services* of *general interest* or the realisation of regulatory activities.

Generally speaking, administrations are part of a richer institutional environment of public and private activity.[35] "Contemporary regulation might be best described as a regime of 'mixed administration' in which private actors and government share regulatory roles."[36] In this regard, there are many "regulatory regimes" and "*services* of *general interest* regimes" dominated by a high degree of interdependence between agencies and non-agency actors. Consistency between public and private actors when both participate in the same regulatory process is a strong argument in favour of the interaction between private law and public law. Working as a team, they all are ensured to follow equivalent rules or principles. For example, a private certifying body (in environmental, water, or reporting activities), when preparing an evaluation, becomes part of the regulatory activity; its contribution is relevant so that the whole process works. Therefore, private entities should meet requirements coming from the culture of administrative law, such as technical competence, expertise, impartiality, openness, or fairness, for example.

The main point here is that private bodies providing services of general interest, participating in regulatory activities, or both, affect the members of the general public to a significant degree. These private activities do not exercise public power, at least in a formal sense. However, if we take a look at the effects or at the results of these activities for the entire society, we might agree that the anti-discrimination principle must be applied when private bodies provide services of general interest, or transparency and expertise principles when they set the standards a product must

[35] Freeman 2000a, p. 816.

[36] Aronson 1997, p. 52, discussing roles of public and private actors in what he calls "mixed" administrations. Freeman 2000b, p. 551 (fn. 15) states: "Private individuals, private firms, financial institutions, public interest organisations, domestic and international standard-setting bodies, professional associations, labor unions, business networks, advisory boards, expert panels, self-regulating organisations, and non-profit groups all help to perform many of the regulatory functions that, at least in legal theory, we assume agencies perform alone."

meet to be imported. Requirements of due process are imposed and arbitrary and unreasonable conduct is not permitted.[37]

3 From a Traditional "Subject-Centred" Administrative Law Towards a Functional and Multi-Disciplinary Approach

3.1 Beyond the Exercise of Governmental Authority. New Frontiers for Administrative Law: Regulatory and Services of General Interest Performed by Private Actors Without Executive Power

As said above, administrative law is the branch of law that governs the *exercise of formal authority* by public actors (mainly administrations, and to a lesser degree other public powers) and, exceptionally, by private actors. State actors must comply with many constitutional and administrative requirements and constraints, including, but not limited to, procedural norms. Private actors, in contrast, remain relatively unregulated by procedural norms.[38] This is the traditional view in both constitutional and administrative law.

However, we are interested in new perspectives for contemporary administrative law, in which private actors perform "administrative" activities.

It is a matter of fact that private actors today perform a huge variety of regulatory tasks and provide *services* of *general interest*. In our view, administrative law science is not allowed to ignore them. This means that the exercise of public power is no longer administrative law's only field of interest – new frontiers are opening for study and research. They consist, in our understanding, of "administrative" actions performed by private actors (Table 2).

In short, it is indispensable that these activities not remain unregulated by public law values. State-society responsibility, sharing and cooperation are now augmented by a partnership and symbiotic role between public and private law. Statutes around the world demonstrate that governance is now considered a common enterprise to be undertaken by public and private actors. The oft-mentioned "privatisation" is often only superficial or incomplete; in most cases, the state remains in the background.

---

[37] See *Forbes v. New South Wales Trotting Club Ltd* (1978–9) 143 CLR 242, cited by Taggart 1997, p. 11.

[38] Freeman 2000a, p. 843.

Table 2 Interaction Between Administrative Law and Private Law: Public Action Subject to Private Law and Private Action Subject to Administrative Law

Administrative Authority	Administration	Private actor	Kind and format of administrative law to be applied
Exercise of administrative authority	Exercise of administrative authority by Administration (derived from statutory provisions) i. e. regulations, adjudications, mandatory self-regulation for standards and co-regulation in implementation, etc.	Exercise of administrative authority by private actor (delegated by legislation) i. e. urban planning, car inspections, etc.	Traditional administrative law is applied both to administration and private actors i. e. throughout administrative procedure acts
	Exercise of administrative authority by administration under private law (derived from private contractual provisions) i. e. a company owned by administration establishes contractual provisions, when contracting with a third party, by which the company enjoys administrative authority in performing the contract: orders, unilateral interpretation etc.		Principles or values of administrative law in collaboration with private law i. e. the company's duty to provide reasoning, proportionality principle, control and review, compensation etc.
Non-mandatory regulatory activities	Regulatory activities by administration without administrative authority i. e. soft law mechanisms	Regulatory activities by private actors without administrative authority (co-regulation, self-regulation etc.) i. e. standardisation, certification, evaluation, monitoring	Adapted and evolved administrative principles and values, depending on the activity, the task and the actor i. e. transparency, public scrutiny, openness, notice and comment procedures, expertise, impartiality, fairness, representation, etc.
Public service activities/ services of general interest	Public services are managed by administration itself (service provided by public sector) i. e. company owned by administration performing public service – urban transportation		Private law and administrative law principles i. e. equality principles, public procurement principles (publication and competition), public selection and recruitment of personnel, etc.
	Public services are contracted out to private providers i. e. contracted urban transportation services		Traditional administrative law i. e. public procurement legislation
		Regulated sectors i. e. telecommunications, water, electricity etc.	Private law and administrative law principles i. e. public procurement principles

3.2 *A Functional Approach: Administrative Law as a Law of Regulatory and Public Service Activities (or Services of General Interest), be the Actors Public or Private*

3.2.1 Beyond the Public/Private Divide

At times, administrative law acquires a functional dimension. It is not just the law of a public or private subject when exercising administrative authority. Subjective criteria can explain the existence of traditional administrative law, but cannot sustain the above-mentioned new lives or spaces, namely the "private life of administration", and the "public life of private actors".

Regulatory responsibilities, on the one hand, and *services* of *general interest*, on the other, are shared in many ways by public and private entities. These activities are *administrative functions* in a broader sense. That is, they are "administrative" tasks, not because they are carried out by an administration, but because they are in some way *administrative in nature*, according to statutes or case law, regardless of whether they are performed by a governmental authority or by private actors. For this reason, one can find case law or legal provisions[39] that have imposed procedural requirements on private actors, based on the fact that they are behaving as public actors.[40] The point here is that we must avoid labelling an activity as essentially public or private. The public-private line is constantly changing: in many areas the public-private divide, responsibilities or roles are elastic. Therefore, this distinction may be a formally, historically and conceptually dubious classification. Rather, statutes should clarify, first and foremost, what must be currently considered an "administrative" function with due regard to all the circumstances involved in benefit of the entire society.

3.2.2 Which Values and Principles are to be Transposed to the Newly Privatised Areas? When and How?

Currently, as already noted, the most important shared "administrative" activities by public and private actors seem to be *services* of *general interest* and regulatory activities.

For this reason, the first challenge for contemporary administrative law is to establish *when* to extend legal requirements to private organisations performing these two "administrative" functions. The second is to analyse *which* requirements are to be extended in each case. The third is *how*, namely, which *mode or format* to use in order to concretise these legal requirements into private law.

In regard to *when*, the lawmaker has the "first word". There are many examples (already mentioned), on the imposition of new legal requirements on private actors –

[39] See the above-mentioned examples, especially the Italian administrative procedure act.
[40] Freeman 2000a, p. 841.

some of them even upheld by case law. The role of administrative law scholars is crucial in this area in order to identify into which regulatory and public service scenarios to extend public law values.

As to *which* criteria are to be extended, these could be classified into two groups. Some of them, stemming from the *rule of law*, are transparency, the duty to give reasons, impartiality, fairness, accountability or review. Others, derived from the *democratic principle*, might be statutory delegation, representativeness, participation, notice and comment, expertise and the like.

Finally, *how* to achieve the "transposition". Such criteria will often be expressed as *general principles*. Since their realisation takes place within, and in collaboration with, private law, these general principles must be specified and adapted accordingly. That is the reason, for example, why European legislation on public procurement only establishes that (private) contracting powers must apply the *principles* of the public contract laws, and not the formal procedures that the statutes establish for administrations.

The main proposal here is to expand public law values into private law.[41] This task entails a *process of adaptation* for traditional administrative law. Not a mere application, but rather, a transfer, export or inoculation of public law values to this area. Therefore, it is a process of seeking and building equivalent rules and principles to be adopted into private law.

Indeed, the transfer of these provisions, values or principles must be an "essentialist" process. It is a distillation. This means that these basic essences (principles or values) should not be mechanically transferred *en bloc*, but adapted. Most important here is the outcome, the end itself. Hence, it is an essentialist transfer of key principles or values in order to guarantee results.

Thus, both co-exist: On the one hand, traditional administrative law, actor-oriented, regulating administrative actions when dressed "in uniform" in the field of services of general interest and regulatory activities; on the other hand, new administrative law, function-oriented, accompanying actors in determined activities under private law.

3.2.3 Lack of Monopoly. A Multi-Disciplinary Approach: Conceptual Bridges Between Public and Private Law

On the one hand, while the principles for "public life" are extracted primarily from administrative law, there is much in common here with constitutional law.[42] The need for private entities performing regulatory tasks to justify their actions against recognised criteria and the inability to exercise the same freedom of action as individuals is a conclusion derived from constitutional law (principle of rule of law, rationality, transparency, accountability, and the like), and administrative law (duty of give reasons, review, control by the public or those affected etc.).

---

[41] To rehash a phrase from the influential work of Freeman 2003.

[42] Taggart 1997, p. 3.

On the other, the metaphors used for describing this functional process ("infuse", "transfer", "adaptation" or "application" from public law to private law) do not mean that *all* these values belong exclusively to public law. Indeed, it would be wrong to suppose that there are no parallels between these branches of the law. In any case, the transfer from public to private law started a long time ago.

Indeed, conflict of interest rules, transparency, representativeness, anti-discriminatory principles and so forth are now customary principles in private law. Increasingly, legislative interventions place limits on the private law's instinctive privileging of self-regarding behaviour. "So much that in particular instances the results derived from private law analysis may well approximate those derived from administrative law analysis. Starting points leading in different directions do not necessarily lead to different end points. At a reasonably high level of abstraction public law and private law share several underlying values".[43] "What we are witnessing in some areas at least is a synthesis or blending of public and private law principles."[44]

For this reason, I believe that the construction of "conceptual bridges" between both systems is methodologically required, in order to analyse systematically the underlying values and principles in services of general interest and/or regulatory activities. For example, in such cases private actors must justify their actions in terms of the general interest, and not their own interests; and the duty to give reasons in a decision-making process should be considered as a basic duty, whether the actor is public or private, even though that duty may manifest itself differently in each circumstance.

3.2.4 Some Values Can be Classified in Two Ways from an Administrative Law Viewpoint: by Organisation and by Procedure

Under those assumptions, a formula to successfully accomplish the above-mentioned task could be to establish *procedural* arrangements (consultations, transparency, duty to give reasons, impartiality and the like) and *organisational and structural* layouts (composition, openness, expertise, representativeness, avoidance of conflicts of interest, etc.).[45] Organisation – the way to be – and procedure – the way to act – are institutions with structural effects.

As has been noted before, if public and private actors interact in different ways in many privatised areas, and they are part of a joint plan of action, to design procedural and organisational arrangements, not only for administrations, but also for non-governmental organisations will give coherence to the whole system. For example,

[43] Oliver 1997; Taggart 1997, p. 5: "There is a good deal of interaction between the two bodies of law, and there is increasing evidence of cross-fertilisation [. . .] Employment law is one area where the influence of public law values can be seen."

[44] Taggart 1997, p. 5–6: "While the distinction between, and the symbolic functions of, private law and public law are unlikely to fall away, the tensions between them is being mediated in ways that look interestingly familiar to both public and private lawyers."

[45] See Barnés 2013, p. 305–338.

an association that establishes professional standards in a self-regulatory regime can no longer act as merely a private association. It must instead be a representative of its entire professional field, it must give reasons why it establishes said standards, and it must act with transparency, among other requirements.

Procedure and organisation could be understood as two *conceptual bridges* between administrative and private law in these areas. Administrative law and private law scholars should be equally interested in both these fields when networked public and private actors provide services of general interest, participate in the regulatory cascade, or do both.

3.3 *Final Remarks: Principles to be Internalised by Private Law*

As said, new domains for administrative law are arising from increasingly relevant fields, such as: the "private life of administration" (i), the "public life of private actors" (ii), the "public life of administration beyond command and control regulations" (iii), the "international and global life of administration" (iv), and the "influential life of administration performing crucial public policies" (v). These fields are not entirely new for administrative law. Nevertheless, they have continued their exponential growth and significance, and, even more importantly, their interactions with other branches of the law.

In many ways, *customary* administrative law has been absent from these "lives". This is because basic and central requirements were not being met, in part or completely, as occurs, for example, when an administration does not act "in uniform", i. e. as merely a private actor (i); when private organisations participate in regulatory process or in public service activities or provide *services* of *general interest* (ii); when an administration enacts soft law, or just gathers, processes and shares information (iii); when an administration does not act within state boundaries (iv); or when an administration (a super-agency) leads and implements significant public policies (v).

However, for a number of reasons, a *new* administrative law is evolving and has a challenging role to play in these areas, in interaction with the other branches of the law. It is an administrative law system based on functional and multi-disciplinary approaches. Values, principles or rules stemming from public law are, and still have to be, adapted according to the peculiarities of each "life", in collaboration with other areas of the law: private law, constitutional law, international law, global administrative law and the like. These public values, principles or rules are determined by the task or function to be accomplished, whether the actor is public or private, whether the actor operates domestically or in the global arena, or whether the actor is vested or not with administrative powers. The question of the scope of these public law values will become a central point of controversy among public-law lawyers.

Regarding the private and public law relationship, when "administrative" actions are performed, mutual collaboration, and, more specifically, the internalisation of public values and norms into private law are needed. In other words, the premise is to "infuse" and to blend private law with public law values.

4 Conclusions

In short: this article does not advocate, as a continental-European lawyer might think, for replacing private law with rival legal norms – "more administrative law", nor for abandoning administrative law – "less administrative law". On the contrary, it calls attention to the mutual benefits to be found in a collaborative work between both of them.

4.1 A Functional Aapproach: Transfer of Public Norms to Private Law to Perform a Variety of Functions

Administrative law is in transition. That being said, however, it can be argued that "Administrative law will continue to be evolutionary and strongly conservative in character",[46] at the same time.

In this article, firstly, I claim that given that administrative law scholars must deal with two different and evolving activities (regulatory and public service activities) – even if they are performed without vested executive power and are subject to private law – our field of study is broader than it used to be.

Secondly, administrative law is also evolving in a functionally oriented manner. I hold, then, that these new functions, performed with the massive involvement of the private sector, are mainly two: the regulatory function and the public service one. If administrative law does not adapt according to the changing conditions of these new "lives" to become, in the pertinent scenarios, more functional – so that these lives can be properly rationalised and regulated (Sect. 1) – it risks going backwards.

Finally, I suggest a way – one perspective among others – of solving the conflicts arising from public-private interactions in the new frontiers and this would be that private law adopts and embraces public values or principles.

Plainly, contemporary administrative law embodies a wide range of formats, apart from the traditional one. Moreover, it is undergoing a transition from a purely subjective definition (in essence, the law that applies to the administration when it exercises authority) to a broader, function-defined approach.

---

[46] Stewart 2003, p. 453. As *Mark Seidenfeld* states, "Stewart is correct in his understanding that administrative law is evolutionary and builds upon prior doctrine without ever jettisoning that doctrine entirely." The Quixotic Quest for a "Unified" Theory of the Administrative State.

4.2 Case by Case Approach

"New administrative law" here, first and foremost, can be understood as a functional law in nature, which may be articulated in principles. We mean by this that public values and principles, not detailed norms and regulations, are to be transported from public law into private law. For instance, professional associations at the European level, which establish codes of conduct under self-regulation regimes, are not expected to apply or incorporate traditional and strict administrative law procedural rules to make decisions. The intention is to not constrain these private organisations as if they were administrations, rather, what is expected of them is that they adapt the public values derived from those rules into private law.

Case by case arrangements are necessary for adapting to different areas and to maintain coherence with the other public actors involved in the same area. On the one side, in the field of private regulatory activities, self-dealing, conflicts of interest, secrecy, irrationality, lack of representation, procedural irregularity, and the like are to be avoided; and, on the other, in the area of *services* of *general interest*, low quality service, lack of universality, lack of competition, discrimination, poor consumer protection, and so forth must be avoided. Each function (regulatory and public service) is different, as well as is each sector. Furthermore, "[w]hen a private actor plays an enforcement role, we might expect it to act differently than when it develops standards. In the former case, we might worry about private motivations that threaten to conflict with a rational enforcement agenda. In the latter case, we might want to minimize self-dealing and anti-competitive behaviour."[47]

All in all, since public policies are implemented through a myriad of regulators and service providers (as is the case of financial market regulation), each requiring a different approach, there is a mission to accomplish: to promote the *coexistence* between the different *formats* of administrative law and the collaboration between public and private law. For instance, a central bank might be subject to strict domestic rules on administrative procedure regarding rulemaking (hard or traditional subjective-centred administrative law); the same central bank will be subject to informal administrative principles when acting before the Basel Committee on Banking Supervision (soft and functional administrative law). In addition, private credit rating agencies are expected to follow similar (administrative in nature) principles when performing their tasks in the same market. As *J. Freeman* states, "[e]ven traditional command and control regulation – a hierarchical arrangement in which the agency dictates and enforces standards – is characterized by informal interdependence between government and private actors."[48]

---

[47] Freeman 2000a, p. 846.

[48] Freeman 2000a, p. 857: "[A]dministration is an enterprise characterized by interdependence among a host of different actors (agencies, private firms, lenders, insurers, customers, non-profits, third party enforcers, and professional associations, for example). Government and non-government actors operate in a context of institutional richness, in relationship to each other, and against a background of legal rules, informal practices and shared understandings. These public-private arrangements defy easy division into purely public and purely private roles."

See also Cassese 2012, p. 608: "Administration, politics, and society now form a triangle; there is

4.3 *Administrative Law as a Legal Heritage and Common Basic System for Private Law when Private Entities Provide Public Services or Participate in the Regulatory Cascade*

The view that we uphold here is not towards the application of private law in lieu of administrative law in certain traditional areas (typically, contracts), nor that of the inclusion of principles of private law within administrative law, but rather one in the opposite direction. On the contrary, I argue that the administrative law system operates as a common heritage for statutes and case law, supplemented by legal research, in order to determine the "public life" principles that private entities should adapt and adopt in certain scenarios. I refer to a collaborative interplay or melange, by virtue of which "public life" principles modify, complete or permeate private law, on the one side; and, on the other, at the same time, private law will transform these principles by its own means and personality. The resultant combination will be different in each case.

4.4 *New Perspectives: Can one Single Theory Completely Explain Administrative Law?*

In my view, there is reason to believe that a broad, common, theoretical basis for administrative law, on the one hand, and a variety of branching, functional modalities of administrative law, on the other, may be compatible.

The question is not about finding one, new foundation or a monolithic theory for administrative law, but, on the contrary, it is about finding connections and interactions between a common basis and different functional modalities. A functional application of public law values to private law in some cases is just one example of that.

Indeed, I believe that exercising executive or administrative authority is not the only foundation of administrative law. Regulatory activities and services of general interest (and more broadly, public service activities), regardless of the exercise of power or of the performer, are also criteria that should be taken into account.

As *S. Cassese* concludes, new "developments make it necessary to abandon the public law regime paradigm, to de-publicize the approach adopted by administrative law scholarship and to study the ambiguities and the richness of the interconnections between public and private law."[49]

no longer a clear dividing line between administration and society; negotiation runs side by side with command and control; as soon as new services require new structures, these new structures establish links with their institutional clients and attract new clients (both internally and externally); decision-making processes are replaced or accompanied by consultation, mediation, Parliament-like procedures, or, simply, muddling through."

[49] Cassese 2012, p. 607. See also Bignami 2011.

It is no longer a zero-sum game: "privatisation" *versus* "publicisation". The two phenomena are fundamentally compatible. It is not about abandoning private regulatory and public service activities to private parties; it is not about constraining private actors performing these tasks as if they were administrative agencies. I argue that one way to deal with this is the collaboration between the two branches of the law. In this regard, private law should internalise and embrace some administrative principles and values, adapted to its flexible operating system. Legislation should extend administrative principles and values to private actors through statutory provisions, contracts, subsidies or grants, and so forth.[50]

A key role to be played by legislator is to inculcate and to preserve public law values in the reconfigured public-private landscape.

The emphasis on public law principles or values allows the growth and influence of administrative law science to transcend its traditionally limited domains. However, it is not about a *public colonisation of private law*. It is about finding complementarity and interplay between administrative law and private law,[51] on the one hand, and building conceptual bridges for these values, that are not, or not entirely, monopolised by public law, on the other.

The illustrations below are meant to be suggestive rather than comprehensive.

References

Aronson, M. (1997). A Public Lawyer's Response to Privatization and Outsourcing. In M. Taggart (Ed.), *The Province of Administrative Law* (pp. 40–70). Oxford: Hart Publishing.

Barnés, J. (2013). Le importan al Derecho Administrativo las organizaciones y los procedimientos sujetos al Derecho Privado? In J. Barnés (Ed.), *Innovación y Reforma en el Derecho Administrativo 2.0* (2nd edn., pp. 305–338). Sevilla: Editorial Derecho Global.

Bignami, F. (2011). From Expert Administration to Accountability Network: A New Paradigm for Comparative Administrative Law. *American Journal of Comparative Law*, *59*(4), 859–908.

Casini, L. (2014). 'Down the rabbit-hole': The projection of the public/private distinction beyond the state. *International Journal of Constitutional Law*, *12*(2), 402–428.

Cassese, S. (2012). New Paths for Administrative Law: A Manifesto. *International Journal of Constitutional Law*, *10*(3), 603–613.

Cassese, S. (2014). *Derecho Administrativo: historia y futuro*. Sevilla: Editorial Derecho Global.

Frankfurter, F. (1941). The Final Report of the Attorney-General's Committee on Administrative Procedure. *Columbia Law Review*, *41*(4), 585–588.

Freeman, J. (2000a). Private Parties, Public Functions and the New Administrative Law. *Administrative Law Review*, *52*(3), 813–858.

Freeman, J. (2000b). The Private Role in Public Governance. *New York University Law Review*, *75*(3), 543–675.

Freeman, J. (2003). Extending Public Law Norms Through Privatization. *Harvard Law Review*, *116*(5), 1285–1352.

[50] From a different perspective, see Freeman 2003.

[51] See Hoffmann-Riem and Schmidt-Aßmann 1996.

Harlow, C. (2009). The 'Hidden Paw' of the state and the publicisation of private law. In D. Dyzenhaus, M. Hunt, & G. Huscroft (Eds.), *A Simple Common Lawyer: Essays in Honour of Michael Taggart* (pp. 75–97). Oxford: Hart Publishing.

Hoffmann-Riem, W., & Schmidt-Aßmann, E. (1996). *Öffentliches Recht und Privatrecht als wechselseitige Auffangordnungen*. Baden-Baden: Nomos.

McLean, J. (2009). *British Idealism and the Administrative State. Unpublished manuscript. Comparative Administrative Law Conference. Yale Law School*. http://www.law.yale.edu/documents/pdf/CompAdminLaw/Janet_McLean_CompAdLaw_paper.pdf. Accessed 2. February 2015

Oliver, D. (1997). The Underlying Values of Public and Private Law. In M. Taggart (Ed.), *The Province of Administrative Law* (pp. 217–242). Oxford: Hart Publishing.

Stewart, R. B. (2003). Essay: Administrative Law in the Twenty First Century. *New York University Law Review*, *78*(2), 437–460.

Taggart, M. (1997). The Province of Administrative Law Determined? In M. Taggart (Ed.), *The Province of Administrative Law* (pp. 1–20). Oxford: Hart Publishing.

Selected National and International Courts

National

Austria	http://www.vfgh.gv.at
Belgium	http://www.const-court.be
Bulgaria	http://www.constcourt.bg
Cyprus	http://www.supremecourt.gov.cy
Czech Republic	http://www.concourt.cz http://www.usoud.cz/
Denmark	http://www.domstol.dk
Estonia	http://www.riigikohus.ee
Finland	http://www.kho.fi
France	http://www.conseil-constitutionnel.fr http://www.conseil-etat.fr
Germany	http://www.bundesverfassungsgericht.de http://www.bverwg.de/ http://www.bundesarbeitsgericht.de/index.htm
Greece	http://www.ste.gr
Hungary	http://www.mkab.hu
Ireland	http://www.supremecourt.ie
Italy	http://www.cortecostituzionale.it http://www.giurcost.org http://www.giustizia-amministrativa.it
Latvia	http://www.satv.tiesa.gov.lv
Lithuania	http://www.lrkt.lt
Luxembourg	http://www.justice.public.lu/fr/jurisprudence/cour-constitutionnelle/index.html
Netherlands	http://www.raadvanstate.nl
Poland	http://www.trybunal.gov.pl
Portugal	http://www.tribunalconstitucional.pt/tc/home.html
Romania	http://www.ccr.ro

H.-J. Blanke et al. (eds.), *Common European Legal Thinking*,
DOI 10.1007/978-3-319-19300-7

Slovakia	http://www.concourt.sk
Slovenia	http://www.us-rs.si
Spain	http://www.tribunalconstitucional.es
United Kingdom	http://www.parliament.uk/business/lords
	http://www.supremecourt.gov.uk
	https://www.justice.gov.uk/courts/rcj-rolls-building/court-of-appeal/criminal-division
Canada	http://www.scc-csc.gc.ca
United States of America	http://www.supremecourt.gov

International

Court of Justice of the European Union	http://curia.europa.eu/
European Court of Human Rights	http://www.echr.coe.int/
International Court of Justice	http://www.icj-cij.org/

Publications by Albrecht Weber

I. Authored Books and Editorships

1. Der UN-Beamte in den USA: Sein völkerrechtlicher Status (Vorrechte und Immunitäten). Diss. Würzburg 1972, 132 Seiten
2. Hahn/Weber: Die OECD – Organisation für wirtschaftliche Zusammenarbeit und Entwicklung, Baden-Baden (Nomos) 1976, 443 Seiten
3. Schutznormen und Wirtschaftsintegration: Zur völkerrechtlichen, europarechtlichen und innerstaatlichen Problematik von „ordre public" und Schutzklauseln, Baden-Baden (Nomos) 1982, 480 Seiten
4. Geschichte der internationalen Wirtschaftsorganisationen, Wiesbaden 1983, 183 Seiten
5. Starck/Weber (Hrsg.), Verfassungsgerichtsbarkeit in Westeuropa. Eine Einführung mit Nationalberichten: Bundesrepublik, Österreich, Schweiz, Frankreich, Italien, Spanien, Portugal, Griechenland und Belgien, Baden-Baden (Nomos) 1986, Teilband I: Berichte, 392 S., Teilband II: Dokumentation, 616 Seiten
6. Rechtsfragen der Durchführung des Gemeinschaftsrechts in der Bundesrepublik, Köln 1987, 134 Seiten
7. Die Umweltverträglichkeitsrichtlinie im deutschen Recht, Köln 1988, 485 Seiten
8. Horn/Weber (Hrsg.), Richterliche Verfassungskontrolle in Lateinamerika, Spanien und Portugal, Baden-Baden (Nomos) 1989, 249 Seiten
9. Fälle zum Völker- und Europarecht. JuS-Schriftenreihe, München (C.H. Beck) 1992, 194 Seiten
10. Gramlich/Weber/Zehetner (Hrsg.), Auf dem Wege zur Währungsunion. Symposium anläßlich des 65. Geburtstags von Prof. H. J. Hahn, Baden-Baden (Nomos) 1992, 149 Seiten
11. Weber (Hrsg.) in Verbindung mit Häde, Gramlich, Zehetner: Währung und Wirtschaft. Das Geld im Recht, Festschrift für H. J. Hahn zum 70. Geburtstag am 15.01.1997. Baden-Baden (Nomos) 1997, 750 Seiten

12. Weber (Hrsg.), Einwanderungsland Bundesrepublik in der Europäischen Union – Gestaltungsauftrag und Regelungsmöglichkeiten, IMIS-Schriften, Bd. 5, Osnabrück (Universitätsverlag Rasch) 1997, 381 Seiten
13. Herausgeber des von der Deutschen Forschungsgemeinschaft seit 1996 geförderten Projekts „Fundamental Rights in Europe and North America" i. V. m. Adam, Bjerkén, Brugger, Casey, Delpérée, Eberle, Favoreu, Filip, Garlicki, Jociene, Kälin, Kommers, Levits, Luciani, Luther, Miranda, Nergelius, Novak, Páczolay, Pavcnik, Pernice, Renoux, Rubio Llorente, Schäffer, Schaffmeister, Scheinin, Schermers, Sinkovec, Skouris, Uibopuu, Wright, Zuleeg; mit Nationalberichten aus 25 Rechtsordnungen (Austria, Belgium, Czech Republic, Denmark, Estonia, Finland, France, Germany, Greece, Hungary, Ireland, Italy, Latvia, Lithuania, Netherlands, Poland, Portugal, Slovenia, Spain, Sweden, Switzerland, United Kingdom, USA; ECJ, ECHR) und Generalberichten zu „Allgemeiner Teil" und Einzelgrundrechten; laufende Veröffentlichung als Loseblattsammlung
    Part A, Den Haag (Kluwer Law International) 2001 ff.;
    Part B: Hungary, Leiden (Martinus Nijhoff) 2006; ECHR, Leiden (Martinus Nijhoff) 2006; Greece, Leiden (Martinus Nijhoff) 2006; Denmark, Leiden (Martinus Nijhoff) 2008; Germany, Leiden (Martinus Nijhoff) 2008
14. Charta der Grundrechte der Europäischen Union – Charte des Droits Fondamentaux de l'Union Européenne – Charter of Fundamental Rights of the European Union, Einführung und Textsynopse, München (Sellier European Law Publishers) 2002, 145 Seiten
15. Weber/Gas, Fälle zum Europarecht. JuS-Schriftenreihe, 2., neu bearbeitete Auflage, München (C.H. Beck) 2003, 200 Seiten
16. Schweitzer/Weber, Handbuch der Völkerrechtspraxis der Bundesrepublik Deutschland, Baden-Baden (Nomos) 2004, 862 Seiten
17. Menschenrechte – Texte und Fallpraxis, München (Sellier European Law Publishers) 2003, 1050 Seiten
18. Starck/Weber (Hrsg.), Verfassungsgerichtsbarkeit in Westeuropa. Eine Einführung mit Nationalberichten: Bundesrepublik, Österreich, Schweiz, Frankreich, Italien, Spanien, Portugal, Griechenland und Belgien, 2. Auflage, Baden-Baden (Nomos) 2007
    Teilband I: Berichte, 376 Seiten; Teilband II: Dokumentation, 705 Seiten
19. Luchterhand/Starck/Weber (Hrsg.), Verfassungsgerichtsbarkeit in Mittel- und Osteuropa, Teilband I (mit Nationalberichten aus Albanien, Bulgarien, Litauen, Polen, Rumänien, Rußländische Föderation, Slowakei, Slowenien, Tschechien, Türkei, Ungarn, Zypern und Generalbericht); Teilband II (mit Dokumentation der Verfassungen und Verfassungsgerichtstexte), Baden-Baden (Nomos) 2007
    Teilband I: Berichte, 356 Seiten; Teilband II: Dokumentation: 389 Seiten
20. Davy/Weber (Hrsg.), Paradigmenwechsel in Einwanderungsfragen? Überlegungen zum neuen Zuwanderungsgesetz, Baden-Baden (Nomos) 2006
21. Europäische Verfassungsvergleichung, München (C.H. Beck) 2010, 447 Seiten

II. Journal Articles and Book Chapters in German

1. Der völkerrechtliche Status des UN-Beamten in den USA, in: Vereinte Nationen 1972, S. 186–190
2. Diplomatische Beziehungen zwischen der Bundesrepublik Deutschland und der DDR? in: Politische Studien 1974, S. 337–351
3. Die Entwicklung des Mutterschutzes durch die internationalen Organisationen, in: Recht der Arbeit 1975, S. 229–232
4. Die neue Weltwirtschaftsordnung: Die Ergebnisse der 7. Sondergeneralversammlung der Vereinten Nationen, in: RIW 1977, S. 21–28
5. Kurzbeiträge in: Wirtschaftswissenschaftliches Studium (1), 1977, S. 48 (Diskontsatzfestsetzung der Bundesbank); WiSt (3), 1977, S. 143–144 (Geldwertsicherungsklauseln); WiSt (8), 1977, S. 399–400 (Weisungen in der Mindestreservepolitik)
6. Die 2. Satzungsnovelle des Internationalen Währungsfonds und das Völkerrecht, in: Festschrift für F. A. Mann, München 1977, S. 807–846
7. Die Rechtsprechung des EuGH zum Vorbehalt der öffentlichen Ordnung und Sicherheit im Bereich der Freizügigkeit, in: EuGRZ 1978, S. 157–160
8. Neuere Tendenzen im Integrationsrecht Lateinamerikas, in: Verfassung und Recht in Übersee 1978, S. 89–101
9. Das nationale Ausländer- und Melderecht in gemeinschaftsrechtlicher Sicht, in: BayVBl. 1978, S. 357–363
10. Der praktische Fall – öffentliches Recht: Die Kreditlimitierungsverordnung, in: JuS 1978, S. 554–559
11. Die Grundrechte im europäischen Beamtenrecht, in: Zeitschrift für Beamtenrecht, 1978, S. 326–333
12. Die Bedeutung des Art. 115 EWGV für die Freiheit des Warenverkehrs, in: EuR 1979, S. 30–47
13. Beteiligung und Rechtsschutz ausländischer Nachbarn im atomrechtlichen Genehmigungsverfahren, in: DVBl. 1980, S. 330–336
14. Vorbescheid und Teilgenehmigung im Atomrecht, in: DÖV 1980, S. 397–405
15. Die spanische Verfassung von 1978, in: JöR 1980, S. 209–278
16. Kommentierung von Art. 248 EWGV, in: Groeben/Boeckh/Thiesing/Ehlermann, Kommentar EWG-Vertrag, 3. Aufl. 1983, S. 1337–1349
17. Verfassungsrechtliche Probleme des Familiennachzugs von Ausländern, in: NJW 1983, S. 1225–1230
18. (mit Benda): Der Einfluß der Verfassung im Prozeßrecht. Deutscher Landesbericht für den Internationalen Kongreß für Zivilprozeßrecht in Würzburg 1983, in: Gilles (Hrsg.), Effektivität des Rechtsschutzes und verfassungsmäßige Ordnung, 1983, S. 1–23; zugleich in: Zeitschrift für Zivilprozeßrecht 1983, S. 285–306
19. Krisenvorsorge und Krisenmanagement im europäischen Währungswesen, in: Zuleeg (Hrsg.), Krisenvorsorge und Krisenmanagement in der Europäischen Gemeinschaft, Baden-Baden 1983, S. 27–45

20. Auslieferung trotz Asylrecht? Verfassungsrechtliche und verfassungspolitische Überlegungen zum Fall Altun, in: ZAR 1984, S. 16–23
21. Anfechtbarkeit und Aufhebbarkeit gemeinschaftswidriger nationaler Verwaltungsakte, in: BayVBl. 1984, S. 321–327
22. Nachrüstung und Grundgesetz, in: JZ 1984, S. 589–595
23. Stellung und Begriff des Hochschullehrers in der Rechtsprechung des BVerfG, in: Maunz/Roellecke/Zeidler, Festschrift für Bundesverfassungsrichter Prof. Faller, München 1984, S. 287–304
24. Das Verwaltungsverfahren im Antidumpingrecht der EG in: EuR 1985, S. 1–21
25. Kanadas Sprachenfrage und der Constitution Act 1982 im Lichte der Entscheidung des kanadischen Supreme Court im Fall „Quebecs Association of Protestant School Boards“, in: EuGRZ 1985, S. 29–33
26. Direkte Demokratie im Landesverfassungsrecht, in: DÖV 1985, S. 178–184
27. Rechtsfragen der grenzüberschreitenden Luftverschmutzung, in: Recht und Wirtschaft, Schriftenreihe Osnabrücker Rechtswissenschaftliche Abhandlungen, 1985, Band I, S. 55–72
28. Verfassungsgerichtsbarkeit in Spanien: in: JöR 1985, S. 245–301
29. Verwaltungskollisionsrecht der Europäischen Gemeinschaften im Lichte neuerer Rechtsentwicklungen, in: EuR 1986, S. 1–28
30. Verfassungsgerichtsbarkeit westeuropäischer Staaten im Vergleich, Generalbericht, in: Starck/Weber (Hrsg.), Verfassungsgerichtsbarkeit in Westeuropa, Bd. I, Baden-Baden 1986, S. 49–120
31. Die Bundesländer und die Reform der Gemeinschaftsverträge, in: DVBl. 1986, S. 800–806
32. Schutzklauseln der Freihandelsabkommen EWG-EFTA, in: Koppensteiner (Hrsg.): Rechtsfragen der Freihandelsabkommen der Europäischen Wirtschaftsgemeinschaft mit den EFTA-Staaten, Wien 1987, S. 267–286
33. Zur Bedeutung der Rechtsvergleichung für die Verfassungsgerichtsbarkeit, dargestellt am Beispiel des Schwangerschaftsabbruchs, in: Festschrift für BVerfG-Präs. Prof. Zeidler, 1987, S. 371–393
34. Zur Umsetzung der Umweltverträglichkeitsrichtlinie im deutschen Recht, UPR 6 (1988), S. 206–215
35. Die Grundrechte im Integrationsprozeß der Gemeinschaft in vergleichender Perspektive, in: JZ 1989, S. 965–973
36. Richterliche Kontrolle bei der Ausführung von Gemeinschaftsrecht durch die Mitgliedstaaten, in: Festschrift 175 Jahre Oberlandesgericht Oldenburg, 1989, S. 699–711
37. Berufsausbildung und Berufszugang für Juristen im EG-Binnenmarkt, in: NVwZ 1990, S. 1–8
38. Die Umweltverträglichkeitsprüfung (Stichwortartikel), Ergänzbares Lexikon des Rechts, 7/870 (1990)
39. Internationales Wirtschaftsverwaltungsrecht (Stichwortartikel), Ergänzbares Lexikon des Rechts, 7/510 (1990)

40. (mit Hellmann) Das Gesetz über die Umweltverträglichkeitsprüfung (UVP-G), in: NJW 1990, S. 1625–1633
41. (mit Eschmann) Methodik der Fallbearbeitung – Öffentliches Recht: Der eigenwillige Abgeordnete, in: JuS 1990, S. 659–661
42. Das amerikanisch-kanadische Freihandelsabkommen vom 2.1.1988, in: RIW 1990, S. 975–982
43. Kommentierung zu Art. 217, Art. 248 EWGV, in: von der Groeben/von Boeckh/Thiesing/Ehlermann, 4. Aufl., Baden-Baden 1991, S. 5471–5484
44. Das Verwaltungsverfahren, in: Schweitzer (Hrsg.), Europäisches Verwaltungsrecht, Wien 1991, S. 55–83
45. Belgien (Stichwortartikel): Recht und Verfassung, in: Staatslexikon der Görres-Gesellschaft, Bd. 6/1992 (7. Aufl.), S. 118–119
46. (mit Eschmann) Der praktische Fall – Öffentliches Recht: Der verhinderte italienische Rechtsreferendar, in: JuS 1992, S. 497–502
47. Kommentierung von §§ 49–57 BVerfGG (Präsidentenanklage), in: Umbach/Clemens (Hrsg.), Bundesverfassungsgerichtsgesetz, Heidelberg 1992, S. 776–795
48. Zur Umsetzung von EG-Richtlinien im Umweltrecht, in: UPR 1992/1, S. 5–9
49. Einwanderungs- und Asylpolitik nach Maastricht, in: ZAR 1993, S. 11–18
50. Die Harmonisierung des europäischen Einwanderungs- und Asylrechts, in: ZRP 1993, S. 170–173

51a Zur Verfassungsstruktur der Europäischen Gemeinschaft nach Maastricht, in: Hrbek (Hrsg.), Der Vertrag von Maastricht in der wissenschaftlichen Kontroverse. Schriftenreihe des Arbeitskreises für Europäische Integration 1993, S. 121–132

51b Zur künftigen Verfassung der Europäischen Gemeinschaft – Föderalismus und Demokratie als Strukturelemente, in: JZ 1993, S. 325–330

52. (mit C. Grewe): Die Reform des Ausländer- und Asylrechts in Frankreich/Die Entscheidung des Conseil Constitutionnel vom 13. August 1993, in: EuGRZ 1993, S. 496–499
53. Die Wirtschafts- und Währungsunion nach dem Maastricht-Urteil des BVerfG, in: JZ 1994, S. 53–61
54. Nichtdiskriminierung und Minderheitenschutz in Kanada in vergleichender Perspektive, in: EuGRZ 1994, S. 537–548
55. Der Vertrag von Maastricht vor dem Verfassungsgericht. – Einige rechtsvergleichende Anmerkungen zum Urteil des BVerfG vom 10.12.1993, in: FS für Benda (1995), S. 421–441
56. Umweltschutz und internationale Wirtschaftsordnung, in: Areopag (Jahrbuch für Kultur und Kommunikation), 1994
57. Verfassungsgerichte in anderen Ländern, Veröffentlichung der Fachtagung der Politischen Akademie (Tutzing) 1993 – Das Jahr des BVerfG. Ein Gericht im Schnittpunkt von Recht und Politik (1995), S. 61–73
58. Die Kontrolle kompetenzwidriger Gemeinschaftsakte – Ringvorlesung anläßlich des 10jährigen Bestehens des Instituts für Europarecht, Köln u. a. 1995, S. 21–33

59. Zur Kontrolle grundrechts- bzw. kompetenzwidriger Rechtsakte der EG durch nationale Verfassungsgerichte, in: FS für Everling, Baden-Baden 1995, S. 1625–1639
60. Die Bedeutung der Regionen für die Verfassungsstruktur der Europäischen Union, in: FS Heymanns Verlag, Köln u. a. 1995, S. 681–693
61. Französisches Staatsangehörigkeitsrecht im Wandel, in: ZAR 1995, S. 147–151
62. Der nationale Verfassungsstaat vor den Herausforderungen der Europäischen Integration, in: Perspectivas Constitucionais, FS anläßlich des 20jährigen Bestehens der portugiesischen Verfassung, Coimbra 1996, S. 769–785
63. Die Bananenmarktordnung unter Aufsicht des Bundesverfassungsgerichts? in: EuZW 1997, S. 165–169
64. Die Währungsunion – Modell für ein Europa mehrerer Geschwindigkeiten?, in: Währung und Wirtschaft – Das Geld im Recht, FS zum 70. Geburtstag von Prof. Dr. Hugo J. Hahn, Baden-Baden 1997, S. 273–283
65. Klassische Einwanderungsländer: USA, Kanada, Australien, in: Weber (Hrsg.), Einwanderungsland Bundesrepublik Deutschland in der Europäischen Union: Gestaltungsauftrag und Regelungsmöglichkeiten, Osnabrück 1997, S. 97–122; Einführung in den Sammelband vom Herausgeber, S. 1 ff.
66. Kommentierung zum EG/EU-Vertrag (Art. 217, 238, 248; R, S), 5. Aufl. 1997, Baden-Baden 1998, S. 289–298, 717–768, 795–808, 1181–1183
67. Möglichkeiten und Grenzen europäischer Asylrechtsharmonisierung vor und nach Amsterdam, in: ZAR 1998, S. 147–152
68. Entwicklungen im europäischen Verwaltungsrecht, in: Ipsen/Stüer (Hrsg.), Öffentliche Verwaltung in Europa. Symposium aus Anlaß des 60. Geburtstags von Professor Dr. Hans-Werner Rengeling, 6. März 1998, ORA Bd. 56, S. 35–59
69. (mit Moos) Rechtwirkungen und Entscheidungen im WTO-Streitbeilegungsverfahren im Gemeinschaftsrecht, in: EuZW 1999, S. 229–236
70. WWU und Euro – Bedeutung für die Rechtsordnungen der Mitgliedstaaten, in: Start in die Wirtschafts- und Währungsunion – Euro für Juristen". 2. Fakultätentag der Rechtswissenschaftlichen Fakultät, Graz 1999, S. 29–64
71. Ansätze zu einem gemeineuropäischen Asylrecht, in: EuGRZ 1999, S. 301–313
72. Entwicklungen zu einem gemeineuropäischen Asylrecht, in: AWR Bulletin 1999, S. 122–127
73. Die europäische Grundrechtscharta – auf dem Weg zu einer europäischen Verfassung, in: NJW 2000, S. 537–544
74. Das neue Staatsangehörigkeitsrecht, in: DVBl. 2000, S. 369–376
75. Die Durchsetzung der Menschen- und Grundrechte in der Bundesrepublik Deutschland, in: Mitteilungen der Deutsch-Israelischen Juristenvereinigung, VIII April 2000, S. 33 ff.
76. (mit Santel) Zwischen Ausländerpolitik und Einwanderungspolitik: Migrations- und Ausländerrecht in Deutschland, in: Bade/Münz (Hrsg.), Migra-

tionsreport 2000. Fakten – Analysen – Perspektiven, Frankfurt 2000, S. 109–140

77. Kommentierung von Art. 32, 59 Abs. 2 GG, in: Umbach/Clemens (Hrsg.), Grundgesetz, Mitarbeiter-Kommentar, Heidelberg 2002
78. Zur Restitution enteigneten Vermögens im Spiegel deutscher und ausländischer Verfassungsjudikatur, in: Ipsen/Schmidt-Jortzig, Recht – Staat – Gemeinwohl, FS für H. Rauschning, Köln u. a. 2001, S. 371–382
79. Asylrecht in Europa, in: Jochen Oltmer (Hrsg.), Migrationsforschung und Interkulturelle Studien: Zehn Jahre IMIS, Osnabrück 2001, S. 115–133
80. Die Zukunft der Grundrechtscharta, in: Stefan Griller/Waldemar Hummer (Hrsg.), Die EU nach Nizza. Ergebnisse und Perspektiven Springer 2002, S. 281–295
81. Grundrechte in der EU, in: Erhard Busek/Waldemar Hummer (Hrsg.), Etappen auf dem Weg zu einer europäischen Verfassung, Wien u. a., 2004, S. 55–70
82. Kommentierung zum EG/EU-Vertrag, 6. Aufl. 2002, Baden-Baden 2003, Art. 50, 51, 52, 53 EUV (Bd. 1, S. 553–556), Art. 290 (S. 1451–1460), Art. 310, 311, 312, 313, 314 EGV (Bd. 4, S. 1751–1804)
83. Die Genfer Flüchtlingskonvention und die Forschung im 21. Jahrhundert, in: AWR Bulletin 3/2002, S. 101–106
84. Regionalismus und Föderalismus als Strukturprinzipien Europas. Einige historische Anmerkungen am Beispiel Deutschlands und Frankreichs, in: Zehetner (Hrsg.), Festschrift für Hans-Ernst Folz, Wien/Graz 2003, S. 369–377
85. Einheit und Vielfalt der europäischen Grundrechtsordnung(en). Zur Inkorporation der Grundrechtscharta in einen europäischen Verfassungsvertrag, in: DVBl. 2003, S. 220–227
86. Die Regionen als verfassungsgeschichtliche Voraussetzung des Europarechts, in: Bauer/Welker (Hrsg.), Europa und seine Regionen. Tagungsband, Köln u. a. 2007, S. 749–762
87. Die Europäisierung des Asyl- und Migrationsrechts und ihre Folgen für die Bundesrepublik, in: Migration, Flüchtlinge und Integration 12/2004
88. Religiöse Symbole in der Einwanderungsgesellschaft, in: ZAR 2/2004, S. 53–60
89. Richterliche Verfassungskontrolle und Verfassungsinterpretation, in: Starck (Hrsg.), Die Rolle der Verfassungsrechtswissenschaft im demokratischen Verfassungsstaat. Zweites deutsch-taiwanesisches Kolloquium vom 26. bis 28. September 2002 in Taipeh, Baden-Baden 2004, S. 93–100
90. (mit Walter) Familiennachzug im europäischen und deutschen Recht, in: RdjB 1/2004, S. 108–128
91. Die Rolle der nationalen Parlamente in der Verfassungsentwicklung der Europäischen Union, in: Wollenschläger/Kreßel/Egger (Hrsg.), Recht – Wirtschaft – Kultur. Festschrift für Hans Hablitzel, Berlin 2005, S. 325–334
92. Typen der Verfassungsgerichtsbarkeit, in: Starck (Hrsg.), Fortschritte der Verfassungsgerichtsbarkeit in der Welt – Teil I. Deutsch-Japanisches Kolloquium

vom 20. bis 24. September 2002 in Tokio und Kioto, Baden-Baden 2004, S. 35–48

93. Zur föderalen Struktur der Europäischen Union im Entwurf des Europäischen Verfassungsvertrags, in: Europarecht 6/2004, S. 841–855
94. Das europäische Flüchtlings- und Migrationsrecht im Lichte des EU-Verfassungsentwurfs, in: Tagungsband 10. Würzburger Europarechtstage, Baden-Baden 2004
95. Interpretationsmethodische Aspekte, in: Tettinger/Stern (Hrsg.), Kölner Gemeinschafts-Kommentar Europäische Grundrechte-Charta, München 2006, S. 220–225
96. Grundrechtsschutz in Europa – Kooperation oder Kooperationsverweigerung, in: Akyürek/Baumgartner/Jahnel/Lienbacher/Stolzlechner (Hrsg.), Staat und Recht in europäischer Perspektive, FS für Heinz Schäffer, Wien 2006, S. 911–922
97. Die neuen Einreise- und Aufenthaltsbeschränkungen im Interesse der nationalen Sicherheit, in: Davy/Weber (Hrsg.), Paradigmenwechsel in der Einwanderungspolitik? Überlegungen zum neuen Zuwanderungsgesetz (Tagungsband), Baden-Baden 2006, S. 246–259
98. Marktfreiheit oder kooperative Gemeinwohlverwirklichung im internationalen Wirtschaftsrecht?, in: Leible/Ruffert (Hrsg.), Völkerrecht und IPR, Jena 2006, S. 71–88
99. Internationales Recht als höheres Recht, in: Starck (Hrsg.), Fortschritte der Verfassungsgerichtsbarkeit in der Welt – Teil II. Deutsch-Japanisches Kolloquium vom 25. bis 30. August 2004 in Göttingen und Osnabrück, Baden-Baden 2006, S. 61–83
100. Verfassungsgerichtsbarkeit als Element europäischer Verfassungslehre und europäischer Staatslehre, in: Grote/Härtel/Hain/Schmidt/Schmitz/Schuppert/Winterhoff (Hrsg.), Die Ordnung der Freiheit. Festschrift für Christian Starck. Tübingen 2007, S. 687–698
101. Der Stabilitätspakt in Bewegung: pactum de negotiando?, in: Gramlich/Häde/Weber/Zehetner (Hrsg.), Juristische Wechselreden. Festgabe für Hugo J. Hahn. Chemnitz 2007, S. 141–150
102. (mit Walter) Der Schutz der nationalen Sicherheit im Aufenthaltsrecht, in: Möllers/van Ooyen (Hrsg.), Jahrbuch öffentliche Sicherheit (JBÖS) 2006/2007, Frankfurt 2007, S 269–279
103. Die Verfassungsgerichtsbarkeit in der Bundesrepublik Deutschland, in: Starck/Weber (Hrsg.), Verfassungsgerichtsbarkeit in Westeuropa, Baden-Baden 2007, S. 37–66
104. Generalbericht: Verfassungsgerichtsbarkeit in Westeuropa, in: Starck/Weber (Hrsg.), Verfassungsgerichtsbarkeit in Westeuropa, Baden-Baden 2007, S. 313–376
105. Regionen im Europäischen Gemeinschaftsrecht: Regionalismus und Ausschuss der Regionen, in: Hufeld/Müller-Graff/Okruch (Hrsg.), Nachbarschaften innerhalb der Europäischen Union, Schriftenreihe des Arbeitskreise Europäische Integration Bd. 62, Baden-Baden 2007, S. 27–38

106. Europarechtliche Aspekte illegaler Migration, in: Becker/Hablitzel/Kressel (Hrsg.), Migration, Beschäftigung und soziale Sicherheit, Berlin 2007, S. 41–51
107. (mit Walter) Der gemeinschaftsrechtliche Schutz der Familie für Flüchtlinge, in: AWR-Bulletin 3/2007, S. 196–205
108. (mit Loer) Interkommunale Zusammenarbeit im Sinne der Zusammenarbeit von kommunalen Gebietskörperschaften mit eigenen Unternehmen (Eigengesellschaften) unter besonderer Berücksichtigung des ausschreibungsfreien Inhouse-Geschäfts, in: Vergaberecht 6/2007, S. 721–733
109. Die Individualverfassungsbeschwerde gegen gerichtliche Urteile, in: Heun/Starck, Verfassungsgerichtsbarkeit im Rechtsvergleich, Tagungsband Drittes deutsch-taiwanesisches Kolloquium vom 2.–3. Oktober 2006 an der Georg-August-Universität Göttingen, Baden-Baden 2007, S. 77–91
110. Vom Verfassungsvertrag zum Vertrag von Lissabon, in: EuZW 1/2008, S. 7–14
111. Europäischer Verfassungsvertrag und partizipative Demokratie, in: Ipsen/Stüer (Hrsg.), Europa im Wandel. Festschrift für Hans-Werner Rengeling, Köln, München 2008, S. 661–672
112. Migration im Vertrag von Lissabon, ZAR 2/2008, S. 55–58
113. Der Schutz der Verfassung durch Revisionsverbote und Notstandsregime in vergleichender Sicht, in: Fischer-Lescano/Grasser/Marauhn/Ronzitti (Hrsg.), Frieden in Freiheit Festschrift für Michael Bothe, Baden-Baden 2008, S. 1229–1241
114. Rechtsstaatsprinzip als gemeineuropäisches Verfassungsprinzip, in: ZÖR 63 (2008), S. 267–292
115. Das Bundesverfassungsgericht – Grundlagen und neuere Entwicklungen, in: Waseda Proceedings of Comparative Law 10/2007, Tokio 2008, S. 201–218
116. Der Raum der Freiheit, der Sicherheit und des Rechts im Vertrag von Lissabon, in: BayVBl. 16/2008, S. 485–489
117. Sitzverlegung von Gesellschaften in einen anderen EU-Mitgliedstaat – Anmerkungen zum Cartesio-Urteil des EuGH vom 6. Dezember 2008, in: Recht und Wirtschaft. Gedächtnisschrift Schindhelm, Köln 2009, S. 615–622
118. Die Europäische Union unter Richtervorbehalt?, in: JZ 4/2010, S. 157–164
119. Klimaschutz nach dem Lissabonner Vertrag, in: Haslinger/Kanonier/S. Zehetner (Hrsg.), Ein Jurist im Spannungsfeld von Wirtschaft, Technik und Recht. Festschrift für Franz Zehetner, Wien 2009, S. 123–131
120. Die Reform der Wirtschafts- und Währungsunion in der Finanzkrise, in: EuZW 24/2011, S. 935–940
121. Richterliche Unabhängigkeit in menschenrechtlicher Perspektive, Teil 1 in: DRiZ Januar 2012, S. 16–18; Teil 2 in: DRiZ Februar 2012, S. 59–61
122. Auf der Suche nach dem europäischen Juristen?, in: JÖR 60/2012, S. 307–316
123. Die Rechtssatzverfassungsbeschwerde in vergleichender Sicht, in: Sachs/Siekmann (Hrsg.), Der grundrechtsgeprägte Verfassungsstaat. FS für Klaus Stern. Berlin 2012, S. 1189 ff.

124. Der Vertrag von Lissabon vor dem polnischen Verfassungsgericht, in: EuGRZ 2012, S. 139–141
125. Die Europäische Union auf dem Wege zur Fiskalunion?, in: DVBl. 13/2012, S. 801–806
126. Menschenrechtlicher Schutz von Bootsflüchtlingen. Bedeutung des Straßburger *Hirsi-Jamaa*-Urteils für den Flüchtlingsschutz, in: ZAR 8/2012, S. 265–270
127. Schutz und Förderung der Roma in der EU in menschenrechtlicher Perspektive, in: ZAR 5–6/2013, S. 188–196
128. Europa- und völkerrechtliche Elemente der Gewährleistung von Haushaltsdisziplin in der Währungsunion, in: EuR 4/2013, S. 375–388
129. Europa- und völkerrechtliche Elemente der Gewährleistung von Haushaltsdisziplin in der Währungsunion, in: Blanke/Pilz (Hrsg.), Die „Fiskalunion", Tübingen 2014, S. 3-23
130. Kommentierung Präambel, Art. 7, Art. 23, Art. 25, Interpretationsmethodische Aspekte, in: Stern/Sachs (Hrsg.), Europäische Grundrechtecharta, Kommentar, München 2015
131. Europäische Wirtschaftsregierung, in: Griller/Obwexer (Hrsg.), Die "schleichende" Reform der EU im Zuge der Bekämpfung der Wirtschafts- und Staatsschuldenkrise , ECSA Tagung Innsbruck 25./26.11.2014. EuR Beiheft 2015

III. Journal Articles and Book Chapters in other Languages

1. Safeguards in International Economic Organizations in Times of Crisis with Special Reference to the EEC, in: German Yearbook of International Law 1984, S. 212–232
2. La participation directe du citoyen à la vie politique, Deutscher Nationalbericht für das Colloque 12. Journées Juridiques Jean Dabin, in Louvain, 1985 in: Référendums, (sous la direction de Francis Delpérée), 1985, S. 325–355
3. The role of Comparative Law in the Civil Liberties Jurisprudence, of German Courts, in: de Mestral/Birks/Bothe/Cotler/Klinck/Morel (Hrsg), The Limitation of Human Rights in Comparative Constitutional Law, 1987, S. 525–548
4. Jurisdicción Constitucional en Europa occidental. Una Comparación, in: Revista de Derecho Constitucional 1986, S. 47–83
5. Le contrôle juridictionnel de la Constitutionalité des lois dans les pays d'Europe Occidentale, in: Annuaire International de Justice Constitutionnelle (AIJC) 1985, S. 39–76
6. The supranationality problem, in: Starck (Hrsg.), Rights, Institutions and Impact of International Law according to the German Basic Law, Baden-Baden 1987, S. 225–241
7. Investment Risks in International Law, in: Oppermann (Hrsg.), Reforming the International Order, Berlin 1987, S. 20–25

8. Fundamental Rights and Judicial Review in Canada, in: JÖR 36/1988, S. 597–620
9. La protección de la propiedad en el Derecho comparado, in: CIVITAS, Revista española de derecho administrativo 1991, S. 477–490
10. Il Diritto Amministrativo Procedimentale nell'ordinamento della Comunità Europea, in: Rivista Italiana di Diritto Pubblico Comunitario (RIDPC) 1992, S. 393–412
11. Allemagne; Nationalbericht, in: Masclet/Maus (Hrsg.), Les constitutions nationales à l'épreuve de l'Europe, Paris 1993, S. 17–25
12. La Révision Constitutionnelle en Allemagne après l'unification allemande et le Traité de Maastricht, in: Revue de Recherche Juridique, Droit Prospectif 3/1993, S. 777–793
13. Comunidad europea: El procedimiento administrativo en el derecho comunitario, in: Barnés (Hrsg.), El procedimiento administrativo en el derecho comparado, 1993, S. 57–90
14. Federalismo e Regionalismo nell'Unione Europea, in: RIDPC 1993, S. 705–722
15. L'équilibre budgetaire dans le droit fédéral allemand, Nationalbericht für Kolloquium Paris-Nanterre, 12 et 13 mai 1992, in: L'èquilibre budgetaire (sous la direction de Tallineau), Paris 1994, S. 231–240
16. Le traité de Maastricht devant les jurisdictions constitutionnelles, in: AIJC 1993, S. 11–30
17. Il trattato di Maastricht sul banco di prova delle corti costituzionali europee, in: RIDPC 1996, S. 1215–1237
18. El control del tratado de Maastricht por la Jurisdicción constitucional desde una perspectiva comparada, in: Revista española de derecho constitucional 1995, S. 31–51
19. L'état social et les droits sociaux en RFA, in: Revue Française de Droit Constitutionnel (RFDC) 1995, S. 677–693
20. (mit C. Grewe) L'arrêt de la Cour constitutionnelle allemande relative au crucifix, in: RFDC 1996, S. 183–188
21. Judicial Review in the Federal Republic of Germany, in: Yong Zhang (Hrsg.), Comparative Studies on the Judicial Review System in East and Southeast Asia, Den Haag u. a. 1997, S. 237–251
22. Nationalbericht Alemaña, in: Eliseo Aja (Hrsg.), Las tensiones entre el Tribunal Constitucional y el Legislador en la Europa actual, Barcelona 1998, S. 53–88
23. Sviluppi nel diritto amministrativo europeo, in: Rivista italiana di diritto pubblico comunitario 1998, S. 589–609
24. Estado social, derechos sociales fundamentales y protección social en la República Federal de Alemaña, in: Muñoz Machado et. al., Las Estructuras del Bienestar en Europa, Madrid 1999, S. 569–578

25. Possibilità e limiti dell'armonizzazione europea del diritto d'asilo prima c dopo Amsterdam, in: Rivista italiana di diritto pubblico comunitario 1998, S. 1003–1019
26. European Monetary Union (EMU) and its Impact on Monetary Relations of Non-Members (including EEA), in: Müller-Graff/Selvig (Hrsg.), EEA-EU Relations, Berlin 1999, S. 147–161
27. La interpretación de la Constitución por la jurisdicción ordinaria en Alemaña (Beitrag zum 20-jährigen Bestehen der spanischen Verfassung), in: Cuadernos de Derecho Publico 1999, S. 41–64
28. La interpretación de la Constitución por la Jurisdicción Ordinaria, in: Revista Canaria de Ciencias Penales 1999, S. 31–47
29. The European Charter of Fundamental Rights, in: Swedish Law Journal of European Law (Europarättslig Tidskrift) 2000, S. 447–453
30. The European Charter of Fundamental Rights, in: German Yearbook of International Law, 43/2001, S. 101–115
31. (mit Gas) République fédérale d'Allmagne – Justice constitutionnelle et subsidiarité, in: Delpérée (Hrsg.), Justice constitutionnelle et subsidiarité, Brüssel 2000, S. 137–177
32. La Carta europea de derechos fundamentales y la protección nacional de los derechos fundamentales. Ordenamientos separados de derechos fundamentales, relación de cooperación o coordinación *cuasifederal*?, in: Aragón/Jiménez/Solozábal (Hrsg.), La democracia constitucional, Festschrift für Rubio Llorente, Madrid 2003, S. 1391–1405
33. La Carta de los Derechos Fundamentales de la Unión Europea, in: Revista Española de Derecho Constitucional 64/2002, S. 79–97
34. Rapport allemand: La réinvention ou l'affaiblissement de l'État ?, in: Milacic (Hrsg.), Tagungsband zum Kolloquium « La Réunion de l'État » in Paris, April 2002, Brüssel 2003, S. 333–344
35. Il futuro della Carta dei Diritti fondamentali dell'Unione europea, in: Rivista Italiana di Diritto Pubblico Comunitario 1/2002, S. 31–45
36. Tipos de jurisdicción constitucional, in: Anuario Iberoamericano de Justicia Constitucional 6/2003, S. 583–599
37. Die Grundrechtsbeschwerde in rechtsvergleichender Sicht, in: F. Fernández Segado (Hrsg.), The Spanish Constitution in the European Constitutional Context (Festschrift zum 25jährigen Bestehen der spanischen Verfassung), Madrid 2003, S. 1217–1231
38. A reforma institucional nas resoluções da Convenção sobre o Futuro da Europa, in: Instituto Europeu da Faculdade de Direito de Lisboa u. a. (Hrsg.), Uma Constituição para a Europa, Colóquio internacional de Lisboa, Maio de 2003, Aldedina 2004, S. 139–158
39. La jurisdicción constitucional de la República federal de Alemania, in: Anuario Iberoamericano de Justicia Constitucional 7/2003, S. 495–538.
40. Notes sur la justice constitutionnelle comparée: Convergences et divergences, in: Annuaire International de Justice Constitutionnelle (AIJC) XIX/2003, S. 29–41

41. Die Regionen als verfassungsrechtliche Voraussetzung des Europarechts, in: Essays in Honour of Georgios I. Kassimatis, Athen u. a., 2004, S. 891–903
42. La Carta Europea de los Derechos Fundamentales desde la perspectiva comparada, in: Pensamiento Constitucional 9/2003, S. 229–241
43. The New Asylum and Immigration Law in Europe – Constitutional and Human Rights Aspects, in: Tagungsband The 4th International Immigration Conference, Warschau 2005, S. 65–73
    The New Asylum and Immigration Law in Europe – Constitutional and Human Rights Aspects, in: AWR-Bulletin 1/2005
44. The Constitutionalization of Unwritten Principles in European Law, in: Riedel (Hrsg.), Constitutionalism – Old Concepts, New Worlds, Berlin 2005, S. 187–197
45. Les droits sociaux constitutionnels en République fédérale d'Allemagne, in: Gay/Mazuyer/Nazet-Alluche (Hrsg.), Les droits sociaux fondamentaux. Entre droits nationaux et droit européen, Brüssel 2006
46. Double ou triple protection des droits fondamentaux en Europe ?, in: Roux/ Ghevontian/Bon/Maus/Soucramanien (Hrsg.), Renouveau du droit constitutionnel (Gedenkschrift Favoreu), Paris 2007, S. 1747–1759
47. La participation des *Länder* allemands aux Communautés européennes dans la perspective du fédéralisme comparé, in: En hommage à Francis Delpérée. Itinéraires d'un constiutionaliste, Bruylant 2007, S. 1719–1730
48. Intervento, in: Falcon (Hrsg.), Il procedimento amministrativo nei diritti europei e nel diritto comunitario, Mailand 2008, S. 339–342
49. El principio de estado de derecho como rincipio constitucional común europeo, in: REDC 2008, S. 27–59
50. A la busca del jurista europeo, Text der Abschiedsvorlesung vom 25.6.2010 in der Übersetzung von Jaime Nicolás Muñiz, in : REDC 3/2011, S. 11–23
51. The Distribution of Competences Between the Union and the Member States, in: Blanke/Mangiameli (Hrsg.), The European Union after Lisbon, Heidelberg 2012, S. 311-321
52. Elementos de derecho europeo e internacional para la garantía de la disciplina presupuestaria en la unión monetaria, in: Revista española de derecho constitucional 2013, S. 39-61
53. Article 5, in: Blanke/Mangiameli (Hrsg.), The Treaty on European Union (TEU), Heidelberg 2013, S. 255–286
54. Article 122, in: Blanke/Mangiameli (Hrsg.), The Treaty on the Functioning of the European Union (TFEU), Heidelberg, i. V.

IV. Reports

1. Bericht über das deutsch-spanische Verfassungskolloquium vom 18.–20.06.1980 in Berlin, in: JZ 1981, S. 38–39
2. Staatsrechtslehrertagung in Trier (1981), in: JZ 1981, S. 849–853

V. Case Notes

1. BVerfG vom 01.09.1976 – VII B 101/76 – (Rechtsnatur von Petitionsbescheiden), in: NJW 1977, S. 594–595
2. BVerfG vom 08.06.1977 (Eigentumsrecht; Interventionsansprüche) in: DÖV, 1978, S. 176–178
3. EuGH vom 27.11.1977 (Bouchereau: Art. 48 EWGV, öffentliche Ordnung) in: NJW, 1978, S. 1105–1106
4. BVerfG vom 26.09.1978 (Aufenthaltserlaubnis, Vertrauensschutz) in: DÖV 1979, S. 370–371
5. BVerfG vom 20.12.1979 (Atomrecht: Mühlheim-Kärlich), in: JZ 1980, S. 314–315
6. BVerfG vom 29.06.1983 (Amtsbezeichnung von Hochschullehrern), in: JZ 1984, S. 323 (327)
7. BVerwG vom 17.12.86 – BVerwG 7 C 29.85 – (KKW Lingen), in: DVBl. 1987, S. 377–380
8. EuGH vom 31.12.1991 (Fall C-18/19, Bahia Kziber), in: Common Market Law Review 28/1991, S. 959–963
9. BVerfG vom 31.10.1991 (Kommunalwahlrecht für Ausländer), in: Revue Française de Droit Constitutionnel, 7/1991, S. 553–555
10. Corte di Giustizia Justizia della Communitá Europea vom 30. Juni 1991 (Causa 59/89), in: Rivista Italiana di Diritto Publico Comunitario 1992, S. 911–921
11. EuGH vom 16.12.1992 (Fall C-237/91, Kazim Kus), in: Common Market Law Review 1994, S. 423–427
12. (mit C. Grewe): Die Reform des Ausländer- und Asylrechts in Frankreich/Die Entscheidung des Conseil Constitutionnel vom 13. August 1993, in: EuGRZ 1993, S. 496–499
13. Italienischer Verfassungsgerichtshof vom 14.11.1997 (Nr. 329, Giurisprudenza Costituzionale, 1997 FASC.6, S. 3335), in: EuGRZ 1999, S. 662-665
14. Strafrechtliche Gleichbehandlung von Glaubensbekenntnissen, Anmerkung zur Entscheidung der Corte Costituzionale, Rom, vom 14.11.1997, EuGRZ 1998, S. 663
15. EGMR vom 10.11.2005 (Leyla Şahin v. Turkey, Application no. 44774/98), in: DVBl. 2006, S. 167–174
16. Die Kontrolle von Nichtvorlagen letztinstanzlicher Gerichte an den EuGH/ Überlegungen aus Anlass von EGMR, Ullens de Schooten, EuGRZ 2012, S. 133-138
17. Der Vertrag von Lissabon vor dem polnischen Verfassungsgericht, in: EuGRZ 2012, S. 139–141

VI. Book Reviews

1. Jütter Heinrich: Förderung und Schutz deutscher Direktinvestitionen in Entwicklungsländern, Baden-Baden 1975, in: Kredit und Kapital 3, 1976, S. 426–428
2. Stollberg, Frank: Die verfassungsrechtlichen Grundlagen des Parteienverbots, Berlin 1976, in: BayVBl, 1977, S. 159–160
3. Kupper, Siegfried: Der innerdeutsche Handel. Rechtliche Grundlagen, politische und wirtschaftliche Bedeutung. Köln 1972. Ehlermann/Kupper/Lambrecht/Ollig: Handelspartner DDR – Innerdeutsche Wirtschaftsbeziehungen, Baden-Baden 1975, in: AöR 102 (1977), S. 151–155
4. Bünten, Wilfried: Staatsgewalt und Gemeinschaftshoheit bei der innerstaatlichen Durchführung des Rechts der Europäischen Gemeinschaften, Berlin 1977, in: BayVBl, 1978, S. 318
5. Roth, Wulf-Henning: Freier Warenverkehr und staatliche Regelungsgewalt in einem Gemeinsamen Markt, München 1977, in: Österreichische Zeitschrift für Rechtsvergleichung, 1978, S. 225–226, zugleich in: Modern Law and Society, 1979, S. 52–53
6. Natermann, Eberhard: Der Eurodollarmarkt in rechtlicher Sicht, in: Österreichisches Bank-Archiv, 1979, S. 72–74
7. Fröhler/Zehetner: Rechtsschutzprobleme bei grenzüberschreitenden Umweltbeeinträchtigungen, Bd. I, 1979, in: BayVBl, 1981, S. 669
8. Carreau/Juillard/Flory: Droit International Economique, Paris 1978, 1980, in: Kredit und Kapital, 1980, S. 282–284
9. Kohler, Beate: Politischer Umbruch in Südeuropa – Portugal, Griechenland, Spanien auf dem Weg zur Demokratie. Europäische Schriften des Instituts für europäische Politik, Bonn 1981, in: DVBl 1982, S. 709
10. Böckenförde/Tomuschat/Umbach: Extremisten im öffentlichen Dienst, Baden-Baden 1982, in: DVBl, 1982, S. 142
11. Hilf, Meinhard: Die Organisationsstruktur der Europäischen Gemeinschaften, in: NJW 22, 1983, S. 1247
12. Mackert, J./Schneider, F. (Hrsg.): Bibliographie zur Verfassungsgerichtsbarkeit des Bundes und der Länder, Bd. 3, in: JZ 1983, S. 623
13. Schnur, Roman: Vive la Rėpublique oderVive la France. Zur Krise der Demokratie in Frankreich 1939/40, Schriften zur Verfassungsgeschichte, Bd. 34. in: DVBl 1984, S. 841
14. Encyclopedia of Public International Law, Bd. 5: International Organisations in General, Bd. 6: Regional Cooperation, Organisations and Problems, in: ZaöRV 1984, S. 364–369
15. Rettberg, Jürgen: Weltwährungsfond und Weltbankgruppe und Unctad. Studien zum internationalen Wirtschaftsrecht und Atomenergierecht. Begründet von Georg Erler. Volkmar Götz, Dietrich Rauschning, Gottfried Zieger (Hrsg.), Bd. 69, Köln 1983, in: DVBl 1985, S. 1195

16. Däubler, Wolfgang: Privatisierung als Rechtsproblem, Reihe Demokratie und Rechtsstaat. in: AöR 106 (1981), S. 496
17. Biskup, Reinhold: Deutschlands offene Handelsgrenze. Die DDR als Nutznießer des EWG-Protokolls über den innerdeutschen Handel, Berlin 1977, in: JZ 1978, S. 120
18. Grimmer: Demokratie und Grundrechte. Schriften zum öffentlichen Recht, Bd. 382, in: AöR 108 (1983), S. 325–326
19. Quick, Reinhard: Exportselbstbeschränkungen und Art. XIX GATT. Studien zum internationalen Wirtschaftsrecht und Atomenergierecht. Begründet von Georg Erler. Volkmar Götz, Dietrich Rauschning, Gottfried Ziegler (Hrsg.) Bd. 67, in: DVBl 1985, S. 1197
20. Isam Kamel Salem: Islam und Völkerrecht. Das Völkerrecht in der islamischen Weltanschauung, in: ZAR 1984, S. 214
21. v. Bothe/Prieur/Ress (Hrsg.): Fachtagung-Colloque Saarbrücken v. 13.–15. Mai 1982. Rechtsfragen grenzüberschreitender Umweltbelastungen. Les problèmes juridiques posés par les pollutions transfrontières, in: DVBl 1984, S. 799
22. Schwan, Hartmut Heinrich: Die deutschen Bundesländer im Entscheidungssystem der Europäischen Gemeinschaften, Beschlußfassung und Durchführung, Schriften zum öffentlichen Recht. Bd. 433, Berlin 1982, in: DÖV 1984, S. 1036
23. Sommermann, Karl Peter: Der Schutz der Grundrechte in Spanien nach der Verfassung von 1978. Ursprünge, Dogmatik, Praxis, Schriften zum öffentlichen Recht, Bd. 472. Berlin/München 1984, in: DVBl 1985, S. 638
24. v. Gerhard Lüke/Georg Ress/Michael R. Will (Hrsg.): Rechtsvergleichung, Europarecht und Staatenintegration, Gedächtnisschrift für Léontin-Jean Constantinesco. Schriftenreihe Annales Universitatis Saraviensis, Rechts- und Wirtschaftswissenschaftliche Abteilung, Bd. 100, in: DVBl 1985, S. 1091–1092
25. J.J. González Encinar: Diccionário Del Sistema Politico Espanol, AKAL. Madrid 1984, in: AöR 111 (1986), S. 663
26. Huthmacher, Karl-Eugen: Der Vorrang des Gemeinschaftsrechts bei indirekten Kollisionen. Eine Studie zum Verhältnis von EG-Recht zu nationalem Vollzugsrecht, dargestellt am Beispiel des Konflikts zwischen materiellem EG-Recht und nationalen Rechtsmittelfristen, Köln 1985. in: DVBl 1985, S. 1028
27. Ingo v. Münch/Andreas Buske: International Law. The essential treaties and other relevant documents, in: DVBl 1986, S. 704
28. Weimar/Schimikowski: Grundzüge des Wirtschaftsrechts, 1983. in: DVBl 1986, S. 790
29. Europa ringt um seine Wirtschaftsverfassung, Liber Amicorum aus Anlaß des 60. Geburtstags von Dr. Karl-Heinz Narjes. 1984. in: DVBl 1986, S. 201
30. Gemeinschaftskommentar zum Asylverfahrensgesetz, 2. Aufl., Loseblatt-Werk, ab 1.7.1986, in: DVBl 1987, S. 542

31. Harz, Annegret, Die Schutzklauseln des Kapital- und Zahlungsverkehrs im EWG-Vertrag, Band 72, in: DVBl. 1987, S. 596
32. Antoniou, Theodora, Europäische Integration und griechische Verfassung; Schriften zum Staats- und Völkerrecht, Bd. 21, 1985, in: DVBl 1987, S. 434
33. Kälin, Walter, Verfassungsgerichtsbarkeit in der Demokratie. Funktionen der staatsrechtlichen Beschwerde, Stämpfli, 1987, in: JZ 1988, S. 553
34. Hummer/Schweitzer, Österreich und die EWG. Neutralitätsrechtliche Beurteilung der Möglichkeiten der Dynamisierung des Verhältnisses zur EWG, Wien 1987, in: DVBl 1988, S. 416
35. Brun-Otto Bryde/Philip Kunig/Thomas Oppermann (Hrsg.), Neuordnung der Weltwirtschaft? Hamburger Herbert-Krüger-Colloquium 1986, in: DVBl 1988, S. 372
36. Karl, Wolfram/Miehsler, Herbert, Internationaler Kommentar zur Europäischen Menschenrechtskonvention, in: DVBl 1988, S. 913
37. Cromme, Franz, Verfassungsvertrag d. Gemeinschaft der Vereinigten Staaten, in: DVBl 1988, S. 800
38. Cruz Villalón, Pedro: La formación del sistema europeo de control de constitucionalidad (1918–1939), Madrid 1987, in: ZaöRV 1988, Bd. 48, S. 540
39. Kohlhase, Einheit in der Vielfalt – Essays zur Europäischen Geschichte, Kultur und Gesellschaft, 1988, 261 S., in: DVBl 1990, S. 176
40. Hundertmark, Dr. Ulrich, Die Durchführung der Umweltverträglichkeitsprüfung, Beiträge zur Umweltgestaltung, Band A 105, DVBl 1990, S. 548
41. Karpen, Ulrich, The Constitution of the Federal Republic of Germany, Baden-Baden 1988, in: DVBl 1990, S. 723
42. Paschen Herbert, Die Rolle der Umweltverträglichkeitsprüfung im Entscheidungsprozeß, Beiträge zur Umweltgestaltung, Band A 113 (1989), in: DVBl 1991, S. 176
43. Schulze-Fielitz, H., Theorie und Praxis parlamentarischer Gesetzgebung – besonders des 9. Deutschen Bundestags (1980–83) –, in: AöR 114/3 (1989), S. 494–497
44. Schweitzer/Hummer, Europarecht, Juristische Lernbücher, Bd. 16, 3. Aufl. 1990, in: NJW 1991, S. 613
45. Langenfeld, Christine, Die Gleichbehandlung von Mann und Frau im Europäischen Gemeinschaftsrecht, in: DVBl 1990, S. 1245–1246
46. Engel, Christoph, Völkerrecht als Tatbestandsmerkmal deutscher Normen, Tübinger Schriften zum internationalen und europäischen Recht, Bd. 19, 359S., in: DVBl 1992, S. 796
47. Streinz, Rudolf, Bundesverfassungsgerichtliche Kontrolle über die deutsche Mitwirkung am Entscheidungsprozeß im Rat der Europäischen Gemeinschaften, Schriften zum europäischen Recht, Bd. 3, in: JZ 1990, S. 1124
48. Landfried, Christine, Constitutional Review and Legislation. An International Comparison, Baden-Baden 1988, in: Der Staat 1/91, S. 146
50. Reports on German Public Law, Hrsg. Rudolf Bernhardt/Ulrich Beyerlin, XIIth International Congress of Comparative Law, 1990, in: AöR 117/I (1992), S. 132

51. Fabricius, Fritz. Streik und Aussperrung im internat. Recht, in: Vierteljahresschrift für Sozial- und Wirtschaftsgeschichte 79, Band 1992, S. 105
52. Handbuch der internat. Rechts- und Verwaltungssprache, in: DVBl. 1991, S. 1384
53. Kloepfer, Michael, Zur Rechtsumbildung durch Umweltschutz, in: AöR 117 (1992), S. 327
54. Prof.Dr. Christian Starck, Grundgesetz und deutsche Verfassungsrechtsprechung im Spiegel ausländischer Verfassungsentwicklung, in: DVBl 1991, S. 887
55. Handbuch der Umweltverträglichkeitsprüfung (HdUVP), Hrsg.: Peter-Christoph Storm und Thomas Bunge, Bielefeld 1991, in: NVwZ 1992, S. 156
56. Reinhard Marx: Asylrecht und Menschenrechte, Bd. 1, Asylrecht Bd. 2 und Bd. 3, 5. Aufl. 1991, in: DVBl 1992, S. 733
57. Kay Hailbronner/Günter Renner: StAngR, Staatsangehörigkeitsrecht, Kommentar, 1991, in: DVBl 1992, S. 851
58. Jörg Luther: Die italienische Verfassungsgerichtsbarkeit. Geschichte, Prozeß, Rechtsprechung. Nomos-Verlag, Baden-Baden 1990. 222 S. Brosch., in: DVBl. 1992, S. 1611
59. Kay Hailbronner, Ausländerrecht, Kommentar, 4. Ergänzungslieferung Juni 1994, C.F. Müller Verlag, Heidelberg, in: DVBl. 1995, S. 816
60. Bertold Humber, Handbuch des Ausländer- und Asylrechts, 1994, Verlag C.H. Beck, München, in: DVBl. 1995, S. 1033
61. Walter Kälin (Hrsg.), Aktuelle Probleme des Menschenrechtsschutzes, 1994, Berichte der Deutschen Gesellschaft für Völkerrecht, Bd. 33, C.F. Müller Verlag, Heidelberg, in: AÖR 1994, S. 3295
62. Streinz, Rudolf, Europarecht, 2. völlig neu überarb. Aufl., C.F. Müller Verlag, Heidelberg 1995, in: JZ 1995, S.
63. Kay Hailbronner, Ausländerrecht, Kommentar, 5. Ergänzungslieferung November 1994, C.F. Müller Verlag, Heidelberg, in: DVBl. 1995, S. 816
64. Kay Hailbronner, Ausländerrecht, Kommentar, 7. Ergänzungslieferung Juli 1995 und 8. Ergänzungslieferung Dezember 1995, C.F. Müller Verlag, Heidelberg, in: DVBl. 1996, S. 448 f.
65. Bertold Huber, Handbuch des Ausländer- und Asylrechts, 3. Ergänzungslieferung Oktober 1995, in: DVBl. 1997, S. 133 f.
66. Bertold Huber, Handbuch der Ausländer- und Asylrechts, 6. Ergänzungslieferung November 1996, in: DVBl. 1997, S. 1348
67. Kay Hailbronner, Rückübernahme eigener und fremder Staatsangehöriger. Völkerrechtliche Verpflichtungen, C.F. Müller Verlag, Heidelberg, in: DVBl. 1998, S. 62 f.
68. M. Schefer, Konkretisierung von Grundrechten durch den US Supreme Court. Zur sprachlichen, historischen und demokratischen Argumentation im Verfassungsrecht, Schriften zum Internationalen Recht, Bd. 82, Duncker & Humblot, Berlin, 1997, in: DVBl. 1997, S. 1399

69. José Martínez Soria, Die Garantie des Rechtsschutzes gegen die öffentliche Gewalt in Spanien, Schriften zum Internationalen Recht, Bd. 85, Duncker & Humblot, Berlin 1997, in: DVBl. 1997, S. 1451
70. Kay Hailbronner, Ausländerrecht – Kommentar, 11. Ergänzungslieferung, März 1997, 12. Ergänzungslieferung, Juni 1997, C.F. Müller Verlag, Heidelberg, in: DVBl. 1998, S. 1308
71. Annette Rey, Einwanderung in Frankreich 1981–1995, Leske und Budrich Verlag, Opladen, 1997, in: ZAR 1998, S. 146
72. Thomas Fleiner-Gerner (Hrsg.), Die multikulturelle und multi-ethnische Gesellschaft. Eine neue Herausforderung an die Europäische Verfassung. Wissenschaftliches Kolloquium zu Ehren des 60. Geburtstages von Peter Häberle in Disentis, Institut du Fédéralisme Fribourg Suisse, 1995, in: DVBl. 1998, S. 976
73. Katja Gelinsky, Der Schutz des Eigentums gemäß Art. 1 des Ersten Zusatzprotokolls zur Europäischen Menschenrechtskonvention,
und
Olaf Müller-Michaels, Grundrechtlicher Eigentumsschutz in der Europäischen Union, in: ZÖR 1998
74. Bertold Huber, Handbuch des Ausländer- und Asylrechts, 8. Ergänzunglieferung, August 1997, C.H. Beck Verlag, in: DVBl.
75. Ruth Lang, Die Mitwirkungsrechte des Bundesrates und des Bundestages in Angelegenheiten der Europäischen Union gemäß Artikel 23 Abs. 2 bis 7 GG, Schriften zum Europäischen Recht, Band 36, Duncker & Humblot, Berlin 1997, in: AöR 1998
77. Franz Cromme, Spezifische Verfassungselemente des Staatenverbundes. Bausteine für die Europäische Union, in: DVBl. 1998, S. 1303
78. Christian Autexier, Introduction au droit public allemand, in: DVBl. 1998
79. Jan Ziekow, Über Freizügigkeit und Aufenthalt. Paradigmatische Überlegungen zum grundrechtlichen Freiheitsschutz in historischer und verfassungsrechtlicher Perspektive, 1997, Mohr (Paul Siebeck) Verlag, 734 Seiten, in: DVBl. 1999
80. Hailbronner/Renner, Staatsangehörigkeitsrecht, 2. Aufl., C. H. Beck 1998, in: DVBl. 1999
81. Peter Häberle (Hrsg.) Jahrbuch des öffentlichen Rechts der Gegenwart, NF 4, Mohr Siebeck, Tübingen, in: DVBl. 1999, S. 340–341
82. Kirsten Wendland, Spanien auf dem Weg zum Bundesstaat? Entstehung und Entwicklung der autonomen Gemeinschaften, Nomos Verlagsgesellschaft, Baden-Baden 1998, in: DVBl. 1999, S. 583–584
83. Peter Häberle (Hrsg.), Jahrbuch des öffentlichen Rechts der Gegenwart, NF 46, Mohr Siebeck, Tübingen, in: DVBl. 1999, S. 1064–1065
84. Astrid Wallrabenstein, Das Verfassungsrecht der Staatsangehörigkeit, Nomos Verlagsgesellschaft, Nomos, Baden-Baden 1999, in: DVBl. 2000
85. Miriam Wolter, Auf dem Weg zu einem gemeinschaftlichen Asylrecht in der Europäischen Union. Rechtsvergleichende Betrachtung des materiellen Asylrechts der EU-Mitgliedstaaten im Hinblick auf eine Vergemeinschaftung

der Materie, Kieler Rechtswissenschaftliche Abhandlungen (NF), Bd. 21, in: DVBl. 2001, S. 357–358
86. Kai Hailbronner, Die allgemeinen Regeln des völkerrechtlichen Fremdenrechts. Bilanz und Ausblick an der Jahrtausendwende. Beiträge anlässlich des Kolloquiums zu Ehren von Prof. Dr. Karl Dohering aus Anlass seines 80. Geburtstags am 17. März 1999 in Konstanz, C.F. Müller, Heidelberg, in: DVBl. 2001, S. 1409–1410
87. Peter Häberle, Europäische Verfassungslehre in Einzelstudien, Nomos, Baden-Baden 1999, in: DVBl. 2002, S. 317–318
88. Kai Hailbronner, Ausländerrecht – Kommentar, 22.–29. Ergänzungslieferung, C.F. Müller Verlag, Heidelberg 2000/2001, in: DVBl. 2002, S. 895–896
89. François Venter, Constitutional Comparison. Japan, Germany, Canada and South Africa as Constitutional States, Kluwer Law International, Den Haag 2000, in: DVBl. 2002, S. 113–114
90. Hailbronner/Klein (Hrsg.), Flüchtlinge – Menschenrechte – Staatsangehörigkeit. Menschenrechte und Migration, C.F. Müller, Heidelberg 2001, in: DVBl. 8/2003, S. 509–510
91. K. Stern (Hrsg.), Zeitgemäßes Zuwanderungs- und Asylrecht – ein Problem der Industriestaaten, Schriften zum Öffentlichen Recht 922, Duncker & Humblot, Berlin 2003, in: DVBl. 7/2004, S. 421
92. Franz Cromme, Verfassungsvertrag der Europäischen Union, Nomos, Baden-Baden 2003, in: DVBl. 9/2005, S. 561–562
93. Peter Häberle, Jahrbuch des Öffentlichen Rechts. NF 51, Mohr Siebeck, Tübingen 2003, in: DVBl. 21/2004, S. 1353
94. Horst Call, Grundrechtsschutz in Schweden unter rechtsvergleichenden Gesichtspunkten. Verlag Duncker & Humblot, Berlin 2003, in: DÖV 2005, S. 220
95. Peter Häberle, Europäische Verfassungslehre, 2. Aufl., Nomos, Baden-Baden 2004, in: DVBl. 6/2005, S. 359
96. Jochen Gebauer, Die Grundfreiheiten des EG-Vertrags als Gemeinschaftsgrundrechte, Verlag Duncker & Humblot, Berlin 1994, in: DÖV 2005, S. 87
97. Hailbronner/Renner†, Staatsangehörigkeitsrecht, 4. Aufl., Beck, München 2005
98. Christoph Ohler, Die Kollisionsordnung des Allgemeinen Verwaltungsrechts, Mohr Siebeck Tübingen 2005, in: DVBl. 2006, S. 759
99. Kay Hailbronner, Ausländer- und Asylrecht. Vorschriftensammlung, 2. Aufl., C. F. Müller, Heidelberg 2005, in: DVBl. 2008
100. Schulze/Zuleeg, Europarecht. Handbuch für die deutsche Rechtspraxis, Nomos, Baden-Baden 2006, in: ZAR 2006
101. Peter Häberle, Europäische Verfassungslehre, 4. aktualisierte und erweiterte Auflage, Nomos, Baden-Baden 2006, in: DVBl. 2007, S. 1095
102. Kay Hailbronner, Asyl- und Ausländerrecht, Kohlhammer, Stuttgart 2006, in: DVBl. 2008, S. 1177

103. Kay Hailbronner, Ausländerrecht. Kommentar, 57. Ergänzungslieferung, C.F. Müller, Heidelberg 2008, in: DVBl. 8/2008, S. 1374
104. Peter Häberle, Europäische Verfassungslehre, 5. Aufl., Nomos, Baden-Baden 2007, in: DVBl. 22/2008, S. 1433
105. Ingo von Münch, Die deutsche Staatsangehörigkeit. Vergangenheit, Gegenwart, Zukunft, De Gruyter Recht, Berlin 2007, in: DVBl. 7/2009, S. 436
106. Nadezda Siskova (Hrsg.), The Process of Constitutionalisation of the EU and Related Issues, Europa Law Publishing 2008, in: DVBl. 22/2009, S. 1436
107. Kay Hailbronner, Ausländerrecht. Kommentar, 58.–65. Ergänzungslieferung, C.F. Müller, Heidelberg, in: DVBl. 8/2010, S. 500–501
108. Waldemar Hummer/Wolfgang Karl, Regionaler Menschenrechtsschutz, 2 Bände, Bd. I: Allgemeiner Schutzbereich, Teilband I/1 Europa, Nomos, Baden-Baden 2009, in: DVBl. 10/2010, S. 641–642
109. Häberle, P.; Verfassungsvergleichung in weltbürgerlicher Absicht; hrsg. von M. Kotzur/L. Michael; Schriften zum Öffentlichen Recht, Band 1127; Duncker & Humblot, Berlin 2009, in: DVBl. 17/2010, S. 1097
110. Franz Cromme, Die Zukunft des Lissabon-Vertrags. Ein kurzgefasster und dynamischer Verfassungsvertrag. Entwurf und Begründung, Nomos, Baden-Baden 2010, in: DVBl. 2/2011, S. 88–89
111. Tobias M. Wagner, Parlamentsvorbehalt und Parlamentsbeteiligungsgesetz. Die Beteiligung des Bundestages bei Auslandseinsätzen der Bundeswehr, Beiträge zum Parlamentsrecht 66, Duncker & Humblot, Berlin 2010, in: DVBl. 5/2011, S. 284
112. Diana-Urania Galetta, Procedural Autonomy of EU Member States: Paradise Lost? A Study on the "Functionalized Procedural Competence" of EU Member States, Springer Verlag, Heidelberg 2010, in: DVBl. 8/2011, S. 483
113. Sebastian Steinharth, Das Institut der Präsidenten- und Ministeranklage in rechtshistorischer und rechtsvergleichender Perspektive. Ursprünge, Erscheinungsformen und bleibende Sinnhaftigkeit von Gerichts- und Impeachmentverfahren zur Durchsetzung gubernativer Verantwortlichkeit. Hannoverisches Forum der Rechtswissenschaft 36, Nomos, Baden-Baden 2010, ZParl 4/2011
114. Simon Burger, Verantwortung und Verantwortlichkeit für die Umsetzung supranationalen Rechts im Bundesstaat. Die horizontale und vertikale Zuordnung der Umsetzungspflichten einschließlich der Haftung, Dissertation Köln, Shaker Verlag, Aachen 2010, in: DVBl. 4/2012, S. 227
115. Daniel Thym, Migrationsverwaltungsrecht, JusPublicum 188, MohrSiebeck, Tübingen 2010, in: DVBl. 5/2012, S. 284–285
116. Manfred A. Dauses, Protection of Fundamental Rights in the Legal Order of the European Union. With Emphasis on the Institutional Protection of those Rights, Peter Lang Verlag, 2010, in: DVBl. 18/2012, S. 1157
117. Jürgen Bast, Aufenthaltsrecht und Migrationssteuerung, Ius Publicum 207, Mohr Siebeck, Tübingen 2011, in: DVBl. 18/2012, S. 1158

118. Daniel Fröhlich, Das Asylrecht im Rahmen des Unionsrechtes. Entstehung eines föderalen Asylregimes in der Europäischen Union, Mohr Siebeck, Tübingen 2011, in: ZAR 8/2012, S. 308
119. Tilman Nagel, Zu den Grundlagen des islamischen Rechts, Veröffentlichungen der Potsdamer Juristischen Gesellschaft 14, Nomos, Baden-Baden 2012, in: ZAR 1/2013, S. 41
120. Janine Osthoff, Weiterentwicklung des internationalen Menschenrechtsschutzes unter dem UN-Menschenrechtsrat? Darstellung und Analyse des UN-Menschenrechtsrats und seines Kontrollregimes, Saarbrücker Studien zum Internationalen Recht 51, Nomos, Baden-Baden 2012, in: ZAR 1/2013, S. 41
121. Maartje Verhoeven, The Costanzo Obligation. The obligations of national authorities in case of incompatibility between national law and European Law, Ius Commune Europaeum 93/2011, intersentia, in: DVBl. 2/2013, S. 97–98
122. Eberhard Eichenhofer, Soziale Menschenrechte im Völker-, europäischen und deutschen Recht, Mohr Siebeck, Tübingen 2012, in: ZAR 5–6/2013, S. 215
123. Reinhard Marx, Handbuch zum Flüchtlingsschutz. Erläuterungen zur Qualifikationsrichtlinie, Luchterhand Verlag, 2. Auflage, Köln 2012, in: ZAR 5–6/2013, S. 216
124. Jürgen Schwarze, Europarecht, Ausgewählte Beiträge, Nomos, Baden-Baden 2012, in: EuR 2013
125. Angelos S. Gerontas, Europäisierung und Internationalisierung des Verwaltungshandelns. Am Beispiel der einwanderungsrechtlichen Rückführungsproblematik, Europäisches Recht, Politik und Wirtschaft 362, Nomos Verlag, Baden-Baden 2011
126. Claudio Franzius/Franz C. Mayer/Jürgen Neyer (Hrsg.), Grenzen der europäischen Integration. Herausforderungen für Recht und Politik; Baden-Baden 2014
127. Kay Hailbronner, Asyl und Ausländerrecht, 3. überarbeitete Auflage, 2014
128. Armin Hatje(Hrsg.), Die Einheit des Europarechts im Zeichen der Krise, EuR Beiheft 2/2013